D0983085

A Textbook of Econometrics

SECOND EDITION

A TEXTBOOK OF ECONOMETRICS

LAWRENCE R. KLEIN

Benjamin Franklin Professor of Economics
Wharton School
University of Pennsylvania

PRENTICE-HALL, INC., Englewood Cliffs, N.J.

Library of Congress Cataloging in Publication Data

Klein, Lawrence Robert.
A textbook of econometrics.

Includes bibliographies.
1.–Econometrics. I.–Title.
HB139.K53–1974 330′.01′82 73–466
ISBN 0-13-912832-8

Printed in the United States of America

10 9 8 7 6 5 4 3 2 1

Prentice-Hall International, Inc., *London*
Prentice-Hall of Australia, Pty. Ltd., *Sydney*
Prentice-Hall of Canada, Ltd., *Toronto*
Prentice-Hall of India Private Limited, *New Delhi*
Prentice-Hall of Japan, Inc., *Tokyo*

Contents

PREFACE ix

Chapter I. THE ECONOMETRIC APPROACH 1

1. The Meaning of Econometrics 1
2. The Sources of Hypotheses Used in Econometrics 2
3. The Concept of Autonomous Relations 19

Chapter II. STATISTICAL GROUNDWORK 25

1. Probability 25
2. Distributions 31
3. Moments 40
4. Particular Distributions 45
5. Statistical Inference 52
6. Pedagogical Note 64

Chapter III. REGRESSION: SINGLE EQUATIONS 66

1. The Principle of Least Squares 66
2. Statistical Testing 80
3. Variations of the Standard Case and Special Problems 85
4. Nonlinear Regression 116

Chapter IV. REGRESSION SYSTEMS OF LINEAR SIMULTANEOUS EQUATIONS 131

1. Introduction 131
2. Identification 137
3. The Principle of Maximum Likelihood 146
4. Single Equation Estimators 150
5. Equation System Estimators 171
6. Some Problems in Estimating Equation Systems 183

Chapter V. SPECIAL CASES AND EXTENSIONS: SYSTEMS OF SIMULTANEOUS EQUATIONS 197

1. Recursive Systems 197
2. Nonlinear Systems 202
3. Serial Correlation 207
4. Specification Problems 210
5. Sampling Experiments 213

Chapter VI. APPLICATIONS IN MACROECONOMICS 226

1. Estimates of the Klein-Goldberger (revised) Model 226
2. Simulation 233
3. Analysis of Economic Policy 248
4. Stochastic Simulation and the Analysis of Business Cycles 252
5. Standard Error of Forecast 260
6. Estimation and Prediction 272

Chapter VII. ECONOMETRIC COMPUTATION 281

1. Introduction 281
2. The OLS Regression Calculations 282
3. Two-Stage-Least-Squares 303
4. Limited Information Maximum Likelihood 304
5. Full Information Maximum Likelihood 306
6. Solution and Simulation Programming 311

Chapter VIII. METHODS OF SECTOR ANALYSIS 321

1. Types of Disaggregation 321
2. Estimation of Sector Models 322
3. Estimation from Cross-Section Data 349
4. A Cross-Section Model of Production of Railway Services 363
5. Pooling of Time Series and Cross-Section Data 374

Chapter IX. SPECIAL PROBLEMS OF ECONOMETRICS 383

1. Errors of Observation and Measurement 383
2. Weighted Regressions from Sample Survey Data 409
3. Varying the Length of Unit Observation Periods 416

INDEX 429

Preface

Twenty years ago, when the original edition was being prepared, there were few systematic treatises on econometrics; the subject was not fully accepted from an academic viewpoint; classes were small; but it was exciting to be preparing material for what seemed to be the wave of the future. Solid development in the 1950's, followed by a veritable explosion in the 1960's, put econometrics in the forefront of economic science.

During the past decade many fine textbooks on econometrics have been made available, and econometrics instruction became a standard part of the economics curriculum in most universities and many colleges. At the same time, econometric knowledge is in great demand for applied work in research institutes, government agencies, international organizations, and business firms. This second edition is being written in an entirely new intellectual environment, where the subject is accorded a cordial reception. It is no longer a matter of struggling for acceptance or recognition.

Developments in technique and methodology, together with refinements in application, have been great during the past twenty years. Among all the good texts that have become available, I still feel that *A Textbook of Econometrics* had something different to offer, especially in the link between theoretical and applied branches of the subject. Although the Text has been out of print for some time, except to those who knew about the Asian edition in English, I had been teaching from notes that followed the original in spirit, but revised the presentation to be in line with recent developments.

In the revision, the idea of presenting some elementary principles of statistics was not markedly changed because these are basic ideas that get used over and again in the chapters on estimation and testing. Only selected concepts from statistics are introduced in order to make the treatment nearly self-contained. This idea required a full chapter's elaboration of that aspect of statistics that has most relevance and meaning for economists, namely regression analysis. The standard case followed by treatment of serial correlation, distributed lags, nonlinearity, heteroscedasticity, dummy variables, variance analysis, and other departures from the classic Markoff Theorem on least squares are taken up at some length.

Next, chapters on estimation of economic relationships in simultaneous equations cover several limited and full information methods (TSLS, IV, LIML, FIML, 3SLS, SLS) including also sampling experiments. This material constitutes a major part of the revision to reflect the enormous activities in estimation methodology following the break-throughs of Theil, Koyck, and others.

Applications and computing are dominated now by the introduction of the electronic computer. Econometricians have been quick and adept in harnessing this powerful tool, which has literally transformed modern econometric practice. Those who labored over computing bottlenecks in the formative years cannot help but marvel at the feats now performed with electronic aids. This development required an entire rewriting of the chapters on applications and computing. Developments are so rapid for this aspect of econometrics, however, that further revision and elaboration will be needed again soon.

The remaining chapters on sector analysis and special problems are not as intensively revised. They are given an up-dating but not complete revision.

Theory, methodology, and hardware have changed greatly; the students have as well. Today, the economics student is far better prepared to take up technical details of econometrics. Mathematical background, together with experience in computer programming, is generally adequate for the requirements of the subject. For this reason, I have deleted the appendix on matrix algebra, that seemed to be wanted twenty years ago. It is now a common expectation that economics students will receive a standard mathematical education, covering elementary analysis and linear algebra.

As econometrics enters a new phase of intricate applications of time series analysis and control theory, some new mathematical tools may need development, and we may turn to these instead of trying to fill the gaps with brief treatment of the algebra of matrices and determinants. These latter subjects are, by now, very well handled in easily accessible mathematical tracts.

The revised lecture notes have benefited greatly from exposure to classroom presentation. Perceptive students have spotted mistakes quickly and greatly improved the entire new presentation.

PHILADELPHIA, DECEMBER, 1972

A Textbook of Econometrics

1

The Econometric Approach

1. THE MEANING OF ECONOMETRICS

Measurement in economics is the subject matter of this volume. That measurement alone is not enough to distinguish econometrics from other branches of economics will be seen from the development in later chapters. We shall not try, however, to develop an elegant definition of econometrics in a single sentence or paragraph; we shall, instead, attempt to give a clearer idea of what the subject is all about from a general discussion in this entire chapter.

Although econometrics deals intimately with measurement, it is not the mere recording of facts; the gathering of factual data is, however, an important first step in the investigation of any empirical econometric problem. Econometrics is not what is commonly known as mathematical economics, although the mathematical formulation of properties from economics is also essential to econometrics, whether theoretical or empirical econometrics or a combination of both types. The purely theoretical approach to econometrics may be envisioned as the development of that body of knowledge that tells us how to go about measuring economic relations. This theory is often developed on a fairly abstract or general basis, so that the results may be applied to any one of a variety of concrete problems that may arise. The empirical work in econometrics deals with actual data and sets out to make numerical estimates of economic relationships. The empirical procedures are direct applications of the methods of theoretical econometrics.

The historical development of mathematical economics has been in the treatment of patterns of human behavior in the economic sphere of life, as though the implied relationships were exactly fulfilled. Such is not the case in econometrics, where random deviations from the patterns suggested by mathematical economics are essential features of the scheme. Econometrics recognizes that social behavior is exceedingly complex and that a limited number of variables related together in fairly simple and elegant equations cannot explain the whole of such behavior. Because life in our social world is subject to much uncertainty, and numerous minute or subjective variables play a role in conditioning human behavior, econometric analysis explicitly introduces random perturbations and leads only to probabilistic conclusions. Observations of the factual data serving as raw material for the econometrician, moreover, are hardly ever precise, thus leading to another type of error, that is, errors of observation. It is often realistic and adequate to regard observational errors as random, and their treatment may be worked into the general probability scheme of the econometric approach.

At least one reason why econometrics deserves separate treatment as a distinct body of knowledge is that the techniques of measurement developed are applied to nonexperimental observations. The inability to perform controlled experiments in most situations is not a difficulty exclusive to econometrics, for it occurs in other social sciences and elsewhere. It does call for yet undeveloped methods of measurement. If controlled experiments were possible, econometrics would undoubtedly be based on the application of standard statistical techniques to economic data, although even in this case some special work would have to be done to adapt statistical procedures to the specific structure of economics.

Because the data used in econometrics are obtained by observing actual economic processes, we may conclude that econometrics is a way of studying history—a very systematic way. We never know what economic behavior will be like in future, unobserved situations, but we try to make as strong a statement as possible about this unknown area on the basis of past history. The econometrician tries to piece together the fundamental aspects of economic behavior by looking at the interrelationships of the quantitative magnitudes generated historically and then tries further to extrapolate past behavior into the unknown future. As we shall see below, a sensible method of extrapolation is not naïve or mechanical, and the econometrician is no less flexible than any other historian who tries to evaluate the future on the basis of the past. Even without the attempts at extrapolation, however, econometrics is interesting as a mere study of the past to show how quantitative magnitudes interacted at that time. This is, in itself, a challenging intellectual problem.

2. THE SOURCES OF HYPOTHESES USED IN ECONOMETRICS

The very general type of discussion of the preceding section is wholly inadequate to convey an impression of the subject matter of econometrics to one who is not already familiar with the field. Some concrete illustrations may be more useful in clarifying the basic ideas. At the microeconomic level, where individual firms and households are the units of analysis, economic theory suggests hypotheses that can be put into mathematical form and then tested from an econometric point of view. It must be emphasized, however, that academic economic theory is only one among alternative sources for the development of hypotheses. It forms a good starting point, but we shall by no means be so narrow as to insist that econometric work be built on this particular foundation.

The traditional theory of the firm tells us that labor input will be demanded by an entrepreneur up to the point at which

marginal productivity of labor = real wage rate

under competitive market conditions. This is an hypothesis that establishes a relationship of the sort that is amenable to econometric methods. Underlying the concept of marginal productivity is a technological relationship showing how inputs are transformed into outputs—the production function. The task for the econometrician is then clear. He will proceed as follows. He first lists the inputs and outputs relevant to the firm being studied. We shall call them n = labor input, c = raw materials input, d = capital input, x = product output. Let us assume, in the first instance, that the firm being analyzed uses only one type of each of the three inputs and produces only one type of output. In many practical cases, it is necessary to subdivide the variables into finer categories. The production function will be written as

$$x = f(n, c, d), \tag{1.2.1}$$

which says nothing more nor less than that the inputs n, c, d are transformed into output x by the function (production process) f. We do not insist, in econometric work, that this relation be exact. We shall reformulate it by writing

$$x = f(n, c, d, u), \tag{1.2.2}$$

where u is a random variable having certain well-defined probabilistic properties. In the following chapter, probability concepts will be introduced in some detail. From empirical observation of the interrelations between x on the one hand and n, c, d on the other and possibly from technological facts supplied by engineers, the econometrician will try to estimate the quantitative properties of f. For example, if f were quadratic, to an adequate empirical approximation, so that the production function could be written as

$$\begin{aligned} x = \alpha_0 + \alpha_1 n + \alpha_2 c + \alpha_3 d + \alpha_4 n^2 + \alpha_5 c^2 + \alpha_6 d^2 \\ + \alpha_7 nc + \alpha_8 nd + \alpha_9 cd + u, \end{aligned} \tag{1.2.3}$$

we would say that the production function is characterized by its parameters $\alpha_0, \alpha_1, \alpha_2, \ldots, \alpha_9$, and that the econometrician's job would be to estimate numerical values for the αs. Other approximations may serve equally well in the range of observed variation of x, n, c, d. One useful type is that estimated in so many cases by C. Cobb and P. H. Douglas:

$$x = An^{\alpha'_1}c^{\alpha'_2}d^{\alpha'_3}u. \tag{1.2.4}$$

This function achieves some of the curvature features of (1.2.3) but is much more economical in its use of parameters.

The firm's engineers may tell the econometrician that there is a fixed technological relationship between raw materials and capital. The variable c may represent fuel consumption by the firm's machines, and d may represent machine hours. If every machine hour requires a fixed input of fuel, then we may append the exact relationship

$$c = \alpha d \tag{1.2.5}$$

to the production function, with the value of α supplied by the engineer. A combination of (1.2.5) with either of the production functions (1.2.3) or (1.2.4), whichever is more satisfactory, enables the econometrician to eliminate one variable, either c or d, and thereby to specify its form more closely.

Let us now return to our hypothesis suggested by economic theory. If (1.2.3) is the form of the production function, then the marginal productivity of labor is given by

$$\alpha_1 + 2\alpha_4 n + \alpha_7 c + \alpha_8 d$$

that is obtained as the partial derivative of x with respect to n in (1.2.3). If (1.2.5) also holds, the marginal productivity of labor could be expressed further as

$$\alpha_1 + 2\alpha_4 n + \alpha_7 \alpha d + \alpha_8 d.$$

The theoretical hypothesis being considered now has the mathematical formulation

$$\frac{\partial x}{\partial n} = \alpha_1 + 2\alpha_4 n + \alpha_7 \alpha d + \alpha_8 d = \frac{w}{p}, \tag{1.2.6}$$

where w = wage rate and p = price of output. Equation (1.2.6) is exact, but more realistically we should suppose that an entrepreneur is not always at his true optimal position, but only within a random error of reaching it. Thus we may have the stochastic relation

$$\alpha_1 + 2\alpha_4 n + \alpha_7 \alpha d + \alpha_8 d = \frac{w}{p} + v, \tag{1.2.7}$$

where v = random variable with definite probability properties. This is the genesis of a genuine econometric relation, representing an hypothesis to be tested against the facts. Equation (1.2.3) is also an econometric relation. It has a technological basis, but (1.2.7) has an economic-theoretical basis. Both (1.2.3) and (1.2.7) are called structural equations. Although (1.2.3) is further termed a technological relation, (1.2.7) is termed a behavior equation representing the economic behavior of an entrepreneur.

In (1.2.3), x, n, c, d are objective and measurable; u is not directly observable. Simultaneously, as the parameters are estimated from the observable variables, the properties of u may be estimated and examined to see whether or not they contradict the assumptions made. The marginal productivity hypothesis in (1.2.7) can be tested from the parameters estimated in (1.2.3), or estimates of the parameters appearing in (1.2.7) can be made directly from observations of n, d, w, p. Again, the properties of the unobserved variable v can be estimated and tested for consistency with the assumptions made. As we shall later see, there is a statistical problem in determining estimates of the parameters of both (1.2.3) and (1.2.7) simultaneously so that they are consistent with each other.

We must caution the reader that the treatment is now at a purely expositional level and that the oversimplified picture of entrepreneurial behavior is not to be interpreted as anything more than an example of the type of relationship that arises in econometrics. A really satisfactory theory of the firm must include more than short-run profit maximization under conditions of certainty and perfectly competitive markets. Econometric techniques are by no means limited to relationships as simple as those in (1.2.3) and (1.2.7), although there are cases where highly complicated relations may be unnecessary.

A simple extension of the static equilibrium theory from which (1.2.3) and (1.2.7) are derived is the formulation of an adjustment equation of the form

$$\lambda\left[(\alpha_1 + 2\alpha_4 n + \alpha_7 \alpha d + \alpha_8 d) - \frac{w}{p}\right] - v = \frac{dn}{dt}. \tag{1.2.7$'$}$$

In this dynamic relationship, the idea is expressed that entrepreneurs will adjust their input of labor by increasing it if marginal productivity exceeds the real wage rate and by reducing it if marginal productivity falls short of the real wage rate. In discrete observational form, dn/dt would be replaced by $\triangle n_t = n_t - n_{t-1}$. Other similar adjustment processes may be formulated as alternatives to be tested against data. The important point to be made is that received equilibrium theory may be a starting point for generalization into more realistic dynamic relationships. Such adjustment processes have actually been estimated for separate sectors of the economy.[1]

A different direction of generalization is to extend the model to the case of imperfectly competitive markets. This is done in Chap. 8, below.

In a manner analogous to the above use of the mathematical formulation of the theory of the firm, we may turn to the theory of consumer behavior to state hypotheses in the household sector of the economy. There are some

[1] Phoebus J. Dhrymes, "A Model of Short-Run Labor Adjustment," in *The Brookings Model: Some Further Results*, ed. J. Duesenberry et al. (Chicago: Rand McNally, 1969), pp. 110–49.

basic reasons, however, why theory is less helpful in this instance. The counterpart of the marginal productivity relations are marginal utility relations of the following sort:

$$\frac{\text{marginal utility of good } A}{\text{marginal utility of good } B} = \frac{\text{price of good } A}{\text{price of good } B}.$$

Relationships like this hold for the individual household. The marginal productivity relations in the theory of the firm can be pushed back to objective, measurable, technological equations (production functions). The subjective nature of individual utility functions, underlying the theory of consumer behavior, immensely decreases the value of marginal utility relations to the econometrician, because the possibility of direct measurement is, for the time being, very unlikely. Perhaps with the aid of psychologists, measurement may become possible in this area in the future. The utility calculus in the theory of consumer behavior may not be entirely valueless in the setting up of hypotheses in the household sector of the economy. If there are n goods in the individual's budget, his behavior, according to the traditional theory, will be described by a set of $n - 1$ of the preceding type of marginal utility equations and by a budget restriction. The latter relation states that expenditures on current goods and services plus savings equal income. We can then make the very general mathematical statement that the individual's demand for any good can be expressed as a function of all the prices confronting him and his income. This intuitive result could undoubtedly have been derived from a variety of thought processes without resorting to the theory of consumer behavior.

The theory does push matters somewhat further, and the results may be of some value to the econometrician. A proposition developed in this theory is that the demand relations must depend on relative prices and real income instead of absolute prices and money income. This may or may not be intuitively obvious. We shall write

$$x_i = g\left(\frac{p_1}{p_i}, \frac{p_2}{p_i}, \ldots, \frac{p_{i-1}}{p_i}, \frac{p_{i+1}}{p_i}, \ldots, \frac{p_n}{p_i}, \frac{y}{p_i}, v\right) \tag{1.2.8}$$

where x_i = quantity demanded of the ith commodity,
p_i = price of the ith commodity,
y = money income,
v = random variable.

The characteristics of g (its parameters) depend on the individual's utility function, for which we have no direct measurements. As we shall later see, a more complete theory allowing for consumer planning over time, asset-debt holding, expectations about incomes or prices, and so on, will lead to somewhat more complex hypotheses; yet the general approach is not essentially different.

A somewhat deeper theorem following from the utility calculus is embedded in the celebrated *Slutsky equation*, sometimes called the fundamental equation of value theory. This equation will be written as

$$\frac{\partial x_i}{\partial p_j} = -x_j \frac{\partial x_i}{\partial y} + \frac{\partial x_i}{\partial p_j}\bigg|_{u=\text{const.}}, \tag{1.2.9}$$

and interpreted as breaking up the variation in quantity demanded with respect to price change into two components: (*a*) the variation of quantity demanded with respect to income change, and (*b*) the variation of quantity demanded with respect to price change for a constant level of utility. This latter expression is sometimes called the substitution effect between goods i and j and is known to have the mathematical property of being symmetrical, that is,

$$\frac{\partial x_i}{\partial p_j}\bigg|_{u=\text{const.}} = \frac{\partial x_j}{\partial p_i}\bigg|_{u=\text{const.}}. \tag{1.2.10}$$

The symbol u in this context refers to utility and not a random variable. The symmetry property leads to the following important result:

$$\frac{\partial x_i}{\partial p_j} + x_j \frac{\partial x_i}{\partial y} = \frac{\partial x_j}{\partial p_i} + x_i \frac{\partial x_j}{\partial y}. \tag{1.2.11}$$

Equation (1.2.11) tells us that the price and income effects of pairs of goods in the individual's budget should be related in a particular fashion. Restrictions are thus imposed by the theory of consumer behavior on the parameters of the demand functions in (1.2.8). A problem for the econometrician is to attempt to measure the parameters of the demand functions and then to see whether they fulfill the conditions of (1.2.11) within a prescribed margin of error. The latter qualification is important, for the ever present random error and stochastic property has been omitted from (1.2.11) in its development by the "exact" methods of mathematical economics. It would be more appropriate to write

$$\frac{\partial x_i}{\partial p_j} + x_j \frac{\partial x_i}{\partial y} = \frac{\partial x_j}{\partial p_i} + x_i \frac{\partial x_j}{\partial y} + v'. \tag{1.2.12}$$

In empirical work we would expect our condition (1.2.12) to be subject to random error, v'. In addition, estimates of the parameters of the demand equations, essential to the empirical determination of expression (1.2.12), are obtained from samples and are hence subject to error. This gives us another reason not to expect exact agreement with the theoretical hypothesis.

Complete statistical expenditure systems that preserve homogeneity (price relative and real income), the consumer's budget restriction, and the Slutsky condition (1.2.11) can be estimated in special cases. The linear case expresses (1.2.8) as

$$x_i = \beta_i - \sum_{j=1}^{n} \alpha_i \beta_j \left(\frac{p_j}{p_i}\right) + \alpha_i \left(\frac{y}{p_i}\right) + v_i; \ \sum_{i=1}^{n} \alpha_i = 1. \tag{1.2.8$'$}$$

The problem of parameter estimation $(\alpha_1, \ldots, \alpha_n, \beta_1, \ldots, \beta_n)$ in this model is not altogether straightforward, but it can be done.[2] Nonlinear methods must be employed, unless some stepwise linear methods can be developed.

Tests of the Slutsky condition can be made in an unrestricted model, that is, one in which demand equations are estimated without imposition of conditions (1.2.12), but the results have not been uniformly satisfactory; therefore, restricted estimates for systems that obey the a priori theoretical conditions are being increasingly used.

Another branch of economic theory that the econometrician must consult is that describing the functioning of markets. An interesting new element is introduced into the situation in this respect, because market theory deals always with collections of individuals and group behavior, as contrasted with some of the patterns of individualistic behavior derived from the standard theories of the firm and consumer behavior.

The essential structure of economic theory is the following. The theory of the firm (profit maximization) shows the behavior of entrepreneurs (producers) in supplying goods to the market and in demanding the services of factors of production. The theory of consumer behavior (utility maximization) shows the decisions of households in demanding goods and services and in supplying labor power. The system is closed by market clearing—the equating of supplies and demands in all markets. Market clearing relations involve the aggregate supply and demand of all individual firms and households participating in each market. In static, exact systems we write

$$\sum_{i=1}^{n_1} x_{ij}^S = \sum_{i=1}^{n_2} x_{ij}^D \tag{1.2.13}$$

as the market clearing condition for the jth commodity, reconciling the aggregate supply of n_1 producers with the aggregate demand of n_2 consumers. A stochastic element can be introduced at the static level by rewriting the market clearing condition as

$$\sum_{i=1}^{n_1} x_{ij}^S = \sum_{i=1}^{n_2} x_{ij}^D + v_j, \tag{1.2.14}$$

where v_j is a random perturbation. In this case, markets are cleared except for random deviations. A more realistic and more interesting picture is given by the dynamic, stochastic scheme

$$\frac{dp_j}{dt} = f\left(\sum_{i=1}^{n_1} x_{ij}^S(t) - \sum_{i=1}^{n_2} x_{ij}^D(t), v_j(t)\right). \tag{1.2.15}$$

Equation (1.2.15) relaxes the overrestrictive condition of continuous market

[2] Robert A. Pollak and Terence J. Wales, "Estimation of the Linear Expenditure System," *Econometrica*, 37 (October, 1969), 611–28. They assume a different stochastic structure for their estimation procedures.

clearance, except for random deviation, imposed by (1.2.14) and states instead that prices, p_j, adjust so as to clear the market, the degree of adjustment depending on the size of the market disequilibrium. In actual practice we do not observe prices and quantities as continuous functions of time. We use average values over a period of time (month, quarter, year, decade, and so on) or discrete observations at successive intervals of time. The discrete analogue of (1.2.15) is

$$p_j(t) - p_j(t-1) = f\left(\sum_{i=1}^{n_1} x_{ij}^S(t) - \sum_{i=1}^{n_2} x_{ij}^D(t), v_j(t)\right). \tag{1.2.16}$$

In (1.2.16), $p_j(t)$ is, let us say, the average price during the tth month, $\sum_{i=1}^{n_1} x_{ij}^S(t)$ is the aggregate amount supplied to the market during the tth month, and $\sum_{i=1}^{n_2} x_{ij}^D(t)$ is the aggregate amount demanded from the market during the tth month. In the dynamic, stochastic case, the market is not necessarily cleared at any particular time point, and the tendency towards clearance is randomly disturbed.

As concrete examples of this type of relation we may cite the following cases: $p_j(t)$ = average monthly rental, and $\sum_{i=1}^{n_1} x_{ij}^S(t) - \sum_{i=1}^{n_2} x_{ij}^D(t)$ = average number of dwelling units vacant during the month. $p_j(t)$ = average monthly wage rate, and $\sum_{i=1}^{n_1} x_{ij}^S(t) - \sum_{i=1}^{n_2} x_{ij}^D(t)$ = average number of persons unemployed during the month.

Many observations of economic data are made exclusively in terms of aggregates of the type $\sum_{i=1}^{n} x_{ij}$ that arise in the theory of market clearing. But if the whole system is to be tied together with the theory of the firm, the theory of consumer behavior, and market clearing simultaneously built in, we must either obtain breakdowns of the aggregates (that is, obtain observations of the individual x_{ij}) or study aggregate relations derived from the individual equations of the theories of the firm and consumer behavior. Both approaches will be studied in this volume. In later chapters, we shall investigate the statistical problems of estimating relationships based on data taken from individual firms or households and the problem of the structure of aggregate relationships. The latter problem, sometimes called the aggregation problem, can be formulated as the attempt to develop behavior patterns of communities of individuals on the basis of the individual behavior patterns.

In the discussion of the theory of the firm we saw the distinction between technological relations and behavior relations, both of which are structural relations. In the theory of consumer behavior, household demand for goods and the associated Slutsky equations are further examples of behavior relations. The market clearing equations are also behavior relations. The first two types of behavior relations refer to entrepreneurial behavior and to household behavior separately. The market clearing equations refer to the joint, interacting behavior of both producers and consumers in their bargaining *vis-à-vis* each other.

The market clearing equations are also interesting in that they introduce dynamic elements into the structure immediately. It is, of course, plausible and empirically necessary to work with dynamic formulations of the technological, entrepreneurial behavior and household behavior relations. There are, in these equations, lags in response of one variable to another, interrelations of some cumulative variables to their rates of change, and diverse other ways in which further dynamization will be achieved.

It is only at a very abstract level that we can use the theoretical scheme discussed thus far to draw up a set of equations describing the operation of an economic system. In reality, the government and various other institutional or legal organs play a great role in economic affairs. This brings additional types of structural relations into the model. We shall call them legal and institutional relations. One of the best examples is the tax laws. For an individual household or corporation there is an equation of the form

$$r = h(y) \tag{1.2.17}$$

stating that governmental revenues, r, in the form of income taxes are collected from this individual on the basis of his income, y. The function h is a mathematical expression for the tax laws. Equation (1.2.17) is not properly a stochastic relation, for people are assumed to obey the laws exactly. They may miscalculate or misreport their income, but they use Eq. (1.2.17) exactly, in most cases, on the legal tax forms. The tax laws, being very complicated, present the econometrician with a function h that is unmanageable for statistical purposes. In choosing some smooth approximation

$$r = h^*(y, v), \tag{1.2.18}$$

an error v is introduced, and we now have a stochastic legal equation instead of that in (1.2.17). At the aggregative level, tax relations are even more approximate and are, for that reason, really stochastic. The estimates of the parameters of h^* are, however, often not obtained by methods of statistical inference applied to sample observations. A smoothing technique applied to a priori information contained in tax laws may be used to estimate the parameters of h^*; thus (1.2.18) may be treated somewhat differently, in a statistical sense, from other structural equations.

The maintenance of fixed proportions between bank reserves and deposits is another type of relation imposed upon the system by legal or institutional restrictions. In some countries, bank reserves are fixed by law; in others, they are maintained above some constant fraction of deposits according to long standing custom that over the course of time becomes a fixed rule—in other words, an institutional relation.

Questions and Problems

1. In the theory of the firm, cost equations, derived from production functions and marginal productivity equations, give a relation between total cost and quantity of output.

   (a) How can the econometrician measure marginal cost concepts from measurements of the production function and marginal productivity equations?

   (b) Formulate hypotheses from economic theory about marginal costs which the econometrician could test.

   (c) Would there be any reason for estimating a cost function instead of production and marginal productivity equations?

2. Extend the theory of consumer behavior to asset holding, borrowing, and household planning over time. What information does the extended theory give about the nature of equations of consumer demand that would be useful to the econometrician who wants to estimate these equations?

3. Various institutional arrangements affect the functioning of the economy. Banks must hold a certain fraction of their liquid assets as reserves against deposits. Unemployment benefits vary with the level of unemployment, the duration of unemployment, and the past earnings of unemployed workers. The government deals in agricultural commodities so as to make the index of prices received *at least* as high as prices paid by farmers; otherwise, agricultural prices are allowed to seek their level governed by the forces of supply and demand. Express these institutional arrangements in the form of mathematical equations, and show how these equations fit into larger systems of the economic process.

The above narrow view of economic theory has by no means proved to be the most satisfactory approach for formulating hypotheses to be used in econometric analysis. That specialized branch of economic theory called business-cycle theory has produced a large number of useful hypotheses without explicit reference to the theories of the firm, consumer behavior, or market clearing. In fact, Professor Tinbergen's great pioneering work in econometrics was entitled *Statistical Testing of Business-Cycle Theories.*[3] One of the main purposes of Tinbergen's work was to examine statistically the existing body of business-cycle theories as exemplified by the content of Professor Haberler's well-known book, *Prosperity and Depression.*[4] A feature of the hypotheses coming from business-cycle theory is that they are usually in aggregative form, referring to a whole industry, groups of industries, groups of households, and so on. Usually, these hypotheses are not derived by first studying individual behavior and then performing rigorous aggregations to the final result.

[3] J. Tinbergen, *Statistical Testing of Business-Cycle Theories*, 2 vols. (Geneva: League of Nations, 1939).

[4] G. Haberler, *Prosperity and Depression* (Geneva: League of Nations, 1937).

Some of the particular aspects stressed in business-cycle writings have been mathematically formulated and can thus be expressed as econometric equations. A few writers have even gone so far as to develop systems of equations attempting to give a complete explanation of cyclical swings in the economy. The macrodynamic mathematical systems are especially suited to econometric analysis.

One of the widely known relations in business-cycle literature is the acceleration principle. It states that

investment expenditures depend on the rate of change of consumption outlays.

In mathematical form we write

$$I = f\left(\frac{dC}{dt}, u\right) \tag{1.2.19}$$

where $I =$ investment, $C =$ consumption, and $u =$ random error. As used in business-cycle theory, the acceleration principle is often applied to an entire economy's investment and consumption. It is also applied to individual industries, and though it may be developed from the rational behavior of an individual firm, it is rarely used on the microeconomic level in business-cycle analysis. If every firm's investment were some function of the rate of change in its *output* (producer or consumer good output), it would be difficult to say what relation would exist between aggregate investment and the rate of change of aggregate consumption. Nevertheless, certain business-cycle theories put forth the hypothesis stated in (1.2.19) on an aggregative basis, and such an equation could be tested and estimated by the application of econometric techniques.

In place of the strict accelerator hypothesis (1.2.19), econometricians have broadly come round to the *flexible* accelerator which can be formulated as

$$\frac{dk}{dt} = I(t) = \lambda(K^*(t) - K(t)) + u(t) \qquad 0 < \lambda < 1 \tag{1.2.19'}$$

where $K^*(t) = \mu X(t)$.

In this relationship, $K^*(t)$ is the *desired* stock of capital, which is assumed to be proportional to the output flow $X(t)$. This assumption is more plausible than to say that the *actual* stock of capital $K(t)$ is proportional to consumption, $C(t)$, [or output $X(t)$] as is implied by (1.2.19). The flexible version states that capital stock is adjusted at rate λ to bring desired capital into line with existing capital. In discrete form, this equation is

$$K(t) - K(t-1) = I(t) = \lambda(K^*(t) - K(t-1)).$$

The dynamic implications of this adjustment process are similar to those mentioned above for employment. The theory of investment can similarly be formulated in terms of profit maximizing equilibrium conditions to define $K^*(t)$.

A complete macrodynamic model of business cycles has been suggested by M. Kalecki. His theory begins by viewing the economy as composed of two broad groups—workers and capitalists. It is assumed that workers consume all their income, that is, contribute nothing to the economy's savings. The gross profits B accruing to the capitalist sector of the economy are split into two components: (*a*) consumption by capitalists C, and (*b*) saving by capitalists A. By definition, A, C, and B are related in the equation

$$B = C + A. \tag{1.2.20}$$

This is an exact accounting relation and is not subject to random disturbance. If independent observations are made for the three variables, the three separate sets of observations may not exactly satisfy equation (1.2.20) because of observational errors. In some studies, statistical observations are prepared for two of the three variables and the remaining variable is determined so as to satisfy (1.2.20) precisely.

A simple linear equation is introduced by Kalecki to explain capitalists' consumption as a function of gross profits.

$$C = C_1 + \lambda B + v_1. \tag{1.2.21}$$

We add the disturbance v_1 to allow for random deviations from the law of consumption behavior. In this relation, C_1 is the minimum level of consumption for this sector of the economy, and λ is the marginal propensity to consume out of gross profits.

Orders of capital goods are denoted by I and deliveries by L. Because it takes time to get capital goods after orders are first placed, there is the equation

$$L(t) = I(t - \theta) + v_2 \tag{1.2.22}$$

that states that investment orders are fulfilled after a lapse of θ time units, subject to a random error v_2. The average amount of unfilled orders existing at time period t is represented by

$$\frac{1}{\theta} \int_{t-\theta}^{t} I(\tau)\, d\tau,$$

and is set equal to profits not consumed, that is, available for accumulation.

$$A(t) = \frac{1}{\theta} \int_{t-\theta}^{t} I(\tau)\, d\tau + v_3. \tag{1.2.23}$$

The existing stock of physical capital K is related to investment by definition in

$$\frac{dK(t)}{dt} = L(t) - U(t), \tag{1.2.24}$$

where $U(t)$ = depreciation. We shall assume $U(t)$ to be a known function of time. The system is then closed by an equation expressing the demand for new capital, investment orders, as a function of gross profits and the existing stock of capital,

$$\frac{I}{K} = \alpha\frac{B}{K} + \beta + v_4. \tag{1.2.25}$$

In this business-cycle theory, there are six unknown variables (B, C, A, L, I, and K) and six relations. Thus, it is a closed system. Empirical work may not be directly possible without some discrete approximation to the continuous variables. Equation (1.2.23) would have to be reformulated in terms of summations instead of integrations, and (1.2.24) would have to be reformulated in terms of differences instead of derivatives. Parenthetically, it may be remarked that much theoretical interest was attached to Kalecki's original presentation of the theory because of the fact that it involved a mixture of discrete differences, derivatives, and integrals. It can be shown that the system reduces to the mixed difference–differential equation

$$\begin{aligned} J'(t) &= \frac{\alpha}{(1-\lambda)\theta}[J(t) - J(t-\theta)] + \beta J(t-\theta) \\ J(t) &= I(t) - U(t), \end{aligned} \tag{1.2.26}$$

if the error terms v_i are neglected.

From the point of view of the econometric problem of measurement and hypothesis testing, Kalecki's theory provides an interesting framework. Making use of the available statistics on consumption, profits, investment orders, investment installation, depreciation, and the stock of capital, we could obtain observations on each variable of the model and try to infer numerical values of the parameters (C_1, λ, θ, α, β) from the sample data. At the same time, we would apply various tests as to whether the theory were essentially consistent with the observed facts, apart from random deviations.

The behavior patterns in Kalecki's business-cycle theory are assumed to be adequately approximated by some simple linear relations. This may or may not be correct. For the most part, a priori analysis of any sort tells us very little about the shape of the relations studied. It tells us such things as (*a*) what are the relevant equations for which to look; (*b*) what variables are involved; and (*c*) what is the direction of effect of one variable on another. The form of the relationship is very much an empirical matter. We shall have to work with relations that are sufficiently complex to explain reality. It will become evident, however, in the chapters on statistical method, that pragmatic considerations will bear heavily on the final choice of the type of equation to use. The limited size of available samples imposes a real restriction on the number of parameters that can be utilized. Although many statistical techniques can be easily used in equations that are nonlinear in the economic variables, they often cannot be used as easily in equations that are nonlinear in the parameters to be estimated. Although the hypothetical models treat the economic variables as unknowns and the parameters as known constants, many statistical problems treat the observed economic variables as a set of known numbers and the parameters as things to be estimated. The random disturbances are regarded as additive in linear equations; this, too, is a simplifying approach in the application of statistical methods.

Questions and Problems

1. The equation of exchange

$$MV = PT,$$

where

M = stock of cash balances
V = velocity of circulation of cash
P = general price level
T = volume of transactions

is widely used in monetary theory. Is this an equation of economic behavior, an institutional restriction, or a definition? If the condition

$$V = \text{constant}$$

is added, does the classification change?

2. A simplified version of the Keynesian system is

a. $C = C(r, Y)$ consumption function
b. $I = I(r, Y)$ investment function
c. $M = L(r, Y)$ liquidity preference function
d. $Y = C + I.$

The variables are

C = consumer expenditures
r = rate of interest
Y = income
I = investment expenditures
M = stock of cash balances.

The stock of cash is fixed by the banking system.

Classify each of the four equations as behavioral, technological, institutional, or definitional. What economic agents are acting in each equation? Modify the system by introducing random disturbances and dynamic variables so that an econometric business-cycle model could be obtained from it.

Very often linear approximation is adequate, but we shall investigate nonlinear systems also. At this stage, it should be remarked that a series of linear segments, if divided finely enough, can be used to approach curved surfaces as closely as we please. To some extent, this principle will be appealed to in our work with linear systems.

The preceding brief discussion on linearity leads conveniently to another possible approach in some econometric problems. Some persons would prefer to choose econometric models on an empirical basis. Rather than start out from an a priori theory such as conventional economic theory or business-cycle theory, they would base everything on an empirical foundation from the start. A possible formulation of an empirical approach is the following: Given a set of observations on n economic variables $y_1, y_2, \ldots y_n$, how many linear relations exist, in some probability sense, among these n variables? If these n variables are linearly related in m equations

$$\begin{aligned} \alpha_{11}y_1 + \alpha_{12}y_2 + \cdots + \alpha_{1n}y_n &= v_1 \\ \alpha_{21}y_1 + \alpha_{22}y_2 + \cdots + \alpha_{2n}y_n &= v_2 \\ &\cdot \\ &\cdot \\ &\cdot \\ \alpha_{m1}y_1 + \alpha_{m2}y_2 + \cdots + \alpha_{mn}y_n &= v_m, \end{aligned} \tag{1.2.27}$$

this set of relations defines an econometric model. Economic theory may be used at a later stage to attach some deeper meaning to each of the m equations, but this approach is essentially empirical. After the number of linearly independent relations among the n variables is established, the values of the parameters are estimated. There are great similarities between this approach and the confluence analysis of R. Frisch[5], or the factor analysis of psychometrics. J. R. N. Stone[6] has attempted to apply factor analysis methods in this way to economic data.

Some economic statisticians are led to seek relationships that exhibit high correlation with apparent persistency, regardless of their ability to explain the behavioral, technological, or other structural process on which these correlation relationships are based. As we shall see in Chap. 4, there are two ways of looking at an economic system—either in terms of its original *structural form* or in terms of its *reduced form*, in which each variable to be explained is expressed as a function of all the explanatory variables of the system. A reduced form equation that does not relate the separate coefficients to an original structure has principally an empirical basis for existence but can be used, somewhat inefficiently, in forecasting applications as long as there are no changes in the system's structure.

[5] R. Frisch, *Statistical Confluence Analysis by Means of Complete Regression Systems* (Oslo: Universitetets Økonomiske Institutt, 1934).

[6] J. R. N. Stone, "On the Interdependence of Blocks of Transactions," Supplement to *Journal of the Royal Statistical Society*, VIII, pt. I (1947), 1–32.

The search for high correlation between such variables as total production (GNP), employment, unemployment, or price level, on the one hand, and explanatory factors such as money supply, government expenditures, government receipts, exports, stock prices, and previous values of these factors, on the other hand, is an increasingly popular form of relatively unguided empirical econometrics. These schemes may work temporarily, especially when not far removed from the sample period that produces high correlation, but it is not likely that they will stand up under repeated use and offer minimal opportunity for the study of economic alternatives other than the setting of different levels for explanatory variables. They do not lend themselves in a flexible way to consideration of changes in structure. This approach tends to take econometric research further from its a priori economic base and move it towards empirical statistical research.

Empirical methods are also used in a less formal manner at the first stage of econometric work. For example, an investigator may observe published records of the orders for industrial equipment and of the deliveries of the same equipment. From these observations he may learn that there is a systematic time lag between orders and deliveries. The lag may vary with the business cycle, but retain some systematic characteristics. When this investigator comes to the problem of econometric model construction, he will build this lag into the system as one of the structural properties. The existence of this lag was not determined on the basis of prior reasoning and thinking about economic processes; it was empirically discovered. After its discovery, however, the investigator will realize that this lag is based on considerations such as the production process in capital goods industries, the organization of markets for capital goods, transportation facilities, and communication facilities. There is a sound basis for treating this lag as a structural property. In this way, a great deal of empirical work will be of the utmost importance in the formulation of hypotheses.

On the other hand, purely empirical methods can, at times, be seriously misleading. Many persons have observed, for example, a strong positive correlation between the statistics on investment and the corresponding statistics on the rate of change of consumption (between the stock of capital and consumption). From this empirical observation they sometimes conclude that there exists a structural relationship in the system explaining investment behavior in terms of the rate of change of consumption—the acceleration principle discussed earlier. The high correlation cannot be denied; it is a fact, but there is a real question whether or not the high correlation can be identified as a relationship revealing entrepreneurial investment behavior. It may very well be part of a technological relationship showing how the input of capital goods is transformed into production.

This problem introduces a basic econometric concept—the concept of identification. The earliest empirical work in econometrics, the estimation of statistical demand curves, uncovered the problem that observed correlations between prices and quantities of commodities did not necessarily reveal the nature of the demand curve. Because supply curves involved the same variables, the observed correlation could be identified with the supply curve, or perhaps with some combination of supply and demand curves. Let us write a demand curve as

$$x = \alpha_0 + \alpha_1 p + u \tag{1.2.28}$$

and the corresponding supply curve as

$$x = \beta_0 + \beta_1 p + v, \tag{1.2.29}$$

where x = quantity demanded and supplied, p = price, and u and v = random disturbances. In general, it will not be possible to identify statistical estimates of a linear relation between x and p as estimates of (1.2.28), (1.2.29) or

$$x(\lambda_1 + \lambda_2) = \alpha_0\lambda_1 + \beta_0\lambda_2 + (\alpha_1\lambda_1 + \beta_1\lambda_2)p + \lambda_1 u + \lambda_2 v, \tag{1.2.30}$$

where λ_1 and λ_2 = constants. Even the added information that the demand curve has a negative slope ($\alpha_1 < 0$) and the supply curve a positive slope ($\beta_1 > 0$) is not enough to provide identification because λ_1 and λ_2 are arbitrary. There do exist restrictions or modifications of the model that lead to identification; they will be fully discussed later. However, at this point it is desirable to introduce the concept of identification, for it shows clearly the limitations of a purely empirical approach. The observed correlation between investment and the rate of change of consumption or output is not sufficient to confirm the existence of the acceleration principle unless this relation can be fitted into the large framework of a complete system in which there is identification. In a linear system, this means one in which it is not possible to derive an equation having the same statistical structure as the equation of the acceleration principle by performing linear combinations of other equations in the system. For example, Eqs. (1.2.28)–(1.2.30) are all alike from the statistical point of view; they are all linear relations in x and p subject to a random disturbance. Equation (1.2.30) is a linear combination of (1.2.28) and (1.2.29) that looks like both of its component equations from a statistical point of view. Similarly, all the equations in (1.2.27) appear the same to a statistician. Unless some a priori restrictions can be imposed on the parameters of this equation system, it will not be identified. Identifying types of restrictions will be discussed in subsequent chapters.

Identification is not a statistical concept, and criteria for the existence of identification must be examined before the methods of statistical estimation are applied. Empirical considerations are not ruled out in the sense that a set of econometric equations is developed on the basis of diverse sorts of information —empirical observation, pure theory, knowledge of institutions, and so on. Whatever the source of information, the equations of the system to be tested and estimated must be examined for fulfillment of the criteria of identification.

Questions and Problems

1. If the components of national income (wages, salaries, profit, interest, rent, and so on) and national expenditure (consumption, investment, government outlays, exports, and so on) are each made simple linear functions of gross national product, we observe that each empirical equation shows a high correlation. Formulate, in mathematical terms, an econometric model based on such empirical equations, and compare the system derived with one explicitly constructed from business-cycle and other economic theory.

3. THE CONCEPT OF AUTONOMOUS RELATIONS

Mathematical systems of n equations in n variables can, under fairly general conditions, be reduced to equivalent systems of $n-1$ equations in $n-1$ variables, $n-2$ equations in $n-2$ variables and so on, or even to one equation in one variable. A simple example of this proposition is the following:

$$x = f(y, u) \tag{1.3.1}$$

$$y = g(x, v) \tag{1.3.2}$$

$$x = f[g(x, v), u] = f^*(x, v, u). \tag{1.3.3}$$

Equations (1.3.1) and (1.3.2) describe a set of two equations in two variables, x and y, with random disturbances u and v. Equation (1.3.3) describes one equation in one variable, x, with the same random disturbances. An econometrician may try to make inferences from sample observations to estimate the parameters of f and g separately, or he may try to estimate the parameters of f^* without decomposing them into separate parameters of f and g. In Kalecki's business-cycle model, Eqs. (1.2.20)–(1.2.25) are the individual structural equations, and (1.2.26) is a single dynamic equation in $J(t)$ derived from the other six. The econometrician could estimate the separate parameters of the individual relations in (1.2.20)–(1.2.25) or start out from an equation like (1.2.26). In the latter case, it may be possible to estimate the parameters of (1.2.26) as composites of the parameters in the underlying structural equations without being able to assign separate values to the ultimate set of structural parameters. In a sense, the set (1.2.20)–(1.2.25) is more basic than (1.2.26) because the latter can always be derived from the former. The reverse process is not generally possible.

It sometimes happens that successive elimination of variables yields a single equation in one variable with complicated probability characteristics. We shall find later that independence, in the probability sense, of successive random disturbances in structural equations greatly simplifies statistical estimation. Often original structural equations, assumed to have independent disturbances, do not reduce to a single equation, by elimination processes, with similarly independent disturbances. For this reason, it may be decided not to eliminate equations and variables from an original structural system. In some cases, however, this complication does not arise, and other considerations govern the degree of desirable elimination.

In the theory of the firm in economics, one may study a firm's behavior pattern from its technological production function and factor demand equations; or, one may combine all these equations by an elimination and substitution process into the firm's supply equation of output. The econometrician is faced with the problem of estimating the parameters of the component equations or of the supply equation alone.

The choice is made according to the criteria that the econometrician seeks to estimate structural equations—technological, behavioristic, legal, institutional, definitional equations—and, among the structural set, an *autonomous* set. An autonomous set is one that, in a comparative sense, is not going to change freely in structure. Let us return again to the case of the theory of the firm. The production function and factor demand equations are

$$x = f(n, c, d, v) \qquad \text{production function} \tag{1.3.4}$$

$$\left.\begin{aligned} \frac{\partial f}{\partial n} - \frac{w}{p} &= v_1 && (1.3.5) \\ \frac{\partial f}{\partial c} - \frac{q}{p} &= v_2 && (1.3.6) \\ \frac{\partial f}{\partial d} - \frac{r}{p} &= v_3 && (1.3.7) \end{aligned}\right\} \quad \text{marginal productivity equations}$$

where $x =$ output, $n =$ employment, $c =$ raw materials, $d =$ capital services, $w =$ wage rate, $q =$ price of raw materials, $r =$ price of capital services, and $vs =$ random disturbances. The supply equation is

$$x = g\left(\frac{w}{p}, \frac{q}{p}, \frac{r}{p}, v_1, v_2, v_3, v\right). \tag{1.3.8}$$

In many concrete cases, depending on the algebra involved, the separate disturbances v, v_1, v_2, v_3 in (1.3.8) may be combined into a new disturbance variable u, such that the supply equation can legitimately be written as

$$x = g\left(\frac{w}{p}, \frac{q}{p}, \frac{r}{p}, u\right). \tag{1.3.9}$$

The function g will often lack autonomy. Equations (1.3.5)–(1.3.7) assume that a competitive market prevails. Suppose that some degree of imperfection enters this market. Then Eqs. (1.3.5)–(1.3.7) will be modified, for example, by the introduction of terms involving the elasticity of demand, and the parameters of g will be affected. The function f, on the other hand, will not be affected by this change. If one has estimates of (1.3.4)–(1.3.7), and this type of change occurs, it is possible to pick out those relations that remain unchanged and to modify, in a precise fashion, those that are to be changed. If the only information at our disposal were that contained in estimates of g in (1.3.9) without knowing explicitly its relation to f, it would be difficult or impossible to say what would happen to parameters of g if markets were to become imperfect. The set (1.3.4)–(1.3.7) is more basic than (1.3.9), which is derived from it. In general, the goal is to estimate a set of relations that will remain valid or change in known ways under a wide variety of circumstances. This will be known as structural estimation.

By insisting on following the approach of structural estimation, we come back to a position made above against excessive reliance on empirical findings unguided by a priori analysis. The goal should be to estimate structural relationships that have a high degree of autonomy. There are various stages of model reduction to forms that establish relationships among variables with coefficients that cannot be directly related to a priori structural information, but if it is at all possible, the econometrician should avoid simply trying to estimate empirical versions of reduced relationships and should try to get at the least ambiguous set of structural coefficients.

Another point in the comments of this chapter on the subject matter of econometrics has to do with statistical methodology. There is no unique way of constructing equation systems to describe economic behavior. It has been stressed above that various sources of information are used. Depending upon the sources referred to, the econometrician will start out with a variety of hypothetical systems before the main statistical work has begun. For any given hypothesis, the relevant empirical data are examined to see whether or not this hypothesis is acceptable. Hypotheses that are inconsistent with the sample observations, in a statistical sense, will be rejected as unacceptable. Those that are consistent will be tentatively accepted. If all but one were rejected, we could accept that one as our definite hypothesis, but experience has shown that the sample data usually employed in econometrics are consistent with a variety of hypotheses. The acceptable group is continuously narrowed down by extrapolation of estimated equations to observations beyond the sample point and repeated examination of independent samples of data. Those equations that do not extrapolate well outside the sample or those that do not stand up under repeated estimation in independent samples are gradually rejected.

4. ECONOMIC DATA, THE RAW MATERIALS OF ECONOMETRICS

Theoretical econometrics can exist entirely in the realm of mathematical analysis, but applied econometrics must pay attention to many aspects of realistic economic life, not the least of which is accurate measurement, in a descriptive sense, of the economy. The preparation of data series is not by itself part of the subject matter of econometrics, but it is of the greatest importance to the econometrician user. Results in applied econometrics are no better in quality than the quality of the main inputs.

The principal sources of economic data used by the applied econometrician are the public bodies who gather information for functional purposes such as taxation, regulation, appraisal, or for descriptive purposes to show people how the economy is performing. Among public data sources, the most important, by far, is the system of national income accounts showing much detail about income flows, expenditures, and payments throughout the economy. In some countries, these data come from the central statistical office; in the United States, from the Bureau of Economic Analysis of the U.S. Department of Commerce.

A full analysis of the national income accounts would be incomplete without indexes of prices, wage rates, interest rates, employment levels, acreages, and other magnitudes collected by departments of Labor, Treasury, Agriculture, and others. An entire set of financial statistics comprising the flow of funds accounts, accounting statements of many financial institutions, and money market rates are also of great importance. The Department of Commerce provides statistics of foreign trade, international payments, and census facts, and the Collector of Internal Revenue provides taxation data.

Many of the masses of statistics supplied from federal agencies are supplemented by those coming from supranational organizations (UN, IMF, IBRD, and so on) or from subnational departments in states and cities. The banking system, insurance companies, industrial companies, trade unions all furnish statistics of economic life, some through government, some through trade associations, and some, independently.

A common characteristic of the "official" data series mentioned so far is that they are usually regularly published and are principally intended for purposes other than econometric analysis. This means that the econometrician is, by and large, a user of secondary source material. The concepts shaping the published statistics will often be alien to economic theory and econometric usage. A great deal of data manipulation or data processing will be required before statistics can actually be used for econometric analysis. This is far from being satisfactory. It would be much better if the econometrician were to play a dual role in original data preparation and in data analysis. But data preparation is so time consuming and expensive that it is handled by another group, one that is made up of specialized statistical economists. It is important, though, for the econometrician to become thoroughly familiar with data concepts and data gathering procedures, for these activities will have a powerful bearing on the subsequent analytical work.

Many economic data are unreliable, not comprehensive, or sparse. These shortcomings do not mean that applied econometrics is hopeless. They mean that the econometrician will have to learn to appreciate the difficulties involved in making statistical inferences from relatively poor data. Economists have great experience in discerning order from chaos when working with imperfect information, and econometricians are fortunate in acquiring the traits of this tradition. It does not follow, however, that unsophisticated methods of econometric analysis should be used simply because the data are poor. Every gain is desperately needed for our understanding of economic life, and econometricians should exploit all avenues even though they lead to modest gains because data are relatively poor. The best possible methods should be used at all times, but the econometrician should not be working away in ignorance of the flaws in his basic input material.

Questions and Problems

1. An interesting problem in economic policy is the specification of measures that would raise the prosperity of the agricultural, compared with the nonagricultural, sector of the economy. If an econometrician is assigned the task of measuring relations that would be helpful in this policy application, what are relevant variables and relationships that he would have to consider? What degree of aggregation over sectors of the economy would be dictated by the nature of the problem?

2. What is the degree of autonomy of cost functions? Compare them in this respect to supply functions, production functions, and marginal productivity functions.

3. In the theory of consumer behavior, demand functions for goods and services are derived from utility functions and budget restrictions. Discuss the relative merits and possibilities of estimating the original relations from which the demand equations are derived. Compare the situation in consumer theory with that in the theory of the firm.

SUGGESTED READINGS

Frisch, R., "Propagation Problems and Impulse Problems in Dynamic Economics," in *Economic Essays in Honour of Gustav Cassel*. London: George Allen and Unwin, Ltd., 1933. One of the original and most informative discussions of macrodynamic systems.

Haavelmo, T., "The Probability Approach in Econometrics," *Econometrica*, XII, Supplement (1944). A comprehensive treatment of the theory of econometrics, based on modern developments in probability theory and statistical inference.

Kalecki, M., "A Macrodynamic Theory of Business Cycles," *Econometrica*, III (1935), 327–44. Development of a macrodynamic model.

Klein, L. R., "The Scope and Limitations of Econometrics," *Applied Statistics*, VI

(1957), 1–18. A Statement of the accomplishments of econometrics and the problems faced in the mid fifties.

———, "The Role of Mathematics in Economics," in *The Mathematical Sciences*, 161–75, COSRIMS. Cambridge: MIT Press, 1969. A survey article on the growth of the mathematical method in economics, covering both mathematical economics and econometrics, written for a general audience.

———, "Whither Econometrics?", *The Journal of the American Statistical Association*, 66 (June, 1971), 415–21. Brief survey of past accomplishments and speculative thoughts on directions of the subject in the seventies.

Koopmans, T., "The Logic of Econometric Business Cycle Research," *The Journal of Political Economy*, XLIX (1941), 157–181. A highly readable discussion of econometric methods in business cycle research, stemming from the discussion surrounding Tinbergen's pioneer contributions.

Marschak, J., "Economic Structure, Path, Policy and Prediction," *American Economic Review*, Supplement, Papers and Proceedings, XXXVII (1947), 81–84. A terse nonmathematical statement on the field of econometric research.

———, "Statistical Inference in Economics: An Introduction," in *Statistical Inference in Dynamic Economic Models*, ed. T. Koopmans. New York: John Wiley & Sons, 1950. A rigorous statement of the econometric problem.

Strotz, R. H., "Econometrics," *International Encyclopedia of the Social Sciences*, IV, 350–59, New York: Macmillan and The Free Press, 1968. A comprehensive statement on the state of the subject for the second edition of the *Encyclopedia.*

Tinbergen, J., *An Econometric Approach to Business Cycle Problems*. Paris: Hermann et Cie., 1937. An econometric model of the Dutch economy, one of the first ever developed.

———, *Statistical Testing of Business-Cycle Theories*. Vol. I: *A Method and Its Application to Investment Activity;* Vol. II: *Business Cycles in the United States of America, 1919–1932*. Geneva: League of Nations, 1939. A pioneering study in empirical construction of an econometric model.

2

Statistical Groundwork

1. PROBABILITY

Before we can go into the problems of econometrics, as such, the underlying statistical theory must be explained; and before we can develop the statistical theory, the underlying theory of probability must be explained. Probability and statistics are basic features of econometric analysis and are essential in distinguishing this type of work from mathematical economics.

The axiomatic foundations of probability that go back, in an absolute sense, to first principles rest upon the mathematical theory of sets. We shall not revert to a set-theoretic treatment in these pages because bounds must be set at some point to the contents of a single volume. For most purposes in econometrics, a less rigorous and less modern treatment of probability theory than that developed from the theory of sets will be entirely adequate. Interested students can easily pursue the subject further from references given in the bibliography.

In real world analogies, probability is given a frequency interpretation of the following sort: in a fixed type of experiment E, a variable v_i is defined as

$v_i = 1$ if the event A occurs on the ith performance of E, and

$v_i = 0$ if the event A does not occur on the ith performance of E.

The probability of the event A, written as $P(A)$, is the limiting value approached by $\sum_{i=1}^{n} \frac{v_i}{n}$ as n grows larger and larger. The mathematical expression is

$$\lim_{n\to\infty} \frac{1}{n} \sum_{i=1}^{n} v_i = P(A). \tag{2.1.1}$$

The mathematical theory of probability achieves its greatest generality and rigor if experiments, events, and frequency ratios are replaced by arbitrary sets of points and measures of sets. A useful calculus can best be developed from the idealized mathematical concepts, yet we cannot escape the concept of relative frequency when we consider probability in the real world.

Most examples of probability concepts have traditionally been concerned with coin tossing, games of chance, drawing of balls from an urn, and so on. We get closer to our own experience by pointing out an example from population statistics. Regard an experiment as a birth and the occurrence of the event A as the birth of a female child. We observe thousands and thousands of performances of this experiment every year and find that the event A occurs slightly less than one-half the time, or that

$$\frac{1}{n}\sum_{i=1}^{n} v_i \longrightarrow 0.487.$$

In any short sequence of births, girls can be born much more or less than 48.7 percent of the time, but this is never the case in thousands of repetitions that are *selected at random for observation.* From the impersonal point of view of a statistician who is going to record a large number of repeated births, the probability of a female birth is 0.487. The subjective probability existing in the minds of the parents is another thing, for they are not going to repeat their experiment thousands of times. However, as statisticians and econometricians we are going to view real world processes as detached, impersonal observers, in the most objective sense.

Some of the more important axioms of probability theory can be expressed as:

(2.1.2) $0 \leq P(A) \leq 1$, for any event A,

(2.1.3) $P(A + B + C + \cdots) = P(A) + P(B) + P(C) + \cdots$ for all mutually incompatible events, $A, B, C, \ldots$. Read $A + B + C + \cdots$ as either A or B or C or .... The set of events $A, B, C, \ldots$ may be finite or infinite (denumerable).

(2.1.4) $P(A + B + C + \cdots) = 1$ where $A + B + C + \cdots$ is an exhaustive set of events, a set that exhausts all possible outcomes of the experiment.

According to (2.1.2), probability is expressed as a positive number from zero to unity. If $P(A) = 0$, we say that the event A is practically impossible (not virtually impossible). The relative frequency of occurrence of A, if $P(A) = 0$, will be exceedingly small after numerous repetitions of the experiment producing the event A. On the other hand, $P(A) = 1$ means that A is practically certain. It is altogether obvious that the relative frequency of the occurrence of an event produced in a repeated experiment cannot be less than zero nor greater than unity.

If the event A cannot occur whenever B occurs nor can B occur whenever A occurs, then the relative frequency of the event A or B must be the sum of the relative frequencies of A and of B. Equation (2.1.3) expresses in probability notation that the probability of either A or B or C or . . . is equal to the sum of the respective probabilities of A, B, C, ... In a special case, let $\bar{A}$ denote the nonoccurrence of A. Obviously A and $\bar{A}$ are incompatible (mutually exclusive) and according to (2.1.3)

$$P(A + \bar{A}) = P(A) + P(\bar{A}).$$

We know, moreover, that either A or $\bar{A}$ must occur with practical certainty; therefore,

$$P(A + \bar{A}) = P(A) + P(\bar{A}) = 1.$$

In this case A and $\bar{A}$ are an exhaustive set of mutually exclusive outcomes of the experiment, and the probability of the occurrence of either one or the other must be unity according to (2.1.4).

Equation (2.1.4) is general in that the exhaustive set of events $A + B + C + \cdots$ need not be mutually exclusive. Equation (2.1.4) merely states that some one out of all possible outcomes must occur with practical certainty.

The notation $P(A + B)$ is interpreted as the probability of either A or B. On the other hand, the notation $P(AB)$ means the probability of *both A and B*. It is the joint probability of two events. The *conditional* probability of B, given the occurrence of A, is defined as

$$P(B \mid A) = \frac{P(AB)}{P(A)}. \tag{2.1.5}$$

Equation (2.1.5) can be rewritten as

$$P(B \mid A)P(A) = P(AB), \tag{2.1.5}$$

which breaks up the probability of the joint occurrence of A and B into two components, the probability of B, given A, and the probability of A, regardless of B.

Given the condition that A and B are mutually exclusive, the axiom contained in (2.1.3) equates $P(A + B)$ to the sum, $P(A) + P(B)$. It seems natural to inquire into the conditions enabling us to write

$$P(AB) = P(A)P(B). \tag{2.1.6}$$

Obviously if

$$P(B) = P(B \mid A), \tag{2.1.7}$$

then (2.1.5) gives

$$P(AB) = P(A)P(B). \tag{2.1.6}$$

Equation (2.1.7) states that the probability of B, given A, is the same as the probability of B, regardless of A; therefore, we interpret (2.1.7) as meaning that A and B are *independent*. The concept of independence is expressed equally well in (2.1.6) or (2.1.7).

An elegant formula connecting $P(A + B)$ and $P(AB)$ with no assumptions about independence or incompatibility is given by

$$P(A + B) = P(A) + P(B) - P(AB). \tag{2.1.8}$$

A geometrical demonstration of the validity of this formula may be of some interest because it will serve also as a basis for demonstrating some of the preceding propositions and will give a hint about the set theoretic approach to probability.

The space E consists of a large collection of elements (points), with A and B as subsets of E. The experiment consists of selecting points at random from E. The event A will be said to occur if a selected point of E belongs to A. Similarly, B occurs if a selected point belongs to B.

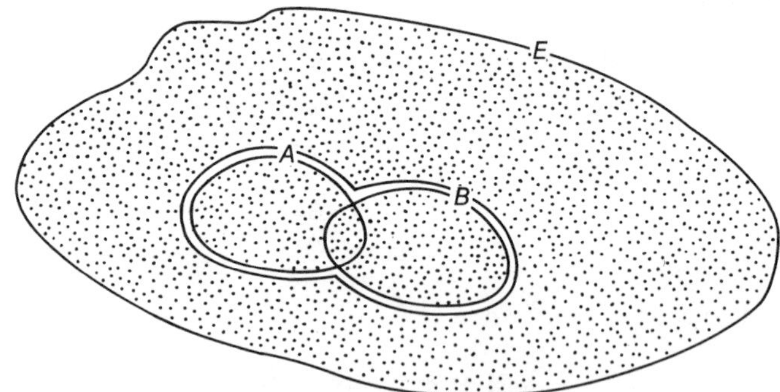

Figure 2.1.1

There are n points in E, n_A in A and n_B in B.

$$P(A) = \frac{n_A}{n}, \qquad \text{and} \tag{2.1.9}$$

$$P(B) = \frac{n_B}{n} \tag{2.1.10}$$

give the elementary probabilities.

The probability that a selected point belongs to either A or B is given by the ratio of the points in the area enclosed by the double line to n. The number of points in this area is evidently equal to $n_A + n_B - n_{AB}$, where n_{AB} is the set of points in the area common to both A and B. Thus

$$\frac{n_A + n_B - n_{AB}}{n} = P(A) + P(B) - P(AB) = P(A + B) \qquad (2.1.11)$$

because

$$P(AB) = \frac{n_{AB}}{n}, \text{ by the definition of } P(AB) \text{ and } n_{AB}. \qquad (2.1.12)$$

If the subsets, A and B, did not intersect, that is, were mutually exclusive, there would be no such area and no points common to them. In this case we would have $n_{AB} = 0$, and

$$P(A + B) = P(A) + P(B) = \frac{n_A + n_B}{n}. \qquad (2.1.13)$$

Conditional probabilities are given a geometrical interpretation as

$$P(A \mid B) = \frac{n_{AB}}{n_B} \qquad (2.1.14)$$

$$P(B \mid A) = \frac{n_{AB}}{n_A}. \qquad (2.1.15)$$

From (2.1.9), (2.1.12), and (2.1.15) we verify

$$P(AB) = P(B \mid A)P(A) \text{ as}$$

$$\frac{n_{AB}}{n} = \frac{n_{AB}}{n_A}\frac{n_A}{n}.$$

Classical examples of the various probability concepts are provided by the calculations of the several chances in the throwing of dice. To achieve the idealized results of the mathematical probability calculus, we assume that we have a perfect die thrown perfectly on a perfectly flat surface. Call A the occurrence of a "three" in the throw of a single die, then $P(A) = \frac{1}{6}$. After many repeated throws, the fraction of cases showing a "three" face should differ little from $\frac{1}{6}$. The occurrence of the turning up of any one of the other five faces of the die carries the same probability. This is the classical case of *equally likely* events. Call B the occurrence of a "two" in the throw of a single die, then

$$P(A + B) = P(A) + P(B) = \tfrac{2}{6} = \tfrac{1}{3}.$$

Of the six equally likely events, one represents the occurrence of A and one represents the occurrence of B; thus, the probability of either A or B is $\frac{2}{6}$. The same result is obtained by regarding A and B as mutually exclusive and adding their respective probabilities,

$$\tfrac{1}{6} + \tfrac{1}{6} = \tfrac{2}{6}.$$

Now consider a new experiment consisting of two throws of the die, A being the turning up of "three" on the first throw and B being the turning up of "two" on the second throw. Enumeration of the possible cases shows

$$P(AB) = P(A)P(B) = \tfrac{1}{36}.$$

There are 36 possible results in the throwing of a single die twice; only one of them consists of a "three" followed by a "two." The result $\frac{1}{36}$ could also be obtained by performing the multiplication $\frac{1}{6} \times \frac{1}{6}$, because A and B are independent events.

Questions and Problems

1. Let $A_1, A_2, A_3, \ldots A_n$ be a set of mutually incompatible events. If for any two events

$$P(A_i + A_j) = P(A_i) + P(A_j),$$

show that

$$P\left(\sum_{i=1}^{n} A_i\right) = \sum_{i=1}^{n} P(A_i).$$

2. Using the formula

$$P(A_1A_2) = P(A_1 \mid A_2)P(A_2),$$

decompose $P(A_1A_2A_3 \ldots A_n)$ into a product of conditional and marginal probabilities such that each conditional probability gives the probability of occurrence of a single event for assumed values of other events, and the marginal probability gives the probability of the other events.

3. The children of a family consist of two boys and one girl. What is the probability that an expected new child will be a boy? Does this question differ from the following: What is the probability that the children of this family, before they have had any births, would ultimately consist of two girls and two boys?

4. What is the probability of throwing "five" with two dice (the sum of the exposed faces)?

5. Show by probability calculations the rationale of ordering winning poker hands in dealing five cards from a deck of 52, as

(a) one pair
(b) two pair
(c) three of a kind
(d) straight (uninterrupted sequence of five cards from lowest to highest)
(e) flush (five cards in one suit)
(f) full house (a pair and three of a kind)
(g) four of a kind
(h) straight flush (uninterrupted sequence of five cards in one suit)
(i) royal flush (ace, king, queen, jack, ten in the same suit).

2. DISTRIBUTIONS

Related to the basic concept of probability is the notion of a probability distribution. If we are concerned with a random variable that can assume values x_i only at discrete points, we associate a probability value p_i to the occurrence of $\xi = x_i$. The probability distribution, in this case, may be written as

$$P(\xi = x_i) = p_i. \tag{2.2.1}$$

The distribution has the further property

$$\sum_i p_i = 1. \tag{2.2.2}$$

For the die casting example we have

$$\begin{aligned} P(\xi = \text{"one"}) &= \tfrac{1}{6} = p_1, \\ P(\xi = \text{"two"}) &= \tfrac{1}{6} = p_2, \\ &\vdots \\ P(\xi = \text{"six"}) &= \tfrac{1}{6} = p_6, \\ p_1 + p_2 + \cdots + p_6 &= 6(\tfrac{1}{6}) = 1. \end{aligned}$$

On the other hand ξ may be a continuous variable, and we write[1]

$$P(a < \xi \leq b) = F(b) - F(a) \tag{2.2.3}$$

[1] Equation (2.2.3), in particular, holds as well for discrete variables. The subsequent development could also be made for discrete variables, if we were to generalize the concept of integration used.

as the probability that ξ is contained in the interval from a to b. $F(b)$ is called the cumulative probability function giving the probability that ξ is contained in the infinite interval from $-\infty$ to b. Similarly, $F(a)$ is the cumulative probability covering the interval from $-\infty$ to a. We define $p(\xi)$ as a *probability density function* if for any a and b

$$P(a < \xi \leq b) = \int_a^b p(\xi)\, d\xi. \tag{2.2.4}$$

By the mean value theorem,

$$\int_a^b p(\xi)\, d\xi = p(\xi')(b - a),$$

where ξ' lies in the interval (a, b). Consider now the interval from x to $x + \Delta x$ ($\Delta x =$ increment of x). The application of the mean value theorem and (2.2.4) to this interval yields

$$\begin{gathered} P(x < \xi \leq x + \Delta x) = p(x + \theta\Delta x)\, \Delta x, \\ 0 < \theta < 1, \\ \text{or} \\ P(x < \xi \leq x + \Delta x) = p(x)\Delta x + o(\Delta x). \end{gathered} \tag{2.2.5}$$

The term $o(\Delta x)$ has the property

$$\lim_{\Delta x \to 0} \frac{o(\Delta x)}{\Delta x} = 0;$$

therefore

$$\lim_{\Delta x \to 0} \frac{P(x < \xi \leq x + \Delta x)}{\Delta x} = p(x), \tag{2.2.6}$$

and we write $p(x)\, dx$ as an infinitesimal *probability element*. The continuous function $p(x)$, the probability density function, satisfies

$$\int_{-\infty}^{\infty} p(x)\, dx = 1. \tag{2.2.7}$$

In other words, the area under the density function must be unity. In the notation of cumulative probabilities we have

$$F(\infty) = 1,$$

and

$$F(-\infty) = 0.$$

Because

$$\lim_{\Delta x \to \infty} \frac{P(x < \xi \le x + \Delta x)}{\Delta x} = \lim_{\Delta x \to 0} \frac{F(x + \Delta x) - F(x)}{\Delta x} = \frac{dF(x)}{dx},$$

we find that

$$\frac{dF(x)}{dx} = p(x) \tag{2.2.8}$$

gives the relation between the cumulative distribution and density function. We may also express the cumulative distribution function by integrating (2.2.8), as

$$F(x) = P(\xi \le x) = \int_{-\infty}^{x} p(y)\, dy.$$

These results hold for the continuous case. For discrete variables we have as the definition of the cumulative distribution function

$$F(x) = P(\xi \le x) = \sum_{x_i \le x} p_i. \tag{2.2.9}$$

Let us now turn to some illustrations to make these ideas as clear as possible. The empirical counterpart of a probability distribution is a relative frequency distribution. The 1969 distribution of United States families by age of head provides a useful example.

Age is a continuous variable, ξ, and is presented in six classes in the Table (2.2.1) only for convenience. If we imagine the fraction of cases (relative frequencies) in an age class to be concentrated at the midpoint, we have the analogue of the discrete distribution in (2.2.1)–(2.2.2). The relative frequencies sum to unity in the table according to (2.2.2).

The cumulative (relative) frequency distribution for the same variable is given in the next table.

In many cases it is found convenient to transform a random variable into another variable and then work with the latter. For example, instead of ξ, it may be preferable to change to

$$\theta = g(\xi). \tag{2.2.10}$$

We shall restrict the transformation function $g(\xi)$ to being monotonic with a unique inverse. If ξ is a random variable, then any function of ξ is also a random variable. In particular, θ is a random variable. The probability element of ξ is expressed as $p(x)\, dx$. What is the corresponding probability element of θ? By (2.2.4), we have

$$P(a < \xi \le b) = \int_{a}^{b} p(\xi)\, d\xi.$$

TABLE (2.2.1)

Distribution of All Heads of Families in the United States by Age, 1969

Age group	*Fraction of cases*
14–24 years	0.07
25–34	0.21
35–44	0.21
45–54	0.21
55–64	0.16
65 and over	0.14
	1.00

Source: U.S. Department of Commerce, Bureau of the Census, *Current Population Reports,* Series P–60, No. 75, December 14, 1970.

TABLE (2.2.2)

Cumulative Distribution of All Heads of Families in the United States by Age, 1969

Age group	*Fraction of cases*
Less than	
25 years	0.07
35	0.28
45	0.49
55	0.70
65	0.86
Oldest family head	1.00

Our problem then is to change the variable of integration from ξ to $\theta = g(\xi)$. This can be done by a well known device for transformation of variables in integral calculus.

$$\int_a^b p(\xi)\, d\xi = \int_{g(a)}^{g(b)} p(\xi) \frac{1}{g'(\xi)}\, d\theta.$$

Following an argument like that used in (2.2.4)–(2.2.5) above, we can write the probability elements of each side as

$$\begin{aligned} p(x)\, dx &= p(x) \left| \frac{1}{g'(x)} \right| dy \\ &= p(x) \left| \frac{dx}{dy} \right| dy, \text{ where} \\ y &= g(x). \end{aligned} \tag{2.2.11}$$

The absolute value of $\left|\frac{dx}{dy}\right|$ is used in (2.2.11) because the function $g(x)$ could have a negative derivative. Probability is confined to positive values. Formula (2.2.11) thus gives a method whereby we may obtain the probability density function of θ from a knowledge of the density function of ξ and the transformation carrying ξ into θ. The density function of ξ is given by $p(x)$. The transformation function g tells us how to replace x by y and how to calculate $\frac{dx}{dy}$. In the right-hand side of (2.2.11), we may ultimately eliminate x by substituting $x = g^{-1}(y)$.

Probability distributions can be generalized into functions of many variables. The bivariate case is sufficiently interesting in itself, however, to justify separate treatment. If we are dealing with two continuous random variables simultaneously, ξ and η, their joint probability element is given in symbolic fashion by

$$P(x < \xi < x + dx, y < \eta < y + dy) = p(x, y)\, dx\, dy. \tag{2.2.12}$$

The volume under this surface, $p(x, y)$, is made equal to unity in

$$\int_{-\infty}^{\infty}\int_{-\infty}^{\infty} p(x, y)\, dy\, dx = 1. \tag{2.2.13}$$

The function $p(x, y)$ in the theory of distributions is the counterpart of $P(AB)$ in the theory of probability of elementary events. $p(x, y)$ is the joint probability of both ξ and η. The bivariate cumulative distribution function is defined as

$$F(x, y) = P(\xi \leq x, \eta \leq y) = \int_{-\infty}^{x}\int_{-\infty}^{y} p(z, w)\, dw\, dz. \tag{2.2.14}$$

The conditional distribution of ξ, given $y < \eta < y + dy$ is written as

$$\begin{aligned} P(x < \xi < x + dx \mid y < \eta < y + dy) &\\ &= \frac{P(x < \xi < x + dx, y < \eta < y + dy)}{P(y < \eta < y + dy)} \\ &= \frac{p(x, y)\, dy\, dx}{\left[\int_{-\infty}^{\infty} p(x, y)\, dx\right] dy} \\ &= \frac{p(x, y)\, dy\, dx}{p^*(y)\, dy} = p_1(x \mid y)\, dx. \end{aligned} \tag{2.2.15}$$

This formula is the analogue of (2.1.5), developed above. The function $p_1(x \mid y)$ is called the conditional probability density function, and $p^*(y)$ is called the marginal probability density function. The former gives the probability that ξ is contained in an interval, given that η is in a certain interval, and the latter gives the probability that η is contained in an interval regardless of the value of

ξ. The integral

$$\left[\int_{-\infty}^{\infty} p(x, y)\, dx\right] dy = p^*(y)\, dy$$

satisfies this definition because it allows the x variable to be anywhere between plus or minus infinity.

The concepts of conditional, marginal, and joint probability distributions are extremely important in future work and must be made clear at the outset. An example from studies of family population characteristics should help to illustrate the meanings of these concepts.

The second half of Table (2.2.3) presents the joint relative frequency dis-

TABLE (2.2.3)

Distribution of Income by Age of Head of Family, 1969
(*Distribution of Family Units*)

Income class	Age groups *14–24*	*25–34*	*35–44*	*45–54*	*55–64*	*65 and over*
Under $3,000	0.147	0.055	0.043	0.047	0.088	0.274
3,000–3,999	0.083	0.037	0.029	0.031	0.046	0.140
4,000–4,999	0.090	0.045	0.034	0.037	0.054	0.106
5,000–5,999	0.110	0.058	0.048	0.041	0.058	0.083
6,000–6,999	0.104	0.075	0.054	0.050	0.064	0.066
7,000–7,999	0.113	0.087	0.066	0.059	0.075	0.060
8,000–9,999	0.167	0.190	0.151	0.125	0.141	0.087
10,000–11,999	0.097	0.170	0.158	0.137	0.110	0.057
12,000–14,999	0.065	0.151	0.178	0.168	0.130	0.049
15,000–24,999	0.022	0.121	0.199	0.239	0.178	0.056
25,000 and over	—	0.012	0.039	0.065	0.056	0.021
	1.00	1.00	1.00	1.00	1.00	1.00
	Joint relative frequency distribution of income and age					
Under $3,000	0.01029	0.01155	0.00903	0.00987	0.01408	0.03836
3,000–3,999	0.00581	0.00777	0.00609	0.00651	0.00736	0.01960
4,000–4,999	0.00630	0.00945	0.00714	0.00777	0.00864	0.01484
5,000–5,999	0.00770	0.01218	0.01008	0.00861	0.00928	0.01162
6,000–6,999	0.00728	0.01575	0.01134	0.01050	0.01024	0.00924
7,000–7,999	0.00791	0.01827	0.01386	0.01239	0.01200	0.00840
8,000–9,999	0.01169	0.03990	0.03171	0.02625	0.02256	0.01218
10,000–11,999	0.00679	0.03570	0.03318	0.02877	0.01760	0.00798
12,000–14,999	0.00455	0.03171	0.03738	0.03528	0.02080	0.00686
15,000–24,999	0.00154	0.02541	0.04179	0.05019	0.02848	0.00784
25,000 and over	—	0.00252	0.00819	0.01365	0.00896	0.00294

Source: U.S. Department of Commerce, Bureau of the Census, *Current Population Reports* Series P-60, No. 75, Tables 16 and 17.

tribution of the income and age. The entries in this table add up to unity. Any cell of the table shows the fraction of cases that simultaneously lie between the age limits of the column heading and the income limits of the row heading. The first half of this table is the conditional relative frequency distribution of income given age. It shows the distribution of income in any given age class. If age is fixed within class limits, then income is distributed (approximately) according to the figures given in the column associated with these class limits. The first half of Table (2.2.3) actually gives six conditional distributions, each corresponding to different age limits. Each of the conditional distributions adds to unity over the range of variation, as illustrated by the fact that each of the column totals is 1.00. In Table (2.2.1) presented earlier, we have an example of the univariate distribution of age. This distribution holds regardless of income level; therefore, it is the marginal relative frequency distribution of age. The cells in the lower half of Table (2.2.3) can be computed as products of elements of the marginal and conditional distributions. The figures in the first column of the second half of the table are equal to the product of the figure in the first row of Table (2.2.1) 0.07 and each of the figures in the first column of the first half of Table (2.2.3) This multiplication process is carried out for discrete intervals, according to the rules given in (2.2.15) for getting a joint distribution from conditional and marginal distributions.

The method of transforming variables in bivariate probability distributions brings in some new problems. The two primary random variables are ξ and η. They are transformed into ϵ and θ by

$$\begin{aligned} \epsilon &= f(\xi, \eta) \\ \theta &= g(\xi, \eta). \end{aligned} \tag{2.2.16}$$

Paralleling the assumption, in the univariate case, that the transformation (2.2.10) is monotonic with a unique inverse, we require here that the bivariate transformation is *one-to-one*. To each pair of admissible values of ξ and η, there corresponds only one pair of values of ϵ and θ. Conversely, to each pair of admissible values of ϵ and θ there corresponds only one pair of values of ξ and η. How is the joint probability element of ϵ and θ related to that of ξ and η?

The result is simply a generalization of (2.2.11), using the technique of transforming variables in multiple integration. The result, stated without proof, is[2]

$$P(a_1 < \xi \leq b_2, a_2 < \eta \leq b_2) = \int_{a_1}^{b_1}\int_{a_2}^{b_2} p(\xi, \eta)\, d\eta\, d\xi.$$

$$\int_{a_1}^{b_1}\int_{a_2}^{b_2} p(\xi, \eta)\, d\eta\, d\xi = \int_{d_1}^{c_1}\int_{d_2(\epsilon)}^{c_2(\epsilon)} p(\xi, \eta)\frac{\partial(\xi, \eta)}{\partial(\epsilon, \theta)}\, d\theta\, d\epsilon.$$

[2] A clear presentation of the general method of transforming variables can be found, for example, in R. S. Burington and C. C. Torrance, *Higher Mathematics* (New York: McGraw-Hill Book Co., 1939), pp. 260–62.

The limits of integration in the (ϵ, θ) plane are chosen to cover, in this plane, the image of the rectangular area $(a_1 < \xi \leq b_1,\ a_2 < \eta \leq b_2)$ from the (ξ, η) plane. The image of the rectangular area is produced by the transformation functions (2.2.16). The expression

$$\frac{\partial(\xi, \eta)}{\partial(\epsilon, \theta)}$$

is called the Jacobian of the transformation carrying ξ and η into ϵ and θ. The transformation is given explicitly in (2.2.16), and the evaluation of the Jacobian leads to

$$\frac{\partial(\xi, \eta)}{\partial(\epsilon, \theta)} = \begin{vmatrix} \dfrac{\partial \xi}{\partial \epsilon} & \dfrac{\partial \xi}{\partial \theta} \\[2ex] \dfrac{\partial \eta}{\partial \epsilon} & \dfrac{\partial \eta}{\partial \theta} \end{vmatrix} = \frac{1}{\dfrac{\partial f}{\partial \xi}\dfrac{\partial g}{\partial \eta} - \dfrac{\partial f}{\partial \eta}\dfrac{\partial g}{\partial \xi}}.$$

The probability elements transform according to

$$p(x, y)\, dx\, dy = p(x, y) \left| \frac{\partial(x, y)}{\partial(w, z)} \right| dw\, dz. \tag{2.2.17}$$

The Jacobian in (2.2.17) is obviously given by

$$\frac{1}{\dfrac{\partial f}{\partial x}\dfrac{\partial g}{\partial y} - \dfrac{\partial f}{\partial y}\dfrac{\partial g}{\partial x}},$$

because x and y are carried into w and z by the two transformations in (2.2.16).

The whole theory of probability distributions carries a straightforward generalization to multivariate schemes. Let $\xi_1, \xi_2, \ldots, \xi_n$ be a set of random variables. The multivariate probability element is defined by

$$\begin{aligned} &P(x_1 < \xi_1 < x_1 + dx_1, x_2 < x_2 + dx_2, \\ &\ldots x_n < \xi_n < x_n + dx_n) = p(x_1, x_2, \ldots, x_n)\, dx_1\, dx_2 \ldots dx_n. \end{aligned} \tag{2.2.18}$$

We call p the joint probability density function. The unit area (volume in n dimensions) restriction becomes

$$\int_{-\infty}^{\infty} \int_{-\infty}^{\infty} \cdots \int_{-\infty}^{\infty} p(x_1, x_2, \ldots, x_n) dx_1\, dx_2 \ldots dx_n = 1. \tag{2.2.19}$$

The relation between marginal and conditional distributions may be written as

$$p_1(x_1 \mid x_2, x_3, \ldots, x_n) p^*(x_2, x_3, \ldots, x_n) = p(x_1, x_2, \ldots, x_n). \tag{2.2.20}$$

The marginal density p^* is also a function of several variables, $n - 1$ in fact, and can be written as the product of conditional and marginal density function. Carrying this process to its ultimate step we find

$$p_1(x_1 \mid x_2, x_3, \ldots, x_n)p_2(x_2 \mid x_3, x_4, \ldots, x_n) \\ p_3(x_3 \mid x_4, x_5, \ldots, x_n). \ldots . p_n(x_n) = p(x_1, x_2, \ldots, x_n), \tag{2.2.21}$$

or

$$\prod_{i=1}^{n} p_i(x_i \mid x_{i+1}, x_{i+2}, \ldots, x_n) = p(x_1, x_2, \ldots, x_n).$$

A cumulative distribution function in n dimensions is obviously

$$F(x_1, x_2, \ldots, x_n) \\ = \int_{-\infty}^{x_1} \int_{-\infty}^{x_2} \cdots \int_{-\infty}^{x_n} (y_1, y_2, \ldots, y_n)\, dy_1\, dy_2 \ldots dy_n. \tag{2.2.22}$$

If the random variables $\xi_1, \xi_2, \ldots, \xi_n$ are transformed into $\eta_1, \eta_2, \ldots, \eta_n$ by the set of equations

$$\eta_i = f_i(\xi_1, \xi_2, \ldots, \xi_n), \qquad i = 1, 2, \ldots, n,$$

then the joint probability element of the ξ_i variables is transformed into the joint probability element of the η_i variables by the relation

$$p(x_1, x_2, \ldots, x_n)\, dx_1\, dx_2 \ldots dx_n \\ = p(x_1, x_2, \ldots, x_n) \left| \frac{\partial(x_1, x_2, \ldots, x_n)}{\partial(y_1, y_2, \ldots, y_n)} \right| dy_1\, dy_2 \ldots dy_n,$$

where

$$y_i = f_i(x_1, x_2, \ldots, x_n), \qquad i = 1, 2, \ldots, n,$$

and

$$\frac{\partial(x_1, x_2, \ldots, x_n)}{\partial(y_1, y_2, \ldots, y_n)} = \begin{vmatrix} \frac{\partial x_1}{\partial y_1} & \frac{\partial x_1}{\partial y_2} & \cdots & \frac{\partial x_1}{\partial y_n} \\ \frac{\partial x_2}{\partial y_1} & \frac{\partial x_2}{\partial y_2} & \cdots & \frac{\partial x_2}{\partial y_n} \\ \vdots & & & \vdots \\ \frac{\partial x_n}{\partial y_1} & \frac{\partial x_n}{\partial y_2} & \cdots & \frac{\partial x_n}{\partial y_n} \end{vmatrix} = \begin{vmatrix} \frac{\partial f_1}{\partial x_1} & \frac{\partial f_2}{\partial x_1} & \cdots & \frac{\partial f_n}{\partial x_1} \\ \frac{\partial f_1}{\partial x_2} & \frac{\partial f_2}{\partial x_2} & \cdots & \frac{\partial f_n}{\partial x_2} \\ \vdots & & & \vdots \\ \frac{\partial f_1}{\partial x_n} & \frac{\partial f_2}{\partial x_n} & \cdots & \frac{\partial f_n}{\partial x_n} \end{vmatrix}^{-1}.$$

Thus

$$\frac{\partial(x_1, x_2, \ldots, x_n)}{\partial(y_1, y_2, \ldots, y_n)}$$

is an nth order Jacobian determinant and is equal to the inverse of the Jacobian of the f_i transformation functions.

We shall not go into bivariate and multivariate extensions for discrete distributions, but the student should have little trouble in performing these generalizations by analogy with the continuous case.

Questions and Problems

1. Given the probability density function $p(x)$ and the corresponding cumulative distribution function

$$z = F(y) = \int_{-\infty}^{y} p(x)\,dx, \qquad \text{(a)}$$

find the density function of z, regarded as a variable related to y by the transformation in (*a*) (probability integral transformation).

2. Plot a graph of the cumulative distribution function corresponding to the six elementary probabilities of the appearance of the different faces on a die, given on p. 31. How would you characterize this function? Is it continuous? Plot also a graph of the cumulative distribution function of a continuous random variable.

3. Lorenz curves of income distribution show the percentage of aggregate income (ordinate) accruing to each percentage of recipients (abscissa). Give an analytical expression for such curves in terms of income distribution or density functions. What is the Lorenz curve of equal income distribution, n percent of recipients having n per cent of total income?

3. MOMENTS

The statistician and mathematician must look for convenient summaries of the contents of probability or frequency distributions. The complete distributions may become unwieldy in analytical work; therefore, we must turn to a method of boiling down the information to bare essentials. Characteristics of a distribution that are commonly used for summary presentation are *moments*. The ith moment of a univariate continuous distribution is defined as

$$E(\xi^i) = \int_{-\infty}^{\infty} x^i\, p(x)\,dx. \tag{2.3.1}$$

Equation (2.3.1) reads, on the left-hand side, "the mathematical expectation of the ith power of the random variable ξ." The right-hand side evaluates the mathematical expectation as the arithmetic mean of the ith powers of the values x assumed by the random variable ξ. If $i = 0$, (2.3.1) becomes

$$\int_{-\infty}^{\infty} p(x)\,dx = 1$$

by (2.2.7) above. A familiar case to all is that for $i = 1$. Then we have

$$E(\xi) = \int_{-\infty}^{\infty} xp(x)\, dx = \mu_1, \tag{2.3.2}$$

in which the mathematical expection of ξ is defined as the mean of the distribution. In the event that the distribution is discrete, we have

$$E(\xi) = \sum_{i=1}^{\infty} x_i p_i, \tag{2.3.3}$$

where we weight each x_i by its chance of occurrence. In calculating arithmetic means from frequency distributions, we go through the steps of (2.3.3) (except that p_i is replaced by the empirical relative frequency), which are finite in number.

The ith moment defined in (2.3.1) is calculated in terms of deviations from a zero origin, that is,

$$E(\xi^i) = E((\xi - 0)^i).$$

But if we choose the mean of the distribution as the point of origin the ith moment becomes

$$E((\xi - \mu_1)^i) = \int_{-\infty}^{\infty} (x - \mu_1)^i p(x) dx, \tag{2.3.4}$$

which is called the ith *central* moment of the distribution. Readers will recognize the second central moment, or variance, of the distribution,

$$E((\xi - \mu_1)^2) = \int_{-\infty}^{\infty} (x - \mu_1)^2 p(x)\, dx = \sigma^2. \tag{2.3.5}$$

By expanding the squared term under the integral sign and integrating term by term we find

$$\int_{-\infty}^{\infty} (x^2 - 2\mu_1 x + \mu_1^2)p(x)\, dx = \int_{-\infty}^{\infty} x^2 p(x)\, dx - \mu_1^2 = E(\xi^2) - \mu_1^2,$$

thus establishing a relation between the second moment about the mean and the first two moments about zero. By applying simple formulas of algebra and calculus, the reader can establish further relationships between higher order moments about the mean and about zero.

The square root of the variance is known as the *standard deviation*, a measure of the dispersion of a distribution. In calculating standard deviations or variances of empirical frequency distributions, one would use the discrete companion to (2.3.5) with relative frequencies replacing the probability densities.

The simplest formula would be

$$\sigma = \sqrt{\sum_i p_i x_i^2 - (\sum_i p_i x_i)^2}. \tag{2.3.6}$$

The first term under the radical is the weighted sum of squares of the distribution, the weights being probabilities of occurrence of x_i, or relative frequencies in empirical work. The second term is simply the square of the weighted sum of the x_i, the square of the mean.

A distribution is completely described by its moments. Some distributions are described by a small or finite number of moments, and others require an unlimited number for a complete description. Other properties of the distribution, besides the moments, are of interest also. The range is relevant. Some distributions go from plus to minus infinity in the x value; others are confined to the positive part of the x axis (0 to $+\infty$); others are confined to a finite range; and so on. The range of a set of empirical data is a measure of dispersion. A frequently used set of characteristics of a distribution is that defining *quartile* points. Perhaps the best known is the *median* point that divides a distribution into two *quantiles*, each quantile associated with 50 percent of the area under the probability distribution. The value of x satisfying

$$\int_x^\infty p(x)\,dx = \int_{-\infty}^x p(x)\,dx = \tfrac{1}{2} \tag{2.3.7}$$

is the median of the distribution. Quartile points are defined by

$$\begin{aligned} \int_{-\infty}^{Q_1} p(x)\,dx &= \tfrac{1}{4}, \\ \int_{-\infty}^{Q_2} p(x)\,dx &= \tfrac{1}{2}, \\ \int_{-\infty}^{Q_3} p(x)\,dx &= \tfrac{3}{4}. \end{aligned} \tag{2.3.8}$$

Q_2, the second quartile point, coincides with the median. Decile and percentile points are analogously defined.

In certain applications it is important to know the relationship of moments of simple functions of variables to the moments of the variables themselves. Two random variables ξ and η are distributed according to $p(x)$ and $f(y)$ respectively. What is the relation between $E(\xi + \eta)$, $E(\xi)$, and $E(\eta)$?

The following relations hold:

$$\begin{aligned} E(\xi + \eta) &= \int_{-\infty}^\infty xp(x)\,dx + \int_{-\infty}^\infty yf(y)\,dy = E(\xi) + E(\eta), \\ E(\xi - \eta) &= E(\xi) - E(\eta), \\ E(a + b\xi + c\eta) &= a + bE(\xi) + cE(\eta), \qquad a, b, c = \text{constants}, \\ E(\xi\eta) &= E(\xi)E(\eta) \qquad \text{if } \xi \text{ and } \eta \text{ are } \textit{independent}. \end{aligned} \tag{2.3.9}$$

The same types of relations can be developed for second moments about the mean as an origin.

$$\begin{aligned} E[(\xi - E(\xi)) \pm (\eta - E(\eta))]^2 &= E(\xi - E(\xi))^2 + E(\eta - E(\eta))^2 \\ &\qquad \text{if } \xi \text{ and } \eta \text{ are independent,} \\ E[a(\xi - E(\xi)) \pm b(\eta - E(\eta))]^2 &= a^2E(\xi - E(\xi))^2 \\ &\quad + b^2E(\eta - E(\eta))^2 \quad \text{if } \xi \text{ and } \eta \text{ are independent.} \end{aligned} \tag{2.3.10}$$

The equations in (2.3.10) state that the variance of a sum or difference of random variables is the sum of the separate variances. The second part of (2.3.10) generalizes this formula to linear combinations. It is essential to remember that these relations hold good only if ξ and η are independent; otherwise, covariances showing interdependence between ξ and η must enter in addition to the variances.

If the last part of (2.3.10) is extended to the case of n independent random variables, $\xi_1, \xi_2, \ldots, \xi_n$ we get

$$\begin{aligned} E\left[\sum_{i=1}^{n} a_i(\xi_i - E(\xi_i))\right]^2 &= \sum_{i=1}^{n} a_i^2 E(\xi_i - E(\xi_i))^2 \\ &= \sum_{i=1}^{n} a_i^2\sigma_i^2, \end{aligned} \tag{2.3.11}$$

where σ_i^2 = variance of ξ_i. In particular if $a_i = 1/n$ and $\sigma_i^2 = \sigma^2$

$$E\left[\frac{1}{n}\sum_{i=1}^{n} (\xi_i - E(\xi_i))\right]^2 = \frac{1}{n}\sigma^2,$$

which is the expression for the variance of a mean of independent random variables. This formula is very important in sampling and other applications.

The formulas for moments admit of a simple extension from univariate to bivariate distributions. In the general bivariate case, moments are defined as

$$E(\xi^i\eta^j) = \int_{-\infty}^{\infty}\int_{-\infty}^{\infty} x^i y^j p(x, y)\,dy\,dx. \tag{2.3.12}$$

If we assign $j = 0$, (2.3.12) becomes

$$\int_{-\infty}^{\infty}\int_{-\infty}^{\infty} x^i p(x, y)\,dy\,dx = \int_{-\infty}^{\infty} x^i p^*(x)\,dx = E(\xi^i),$$

where p^* is the marginal density function of x. From the marginal distribution, we can get the univariate moments. Another interesting case arises when we have $i = j = 1$. The moment for this case, about the respective mean values, is

$$\begin{aligned} &E[(\xi - E(\xi))(\eta - E(\eta))] \\ &\quad = \int_{-\infty}^{\infty}\int_{-\infty}^{\infty} (x - \mu_1)(y - \mu_2)p(x, y)\,dy\,dx, \end{aligned} \tag{2.3.13}$$

where $\mu_1 = E(\xi)$ and $\mu_2 = E(\eta)$.[3] The variances of ξ and η are defined as

$$\begin{aligned} E(\xi - E(\xi))^2 &= \int_{-\infty}^{\infty} (x - \mu_1)^2 p^*(x)\, dx, \\ E(\eta - E(\eta))^2 &= \int_{-\infty}^{\infty} (y - \mu_2)^2 p^{**}(y)\, dy. \end{aligned} \tag{2.3.14}$$

The starred functions are marginal density functions of ξ and η respectively. The correlation between ξ and μ is then given by

$$\rho = \frac{E[(\xi - E(\xi))(\eta - E(\eta))]}{\sqrt{E(\xi - E(\xi))^2 E(\eta - E(\eta))^2}} \tag{2.3.15}$$

We shall find these concepts of the greatest importance in empirical investigations.

There is no reason to stop at the bivariate case, for all the moment concepts carry over in a straightforward manner to multivariate schemes. The general formula for moments of a joint distribution of $\xi_1, \xi_2, \ldots, \xi_n$ is

$$\begin{aligned} &E(\xi_1^{i_1}\xi_2^{i_2} \cdots \xi_n^{i_n}) \\ &= \int_{-\infty}^{\infty}\int_{-\infty}^{\infty} \cdots \int_{-\infty}^{\infty} x_1^{i_1}x_2^{i_2} \ldots x_n^{i_n} p(x_1, x_2, \ldots, x_n)\, dx_1\, dx_2 \ldots dx_n. \end{aligned} \tag{2.3.16}$$

Questions and Problems

1. Develop a general formula for expressing the kth moment of a distribution about the mean in terms of moments about zero.

2. Define moments of a discrete distribution.

3. The random variables $\xi_1, \xi_2, \ldots, \xi_n$ are not *independent*. Show that

$$\sigma_{i\pm j}^2 = \sigma_i^2 \pm 2\rho_{ij}\sigma_i\sigma_j + \sigma_j^2,$$

where

$$\begin{aligned} \sigma_i^2 &= \text{variance of } \xi_i, \\ \sigma_{i\pm j}^2 &= \text{variance of } \xi_i \pm \xi_j, \\ \rho_{ij} &= \text{correlation between } \xi_i \text{ and } \xi_j. \end{aligned}$$

Extend this result to the variance of the sum of n dependent random variables.

4. The random variables $\xi_1, \xi_2, \ldots, \xi_n$ have the joint density function $p(x_1, x_2, \ldots, x_n)$. Express the ith moment of ξ_j in terms of a univarlate marginal distribution and a joint distribution.

[3] In the present context, μ_2 is not to be confused with the second central moment of a univariate distribution. Many authors use μ_i for the ith central moment of a univariate distribution.

4. PARTICULAR DISTRIBUTIONS

The ideas of probability distributions and related concepts have been presented in fairly general terms in the preceding section. We now turn to a discussion of some specific distributions, including those that are likely to arise in econometric work.

A previous example of the density function describing the chances of obtaining a particular face up on a perfect die gave the result

$$p_i = \tfrac{1}{6}, \qquad i = 1, 2, \ldots, 6. \tag{2.4.1}$$

This function could be represented graphically as six equally spaced ordinates of equal height. The entire density of the distribution function is concentrated at the six discrete points. This function is called the rectangular or uniform distribution. The continuous rectangular density function is represented as

$$p(x)\,dx = \frac{1}{b - a}\,dx, \qquad a \leq x \leq b,\, a < b. \tag{2.4.2}$$

The variable x is confined to the finite range (a, b). a and b are two constants defining the limits of the range of x. Because $a < b$, $\dfrac{1}{b - a}$ is always positive. Furthermore,

$$\int_{-\infty}^{\infty} p(x)\,dx = \int_a^b p(x)\,dx = \frac{1}{b - a}\int_a^b dx = 1;$$

thus the function in (2.4.2) has the properties of a probability density function.

Another important discrete distribution is known as the binomial distribution. Suppose that the possible outcomes of any trial in an experiment can be classified as either a success or a failure, with no other possibilities. Let the probability of a success be p and the probability of a failure be $q = 1 - p$. The experiment consists of n independent trials. In the n trials, exactly r successes and $n - r$ failures can occur in a number of ways, depending upon the order in which the mutually exclusive outcomes take place. There are

$$\frac{n!}{r!(n - r)!} = {}_nC_r$$

orders of the outcomes. This expression is the formula for the number of combinations of n things taken r at a time. The probability of any particular order is

$$p^r q^{n-r}$$

because the multiplication rule for probabilities of independent events applies.

There are thus ${}_nC_r$ mutually exclusive events, each having the probability

$$p^r q^{n-r}.$$

The probability of exactly r successes in n independent trials is

$$f(r) = \frac{n!}{r!(n-r)!} p^r q^{n-r}. \tag{2.4.3}$$

The variable r ranges from 0 to n, that is, there can be any number of successes between 0 and n. The distribution in (2.4.3) is called the binomial distribution because $f(r)$ is a typical term of the binomial expansion of

$$(p+q)^n = p^n + np^{n-1}q + \frac{n(n-1)}{2!} p^{n-2}q^2 + \cdots + \frac{n!}{r!(n-r)!} p^r q^{n-r} + \cdots + q^n.$$

The expression for $f(r)$ is the $(r + 1)$st term of this biomial expansion. It follows that

$$\sum_{r=0}^{n} f(r) = 1$$

because

$$\sum_{r=0}^{n} f(r) = \sum_{r=0}^{n} {}_nC_r p^r q^{n-r} = (p+q)^n = 1^n = 1.$$

Simple calculations lead to the following important results with the binomial distribution:

$$E(r) = \sum_{r=0}^{n} rf(r) = np,$$
$$E\left(\frac{r}{n}\right) = p. \tag{2.4.4}$$

$$\sigma_r^2 = E(r-np)^2 = \sum_{r=0}^{n} (r-np)^2 f(r) = npq,$$
$$\sigma_{r/n}^2 = \frac{pq}{n}. \tag{2.4.5}$$

These formulas for the first two moments are extensively used in sampling theory and practice. Sampling statisticians may set out to estimate the fraction of the national population holding \$3,000 or more of liquid assets (bank deposits plus government bonds). Regard a purely random sample as an experiment and a *success* represented by the drawing of an individual actually holding \$3,000 or more of liquid assets. A *failure* is the drawing of an individual holding less than \$3,000 of liquid assets. The probability of finding exactly r persons holding

\$3,000 or more of liquid assets in a sample of n is given by (2.4.3). Equation (2.4.4) tells us that the mathematical expectation of the *fraction* of successes in n trials is equal to the probability of a success. In any particular sample, the fraction of successes r/n will not equal p, but on the average it will. The fraction r/n will be dispersed about p according to the formula in (2.4.5). The sampling statistician calculates the fraction of individuals in his sample holding \$3,000 or more of liquid assets as an estimate of p, but he wants to know how reliable this estimate is—how it would be dispersed about the value of p in many repeated samples. In other words, he wants to estimate the sampling error or sampling variability. Formula (2.4.5) tells him that as his sample is increased, the variability of his estimate is decreased. It also tells him the necessary size of sample to be used to achieve a certain reliability for any given set of p and q. He does not know p and q in advance, but he often knows their values closely enough to make use of (2.4.5).

In the binomial distribution, r represents the values that the random variable being treated can assume, and $(0, n)$ represents the range of variation of r. The parameters of the distribution are p and q, but because p and q add up to unity, there is, in effect, only one parameter. The parameter is an unknown population value that is usually the object of statistical inference.

The binomial distribution is developed from a set of first principles using probability theory and some particular experimental situation. This basic distribution serves as a transition element to two other well-known distributions, the Poisson distribution and the normal distribution. Both of these latter distributions can be derived from elementary probability processes, but they are also limiting cases of the binomial distribution. The Poisson distribution, also a discrete distribution, is obtained from the binomial distribution by setting

$$p = \frac{\lambda}{n}, \tag{2.4.6}$$

where $p =$ the parameter of the binomial distribution, $n =$ total number of events (successes and failures), and $\lambda =$ positive constant. By (2.4.6), as n increases, the probability of success falls. If (2.4.6) holds, then

$$\lim_{n\to\infty} \frac{n!}{r!(n-r)!} p^r(1-p)^{n-r} = \frac{\lambda^r}{r!} e^{-\lambda}.$$

The right-hand expression represents the Poisson distribution. Proofs of this limiting result can be found in standard statistical treatises among the references at the end of this chapter.

The theorem establishing the normal distribution as the limiting case of the binomial distribution is stated as follows: For an arbitrary $a < b$,

$$\lim_{n\to\infty} P\left(a < x = \frac{r-np}{\sqrt{npq}} \leq b\right) = \frac{1}{\sqrt{2\pi}} \int_a^b e^{-x^2/2}\, dx.$$

In this statement the variable r has been transformed by subtracting its mean value np and dividing the result by the standard deviation, $\sqrt{npq}$. This is called a standardized variable because it has a zero mean and unit standard deviation. The subtraction of np is called a transformation of location, and the division by $\sqrt{npq}$ is called a transformation of scale. The standardized variable x follows the binomial distribution for finite values of n, but as n becomes indefinitely large, x follows the normal distribution

$$\frac{1}{\sqrt{2\pi}} e^{-x^2/2},$$

one of the most important distributions in statistics. The proof of the theorem showing the normal as a limiting case of the binomial distribution can also be found in suggested readings listed at the end of this chapter and will not be given here.

The above form of the normal distribution is derived as a limiting case of the binomial distribution when the variable of the latter distribution is standardized. The variable x in the normal distribution is also standardized. To get to the unstandardized case, we use the result of (2.2.11), showing how the probability distribution of one variable may be derived from the probability distribution of another when a transformation function connects the two variables. We have

$$p(x)\,dx = \frac{1}{\sqrt{2\pi}} e^{-x^2/2}\,dx. \tag{2.4.7}$$

Because x is standardized, it is related to an unstandardized variable y by the equation

$$x = \frac{y-\mu}{\sigma}, \tag{2.4.8}$$

where $\mu = E(y)$ and $\sigma^2 = E(y-\mu)^2$.
From (2.4.8), we get

$$\left|\frac{dx}{dy}\right| dy = \left|\frac{1}{\sigma}\right| dy.$$

Substituting these results into (2.2.11), we find

$$\frac{1}{\sqrt{2\pi}} e^{-x^2/2} dx = \frac{1}{\sqrt{2\pi}\sigma} e^{-[(y-\mu)^2/2\sigma^2]}\,dy. \tag{2.4.9}$$

The right-hand side of (2.4.9) is the normal density function in unstandardized form. This distribution depends on two parameters, $\mu =$ mean and $\sigma^2 =$ variance.

Elementary calculations show that

$$\begin{aligned}
&\frac{1}{\sqrt{2\pi}\sigma}\int_{-\infty}^{\infty} e^{-[(y-\mu)^2/2\sigma^2]}\,dy = 1,\\
&\frac{1}{\sqrt{2\pi}\sigma}\int_{-\infty}^{\infty} ye^{-[(y-\mu)^2/2\sigma^2]}\,dy = \mu, \qquad (2.4.10)\\
&\frac{1}{\sqrt{2\pi}\sigma}\int_{-\infty}^{\infty} (y-\mu)^2 e^{-[(y-\mu)^2/2\sigma^2]}\,dy = \sigma^2.
\end{aligned}$$

The first part of (2.4.10) states that the normal distribution, as written in (2.4.9), contains a unit area under the curve. The second part states that μ is interpreted as the mean of y, and the third part that σ^2 is interpreted as the variance of y. The normal distribution is bell shaped and symmetrical about the point $y = \mu$. This distribution derives its importance in large part from the fact that variables generated according to simple random schemes often follow the normal law. It has wide empirical and theoretical use.

A remarkable property of the normal distribution is that sums and differences of normally distributed variables are also normally distributed. In fact, any linear function of normal variables is also a normally distributed variable. A much more general result is contained in the celebrated central limit theorem: If the random variables $\{\xi_i\}$ are independent, the distribution of their sum, $\xi = \xi_1 + \xi_2 + \cdots + \xi_n$, tends to the normal distribution as $n \longrightarrow \infty$, subject to some general mathematical restrictions. The restrictions need not detain us, and it must be emphasized that no assumption is made about the distributions of the $\{\xi_i\}$. They can be virtually anything as long as the $\{\xi_i\}$ are independent. The central limit theorem gives a very strong justification for the widespread use of the normal distribution.

The two-dimensional normal density function is written as

$$\frac{1}{2\pi\sigma_x\sigma_y\sqrt{1-\rho^2}}\exp\left\{-\frac{1}{2(1-\rho^2)}\left[\frac{(x-\mu_x)^2}{\sigma_x^2} - \frac{2\rho(x-\mu_x)(y-\mu_y)}{\sigma_x\sigma_y} + \frac{(y-\mu_y)^2}{\sigma_y^2}\right]\right\} dx\,dy.$$

The parameter ρ is the correlation between x and y. In the bivariate normal case, if $\rho = 0$, the variables are also independent; the expression for the joint distribution becomes the product of two univariate normal distributions. The normal distribution can be extended to any finite number of dimensions.

The income distribution is an important case arising in econometric work but is seen at a glance to be quite different from the normal distribution. The income distribution lacks the symmetry of the normal distribution. Various empirical data suggest, though, that a simple transformation of income variables to logarithms yields a normal distribution. Suppose that we are dealing only with positive incomes, then log y (y = income) is said to be normally distributed,

$$p(\log y)\, d\log y = \frac{1}{\sqrt{2\pi}\sigma} \exp\left[-\frac{(\log y - \mu)^2}{2\sigma^2}\right] d\log y. \qquad (2.4.11)$$

The parameter μ is the mean of log y; in other words, the logarithm of the geometric mean of y. The variance parameter σ^2 is the variance of log y. What is the distribution of y = income? Again, we apply the expression in (2.2.11). Let $x = \log y$. Then x is normally distributed as in (2.4.11), and

$$\frac{dx}{dy} = \frac{1}{y}.$$

The probability density of y is given by

$$\frac{1}{\sqrt{2\pi}\, y\sigma}\, e^{-[(\log y-\mu)^2/2\sigma^2]}\, dy.$$

The graph of this curve has the skew properties of the income distribution.

We should allow for the possibility that income can be negative—for example, through business losses. Because we cannot form the logarithm of negative numbers, we redefine the origin of y to make all quantities positive. In this case,

$$x = \log(y - \alpha)$$

where α = minimum income of the population. The density function of y is now

$$\frac{1}{\sqrt{2\pi}\sigma(y - \alpha)}\, e^{-[(\log(y-\alpha)-\mu)^2/2\sigma^2]}\, dy.$$

These distributions are called the logarithmic normal distributions. They can be generated by interesting probability processes, which have some applicability to the description of the generation of income distributions.

If income in two successive periods is classified by bracket position in each period according to the notation

N_{ij} = number of income receivers moving from class i in period t to class j in period $t + 1$,

we may write the identity

$$N_{j,t+1} = N_{1j} + N_{2j} + \cdots + N_{nj} \qquad (2.4.12)$$

This simply states that all the occupants of income class j in period $t + 1$ came from one of the n possible classes in period t. Next, define

$$p_{ij} = \frac{N_{ij}}{N_{it}},$$

the fraction of units in class i (period t) who moved into class j (period $t + 1$). These are called *transition probabilities*. The identity (2.4.12) can be rewritten as

$$N_{j,t+1} = \sum_{i=1}^{n} p_{ij} N_{it}. \tag{2.4.13}$$

If the p_{ij} were constant, we could solve the linear equation system in (2.4.13) to show how the distribution at time t is transformed into a distribution at time $t + 1$. The *limit* distribution is the solution that is found when

$$N_{j,t+1} = N_{j,t} = N_j.$$

A more interesting case to consider is one of systematic variation in the p_{ij}. It is reasonable to assume that p_{ij} depends on some measure of difference between j and i. Aitchison and Brown divide the income scale into units of equal arithmetic width, so that the class limits follow an arithmetic progression. They have shown that if

$$p_{ij} = f\left(\frac{j}{i}\right),$$

with a special definition for $j = 1$

$$p_{i1} = 1 - \sum_{j=2}^{n} f\left(\frac{j}{i}\right),$$

the limiting distribution from the difference equations in (2.4.13) is the logarithmic normal distribution.[4]

Their analysis was an adaption of a theorem of Champernowne, who assumed

$$p_{ij} = f(j - i)$$

$$p_{i1} = 1 - \sum_{j=2}^{n} f(j - i)$$

where the class limits grow in geometric progression. Champernowne showed that the limit distribution in this case is the Pareto distribution.[5]

$$p(y) = Ay^{-\alpha}$$

$p(y)$ = fraction of units with income in excess of y.

[4] J. Aitchison and J. A. C. Brown, *The Lognormal Distribution* (Cambridge: Cambridge University Press, 1957).

[5] D. G. Champernowne, "A Model of Income Distribution," *Economic Journal*, LXIII (1953), 318–51.

The student should note that this is a cumulative distribution function, but it shows the relative frequency *greater than* instead of *less than*. This is the traditional way that the Pareto distribution was stated since it was first discovered as an empirical regularity.

The logarithm of the fraction of units with income in excess of some value is a negatively sloped linear function of the logarithm of that income level. The density function is

$$p(y) = \alpha A y^{-(\alpha+1)}.$$

Questions and Problems

1. Determine the mean and variance of a Poisson distribution.

2. The n-dimensional generalization of the binomial distribution is the multinomial distribution

$$f(r_1, r_2, \ldots, r_k) = \frac{n!}{r_1!r_2! \cdots r_k!} p_1^{r_1} p_2^{r_2} \cdots p_k^{r_k},$$

the general term in the expansion of

$$(p_1 + p_2 + \cdots + p_k)^n.$$

Show that

$$\sum_{r_1} \cdots \sum_{r_k} f(r_1, r_2, \ldots, r_k) = 1,$$
$$r_1 + r_2 + \cdots + r_k = n.$$

Find an expression for the mean and variance of the multinomial distribution.

3. Show that moments of the normal distribution of order three or higher can be expressed in terms of the first two moments alone.

4. Express the first moment (arithmetic mean) of the logarithmic normal distribution in terms of the parameters of the distribution and see whether your result agrees with the general theorem that the geometric mean of a series of positive quantities never exceeds the arithmetic mean.

5. The area under the normal distribution between successive ordinates is widely tabulated for the case of zero mean and unit variance. How can these tables be used to find the area between two ordinates under a normal curve with nonzero mean and nonunit variance?

5. STATISTICAL INFERENCE

Statistical inference is a method of inferring population characteristics on the basis of observed samples of information. This is one aspect of mathematical statistics that finds wide application in econometrics. First, let us consider the problem of *estimation* within the larger scope of statistical inference.

Assume that we are given a sample of observations, $x_1, x_2, \ldots, x_n$, of the random variable ξ, which is distributed according to the probability density function

$$p(x \mid \theta)$$

where θ is a population parameter. θ is an unknown constant that it is desired to estimate, and, in order to do so, we form an estimating function of the sample observations

$$\text{est. } \theta = f(x_1, x_2, \ldots, x_n). \tag{2.5.1}$$

Although θ is an unknown constant, est. θ is a random variable because it is some function of the random variables $x_1, \ldots, x_n$. As an illustration of what is meant here, let θ be the population mean

$$E(x) = \theta = \int_{-\infty}^{\infty} xp(x \mid \theta)\, dx. \tag{2.5.2}$$

The function $p(x \mid \theta)$ is said to be completely specified by the value of its mean, θ. An intuitively desirable estimate of θ would be the sample mean; in other words,

$$\text{est. } \theta = \frac{1}{n} \sum_{i=1}^{n} x_i. \tag{2.5.3}$$

The function f thus has the concrete expression given in (2.5.3). However, unless we have established some theory of estimation, we do not know whether the sample mean is actually a desirable or undesirable estimate of θ.

An important property of estimates is that of being *unbiased.* If $f(x_1, x_2, \ldots, x_n)$ is an estimate of θ, we say that it is an unbiased estimate provided

$$E[f(x_1, x_2, \ldots, x_n)] = \theta \tag{2.5.4}$$

for any set of sample values $x_1, x_2, \ldots, x_n$. Obviously, it is meaningful to form the mathematical expectation of f, because this function is a random variable and is distributed according to some probability density function. In the previous illustration, it follows that the sample mean is an unbiased estimate of the population mean.

$$E\left(\frac{1}{n} \sum_{i=1}^{n} x_i\right) = \frac{1}{n} \sum_{i=1}^{n} E(x_i) = 0 \tag{2.5.5}$$

because all the x_i are drawn from the same population with expected value $= \theta$.

For any distribution function the sample mean is an unbiased estimate of the population mean and, in particular, the sample mean is an unbiased estimate of θ from the distribution in (2.5.2).

The property of being unbiased refers to the first moment of the distribution of the estimating function. Another criterion can be developed by considering the second moment of this distribution. We say that f is the *best unbiased estimate* of θ if

$$\sigma_f^2 = E[f(x_1, x_2, \ldots, x_n) - \theta]^2 = \text{minimum}. \tag{2.5.6}$$

Among the class of all unbiased estimates, which may be quite numerous, we seek the one that has the smallest variance. We may, for simplicity, restrict the estimating functions to those that are linear in the observations. In this case, we look for *best linear unbiased estimates.*

The criteria of unbiasedness and minimum variance are, of course, arbitrary, but they do seem to be reasonable. They are properties that most statisticians think should be possessed by estimates, and they restrict the possible estimating functions to a manageable number of interesting cases. These two properties are supposed to hold regardless of the sample size.

If the model underlying the development of the two criteria for estimates is generalized, we have the following situation: Let $\xi_1, \xi_2, \ldots, \xi_m$ be m random variables jointly distributed according to

$$p(x_1, x_2, \ldots, x_m \mid \theta_1, \theta_2, \ldots, \theta_r).$$

The sample observations of the ξ_i are denoted by $x_{11}, \ldots, x_{1n}, \ldots, x_{m1}, \ldots, x_{mn}$, and the estimating functions are

$$\text{est. } \theta_i = f_i(x_{11}, \ldots, x_{1n}, \ldots, x_{m1}, \ldots, x_{mn}), \; i = 1, 2, \ldots, r. \tag{2.5.7}$$

The f_i functions are unbiased estimates of the parameters θ_i if

$$E(f_i) = \theta_i, \qquad i = 1, 2, \ldots, r, \tag{2.5.8}$$

for any set of sample values. It often happens in econometric analysis that it is simple to obtain estimates satisfying an equation like (2.5.8) on the condition that certain sample values are fixed, but if these values are random variables they cannot be fixed in advance, and these simpler estimating functions have to be ruled out. If, for example, we have

$$E[f_j(x_{11}, \ldots, x_{mn}) \mid x_{k1}, \ldots, x_{kn}] = \theta_j \tag{2.5.9}$$

for the jth parameter, we should not call f_j an unbiased estimate. The expression on the left hand side of (2.5.9) reads, "the expected value of f_j, given the n sample values of x_k." This is a conditional expectation, but we are after unconditional expectations in our concept of unbiasedness.

Frequently, it is difficult to obtain unbiased or best unbiased estimates of parameters, but in many cases it is possible to obtain, instead, estimates that have similar properties asymptotically, that is, as the sample size tends towards infinity. Referring now to (2.5.1), we define $f(x_1, x_2, \ldots x_n)$ to be a *consistent estimate* of θ if

$$\lim_{n \to \infty} P(|f - \theta| > \epsilon) = 0 \tag{2.5.10}$$

for an arbitrary $\epsilon > 0$.

We say that f converges stochastically to θ as the sample size tends toward infinity. We might also write this as

$$\operatorname*{plim}_{n \to \infty} f(x_1, x_2, \ldots, x_n) = \theta;$$

the "limit in probability of f is θ." The sample mean is a consistent, as well as unbiased, estimate of the population mean.

The other asymptotic property of estimates is called *efficiency*. The statistic f is an efficient estimate of θ if, as the sample size increases towards infinity, the distribution of f tends towards the normal distribution with mean θ, and variance less than that of any other statistic that is also asymptotically normally distributed with mean θ. As the sample size gets larger and larger, the distribution of f must approach normality with a mean equal to the parameter being estimated by f. Among the class of estimators of θ having a normal distribution as a limiting distribution, the efficient statistic has minimum variance. The reader can see that this joint criterion is similar to that of a best unbiased estimate except for two features: (*a*) The efficiency criterion applies only in the limit as $n \longrightarrow \infty$, and the condition for best unbiasedness holds for all size samples; and (*b*) the efficiency criterion seeks minimum variance only among normally distributed estimates, but the condition for best unbiasedness makes no restrictions on the distribution function of the estimates. Because the distributions of many estimates tend to normality in the limit, the definition of efficiency is useful.

A particular type of estimate that has been used widely in statistical analysis is called a *maximum likelihood* estimate. It is obtained by expressing the joint distribution function of sample observations in terms of the parameters to be estimated, and then maximizing the distribution function with respect to the unknown parameters. The solutions of the maximization equations express the estimation functions as relations between the estimated parameters and the observations. Maximum likelihood estimates assign those values to unknown parameters that make the probability of obtaining the observed sample as large as possible. A mathematical formulation follows. Let $x_1, x_2, \ldots x_n$ be a set of sample observations drawn from the probability density function

$$p(x \mid \theta)\, dx.$$

If all the observations are independent of each other, the joint distribution of the sample (the likelihood function) is

$$p(x_1 \mid \theta)p(x_2 \mid \theta) \ldots p(x_n \mid \theta)\, dx_1\, dx_2 \ldots dx_n;$$

more generally it is

$$L^*(x_1, x_2, \ldots, x_n \mid \theta)\, dx_1, dx_2, \ldots, dx_n.$$

The maximum likelihood estimate obtained is that value of θ satisfying

$$\frac{dL^*}{d\theta} = 0. \tag{2.5.11}$$

In many problems, results are simplified by maximizing log L^* ($= L$) instead of L^*. Because the logarithm of a positive quantity is an increasing function of the quantity, the same value of θ is obtained by maximizing either L^* or log L^*. In cases where the distribution function depends on many parameters, we make the straightforward generalization of maximizing the likelihood function with respect to the several parameters simultaneously.

Great virtues of maximum likelihood estimates are that they possess the properties of consistency and efficiency, under fairly weak mathematical restrictions.

For illustrative purposes, we show the maximum likelihood estimates of the parameters of a normal distribution. A set of n independent sample values $x_1, x_2, \ldots, x_n$ are drawn from the normal population

$$\frac{1}{\sqrt{2\pi}\sigma} e^{-[(x-\mu)^2/2\sigma^2]}.$$

The likelihood function is

$$\begin{aligned} L^*(x_1, x_2, \ldots, x_n \mid \sigma, \mu) &= \left(\frac{1}{\sqrt{2\pi}\sigma}\right)^n e^{-\sum_{i=1}^{n}[(x_i-\mu)^2/2\sigma^2]}, \\ \log L^* = L &= -n(\log \sqrt{2\pi} + \log \sigma) - \frac{1}{2\sigma^2}\sum_{i=1}^{n}(x_i - \mu)^2. \end{aligned} \tag{2.5.12}$$

Maximization conditions for log L^* are

$$\frac{\partial L}{\partial \sigma} = -\frac{n}{\sigma} + \frac{1}{\sigma^3}\sum_{i=1}^{n}(x_i - \mu)^2 = 0, \tag{2.5.13}$$

$$\frac{\partial L}{\partial \mu} = \frac{1}{\sigma^2}\sum_{i=1}^{n}(x_i - \mu) = 0. \tag{2.5.14}$$

These two equations in μ and σ serve to determine the maximum likelihood values $\hat{\mu}$ and $\hat{\sigma}$. First solve (2.5.14) for

$$\hat{\mu} = \frac{1}{n}\sum_{i=1}^{n} x_i. \tag{2.5.15}$$

Then substitute this value for μ in (2.5.13) to get

$$\hat{\sigma}^2 = \frac{1}{n}\sum_{i=1}^{n} (x_i - \hat{\mu})^2. \tag{2.5.16}$$

Equations (2.5.15) and (2.5.16) show that the sample mean and sample variance are maximum likelihood estimates of μ and σ^2, the population mean and variance of the normal distribution. Oftentimes, as we shall see in later chapters, maximum likelihood estimation does not lead to equations that are so easily solved.

Maximum likelihood estimates may be called point estimates because they determine a set of numerical values as estimates of unknown population characteristics. We get some idea about the reliability of the point values by calculating the variances of maximum likelihood estimates. If the estimates are calculated for distribution functions depending on a single parameter, as in (2.5.11), the quantity

$$-\left.\frac{\partial^2 L}{\partial \theta^2}\right|_{\theta=\hat{\theta}}$$

converges, in probability, to the inverse of the variance of $\hat{\theta}$, the maximum likelihood estimate of θ, as $n \longrightarrow \infty$. If the likelihood function depends on m parameters $\theta_1, \theta_2, \ldots, \theta_m$, the matrix

$$\left\| -\left.\frac{\partial^2 L}{\partial \theta_i \, \partial \theta_j}\right|_{\substack{\theta_1=\hat{\theta}_1 \\ \cdots \\ \theta_m=\hat{\theta}_m}} \right\|^{-1}$$

gives the asymptotic variances and covariances of the maximum likelihood estimates. The diagonal terms of the matrix are the asymptotic variances of the $\hat{\theta}_i$.

A more general way of looking at the estimation problem is to attempt to construct interval, instead of point, estimates of population characteristics. Interval estimation involves making probability statements that a range of values covers the true value to be estimated in repeated samples. This is in sharp contrast to point estimation, as such, although point estimates combined with sampling variances often lead to intervals of the type in which we are interested. A theory of interval estimation is known as the theory of *confidence intervals*.

To estimate the single parameter of

$$p(x \mid \theta),$$

we form two functions of the sample observations,

$$f_1(x_1, x_2, \ldots, x_n) \qquad \text{and}$$
$$f_2(x_1, x_2, \ldots, x_n)$$

such that

$$P(f_1 \leq \theta \leq f_2) = \epsilon \tag{2.5.17}$$

where ϵ is a predetermined confidence coefficient. In a particular case, ϵ may be 0.95 or 0.99 depending on the requirements for precision. Equation (2.5.17) gives the probability that the interval from f_1 to f_2 covers the true value θ. This interval is called a confidence interval. The concept is readily extended to the simultaneous estimation of many parameters. Later, we shall try to develop confidence intervals for estimation of parameters in econometric models.

A related problem that falls under a different branch of statistical inference is known as the testing of hypotheses. A statistical hypothesis can always be formulated as a statement about the probability distribution of the variable at hand. Examples of hypotheses about the density function

$$p(x \mid \theta)$$

are

$$H_1 : \theta = 0$$
$$H_2 : \theta > 0$$
$$H_3 : \theta = \theta_0$$
etc.

Another hypothesis may be that x is distributed according to $p^*(x \mid \eta)$ instead of $p(x \mid \theta)$.

The set of all possible hypotheses about the distribution of x is called Ω. The statistical hypothesis to be tested is that the true distribution of x is a member of ω, a subclass of Ω. Ω may consist of all probability distributions expressed by

$$p(x \mid \theta), -\infty < \theta < \infty,$$

and ω may consist of the subclass

$$p(x \mid \theta) \qquad \theta = 0.$$

In this example, the subclass ω contains a single element, and the hypothesis is said to be *simple*. If we had, instead, set up ω to be

$$p(x \mid \theta), \qquad \theta_1 \leq \theta \leq \theta_2, \qquad \theta_1 < \theta_2,$$

the hypothesis would be *composite* instead of simple.

The next step is to set up a *critical region* such that if the set of observed sample values falls in this region, we reject the hypothesis that the true distribution is a member of ω. The criteria underlying the design of the critical region are the following: Errors may be committed in making statistical decisions about the acceptance or rejection of hypotheses. The critical region is designed to keep these errors small or within prescribed limits. The errors may be of two types, namely, the rejection of true hypotheses (type I error) or the acceptance of false hypotheses (type II error). Decisions that lead to acceptance of true hypotheses or rejection of false hypotheses do not result in errors. It is desired to have both types of errors small, but of course it makes no sense, mathematically, to attempt to minimize the two errors simultaneously. Instead, the theory seeks a minimization of the probability of type II errors for a given probability of type I error.

Let the critical region be denoted by w. The probability that the sample observation falls in w, given the truth of hypothesis H, will be written as

$$P(w \mid H).$$

Let H_1 = hypothesis to be tested, and
H_2 = the only alternative to H_1.
Ω consists of H_1 and H_2; ω consists of H_1.

$$P(w \mid H_1) = \alpha = \text{probability of type I error.} \tag{2.5.18}$$

The probability α is called the size of the critical region and is usually taken to be small at about 0.05 or 0.01.

$$1 - P(w \mid H_2) = \text{probability of type II error} = \text{minimum.} \tag{2.5.19}$$

For a given α, the probability in (2.5.19) is to be made a minimum. The expression $P(w \mid H_2)$ is called the power function of the test, showing the chance of avoiding type II errors. Where H_1 and H_2 are equivalent to the assignment of different values to θ, the parameter of a probability distribution,

$$H_1 : \theta = \theta_1$$
$$H_2 : \theta \neq \theta_1$$

a probability of the form $P(w \mid H) = P(w \mid \theta)$ may be viewed as a function of

θ. For *unbiased tests*, at $\theta = \theta_1$, the graph of this function is a minimum at the level α. At any other point along the θ axis, the corresponding ordinate of the curve shows the probability of avoiding a type II error for any alternative hypothesis to $H_1 : \theta = \theta_1$. These ordinates may be said to show the power of the test with respect to the alternative hypotheses represented by the associated abscissae. The curve drawn in the graph represents a certain test of H_1 against the alternatives $\theta > \theta_1$ and $\theta < \theta_1$. Any other test of H_1 with a power function passing through the point (θ_1, α), that is, with the same size critical region, might be compared with the original test. If for all values of $\theta \neq \theta_1$, the power function of other tests lies below the function graphed above, the original test is called uniformly more powerful. This condition is expressed as

$$P(w' \mid \theta_1) = P(w \mid \theta_1) = \alpha, \tag{2.5.20}$$

$$P(w' \mid \theta) < P(w \mid \theta), \quad \text{for all } \theta \neq \theta_1, w' \neq w. \tag{2.5.21}$$

The test based on critical region w is preferred to that based on w'.

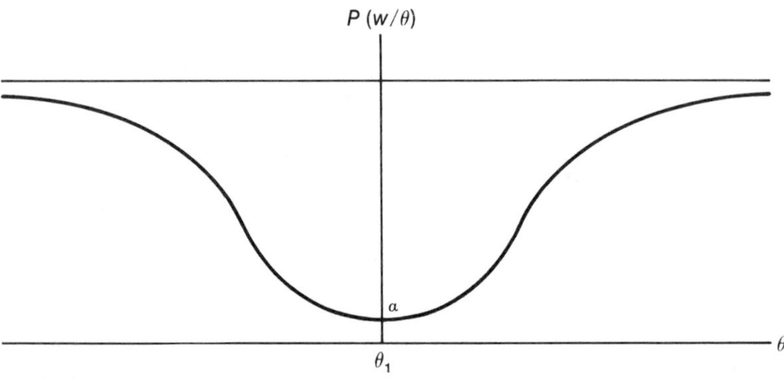

Figure 2.5.1

In most cases uniformly more or most powerful tests do not exist. Sometimes one test has higher power than others over a certain range of variation of the parameters. The usual procedure, however, is to devise tests that have some desirable properties but that are not uniformly most powerful. This brings the student to a large technical literature on the theory of the testing of hypotheses, which we are not going to pursue further at this stage of our work.

In the applications of later chapters, it will be seen that many tests of hypotheses cannot be carried out unless estimation of parameters is also done simultaneously. Indeed, the methods of estimating and testing will be seen to involve the same steps in many problems. A relation between the theory of confidence intervals and the theory of hypothesis testing is that a set of acceptable hypotheses for a given size critical region specifies a set or interval of parameter values. This set or interval is also a confidence interval or confidence set with confidence coefficient equal to one minus the size of the critical region.

A unification and generalization of the entire theory of statistical inference is provided by the theory of statistical decision functions. Whether we are estimating parameters or testing hypotheses, we are making statistical decisions. Rules and principles of such decisions form the subject matter of the theory of statistical decision functions.

In addition to the sample space [regions of all possible sample values—in many univariate problems the range of real numbers $(-\infty, +\infty)$] and the class of all admissible hypotheses $\mathbf{\Omega}$, we consider a space D of all possible statistical decisions. The elements of D, denoted by d, represent the totality of decisions that the statistician can make about some particular problem. The choice of a decision d is associated with the subclass ω of $\mathbf{\Omega}$ in such a way that d means the acceptance of the hypothesis that the true distribution of the random variable x is a member of ω. The parallel treatment with the preceding outline of the theory of testing hypotheses is obvious.

The statistician observes the sample of observations

$$x_1, x_2, \ldots, x_n.$$

His decision problem is to construct the function

$$d(x_1, x_2, \ldots, x_n)$$

so that he can use the observations to determine the decision he should make. Decisions can be right or wrong, and criteria must be designed to attach degrees of importance to various wrong decisions in order to guide the statistician in his choice. If the probability density function of x is

$$p(x \mid \theta),$$

we shall associate a weight function

$$W(\theta, d)$$

with every pair, θ and d, to express the cost involved in making decision d where θ is the true parameter of the probability density of x. The nature of the weight function can be seen in the context of an example already discussed. The class of admissible hypotheses Ω consists of two elements,

$$H_1 : \theta = 0$$
$$H_2 : \theta \neq 0.$$

The subset ω consists of H_1 alone. There are two possible decisions, to accept H_1 or to accept H_2. The first decision is written as d_1 and the second as d_2. The form of the weight function is then

$$W(\theta = 0, d_1) = 0$$
$$W(\theta = 0, d_2) = c_1$$
$$W(\theta \neq 0, d_1) = c_2$$
$$W(\theta \neq 0, d_2) = 0.$$

We attach no cost to correct decisions, and the costs c_1 and c_2 to wrong decisions, errors of type I and II. Weight functions are not necessarily discontinuous as we have made them in this example. Perhaps d_1 is not a bad decision for practical purposes when θ is small in absolute value, and the cost mounts under this decision as θ assumes values farther away from zero. The set of admissible hypotheses could be made more detailed to include values of θ within each of several class intervals and a gradually changing weight attached to successive errors.

Given the set of admissible hypotheses, the space of decisions D and the sample space, we can define

$$\begin{aligned} E\{W[\theta, d(x_1, \ldots, x_n)]\} &= r[\theta, d(x_1, \ldots, x_n)] \\ &= \int_{-\infty}^{\infty} \cdots \int_{-\infty}^{\infty} W[\theta, d(x_1, \ldots, x_n)] p^*(x_1, \ldots, x_n \mid \theta)\, dx_1 \ldots, dx_n \end{aligned} \tag{2.5.22}$$

as the *risk function.* If each variable of the sample has the same density, and if all variables are mutually independent, we can write

$$p^*(x_1, \ldots, x_n \mid \theta) = \prod_{i=1}^{n} p(x_i \mid \theta).$$

The risk function $r(\theta, d)$, defined above, plays an important role in decision function theory. The statistician has no control over θ, one of the arguments of the risk function, but he does control d. The parameter θ is said to be given by "the state of nature." A conservative approach which is often used is to choose the function $d = d(x_1, \ldots, x_n)$ so as to minimize the risk under the assumption that the state of nature gives the least favorable value of θ. This is called a *minimax* solution for the selection of the decision function. Mathematically, we select that decision function $d^*(x_1, \ldots, x_n)$ satisfying

$$\max_{\theta \in \Omega} r(\theta, d^*) = \min_{d \in D} \max_{\theta \in \Omega} r(\theta, d). \tag{2.5.23}$$

The analogy with the theory of games is immediately evident. In that theory (zero sum, two person games), we have a gain function $G(x, y)$ and two players, one choosing x among all possible alternatives open to him and the other y among all possible alternatives open to him. Neither player knows what the other is going to do. The first player gains the amount $G(x, y)$ and the second $-G(x, y)$. This makes the game of the zero sum type, the gain of one being the loss of the other. The first player attempts to maximize G and the second attempts to minimize G (maximize $-G$). The game is said to be determined, that is, have a definite solution, if

$$\max_x \min_y G(x, y) = \min_y \max_x G(x, y).$$

Each player assumes that the other's strategy will be the least favorable to himself and attempts to make his own position optimal under this assumption. If max min and min max of G are the same, the adoption of these rules of behavior leads to a determinate situation.

In the theory of statistical decision functions, the two players are the statistician and nature. In place of the gain function, we have the risk function dependent on two variables or functions, one selected by each player. As in the theory of games, the statistician assumes that his opponent, nature, will present him with the least favorable probability distribution and attempts to minimize the risk subject to this assumption. The statistician minimizes risk through his choice of a decision function.

An interesting result in game theory is that a wide class of zero sum, two person games are determined if each player chooses his strategy by a chance mechanism and the gain function is defined as

$$G^*(x^*, y^*) = E[G(x, y)] = \int_{-\infty}^{\infty} \int_{-\infty}^{\infty} G(x, y)p(x, y)\, dx\, dy,$$

where x^* and y^* are chance strategies. For the expected value of gain we have

$$\max_{x^*} \min_{y^*} G^*(x^*, y^*) = \min_{y^*} \max_{x^*} G^*(x^*, y^*).$$

For randomized selection of decision functions by the statistician, the inference problem can be made to coincide with the fully determined zero sum, two person game. Nature's randomized choice of the underlying probability distribution is known as the a priori distribution of probabilities occurring in the celebrated theorem of Bayes, basic to classical theories of probability and inference.

In line with our preceding exposition of statistical methods, we have presented the theory of decision functions in terms of parametric density functions, that is, functions that depend explicitly on a finite number of parameters. Hypotheses are specifications of values of these parameters, and estimation is concerned with determining these parameters from sample observations. The theory is capable of immediate generalization to nonparametric, multivariate distributions. Ω and ω are regarded simply as classes of distribution functions, and instead of writing θ in the argument of the weight or risk functions, we write

$$W[p^*(x_1, \ldots, x_n), d(x_1, \ldots, x_n)]; r[p^*(x_1, \ldots, x_n), d(x_1, \ldots, x_n)]$$

where p^* is an expression for a nonparametric density function. In many problems occurring in other parts of this chapter as well as here, the entire approach can be generalized by using the cumulative distribution function instead of a continuous density function. In cases where the density function is discontinuous, the cumulative distribution still retains certain essential continuity properties.

The theory of statistical decision functions may seem to be unduly subjective, dependent on the statistician's personal choice of a weight function. It may also seem to be arbitrary in the choice of the minimax criterion among numerous plausible alternatives. However, much of the theoretical development of the subject is devoted to the search for rules of inference that hold for a wide variety of simple weight functions. Conditions are also developed for the coincidence of minimax solutions of decision problems with Bayes' solutions that would occur if we, in fact, knew the a priori distribution of probability laws in Ω. Bayes' theorem gives a logical method of making probability inferences if the a priori probabilities are known. They seldom are known and this is the objection to the use of this theorem for most problems of statistical inference. A major contribution of decision function theory is to show the relation of various inferences to Bayes' type solutions. The beauty of the theory is that it includes hypothesis testing and estimation methods as special cases of a more general approach to inference.

6. PEDAGOGICAL NOTE

The purpose of this chapter has not been to teach probability and statistics to students of econometrics. We have merely tried to acquaint students with those branches of these allied subjects that will be of use in econometric work. It should give one a taste of the sort of material that must be mastered by those who will aspire to do serious, scholarly work in the field of econometrics. For them there is no alternative to careful study of treatises dealing with probability theory and mathematical statistics as separate subjects. Basic works in these fields are listed in the bibliography. It is hoped that sufficient ideas have been put across so that the work of later chapters will be more understandable to those studying econometrics for the first time. Regression analysis is the branch of statistics that is most used in econometrics. The next chapter gives full treatment to the subject.

Questions and Problems

1. The sample mean is an unbiased estimate of the population mean of any distribution. The sample mean, being computed from observations of a random variable, is itself a random variable following some distribution. Calculate the variance of the sample mean. Assuming the parent population to be a normal distribution, calculate the variance of the maximum likelihood estimate of the mean.

2. Suppose that several intervals provide estimates of the same parameter with equal confidence coefficients. What criteria would you propose for selecting among these intervals?

3. In simple applications of statistics to industrial inspection, a lot of material is rejected if more than a preassigned fraction of inspected items proves to be defective. The underlying distribution is assumed to be binomial. Rationalize and restate this inspection program in terms of the theory of testing hypotheses.

4. What intuitive criteria would you select for testing hypotheses in cases where uniformly most powerful tests do not exist?

5. Construct two examples, one showing the use of the theory of statistical decision functions for testing an hypothesis and the other showing the use of the theory for estimating a parameter.

SUGGESTED READINGS

INTRODUCTORY TEXTS:

Feller, W., *An Introduction to Probability Theory and its Applications.* 2nd ed. New York: Wiley, 1957.

Hoel, P. G., *Introduction to Mathematical Statistics.* New York: Wiley, 1962.

Mood, A. M. and F. A. Graybill, *Introduction to the Theory of Statistics* (2nd ed.) New York: McGraw-Hill, 1963.

Neyman, J., *First Course in Probability and Statistics.* New York: Holt, 1950.

ADVANCED TEXTS:

Anderson, T. W., Jr., *Introduction to Multivariate Statistical Analysis.* New York: Wiley, 1958.

Cramér, H. *Mathematical Methods of Statistics.* Princeton: Princeton University Press, 1946.

Kendall, M. G. and A. Stuart, *The Advanced Theory of Statistics.* 3 vols. London: Griffin & Co., 1966.

Wald, A., *Statistical Decision Functions.* New York: Wiley, 1950.

Wilks, S. S., *Mathematical Statistics.* New York: Wiley, 1962.

3

Regression: Single Equations

For the econometrics of estimating economic relationships, and this is a major part of the subject, the most important statistical tool is regression analysis. We shall be concerned with substantial generalizations of this subject, but the single equation regression shows most of the underlying ideas and problems clearly. In this chapter, we shall take up the statistical theory of single equation regression methods to form a basis for equation system estimation in the next chapter.

1. THE PRINCIPLE OF LEAST SQUARES (LS)

The time-honored method of least squares is probably one of the most widely used tools of quantitative economic research. It finds formal mathematical statement in the Markoff Theorem.[1] A statement, for our purposes, would be as follows: Let us assume that we have sample observations on the stochastic variable y_t and the known numbers $x_{1t}, \ldots, x_{nt}$. The sample values are denoted by $t = 1, \ldots, T$. The x_{it} variables are nonstochastic observations on explanatory variables in the relation

$$y_t = \alpha_1 x_{1t} + \ldots + \alpha_n x_{nt} + e_t, \tag{3.1.1}$$

in which the nonobserved random error, e_t, is given by some unknown probability distribution with finite variance. We shall assume $E\, e_t = 0$, $E\, e_t^2 = \sigma_e^2 < \infty$ and $E\, e_t e_{t'} = 0$ if $t \neq t'$. The coefficients, α_i, are unknown constants. The

[1] F. N. David and J. Neyman, "Extension of the Markoff Theorem on Least Squares," *Statistical Research Memoirs*, (London: Department of Statistics, University of London, University College, December, 1938), II, 105–16.

x_{it} are not constant, but they are fixed and known to the investigator for the sample at hand, or any similarly drawn sample. The estimates of α_i, called a_i, that satisfy

$$\sum_{t=1}^{T}(y_t - \alpha_1 x_{1t} - \ldots - \alpha_n x_{nt})^2 = \sum_{t=1}^{T} e_t^2 = \text{minimum}$$

are *best linear unbiased estimates.*

$$a_i = \text{B.L.U.E. } \alpha_i.$$

An *unbiased estimate of* σ^2 is given by

$$S_e^2 = \text{U.E. } \sigma_e^2 = \frac{1}{T-n}\sum_{t=1}^{T}(y_t - a_1 x_{1t} - \ldots - a_n x_{nt})^2. \tag{3.1.2}$$

We shall pause to discuss the meaning of this theorem before passing to its implementation. In the first place, this is a linear theory. As statistician, the econometrician regards y_t and x_{it} to be given *observed* numbers *for the sample* and regards the unknown constants α_i, σ_e^2 as variables to be determined. Later, when the econometrician becomes economist in applying this result to substantive problems of economics, he regards the coefficients a_i to be known, and y_t, x_{it} as variables. In both situations, the above equation is linear. It is linear in parameters if y_t, x_{it} are given. It is linear in variables if the coefficients are given. The important kind of linearity for the Markoff Theorem is the former, linearity in parameters. This theory would hold even if the economic variables did not enter linearly, provided that the α_i did.

There is no restriction in assuming

$$E\, e_t = 0, \tag{3.1.3}$$

provided we make one of the x_{it} unity.[2] Then the vanishing of the expected value of e_t is simply compensated by the value of α_i associated with the unit x_{it}. We make no assumption about the parametric form of the probability distribution of e_t, other than to specify that it has a finite and constant variance. We assume that the sample (of e_t) is drawn in such a way that the different values of e_t are mutually independent.

A consequence of the assumption that x_{it} are nonstochastic and $E\, e_t = 0$ is

$$E\, e_t x_{it} = 0. \tag{3.1.4}$$

[2] The usual development of correlation theory, both bivariate and multivariate, follows the practice of expressing variables as deviations from their means in linear equations, with explicit constant terms. In former days, when computing was done more laboriously, by hand, there was possibly an advantage in this form of expression. It is more symmetrical and simpler, however, to treat all coefficients alike, and in the days of the modern computer there is a distinct gain in measuring all variables as deviations from *zero* and not including a separate constant term in the equations. In a later chapter on computing, we shall make these points clearer.

This condition plays an important role in the determination of least squares bias within the context of equation system models. In the present case, it assures that the estimates obtained by the method of least squares will be unbiased.

We could relax the assumption that the x_{it} are nonstochastic and retain some of the desirable properties of least squares estimators. If they are stochastic, we would want to assume

$$E\, e_t x_{it} = 0, \tag{3.1.4}$$

or the weaker condition,

$$\text{plim}\; e_t x_{it} = 0 \tag{3.1.5}$$

for consistency, if not unbiasedness.

The typical model to which the single regression equation applies is a controlled experiment in which all variables except one (y_t) are fixed and controlled throughout the experiment (x_{it}) by the investigator. There is, however, experimental error acting as a disturbance on the relationship. The disturbance can also be looked upon as an error of observation of y_t.

In the formula for the estimate of variance, it should be noted that $(y_t - a_1x_{1t} - \ldots - a_nx_{nt})^2$ is summed over all $t = 1, \ldots, T$ but divided by $T - n$, the *number of degrees of freedom*, because in the sample of T we have made use of n parameters $a_1, \ldots, a_n$ to determine S_e^2.

The form of the estimates

There is yet another sense in which this theory is linear. We shall find that the a_i are determined as the solution of a system of linear equations and that the a_i can be expressed as a linear function of the e_t. In the expression B.L.U.E., they are *linear* estimates.

For simplicity, let us begin with a simple bivariate regression of y_t on x_t. Let us also assume that the constant term (associated with a unit variable) is zero and that the means of y_t and x_t are also zero. We are then faced with estimation of

$$y_t = \alpha x_t + e_t. \tag{3.1.6}$$

The expression

$$S = \sum_{t=1}^{T} (y_t - \alpha x_t)^2,$$

regarded as a function of α, is to be minimized over the sample. We have

$$\frac{dS}{d\alpha} = 2 \sum_{t=1}^{T} (y_t - \alpha x_t)(-x_t) = 0, \tag{3.1.7}$$

or

$$\sum_{t=1}^{T} y_t x_t = \alpha \sum_{t=1}^{T} x_t^2, \tag{3.1.8}$$

with solution

$$a = \text{B.L.U.E.}\alpha = \frac{\sum_{t=1}^{T} y_t x_t}{\sum_{t=1}^{T} x_t^2} \tag{3.1.9}$$

The residuals from the computed regression

$$y_t - ax_t = r_t \tag{3.1.10}$$

give an estimate of σ_e^2 in[3]

$$S_e^2 = \frac{1}{T-1}\sum_{t=1}^{T} r_t^2. \tag{3.1.11}$$

The associated normalized statistic is the correlation coefficient r_{yx} that is evaluated from the formula

$$r_{yx}^2 = 1 - \frac{S_e^2}{S_y^2}, \tag{3.1.12}$$

where

$$S_y^2 = \frac{1}{T}\sum_{t=1}^{T} y_t^2.$$

The total variation in y is given by S_y^2. Because we are assuming that the mean of y is zero in this formulation, there is no need to adjust S_y^2 for the degrees of freedom used up in estimating S_y^2. The variation in y that is explained by the regression is $\frac{1}{T}\sum_{t=1}^{T}(ax_t)^2$, and the unexplained variation is S_e^2. r_{xy}^2 is interpreted as the percentage of variation in y_t that is "explained" by variation in x_t.

If we did not correct S_e^2 for degrees of freedom (calling it S_e^{*2}), we would have

$$r_{yx}^2 = \frac{S_y^2 - S_e^{*2}}{S_y^2} = \frac{\sum y^2 - \sum (y - ax)^2}{\sum y^2} = \frac{2a\sum yx - a^2 \sum x^2}{\sum y^2}.$$

But we found a to be given by

$$a = \frac{\sum yx}{\sum x^2};$$

therefore we have

$$r_{yx}^2 = \frac{\dfrac{2(\sum yx)^2}{\sum x^2} - \dfrac{(\sum yx)^2}{(\sum x^2)^2}\sum x^2}{\sum y^2}$$

$$r_{yx}^2 = \frac{(\sum yx)^2}{\sum x^2 \sum y^2}$$

[3] Were it not for the fact that the constant term is assumed to be zero, we would have $T - 2$ in the denominator of the expression for S_e^2.

or

$$r_{yx} = \pm \frac{\sum yx}{\sqrt{\sum x^2 \sum y^2}}, \tag{3.1.13}$$

This is the well known Pearson product-moment formula for the correlation coefficient. It is the form given in the preceding chapter in terms of definitions of moments of bivariate distributions.

It is evident that α is estimated by a from a linear equation (one equation in one variable) and that a is a linear function of y_t, given x_t. We shall express a in terms of α and e by

$$a = \frac{\sum yx}{\sum x^2} = \frac{\sum (\alpha x + e)x}{\sum x^2} = \alpha + \frac{\sum ex}{\sum x^2}. \tag{3.1.14}$$

Because the x_t are fixed variates (under experimental control), we have

$$E\,a = \alpha + \frac{E \sum ex}{\sum x^2} = \alpha. \tag{3.1.15}$$

This follows from the basic assumption

$$E\,ex = 0. \tag{3.1.4}$$

We have thus established that a is an unbiased estimate of α.

The estimate a is a function of sample observations and, therefore, of e_t, hence a is a random variable with a distribution that is closely related to the distribution of e_t. We can, therefore, evaluate est. var $a = S_a^2$ from

$$E(a - \alpha)^2 = E\left[\frac{\sum ex}{\sum x^2}\right]^2 = \frac{\sigma_e^2 \sum x^2}{(\sum x^2)^2} = \frac{\sigma_e^2}{\sum x^2}. \tag{3.1.16}$$

In this evaluation, we have made use of the property

$$E\,e_t e_{t'} = 0, \quad t \neq t'. \tag{3.1.17}$$

For future use, we derive the expression

$$E(a - \alpha) \sum_{t=1}^{T} e_t x_t = E \frac{(\sum e_t x_t)(\sum e_t x_t)}{\sum x_t^2} = \sigma_e^2. \tag{3.1.18}$$

The least squares estimate a, under present stringent assumptions, has been shown to be a linear estimate and unbiased. It remains to be shown that it is *best* among such linear unbiased estimates, that is, that

$$E(a - \alpha)^2 \leq E(a^* - \alpha)^2,$$

where a^* is any other linear unbiased estimate of α.

We can express a^* as

$$a^* = \sum_{t=1}^{T} \left[\frac{x_t}{\sum x_t^2} + \delta_t \right] y_t,$$

where δ_t is nonstochastic. Therefore a^* is a different linear estimate of α. By the condition of unbiasedness, we have

$$E(a^*) = E\left[\sum \left(\frac{x_t}{\sum x_t^2} + \delta_t \right)(\alpha x_t + e_t) \right]$$

$$= \alpha + E\left(\alpha \sum \delta_t x_t + \frac{\sum x_t e_t}{\sum x_t^2} + \sum \delta_t e_t \right)$$

$$E \sum \delta_t x_t = 0; \quad E \sum \delta_t e_t = 0. \tag{3.1.19}$$

The variance of a^* is

$$E(a^* - \alpha)^2 = \frac{\sigma_e^2}{\sum x_t^2} + \sigma_e^2 \sum \delta_t^2 + 2\sigma_e^2 \frac{\sum \delta_t x_t}{(\sum x_t^2)}. \tag{3.1.20}$$

Because the last term on the right vanishes (condition of unbiasedness) and the second term is positive, we find that a is best among all linear unbiased estimators.

The reader may want to be convinced that we are not using a "straw man" in choosing the best among linear unbiased estimates. In contrast to the least squares estimate,

$$a = \frac{\sum_{t=1}^{T} y_t x_t}{\sum_{t=1}^{T} x_t^2}, \tag{3.1.9}$$

we might consider

$$\tilde{a} = \frac{\sum_{t=1}^{T} y_t}{\sum_{t=1}^{T} x_t}, \tag{3.1.21}$$

or

$$a^* = \frac{y\min + y\max}{x\min + x\max}, \tag{3.1.22}$$

where (y min, x min) and (y max, x max) are pairs associated with minimum and maximum sample values of x_t. Many other examples of linear unbiased estimates are possible.

The estimate of *var e* given above is not a linear estimate; so we shall not classify it as B.L.U.E., but we do say that it is unbiased.

$$E \sum r_t^2 = E \sum (y_t - a x_t)^2 = E \sum (y_t - \alpha x_t - (a - \alpha) x_t)^2$$
$$= E \sum (e_t - (a - \alpha) x_t)^2 = E \sum e_t^2 - 2E(a - \alpha) \sum e_t x_t + E(a - \alpha)^2 \sum x_t^2.$$

Using the above results for $E(a-\alpha)^2$ and $E(a-\alpha)\sum_{t=1}^{T} e_t x_t$, we get

$$E\sum r_t^2 = T\sigma_e^2 - 2\sigma_e^2 + \frac{\sigma_e^2}{\sum x_t^2}\sum x_t^2 = (T-1)\sigma_e^2$$

or

$$E\frac{1}{T-1}\sum (y_t - ax_t)^2 = E\,S_e^2 = \sigma_e^2. \tag{3.1.23}$$

The bivariate results generalize readily. The general regression problem in which the parameters of

$$y_t = \alpha_1 x_{1t} + \cdots + \alpha_n x_{nt} + e_t \tag{3.1.1}$$

are estimated under the stated assumptions is developed as follows: Form

$$S = \sum_{t=1}^{T} (y_t - \alpha_1 x_{1t} - \cdots - \alpha_n x_{nt})^2$$

and minimize S with respect to (*w.r.t.*) α_i. The conditions for a minimum are

$$\frac{\partial S}{\partial \alpha_i} = -2\sum_{t=1}^{T} (y_t - \alpha_1 x_{1t} - \cdots - \alpha_n x_{nt})(x_{it}) = 0$$

or

$$\sum_{t=1}^{T} y_t x_{it} = \alpha_1 \sum_{t=1}^{T} x_{1t} x_{it} + \cdots + \alpha_n \sum_{t=1}^{T} x_{nt} x_{it}, \qquad i = 1, \ldots, n. \tag{3.1.24}$$

These are n linear equations in n unknown parameters. They are the *normal* equations of least squares regression theory.

It may be instructive to give two alternative matrix expressions for these equations. The coefficients in the linear equation system (the "normal" equations) are sample moments. Moment matrices are denoted as

$$M_{xx} = \left(\sum_{t=1}^{T} x_{it} x_{jt}\right) = \begin{bmatrix} \sum x_{1t}^2 & \sum x_{1t}x_{2t} & \cdots & \sum x_{1t}x_{nt} \\ \sum x_{2t}x_{1t} & \sum x_{2t}^2 & \cdots & \sum x_{2t}x_{nt} \\ \vdots & & & \\ \sum x_{nt}x_{1t} & \sum x_{nt}x_{2t} & \cdots & \sum x_{nt}^2 \end{bmatrix}$$

$$M_{xy} = \left(\sum_{t=1}^{T} x_{it} y_t\right) = \begin{bmatrix} \sum x_{1t}y_t \\ \sum x_{2t}y_t \\ \vdots \\ \sum x_{nt}y_t \end{bmatrix}.$$

It will, of course, be noted that M_{xx} is square and symmetrical, and M_{xy} is columnar. In more general formulations, at a later stage, we shall deal with several y_t variables simultaneously. Then M_{xy} will be rectangular.

Writing $\alpha = \begin{bmatrix} \alpha_1 \\ \cdot \\ \cdot \\ \cdot \\ \alpha_n \end{bmatrix}$ as a column vector, we have

$$M_{xx}\alpha = M_{xy} \tag{3.1.25}$$

with solution

$$a = \text{B.L.U.E.}\alpha = M_{xx}^{-1}M_{xy}. \tag{3.1.26}$$

The other matrix formulation in frequent use is based on the definitions[4]

$$X = \begin{bmatrix} x_{11} & x_{21} & \cdots & x_{n1} \\ x_{12} & x_{22} & \cdots & x_{n2} \\ \cdot & \cdot & & \cdot \\ \cdot & \cdot & & \cdot \\ \cdot & \cdot & & \cdot \\ x_{1T} & x_{2T} & \cdots & x_{nT} \end{bmatrix}$$

$$y = \begin{bmatrix} y_1 \\ y_2 \\ \cdot \\ \cdot \\ \cdot \\ y_T \end{bmatrix},$$

with the identities

$$X'X = M_{xx}, \qquad X'y = M_{xy}.$$

These matrix operations imply the evaluation of moments as well as the laying out of a matrix of coefficients in a linear equation system. Our system of normal equations is

$$\begin{aligned} X'X\alpha &= X'y, \\ a &= (X'X)^{-1}X'y. \end{aligned} \tag{3.1.27}$$

Having estimates of the α-coefficients from the normal equations, we can estimate the variance of error by the residual variance from the computed regression in the sample period.

$$S_e^2 = \text{U.E. } \sigma_e^2 = \frac{1}{T-n}\sum_{t=1}^{T} r_t^2 = \frac{1}{T-n}\sum_{t=1}^{T}(y_t - a_1x_{1t} - \cdots - a_nx_{nt})^2. \tag{3.1.28}$$

[4] In matrix X we have kept the t-subscript in its customary second position, x_{it}, although it is usual to have the row designation first.

The corresponding correlation measure is

$$R^2 = 1 - \frac{S_e^2}{S_y^2} \tag{3.1.29}$$

where

$$S_y^2 = \frac{1}{T-1}\sum_{t=1}^{T}(y_t - \bar{y})^2. \tag{3.1.30}$$

Proofs of best and unbiased properties of these multiple regression estimates are simply straightforward extensions of those developed in detail for the bivariate case, and we shall not present them here. We shall, however, develop an expression for the estimated variance of the coefficient estimates.

From the normal equations we can solve explicitly for a_i in the form

$$a_i = \frac{1}{|M_{xx}|}\begin{vmatrix} \sum x_{1t}^2 & \cdots & \sum x_{1t}y_t & \cdots & \sum x_{1t}x_{nt} \\ \vdots & & \vdots & & \vdots \\ \sum x_{nt}x_{1t} & \cdots & \sum x_{nt}y_t & \cdots & \sum x_{nt}^2 \end{vmatrix} \tag{3.1.31}$$

$$a_i = \frac{\sum_{j=1}^{n} |M_{xx}|_{ji} \sum_{t=1}^{T} x_{jt}y_t}{|M_{xx}|}$$

where $|M_{xx}|$ is the determinant of M_{xx} and $|M_{xx}|_{ji}$ is the ji cofactor. Because $|M_{xx}|$ and its cofactor depend only on moments of the x_{it}, the expression for a_i is a linear function of y_t with weights being

$$\frac{\sum_{j=1}^{n} |M_{xx}|_{ji} x_{jt}}{|M_{xx}|}.$$

If we substitute

$$y_t = \sum_{k=1}^{n} \alpha_k x_{kt} + e_t$$

into the expression for a_i, we get

$$a_i = \frac{\sum_{j=1}^{n} |M_{xx}|_{ji} \sum x_{jt}(\sum \alpha_k x_{kt})}{|M_{xx}|} + \frac{\sum_{j=1}^{n} |M_{xx}|_{ji} \sum x_{jt}e_t}{|M_{xx}|}.$$

Using theorems on determinants (expansions by cofactors of same and different columns), we find

$$a_i = \alpha_i + \frac{\sum_{j=1}^{n} |M_{xx}|_{ji} \sum x_{jt}e_t}{|M_{xx}|}, \tag{3.1.32}$$

from which we evaluate

$$E(a_i - \alpha_i)^2 = \sigma_e^2 \frac{|M_{xx}|_{ii}}{|M_{xx}|}. \tag{3.1.33}$$

In analogy with the bivariate result, we note that the variance of a_i is the product of σ_e^2 (as before) and a reciprocal element. In this case, the reciprocal element is the diagonal term of the inverse matrix of moments

$$M_{xx}^{-1} = \frac{1}{|M_{xx}|}[|M_{xx}|_{ij}].$$

This is a one-element matrix for the bivariate case; hence, the corresponding reciprocal element is simply $\frac{1}{\sum x_t^2}$.

Questions and Problems

1. Show that the estimate of the general linear regression equation

$$y_t = \sum_{i=1}^{n} a_i x_{it} + r_t$$

is satisfied with r_t (residual) $= 0$ at the point of sample means, $\bar{y}_t$ and $\bar{x}_{it}$.

2. Demonstrate that the log linear regression of y_t on x_t provides a B.L.U.E. of α in the relationship

$$y_t = Ax_t^{\alpha} e_t.$$

3. Show that the coefficient of multiple correlation, R^2, can be evaluated as the simple (product moment) correlation between actual and computed value of the dependent variable, that is, between y_t and $\sum_{i=1}^{n} a_i x_{it}$.

Alternative approaches to least squares

The most straightforward method of deriving results in the method of least squares is to determine the minimal value of

$$S^2 = \sum_{t=1}^{T} e_t^2 = \sum_{t=1}^{T} (y_t - \sum_{i=1}^{n} \alpha_i x_{it})^2$$

$w.r.t.\alpha_i$.

It is revealing to look at the same estimators from other points of view. We noted previously that our assumptions about the error structure led us to impose the restrictions

$$E\, e_t x_{it} = 0. \tag{3.1.4}$$

If we give sample interpretation to this, we should have

$$\sum_{t=1}^{T} e_t x_{it} = 0. \tag{3.1.34}$$

If we write

$$y_t = \alpha_1 x_{1t} + \cdots + \alpha_n x_{nt} + e_t, \tag{3.1.1}$$

multiply both sides by x_{it}

$$y_t x_{it} = \alpha_1 x_{1t} x_{it} + \cdots + \alpha_n x_{nt} x_{it} + e_t x_{it},$$

and sum over t, we have (imposing the restriction)

$$\sum_{t=1}^{T} y_t x_{it} = \alpha_1 \sum_{t=1}^{T} x_{1t} x_{it} + \cdots + \alpha_n \sum_{t=1}^{T} x_{nt} x_{it}. \tag{3.1.24}$$

This gives us the same normal equations for estimating $\alpha_1, \ldots \alpha_n$. We can thus interpret these estimators as those that give sample display of the assumption in (3.1.4).

An important consequence of this result is that residuals (r_t) from sample regressions are uncorrelated with any of the x_{it} variables used in forming the least squares regressions

$$\sum_{t=1}^{T} r_t x_{it} = 0. \tag{3.1.35}$$

This is the numerator of the product-moment formula for correlation between r_t and any x_{it}. We shall make use of this result later.

For another interpretation of least squares theory, let us assume that the random error e_t follows the normal distribution

$$p(e_t)de_t = \frac{1}{\sqrt{2\pi}\,\sigma_e} \exp\left(-\frac{e_t}{2\sigma_e}\right)^2 de_t. \tag{3.1.36}$$

If all the e_t are mutually independent

$$E\, e_t e_{t'} = 0, \quad t \neq t',$$

we have

$$P(e_1 \ldots e_T)de_1 \ldots de_T = \left(\frac{1}{\sqrt{2\pi}\,\sigma_e}\right)^T \exp\left[-\frac{1}{2\sigma_e^2} \sum_{t=1}^{T} e_t^2\right] de_1 \ldots de_T. \tag{3.1.37}$$

We shall regard the equation to be estimated as a transformation relationship, showing how e_t is transformed into $y_t - \sum_{i=1}^{n} \alpha_i x_{it}$. We can thus replace e_t by its equivalent expression in terms of y_t and x_{it} in the joint probability density function to get

$$p(y_1,\ldots,y_T\,|\,x_{11},\ldots,x_{nT})dy_1,\ldots,dy_T = p(e_1,\ldots,e_T)\left|\frac{\partial(e_1\ldots,e_T)}{\partial(y_1\ldots,y_T)}\right|dy_1\ldots,dy_T$$

$$= \left(\frac{1}{\sqrt{2\pi}\,\sigma_e}\right)^T \exp\left[-\frac{1}{2\sigma_e^2}\sum_{t=1}^{T}(y_t - \sum_{i=1}^{n}\alpha_i x_{it})^2\right]dy_1\ldots\ dy_T. \tag{3.1.38}$$

The joint probability density *assumed* to hold for the T unobserved values of e_t has been transformed into a conditional joint probability density of y_t, given all the x_{it}. The stochastic structure of the relationship, therefore, gives a conditional probability for the endogenous variables in terms of the actual given sample of predetermined variables. This provides a useful framework in which to place the variables in the endogenous and predetermined or exogenous category and reveals the role of the latter in the probability set up.

Another point to observe in this formulation is that the probability density now depends directly on α_i, the coefficients to be estimated. The logarithm of the joint density function can be expressed as

$$L(\alpha_1\ldots,\alpha_n\sigma_e^2) = -T\log\sqrt{2\pi} - T\log\sigma_e - \frac{1}{2\sigma_e^2}\sum_{t=1}^{T}(y_t - \sum_{i=1}^{n}\alpha_i x_{it})^2. \tag{3.1.39}$$

We follow the procedures shown in the previous chapter by defining maximum likelihood estimates of the unknown parameters as those values of $\alpha_1,\ldots,\alpha_n$, σ_e^2 that maximize L. We have

$$\frac{\partial L}{\partial \alpha_j} = -\frac{1}{\sigma_e^2}\sum_{t=1}^{T}(y_t - \sum_{i=1}^{n}\alpha_i x_{it})(-x_{jt}) = 0, \qquad j = 1,\ldots,n.$$

$$\frac{\partial L}{\partial \sigma_e} = -\frac{T}{\sigma_e} + \frac{1}{\sigma_e^3}\sum_{t=1}^{T}(y_t - \sum_{i=1}^{n}\alpha_i x_{it})^2 = 0.$$

The first n equations are the normal equations of least squares theory,

$$\sum_{t=1}^{T} y_t x_{jt} = \hat{\alpha}_1\sum_{t=1}^{T} x_{1t}x_{jt} + \cdots + \hat{\alpha}_n\sum_{t=1}^{T} x_{nt}x_{jt}, \tag{3.1.24}$$

and we shall denote $\hat{\alpha}_i$ as the solutions to this system of linear simultaneous equations.

The final equation, maximizing L, is

$$\hat{\sigma}_e^2 = \frac{1}{T}\sum_{t=1}^{T}(y_t - \sum_{i=1}^{n}\hat{\alpha}_i x_{it})^2. \tag{3.1.40}$$

It is to be noted that the denominator in the expression for $\hat{\sigma}_e^2$ is T, although it was $T - n$ in the previous formula for S_e^2. Maximum likelihood theory is basically a large sample theory, and it contains no corrections for degrees of freedom used up in the estimation process.

The properties of maximum likelihood estimates are those of consistency and efficiency. Consistency has been defined as a large sample concept; therefore, maximum likelihood estimates may be biased (in small samples), yet consistent.

Maximum likelihood estimators may be defined for probability distributions other than the normal distribution, but they take on a particularly simple and manageable form in the case of the normal distribution. It becomes apparent why least squares is an attractive principle, in this respect, for it maximizes the exponent of the likelihood function. Another attractive property of the normal distribution in this approach to regression comes about through the *reproductive* property of the normal distribution. Sums, differences, and general linear functions of normal variables are also normal variables. Because the present estimators are linear estimators, as shown above,[5]

$$\hat{\alpha}_i = \sum_{t=1}^{T} w_{it} e_t,$$

the normality of the error distribution of e_t means that $\hat{\alpha}_i$ will be normally distributed. This is true for samples of any size. If the e_t are not normal, linear estimators, under our present assumptions, would tend toward normality with increasing sample size, but if the e_t are normal, our least squares estimators of α_i (looked at from any of the points of view we have discussed) are normally distributed for samples of any size. This is important in making significance tests for coefficients.

We found it convenient and natural to combine the discussion of normality of the e_t with the method of maximum likelihood estimation, but, as was remarked earlier, this method could be applied to other parametric distributions, although it is not common to do so in the context of regression theory. More important, however, is the fact that the theory of least squares estimation can be carried through, in a more powerful manner, if the errors e_t are normally distributed. In place of maximum likelihood formulas, we may use those leading to unbiased estimates of σ_e^2. Instead of

$$\hat{\sigma}_e^2 = m.l.\sigma_e^2 = \frac{1}{T} \sum_{t=1}^{T} (y_t - \sum_{i=1}^{n} \hat{\alpha}_i x_{it})^2,$$

we would have

$$S_e^2 = \text{U.E.}\sigma_e^2 = \frac{1}{T-n} \sum_{t=1}^{T} (y_t - \sum_{i=1}^{n} \alpha_i x_{it})^2.$$

Under the assumptions made here, both $\hat{\alpha}_i$ and a_i are the same estimators. They are the same functions of the sample observations. From the general properties of *m.l.* estimators, we can say that $\hat{\alpha}_i$ are consistent and efficient (the same is true of $\hat{\sigma}_e^2$), but they are also B.L.U.E. of α_i under the conditions of the Markoff

[5] The weights, w_{it}, are determinantal expressions in the moments of the x_{it}.

theorem. If the distribution of the e_t were not normal, this would not affect the values of the a_i, and they would remain as B.L.U.E. of α_i. In general, the $\hat{\alpha}_i$ would be different if we dropped the normality assumption. The great advantage of normality is that it tells us that a_i and $\hat{\alpha}_i$ are normally distributed for samples of any size, because both are (identical) linear functions of the e_t.

According to maximum likelihood theory, if the log likelihood function is

$$L(\theta_1, \ldots, \theta_n)$$

the asymptotic variance-covariance matrix of $\hat{\theta}_1, \ldots, \hat{\theta}_n$ is given by

$$\left\| \operatorname{cov} \hat{\theta}_i \hat{\theta}_j \right\| = \left\| -E \frac{\partial^2 L}{\partial \theta_i \partial \theta_j} \bigg|_{\theta_i = \hat{\theta}_i} \right\|^{-1}. \tag{3.1.41}$$

Because

$$\frac{\partial^2 L}{\partial \alpha_j \partial \sigma_e} \bigg|_{\substack{\alpha_j = \hat{\alpha}_j \\ \sigma_e = \hat{\sigma}_e}} = 0,$$

we can deal with the asymptotic covariance matrix of $\hat{\alpha}_i$ alone, apart from the variance of $\hat{\sigma}_e^2$. By direct evaluation we have

$$-E \frac{\partial^2 L}{\partial \alpha_i \partial \alpha_j} = E \frac{1}{\sigma_e^2} \sum_{t=1}^{T} x_{it} x_{jt}, \tag{3.1.42}$$

leading to the result

$$\left\| \operatorname{cov} \hat{\alpha}_i \hat{\alpha}_j \right\| = \hat{\sigma}_e^2 \left\| \sum_{t=1}^{T} x_{it} x_{jt} \right\|^{-1}. \tag{3.1.43}$$

This is the same as the general result for the basic theorem of least squares, except that $\hat{\sigma}_e^2$ is used instead of S_e^2. In large samples this difference would not be important.

Summary of estimation of a single equation multivariate regression

Sample estimates of the coefficients in the linear regression

$$y_t = \sum_{i=1}^{n} \alpha_i x_{it} + e_t \tag{3.1.1}$$

can be determined from either of the following three prescriptions:

i. $\sum_{t=1}^{T} e_t^2 = \min.$ — principle of least squares

ii. $\sum_{t=1}^{T} e_t x_{it} = 0$ — independence of errors and explanatory variables

iii. $\left(\frac{1}{\sqrt{2\pi}\,\sigma_e}\right)^T \exp\left[-\frac{1}{2\sigma_e^2} \sum_{t=1}^{T} e_t^2\right] = \max.$ — principle of maximum likelihood—normal distribution

The errors are assumed to have zero mean, to have constant variance, to be mutually independent, and to be independent of the explanatory variables. The explanatory variables are assumed to be fixed variables—not to vary in repeated samples.

The estimates of error variance and sampling errors of coefficients are the same in all methods except that iii is an asymptotic method and does not adjust for degrees of freedom used up in estimating coefficients.

Questions and Problems

1. What are the second order conditions for maximization of the likelihood function associated with the general linear regression?

2. Show that

$$E(y_t/x_{1t}, x_{2t}, \ldots, x_{nt}) = \sum_{i=1}^{n} \hat{\alpha}_i x_{it}.$$

3. What is the form of the likelihood function for linear regression with normal error, if the errors are assumed to be serially correlated?

2. STATISTICAL TESTING

We have dealt so far with the strict problem of *estimating* α_i and σ_e^2 in the linear relationship

$$y_t = \sum_{i=1}^{n} \alpha_i x_{it} + e_t. \tag{3.1.1}$$

We have also dealt with estimation of $S_{a_i}^2$, where a_i is an estimate of α_i. We have not, however, shown how the estimates of $S_{a_i}^2$ might be used in testing hypotheses about the relationship.

Testing may take various forms in econometrics, but the most usual question to be considered is whether a variable has a nonzero coefficient in a linear equation. This is equivalent to testing whether there is any linear relationship or not with this particular variable. Let us consider x_{jt} in the linear equation, with estimated coefficient a_j. The standard error of this coefficient is S_{a_j}. The ratio

$$t = \frac{a_j - a_j^0}{S_{a_j}} \tag{3.2.1}$$

will follow the t-distribution if the errors are normally distributed. In testing for zero values, we choose

$$a_j^0 = 0.$$

A critical value for t must also be chosen, say the value of t corresponding to a probability level of 0.05. Our hypotheses are

$$H_0 : \alpha_j = 0; \qquad H_1 : \alpha_j \neq 0.$$

The probability of type I error, the rejection of H_0 (null hypothesis) when it is, in fact, true is given by

$$P(|t| > t_{.05} \mid H_0) = 0.05.$$

If we find our sample values to be such that

$$\left| \frac{a_j}{S_{a_j}} \right| > t_{.05},$$

we say that the observed point falls in the critical region for rejection of H_0. We conclude, statistically, that the parameter is not zero and that there is a significant linear effect of x_{jt} on y_t.

From the corresponding viewpoint of confidence interval construction, we would say that the interval

$$a_j \pm t_{.05} S_{a_j}$$

does not include zero. If zero is an inadmissible value, at the stated level of confidence, we accept the conclusion that $a_j \neq 0$.

Suppose that the results of the test have gone the other way, that

$$\left| \frac{a_j}{S_{a_j}} \right| \leq t_{.05},$$

say

$$\left| \frac{a_j}{S_{a_j}} \right| = t_{.05+\delta}.$$

We would then have concluded that the probability is larger than 0.05 of having $\left| \frac{a_j}{S_{a_j}} \right| > t_{.05+\delta}$, under the null hypothesis. In these conditions, we would be willing to accept H_0, for the probability is plausibly large for having the sample values we found if H_0 were true. Thus for small t-ratios (smaller than a critical value) we accept H_0, and for large t-ratios we reject H_0. The confidence interval would, in fact, include zero if

$$\left| \frac{a_j}{S_{a_j}} \right| \leq t_{.05}.$$

How should we interpret an insignificant estimate, that is, one with a "small" t-ratio or one that leads to acceptance of H_0? One interpretation is that we cannot reject the hypothesis that $\alpha_j = 0$; therefore, we accept the finding

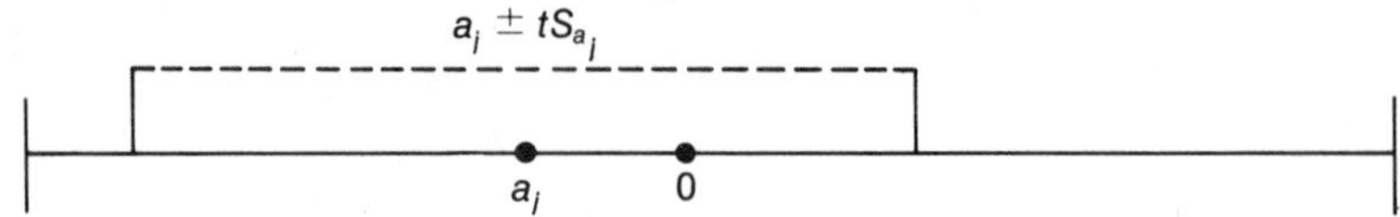

Figure 3.2.1 Confidence interval (insignificant coefficient)

that the influence of x_{jt} on y_t is nil. But we cannot, at the same time, reject other values at the opposite (nonzero) end of the confidence interval, and these might have far from nil effect. In Fig. (3.2.1), we cannot reject, by similar tests, positive or negative values substantially distant from a_j. The most that we can say is that the effect of x_{jt} on y_t is uncertain. It could be fairly large (positive or negative), or it could be nil. To say, with some confidence, that an effect is small, we would need to have a point estimate that is small, on some absolute standard, together with a large t-ratio. In this case, the variable has a significant effect as far as explanatory power in the relationship is concerned, but it has a small effect from the point of view of economic importance. On the same scale as in Fig. (3.2.1), its confidence interval would have to be as in Fig. (3.2.2).

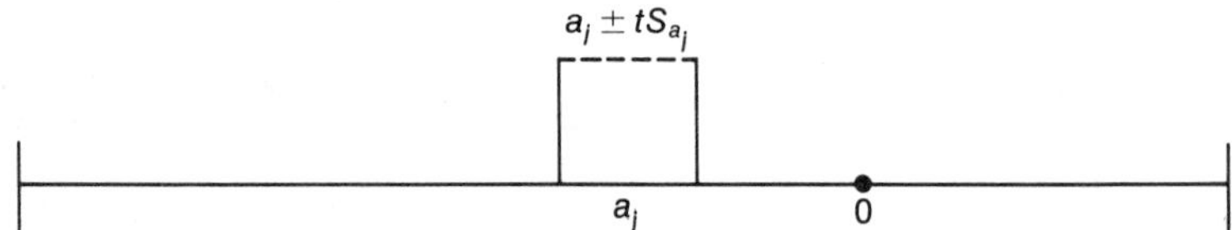

Figure 3.2.2 Confidence interval (significant coefficient)

We must distinguish between statistical significance in terms of degree of relationship and economic significance in terms of magnitude of the regression coefficient. The greater the degree of correlation, the greater will be the t-ratio, with the exception of collinearity effects, to be studied below. It is perhaps instructive to show this for the bivariate case studied above.

$$a = \frac{\sum yx}{\sum x^2}$$

$$r = \frac{\sum yx}{\sqrt{\sum x^2}\sqrt{\sum y^2}}$$

$$t = \frac{a}{S_e/\sqrt{\sum x^2}} = r\frac{\sqrt{\sum y^2}}{\sqrt{\sum x^2}}\frac{\sqrt{\sum x^2}}{S_e} = r\frac{\sqrt{\sum y^2}}{S_e}. \tag{3.2.2}$$

We have also

$$r^2 = 1 - \frac{S_e^2(T-1)}{\sum y^2}$$

$$\frac{\sqrt{\sum y^2}}{S_e} = \frac{\sqrt{T-1}}{\sqrt{1-r^2}};$$

so

$$t = \frac{r(\sqrt{T-1})}{\sqrt{1-r^2}}, \tag{3.2.3}$$

and the t-ratio, for $\alpha^0 = 0$, is seen to vary directly with r, the degree of correlation. This shows that *significance* in conventional testing means significant degree of correlation and not significant magnitude of regression coefficient.

The tests of significance and confidence intervals that we have been considering have been two-sided, or symmetrical, about the point estimates. We have, in fact, been considering the absolute value of t in these tests; whereas, one-sided tests may be more appropriate. In many, if not most, econometric relationships, we have a priori notions about the qualitative nature of parameters; that is, we do not admit positive own-price elasticities for most goods or negative marginal productivities, and so on. This being so, we may be more interested in testing whether a parameter estimate is significantly *greater* than zero or significantly *less* than zero, instead of whether it is significantly *different* from zero.

Suppose that $a_j^0 = 0$ so that

$$t = \frac{a_j}{S_{a_j}};$$

we then consider

$$P(t > t_{.10} \mid H_0) = 0.05;$$

$t_{.10}$ is the usual value of t, taken from the distribution

$$P(|t| > t_{.10} \mid H_0) = 0.10.$$

The t-test, as described above, in either its one-tail or two-tail form, is widely applied in econometric regression analysis. But it is formulated under the null hypothesis, $H = H_0$. The procedures followed guard against type I errors in hypothesis testing by making the probability as low as 0.05 (or some other preassigned value) of rejecting H_0 when it is true, but, as explained in the preceding chapter, we can also make type II errors by accepting false hypotheses. We have to consider the probability of avoiding a type II error that is given by

$$P(|t| > t_{.05} \mid H_1).$$

There are an infinite number of values of α_j under H_1, and this probability will be different, in general, for each one. If the test is two-sided, permitting both negative and positive values for α_j under H_1, we can say that this probability of avoiding type II errors will not be uniformly greater than the probabilities given by any critical region other than that adopted, $|t| > t_{.05}$. On the other hand, if we made a one-sided test, restricting the α_j under H_1 to be either only positive or only negative, the one-sided test proposed would be a uniformly most powerful test in the sense that we would have minimum probability of type II error among all tests with 5 percent probability of committing type I error.

Economists frequently make hypotheses about functions of parameters as well as about individual parameter values. The acceleration principle implies, in some forms, that rate of change variables are the relevant ones to consider; in other words, that

$$\alpha_j = -\alpha_{j+1}.$$

Or we might test that

$$\sum_{j=1}^{n} \alpha_j < 1$$

for some kind of stability condition, possibly dynamic stability (long-run propensity to spend) or comparative static stability (diminishing returns). The variance of any linear function of coefficients, including ordinary sums and differences, is given by

$$S^2_{\sum_{i=1}^{n} w_i a_i} = \sum_{i=1}^{n} w_i^2 S^2_{a_i} + 2 \sum_{i<j} w_i w_j S_{a_i a_j}. \tag{3.2.4}$$

The w_i are *known* weights, and the $S_{a_i a_j}$ are covariances between parameter estimates. We estimate $S^2_{a_i}$ from the inverse moment matrix by multiplying S^2_e by the i-th diagonal element of

$$M_{xx}^{-1} = \left\| \sum_{t=1}^{T} x_{it} x_{jt} \right\|^{-1}.$$

We analogously estimate $S_{a_i a_j}$ by multiplying S^2_e by the i, j off-diagonal element of M_{xx}^{-1}. A t-test can be applied to

$$t = \frac{\sum w_i a_i - \sum w_i a_i^0}{S_{\sum w_i a_i}}.$$

When we test an hypothesis about a single parameter or a functional value of parameters, we construct a confidence interval along a straight line, where successive values of the parameter or function can be arrayed. A more general approach, however, is to construct a confidence region for the joint hypotheses about two or more parameter values. In place of a linear interval, we shall deal with a confidence ellipsoid. As in the interval case, we shall center the ellipsoid at the estimate $a_1, \ldots, a_n$ with the equation

$$\sum_{i,j} m_{ij}(\alpha_i - a_i)(\alpha_j - a_j) = n\, S^2_e\, F_{n,T-n,\alpha} \tag{3.2.5}$$

where

$$m_{ij} = \sum_{t=1}^{T} x_{it} x_{jt}$$

and $F_{n,T-n,\alpha}$ is taken from the F-distribution for n and $T-n$ degrees of freedom at the α probability level. We can write the corresponding probability criterion as

$$P\left(\frac{1}{nS_e^2}\sum m_{ij}(a_i - \alpha_i)(a_j - \alpha_j)\right) < F_{n,T-n,.95} = .95.$$

In this case, we have written the probability equation in terms of the level of confidence, although for the t-test we stated it as the probability of type I error.

Questions and Problems

1. Discuss the idea that testing of economic hypotheses from nonexperimental data enables one to reject false hypotheses but does not necessarily enable one to accept true hypotheses.

2. Compare the t and F tests for significance (different from zero) of the effect of x_t on y_t in the regression model

$$y_t = \alpha + \beta x_t + e_t, \qquad t = 1, 2, \ldots, T.$$

3. VARIATIONS OF THE STANDARD CASE AND SPECIAL PROBLEMS

Procedures for estimating multiple regression equations have become highly standardized and are often carried out without much regard to the underlying theory. This background theory, however, is important in interpreting results and in dealing with complications that arise. The theory in question is centered about the probability structure of the random errors in the equation. Although the least squares regression estimates can usually be readily calculated as numerical magnitudes, the interpretation of the numbers as best linear unbiased estimates, as maximum likelihood estimates, or as estimates with some sort of desirable properties is not possible unless the random errors satisfy strong assumptions. Assumptions that are adequate for giving interpretations of the results have been made in the preceding sections. We now consider the weakening of these assumptions.

a. Generalized least squares[6]

The basic theorem of least squares that serves as the model for most regression analysis is based on the assumptions

$$E\,e_t^2 = \sigma_e^2 < \infty, \quad E\,e_t e_{t'} = 0 \text{ if } t \neq t'.$$

[6] This generalization is known as Aitken's generalization of the Markoff Theorem. A. C. Aitken, "On Least Squares and Linear Combinations of Observations," *Proceedings of the Royal Society of Edinburgh*, 55 (1934–35), 42–48.

All e_t are mutually independent drawings from the same probability distribution with constant variance. Now, let us suppose that the e_t are all drawn from different populations and that the drawings are not necessarily mutually independent. We then have

$$E\begin{bmatrix} e_1 \\ \cdot \\ \cdot \\ \cdot \\ e_T \end{bmatrix}(e_1, \ldots, e_T) = \begin{bmatrix} \sigma_{11} & \sigma_{12} & \cdots & \sigma_{1T} \\ \sigma_{21} & \sigma_{22} & \cdots & \sigma_{2T} \\ \cdot & & & \\ \cdot & & & \\ \cdot & & & \\ \sigma_{T1} & \sigma_{T2} & \cdots & \sigma_{TT} \end{bmatrix}$$

or

$$E\, ee' = \textstyle\sum.$$

The elements of $\sum$ are variances and covariances of individual e_t. By contrast, in the standard case we have

$$E\, ee' = \sigma_e^2\, I;$$

all diagonal elements are the same $(= \sigma_e^2)$, and all off-diagonal elements are zero.

Instead of minimizing $\sum_{t=1}^{T} e_t^2$, as in the standard case, we minimize $\sum_{j=1}^{T}\sum_{i=1}^{T} \sigma^{ij}\, e_i e_j$, a quadratic form in e_t, with coefficients σ^{ij} defined as elements of $\sum^{-1}$, the inverse matrix of $\sum$. The quadratic form to be minimized may be written, in matrix notation, as

$$S = e' \textstyle\sum^{-1} e = (y - X\alpha)' \sum^{-1} (y - X\alpha).$$

Differentiating with respect to elements of α, we have

$$2X' \textstyle\sum^{-1} y - 2X' \sum^{-1} X\alpha = 0$$

or

$$a = (X' \textstyle\sum^{-1} X)^{-1} (X' \sum^{-1} y). \qquad (3.3.1)$$

This is an unbiased estimator if $\sum$ is known a priori. This can be seen if we substitute from

$$y = X\alpha + e$$

to get

$$a = (X' \textstyle\sum^{-1} X)^{-1} X' \sum^{-1} X\alpha + (X' \sum^{-1} X)^{-1} X' \sum^{-1} e$$

$$a = \alpha + (X' \textstyle\sum^{-1} X)^{-1} X' \sum^{-1} e. \qquad (3.3.2)$$

Because the elements of X are fixed variables and $\sum$ is assumed to be known, we have

$$E\,a = \alpha.$$

In addition, if all these assumptions are met, a is a best linear unbiased estimate of α.

This formulation is more general than our previous formulation, but it requires a large amount of a priori information on the elements of $\sum$. It shows us how to proceed with estimation in case $\sum$ is known. Our task now is to investigate what might be done by way of generalizing the standard case when elements of $\sum$ are not known, but the framework of Aitken's generalized formulation will be useful in showing what we might do if we can obtain estimates of $\sum$. In special cases, we might have some a priori information about $\sum$, but usually we must proceed on the assumption that its elements are not known.

b. Interdependence of errors

We first consider the dropping of the assumption

$$E\,e_t e_{t'} = 0, \quad t \neq t'.$$

In this case, $\sum$ is no longer diagonal and the procedures discussed can be looked upon as estimates where

$$E\,ee' = \begin{bmatrix} \sigma_e^2 & \cdots & \sigma_{1T} \\ \cdot & & \cdot \\ \cdot & & \cdot \\ \cdot & & \cdot \\ \sigma_{T1} & \cdots & \sigma_e^2 \end{bmatrix}.$$

We assume that variances are constant, but that covariances among different elements of e are nonzero. The assumption that covariances are zero greatly simplified our previous results. For example, in forming maximum likelihood estimators, we assumed

$$p(e_1, \ldots, e_T) = p(e_1), \ldots, p(e_T).$$

This simplified the expression for the likelihood function. Even though we can form estimates from $\sum_{t=1}^{T} e_t^2 = \min$, when we do not have

$$E(e_t e_{t'}) = 0, \quad t \neq t'$$

our previous formulas for S_{a_i} would not hold. Our propositions about consistency would not be impaired, but our propositions about efficiency would. If the random errors are mutually dependent, our samples are not as large as enumeration of the number of observations would imply. We must, therefore, seek some more efficient form of regression.

Let us consider two possible forms of sample variation—time variation (e_t: $t = 1, \ldots, T$) and spatial variation (e_s: $s = 1, \ldots, S$). A random time series has a jagged, irregular form, and its elements may be assumed to be temporally independent. Examples of nonindependent (or dependent) time series would be trends, cycles, or combinations of the two. Possibly the simplest kind of dependent series is

$$e_t = \rho e_{t-1} + v_t, \tag{3.3.3}$$

where

$$Ev_t v_{t'} = 0, \qquad t \neq t',$$

and

$$|\rho| < 1.$$

The latter condition assures that var e_t determined from a solution of the autoregressive equation in e_t has finite variance. The assumption of dependence among errors could be achieved in a less simple way by assuming

$$e_t = \sum_{i=1}^{p} \rho_i e_{t-i} + v_t$$

or

$$e_t = f(e_t, \ldots e_{t-p}, v_t)$$

or an infinite variety of time-dependent relationships. We shall, however, confine attention here to

$$e_t = \rho e_{t-1} + v_t. \tag{3.3.3}$$

This means that the independence assumptions are transferred from e_t to v_t, and we say that the errors satisfy a first order autoregressive process. The variance-covariance matrix for Aitken estimators is

$$\sigma_e^2 \Sigma = \sigma_e^2 \begin{bmatrix} 1 & \rho & \cdots & \rho^{T-1} \\ \rho & 1 & \cdots & \rho^{T-2} \\ \vdots & \vdots & & \vdots \\ \rho^{T-1} & \rho^{T-2} & \cdots & 1 \end{bmatrix}. \tag{3.3.4}$$

There are thus only two variance-covariance parameters, σ_e^2 and ρ.

In the case of spatial variation, there is no natural way to order the observations. Instead of assuming, in the ideal case, that items adjacent (or near) in time are independent, we assume that items near in space are independent. In the time case a form of independence was taken to mean $\rho = 0$, or that the autoregressive parameter is zero. In spatial models we take the analogue assumption to mean that items nearby in space are independent—that there is no within-class (or between-class) association. If we permit within-class association, we have a situation like that of autoregressive errors in time series analysis. Suppose that there are q classes or groups

$$\begin{matrix} e_{11} & \cdots & e_{1S_1} \\ e_{21} & \cdots & e_{2S_2} \\ & \vdots & \vdots \\ e_{q1} & \cdots & e_{qS_q} \end{matrix}$$

Let us assume that there is a lack of independence within groups but independence between groups.

$$Ee_{ij}e_{ik} = \sigma_{ijk} \neq 0, \qquad j, k = 1, 2, \dots S_i$$

and

$$Ee_{ij}e_{lk} = 0, \qquad i \neq l.$$

This specification yields a variance-covariance matrix of error

$$E\,ee' = \begin{Vmatrix} \Sigma_1 & 0 & 0 & \cdots & 0 \\ 0 & \Sigma_2 & 0 & \cdots & 0 \\ 0 & 0 & \Sigma_3 & \cdots & 0 \\ \vdots & \vdots & \vdots & & \vdots \\ 0 & 0 & 0 & \cdots & \Sigma_q \end{Vmatrix}. \tag{3.3.5}$$

This matrix is block-diagonal with

$$\Sigma_i = \| \sigma_{ijk} \|.$$

If the variance-covariance elements in the different nonzero blocks are the same from block to block, we have a matrix similar to that of the autoregressive case, for as t grows, and $|\rho| < 1$, ρ^t falls. After sufficiently large t, $\rho^t \sim 0$, and we have a matrix that is close to being block-diagonal. It is not, however, precisely the same.

We shall confine our attention here to the time series case, with autocorrelated errors. Our problem will be formulated as the estimation of $\alpha_1, \dots, \alpha_n$, σ and ρ from

$$y_t = \sum_{i=1}^{n} \alpha_i x_{it} + e_t$$

$$e_t = \rho e_{t-1} + v_t,$$

where

$$E\, v_t v_{t'} = 0, \qquad t \neq t',$$

and

$$E\, e_t x_{it} = 0.$$

There are several alternative approaches open for the estimation of this linear stochastic equation with autocorrelated disturbances. A straightforward approach seems to be elimination of e_t and replacement by v_t, transforming as follows:

$$y_t = \sum_{i=1}^{n} \alpha_i x_{it} + e_t$$

$$\rho y_{t-1} = \rho \sum_{i=1}^{n} \alpha_i x_{it-1} + \rho e_{t-1}.$$

Subtracting the bottom equation from the top, we have

$$y_t - \rho y_{t-1} = \sum_{i=1}^{n} \alpha_i (x_{it} - \rho x_{i,t-1}) + e_t - \rho e_{t-1}, \tag{3.3.6}$$

or

$$y'_t = \sum_{i=1}^{n} \alpha_i x'_{it} + v_t$$

where

$$y'_t = y_t - \rho y_{t-1},$$

$$x'_{it} = x_{it} - \rho x_{i,t-1}.$$

We note that if each variable is autoregressively transformed by the same transformation that the e_t and v_t satisfy, we have an equation in y'_t and x'_{it} that now meets the assumptions of the standard case. We can, therefore, transform all our variables to y'_t and x'_{it}; then, proceed as before with least squares theory applied to $\sum_{t=1}^{T} v_t^2$. This procedure would require, however, prior knowledge of ρ. It would be an Aitken estimation of α. The transformations suggested rationalize the frequent use of first differences, for if $\rho = 1$, we have

$$y'_t = y_t - y_{t-1}$$

$$x'_{it} = x_{it} - x_{i,t-1}.$$

Thus if we are dealing with a case in which the errors are highly autocorrelated ($\rho \sim 1.0$) and observe strong positive correlation in sample residuals, a transformation of data to first differences is often recommended to obtain serially uncorrelated residuals. The theory, of course, is in terms of the true (unobserved) errors, but the practical testing is in terms of sample residuals.

Let us suppose now that ρ is not known in advance and that there is no reason to assume that it is close to unity. We could pose this problem: Find estimates of α_i and ρ that minimize

$$\sum_{t=1}^{T} v_t^2 = \sum_{t=1}^{T} \{(y_t - \rho y_{t-1}) - \sum \alpha_i(x_{it} - \rho x_{i,t-1})\}^2.$$

This formulation fails to meet the assumption of linearity; so we cannot proceed in the ordinary way with least squares regression methods. The function to be fitted to the sample data, after autoregressive transformation of variables, is no longer linear in parameters. It depends nonlinearly on ρ and α_i; it is a function of $\rho\alpha_i$. Nonlinear methods, generally, will be discussed below. Here, we shall indicate some special procedures for estimating α_i and ρ.

A linear method of successive approximation will produce estimates that (approximately) minimize $\sum v_t^2$, but the linear calculations have to be repeated, a few times at least, before the requisite estimates can be obtained. With electronic computing aids, this approach is not difficult, but it is laborious as a hand calculation.

For any initial estimated value of $\rho = r_0$, transform the observations

$$y'_{0t} = y_t - r_0 y$$
$$x'_{i0t} = x_{it} - r_0 x_{i,t-1}.$$

Regress y'_{0t} on the x'_{i0t} to obtain regression coefficients a_{i0}. Next, compute residuals

$$y_t - \sum_{i=1}^{n} a_{i0} x_{it} = \hat{e}_{0t},$$

and from these, compute r_1 as

$$r_1 = \frac{\sum_{t=2}^{T} \hat{e}_{0t}\hat{e}_{0,t-1}}{\sum_{t=2}^{T} \hat{e}_{0,t-1}^2}.$$

Again, transform the observations

$$y'_{1t} = y_t - r_1 y_{t-1}$$
$$x'_{i1t} = x_{it} - r_1 x_{i,t-1},$$

and regress y'_{1t} on the x'_{i1t} to get estimates a_{i1}. From a new set of residuals,

$$y_t - \sum_{i=1}^{n} a_{i1} x_{it} = \hat{e}_{1t}$$

we find

$$r_2 = \frac{\sum_{t=2}^{T} \hat{e}_{1t}\hat{e}_{1,t-1}}{\sum_{t=2}^{T} \hat{e}_{1,t-1}^2}$$

and continue iteratively until the estimates of ρ and α_i remain the same (within prescribed limits of accuracy) on successive rounds.

This method was originally proposed by Cochrane and Orcutt.[7] It was later shown by Sargan to converge to a local minimum for $\sum v_t^2$.[8] The relative minimum of $\sum v_t^2$ in the sample space is not necessarily unique, and Sargan has proved convergence only to a relative minimum. Convergence may not be fast, but if the investigator has good a priori notions about the value of ρ and starts from a good initial approximation, r_0, convergence will be improved.

As long as $Ee_t x_{it} = 0$, we shall have consistent estimates of α_i on each round of the Cochrane-Orcutt procedure, and the regression residuals used to estimate ρ on each iterative round will be consistently estimated. Thus, both α_i and ρ will be consistently estimated by this approach. To avoid the possibility of convergence to a local minimum that is not an absolute minimum, starting values, r_0, should be systematically varied over the interval

$$-1 < r_0 < 1,$$

and if convergence to a relative minimum is not unique, the smallest of the relative minima should be chosen as the desired estimate.

If we, in fact, vary r systematically over the whole interval

$$-1 < r < 1,$$

we can directly find the "best" estimators of α and ρ. Suppose that we search the interval from -1 to $+1$ in steps of 0.1.

$$-.9, -.8, -.7, \ldots, 0, +.1, +.2, \ldots, +.7, +.8, +.9$$

For each possible value of ρ at these interval points, transform to y_t' and x_{it}' and estimate α_i by least squares regressions of y_t' on x_{it}'. In the neighborhood of the value of ρ that gives the smallest residual sum of squares, search an interval for values of ρ in smaller steps, say 0.01. Again, transform to y_t' and x_t' for each assumed value of ρ, and estimate α_i by regression of y_t' on x_{it}'. When we have located an optimal value of ρ, accurate to as many decimal places as we like, we can terminate the search. The estimates of α_i and ρ that give the smallest sum of squared residuals in this search are our estimates. For normally distributed errors, they are maximum likelihood estimates. They have the advantage of leading us to a *global* optimum and not simply to a *local* optimum. The search method is fast and simple for a first order autoregressive process in which there is only one unknown parameter on which the search is carried out.

[7] D. Cochrane and G. H. Orcutt, "Application of Least Squares Regression to Relationships Containing Autocorrelated Error Terms," *Journal of the American Statistical Association*, 44 (1949), 32–61.

[8] J. D. Sargan, *Colston Papers*, Vol. XVI (London: Butterworths Scientific Publications, 1964).

If there are two autoregressive parameters

$$e_t = \rho_1 e_{t-1} + \rho_2 e_{t-2} + v_t, \tag{3.3.7}$$

we can use analogous methods. The Cochrane-Orcutt iteration method uses the transformation

$$y'_t = y_t - \rho_1 y_{t-1} - \rho_2 y_{t-2}$$
$$x'_{it} = x_{it} - \rho_1 x_{i,t-1} - \rho_2 x_{i,t-2}.$$

From the residuals at each iterative stage, we must estimate two autoregressive parameters, transform the data, and regress y'_t on x'_{it} to estimate α_i.

It is still feasible to search the parameter space for estimates of both ρ_1 and ρ_2. For a given value of ρ_1, search for ρ_2 in intervals of 0.1 (or possibly 0.2 to 0.25). If this is done for each of several values of ρ_1, we cover variation of both parameters.

In the case of one parameter, we restrict ourselves to the interval

$$-1 < \rho < +1,$$

Where we have two parameters, our region is defined as one in which ρ_1 and ρ_2 are confined to an area such that the solution of the finite difference equation

$$e_t = \rho_1 e_{t-1} + \rho_2 e_{t-2} \tag{3.3.8}$$

is stable. This will be the case if the roots of the characteristic equation

$$\lambda^2 - \rho_1 \lambda - \rho_2 = 0 \tag{3.3.9}$$

are less than unity in absolute value. This will be so if

$$\begin{aligned} &|\lambda_1| < 1, |\lambda_2| < 1, \text{ where} \\ &\lambda_1 = \frac{\rho_1 + \sqrt{\rho_1^2 + 4\rho_2}}{2} \\ &\lambda_2 = \frac{\rho_1 - \sqrt{\rho_1^2 + 4\rho_2}}{2}. \end{aligned} \tag{3.3.10}$$

We may also write

$$\begin{aligned} +\rho_1 &= \lambda_1 + \lambda_2 \\ -\rho_2 &= \lambda_1 \lambda_2. \end{aligned} \tag{3.3.11}$$

The maximum value of ρ_1 is 2, and the minimum is -2. The extremes for ρ_2 are $+1$ and -1. The area of search for values of ρ_1 and ρ_2 that simultaneously satisfy the stability conditions is depicted in Fig. (3.3.1).[9] It is the triangle with

[9] G. M. Jenkins and D. G. Watts, *Spectral Analysis and Its Applications* (San Francisco: Holden-Day, 1968) p. 229.

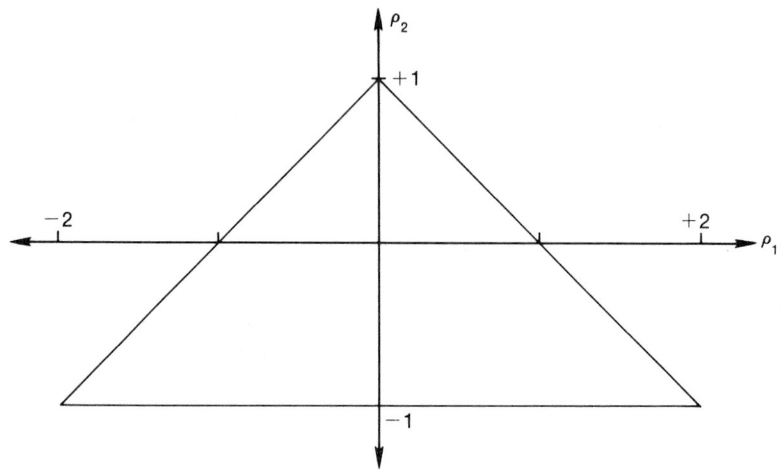

Figure 3.3.1 Stability Region for Second Order Autoregression

height between +1 and −1, the limits on a scale of ρ_2, and base between +2 and −2, the limits on the scale of ρ_1. The sides each have unit slope.

With more than two autoregressive parameters, the search procedure is too tedious. An iterative technique is then required. A direct algebraic method of estimating ρ and α_1 can also be devised for the first order case. From the transformed regression

$$y_t - \rho y_{t-1} = \sum_{i=1}^{n} \alpha_i (x_{it} - \rho x_{it-1}) + v_t$$

$$y'_t = \sum_{i=1}^{n} \alpha_i x'_{it} + v_t$$

we can minimize $\sum v_t^2$ with respect to ρ and α_i to get transformed normal equations

$$\sum_{t=2}^{T} y'_t x'_{jt} = \sum_{t=2}^{T} \sum_{i=1}^{n} \alpha_i x'_{it} x'_{jt} \tag{3.3.12}$$

and

$$\sum_{t=2}^{T} [(y_t - \rho y_{t-1}) - \sum_{i=1}^{n} \alpha_i (x_i - \rho x_{i,t-1})](y_{t-1} - \sum_{i=1}^{n} \alpha_i x_{i,t-1}) = 0.$$

From the transformed normal equations, we can express α_i as functions of ρ. These functions will be ratios of two polynomials in ρ.

$$\alpha_i = \frac{P_1(\rho)}{P_2(\rho)}. \tag{3.3.13}$$

Each polynomial in this expression will be of degree $2n$. If we substitute in the remaining equation of the optimizing set that involves terms of the form $\alpha_i \alpha_j \rho$, we have a final polynomial of degree $4n + 1$

$$P(\rho) = 0. \tag{3.3.14}$$

Among the roots of this polynomial, we are interested in real values of ρ that are associated with a characteristic equation that has roots between -1 and $+1$. Again, with adequate electronic computing facilities, we could extract all relevant roots and choose that one that, together with estimates of α_i, minimize $\sum v_t^2$.

If we estimate the linear structural relation on the assumption that $E(e_t e_{t'}) = 0$, $t \neq t'$, and have no a priori conviction that this hypothesis must be true, we can test the validity of this assumption by forming serial correlation statistics of the residuals. A statistic proposed by von Neumann is

$$\frac{\delta^2}{s^2} = \frac{\sum_{t=2}^{T} (e_t - e_{t-1})^2}{\sum_{t=1}^{T} e_t^2} \frac{T}{T-1}. \tag{3.3.15}$$

We find, on expansion, that this is

$$\frac{\delta^2}{s^2} = \frac{T}{T-1} \frac{\sum_{t=2}^{T} e_t^2 - 2\sum_{t=2}^{T} e_t e_{t-1} + \sum_{t=2}^{T} e_{t-1}^2}{\sum_{t=1}^{T} e_t^2} \cong \frac{2T(1 - r_{-1})}{T-1} \tag{3.3.16}$$

where

$$r_{-1} = \frac{\sum_{t=2}^{T} e_t e_{t-1}}{\sqrt{\sum_{t=2}^{T} e_t^2 \sum_{t=2}^{T} e_{t-1}^2}}.$$

If we ignore end-point effects in $e_1 \ldots e_T$; $e_2 \ldots e_T$; and $e_1 \ldots e_{T-1}$, the formula for δ^2/S^2 in terms of r_{-1} holds exactly. For serial independence ($r_{-1} = 0$), we should have

$$\frac{\delta^2}{S^2} = \frac{2T}{T-1}. \tag{3.3.17}$$

Probabilities for the distribution of δ^2/S^2 under the hypothesis

$$H_0\colon Ee_t e_{t'} = 0, \qquad t \neq t'$$

are tabulated in the form[10]

$$Pr\left(\frac{\delta^2}{S^2} < k \mid H_0\right) = \int_0^k p\left(\frac{\delta^2}{S^2}\right) d\left(\frac{\delta^2}{S^2}\right). \tag{3.3.18}$$

[10] B. I. Hart and J. von Neumann, "Tabulation of the Probabilities for the Ratio of the Mean Square Successive Difference to the Variance," *Annals of Mathematical Statistics*, XIII (June, 1942), 207–14.

Values near 2.1 indicate acceptance of H_0. For different probability levels and sample sizes, values of δ^2/S^2 computed from sample residuals can be tested for temporal independence. Generally speaking, values between 1.7 and 2.5 will suggest acceptance of the independence assumption, H_0. Values much below this critical level (1.0 and lower) indicate the presence of positive first order serial correlation as a form of nonindependence. Large values (3.0 or more) indicate the presence of negative first order serial correlation. This form of nonindependence is less prevalent in economic time series than is the former.

The von Neumann statistic would be best suited to a test of independence among the true errors, e_t. We must evaluate the test statistics from computed residuals. J. Durbin and G. Watson have devised a test for independence of residuals from computed regressions.[11] This statistic is

$$d = \frac{T-1}{T}\frac{\delta^2}{S^2} = \frac{\sum_{t=2}^{T}(\text{res}_t - \text{res}_{t-1})^2}{\sum_{t=1}^{T}(\text{res})_t^2}. \tag{3.3.19}$$

They find distributions for pairs T, n (number of sample observations, number of estimated parameters) of two statistics d_L and d_U that contain d in an interval. Critical values of d_L and d_U are lower and upper critical levels for specified probability values. We denote these as $d_{L,p}$ and $d_{U,p}$. We then have the test procedure:

If $d \geq d_{U,p}$	accept H_0
$d_{L,p} < d < d_{U,p}$	inconclusive
$d \leq d_{L,p}$	reject H_0.

In principle, the Durbin-Watson test makes superior use of the von Neumann statistic for application to the specific problem of error independence in regression analysis, but in practice it is often an inconclusive test.

Questions and Problems

1. What is the difference between the method of generalized least squares (Aitken estimation) of the linear regression model with autoregressive errors and the Cochrane-Orcutt iteration method of estimation?

2. Show how the search method of estimation of the second order case [two autoregressive parameters as in (3.3.7)] can be implemented by searching directly over values of λ_1 and λ_2 such that $|\lambda_1|$ and $|\lambda_2| < 1$.

[11] J. Durbin and G. S. Watson, "Testing for Serial Correlation in Least Squares Regression," *Biometrika*, XXXVII and XXXVIII (December, 1950; June, 1951), 409–28, 159–78.

3. Would the omission of a relevant variable in the specification of a linear equation result in serially correlated residuals? Would the misspecification of a nonlinear function as being approximately linear result in serially correlated residuals?

b. 1. *Lag Distributions.* The problems caused by lack of independence among errors are not problems of consistency or bias mainly, but are problems of efficiency. Even if we proceed in the usual way for the standard case as though $\rho = 0$, when it really does not, we would obtain regression coefficients that are asymptotically unbiased.[12] There is an interesting case, however, in which serial correlation of errors gives rise to a problem of inconsistency. Consider the distributed lag relation

$$y_t = \sum_{i=1}^{p} \alpha_i x_{t-i} + e_t \tag{3.3.20}$$

in which y_t is linearly explained by p lags in x_t. For several reasons, but especially those having to do with multicollinearity discussed below, we might want to specify relations among the α_i in a *lag distribution.*

Among the plausible distributions, the type known as the Koyck lag distribution is[13]

$$y_t = \alpha \sum_{i=0}^{\infty} \lambda^i x_{t-i} + e_t, \tag{3.3.21}$$

or

$$y_t = \alpha x_t + \alpha\lambda x_{t-1} + \alpha\lambda^2 x_{t-2} + \cdots + e_t.$$

The coefficients are thus α, $\alpha\lambda$, $\alpha\lambda^2$, $\alpha\lambda^3$, and so on. In contrast with the unrestricted scheme $\alpha_1, \alpha_2, \alpha_3, \ldots, \alpha_p$, this is an infinite distribution; however, this difference is not practically significant because if $|\lambda| < 1$, after enough periods have elapsed, $\alpha\lambda^i \longrightarrow 0$. We have, therefore, an effective cutoff in the lag distribution.

Having restricted the successive coefficients of the lagged values of x_t to conform to the geometric distribution pattern, we have only two unknown parameters, α and λ, instead of p parameters. Koyck transformed the problem in the following way:

$$\begin{aligned} y_t &= \alpha x_t + \alpha\lambda x_{t-1} + \alpha\lambda^2 x_{t-2} + \cdots + e_t \\ \lambda y_{t-1} &= \alpha\lambda x_{t-1} + \alpha\lambda^2 x_{t-2} + \cdots + \lambda e_{t-1}. \end{aligned}$$

Subtracting, we get

$$y_t - \lambda y_{t-1} = \alpha x_t + e_t - \lambda e_{t-1}$$

[12] See H. Wold, "On Least Squares Regression with Autocorrelated Variables and Residuals," *Bulletin of the International Institute of Statistics*, 32, II (1950), 277–89.

[13] L. M. Koyck, *Distributed Lags and Investment Analysis* (Amsterdam: North-Holland Publishing Company, 1954).

or

$$y_t = \alpha x_t + \lambda y_{t-1} + (e_t - \lambda e_{t-1}). \tag{3.3.22}$$

This appears to be a linear regression with transformed error $e_t - \lambda e_{t-1}$. These error terms are not serially independent, however, because

$$\sum (e_t - \lambda e_{t-1})(e_{t-1} - \lambda e_{t-2}) = \sum (e_t e_{t-1} - \lambda e_t e_{t-2} - \lambda e_{t-1}^2 + \lambda^2 e_{t-1} e_{t-2}).$$

If the series e_t is serially uncorrelated, all terms on the right-hand side vanish except $-\lambda \sum e_{t-1}^2$. This being a sum of squares is, in general, not zero.

We have not yet dropped the assumption that the explanatory variables x_t and e_t are independent. We have

$$E\, e_t x_t = 0, \tag{3.1.4}$$

but we do not have

$$E\, e_t y_t = 0.$$

The problem with the treatment of

$$y_t = \alpha x_t + \lambda y_{t-1} + e_t - \lambda e_{t-1}$$

as an ordinary regression problem is that the combined error is not independent of y_{t-1}, for

$$E\, y_{t-1} e_{t-1} \neq 0.$$

We would have to assume this to be zero in obtaining a least squares regression of y_t on x_t and y_{t-1}.

A simple linear method of dealing with this problem is related to one of the alternative interpretations of least squares theory. Instead of forming the estimation equations by multiplying each side by y_{t-1} and summing, we might use x_{t-1} instead and form, together with a similar use of x_t, the estimation equations

$$\begin{aligned} \sum_{t=1}^{T} y_t x_t &= \alpha \sum_{t=1}^{T} x_t^2 + \lambda \sum_{t=1}^{T} y_{t-1} x_t, \\ \sum_{t=1}^{T} y_t x_{t-1} &= \alpha \sum_{t=1}^{T} x_t x_{t-1} + \lambda \sum_{t=1}^{T} y_{t-1} x_{t-1}. \end{aligned} \tag{3.3.23}$$

These will give consistent estimates of α and λ since[14]

$$Ex_{t-i} e_t = 0 \text{ for all } i.$$

This is not an efficient procedure, but it leads to very simple calculations. The extension of this method to more variables is evident.

[14] N. Liviatan, "Consistent Estimation of Distributed Lags," *International Economic Review*, 4 (January, 1963), 44–52.

The efficiency of this method can be improved if estimation is carried out in two stages. In the first stage, consistent estimates by the previous method are obtained. Call them $\tilde{\alpha}$ and $\tilde{\lambda}$. Computed values of y_t are denoted as

$$\tilde{y}_t = \tilde{\alpha} \sum_{i=0}^{\infty} \tilde{\lambda}^i x_{t-i}, \tag{3.3.24}$$

and computed residuals as

$$\begin{aligned} \tilde{v}_t &= y_t - \tilde{\alpha} x_t - \tilde{\lambda} y_{t-1} \\ \tilde{e}_t &= y_t - \tilde{y}_t = \sum_{i=0}^{\infty} \tilde{\lambda}^i \tilde{v}_{t-i}. \end{aligned} \tag{3.3.25}$$

From the consistently estimated residuals, we obtain

$$(E\tilde{v}_t\tilde{v}_{t'}) = \tilde{\Omega} = \tilde{\sigma}_e^2 \begin{pmatrix} 1+\tilde{\lambda}^2 & -\tilde{\lambda} & \cdots & 0 \\ -\tilde{\lambda} & 1+\tilde{\lambda}^2 & \cdots & 0 \\ \vdots & \vdots & \vdots & \vdots \\ \vdots & \vdots & 1+\tilde{\lambda}^2 & -\tilde{\lambda} \\ 0 & 0 & -\tilde{\lambda} & 1+\tilde{\lambda}^2 \end{pmatrix} \tag{3.3.26}$$

and can estimate $\tilde{\Omega}$ from estimates $\tilde{\sigma}^2$ and $\tilde{\lambda}$. Aitken least squares estimators, using $\tilde{\Omega}$ are computed from the regression of y_t on x_t and $\tilde{y}_{t-1}$.[15]

The estimates of α, λ are

$$\begin{pmatrix} \hat{\alpha} \\ \hat{\lambda} \end{pmatrix} = \left[\begin{pmatrix} x' \\ \tilde{y}'_{-1} \end{pmatrix} \tilde{\Omega}^{-1}(x, y_{-1}) \right]^{-1} \begin{pmatrix} x' \\ \tilde{y}'_{-1} \end{pmatrix} \tilde{\Omega}^{-1} y, \tag{3.3.27}$$

where x and y are column vectors of sample observations. The second step of this two-step procedure improves the efficiency of the estimates derived in the first step.

These methods for estimating distributed lags can be applied where the original errors, e_t, may be serially correlated, even before transformation. If the e_t are mutually independent, the transformed error, $e_t - \lambda e_{t-1}$, will be serially correlated. For the case of zero (or otherwise known) serial dependence among the e_t, we can obtain estimates of α and λ by minimizing

$$S = \frac{1}{1+\lambda^2} \sum_{t=1}^{T} (y_t - \alpha x_t - \lambda y_{t-1})^2 \tag{3.3.28}$$

[15] T. Amemiya and W. Fuller, "A Comparative Study of Alternative Estimators in a Distributed Lag Model," *Econometrica*, 35 July-October, 1967, 509–29. See also E. J. Hannan, "The Estimation of Relationships Involving Distributed Lags," *Econometrica*, 33 (January, 1965), 206–24.

with respect to α and λ. Instead of weighting the sum of squares by the reciprocal of variance, as is usually done, we weight by $\sigma^2(1 + \lambda^2) = \text{var}(e_t - \lambda e_{t-1})$. Because λ appears in both the reciprocal factor $\frac{1}{1 + \lambda^2}$ and as a coefficient in the equation, we cannot ignore it in the minimization of S. This method leads to a quadratic equation for estimating λ.[16]

$$\lambda^2\left(\frac{\sum x_t y_{t-1} \sum y_t x_t}{\sum x_t^2} - \sum y_t y_{t-1}\right) + \lambda\left\{\sum y_t^2 - \sum y_{t-1}^2 + \frac{(\sum x_t y_{t-1})^2 - (\sum y_t x_t)^2}{\sum x_t^2}\right\} + \left(\sum y_t y_{t-1} - \frac{\sum x_t y_{t-1} \sum y_t x_t}{\sum x_t^2}\right) = 0 \tag{3.3.29}$$

Having an estimate of λ, we obtain

$$a = \text{est. } \alpha = -\frac{\hat{\lambda} \sum x_t y_{t-1} + \sum x_t y_t}{\sum x_t^2}. \tag{3.3.30}$$

This is a consistent but not an efficient method of estimating α and λ.

The Koyck distribution is special because it has monotonically decreasing weights as the lag lengthens. In a later section, this distribution will be modified and generalized beyond this shape of the lag distribution. Finite length polynomial lag distributions have been introduced by Shirley Almon.[17] These can have a humped, or more complicated, shape. They will not generally have the bell shape with high contact at end points that is typical of probability density functions, but they serve well for graduating many types of lag distributions.

For the two-variable model, with lag distribution, we have

$$y_t = \sum_{i=0}^{p} w_i x_{t-i} + e_t. \tag{3.3.31}$$

The lag is specified, in advance of estimation, to be of finite length p. The weights, w_i, are assumed to be graduated by a polynomial of the s-th order.

$$w_i = a_0 + a_1 i + a_2 i^2 + \cdots + a_s i^s. \tag{3.3.32}$$

If we substitute (3.3.32) into (3.3.31), we obtain

$$y_t = a_0 \sum_{i=0}^{p} x_{t-i} + a_1 \sum_{i=0}^{p} i x_{t-i} + \cdots + a_s \sum_{i=0}^{p} i^s x_{t-i} + e_t. \tag{3.3.33}$$

[16] L. R. Klein, "The Estimation of Distributed Lags," *Econometrica*, 26 (October, 1958), 553–65. The criterion function is stated differently but leads to the same quadratic in λ that we get by minimizing S.

[17] Shirley Almon, "The Distributed Lag between Capital Appropriations and Expenditures," *Econometrica*, 33 (January, 1965), 178–96.

If the variables are transformed by

$$x_{0t} = \sum_{i=0}^{p} x_{t-i}$$

$$x_{1t} = \sum_{i=0}^{p} i x_{t-i}$$

$$\vdots$$

$$x_{st} = \sum_{i=0}^{p} i^s x_{t-1},$$

the problem becomes one of simply regressing y_t on $x_{0t}, x_{1t}, \ldots, x_{st}$ to estimate regression coefficients $a_0, a_1, \ldots, a_s$. Having estimates of a_s, we can find estimates of w_i from (3.3.32) and substitute them into (3.3.31).

It should be noted that $x_{0t}, x_{1t}, \ldots, x_{st}$ are likely to be intercorrelated, thus giving rise to the problems dealt with below, under the heading of multicollinearity. We are interested primarily in estimates of w_i, however, and not in a_i, by themselves. Collinearity among the x_{it} may lead to large sampling errors in the estimates of a_i (demonstrated below) but this need not imply large sampling errors in the estimates of w_i because

$$\text{var } w_i = \sum_{j=0}^{s} i^{2j} \text{ var } a_j + 2 \sum_{j<k} i^{j+k} \text{ cov } a_j a_k.$$

Many of the covariance terms are likely to be negative, thus restraining the variance of est. w_i even though the individual est. a_i have large variance.

The estimates can be further simplified if certain points of the lag distribution are constrained to be zero—say, at the beginning and end points. The results are particularly simple for quadratic polynomials (parabolas) in this case.

$$w_i = a_0 + a_1 i + a_2 i^2$$

$$w_i = 0 \text{ if } i = 0\text{; therefore } a_0 = 0.$$

$$w_i = 0 \text{ if } i = p\text{; therefore } a_1 = -pa_2.$$

The transformed equation is

$$y_t = a_2 \sum_{i=0}^{p} (i^2 - pi)\, x_{t-i} + e_t.$$

If a_2 is negative, this will form a distribution with shape $\cap$ and if a_2 is positive, the distribution will have the shape $\cup$.

The extension of this method to multiple lag distributions

$$y_t = \sum_{j=1}^{n} \sum_{i=0}^{p} w_{ji} x_{j,t-i} + e_t \tag{3.3.34}$$

is obvious.

Lag distributions may take many forms. The simple geometric distribution studied here is widely used and leads to more general methods of regression estimation because of serial dependence among the error terms. Many other forms of lag distribution are to be considered, and many of these lead to other complications such as strong nonlinearities. The treatment of these will be given later. At the same time, general nonlinear methods for dealing with estimation of the Koyck lag distribution will be considered.

In testing for serial correlation of disturbances in relationships where there is a lagged dependent variable among the predetermined set, as is the case in the transformed treatment of the Koyck lag distribution, it should be noted that there is significant bias in the usual serial correlation statistics.[18] Thus the Durbin-Watson test mentioned above is not satisfactory for testing against serial correlation of disturbances from a regression model such as

$$y_t = ax_t + \lambda y_{t-1} + (e_t - \lambda e_{t-1}).$$

c. Heteroscedasticity

In the case of serial correlation of errors, we deal with nonzero off-diagonal terms of the matrix expression for Eee' but have constant variances along the diagonal. This departs from the standard case where the off-diagonal terms are zero. We now take up a modification of the diagonal terms, leaving the off-diagonal terms as zero. This is the usual case of heteroscedastic disturbances where the variance changes systematically with independent variables of the regression, or with time.

$$E\,ee' = \sigma_e^2 \begin{bmatrix} \mu_1 & 0 & \cdots & 0 \\ 0 & \mu_2 & & 0 \\ \cdot & & & \cdot \\ \cdot & & & \cdot \\ \cdot & & & \cdot \\ 0 & 0 & \cdots & \mu_T \end{bmatrix}. \tag{3.3.35}$$

Heteroscedasticity is likely to occur in samples based on spatial variation, in which the size of economic units being observed changes over a wide range in the sample. If the sample consists of very large and very small firms or very rich and very poor households, we may find a systematic variation in σ_e^2 as we move along the line of relationship. Large units often have more possibility of choice and higher variability than do small units.

In two-dimensional scatter diagrams, the situation may be as depicted on the opposite page. Transformations of scale to $(\log y, \log x)$, $(\sqrt{y}, \sqrt{x})$, $(y/x, 1/x)$, or another combination sometimes changes a hetero- into a homo-

[18] See E. Malinvaud, "Estimation et Prévision dans les Modèles Économiques Autorégressifs," *Revue de l'Institut International de Statistique*, Vol. XXIX, 1961.

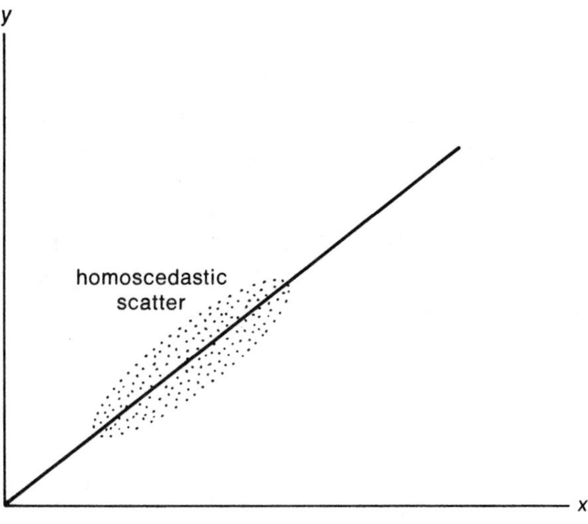

Figure 3.3.2

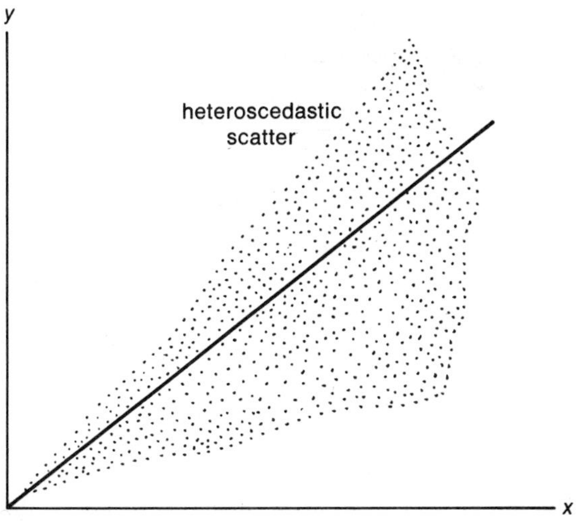

Figure 3.3.3

scedastic scatter. If so, then the transformed relation, if linear in the parameters, can be estimated as in the standard case.

Alternatively, if we know the μ_t in the matrix Eee', we can write

$$\frac{y_t}{\sqrt{\mu_t}} = \sum_{i=1}^{n} \alpha_i \left(\frac{x_t}{\sqrt{\mu_t}}\right) + \frac{e_t}{\sqrt{\mu_t}}, \tag{3.3.36}$$

and

$$\text{var}\left(\frac{e_t}{\sqrt{\mu_t}}\right) = \sigma_e^2 \frac{\mu_t}{\mu_t} = \sigma_e^2.$$

Transformation of variables or weighting by known factors $1/\sqrt{\mu_t}$ and then application of standard regression procedures amount to the direct computation of Aitken estimators. In many cases, the appropriate transformation to use becomes apparent on examination of scatter diagrams, but experience will often lead to an approximate set of weights $1/\sqrt{\mu_t}$, and it is by no means an empty matter to consider the treatment of the heteroscedastic disturbances.

Questions and Problems

1. The stock adjustment form of the investment function is

$$K_t - K_{t-1} = I_t = \lambda(K_t^* - K_{t-1})$$
$$K_t^* = \alpha X_t$$

where

$$K_t = \text{stock of capital at end of period } t$$
$$K_t^* = \text{"desired" stock of capital}$$
$$I_t = \text{net investment}$$
$$X_t = \text{output level}$$

This can be transformed to

i. $$I_t = \alpha\lambda X_t - \lambda K_{t-1}.$$

A distributed lag formulation would, on the other hand, be

$$K_t = \beta \sum_{i=0}^{\infty} \mu^i X_{t-i},$$

which can be transformed to

ii. $$K_t = \beta X_t + \mu K_{t-1}$$
$$I_t = \beta X_t + (\mu - 1)K_{t-1}.$$

Derive i. and ii. from *stochastic* formulations and compare their error properties. The two equations have the same deterministic form, but do they have identical implications for estimation?

2. In family budget samples, it often appears that the variance of saving is proportional to the square of income. How should this information be used in specifying the form of an Engel curve of saving to be estimated from a sample?

d. Multicollinearity

Collinear movements of many economic series, either through time or space, is very common. If x_{it} and x_{jt}, both explanatory variables in

$$y_t = \sum_{i=1}^{n} \alpha_i x_{it} + e_t \tag{3.1.1}$$

tend to move together so that they have high linear correlation, the whole set of estimates may be disturbed, especially those of α_i and α_j, the separate effects of the two collinear variables. The problem is much more general. Any linear relation among some or all x_{it}

$$\sum_{k=1}^{n'} \beta_k x_{kt} = u_t$$

can lead to problems of multicollinearity.

If samples of economic data could be collected from controlled experiments, we would undoubtedly choose efficient designs in order to isolate separate effects of all x_{it}. Some kinds of randomized and orthogonalized schemes, as are used in the design of experiments, would be appropriate. We must, however, recognize the fact that samples are not chosen that way in economics, and we have, in economic time series analysis, different elements of x_{it} moving with common trends and cycles. There is a concept, such as *the business cycle* or *the rate of growth*, that pervades most of our economic time series simultaneously.

To show the effects of multicollinearity on regression estimates, let us scale all variables to have zero mean and unit variance. This can be done by using the transformations

$$\frac{y_t - \bar{y}}{S_y}, \frac{x_{it} - \bar{x}_i}{S_i}.$$

From each variable, we subtract the sample mean and divide by the sample standard deviation. In this notation we have

$$a_i = \frac{\begin{vmatrix} 1 & r_{12} & \cdots & r_{1y} & \cdots & r_{1n} \\ r_{12} & 1 & \cdots & r_{2y} & \cdots & r_{2n} \\ \cdot & \cdot & & \cdot & & \cdot \\ \cdot & \cdot & & \cdot & & \cdot \\ \cdot & \cdot & & \cdot & & \cdot \\ r_{1n} & r_{2n} & \cdots & r_{ny} & \cdots & 1 \end{vmatrix}}{\begin{vmatrix} 1 & r_{12} & \cdots & r_{1i} & \cdots & r_{1n} \\ r_{12} & 1 & \cdots & r_{2i} & \cdots & r_{2n} \\ \cdot & \cdot & & \cdot & & \cdot \\ \cdot & \cdot & & \cdot & & \cdot \\ \cdot & \cdot & & \cdot & & \cdot \\ r_{1n} & r_{2n} & \cdots & r_{ni} & \cdots & 1 \end{vmatrix}}. \tag{3.3.37}$$

In this expression, a_i is the estimated regression coefficient of x_{it}, r_{iy} is the correlation between x_{it} and y_t, and r_{ij} is the correlation between x_{it} and x_{jt}.

If two elements of the vector $(x_{1t}, x_{2t}, \ldots, x_{nt})$ are perfectly correlated, so that $r_{ij} = 1$, the i-th and j-th rows (or columns) of the denominator would be identical, and the determinant would vanish.

$$\begin{matrix} r_{i1} & r_{i2} & \cdots & r_{ii} & \cdots & r_{ij} & \cdots & r_{in} \\ r_{j1} & r_{j2} & \cdots & r_{ji} & \cdots & r_{jj} & \cdots & r_{jn} \end{matrix}$$

In these arrays,

$$r_{ii} = 1, \qquad r_{ij} = 1, \qquad r_{jj} = 1.$$

Correlation between x_{it} or x_{jt}, on the one hand, and the remaining variables, on the other hand, would be identical because perfectly correlated variables must have equal correlation with other variables. Similarly, the i-th and j-th rows of the numerator would be the same.

$$\begin{matrix} r_{i1} & r_{i2} & \cdots & r_{iy} & \cdots & r_{ij} & \cdots & r_{in} \\ r_{j1} & r_{j2} & \cdots & r_{jy} & \cdots & r_{jj} & \cdots & r_{jn}. \end{matrix}$$

In the i-th column positions, we have r_{iy} and r_{jy}, but these are identical if $r_{ij} = 1$. We, therefore, find that if any pair (x_{it}, x_{jt}) are *perfectly correlated*, the estimate of α_i becomes.

$$a_i = \frac{0}{0}. \tag{3.3.38}$$

The same indeterminate value would be obtained if any exact linear relationship existed among $x_{1t}, x_{2t}, \ldots, x_{nt}$.

In the limiting case, perfect correlation, we cannot determine a_i. This is as it should be, for if two elements, x_{it} and x_{jt}, are perfectly correlated, we cannot assess their separate effects on y_t. Our formula for sampling error estimate is

$$S_{a_i}^2 = S_e^2 \frac{|M_{xx}|_{ii}}{|M_{xx}|}. \tag{3.1.33}$$

If we delete the i-th row and column of the M_{xx} matrix in the numerator, we shall *not* find that this determinant vanishes by virtue of the perfect correlation between x_{it} and x_{jt}, but the denominator is the same as that in the expression for a_i; therefore

$$S_{a_i}^2 = \frac{S_e^2 |M_{xx}|_{ii}}{0} \longrightarrow \infty. \tag{3.3.39}$$

This also is an intuitively plausible result. Associated with the indeterminate value of a_i is an infinite sampling variance.

Another result of some interest and use in dealing with the problem of multicollinearity is that the overall correlation or residual variance is not affected by perfect collinearity even though the estimates of regression coefficients are indeterminate.

Suppose that $r_{12} = 1$ and that the regression

$$y_t = a_2 x_{2t} + \cdots + a_n x_{nt} + (\text{res.})_t$$

has been estimated. Residuals from the computed regression are denoted as $(\text{res.})_t$. It is a property of least squares regression (by one of our interpretations) that there is no correlation between any $x_{2t} \ldots x_{nt}$ and $(\text{res.})_t$.

$$\sum (\text{res.})_t \, x_{it} = 0 \qquad i = 2, \ldots, n.$$

If we consider recomputing the regression with x_{1t} added, in the presence of x_{2t}, while $r_{12} = 1$, we observe

$$\sum (\text{res.})_t \, x_{1t} = 0.$$

Because x_{1t} is perfectly correlated with x_{2t}, it must have the same correlation, as x_{2t} has, with $(\text{res.})_t$. Because x_{1t} has no correlation with $(\text{res.})_t$, it can add nothing to the overall correlation and cannot change the estimated residual variance.

These remarks and observations refer to idealized situations in which $r_{ij} = 1$; that is, there is perfect collinearity. In practice, we deal with high values of r_{ij}, say

$$0.5 < |r_{ij}| < 1.$$

In these cases we do not have 0/0 for parameter estimates or infinite variance.

When intercorrelations are high, but not unity, or, more generally, when there are *approximate* linear relationships among the x_{it}, we get specific numerical results for the parameter estimates, a_i, and the question is how to interpret these numbers and how to recognize when multicollinearity is a problem.

First, we have a computational problem. To compute the a_i or other regression statistics, we must invert the moment (correlation) matrix

$$R = \begin{pmatrix} 1 & r_{12} & \cdots & r_{1n} \\ \cdot & \cdot & & \cdot \\ \cdot & \cdot & & \cdot \\ \cdot & \cdot & & \cdot \\ r_{n1} & r_{n2} & \cdots & 1 \end{pmatrix}.$$

As multicollinearity is strong, but not complete, the determinant of this matrix approaches zero, without being zero. An inverse matrix will generally exist if

$$|R| = \epsilon \neq 0,$$

but it may be hard to determine. In small order problems, say $n = 2, 3, 4, \ldots$ we can usually carry enough digits of computational accuracy to ensure that R^{-1} is correctly evaluated in a numerical sense. However, if n is large, say 8 or more, so much accuracy is lost in the successive stages of ordinary calculation procedures that we cannot even evaluate R^{-1} with required precision. Many criteria can be brought to bear on the accuracy of the numerical evaluation. If R is symmetric, R^{-1} must be symmetric. The diagonal terms of R^{-1} must be positive. In later problems, where we must evaluate sets of such regressions using $x_{1t}, \ldots, x_{nt}$ repeatedly, we shall find more of these criteria that need to be satisfied, and it is simply a practical observation that even high powered electronic computers cannot successfully evaluate R^{-1} when $|R| = \epsilon \neq 0$, for small epsilon. We then say that R is ill conditioned. The ultimate test of evaluation is checking to see whether

$$R R^{-1} = I,$$

where I is the unit matrix.

The formula for standard errors of estimated regression coefficients shows that if multicollinearity is high but not complete, in the sense of unit correlation, we shall have small denominators in the expressions for $S_{a_i}^2$. There will be a tendency for $S_{a_i}^2$ to be large unless the overall fit of the equation is so strong that S_e^2 is also near zero. When intercorrelation is high relative to the overall multiple correlation of the function being estimated, the tendency of the denominator to approach zero will dominate the tendency of the numerator to approach zero, and the standard errors will be large. Large, in this context, will mean size in relation to the coefficient, that is, insignificant t-ratios. When an equation appears to fit data reasonably well ($R^2 = 0.7 - 0.9$), and the gross correlations are equally high but many or most t-ratios small (say, less than unity), we have good indications that multicollinearity is present.

Short of drawing a fresh sample in which the collinear relationships are ruptured, we try to deal with the problem by deleting all but one of the collinear variables from the regression, by imposing some a priori restrictions on the parameters, or by carrying coefficients that are insignificant, by t-test, if the estimated coefficients have not become ridiculous in terms of a priori information.

Questions and Problems

1. In the estimation of demand equations in which quantity is to be explained as a function of relative prices and real income, it is frequently found that income and price movements are highly correlated. Explain how family budget statistics might be used to overcome this problem of multicollinearity in demand analysis.

If similar collinearity occurs between relative price and activity levels in export or import equations, what can the econometrician do in this case?

2. Explain how the existence of the business cycle and growth trend induce multicollinearity in economic time series.

e. Qualitative Variables

Most of the statistician's useful information comes to him as numerical observation on variables y_t or x_{it}. Usually these form a continuous gradation, but they could be discrete, confined to integral values, or bounded at finite limits. As long as the observations are numerical, there is no problem. They can be incorporated into the regression framework as we have been using it here. Suppose, however, that the statistician has classificatory or qualitative information that he feels, a priori, has relevance for the explanation that he is trying to give in the form of a regression equation. Should he ignore such information simply because it is not apparently numerical?

We may observe that married people buy some kinds of household durables more frequently than do single individuals, or that people in one region buy more frequently than people in another region. If this information is plausible and has large effect on the outcome of demand analysis, it should be brought into the estimation of demand relationships by regression methods.

In some cases, we have a kind of associated measurement in this problem. We have frequency counts on the number of cases in a given classification that perform some economic act. In aggregating individual relationships, we may use these percentages as measured macroeconomic variables. At the individual level, however, we generally use a different treatment, called the use of *dummy variables*. In dichotomous classification, we have

$D_i = 1$ if the i-th unit is in a given class.
$D_i = 0$ if the i-th unit is not in this class.

One variable with two discrete values serves to measure the significance of a single dichotomous classification. Such variables may be

D_{mi} married; not married
D_{ri} white race; non white race
D_{1i} lives north of a boundary; lives south of a boundary
D_{ai} 60 years or older; under 60 years of age.

An endless list of possible dichotomies that arise in practice could be cited.

As long as we deal with a dichotomy and linear relations, it would not matter which two numerical values were chosen for D_i because any pair of values (0, 1) can be transformed into any other pair by a linear function.

$$Z = a + b\,D. \tag{3.3.40}$$

For $D = 1$ and $D = 0$, we would have

$$Z = a + b\,(0)$$
$$Z = a + b\,(1); \tag{3.3.41}$$

thus, by a suitable choice of a and b we can always transform the pair (0,1) into any two predetermined quantities, the first of which is a and the second of which is $a + b$.

An additional dummy variable in a linear function simply makes a parallel shift of that function.

$$y_j = \sum_{i=1}^{n} \alpha_i x_{ij} + \alpha D_j + e_j \qquad j = 1, 2, \ldots, N \tag{3.3.42}$$

For all j, such that when the corresponding observation is in a given class and $D_j = 1$, the function is shifted by the amount α as compared with observations outside the given class. The constant term, apart from the introduction of D, is, let us say, α_1 corresponding to $x_{1j} \equiv 1$ for all j. This, too, is a dummy variable, but its value is only unity. For x_{1j} and some other variable x_{2j} that is not in the *dummy* category, we would have the picture depicted in Fig. 3.3.4. This picture emerges in time series analysis for prewar and postwar observations or prestrike and poststrike observations.

The shift indicated by the dummy variable could be in either direction. It is simply a shift of the constant term in the equation, but it could equally well be a shift in the slope of an equation. In the bivariate case, we could have

$$y_j = \alpha_1 + \alpha_2 x_{2j} + \alpha D_j + \beta D_j x_{2j} + e_j. \tag{3.3.43}$$

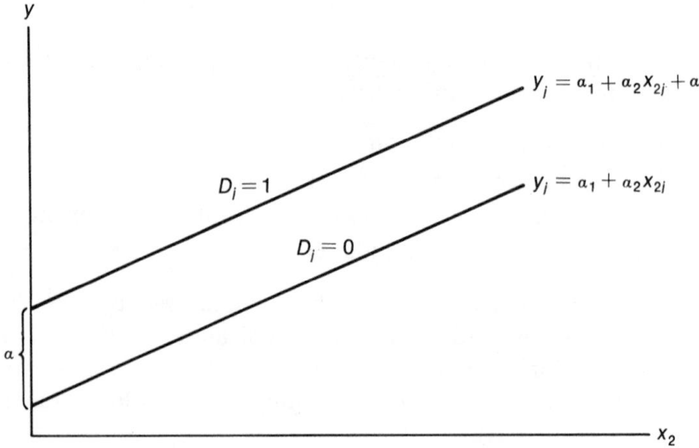

Figure 3.3.4 Additive Dummy Variable

In this case, the constant term becomes

$$\alpha_1 + \alpha$$

when $D_j = 1$, and the slope becomes

$$\alpha_2 + \beta.$$

These two characteristics are α_1 and α_2, respectively, when $D_j = 0$.

Dichotomous classifications call for the introduction of a single dummy variable that assumes one of two values, say 1 or 0. In general, we may contemplate dealing with a characteristic that may be subdivided into n classes. In that case we need n–1 dummy variables.

$$\begin{aligned}
D_{i1} &= 1 \text{ if the } i\text{-th unit is in the first class} \\
D_{i1} &= 0 \text{ if the } i\text{-th unit is not in the first class} \\
D_{i2} &= 1 \text{ if the } i\text{-th unit is in the second class} \\
D_{i2} &= 0 \text{ if the } i\text{-th unit is not in the second class} \\
&\ \vdots \\
D_{i,n-1} &= 1 \text{ if the } i\text{-th unit is in the } (n-1)\text{st class} \\
D_{i,n-1} &= 0 \text{ if the } i\text{-th unit is not in the } (n-1)\text{st class} \\
D_{in} &= 1 \text{ if } D_{i1}, D_{i2}, \ldots, D_{i,n-1} = 0 \\
D_{in} &= 0 \text{ if any of } D_{i1}, D_{i2}, \ldots, D_{i,n-1} = 1
\end{aligned}$$

As long as the classes are mutually exclusive and exhaust the set of possible classifications, the n – th variable is known when the other $n - 1$ are known. For the study of seasonal variation, we have[19]

$$\begin{aligned}
D_s &= 1 && \text{during summer} \\
D_s &= 0 && \text{during fall, winter, spring} \\
D_f &= 1 && \text{during fall} \\
D_f &= 0 && \text{during winter, spring, summer} \\
D_w &= 1 && \text{during winter} \\
D_w &= 0 && \text{during spring, summer, fall.}
\end{aligned}$$

When we have

$$D_s = D_f = D_w = 0$$

it must be spring; so, the fourth seasonal classification is known in this case. If either $D_s = 1$, or $D_f = 1$, or $D_w = 1$, it must not be spring; so, the other value of the fourth seasonal classification is known. The pattern of these dummy

[19] Cf. chap. 9.

variables is

D_s	D_f	D_w
1	0	0
0	1	0
0	0	1
0	0	0
1	0	0
0	1	0
0	0	1
0	0	0
etc.;		

therefore

$$\sum_t D_{st}D_{ft} = \sum_t D_{st}D_{wt} = \sum_t D_{ft}D_{wt} = 0.$$

For seasonal variation, marital status, sex, and many other social characteristics, the use of dummy variables seems to be a natural method of quantification. They may, however, be recommended even in cases where there is a seemingly straightforward method of quantitative measurement. Consider, for example, age. This variable may be important in explaining the receipt of income, its disposition among categories of expenditure, savings, asset holding, and similar economic processes. We could write

$$y_j = \alpha_0 + \alpha_1 A_j + \alpha_2 A_j^2 + e_j \tag{3.3.44}$$

to measure the relationship between a family's income (y_j) and the age of its head (A_j), where the latter is chronological age in calendar years. The effect of age in this case is undoubtedly not linear so that we added the quadratic term A_j^2. Possibly a different nonlinear specification of the relationship would be superior, but this may be a fair approximation. An alternative approach, using dummy variables, would be

$$y_j = \beta_0 + \beta_1 D_{1j} + \cdots + \beta_p D_{pj} + e_j. \tag{3.3.45}$$

$D_{ij} = 1$ if the head of the j-th unit is in the i-th age class
$D_{ij} = 0$ if the head of the j-th unit is not in the i-th age class.

Age is subdivided into $p + 1$ classes. To be very practical, these might be

Class 1, 18–24 years
2, 25–34 years
3, 35–44 years
4, 45–54 years
5, 55–64 years
6, 65 years or older.

With uniform increases in β_i as we move up the age classification, we have a linear affect of chronological age (neglecting the uneven sizes of classes 1 and 6). Nonlinearity would be revealed by disparate changes in size and sign from one value of β_i to the next. This permits a very general form of nonlinearity, but it uses many parameters. If there were six age classes, we would have to estimate five separate β_i parameters besides the constant term. This method, however, is very general, permitting many such variables and in different combinations with other variables to show nonlinear or interaction effects.

Questions and Problems

1. Show the relationship between the exclusion of a single unusual (or outlying) observation (y_k, x_k) in the relationship

$$y_i = \alpha + \beta x_i + e_i, \qquad i = 1, 2, \ldots, N,$$

and the fitting of

$$\begin{aligned} y_i &= \alpha + \beta x_i + \gamma d_i + e_i \\ d_i &= 1 \qquad\qquad i = k \\ d_i &= 0 \qquad\qquad i \neq k. \end{aligned}$$

2. Indicate how dummy variables may be used to test for the existence of structural change within a sample. Explain the test procedure.

f. The Analysis of Variance

A traditional method of dealing with qualitative classifications is the *analysis of variance*. This method has also been used to develop tests of regression equations. We can, however, give a regression interpretation of this method of analysis through the use of dummy variables.

Suppose that we have observations on a variable x arranged in p classifications,

$$\begin{matrix} x_{11} & x_{12} & \cdots & x_{1p} \\ \vdots & \vdots & & \vdots \\ x_{n_1 1} & x_{n_2 2} & \cdots & x_{n_p p}. \end{matrix}$$

In all, there are $n = n_1 + n_2 + \ldots . n_p$ observations, and the number of cases in the different classes is not constant. The sum of squared deviations about the mean of the whole sample can be written as

$$\begin{aligned} \sum_{j=1}^{p}\sum_{i=1}^{n_j}(x_{ij} - \bar{x})^2 &= \sum_{j=1}^{p}\sum_{i=1}^{n_j}(x_{ij} - \bar{x}_j + \bar{x}_j - \bar{x})^2 \\ &= \sum_{j=1}^{p}\sum_{i=1}^{n_j}(x_{ij} - \bar{x}_j)^2 + \sum_{j=1}^{p} n_j(\bar{x}_j - \bar{x})^2, \end{aligned} \tag{3.3.46}$$

where $\bar{x}$ is the mean of all observations and $\bar{x}_j$ is the mean of the j-th class. In deriving the second expression in this identity, we have made use of the fact that

$$\sum_{j=1}^{p} \sum_{i=1}^{n_j} (x_{ij} - \bar{x}_j)(\bar{x}_j - \bar{x}) = \sum_{j=1}^{p} (\bar{x}_j - \bar{x}) \sum_{i=1}^{n_j} (x_{ij} - \bar{x}_j) = 0. \qquad (3.3.47)$$

This must be so because $\sum_{i=1}^{n_j} (x_{ij} - \bar{x}_j)$ vanishes.

We therefore have a way of decomposing total variability (in the square) as variability *within* a group about group means.

$$\sum \sum (x_{ij} - \bar{x}_j)^2,$$

and variability between groups about the total mean,

$$\sum (\bar{x}_j - \bar{x})^2.$$

The ratio

$$\frac{\frac{1}{p-1} \sum n_j(\bar{x}_j - \bar{x})^2}{\frac{1}{n-p} \sum \sum (x_{ij} - \bar{x}_j)^2}$$

is distributed as F with $p - 1$ and $n - p$ degrees of freedom; thus, the significance of the p classifications can be tested from this statistic and its probability tabulation.

A regression interpretation of the classification can be developed from

$$x_i = \beta_0 + \beta_1 D_{i1} + \cdots + \beta_{p-1} D_{i,p-1} + e_i \qquad (3.3.48)$$
$$D_{ij} = 1 \text{ if the } i\text{-th observation is in the } j\text{-th class}$$
$$D_{ij} = 0 \text{ otherwise.}$$

We can test the significance of any individual β_j or of the whole set. If $\beta_1 = \cdots = \beta_{p-1} = 0$, we have no influence of the classification scheme on the x_i, and we would say that the overall correlation is not significant. To test this, we would compute the same F statistic and test it for significance.

Two-way and higher order schemes of analysis of variance are less easily developed in practical problems of econometrics because they require, in order to get a simple decomposition of the total sum of squares, that the number of observations per cell be constant. This is unlikely to be the case in samples of economic data. The decomposition of variance is especially easy for a one-way classification. That scheme is independent of the number of observations in each class. In schemes of multiple classification, the decomposition of total variance does not simplify, but the regression interpretation of variance analysis remains.

Suppose that we have two ways of classifying data

Column classification C

Row classification R	1	2	. . . .	p
1	$x_{1,11}$	$x_{1,12}$		$x_{1,1p}$
.	.	.		.
.	.	.		.
.	.	.		.
.	$x_{n_{11}\,11}$	$x_{n_{12}\,12}$		$x_{n_{1p},1p}$
.	.	.		.
.	.	.		.
.	.	.		.
.	$x_{1,r1}$	$x_{1,r2}$		$x_{1,rp}$
r	.	.		.
	.	.		.
	.	.		.
	$x_{n_{r1},r1}$	$x_{n_{r2},r2}$		$x_{n_{rp},rp}$

If all n_{ij} are equal, we can use standard analysis of variance formulas. With one observation per cell we have

$$\sum_{i=1}^{r}\sum_{j=1}^{p}(x_{1,ij}-\bar{x})^2 = \sum_{i=1}^{r}\sum_{j=1}^{p}(x_{1,ij}-\bar{x}_{.j}-\bar{x}_{i.}+\bar{x})^2 + p\sum_{i=1}^{r}(x_{i.}-\bar{x})^2 + r\sum_{j=1}^{p}(x_{.j}-\bar{x})^2. \tag{3.3.49}$$

In this expression, $x_{i.}$ is the mean of values in the i-th row and $x_{.j}$ is the mean of values in the j-th column.

For an arbitrary number of observations per cell, we can form the regression

$$x_i = \beta_0 + \sum_{j=1}^{p-1}\beta_j C_{ij} + \sum_{j=1}^{r-1}\gamma_j R_{ij} + \sum_{j=1}^{rp-1}\delta_j (RC)_{ij} + e_i. \tag{3.3.50}$$

The dummy variables are

$C_{ij} = 1$ if the i-th observation is in the j-th C class
$C_{ij} = 0$ otherwise
$R_{ij} = 1$ if the i-th observation is in the j-th R class
$R_{ij} = 0$ otherwise
$(RC)_{ij} = 1$ if the i-th observation is in the j-th cell of R and C jointly classified
$(RC)_{ij} = 0$ otherwise.

The significance of the R and C variables tests for main effects; the significance of the RC variables tests for interaction effects.

There will, indeed, be a large number of parameters to be estimated in such a scheme. Although the regression interpretation is straightforward, there is an enormous simplification if there are equal numbers per cell so that standard analysis of variance methods can be used. As the number of variables of classification increases, the number of possible interactions rises rapidly. Of course, different parametric specifications can be assumed, and, in main effects or interaction effects, groupings can be deleted or combined in order to reduce the number of parameters to be estimated.

Questions and Problems

1. If there are unequal frequencies in the cells of a joint classification, would we be justified in replacing cell entries with cell means and regarding the table as consisting of one (mean) entry per cell?

2. Show how a typical linear regression analysis provides a decomposition of variance like that used in analysis of variance.

4. NONLINEAR REGRESSION

This is more than just a variation on the standard procedure; it opens up a whole new field of analysis. Nonlinear relationships have long been dealt with in econometrics, but these usually have the property that, by suitable transformation, they can be converted into linear relationships, that is, linear in the parameters. Log-linear relationships are one of the most familiar of this variety,

$$y_t = \alpha_0 x_{1t}^{\alpha_1} \ldots x_{nt}^{\alpha_n} e_t. \tag{3.4.1}$$

This transforms to

$$\log y_t = \log \alpha_0 + \sum_{i=1}^{n} \alpha_i \log x_{it} + \log e_t. \tag{3.4.2}$$

By redefining variables to be $\log y_t$ and $\log x_{it}$, we can now proceed with linear methods of estimation as developed above. It should be noted that if we do nothing more than alter the probability structure from multiplicative to additive errors

$$y_t = \alpha_0 x_{1t}^{\alpha_1} \ldots x_{nt}^{\alpha_n} + e_t, \tag{3.4.3}$$

we have a nonlinear model that cannot be transformed as above.

Logistic, probit, and other nonlinear forms have been used in econometrics, and these are not subject to estimation by the usual linear methods.

An interesting field of application of nonlinear methods will be the treatment of lag distributions. The Koyck-type lag studied above

$$y_t = \alpha \sum_{i=0}^{\infty} \lambda^i x_{t-i} + e_t$$

transforms readily to the linear form

$$y_t = \alpha x_t + \lambda y_{t-1} + e_t - \lambda e_{t-1}.$$

The seeming gain in simplicity in this transformation to linear form is lost by the corresponding transformation of the error terms. We considered earlier the use of linear methods to overcome these difficulties. We now consider a direct attack on the problem by nonlinear methods.

It will be convenient to introduce operator notations $Iy_t = y_t$, $Ix_t = x_t$, $Ly_t = y_{t-1}$, $Lx_t = x_{t-1}$, etc. Using the expansion for $|\lambda| < |$,

$$\frac{1}{I - \lambda L} = I + \lambda L + \lambda^2 L^2 + \lambda^3 L^3 + \dots,$$

we can write

$$y_t = \frac{\alpha x_t}{I - \lambda L} + e_t \tag{3.4.4}$$

for

$$y_t = \alpha \sum_{i=0}^{\infty} \lambda^i x_{t-i} + e_t.$$

Maximum likelihood (or least squares, in the present context) estimates of α and λ are given by values that satisfy

$$S(\alpha, \lambda) = \sum_{t=1}^{T} \left(y_t - \frac{\alpha x_t}{I - \lambda L}\right)^2 = \min.$$

The corresponding normal equations are

$$\begin{aligned} \sum_{t=1}^{T} \left(y_t - \frac{\alpha x_t}{I - \lambda L}\right) \frac{x_t}{I - \lambda L} &= 0, \\ \sum_{t=1}^{T} \left(y_t - \frac{\alpha x_t}{I - \lambda L}\right) \frac{L x_t}{(I - \lambda L)^2} &= 0. \end{aligned} \tag{3.4.5}$$

In engineering applications of the same methods, Steiglitz and McBride have suggested the following iterative algorithm for solving these nonlinear equations:[20]

Define filtered values of the variables as

$$y^* = \frac{y_t}{I - \lambda L}; \; x_t^* = \frac{x_t}{I - \lambda L}, \; x_t^{**} = \frac{x_t^*}{I - \lambda L} = \frac{x_t}{(I - \lambda L)^2}.$$

[20] K. Steiglitz and L. E. McBride, "A Technique for the Identification of Linear Systems," *IEEE Transactions on Automatic Control*, AC-10 (October, 1965), 461–64.

We can now write the normal equations as

$$\begin{aligned}\sum_{t=1}^{T}(y_t^* - \lambda y_{t-1}^* - \alpha x_t^*)x_t^* &= 0,\\ \sum_{t=1}^{T}(y_t^* - \lambda y_{t-1}^* - \alpha x_t^*)x_{t-1}^{**} &= 0.\end{aligned} \tag{3.4.5*}$$

For the zero-th iteration choose a starting estimate λ^0, obtained as a consistent estimator by the method of instrumental variables, discussed above, or some other easily applied consistent method. Prefilter y and x by using λ^0 to obtain

$$\sum_{t=1}^{T}(y_t^{(0)*} - \lambda y_{t-1}^{(0)*} - \alpha x_t^{(0)*})x_t^{(0)*} = 0,$$

$$\sum_{t=1}^{T}(y_t^{(0)*} - \lambda y_{t-1}^{(0)*} - \alpha x_t^{(0)*})x_{t-1}^{(0)**} = 0,$$

where $y_t^{(0)*} = \dfrac{y_t}{I - \lambda^{(0)}L}$, etc. From these two linear equations, estimate $\lambda^{(1)}, \alpha^{(1)}$. Prefilter y and x with $\lambda^{(1)}$ and obtain estimates of $\alpha^{(2)}$, $\lambda^{(2)}$. This procedure procedure should be continued until

$$|\lambda^{(r)} - \lambda^{(r-1)}| < \epsilon,$$

$$|\alpha^{(r)} - \alpha^{(r-1)}| < \epsilon,$$

for arbitrarily small and preassigned ϵ.

The same method can be employed by replacing x_{t-1}^{**} by y_{t-1}^{**} in the second of the two normal equations.

$$\sum_{t=1}^{T}(y_t^* - \lambda y_{t-1}^* - \alpha x_t^*)y_{t-1}^* = 0.$$

In this case, we are simply regressing y_t^* on y_{t-1}^* and x_t^*. For a given value of λ used in prefiltering, the term

$$\frac{y_{t-1}}{1 - \lambda^{(0)}L} = y_{t-1}^{(0)*}$$

will be independent of e_t, provided e_t is not serially correlated; therefore, $y_{t-1}^{(0)*}$ is a proper instrumental variable, as is any $y_{t-1}^{(r)*}$, and this alternative method is consistent. It appears to have better convergence because at each stage of the iteration process the matrix of the equation system (normal equations) is a symmetric moment matrix and is positive definite. This assures convergence.

The Steiglitz-McBride method is very attractive and apparently leads to maximum likelihood estimates for normal e_t, but it has an important drawback. The sums y_t^*, x_t^*, x_t^{**}, etc. are infinite sums, yet they are evaluated from finite sample series. If $|\lambda|$ is small enough, the terms that are "thrown away" in finite summation may be negligible, but we cannot be sure of this point. In any event we can assume $x_t = \bar{x}$ for $t < 1$. This means that all presample observations in the infinite sum are assigned a given value, such as the sample mean. Other approximate assignments of x_t for $t < 1$ may be x_1 or x_1 extrapolated backwards according to a simple trend.

An alternative approach that gets round this defect of the Steiglitz-McBride iteration method can be developed by using search methods. Let us rewrite the basic equation as

$$y_t = \alpha \sum_{i=0}^{t-1} \lambda^i x_{t-i} + \lambda^t \eta_0 + e_t, \tag{3.4.6}$$

where

$$\eta_t = \alpha \sum_{i=0}^{\infty} \lambda^i x_{t-i}. \tag{3.4.7}$$

To minimize the sum of squares

$$S(\alpha, \lambda, \eta_0) = \sum_{t=1}^{T} (y_t - \alpha \sum_{i=0}^{t-1} \lambda^i x_{t-i} + \lambda^t \eta_0)^2,$$

we first choose a value for λ in the interval $-1 < \lambda < 1$, redefine new variables

$$\begin{aligned} z_t &= \sum_{i=0}^{t-1} \lambda^i x_{t-i}, \\ w_t &= \lambda^t, \end{aligned} \tag{3.4.8}$$

minimize

$$S(\alpha, \lambda, \eta_0) = \sum_{t=1}^{T} (y_t - \alpha z_t - \eta_0 w_t)^2 \tag{3.4.9}$$

w.r.t. α, η_0 for the given value of λ. We can systematically search for values of λ in the stated interval, each time minimizing *w.r.t.* α, η_0, until we find a minimum for S. This has the advantage over other methods of providing a global minimum. It also involves only finite sums. By searching the parameter space and making linear estimates at each search point, it provides a solution to a nonlinear problem in three parameters.

These methods, filtering and search, can also be used to solve a more intractable problem, namely, the simultaneous estimation of more than one distributed lag. Consider

$$y_t = \alpha_1 \sum_{i=0}^{\infty} \lambda^i x_{t-i} + \alpha_2 \sum_{i=0}^{\infty} \mu^i z_{t-i} + e_t. \tag{3.4.10}$$

As a search problem, we could choose values of λ, μ in a two-dimensional grid $-1 < \lambda < 1$, $-1 < \mu < 1$ and regress y_t on values

$$\sum_{i=0}^{t-1} \lambda^i x_{t-i}, \lambda^t, \sum_{i=0}^{t-1} \mu^i z_{t-i}, \mu^t.$$

The corresponding equation to be estimated is

$$y_t = \alpha_1 \sum_{i=0}^{t=1} \lambda^i x_{t-i} + \eta_0 \lambda^t + \alpha_2 \sum_{i=0}^{t=1} \mu^i z_{t-i} + \zeta_0 \mu^t + e_t. \qquad (3.4.11)$$

Values of λ and μ are searched in the appropriate area, until we find estimates of $\alpha_1, \alpha_2, \eta_0, \zeta_0$, with a minimal sum of squared residuals up to a given degree of precision in values for λ, μ.

We can also use the filtering method, again truncating sums from the beginning of the same sample run and using a mean for $x_0, x_{-1}, x_{-2} \ldots;$ $z_0, z_{-1}, z_{-2} \ldots$. We write

$$y_t = \frac{\alpha_1}{I - \lambda L} x_t + \frac{\alpha_2}{I - \mu L} z_t + e_t, \qquad (3.4.12)$$

and define

$$y_t^* = \frac{y_t}{I - \lambda L}, \; x_t^* = \frac{x_t}{I - \lambda L}, \; z_t^+ = \frac{z_t}{I - \mu L},$$

$$y_t^+ = \frac{y_t}{I - \mu L}, \; x_t^{**} = \frac{x_t^*}{I - \lambda L}, \; z_t^{++} = \frac{z_t^+}{I - \mu L},$$

$$y_t^{+*} = \frac{y_t}{(I - \mu L)(I - \lambda L)}.$$

The minimand is

$$S(\alpha_1, \alpha_2, \lambda, \mu) = \sum_{t=1}^{T} \left(y_t - \frac{\alpha_1}{I - \lambda L} x_t - \frac{\alpha_2}{I - \mu L} z_t \right)^2$$

$$= \sum_{t=1}^{T} (y_t^{*+} - (\lambda + \mu) y_{t-1}^{*+} + \lambda \mu y_{t-2}^{*+} - \alpha_1 x_t^* - \alpha_2 z_t^+)^2.$$

The associated normal equations are

$$\begin{aligned}
&\sum_{t=1}^{T} [y_t^{*+} - (\lambda + \mu) y_{t-1}^{*+} + \lambda \mu y_{t-2}^{*+} - \alpha_1 x_t^* - \alpha_2 z_t^+] x_t^* = 0 \\
&\sum_{t=1}^{T} [y_t^{*+} - (\lambda + \mu) y_{t-1}^{*+} + \lambda \mu y_{t-2}^{*+} - \alpha_1 x_t^* - \alpha_2 z_t^+] z_t^+ = 0 \\
&\sum_{t=1}^{T} [y_t^{*+} - (\lambda + \mu) y_{t-1}^{*+} + \lambda \mu y_{t-2}^{*+} - \alpha_1 x_t^* - \alpha_2 z_t^+] x_{t-1}^{**} = 0 \\
&\sum_{t=1}^{T} [y_t^{*+} - (\lambda + \mu) y_{t-1}^{*+} + \lambda \mu y_{t-2}^{*+} - \alpha_1 x_t^* - \alpha_2 z_t^+] z_{t-1}^{++} = 0.
\end{aligned} \qquad (3.4.13)$$

We could also replace x_{t-1}^{**} by y_{t-1}^{*+} and z_{t-1}^{++} by y_{t-2}^{*+} as in the previous case and still retain consistency, while gaining symmetry in the moment matrix.

The iteration procedure is obvious, choose (consistent) starting estimates $\lambda^{(0)}$, $\mu^{(0)}$ and evaluate prefiltered quantities y_t^{*+}, y_{t-1}^{*+}, y_{t-2}^{*+}, x_t^*, z_t^+, x_{t-1}^{**}, z_{t-1}^{++}. The linear normal equation system in these prefiltered quantities provides estimates of $\lambda + \mu$, $\lambda\mu$, α_1, α_2. From

$$\text{est}\ (\lambda + \mu) = r_1,\ \text{est}\ \lambda\mu = r_2, \tag{3.4.14}$$

we can find estimates of λ and μ as

$$\text{est}\ \lambda = \frac{r_1 \pm \sqrt{r_1^2 - 4r_2}}{2}, \tag{3.4.15}$$

$$\begin{aligned} \text{est}\ \mu &= r_1 - \text{est}\ \lambda, \\ &= \frac{r_1 \mp \sqrt{r_1^2 - 4r_2}}{2}. \end{aligned} \tag{3.4.16}$$

Because there are two possible values, we choose that pair that minimizes the residual sum of squares.

The solution of the quadratic formula expressions of λ and μ can be avoided if we write the normal equations (equivalently) as

$$\begin{aligned} &\sum_{t=1}^{T} (y_t^* - \lambda y_{t-1}^* \qquad\qquad - \alpha_1 x_t^* - \alpha_2 z_t^+) x_t^* = 0 \\ &\sum_{t=1}^{T} (y_t^+ \qquad\qquad - \mu y_{t-1}^+ - \alpha_1 x_t^* - \alpha_2 z_t^+) z_t^+ = 0 \\ &\sum_{t=1}^{T} (y_t^* - \lambda y_{t-1}^* \qquad\qquad - \alpha_1 x_t^* - \alpha_2 z_t^+) x_{t-1}^{**} = 0 \\ &\sum_{t=1}^{T} (y_t^+ \qquad\qquad - \mu y_{t-1}^+ - \alpha_1 x_t^* - \alpha_2 z_t^+) z_{t-1}^{++} = 0. \end{aligned} \tag{3.4.17}$$

These equations are purely linear in $\alpha_1, \alpha_2, \lambda, \mu$. They are obviously much simpler when extended for the general case

$$y_t = \sum_{i=1}^{n} \frac{\alpha_i}{I - \lambda_i L} x_{it} + e_t \tag{3.4.18}$$

because they avoid complicated cross-prefiltering and the solution of nonlinear equations of higher order in transforming computed coefficients into structural parameters of lag distributions. The search method becomes impractical for $n \geq 3$; therefore, the simplified form of iteration should be used.

A more general form of the lag distribution is

$$y_t = \frac{N(L)}{D(L)} x_t + e_t \tag{3.4.19}$$

in which a numerator polynomial

$$N(L) = n_0 + n_1 L + n_2 L^2 + n_3 L^3 + \dots$$

of specified degree is combined with a denominator polynomial, also of specified degree,

$$D(L) = I + d_1 L + d_2 L^2 + d_3 L^3 + \dots$$

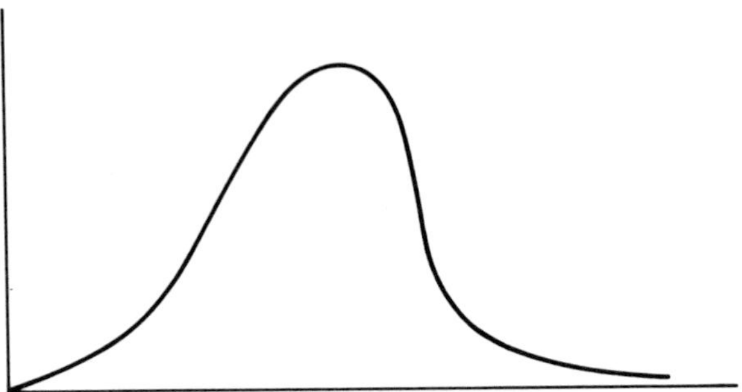

Figure 3.4.1 Humped Lag Distribution

to form the rational function lag distribution $\frac{N(L)}{D(L)}$. This permits a wide variety of possible shapes to the distribution, one of the most useful being the unimodal, humped shape. The normal equations are[21]

$$\begin{aligned} &\sum_{t=1}^{T}\left(y_t - \frac{N(L)}{D(L)}x_t\right)\frac{L^j x_t}{D(L)} = 0 \qquad j = 0, 1, 2, \ldots \\ &\sum_{t=1}^{T}\left(y_t - \frac{N(L)}{D(L)}x_t\right)\frac{N(L)L^j x_t}{[D(L)]^2} = 0 \qquad j = 1, 2, \ldots \end{aligned} \tag{3.4.20}$$

The first set are obtained by minimizing $\sum_{t=1}^{T} e_t^2$ *w.r.t.* n_j, the coefficients of the numerator polynomial, and the second set are obtained by minimizing $\sum_{t=1}^{T} e_t^2$ *w.r.t.* d_j, the coefficients of the denominator polynomial. As in the treatment of the special case above, we define prefiltered values

$$x_t^* = \frac{x_t}{D(L)},\ y_t^* = \frac{y_t}{D(L)},\ x_t^{**} = \frac{N(L)x_t}{[D(L)]^2} = \frac{N(L)}{D(L)}x_t^*.$$

We can then rewrite the normal equations as

$$\begin{aligned} &\sum_{t=1}^{T}(D(L)y_t^* - N(L)x_t^*)x_{t-j}^* = 0, \qquad j = 0, 1, 2, \ldots, \\ &\sum_{t=1}^{T}(D(L)y_t^* - N(L)x_t^*)x_{t-j}^{**} = 0, \qquad j = 1, 2, \ldots. \end{aligned} \tag{3.4.21}$$

The iterative procedure is now evident. From preliminary estimates of $N(L)$ and $D(L)$, by some consistent method of estimation such as instrumental vari-

[21] See P. J. Dhrymes, L. R. Klein, K. Steiglitz, "Estimation of Distributed Lags," *International Economic Review*, 11 (June, 1970), 235–50.

ables, we obtain prefiltered values and the normal equations

$$\sum_{t=1}^{T}(D(L)y_t^{(0)*} - N(L)x_t^{(0)*})x_{t-j}^{(0)*} = 0,$$
$$\sum_{t=1}^{T}(D(L)y_t^{(0)*} - N(L)x_t^{(0)*})x_{t-j}^{(0)**} = 0. \tag{3.4.22}$$

These are linear equations in the unknown coefficients $n_0, n_1, n_2, \ldots d_1, d_2, \ldots$. The first round iterative estimates $n_0^{(1)}, n_1^{(1)}, n_2^{(1)}, \ldots, d_1^{(1)}, d_2^{(1)}, \ldots$ are obtained by solving (3.4.22). If the zero-th round estimates are consistent, the first round estimates will also be consistent. We obtain prefiltered values $y_t^{(1)*}$, $x_t^{(1)*}$, and $x_t^{(1)**}$ to be used in forming the normal equations for calculation of the second round estimates, and so on. When the individual coefficients have converged

$$\left|\frac{n_j^{(r)} - n_j^{(r-1)}}{n_j^{(r-1)}}\right| < \epsilon, \left|\frac{d_j^{(r)} - d_j^{(r-1)}}{d_j^{(r-1)}}\right| < \epsilon,$$

we cease iterating. In large complicated systems convergence may be a delicate matter, but the closely related estimates with y_{t-j}^{**} replacing x_{t-j}^{**} in the second of the two normal equations give us symmetrical moment matrices obtained by regressing y_t^* on $y_{t-1}^*, y_{t-2}^*, \ldots x_t^*, x_{t-1}^*, x_{t-2}^*, \ldots$. This case does converge in prefiltered iterations and gives consistent estimates, provided that we start with consistent estimators and provided that the original errors, e_t, are not serially correlated.

We remarked above that expressions like

$$\frac{x_t}{I - \lambda L}$$

were infinite sums and were approximated by finite sums over the sample period. Similarly

$$\frac{x_t}{D(L)}$$

are infinite sums and must also be approximated in the extended case.

Two special cases should be noted. (1) The Koyck lag distribution need not be introduced for all values of x_t. We could start after the p-th lag as in

$$y_t = \sum_{i=0}^{p} \alpha_i x_{t-i} + \alpha \sum_{i=p}^{\infty} \lambda^{i-p} x_{t-i-1} + e_t. \tag{3.4.23}$$

The infinite sum

$$\sum_{i=p}^{\infty} \lambda^{i-p} x_{t-i-1}$$

can be split into

$$\sum_{i=p}^{t+p-1} \lambda^{i-p} x_{t-i-1} + \sum_{i=t+p}^{\infty} \lambda^{i-p} x_{t-i-1},$$

or

$$\sum_{i=p}^{t+p-1} \lambda^{i-p} x_{t-i-1} + \lambda^t \sum_{i=p}^{\infty} \lambda^{i-p} x_{-i-1}.$$

We can use the search technique again for values of λ in the interval $-1 < \lambda < +1$. In this case we estimate $\alpha_0, \alpha_1, \ldots, \alpha_p, \alpha$ and $\sum_{i=p}^{\infty} \lambda^{i-p} x_{-i-1}$ for each selected value of λ. In this extended form, the modified Koyck lag can be used to obtain quite general shapes for the lag distribution.

(2) The other case is the Pascal distribution, suggested by Solow.[22] It takes the form

$$y_t = \frac{N(L)x_t}{(I - \lambda L)^r} + e_t. \tag{3.4.24}$$

The exponent r is an integer, and the denominator is an r-th order polynomial. This is just a special case in which

$$D(L) = (I - \lambda L)\,(I - \lambda L) \ldots (I - \lambda L) = (I - \lambda L)^r.$$

The prefiltering and iterative procedures of Steiglitz and McBride seem to be natural tools to use here. It is merely a simpler application in which the denominator polynomial of the rational lag distribution has only one parameter.

A generalization of the treatment of lag distributions occurs when we recognize that the error term may, in fact, be autocorrelated. We might assume

$$e_t = \frac{u_t}{R(L)}$$

where

$$Eu_t u_{t-j} = 0, \qquad j \neq 0.$$

In this case we have

$$u_t = R(L)e_t = e_t - r_1 e_{t-1} - r_2 e_{t-2} + \ldots.$$

The recommended treatment of the relationship

$$y_t = \frac{N(L)}{D(L)} x_t + \frac{u_t}{R(L)} \tag{3.4.25}$$

would be to use prefiltering iterative methods on

$$R(L)y_t = \frac{R(L)N(L)}{D(L)} x_t + u_t. \tag{3.4.26}$$

[22] R. Solow, "On a Family of Lag Distributions," *Econometrica*, 28 (April, 1960), 393–406.

If $R(L)$ is of order, at most, 2, we can search the permissible region of the parameter space for different pairs (r_1, r_2) and use prefiltering methods on

$$\begin{aligned} y'_t &= R(L)\, y_t \\ x'_t &= R(L)\, x_t. \end{aligned} \tag{3.4.27}$$

If there are more unknown parameters in $R(L)$, we should first obtain preliminary estimates of $N(L)$ and $D(L)$ by a consistent method such as instrumental variables. From the residuals

$$y_t - \frac{N^{(0)}(L)}{D^{(0)}(L)} x_t = \hat{e}_t^{(0)}, \tag{3.4.28}$$

we can estimate $r_i^{(0)}$ by autoregression ($\hat{e}_t^{(0)}$ on $\hat{e}_{t-1}^{(0)}, \hat{e}_{t-2}^{(0)}, \hat{e}_{t-3}^{(0)}$,), transform

$$\begin{aligned} y_t^{(0)\prime} &= R^{(0)}\,(L)\, y_t \\ x_t^{(0)\prime} &= R^{(0)}\,(L)\, x_t \end{aligned} \tag{3.4.29}$$

Prefilter, iterate, and obtain new coefficients $N^{(1)}\,(L)$, $D^{(1)}\,(L)$. Again, we can compute new residuals and new autoregressions, continuing these methods until convergence is obtained.

Questions and Problems

1. Prove that the Steiglitz-McBride iteration method, for a simple case of the Koyck lag distribution, provides a consistent estimate of α, λ on the r-th iteration if the estimates were consistent on the $(r - 1)$st iteration.
2. Show that the normal equations in (3.4.13) and (3.4.17) are equivalent.
3. Develop a search procedure for estimating the model

$$y_t = \frac{\alpha}{I - \lambda L} x_t + \frac{u_t}{I - \rho L}.$$

Lag distributions are but one of many situations in which nonlinear regression methods will be found useful. The theory of production in economics has generally been based on the assumption of nonlinear relationships, but applications have usually been with linear or log-linear functions.

It was remarked above that the Cobb-Douglas form of production function could be readily transformed to a relationship that was linear in the unknown parameters. In its traditional two-factor form we have

$$x_t = AN_t^{\alpha} K_t^{\beta} e_t, \tag{3.4.30}$$

$X =$ output,

$N =$ labor employed,

$K =$ stock of capital.

This function has recently been replaced in many studies by the CES function (constant elasticity of substitution).

$$X_t = B(\delta N_t^{-\rho} + (1-\delta)K_t^{-\rho})^{\gamma/\rho} e_t. \tag{3.4.31}$$

In this relationship we have four parameters—B, δ, ρ, γ—in nonlinear form. Some authors used approximate linear methods or linear models that would be suitable only under restrictive assumptions. Using nonlinear methods, these parameters can be directly estimated using assumptions no stronger than those associated with production functions that are linear in the parameters.[23]

Let us suppose that we have the problem of estimating the general nonlinear relationship

$$y_t = f(x_{1t}, \ldots, x_{nt}; \alpha_1, \ldots, \alpha_r) + e_t. \tag{3.4.32}$$

In the nonlinear form, without further specification we cannot say how many parameters are to be estimated. We simply write $\alpha_1, \ldots, \alpha_r$ without requiring $r = n$. There are two basic approaches to the estimation of α_i.

1. First order Taylor expansion.[24] Consider f as a function of $\alpha_1, \ldots, \alpha_r$ and choose (guess) an initial vector of estimates $a_{10}, \ldots, a_{r0}$. Expand f about this initial vector and discard all but linear terms. We have

$$f_0 = f(x_{1t}, \ldots, x_{nt}; a_{10}, \ldots, a_{r0}) + \sum_{i=1}^{r} \left.\frac{\partial f}{\partial \alpha_i}\right|_{\alpha = a_0} (\alpha_i - a_{i0}). \tag{3.4.33}$$

Form the criterion

$$S_0(\alpha, \ldots, \alpha_r) = \sum_{t=1}^{T} (y_t - f_0)^2,$$

and minimize *w.r.t.* α_i. This will yield a set of linear normal equations in α_i

$$\frac{\partial S_0}{\partial \alpha_i} = -2 \sum_{t=1}^{T} (y_t - f_0) \left.\frac{\partial f}{\partial \alpha_i}\right|_{\alpha = a_0} = 0,$$

or

$$\begin{aligned} \sum_{t=1}^{T} y_t f_i'(x_t, a_0) &= \sum_{t=1}^{T} f(x_t, a_0) f_i'(x_t, a_0) \\ &\quad + \sum_{t=1}^{T} \sum_{j=1}^{r} f_j'(x_t, a_0) f_i'(x_t, a_0)(\alpha_j - a_{j0}), \end{aligned} \tag{3.4.34}$$

with the obvious notation

$$f(x_t, a_0) = f(x_{1t}, \ldots, x_{nt}; a_{10}, \ldots, a_{r0}),$$

$$f_i'(x_t a_0) = \left.\frac{\partial f}{\partial \alpha_i}\right|_{\alpha = a_0}.$$

[23] See R. G. Bodkin and L. R. Klein, "Nonlinear Estimation of Aggregate Production Functions," *Review of Economics and Statistics*, XLIX (February, 1967) 28–44.

[24] See H. O. Hartley, "The Modified Gauss-Newton Method for the Fitting of Nonlinear Regression Functions by Least Squares," *Technometrics*, 3 (May, 1961), 269–80.

To evaluate the terms of these linear equations, it is necessary to compute $f(x_t, a_0)$ and $f'_i(x_t, a_0)$ as nonlinear functions of the sample and initial parameter values. This makes terms like $\sum y_t f'_i(x_t, a_0)$, $\sum f(x_t, a_0) f'_i(x_t, a_0)$, and $\sum f'_j(x_t, a_0), f'_i(x_t, a_0)$ numerical quantities.

The solution of the linear equations gives a vector estimate $a_{11}, \ldots, a_{r1}$. We now form

$$f_1 = f(x_{1t}, \ldots, x_{nt}; a_{11}, \ldots, a_{r1}) + \sum_{i=1}^{r} \frac{\partial f}{\partial \alpha_i}\bigg|_{\alpha=a_1} (\alpha_i - a_{i1}) \tag{3.4.35}$$

and the criterion

$$S_1(\alpha_1, \ldots, \alpha_r) = \sum_{t=1}^{T} (y_t - f_1)^2.$$

As before, we minimize S_1 *w.r.t.* α_i, obtaining a new set of normal equations

$$\sum_{t=1}^{T} y_t f'_i(x_t, a_i) = \sum_{t=1}^{T} f(x_t, a_1) f'_i(x_t, a_1) + \sum_{t=1}^{T} \sum_{j=1}^{r} f'_j(x_t, a_1) f'_i(x_t, a_1)(\alpha_j - a_{j1}). \tag{3.4.36}$$

From these linear equations we compute $a_{12}, \ldots, a_{r2}$, and continue iteratively. When we find

$$\left| \frac{a_{ip} - a_{i,p-1}}{a_{i,p-1}} \right| < \epsilon \text{ for all } i,$$

where ϵ is a pre-assigned small quantity, we stop the iterations and call a_{ip} the set of estimates of α_i.

The method requires evaluation of first derivatives of f, evaluation of coefficients in normal equations, and repeated solution of normal equations. If the derivatives of f are not difficult to evaluate, this method is actually quite feasible and fast in large scale computers. Although it appears to be tedious and formidable, it is not so if modern computing facilities are used.

2. Second order Taylor expansions: Form the criterion

$$S(\alpha_1, \ldots, \alpha_r) = \sum_{t=1}^{T} (y_t - f)^2$$

and minimize *w.r.t.* α_i, to obtain

$$S'_i(\alpha_1, \ldots, \alpha_r) = \frac{\partial S}{\partial \alpha_i} = -\sum_{t=1}^{T} (y_t - f) \frac{\partial f}{\partial \alpha_i} = 0. \tag{3.4.37}$$

Choose an initial estimate $a_{10}, \ldots, a_{r0}$ and set the first-order Taylor expansion of S'_i about this vector equal to zero.

$$S'_i(a_{10}, \ldots, a_{r0}) + \sum_{i=1}^{r} \frac{\partial S'_i}{\partial \alpha_i}\bigg|_{\alpha=a_0} (\alpha_i - a_{i0}) = 0.$$

In terms of the f-function, this becomes

$$\begin{aligned}\sum_{t=1}^{T}(y_t - f(x_t, a_0))f_i'(x_t, a_0) + \sum_{t=1}^{T} y_t \sum_{j=1}^{r} f_{ij}''(x_t, a_0)(\alpha_j - a_{j0}) \\ - \sum_{t=1}^{T}\sum_{j=1}^{r}[f_j'(x_t, a_0)f_i'(x_t, a_0) + f(x_t, a_0)f_{ij}''(x_t, a_0)](\alpha_j - a_{j0}) = 0.\end{aligned} \tag{3.4.38}$$

These linear equations can be solved for a_{i1} as estimates of α_i, but it is now required to evaluate second derivatives of f at a_0, and, generally, to evaluate more numerical coefficients to get the linear equation system in parameter estimates. Having first round estimates of a_{i1}, we expand S_i' about these values to get a linear system in a_{i2}, etc. We stop when $\left|\dfrac{a_{ip} - a_{i,p-1}}{a_{i,p-1}}\right| < \epsilon$, for all i. Apart from the estimation of S_{ij}'', the calculations required are much the same as in method 1., and this method is probably quick in terminating the iterations. The second method is known as scoring and has been used in statistical estimation for some time.

In the iteration procedure, we have formed each successive estimate from the relationship

$$a_{ip} = a_{i,p-1} + \Delta a_{ip},$$

where Δa_{ip} is the difference between the value obtained as a solution to the linear approximation equations on the p-th round and the value assumed to be the approximation at the start of that round [$(p - 1)$st round]. Another choice for the solution value on the p-th round is

$$a_{ip} = a_{i,p-1} + h\Delta a_{ip}.$$

If $h \neq 1$, this means that the value chosen as a possible solution on the p-th round is the value so chosen on the $(p - 1)$st round plus h times the difference between the solution of the linearly approximated equations (not the same thing as a_{ip}) and the starting value on the p-th round. The step size h can be varied during the computation process so as to bring the result closer to the correct solution without undue over or undershooting this solution.

As we saw earlier in the discussion of maximum likelihood methods of estimation in linear regression equations, the variance-covariance matrix of regression coefficients can be written

$$\left\|\operatorname{cov} a_i a_j\right\| = \left\| - E\frac{\partial^2 L}{\partial\alpha_i \partial\alpha_j}\bigg|_{\alpha=a}\right\|^{-1}. \tag{3.4.39}$$

The same formula may be used in the present context of nonlinear estimation, assuming normally distributed e_t, and this will become

$$\|\operatorname{cov} a_i a_j\| = S_e^2 \,\|S_{ij}''(a_{1p} \ldots a_{rp})\|^{-1}. \tag{3.4.40}$$

From the mean residual variation

$$S_e^2 = \frac{1}{T}\sum_{t=1}^{T}(y_t - f(x_t, a_p))^2,$$

we have an estimate

$$S_e^2 = \text{est}\,\sigma_e^2.$$

We could adjust for degrees of freedom used up in small samples and compute

$$\frac{1}{T-r}\sum_{t=1}^{T}(y_t - f(x_t, a_p))^2$$

for the adjusted value of S_e^2.

It should be noted that S''_{ij} will be evaluated at each stage of the iteration process in method 2.; therefore, it will be readily available for computation of $\|\text{cov}\, a_i a_j\|$.

Questions and Problems

1. In estimating the linear structural relation with first order autoregressive disturbances

$$y_t = \alpha + \beta x_t + e_t$$
$$e_t = \rho e_{t-1} + u_t,$$

the final equation to be estimated

$$y_t = \alpha(1-\rho) + \beta(x_t - \rho x_{t-1}) + \rho y_{t-1} + u_t,$$

is nonlinear in the parameters. Compare the iteration procedures using Taylor expansions with the Cochrane-Orcutt method for this case.

2. The estimation of

$$y_t = A\, x_{1t}^{\alpha_1} x_{2t}^{\alpha_2} e_t$$

is treated as a linear problem, while estimation of

$$y_t = A x_{1t}^{\alpha_1} x_{2t}^{\alpha_2} + e_t$$

is a nonlinear problem. Discuss the differences between two cases and point out their relevance in applied econometrics.

SUGGESTED READINGS

Almon, S., "The Distributed Lag between Capital Appropriations and Expectations", *Econometrica*, 33 (January, 1965), 178–96. An innovative article on the use of polynomial lag distributions.

Dhrymes, P. J., *Distributed Lags: Problems of Estimation and Formulation*, San Francisco: Holden Day, 1971. A modern treatment of the estimation of distributed lags by a wide variety of methods.

Ezekiel, M. and K. A. Fox, *Methods of Correlation and Regression Analysis*, New York: John Wiley & Sons, 1959, 3rd edition. A classic of long standing that gives good understanding of regression methods in economics.

Goldberger, A. S., *Topics in Regression Analysis*, New York: Macmillan, 1968. A novel treatment of the regression problem.

Griliches, Z., "Distributed Lags: A Survey", *Econometrica*, 35 (January, 1967) 16–49. An expository paper on different approaches to the estimation and interpretation of lag distributions.

Hartley, H. O., "The Modified Gauss-Newton Method for the Fitting of Nonlinear Regression Functions by Least Squares", *Technometrics*, 3 (May, 1961) 269–80. A basic paper on the use of approximation and iteration methods for estimating nonlinear regressions.

Jorgenson, D., "Rational Distributed Lag Functions", *Econometrica*, 34 (January, 1966), 135–49. Generalizes for economists the Pascal-type lag distribution to the rational function lag distribution used in engineering.

Kendall, M. G., and A. Stuart, *The Advanced Theory of Statistics*, London: Griffin & Co., 1966, 3 vols. Provides a statistical treatment of regression and variance analysis.

Kmenta, J., *Elements of Econometrics*, New York: Macmillan, 1971. An excellent exposition of the statistical theory of regression analysis and its interpretation for use in economics.

Malinvaud, E., "The Consistency of Nonlinear Regressions", *Annals of Mathematical Statistics*, 41, (June, 1970), 956–69. Goes beyond the problem of computing estimates of nonlinear regressions and takes up the conditions for consistency in estimation.

Solow, R. M., "On a Family of Lag Distributions", *Econometrica*, 28, (April, 1960), 393–406. Introduces the Pascal-type lag distribution in economics as a significant generalization in the shape of the distribution.

4

Regression Systems of Linear Simultaneous Equations

1. INTRODUCTION

The Walrasian concept of an economic system portrays an economy as a set of simultaneous equations. The nonexperimental and imperfectly controllable nature of our observational data on this system, among other causes, prevents our making universal application of the single equation regression methods of the previous chapter in the estimation of economic relationships. It is, of course, evident that many economic relationships are of the single equation type, but most are probably not.

If we consider the problem of estimating crop yield as a function of meteorological data on rainfall and temperature, it may be acceptable to form a regression estimate of

$$y_t = \alpha_0 + \alpha_1 r_t + \alpha_2 C_t \tag{4.1.1}$$

where y_t = crop yield, in bushels per acre, during season t
r_t = rainfall, in inches, during season t
C_t = average temperature, in centigrade degrees, during season t.

The variables r_t and C_t are not controlled, and the data are not experimental, but these explanatory variables are generated by a different probability and explanatory mechanism detailing cloud formation, wind velocities, and general meteorological dynamics so that we can say

$$Er_te_t = EC_te_t = 0.$$

In this case, we have stochastic explanatory variables, but they satisfy the conditions for consistency in least squares regression, and the methods of the previous chapter would be applicable.

The yield relationship posited may not be satisfactory for a variety of reasons. The functional relationship may not be linear. This is especially so because rainfall may surpass a saturation state. Also, the variables r_t and C_t may not be specific enough. Possibly, rainfall in certain strategic periods of the growing season may be a more correct variable. Or certain combinations of rainfall and temperature may be more important than others for crop yield. These deficiencies in the relationship can be accounted for by redefining and respecifying the variables and the parameters of their relationship with y_t. At worst, we may be involved with the estimation of a nonlinear relationship of the types considered in the preceding chapter for which the simple criterion

$$\sum_{t=1}^{T} e_t^2 = \min.$$

could still be used.

If we decide, though, that important variables have been neglected in this relationship, our modifications of the equation to take them into account will be different. Let us suppose that applications of fertilizer to the acreage will substantially improve yields. Then we would have

$$y_t = \alpha_0 + \alpha_1 r_t + \alpha_2 C_t + \alpha_3 f_t + e_t, \tag{4.1.2}$$

where

$$f_t = \text{fertilizer application, in pounds, during season } t.$$

If the data from which this equation is to be estimated are from an experimental plot, the fertilizer applications can be varied and controlled to suit the experimentalist's needs. In this case, we can, in fact, treat the f_t as a set of known numbers. Thus, either from the assumption of stochastic independence or experimental control we have

$$Er_t e_t = EC_t e_t = Ef_t e_t = 0,$$

and least squares regression is the indicated method of estimation of α_i.

The situation would be much the same if we were to introduce manpower or machinery use in the yield equation. For an experimental plot, these can be controlled variates and treated as a set of known numbers, as in the specification of the Markoff Theorem.

Suppose, however, that our yield data are not readings from an experimental plot with controlled dosages of f_t or controlled inputs of manpower and machines. If the y_t are nonexperimental readings from yields in the agricultural sector as a whole, actual outputs per acre, and the inputs of fertilizer (also manpower and machines) depend on market prices of these inputs, that, in turn, depend on agricultural output, fertilizer supply, and the whole nonexperimental outcome of the actual economy; then we have a true Walrasian situation in which many of the variables are jointly interdependent. Our basic model will then become one involving a whole system of simultaneous equations. Our techniques must differ because in these circumstances it is no longer appropriate to assume

$$E f_t e_t = 0$$

when f_t is not a controlled variable. Single equation least squares regression estimates then lose their property of consistency.

Concepts in a Simultaneous Equation Model

To make the statement of our model clear, let us define some important concepts in simultaneous equation systems.

Endogenous or Dependent Variable

Endogenous variables are random variables that have a probability distribution whose parameters are elements in the system being estimated. In general, we have

$$E\, y_t e_t \neq 0,$$

where y_t is an endogenous variable and e_t is a random disturbance. Endogenous variables have an effect on the system being studied and are affected by the system being studied.

Exogenous or Independent Variable

Exogenous variables are either a set of known numbers, that is, fixed variates without a probability distribution or random variables that have a marginal probability distribution with parameters that are not elements of the system being estimated. In linear systems and in some nonlinear systems, we have

$$E\, x_t e_t = 0,$$

as a condition *imposed* on the exogenous variable x_t and the random error e_t. Exogenous variables have an affect on the system but are not affected by the system.

Predetermined Variable

An exogenous variable is predetermined, but lagged values of endogenous variables are also predetermined. In a linear system,

$$E\, y_{t-1} e_t = 0$$

provided the errors e_t are mutually independent; that is,

$$E\, e_t e_{t'} = 0, \qquad t \neq t'.$$

This can be seen in the following way: the solution to a linear system will make the stochastic part of y_{t-1} a linear function of $e_{t-1}, e_{t-2}, e_{t-3}, \ldots e_0$, where the e_{t-i} include all disturbances in the whole system. If the e_t are mutually independent and y_{t-1} depends linearly on $e_{t-1}, e_{t-2}, \ldots e_0$; then,

$$E\, y_{t-1} e_t = 0.$$

Linear Model

$$Ay_t + A_1 y_{t-1} + \cdots + A_p y_{t-p} + Bx_t = e_t \tag{4.1.3}$$

$$A = \begin{pmatrix} \alpha_{11} & \cdots & \alpha_{1n} \\ \cdot & & \cdot \\ \cdot & & \cdot \\ \cdot & & \cdot \\ \alpha_{n1} & \cdots & \alpha_{nn} \end{pmatrix}$$ square matrix of coefficients $n \times n$

$$y_t = \begin{pmatrix} y_{1t} \\ \cdot \\ \cdot \\ \cdot \\ y_{nt} \end{pmatrix}$$ Column vector of dependent (endogenous) variables

$$A_i = \begin{pmatrix} \alpha_{11i} & \cdots & \alpha_{1ni} \\ \cdot & & \cdot \\ \cdot & & \cdot \\ \cdot & & \cdot \\ \alpha_{n1i} & \cdots & \alpha_{nni} \end{pmatrix}$$ square matrix of coefficients $n \times n$
$i = 1, 2, \ldots, p$

$$y_{t-i} = \begin{pmatrix} y_{1,t-i} \\ \cdot \\ \cdot \\ \cdot \\ y_{n,t-i} \end{pmatrix}$$ column vector of predetermined (lagged dependent) variables.

$$B = \begin{pmatrix} \beta_{11} & \cdots & \beta_{1m} \\ \cdot & & \cdot \\ \cdot & & \cdot \\ \cdot & & \cdot \\ \beta_{n1} & \cdots & \beta_{nm} \end{pmatrix}$$ rectangular matrix of coefficients $n \times m$

$$x_t = \begin{pmatrix} x_{1t} \\ \cdot \\ \cdot \\ \cdot \\ x_{mt} \end{pmatrix}$$ column vector of independent (exogenous) variables

$$e_t = \begin{pmatrix} e_{1t} \\ \cdot \\ \cdot \\ \cdot \\ e_{nt} \end{pmatrix}$$ column vector of random errors.

A typical equation, the $i^{-\text{th}}$, in this linear dynamic system is

$$\sum_{j=1}^{n} \alpha_{ij} y_{jt} + \sum_{j=1}^{n} \sum_{k=1}^{p} \alpha_{ijk} y_{j,t-k} + \sum_{j=1}^{m} \beta_{ij} x_{jt} = e_{it}.$$

There are some general features of the typical linear simultaneous equation model that should be considered immediately before we take up problems of estimation. In the first place, the lag structure need not be explicitly included at this time if we assume

$$E\, e_{it} e_{jt'} = 0, \qquad t \neq t'.$$

If there is no serial dependence among elements of e_t, we can treat the y_{t-i} like other predetermined variables, the x_t, in large samples. In one of the earliest and most basic papers in the modern approach to econometrics, Mann and Wald showed the consistency and efficiency of treating lagged dependent variables as though they were exogenous variables.[1] We can thus treat estimation problems, in the context of no serial dependence, from the simpler model

$$Ay_t + Bx_t = e_t. \tag{4.1.5}$$

The lag structure of y_{t-i} cannot be ignored in other problems, but here we shall simply define elements of y_{t-i} as newly defined elements of x_t. The same is true of lagged exogenous variables. They can be simply classified as newly defined exogenous variables.

The model

$$Ay_t + Bx_t = e_t \tag{4.1.5}$$

can be extended to

$$\begin{aligned} Ay_t + Bx_t &= e_t \\ \Gamma x_t &= u_t. \end{aligned} \tag{4.1.6}$$

The second system of linear equations is appended to show how the x_t may be determined in a separate model that is independent of the model of the economy. The relations

$$\Gamma x_t = u_t$$

will not be investigated by the econometrician. They are the laws governing meteorology, political processes, and other extra economic events in a separate mechanism. If some elements of x_t are fixed variates, these are not determined in this added linear system. The added system determines the stochastic exogenous variables.

[1] H. B. Mann and A. Wald, "On the Statistical Treatment of Linear Stochastic Difference Equations," *Econometrica*, 11, (1943), 173–220.

The matrices A and B are written as though they are quite dense, although in practice they often are sparse. Some variables appear in only one or two equations of the Walrasian system, and others appear in many. In principle, everything depends on everything else, but that is really too sweeping and does not stand up in any significant sense. Many interrelations are so remote or weak that we may as well consider the associated α_{ij} or β_{ij} to be zero.

In fact, if all the relevant matrices are fully dense, that is, contain no zeros, every equation in the system looks like every other. It is a linear equation with *unknown* coefficients associating the elements of y_t and x_t in a stochastic relationship. We need specific a priori information in order to distinguish one equation from another and to determine (identify) its economic meaning. Zeros are one set of a priori valuations of elements of A and B, but others are relevant as well. This leads us to the problem of identification.

Questions and Problems

1. In the linear system

$$\begin{aligned} Ay_t + Bx_t &= e_t \\ \Gamma x_t &= u_t, \end{aligned}$$

show that the definition of exogeneity

$$E\, x_{it}e_{jt} = 0, \qquad \text{all } i, j$$

is equivalent to

$$E\, e_{it}u_{jt} = 0.$$

2. Give examples of exogenous variables in models of
   (a) a national economy
   (b) world trade
   (c) a commodity market
   (d) a system of consumer demand.
3. In the transformation of the lag distribution

$$y_t = \alpha \sum_{i=0}^{\infty} \lambda^i x_{t-i} + e_t$$

to the expression

$$\begin{aligned} y_t &= \alpha x_t + \lambda y_{t-1} + (e_t - \lambda e_{t-1}) \\ &= \alpha x_t + \lambda y_{t-1} + v_t, \end{aligned}$$

show why y_{t-1} cannot be treated as a predetermined variable for least squares regression estimation.

Under what condition should y_{t-1} be treated as predetermined in the adaptive model

$$\begin{aligned} y_t - y_{t-1} &= \mu(y_t^* - y_{t-1}) + e_t \\ y_t^* &= \beta x_t + u_t? \end{aligned}$$

2. IDENTIFICATION

First, let us consider the criteria for identification in a linear system, then we shall consider more general concepts. The i-th equation in the linear system

$$Ay_t + Bx_t = e_t$$

is written as

$$\sum_{j=1}^{n_i} \alpha_{ij} y_{jt} + \sum_{j=1}^{m_i} \beta_{ij} x_{jt} = e_{it}, \tag{4.2.1}$$

where $n_i \leq n$ and $m_i \leq m$. There are n endogenous variables in the whole system and m predetermined variables. In the i-th equation, we have n_i endogenous variables and m_i predetermined variables. Because some elements of y_t and x_t may be absent from the list of variables in the i-th equation, we shall usually have $n_i < n$ and $m_i < m$ in a system of any size. It is the presence of zero coefficients or other linear *restrictions* on the α_{ij} and β_{ij} that serve to identify the i-th equation.

If it is impossible to reproduce the *statistical form* of the i-th equation by linear combination of some or all the equations of the system, we say that the i-th equation is identified. By reproduction of the *statistical form* of the i-th equation, we mean the derivation of an equation expressing a stochastic linear relation among the same variables that appear with nonzero coefficients in the i-th equation and having the same linear restrictions that occur among the parameters of the i-th equation.

Examples of Identification Criteria

Consider the simple macromodel of the most elementary Keynesian type:

$$\begin{aligned} C_t &= \alpha_0 + \alpha_1 Y_t + e_{1t} \\ I_t &= \beta_0 + \beta_1 Y_t + e_{2t} \\ Y_t &= C_t + I_t \\ Y &= \text{income} \\ C &= \text{consumption} \\ I &= \text{investment.} \end{aligned} \tag{4.2.2}$$

By substitution of the third (identity) equation into the first, we have

$$\begin{aligned} I_t &= -\alpha_0 + (1 - \alpha_1) Y_t - e_{1t} \\ I_t &= \beta_0 + \beta_1 Y_t + e_{2t}. \end{aligned} \tag{4.2.3}$$

These two equations have the same statistical form, both being linear stochastic relations between I_t and Y_t with unknown coefficients, and any linear combination of them will also have the same statistical form. We, therefore, say that neither of these two equations is identified.

Let us now modify this system by introducing exogenous public investment (G_t)

$$\begin{aligned} C &= \alpha_0 + \alpha_1 Y_t + e_{1t} \\ I_t &= \beta_0 + \beta_1 Y_t + e_{2t} \\ Y_t &= C_t + I_t + G_t. \end{aligned} \tag{4.2.4}$$

By substitution, we now have

$$\begin{aligned} I_t &= -\alpha_0 + (1 - \alpha_1)\, Y_t - G_t - e_{1t} \\ I_t &= \beta_0 + \beta_1 Y_t + e_{2t}. \end{aligned} \tag{4.2.5}$$

There are two distinctive features in this system. In the first equation, the coefficient of G_t is (-1). In the second, it is zero. Any linear combination of these two equations will not generally have either a zero or (negative) unit coefficient of G_t; therefore, both are identified.

Now, let us modify our investment hypothesis by introducing the accelerator principle, so that the system is

$$\begin{aligned} C_t &= \alpha_0 + \alpha_1 Y_t + e_{1t} \\ I_t &= \beta_0 + \beta_1 (Y_t - Y_{t-1}) + e_{2t} \\ Y_t &= C_t + I_t + G_t. \end{aligned} \tag{4.2.6}$$

Substituting, again, we have

$$\begin{aligned} I_t &= \alpha_0 + (1 - \alpha_1) Y_t - G_t - e_{1t} \\ I_t &= \beta_0 + \beta_1 Y_t - \beta_1 Y_{t-1} + e_{2t}. \end{aligned} \tag{4.2.7}$$

There are now four *restrictions* to note in these two equations. In the first, we have the restriction that the coefficient of G_t is known, a priori, to be (-1). We also note that the coefficient of Y_{t-1}, a predetermined variable, is zero. In the second equation, the coefficient of G_t is zero and the coefficient of Y_{t-1} is equal but opposite in sign to that of Y_t. Linear combination of these two equations will, in general, violate the conditions imposed on one or the other; therefore, it is not possible to duplicate an equation with the same statistical form as either, and we say that both are identified.

We shall now introduce a new concept, that of *reduced form* of a system. This is an alternative way of writing a system so that each endogenous variable is expressed as a function of predetermined variables alone. In the general linear system, it is

$$\begin{aligned} Y_t &= -A^{-1}Bx_t + A^{-1}e_t \\ &= \Pi x_t + v_t \end{aligned} \tag{4.2.8}$$

where

$$\Pi = -A^{-1}B;\ v_t = A^{-1}e_t.$$

In our third example (4.2.6), it is

$$\begin{aligned} Y_t &= \frac{\alpha_0 + \beta_0}{1 - \alpha_1 - \beta_1} + \frac{G_t}{1 - \alpha_1 - \beta_1} - \frac{\beta_1}{1 - \alpha_1 - \beta_1} Y_{t-1} + \frac{e_{1t} + e_{2t}}{1 - \alpha_1 - \beta_1} \\ I_t &= \frac{\alpha_0\beta_1 + \beta_0(1 - \alpha_1)}{1 - \alpha_1 - \beta_1} + \frac{\beta_1 G_t}{1 - \alpha_1 - \beta_1} - \frac{\beta_1(1 - \alpha_1)}{1 - \alpha_1 - \beta_1} Y_{t-1} \\ &\quad + \frac{\beta_1 e_{1t} + (1 - \alpha_1)e_{2t}}{1 - \alpha_1 - \beta_1}. \end{aligned} \tag{4.2.9}$$

The reduced form equations corresponding to the other two models can be determined from these. If the values of Y_{t-1} are suppressed, we have the reduced form equations for the second version (4.2.4). If the values of both G_t and Y_{t-1} are suppressed, we have the reduced form equations for the first version (4.2.2).

There are six elements in the Π-matrix above ($-A^{-1}B$), yet there are only four elements in A and B together. These are α_0, α_1, β_0, β_1. In the third model, we have more than enough elements in Π to determine the four structural coefficients from them. This is the case of *overidentification.* In the second model, there are only four elements in Π and four in A, B, and we can transform uniquely from knowledge of the elements of Π to knowledge of the elements of A, B provided there are no singularities in the transformation. The four elements of Π are

$$\Pi = \begin{pmatrix} \pi_{11} & \pi_{12} \\ \pi_{21} & \pi_{22} \end{pmatrix} = \frac{1}{1 - \alpha_1 - \beta_1}\begin{pmatrix} \alpha_0 + \beta_0 & 1 \\ \alpha_0\beta_1 + \beta_0(1 - \alpha_1) & \beta_1 \end{pmatrix}. \tag{4.2.10}$$

From knowledge of π_{12} and π_{22} we can determine β_1,

$$\frac{\pi_{22}}{\pi_{12}} = \beta_1 \tag{4.2.11}$$

If we know β_1 and π_{12}, we can determine α_1 from

$$\pi_{12} = \frac{1}{1 - \alpha_1 - \beta_1}. \tag{4.2.12}$$

From the two equations; linear in α_0 and β_0, given α_1, β_1, π_{11}, π_{21}; we can solve for α_0 and β_0

$$\begin{aligned} \pi_{11}(1 - \alpha_1 - \beta_1) &= \alpha_0 + \beta_0 \\ \pi_{21}(1 - \alpha_1 - \beta_1) &= \alpha_0\beta_1 + \beta_0(1 - \alpha_1). \end{aligned} \tag{4.2.13}$$

As long as $1 - \alpha_1 - \beta_1 \neq 0$, we can transform uniquely from elements of Π to elements of A, B. In this case, the model is *exactly identified.*

In the first model, we have both G_t and Y_{t-1} deleted; so there are only two reduced form coefficients, $\pi_{11}\ \pi_{21}$, but there are four unknown elements of A (B does not exist in this case). We have too little information in the Π-matrix to determine the elements of the A-matrix, and the system is *underidentified.*

General Treatment of Zero-type Restrictions in the Linear Case

The $i^{\text{-th}}$ equation in the system considered is

$$\sum_{j=1}^{n_i} \alpha_{ij} y_{jt} + \sum_{j=1}^{m_i} \beta_{ij} x_{jt} = e_{it} \tag{4.2.1}$$

The reduced form for the $j^{\text{-th}}$ variable is

$$y_{jt} = \sum_{k=1}^{m} \pi_{jk} x_{kt} + v_{jt}. \tag{4.2.14}$$

Multiply both sides by α_{ij} and sum from 1 to n_i

$$\sum_{j=1}^{n_i} \alpha_{ij} y_{jt} = \sum_{j=1}^{n_i} \sum_{k=1}^{m} \alpha_{ij} \pi_{jk} x_{kt} + \sum_{j=1}^{n_i} \alpha_{ij} v_{jt}. \tag{4.2.15}$$

We now have two expressions for $\sum_{j=1}^{n_i} \alpha_{ij} y_{jt}$, one in (4.2.1), the other in (4.2.15); therefore, we equate coefficients of the right-hand side variables, term by term, to get

$$\beta_{ik} = -\sum_{j=1}^{n_i} \alpha_{ij} \pi_{jk} \qquad k = 1, 2, \ldots, m_i \tag{4.2.16}$$

$$0 = \sum_{j=1}^{n_i} \alpha_{ij}\, \pi_{jk} \qquad k = m_i + 1, \ldots, m. \tag{4.2.17}$$

In order to determine the α_{ij} uniquely from knowledge of the π_{jk}, the set of homogeneous linear equations in (4.2.17) must have a matrix of coefficients with rank less than n_i. We must have

$$\text{rank} \begin{pmatrix} \pi_{1,\, m_i+1} & \cdots & \pi_{1,\, m} \\ \cdot & & \cdot \\ \cdot & & \cdot \\ \cdot & & \cdot \\ \pi_{n_i,\, m_i+1} & \cdots & \pi_{n_i,\, m} \end{pmatrix} \leq n_i - 1,$$

otherwise, the only solution would be $\alpha_{ij} = 0$ for $j = 1, 2, \ldots, n_i$. If rank $< n_i - 1$, we cannot determine ratios of elements of α_{ij} uniquely. Except for the choice of one variable to have unit coefficient, we want to have unique values of α_{ij}; therefore,

$$\text{rank}\begin{pmatrix} \pi_{1,\,m_i+1} & \cdots & \pi_{1,\,m} \\ \vdots & & \vdots \\ \pi_{n_i,\,m_i+1} & \cdots & \pi_{n_i,\,m} \end{pmatrix} = n_i - 1. \tag{4.2.18}$$

This is a necessary and sufficient condition for identification in a linear system with zero-type restrictions.

In order for a solution for ratios of α_{ij} to exist, it is necessary that

$$\begin{pmatrix} \pi_{1,\,m_i+1} & \cdots & \pi_{1,\,m} \\ \vdots & & \vdots \\ \pi_{n_i,\,m_i+1} & \cdots & \pi_{n_i,\,m} \end{pmatrix}$$

have at least $n_i - 1$ columns. This condition may be written as

$$m - m_i \geq n_i - 1. \tag{4.2.19}$$

The number of excluded predetermined variables in the i-th equation must be at least as large as the number of included dependent variables less one. An equivalent expression is

$$m - m_i + n - n_i \geq n - 1$$

or the total number of variables excluded from the i-th equation (predetermined or dependent) must be at least as great as the number of dependent variables in the whole system, less one.

It is evident that if

$$m - m_i = n_i - 1,$$

we can solve for unique ratios of the α_{ij} in

$$0 = \sum_{j=1}^{n_i} \alpha_{ij}\pi_{jk} \qquad k = m_i + 1, \ldots, m. \tag{4.2.17}$$

provided the rank of the coefficient matrix is $n_i - 1$. This is the condition of exact identification. For

$$m - m_i > n_i - 1$$

we have a necessary condition for overidentification.

General Linear Homogeneous Restrictions

For more general, that is, linear homogeneous, restrictions we write

$$(\alpha_{i1}, \ldots, \alpha_{in}, \beta_{i1}, \ldots, \beta_{im})\Phi_i = 0 \tag{4.2.20}$$

where Φ is a matrix of *known* coefficients with $m + n$ rows and as many columns as are necessary to express all the restrictions. In the examples cited above, we have for the first equation in (4.2.2)

$$(1 \quad -\alpha_0 \quad -\alpha_1 \quad -\alpha_2)\begin{pmatrix} 0 \\ 0 \\ 0 \\ 1 \end{pmatrix} = 0$$

$$-\alpha_2 = 0,$$

that expresses the fact that I_t does not appear in the first equation.[2] In (4.2.4), our restrictions take the form

$$(1 \quad -\alpha_0 \quad -\alpha_1 \quad -\alpha_2 \quad -\gamma_1)\begin{pmatrix} 0 & 0 \\ 0 & 0 \\ 0 & 0 \\ 1 & 0 \\ 0 & 1 \end{pmatrix} = 0$$

$$-\alpha_2 = 0; \; -\gamma_1 = 0.$$

These say that neither I_t nor G_t appears in the first equation.

Let us now consider the second equation of (4.2.6). The restrictions are expressed as

$$(1 \quad -\beta_0 \quad -\beta_1 \quad -\beta_2 \quad -\delta_1 \quad -\delta_2)\begin{pmatrix} 0 & 0 & 0 \\ 0 & 0 & 0 \\ 0 & 0 & 1 \\ 1 & 0 & 0 \\ 0 & 1 & 0 \\ 0 & 0 & 1 \end{pmatrix} = 0$$

$$-\beta_2 = 0; \; -\delta_1 = 0; \; -\beta_1 - \delta_2 = 0.$$

The first says that C_t does not enter this equation, the second that G_t does not enter this equation, and the third that the coefficient of Y_{t-1} is $-\beta_1$. This last restriction is not of the zero-type, but is a linear homogeneous restriction.

A necessary and sufficient condition for the identifiability of the i-th equation

[2] Because we have included constant terms in our examples, Φ has an extra row.

in the system

$$Ay_t + Bx_t = e_t$$

is

$$\text{rank}\,(A\ B)\,\Phi_i = n - 1, \tag{4.2.21}$$

and a necessary (not sufficient) condition is

$$\text{rank}\,\Phi_i = n - 1. \tag{4.2.22}$$

Degree of Identification

For the linear model, we have been able to give a complete mathematical statement of conditions for identification. This treatment gives the appearance of an exact concept. Identification is either present or absent; either exactly or overidentified, if present. There is, however, a meaning to the degree of identification that goes beyond the counting of restrictions or rank of a matrix.

If identification is achieved by excluding variables from some equations and including them in others, these variables must make a difference to the statistical explanation of the system to give meaning to their exclusion from particular equations. We could always satisfy formal conditions for identification by including trivial variables in the system and leaving them out of an equation that is being tested for identification. Similarly, other kinds of linear homogeneous restrictions that serve to establish identification must be of *significance* if identification is to be strong.

Related to the possibility of trivial or weak identification we have the position of T. C. Liu, who argues that we may be unjustified in deviating from the general position that everything depends on everything else in an interrelated general equilibrium economy.[3] He questions the specifications of models whereby restrictions are imposed on particular parameters or groups of them. His position is that econometric models are generally underidentified and that the most we can do is to estimate reduced forms without a priori restrictions.

F. Fisher has examined this argument from the point of view that certain variables may enter equations with very small coefficients, ϵ_{ij}. If the ϵ_{ij} are very small but nonzero, as required by Liu, do we lose identification? Fisher shows that there is approximate identification to correspond with approximate (ϵ_{ij}) effects of variables in specific equations.

Although some particular equation may be identified by the criteria stated above, even strongly identified, the system as a whole may not be identified because other individual equations of the system are not identified.

It is also worth pointing out that the full (rank) conditions for identification involve the properties of determinants of structural parameters. These properties may be satisfied for some values of parameters and not for others.

[3] T. C. Liu, "Underidentification, Structural Estimation, and Forecasting," *Econometrica*, 28 (October, 1960), 855–65.

Because we do not know the true values—that is the purpose of our whole approach to estimation through statistical inference—we cannot know, in general, whether our systems are definitely identified. Our only fairly certain information comes from the *necessary* conditions and not the full rank conditions.

Identification in the General Case

The complete theorems for identification have been stated for linear restrictions in linear systems, but the concept is much more general. The basic question being posed in the matter of identification is whether the probability distribution of jointly dependent (endogenous) variables could have been produced by a unique set of parameters.

A fundamental way of considering the structural equations of an economy is to regard them as *transformation* equations showing us how to transform from the (unobserved) random errors to the (observed) dependent variables. More particularly, they show us how to transform the probability distributions of the errors into probability distributions of the dependent variables. Let us write our system generally as

$$f_i(y_{1t}, \ldots, y_{nt}; x_{1t}, \ldots, x_{mt}) = e_{it}, \qquad i = 1, 2, \ldots, n. \tag{4.2.23}$$

The joint probability density of e_{it} over the T-element sample is

$$p(e_{11}, \ldots, e_{1T}, \ldots, e_{n1}, \ldots, e_{nT}).$$

In Chap. 2, we found that a probability distribution of one set of variables can be transformed into another distribution of a functionally related set of variables, and we shall use the structural equations of the model for these functional relationships. Using the techniques of transforming probability distributions, we have, as the density function of $y_{11}, \ldots, y_{nT}$ (given $x_{11}, \ldots, x_{mT}$),

$$p(e_{11}, \ldots, e_{nT}) \left| \frac{\partial(e_{11}, \ldots, e_{nT})}{\partial(y_{11}, \ldots, y_{nT})} \right| = p(f_1, \ldots, f_n) \left| \frac{\partial(e_{11}, \ldots, e_{nT})}{\partial(y_{11}, \ldots, y_{nT})} \right|. \tag{4.2.24}$$

In general terms, we shall write

$$g(y_{11}, \ldots, y_{nT} \mid x_{11}, \ldots, x_{mT}; \theta_1, \ldots, \theta_r)$$

as the joint density function of our observed sample of y_{it}, given the observed sample of x_{it} and the r parameters $\theta_1, \ldots, \theta_r$. The parameters of this distribution are combinations of the parameters in the density function p and in the Jacobian of the transformation. The latter depend, in turn, on the parameters of the structural equations.

Consider now the set of all parameter values that lead to *identical* probabilities of obtaining the observed sample. If $\theta'_1, \ldots, \theta'_r$ and $\theta''_1, \ldots, \theta''_r$ are two members of this set we would have

$$g(y_{11}, \ldots, y_{nT} \mid x_{11}, \ldots, x_{mT}; \theta'_1, \ldots, \theta'_r) \equiv g(y_{11}, \ldots, y_{nT} \mid x_{11}, \ldots, x_{mT}; \theta''_1, \ldots, \theta''_r) \tag{4.2.25}$$

for all possible samples of y_{it} and x_{it}.

Because $\theta'_1, \ldots, \theta'_r$ and $\theta''_1, \ldots, \theta''_r$ define models that give rise to identical probabilities of obtaining the observed samples, the statistician would not be able to choose one set of parameter values over the other as the true or correct set. There may be many such sets of parameter values giving rise to equal probabilities of obtaining the observed samples.

Different situations may be classified as follows:

1. There is a unique set of parameters satisfying the above identity. We would say that for any pair $\theta'_1, \ldots, \theta'_r$ and $\theta''_1, \ldots, \theta''_r$ satisfying the identity, we have

$$\theta'_i = \theta''_i \qquad i = 1, 2, \ldots, r.$$

In this case, all parameters and all equations are identified.

2. For any two sets satisfying the identity, we have

$$\begin{aligned} \theta'_{r_1} &= \theta''_{r_1} \\ \theta'_{r_2} &= \theta''_{r_2} \\ &\vdots \\ \theta'_{r_s} &= \theta''_{r_s} \end{aligned}$$

In this case, a subset of parameters $\theta_{r_1}, \ldots, \theta_{r_s}$ $(s < r)$ is identified. Either individual parameters or those belonging to an entire structural equation may be in the identified set.

3. Lack of identification may be finite, in which case there is only a finite number (w) of distinct sets $\theta'_1, \ldots, \theta'_r; \theta''_1, \ldots, \theta''_r; \ldots \theta^w_1, \ldots, \theta^w_r$ satisfying the identity.

These are general conceptual criteria but are not easy to apply in practical cases. In terms of this concept of identification though, we can see how specific nonlinearities and restrictions on the variance-covariance matrix $(Ee_{it}e_{jt})$ may lead to identification.

Questions and Problems

1. Consider a linear supply-demand model.

$$\begin{aligned} S_t &= \alpha_0 + \alpha_1 P_t + e_t \\ D_t &= \beta_0 + \beta_1 P_t + u_t \\ S_t &= D_t \end{aligned}$$

Is this system identified?

2. Discuss identification in the "cobweb" model of supply and demand.

3. Derive the reduced form expression for the general dynamic linear model

$$\sum_{i=0}^{P} A_i y_{t-i} + Bx_t = e_t.$$

3. THE PRINCIPLE OF MAXIMUM LIKELIHOOD (ML)

In a general discussion of methods of statistical estimation in Chap. 2, we have defined the principle of *maximum likelihood* and have also used it in Chap. 3 for the estimation of single equations. We now consider application of this principle to the estimation of econometric systems.

As a result of its properties of consistency, efficiency, and sufficiency in large samples, maximum likelihood theory has played a normative role in econometric estimation, in some respects almost like the role played by perfect competition in economic analysis. With strict enough assumptions, both approaches are normative in their own contexts yet both are hard to realize in practice, partly because of the restrictiveness of the assumptions, and partly because of the difficulties of execution even under strict assumptions. In the case of maximum likelihood theory, it has been the difficulty of computation that has led to its inapplicability, but these difficulties are rapidly being overcome.

The method of maximum likelihood is not necessarily tied to the linearity of the relationships being estimated (either as functions of the variable or the parameters), therefore, we shall first give a general formulation. As above, our equation system is

$$f_i(y_{1t}, \ldots, y_{nt}; x_{1t}, \ldots, x_{mt}) = e_{it} \qquad i = 1, 2, \ldots, n \tag{4.3.1}$$

and the likelihood function is

$$\begin{aligned} L^* &= p(e_{11}, \ldots, e_{nT}) \left| \frac{\partial(e_{11}, \ldots, e_{nT})}{\partial(y_{11}, \ldots, y_{nT})} \right| = p(f_1, \ldots, f_n) \left| \frac{\partial(e_{11}, \ldots, e_{nT})}{\partial(y_{11}, \ldots, y_{nT})} \right| \\ &= g(y_{11}, \ldots, y_{nT} \mid x_{11}, \ldots, x_{mT}; \theta_1, \ldots, \theta_r). \end{aligned} \tag{4.3.2}$$

If the $e_{1t}, \ldots, e_{nt}$ are jointly normally distributed and serially independent, we have the specific form

$$\begin{aligned} L^* &= g(y_{11}, \ldots, y_{nT} \mid x_{11}, \ldots, x_{mT}; \theta_1, \ldots, \theta_r) \\ &= \prod_{t=1}^{T} \left| \frac{\partial(f_1, \ldots, f_n)}{\partial(y_{1t}, \ldots, y_{nt})} \right| \left(\frac{1}{\sqrt{2\pi}} \right)^{-Tn} |\Sigma|^{-T/2} \exp\left\{ -\frac{1}{2} \sum_{t=1}^{T} f' \Sigma^{-1} f \right\}, \end{aligned} \tag{4.3.3}$$

or by forming logarithms

$$L = \sum_{t=1}^{T} \log |J_t| - Tn \log \sqrt{2\pi} - \frac{T}{2} \log |\Sigma| - \frac{1}{2} \sum_{t=1}^{T} f' \Sigma^{-1} f,$$

where

$$\text{Jacobian} = J_t = \frac{\partial(f_1, \ldots, f_n)}{\partial(y_{1t}, \ldots, y_{nt})}$$

$$\text{variance-covariance matrix} = \Sigma = \| E(e_{it}e_{jt}) \| = \| \sigma_{ij} \|.$$

$$f' = (f_1, f_2, \ldots, f_n)$$

The elements of Σ are parameters and are represented by some of the θ_i in the joint density function g. The parameters of the structural functions f_i are the remaining elements in $\theta_1, \ldots, \theta_r$ that are otherwise unspecified in this general presentation.

The method of maximum likelihood would be formulated as the finding of roots of

$$\frac{\partial L}{\partial \theta_i} = 0 \qquad i = 1, 2, \ldots, r.$$

In the present representation, we would have

$$\frac{\partial L}{\partial \theta_i} = \sum_{t=1}^{T} \frac{1}{|J_t|} \frac{\partial |J_t|}{\partial \theta_i} - \frac{T}{2|\Sigma|} \frac{\partial |\Sigma|}{\partial \theta_i} - \frac{1}{2} \frac{\partial}{\partial \theta_i} \sum_{t=1}^{T} f' \Sigma^{-1} f = 0 \qquad (4.3.4)$$

This can be simplified by the methods of stepwise maximization.[4] The maximization of L *w.r.t.* those θ_i that are elements of Σ will yield estimation equations of the form

$$\hat{\sigma}_{ij} = \frac{1}{T} \sum_{t=1}^{T} \hat{f}_i \hat{f}_j,$$

where $\hat{f}_i$ are the values of f_i computed for optimal (maximizing) parameter values $\hat{\theta}_1, \ldots, \hat{\theta}_r$. Thus, at the optimal point in the parameter space we find

$$\frac{1}{T} \sum_{t=1}^{T} \hat{f}' \hat{\Sigma}^{-1} \hat{f} = n.$$

Our problem is, therefore, reduced to that of finding $\hat{f}_i$ and then evaluating $\hat{\Sigma}$ as a function of $\hat{f}_i$. The optimum values of $\hat{\theta}_i$ and, hence, $\hat{f}_i$ must be those that maximize

$$L_c = \sum_{t=1}^{T} \log |J_t| - \frac{T}{2} \log |\Sigma|, \qquad (4.3.5)$$

when the elements of Σ are defined as $\frac{1}{T} \sum_{t=1}^{T} f_i f_j$. This is known as the *concentrated* form of the likelihood function. The maximum likelihood equations are,

[4] For somewhat simpler reasons, it was seen in Chap. 3 that the maximum likelihood method of estimation of the coefficients and variance of a single linear regression equation could be carried out in two steps. In the first step, estimates of regression coefficients are determined, and, from these, estimates of the variance of error are found in the second step.

therefore,

$$\frac{\partial L_c}{\partial \theta_i} = \sum_{t=1}^{T} \frac{1}{|J_t|} \frac{\partial |J_t|}{\partial \theta_i} - \frac{1}{2} \frac{T}{|\Sigma|} \frac{\partial |\Sigma|}{\partial \theta_i} = 0, \tag{4.3.6}$$

$$\hat{\sigma}_{ij} = \frac{1}{T} \sum_{t=1}^{T} \hat{f}_i \hat{f}_j. \tag{4.3.7}$$

In the general case, these are difficult nonlinear equations to be solved. Even specification of the system to be linear cannot make this problem simple for both the expressions

$$\sum_{t=1}^{T} \frac{1}{|J_t|} \frac{\partial |J_t|}{\partial \theta_i} \qquad \text{and} \qquad \frac{T}{|\Sigma|} \frac{\partial |\Sigma|}{\partial \theta_i}$$

are nonlinear functions of θ_i even if the original equation system is linear. In the single equation case of Chap. 3, the equations were, in fact, linear because $|J_t| = 1$ and $\Sigma = \frac{1}{T} \sum_{t=1}^{T} f^2$ in that instance.

In a linear model, we have

$$f = Ay_t + Bx_t = e_t, \tag{4.3.8}$$

and the log likelihood function is

$$L = T \log |A| - Tn \log \sqrt{2\pi} - \frac{T}{2} \log |\Sigma| - \frac{1}{2} \sum_{t=1}^{T} (Ay_t + Bx_t)' \Sigma^{-1} (Ay_t + Bx_t). \tag{4.3.9}$$

The concentrated form is

$$\frac{1}{T} L_c = \log |A| - \frac{1}{2} \log |\Sigma|, \tag{4.3.10}$$

where

$$\Sigma = \frac{1}{T} \sum_{t=1}^{T} (Ay_t + Bx_t)(Ay_t + Bx_t)' = \left\| \frac{1}{T} \sum_{t=1}^{T} \left(\sum_{k=1}^{n} \alpha_{ik} y_{kt} + \sum_{k=1}^{m} \beta_{ik} x_{kt} \right) \left(\sum_{l=1}^{n} \alpha_{jl} y_{lt} + \sum_{l=1}^{m} \beta_{jl} x_{lt} \right) \right\|.$$

In this form, A is a constant Jacobian matrix, but its determinant, $|A|$, is generally a nonlinear function of the α_{ij}, as is $\frac{\partial |A|}{\partial \alpha_{ij}}$. It is clear that the parameters of the system, A, B, are parameters of L_c *w.r.t.* which the likelihood function is to be maximized.

In finding maximum likelihood estimates, there is no restriction imposed on the ratios of coefficients in each linear equation if we adopt some rule of normalization. That is to say, the $i^{\text{-th}}$ equation,

$$\sum_{k=1}^{n} \alpha_{ik} y_{kt} + \sum_{k=1}^{m} \beta_{ik} x_{kt} = e_{it}$$

could be multiplied by an arbitrary constant λ_i

$$\lambda_i \sum_{k=1}^{n} \alpha_{ik} y_{kt} + \lambda_i \sum_{k=1}^{m} \beta_{ik} x_{kt} = \lambda_i e_{it}.$$

If this transformed equation were to replace the original in the likelihood function, the estimated ratios of coefficients in the $i^{\text{-th}}$ equation would be unchanged. We usually make one coefficient in each linear equation unity and use this as a rule of normalization. The invariance property of maximum likelihood estimation means that any alternative choice of the coefficient to be set equal to unity would yield the same set of ratios of coefficients. The method, therefore, is invariant under a change of normalization units.

In evaluating $\frac{\partial \log |A|}{\partial \alpha_{ij}}, \frac{\partial \log |\Sigma|}{\partial \alpha_{ij}}, \frac{\partial \log |\Sigma|}{\partial \beta_{ij}}$, that form the basis of the maximum likelihood estimating equations, we must recognize that many elements of the A and B matrices are restrained. We must deal with *identified* systems in obtaining structural estimates, and the restrictions on A and B are the identifying restrictions discussed in the preceding section. The problem can either be organized for computational purposes as a constrained maximization problem, or we can substitute the restraints into the system, derive constrained expressions for A and B, and then maximize as in an unconstrained problem.

To find the estimated variance-covariance matrix of coefficients, we evaluate

$$\begin{pmatrix} \left\| -E\frac{\partial^2 L_c}{\partial \alpha_{ij} \partial \alpha_{kl}} \right\| & \left\| -E\frac{\partial^2 L_c}{\partial \alpha_{ij} \partial \beta_{kl}} \right\| \\ \left\| -E\frac{\partial^2 L_c}{\partial \alpha_{ij} \partial \beta_{kl}} \right\| & \left\| -E\frac{\partial^2 L_c}{\partial \beta_{ij} \partial \beta_{kl}} \right\| \end{pmatrix}^{-1}. \tag{4.3.11}$$

The beauty of this approach is that it gives us a complete set of variances and covariances between different parameters in the same equation and even between parameters in different equations. It is, of course, only an asymptotically valid formula.

Although the maximum likelihood method has the desirable properties of maximum likelihood generally, is invariant with changes in normalization (ways of writing a system), takes into account all restrictions between and within equations, and gives a complete variance-covariance matrix of estimates for the entire system; it has two significant drawbacks. (1) It is difficult to compute. This is partly due to the nonlinearity of the estimation equations and partly due to its simultaneity. The system of maximum likelihood equations that must be solved simultaneously is of the order of the total number of parameters (excluding error variances and covariances) in the system. This number may be very large indeed. (2) The simultaneity aspect, though desirable, may be very sensitive. If there is an error in *specification* of the model being estimated (wrong restrictions, wrong variables), we may find that estimates *throughout* the system are disturbed because of this error. One must have a strong a priori specification of the model being estimated before maximum likelihood methods are employed. Single equation methods, in the context of a simultaneous system, may be less sensitive to specification error in the sense that those parts of the system that are correctly specified may not be affected appreciably by errors in specification in another part. We shall now consider various single equation alternatives.

Questions and Problems

1. Show that maximum likelihood estimates of a linear equation system may be derived either by maximizing the joint probability of reduced form errors or of structural equation errors.
2. Discuss maximum likelihood estimation in the exactly identified case.
3. What is the appropriate Jacobian expression for the likelihood function of the reduced form equations of a linear system?

4. SINGLE EQUATION ESTIMATORS

The section heading, *Single Equation Estimators*, does not mean that we are reverting to the discussion of the preceding chapter. This expression is meant, in this chapter, to deal with the subject of estimating a single equation that is imbedded in a larger system of equations. We shall deal with methods that estimate any single equation in a whole system, and we shall be concerned with single equations whose specification does not meet the assumptions of the previous chapter. We shall be dealing here with single equations that contain more than one endogenous variable associated with unknown parameters and to apply the least squares regression methods of the preceding chapter would involve us in least squares bias.

The Method of Instrumental Variables (IV)

The reader will recall that one of the principles of the preceding chapter for estimation of

$$y_t = \sum_{i=1}^{n} \alpha_i x_{it} + e_t$$

was to impose the sample condition

$$\sum_{t=1}^{T} x_{it} e_t = 0$$

as a representation of the population assumption

$$Ex_{it}\, e_t = 0.$$

If we now consider the $i^{\text{-th}}$ equation of the system,

$$Ay_t + Bx_t = e_t,$$

that will be written as

$$y_{1t} = \sum_{j=2}^{n_i} \alpha_{ij} y_{jt} + \sum_{j=1}^{m_i} \beta_{ij} x_{jt} + e_{it}, \qquad n_i \le n;\ m_i \le m,$$

we cannot assume

$$E\, y_{jt} e_{it} = 0 \qquad j = 2, \ldots, n_i.$$

The dependence between endogenous variables y_{jt} and e_{it} will cause least squares estimators of α_{ij} and β_{ij} to be biased, and this bias will not become small with increases in sample size.

If the x_{jt} $(j = 1, 2, \ldots, m_i)$ are exogenous variables, we have

$$Ex_{jt}e_{it} = 0, \qquad j = 1, 2, \ldots, m_i.$$

We need $n_i - 1$ similar conditions to replace

$$Ey_{jt}e_{it} \neq 0 \qquad j = 2, \ldots, n_i.$$

Among the $m - m_i$ exogenous or predetermined variables in the system that are not included in the vector $(x_{1t}, \ldots, x_{m_it})$, let us choose

$$x_{m_i+1,t}, \ldots, x_{m_i+n_i-1,t}$$

all with the property of exogenous variables

$$Ex_{jt}e_{it} = 0 \qquad j = m_i + 1, \ldots, m_i + n_i - 1.$$

We then form the normal equations

$$\sum_{t=1}^{T} y_{1t}x_{lt} = \sum_{t=1}^{T}\sum_{j=2}^{n_i} \alpha_{ij} y_{jt} x_{lt} + \sum_{t=1}^{T}\sum_{j=1}^{m_i} \beta_{ij} x_{jt} x_{lt} \qquad l = m_i + 1, \ldots, m_i + n_i - 1$$

$$\sum_{t=1}^{T} y_{1t}x_{kt} = \sum_{t=1}^{T}\sum_{j=2}^{n_i} \alpha_{ij} y_{jt} x_{kt} + \sum_{t=1}^{T}\sum_{j=1}^{m_i} \beta_{ij} x_{jt} x_{kt}. \qquad k = 1, 2, \ldots, m_i \tag{4.4.1}$$

We now have $m_i + n_i - 1$ equations in $m_i + n_i - 1$ unknown coefficients $\alpha_{ij}(j = 2, \ldots, n_i)$; $\beta_{ij}(j = 1, \ldots, m_i)$.

These give *consistent* estimates of the parameters. To show this, we shall use the matrix notation of regression analysis introduced in the previous chapter

$$y = Y_i\alpha_i + X_i\beta_i + e_i \tag{4.4.2}$$

$$y = \begin{pmatrix} y_{11} \\ \cdot \\ \cdot \\ \cdot \\ y_{1T} \end{pmatrix}; \quad Y_i = \begin{pmatrix} y_{21} & \cdots & y_{n_i1} \\ \cdot & & \cdot \\ \cdot & & \cdot \\ \cdot & & \cdot \\ y_{2T} & \cdots & y_{n_iT} \end{pmatrix}; \quad X_i = \begin{pmatrix} x_{11} & \cdots & x_{m_i1} \\ \cdot & & \cdot \\ \cdot & & \cdot \\ \cdot & & \cdot \\ x_{1T} & \cdots & x_{m_iT} \end{pmatrix};$$

$$\alpha_i = \begin{pmatrix} \alpha_{i2} \\ \cdot \\ \cdot \\ \cdot \\ \alpha_{in_i} \end{pmatrix}; \quad \beta_i = \begin{pmatrix} \beta_{i1} \\ \cdot \\ \cdot \\ \cdot \\ \beta_{im_i} \end{pmatrix}; \quad e_i = \begin{pmatrix} e_{i1} \\ \cdot \\ \cdot \\ \cdot \\ e_{iT} \end{pmatrix}$$

$$Z_i = \begin{pmatrix} x_{m_i+1,1} & \cdots & x_{m_i+n_i-1,1} \\ \cdot & & \cdot \\ \cdot & & \cdot \\ \cdot & & \cdot \\ x_{m_i+1,T} & \cdots & x_{m_i+n_i-1,T} \end{pmatrix}.$$

The normal equations are

$$\begin{pmatrix} Z'_iy \\ X'_iy \end{pmatrix} = \begin{pmatrix} Z'_iY_i & Z'_iX_i \\ X'_iY_i & X'_iX_i \end{pmatrix} \begin{pmatrix} \alpha_i \\ \beta_i \end{pmatrix}. \tag{4.4.3}$$

We define $a_i =$ est. α_i and $b_i =$ est. β_i as the solutions to this system of equations

$$\begin{pmatrix} a_i \\ b_i \end{pmatrix} = \begin{pmatrix} Z'_iY_i & Z'_iX_i \\ X'_iY_i & X'_iX_i \end{pmatrix}^{-1} \begin{pmatrix} Z'_iy \\ X'_iy \end{pmatrix}. \tag{4.4.4}$$

By substituting for y, we have

$$\begin{aligned} \begin{pmatrix} a_i \\ b_i \end{pmatrix} = & \begin{pmatrix} Z'_iY_i & Z'_iX_i \\ X'_iY_i & X'_iX_i \end{pmatrix}^{-1} \begin{pmatrix} Z'_i(Y_i\alpha_i + X_i\beta_i) \\ X'_i(Y_i\alpha_i + X_i\beta_i) \end{pmatrix} \\ & + \begin{pmatrix} Z'_iY_i & Z'_iX_i \\ X'_iY_i & X'_iX_i \end{pmatrix}^{-1} \begin{pmatrix} Z'_ie_i \\ X'_ie_i \end{pmatrix} \end{aligned} \tag{4.4.5}$$

$$\begin{pmatrix} a_i \\ b_i \end{pmatrix} = \begin{pmatrix} \alpha_i \\ \beta_i \end{pmatrix} + \begin{pmatrix} Z'_iY_i & Z'_iX_i \\ X'_iY_i & X'_iX_i \end{pmatrix}^{-1} \begin{pmatrix} Z'_ie_i \\ X'_ie_i \end{pmatrix}. \tag{4.4.6}$$

Because

$$\operatorname*{plim}_{T\to\infty} \begin{pmatrix} Z'_iY_i & Z'_iX_i \\ X'_iY_i & X'_iX_i \end{pmatrix}^{-1} \begin{pmatrix} Z'_ie_i \\ X'_ie_i \end{pmatrix} = 0, \tag{4.4.7}$$

we have

$$\operatorname*{plim}_{T\to\infty}\begin{pmatrix} a_i \\ b_i \end{pmatrix} = \begin{pmatrix} \alpha_i \\ \beta_i \end{pmatrix}. \tag{4.4.8}$$

Note that we cannot claim

$$E\begin{pmatrix} a_i \\ b_i \end{pmatrix} = \begin{pmatrix} \alpha_i \\ \beta_i \end{pmatrix}$$

because endogenous variables appear in

$$\begin{pmatrix} Z_i'Y_i & Z_i'X_i \\ X_i'Y_i & X_i'X_i \end{pmatrix}^{-1},$$

and the expected value of such a function of variables is not the function of expected values. We can say, however, that the probability limit of a continuous function of random variables is that function of probability limits.

Because we are proving only consistency and not unbiasedness, we could have made the weaker assumptions

$$\operatorname{plim}\left(\frac{1}{T}\sum_{t=1}^{T} x_{jt}e_t\right) = 0 \qquad j = 1, \ldots, m_i + n_i - 1.$$

This would permit the use of lagged endogenous variables and other predetermined variables as well as purely exogenous variables in the instrumental group.

To recapitulate, we may follow least squares rules in forming normal equations, that is, to multiply both sides of the equation to be estimated by each explanatory variable in turn, sum over sample observations, and neglect error terms, with the following exception: in place of endogenous explanatory variables, we use instrumental variables chosen from the set of predetermined variables in the system but not in the equation being estimated. We see, by this rule, that we have a single equation method of estimation but that it is modified by taking into account some properties of the system as a whole. We do not, however, make use of the knowledge of a priori specification in the rest of the system beyond recognizing those variables that are present.

There are several properties of instrumental variable estimators that should be recognized. They are consistent but not efficient. They must necessarily lack efficiency because they make use of only a limited amount of a priori information. Such estimators are not unique. Except in the special case where

$$m - m_i = n_i - 1$$

that we recognize as the necessary condition for exact identification, we shall have a surplus of predetermined variables in identified systems to choose as instruments. The method, therefore, has a certain degree of arbitrariness. If we recognize, also, that instruments other than $x_{m_i+1}, \ldots, x_m$ are eligible, the degree of arbitrariness is more apparent. Lags of $x_1, \ldots, x_m$ may also be used as instruments, as may variables that are outside the system.

In addition to arbitrariness from choice of instruments, there may be arbitrariness in choice of normalization. It depends on how we choose the instruments. With a fixed set of instruments that do not vary with changes in the way the equation is written, the results do not vary in an essential way if we write the equation as

$$y_{2t} = \alpha'_{i1} y_{1t} + \sum_{j=3}^{n_i} \alpha'_{ij} y_{jt} + \sum_{j=1}^{m_i} \beta'_{ij} x_{jt} + e'_{it}. \tag{4.4.9}$$

If, however, we associate one instrument with each particular variable and delete the instrument for the left-hand side variable, the method applied to this form yields an estimate a'_{i1} such that, in general,

$$\frac{1}{a'_{i1}} \neq a_{i2}$$

$$-\frac{a'_{ij}}{a'_{i1}} \neq a_{ij} \qquad j = 3, \ldots, n_i$$

$$-\frac{b'_{ij}}{a'_{i1}} \neq b_{ij} \qquad j = 1, \ldots, m_i.$$

In this sense, the results are not invariant under a rule of normalization.

Unless the instruments are weakly related to $x_{1t}, \ldots, x_{m_it}$ and strongly related to $y_{1t}, \ldots, y_{n_it}$, they will not give very efficient estimates.

It is worthwhile pointing out an example of instrumental variables that has been used in other contexts under other names. Consider the simple relationship

$$y_{1t} = \alpha_1 + \alpha_2 y_{2t} + e_t, \tag{4.4.10}$$

that is part of a larger system. Order the sample pairs of observations by size of y_{2t} (let T be even)

$$\text{I.}\quad \begin{array}{c} y_{1t_1}, y_{2t_1} \\ y_{1t_2}, y_{2t_2} \\ \vdots \\ y_{1,T/2}, y_{2,T/2} \end{array} \qquad \text{II.}\quad \begin{array}{cc} y_{1,T/2+1} & y_{2\ T/2+1} \\ y_{1,T/2+2} & y_{2,T/2+2} \\ \vdots & \vdots \\ y_{1}, {}_{t_T} & y_{2}, {}_{t_T}. \end{array}$$

In each group, compute means

$$\bar{y}_{1I}, \bar{y}_{2I}; \bar{y}_{1,II}, \bar{y}_{2,II}.$$

If we estimate α_1 and α_2 by the coefficients that determine the line through the two mean points, we have

$$\begin{aligned}\text{est } \alpha_1 &= a_1 = \bar{y}_{1I} - a_2\bar{y}_{2I} \\ \text{est } \alpha_2 &= a_2 = \frac{\bar{y}_{1I} - \bar{y}_{1II}}{\bar{y}_{2I} - \bar{y}_{2II}}.\end{aligned} \tag{4.4.11}$$

By defining the instrumental variable (also a dummy variable)

$$z_t = 1 \text{ if } y_2 \text{ is in group I}$$
$$z_t = -1 \text{ if } y_2 \text{ is in group II,}$$

we get

$$\sum_{t=1}^{T} y_{1t}z_t = \alpha_1 \sum_{t=1}^{T} z_t + \alpha_2 \sum_{t=1}^{T} y_{2t}z_t. \tag{4.4.12}$$

We have constructed z_t so that $\sum_{t=1}^{T} z_t = 0$, and we assume

$$Ez_te_t = 0.$$

We find

$$\text{est } \alpha_2 = a_2 = \frac{\bar{y}_{1I} - \bar{y}_{1II}}{\bar{y}_{2I} - \bar{y}_{2II}} \tag{4.4.13}$$

as above. In order to realize the assumption of independence between z_t and e_t, we must classify y_{1t} and y_{2t} into groups such that the classification is independent of e_t. In this case, there is only one line, regardless of normalization, and the results are invariant for choice of left-hand side variable.

This method of estimation, also known as the method of subgroup averages, is thus seen to be a special case of instrumental variables. Other dummy variable type classifications could be interpreted as examples of instrumental variables.

The Method of Two Stage Least Squares (TSLS)

In estimating the single equation

$$y_{1t} = \sum_{j=2}^{n_i} \alpha_{ij}y_{jt} + \sum_{j=1}^{m_i} \beta_{ij}x_{jt} + e_{it}$$

by the method of instrumental variables, we noted that there was an element of arbitrariness in the choice of instruments. If there is significant overidentification

$$m - m_i > n_i - 1,$$

we may look for a method of combining $x_{m_i+1}, \ldots, x_m$ in an efficient way into just $n_i - 1$ instruments. Because the instruments replace $y_{2t}, \ldots, y_{n_i t}$ in the standard rules for forming normal equations, we might consider

$$\hat{y}_{jt} = \sum_{k=1}^{m} p_{jk} x_{kt} \qquad j = 2, \ldots, n_i \tag{4.4.14}$$

as an efficient set of instrumental variables, where the p_{jk} are least squares regression coefficients of the y_{jt} on all the elements of $x_t = (x_{1t}, \ldots, x_{mt})$. These are efficient instruments because the y_{jt} are replaced by *best-fitting* linear combinations of all the unlagged instruments in the system. These best-fitting linear combinations of instruments are the least squares regressions of y_{jt} on all the x_{kt}. It will be noticed that these linear combinations are unrestricted estimates of the reduced form equations for $y_{2t}, \ldots, y_{n_i t}$.

The normal equations are, therefore,

$$\begin{aligned} \sum_{t=1}^{T} y_{1t}\hat{y}_{lt} &= \sum_{t=1}^{T}\sum_{j=2}^{n_i} \alpha_{ij} y_{jt}\hat{y}_{lt} + \sum_{t=1}^{T}\sum_{j=1}^{m_i} \beta_{ij} x_{jt}\hat{y}_{lt}, \qquad l = 2, \ldots, n_i \\ \sum_{t=1}^{T} y_{1t}x_{kt} &= \sum_{t=1}^{T}\sum_{j=2}^{n_i} \alpha_{ij} y_{jt}x_{kt} + \sum_{t=1}^{T}\sum_{j=1}^{m_i} \beta_{ij} x_{jt}x_{kt}, \qquad k = 1, 2 \ldots, m_i. \end{aligned} \tag{4.4.15}$$

These are just sufficient to determine the $m_i + n_i - 1$ unknown coefficients α_{ij} and β_{ij} provided the (moment) matrix of coefficients is nonsingular.

This extension of the usual applications of the instrumental variable method can be carried a step further by making use of identities from least squares theory, namely,

$$\begin{aligned} \sum_{t=1}^{T} y_{jt}\hat{y}_{lt} &= \sum_{t=1}^{T} \hat{y}_{jt}\hat{y}_{lt} \\ \sum_{t=1}^{T} y_{jt}x_{kt} &= \sum_{t=1}^{T} \hat{y}_{jt}x_{kt}. \end{aligned} \tag{4.4.16}$$

These identities hold because any x_{kt} has zero correlation with the residuals from the regression of y_{lt} on $x_{1t}, \ldots, x_{mt}$. The equations

$$\begin{aligned} \sum_{t=1}^{T} y_{1t}\hat{y}_{lt} &= \sum_{t=1}^{T}\sum_{j=2}^{n_i} \alpha_{ij} \hat{y}_{jt}\hat{y}_{lt} + \sum_{t=1}^{T}\sum_{j=1}^{m_i} \beta_{ij} x_{jt}\hat{y}_{lt} \\ \sum_{t=1}^{T} y_{1t}x_{kt} &= \sum_{t=1}^{T}\sum_{j=2}^{n_i} \alpha_{ij} \hat{y}_{jt}x_{kt} + \sum_{t=1}^{T}\sum_{j=1}^{m_i} \beta_{ij} x_{jt}x_{kt}, \end{aligned} \tag{4.4.17}$$

are immediately recognizable as the normal equations for the regression of y_{1t} on $\hat{y}_{2t}, \ldots, \hat{y}_{n_i t}, x_{1t}, \ldots, x_{m_i t}$,

$$y_{1t} = \sum_{j=2}^{n_i} \alpha_{ij}\hat{y}_{jt} + \sum_{j=1}^{m_i} \beta_{ij}x_{jt} + e_{it}.$$

This method is called the method of *two stage least squares*. In the first stage we form

$$y_{jt} = \sum_{k=1}^{m} \pi_{jk} x_{kt} + v_{jt} \qquad j = 2, \ldots, n_i$$

and estimate the least squares regression values

$$\hat{y}_{jt} = \sum_{k=1}^{m} p_{jk} x_{kt} \qquad j = 2, \ldots, n_i$$

where the p_{jk} are LS estimates of π_{jk} in the reduced form equations.

In the second stage we form

$$y_{1t} = \sum_{j=2}^{n_i} \alpha_{ij} \hat{y}_{jt} + \sum_{j=1}^{m_i} \beta_{ij} x_{jt} + e_{it}$$

and estimate the least squares regression equations

$$y_{1t} = \sum_{j=2}^{n_i} a_{ij} \hat{y}_{jt} + \sum_{j=1}^{m_i} b_{ij} x_{jt} + (\text{res.})_{it},$$

where the a_{ij} and b_{ij} are LS estimates of α_{ij} and β_{ij}, respectively.

The estimate of the variance of error, $S^2_{e_i}$ is obtained from

$$S^2_{e_i} = \frac{1}{T - n_i - m_i + 1} \sum_{t=1}^{T} \left(y_{1t} - \sum_{j=2}^{n_i} a_{ij} y_{jt} - \sum_{j=1}^{m_i} b_{ij} x_{jt} \right)^2. \qquad (4.4.18)$$

The reader should note that we use y_{jt} and not $\hat{y}_{jt}$ in computing $S^2_{e_i}$. If we had used $\hat{y}_{jt}$, we would have *underestimated* $S^2_{e_i}$, for we obtained *least* squares estimates for the sample values $\hat{y}_{2t}, \ldots, \hat{y}_{n_it}$.

The variance-covariance matrix of coefficient estimates is obtained from

$$S^2_{e_i} \begin{pmatrix} \|\Sigma \hat{y}_{jt} \hat{y}_{lt}\| & \|\Sigma x_{jt} \hat{y}_{lt}\| \\ \|\Sigma \hat{y}_{jt} x_{kt}\| & \|\Sigma x_{jt} x_{kt}\| \end{pmatrix}^{-1}, \qquad (4.4.19)$$

where the inverse matrix is determined from the moment matrix of the variables $\hat{y}_{2t}, \ldots, \hat{y}_{n_it}, x_{1t}, \ldots, x_{m_it}$.

We can now give a complete presentation of these results in the matrix notation used previously for the IV method

$$\begin{aligned} y &= Y_i \alpha_i + X_i \beta_i + e_i \\ Y_i &= X \pi_i + v_i. \end{aligned} \qquad (4.4.20)$$

In addition to the previous notation, we use

$$X = \begin{pmatrix} x_{11} & \cdots & x_{m_i 1} & x_{m_i+1,1} & \cdots & x_{m1} \\ \vdots & & \vdots & \vdots & & \vdots \\ x_{1T} & \cdots & x_{m_i T} & x_{m_i+1,T} & \cdots & x_{mT} \end{pmatrix}$$

$$\pi_i = \begin{pmatrix} \pi_{21} & \cdots & \pi_{n_i 1} \\ \vdots & & \vdots \\ \pi_{2m} & \cdots & \pi_{n_i m} \end{pmatrix}; \quad v_i = \begin{pmatrix} v_{21} & \cdots & v_{n_i 1} \\ \vdots & & \vdots \\ v_{2T} & \cdots & v_{n_i T} \end{pmatrix}.$$

Note that the matrix X has m columns to include all predetermined variables in the system.

In the first stage we estimate π_i as

$$p_i = (X'X)^{-1}X'Y_i \tag{4.4.21}$$

and the $\hat{Y}_i$ as

$$\hat{Y}_i = Xp_i = X(X'X)^{-1}X'Y_i. \tag{4.4.22}$$

In the second stage we have the normal equations

$$\begin{pmatrix} \hat{Y}'_i y \\ X'_i y \end{pmatrix} = \begin{pmatrix} \hat{Y}'_i \hat{Y}_i & \hat{Y}'_i X_i \\ X'_i Y_i & X'_i X_i \end{pmatrix} \begin{pmatrix} \alpha_i \\ \beta_i \end{pmatrix}, \tag{4.4.23}$$

and the estimates of α_i, β_i are

$$\begin{pmatrix} a_i \\ b_i \end{pmatrix} = \begin{pmatrix} \hat{Y}'_i \hat{Y}_i & \hat{Y}'_i X_i \\ X'_i Y_i & X'_i X_i \end{pmatrix}^{-1} \begin{pmatrix} \hat{Y}'_i y \\ X'_i y \end{pmatrix}. \tag{4.4.24}$$

By using the LS identities

$$\begin{aligned} \hat{Y}'_i X_i &= Y'_i X_i \\ \hat{Y}'_i \hat{Y}_i &= [X(X'X)^{-1}X'Y_i]' \ [X(X'X)^{-1}X'Y_i] \\ &= Y'_i X(X'X)^{-1}X'X(X'X)^{-1}X'Y_i = Y'_i X(X'X)^{-1}X'Y_i, \end{aligned}$$

we can also express these estimates as

$$\begin{pmatrix} a_i \\ b_i \end{pmatrix} = \begin{pmatrix} Y'_i X(X'X)^{-1}X'Y_i & Y'_i X_i \\ X'_i Y_i & X'_i X_i \end{pmatrix}^{-1} \begin{pmatrix} Y'_i X(X'X)^{-1}X'y \\ X'_i y \end{pmatrix}. \tag{4.4.25}$$

This is a good form for efficient computational procedures because it is expressed entirely in terms of original sample observations on y, Y_i, X_i, X. The inverse moment matrix

$$\begin{pmatrix} Y_i'X(X'X)^{-1}X'Y_i & Y_i'X_i \\ X_i'Y_i & X_i'X_i \end{pmatrix}^{-1} \tag{4.4.26}$$

when multiplied by $S_{e_i}^2$ gives the variance-covariance matrix of parameter estimates.

Because the IV method of estimation is consistent and because TSLS has been shown to be a special case of IV, in which the instrumental variables are

$$Z = \hat{Y}_i,$$

we see that TSLS is also consistent. The elements of $\hat{Y}_i$ are linear combinations of predetermined variables, such as those in Z, and the coefficients of the linear combinations are consistent estimators of true weights,

$$\begin{aligned} p_i &= \text{est } \pi_i \\ \text{plim } p_i &= \pi_i, \end{aligned}$$

it is evident that TSLS is consistent by virtue of the consistency of IV. It is more efficient in the sense that it makes use of more information from the X matrix, beyond that contained in Z. Because the $\hat{Y}_i$ are more closely related to Y_i than are any other linear combination of elements of X in replacing the Y_i, the efficiency of the $\hat{Y}_i$ as instrumental variables among elements of X cannot be improved upon.

Historical Note

The method of TSLS was originally proposed by H. Theil, although similar ideas, less systematically developed and based more on the IV approach, were discussed elsewhere. Because Theil's approach to the derivation of these estimates was different, it is of some interest to examine it for added insight into this technique.[5]

Our problem is to estimate

$$y_{1t} = \sum_{j=2}^{n_i} \alpha_{ij} y_{jt} + \sum_{j=1}^{m_i} \beta_{ij} x_{jt} + e_{it}.$$

Let us multiply both sides by all elements of $(x_{1t}, \ldots, x_{mt})$ and sum over t to get

$$\sum_{t=1}^{T} y_{1t} x_{kt} = \sum_{t=1}^{T} \sum_{j=2}^{n_i} \alpha_{ij} y_{jt} x_{kt} + \sum_{t=1}^{T} \sum_{j=1}^{m_i} \beta_{ij} x_{jt} x_{kt} + \sum_{t=1}^{T} e_{it} x_{kt}. \tag{4.4.27}$$

[5] H. Theil, *Economic Forecasts and Policy* (Amsterdam: North-Holland Publishing Co., 1958), pp. 336–38. Yet another approach is independently developed by R. L. Basmann, "A Generalized Classical Method of Linear Estimation of Coefficients in a Structural Equation," *Econometrica*, 25 (Jan. 1957), 77–83.

In obvious moment notation this is

$$m_{yx_k} = \sum_{j=2}^{n_i} \alpha_{ij} m_{y_j x_k} + \sum_{j=1}^{m_i} \beta_{ij} m_{x_j x_k} + m_{e_i x_k} \qquad k = 1, 2, \ldots, m, \tag{4.4.28}$$

where

$$\sum_{t=1}^{T} y_t x_{kt} = m_{yx_k}, \text{ etc.}$$

There are m equations in $m_i + n_i - 1$ unknown parameters and, as noted previously, if

$$m = m_i + n_i - 1$$

we have exact identification, in which case many of the estimates we are considering give the same values.

If

$$m > m_i + n_i - 1,$$

we treat this as a regression formulation in which the m sets of moments are treated like m separate observations on variables. In other words, a parallel is drawn between

$$\begin{aligned} y_1 &= \sum_{j=1}^{n} \gamma_j z_{j1} + e_1 \\ y_2 &= \sum_{j=1}^{n} \gamma_j z_{j2} + e_2 \\ &\;\;\vdots \\ y_T &= \sum_{j=1}^{n} \gamma_j z_{jT} + e_T \end{aligned}$$

and

$$\begin{aligned} m_{yx_1} &= \sum_{j=2}^{n_i} \alpha_{ij} m_{y_j x_1} + \sum_{j=1}^{m_i} \beta_{ij} m_{x_j x_1} + m_{e_i x_1} \\ m_{yx_2} &= \sum_{j=2}^{n_i} \alpha_{ij} m_{y_j x_2} + \sum_{j=1}^{m_i} \beta_{ij} m_{x_j x_2} + m_{e_i x_2} \\ &\;\;\vdots \\ m_{yx_m} &= \sum_{j=2}^{n_i} \alpha_{ij} m_{y_j x_m} + \sum_{j=1}^{m_i} \beta_{ij} m_{x_j x_m} + m_{e_i x_m}. \end{aligned}$$

In the latter formulation, moments of the variables replace the variables themselves as observations: m replaces T; $m_i + n_i - 1$ replaces n; and moments of e_i and x replace values of e. If x is nonstochastic, the variance of the error terms in the moment formulation is

$$\sigma_e^2 \, ||m_{x_i x_j}||.$$

The elements of the disturbance vector $m_{e_i x_k}$ are not uncorrelated with $m_{y_j x_k}$, but

$$\operatorname{plim} \sum_{k=1}^{m} m_{y_j x_k} m_{e_i x_k} = 0.$$

We apply Aitken's generalized method to the system of moment relationships under these conditions, and the result is TSLS estimators of α_{ij} and β_{ij}.

Estimators of the k Class

The TSLS equations can be transformed by using the identity

$$Y_i = \hat{Y}_i + \hat{V}_i$$
$$Y_i'Y_i = (\hat{Y}_i' + \hat{V}_i')(\hat{Y}_i + \hat{V}_i) = \hat{Y}_i'\hat{Y}_i + \hat{V}_i'\hat{V}_i.$$

The terms $\hat{V}_i'\hat{Y}_i$ and $\hat{Y}_i'\hat{V}_i$ vanish by virtue of the zero correlation between the elements of X and residuals of the regression of Y_i on X (the elements of $\hat{V}_i$).

We can therefore write

$$\begin{pmatrix} a_i \\ b_i \end{pmatrix} = \begin{pmatrix} Y_i'Y_i - \hat{V}_i'\hat{V}_i & Y_i'X_i \\ X_i'Y_i & X_i'X_i \end{pmatrix}^{-1} \begin{pmatrix} (Y_i' - \hat{V}_i')y \\ X_i'y \end{pmatrix}. \tag{4.4.29}$$

Theil introduced the idea of a scalar k, defining the k-class estimators

$$\begin{pmatrix} a_i \\ b_i \end{pmatrix}_k = \begin{pmatrix} Y_i'Y_i - k\hat{V}_i'\hat{V}_i & Y_i'X_i \\ X_i'Y_i & X_i'X_i \end{pmatrix}^{-1} \begin{pmatrix} (Y_i' - k\hat{V}_i')y \\ X_i'y \end{pmatrix}. \tag{4.4.30}$$

When $k = 0$ we have LS estimates, and when $k = 1$, we have TSLS estimates. For any k such that

$$\operatorname{plim}(k - 1) = 0 \tag{4.4.31}$$

we have consistent estimators of the k-class. If k approaches 1 in probability, the k class estimator approaches the TSLS estimator and is thus consistent, like the TSLS estimator. Nagar has also studied the double k class of estimators

$$\begin{pmatrix} a_i \\ b_i \end{pmatrix}_{k_1 k_2} = \begin{pmatrix} Y_i'Y_i - k_1\hat{V}_i'\hat{V}_i & Y_i'X_i \\ X_i'Y_i & X_i'X_i \end{pmatrix}^{-1} \begin{pmatrix} (Y_i' - k_2\hat{V}_i')y \\ X_i'y \end{pmatrix}. \tag{4.4.32}$$

Obviously LS estimates, with $k = 0$, are not consistent, and $\operatorname{plim}(0 - 1) \neq 0$. The two common nonstochastic choices of k are 0 and 1, but k may also be stochastic. A case of particular interest is the method of *limited information maximum likelihood*, in which $k = (1 + \nu)$, and ν is the smallest root of a determinantal equation

$$|\hat{V}_{i*}'\hat{V}_{i*} - (1 + \nu)\hat{V}_i'\hat{V}_i| = 0. \tag{4.4.33}$$

The notation $\hat{V}_{i*}$ gives the Txn_i matrix of residuals from the regression of y_{1t}, $y_{2t}, \ldots, y_{n_it}$ on $x_{1t}, x_{2t}, \ldots, x_{m_it}$ and $\hat{V}_i$ gives the regression of $y_{1t}, y_{2t}, \ldots, y_{n_it}$ on $x_{1t}, x_{2t}, \ldots, x_{mt}$. Note that *all* n_i elements of the y-vector associated with the i-th equation, including y_{1t}, are used in getting $\hat{V}_{i*}$ and that only the m_i elements of $x_{1t}, \ldots, x_{mt}$ appearing in the i-th equation are used as independent variables in this regression. $\hat{V}_i$ are defined as above, except that y_{1t} as well as $y_{2t}, \ldots, y_{n_it}$ is regressed on $x_{1t}, \ldots, x_{mt}$.

We now turn to a derivation and discussion of this particular member of the k-class (LIML).

The Method of Limited Information Maximum Likelihood (LIML)

This method could be approached in various ways, but as it is basically a maximum likelihood method we shall approach it from that viewpoint. This method was originally formulated as a simplification of FIML, and we shall approach it in that spirit.[6]

First let us note that the invariance property of maximum likelihood permits us to maximize either

$$Pr(e_{11}, \ldots, e_{nT}) \text{ subject to } Ay_t + Bx_t = e_t$$
$$\text{w.r.t. } \alpha_{ij}, \beta_{ij}, \sigma_{ij}$$

or equivalently

$$Pr(v_{11}, \ldots, v_{nT}) \text{ subject to } y_t = -A^{-1}Bx_t + v_t$$
$$\text{w.r.t. } \alpha_{ij}, \beta_{ij}, \sigma_{ij}.$$

We shall get the same estimates in both cases.

It is convenient to approach the LIML method through the maximization process applied to the reduced forms

$$y_t = -A^{-1}Bx_t + v_t$$

rather than the original structural set.

In this derivation we shall proceed as in the FIML case and *not* designate any particular variable as "dependent", that is, written with a unit coefficient. As we showed in the discussion of identification, the restrictions on

$$\sum_{j=1}^{n_i} \alpha_{ij} y_{jt} + \sum_{j=1}^{m_i} \beta_{ij} x_{jt} = e_{it}$$

[6] T. W. Anderson and H. Rubin, "Estimation of the Parameters of a Single Equation in a Complete System of Stochastic Equations," *The Annals of Mathematical Statistics*, XX (1949), 46–63.

with reduced form

$$y_{jt} = \sum_{k=1}^{m} \pi_{jk} x_{kt} + v_{jt}$$

are

$$\begin{aligned} \beta_{ik} &= -\sum_{j=1}^{n_i} \alpha_{ij}\pi_{jk} \qquad k = 1, 2, \ldots, m_i \\ 0 &= \sum_{j=1}^{n_i} \alpha_{ij}\pi_{jk} \qquad k = m_i + 1, \ldots, m. \end{aligned} \tag{4.4.34}$$

The first set of m_i equations, in (4.4.34), are not really restrictions because they simply show how the m_i parameters $\beta_1, \ldots, \beta_{m_i}$ depend on α_{ij} and π_{jk}. The second set are, in fact, restrictions.

We formulate LIML estimates as those that maximize

$$p(v_{11}, \ldots, v_{n_iT}) = g(y_{11}, \ldots, y_{n_iT} \mid x_{11}, \ldots, x_{mT})$$

subject to

$$0 = \sum_{j=1}^{n_i} \alpha_{ij}\pi_{jk} \qquad k = m_i + 1, \ldots, m$$

w.r.t. $\alpha_{ij}, \pi_{jk}, \sigma_{v_iv_j}$. Estimates of the β_{ik} will be obtained from

$$\hat{\beta}_{ik} = -\sum_{j=1}^{n_i} \hat{\alpha}_{ij}\hat{\pi}_{jk},$$

where $\hat{\alpha}_{ij}$ and $\hat{\pi}_{jk}$ are determined from the LIML equations.

These are *limited information* methods because they deal with only a part of the likelihood function. They are based on the maximization of the joint probability of $y_{1t}, \ldots, y_{n_it}$ and not on all the y_{it}. In addition, only a portion of the system's restrictions are used. The zero-type restrictions

$$0 = \sum_{j=1}^{n_i} \alpha_{ij}\pi_{jk} \qquad k = m_i + 1, \ldots, m$$

placed on the coefficients in the i-th equation are used, *and all other restrictions are ignored.* It is the ignoring of restrictions on other equations in the system that makes this a *limited information* method and not a *full information* method. By ignoring all the restrictions on other equations, the estimation problem is considerably simplified over that of FIML.

Although only zero-type restrictions are included in the above set, other linear homogeneous restrictions are taken into account through direct substitution. If there is a restriction of the form

$$\sum_{l=1}^{n_{ri}} r_{il}\alpha_{il} + \sum_{l=1}^{m_{ri}} r'_{il}\beta_{il} = 0, \tag{4.4.35}$$

we shall simply define a new variable

$$y_{n_i+1,t} = -y_{1t}\frac{\sum_{l=2}^{n_{ri}} r_{il}\alpha_{il} + \sum_{l=1}^{m_{ri}} r'_{il}\beta_{il}}{r_{i1}} + \sum_{l=2}^{n_{ri}} \alpha_{il}y_{lt} + \sum_{l=1}^{m_{ri}} \beta_{il}x_{lt}. \tag{4.4.36}$$

Single equation methods deal with incomplete systems in any case, and our equation will now have a new variable in place of others that appear separately in the system already.

Some examples may make the understanding of these issues clearer. Let us suppose that consumer spending, C_t, is a function of wage, W_t, and nonwage income, P_t, as separate variables. Let us suppose, also, that lagged consumption is a relevant variable in explaining short-run consumption. The function will then have the form

$$C_t = \alpha_0 + \alpha_1 W_t + \alpha_2 P_t + \alpha_3 C_{t-1} + e_t. \tag{4.4.37}$$

Let us suppose further that W_t has two parts, private wages and public wages

$$W_t = W_{1t} + W_{2t}, \tag{4.4.38}$$

so that we write

$$C_t = \alpha_0 + \alpha_{11} W_{1t} + \alpha_{12} W_{2t} + \alpha_2 P_t + \alpha_3 C_{t-1} + e_t. \tag{4.4.39}$$

In terms of our more general notation

$$y_{1t} = \sum_{j=2}^{n_i} \alpha_{ij} y_{jt} + \sum_{j=1}^{m_i} \beta_{ij} x_{jt} + e_{it},$$

we have the correspondences

$$C_t = y_{1t},\ 1 = y_{2t},\ W_{1t} = y_{3t},\ P_t = y_{4t},\ W_{2t} = x_{1t},\ C_{t-1} = x_{2t}$$
$$\alpha_0 = \alpha_{i2},\ \alpha_{11} = \alpha_{i3},\ \alpha_2 = \alpha_{i4},\ \alpha_{12} = \beta_{i1},\ \alpha_3 = \beta_{i2}.$$

In this formulation, W_{2t} and C_{t-1} are predetermined variables; the others are jointly dependent. By virtue of the fact that this single consumption equation is included in a large simultaneous system, we have many other dependent and predetermined variables in the system as a whole that are not included in this equation. They account for zero-type restrictions on the α_{ij} and β_{ij}. In the larger system, production at the *private* level will deal with private wage payments W_{1t} separately. Public activity, treated exogenously, will deal with W_{2t} separately. We, therefore, need the restriction

$$\alpha_{11} = \alpha_{12} = \alpha_1. \tag{4.4.40}$$

In using the LIML method of estimation, this more general type of linear homogeneous restriction is implicitly brought to bear in the calculations by redefining

$$W_t = W_{1t} + W_{2t} \tag{4.4.38}$$

as a single variable in the jointly dependent group. In place of

$$W_{1t} = y_{3t} \text{ and } W_{2t} = X_{1t}$$

with coefficients

$$\alpha_{11} = \alpha_{i3} \quad \text{and} \quad \alpha_{12} = \beta_{i1},$$

we have

$$W_t = y'_{3t} \tag{4.4.41}$$

a new dependent variable, with coefficient

$$\alpha_1 = \alpha'_{i3}. \tag{4.4.42}$$

We then carry through consumption calculations with the restriction that $W_{1t} + W_{2t}$ are combined into one single dependent variable. In other equations, not being estimated at this stage, we treat W_{1t} and W_{2t} as separate variables.

Another such example is given by the strict accelerator theory of investment. In this case we have

$$I_t = \beta_0 + \beta_1 X_t + \beta_2 X_{t-1} + v_t. \tag{4.4.43}$$

Our restriction is obtained from the specification

$$I_t = \beta_0 + \beta(X_t - X_{t-1}) + v_t, \tag{4.4.43)'$$

implying

$$\beta_1 = -\beta_2. \tag{4.4.44}$$

We take this restriction into account by defining $X_t - X_{t-1}$ as a new endogenous variable and keeping X_t and X_{t-1} in the fixed relationship $X_t - X_{t-1}$ for calculations of the investment function.

The justification for this method of accounting for nonzero-type restrictions arises from the properties of estimates in *incomplete* systems. These have been shown to be consistent and asymptotically efficient.[7] Although these results were first developed for application to LIML estimates, the same principles for taking account of general restrictions apply to the whole k-class, including TSLS, and to IV estimates.

Our approach to LIML estimation is, then: (1) to maximize the likelihood function derived from the joint distribution of reduced form disturbances subject to the zero-type restriction imposed on the equation being estimated; (2) to

[7] H. Chernoff and H. Rubin, "Asymptotic Properties of Limited-Information Estimates under Generalized Conditions," *Studies in Econometric Method*, ed. William C. Hood and T. C. Koopmans (N.Y.: Wiley, 1953).

take other linear homogeneous restrictions into account by redefining variables. This procedure must be repeated for each equation of the system, and the restrictions used in the maximization process apply only to the equation being estimated.

We shall follow Anderson and Rubin in our derivation of LIML estimating equations. First, we shall divide the vector of predetermined variables into two orthogonal parts,

$$x_{1t}, \ldots, x_{m_i t},$$

and

$$z_{m_i+1,t}, \ldots, z_{mt}$$

such that the correlations between all z_{jt} and x_{it} are zero. If this is not so in the sample at hand, the data can always be transformed by regressing the z's on the x's and using the residuals from the regressions as predetermined variables from outside the i-th equation. These regression residuals will necessarily be orthogonal to $x_{1t}, \ldots, x_{m_i t}$ by the fundamental properties of least squares regressions that we developed in the preceding chapter.

The reduced forms are thus, in matrix notation,

$$y_t = \Pi_{yx}x_t + \Pi_{yz}z_t + v_t \tag{4.4.45}$$

and the restrictions are

$$\alpha_i'\Pi_{yz} = 0. \tag{4.4.46}$$

The restrained likelihood function is

$$\begin{aligned} e^L = \left(\frac{1}{\sqrt{2\pi}}\right)^{Tn_i} |\Sigma_{vv}|^{-T/2} \exp\Big\{-\frac{1}{2}\sum_{t=1}^{T}(y_t' - x_t'\Pi_{yx}' - z_t'\Pi_{yz}')\,\Sigma_{vv}^{-1}(y_t \\ -\Pi_{yx}x_t - \Pi_{yz}z_t) + \alpha_i'\Pi_{yz}\lambda\Big\}. \end{aligned} \tag{4.4.47}$$

The unknown parameters are σ_{ij}, the elements of Σ_{vv}; the π_{ij}, the elements of Π_{yx} and Π_{yz}; and α, the coefficients of y_{jt} in the structural equation. The derivatives of L *w.r.t.* these parameters give

$$\begin{aligned} \Sigma_{vv} = M_{yy} - M_{yx}\Pi_{yx}' - M_{yz}\Pi_{yz}' - \Pi_{yx}M_{yx}' - \Pi_{yz}M_{yz}' \\ + \Pi_{yx}M_{xx}\Pi_{yx}' + \Pi_{yz}M_{zz}\Pi_{yz}' \qquad (w.r.t.\sigma_{ij}) \end{aligned} \tag{4.4.48}$$

$$0 = \Sigma_{vv}^{-1}(M_{yz} - \Pi_{yz}M_{zz}) + \alpha_i\lambda' \qquad (w.r.t.\pi_{ij}, j = m_i + 1, \ldots, m) \tag{4.4.49}$$

$$0 = \Sigma_{vv}^{-1}(M_{yx} - \Pi_{yx}M_{xx}) \qquad (w.r.t.\pi_{ij}, j = 1, \ldots, m_i) \tag{4.4.50}$$

$$0 = \Pi_{yz}\lambda \qquad (w.r.t.\alpha_{ij}). \tag{4.4.51}$$

The values of the parameter estimates satisfying these equations and the restraint will be denoted as $\hat{\Sigma}_{vv}$, $\hat{\Pi}_{yx}$, $\hat{\Pi}_{yz}$, $\hat{\alpha}_i$, and $\hat{\lambda}$. In addition, we shall use a normalizing condition

$$\alpha_i'\Sigma_{vv}\alpha_i = 1. \tag{4.4.52}$$

The first equations in this set express the estimated variance-covariance matrix of reduced form errors as the sample variance-covariance matrix of *residuals* from *estimated* reduced forms. The next two sets of equations are simply normal equations generalizing those for single equation least squares regressions and taking the restrictions into account. The final set arises purely from the restraints. The orthogonality of x_t and z_t simplify the derivation in that we do not have to use any terms involving elements of M_{xz}.

We solve for $\hat{\Pi}_{yx}$ as

$$\hat{\Pi}_{yx} = M_{yx}M_{xx}^{-1}, \tag{4.4.53}$$

and for $\hat{\Pi}_{yz}$ as

$$\begin{aligned}\hat{\Pi}_{yz} &= M_{yz}M_{zz}^{-1} + \hat{\Sigma}_{vv}\hat{\alpha}_i\hat{\lambda}'M_{zz}^{-1} \\ &= P_{yz} + \hat{\Sigma}_{vv}\hat{\alpha}_i\hat{\lambda}'M_{zz}^{-1}.\end{aligned} \tag{4.4.54}$$

In this latter expression we have substituted P_{yz} for $M_{yz}M_{zz}^{-1}$; these are ordinary regression coefficients of elements of y_t on z_t.

We now multiply the expression for $\hat{\Pi}_{yz}$ by $\hat{\alpha}_i'$ to get

$$\hat{\alpha}_i'\hat{\Pi}_{yz} = \hat{\alpha}_i'P_{yz} + \hat{\alpha}_i'\hat{\Sigma}_{vv}\hat{\alpha}_i\hat{\lambda}'M_{zz}^{-1} = 0. \tag{4.4.55}$$

This expression vanishes by virtue of the restrictions in (4.4.46)

$$\alpha_i'\Pi_{yz} = 0.$$

We use the normalization condition and rearrange, solving for $\hat{\lambda}'$ as

$$\hat{\lambda}' = -\hat{\alpha}_i'P_{yz}M_{zz}. \tag{4.4.56}$$

We can thus express $\hat{\Pi}_{yz}$ as

$$\begin{aligned}\hat{\Pi}_{yz} &= P_{yz} + \hat{\Sigma}_{vv}\hat{\alpha}_i\hat{\lambda}'M_{zz}^{-1} \\ &= P_{yz} - \hat{\Sigma}_{vv}\hat{\alpha}_i\hat{\alpha}_i'P_{yz}M_{zz}M_{zz}^{-1} \\ &= (I - \hat{\Sigma}_{vv}\hat{\alpha}_i\hat{\alpha}_i')P_{yz}.\end{aligned} \tag{4.4.57}$$

The expressions for $\hat{\Pi}_{yz}$, and $\hat{\Pi}_{yx}$ will now be substituted into the formula (4.4.48) for $\hat{\Sigma}_{vv}$, to obtain

$$\begin{aligned}\hat{\Sigma}_{vv} = M_{yy} &- M_{yx}M_{xx}^{-1}M_{yx}' - M_{yz}M_{zz}^{-1}M_{yz}' + M_{yz}M_{zz}^{-1}M_{yz}'\hat{\alpha}_i\hat{\alpha}_i'\hat{\Sigma}_{vv} \\ &- M_{yx}M_{xx}^{-1}M_{yx}' - M_{yz}M_{zz}^{-1}M_{yz}' + \hat{\Sigma}_{vv}\hat{\alpha}_i\hat{\alpha}_i'M_{yz}M_{zz}^{-1}M_{yz}' \\ &+ M_{yx}M_{xx}^{-1}M_{xx}M_{xx}^{-1}M_{yx}' + M_{yz}M_{zz}^{-1}M_{zz}M_{zz}^{-1}M_{yz}' \\ &- \hat{\Sigma}_{vv}\hat{\alpha}_i\hat{\alpha}_i'M_{yz}M_{zz}^{-1}M_{zz}M_{zz}^{-1}M_{yz}' \\ &- M_{yz}M_{zz}^{-1}M_{zz}M_{zz}^{-1}M_{yz}'\hat{\alpha}_i\hat{\alpha}_i'\hat{\Sigma}_{vv} \\ &+ \hat{\Sigma}_{vv}\hat{\alpha}_i\hat{\alpha}_i'P_{yz}M_{zz}P_{yz}'\hat{\alpha}_i\hat{\alpha}_i'\hat{\Sigma}_{vv}.\end{aligned} \tag{4.4.58}$$

Collecting terms, we have

$$\begin{aligned}\hat{\Sigma}_{vv} = M_{yy} - M_{yx}M_{xx}^{-1}M'_{yx} - M_{yz}M_{zz}^{-1}M'_{yz} \\ + \hat{\Sigma}_{vv}\hat{\alpha}_i(\hat{\alpha}'_i P_{yz} M_{zz} P'_{yz}\hat{\alpha}_i)\hat{\alpha}'_i\hat{\Sigma}_{vv}.\end{aligned} \tag{4.4.59}$$

Let

$$W_{yy} = M_{yy} - M_{yx}M_{xx}^{-1}M'_{yx} - M_{yz}M_{zz}^{-1}M'_{yz}; \tag{4.4.60}$$

this is the variance-covariance matrix of unrestricted reduced form residuals. Also let

$$\begin{aligned}\mu &= \hat{\alpha}'_i P_{yz} M_{zz} P'_{yz}\hat{\alpha}_i \\ &= \hat{\alpha}'_i M_{yz} M_{zz}^{-1} M_{zz} M_{zz}^{-1} M'_{xz}\hat{\alpha}_i.\end{aligned} \tag{4.4.61}$$

Observe that μ is a scalar quantity. We can rewrite the expression for $\hat{\Sigma}_{vv}$ as

$$\hat{\Sigma}_{vv} = W_{yy} + \mu\hat{\Sigma}_{vv}\hat{\alpha}_i\hat{\alpha}'_i\hat{\Sigma}_{vv} \tag{4.4.62}$$

or

$$\begin{aligned}\hat{\Sigma}_{vv}\hat{\alpha}_i &= W_{yy}\hat{\alpha}_i + \mu\hat{\Sigma}_{vv}\hat{\alpha}_i(\hat{\alpha}'_i\hat{\Sigma}_{vv}\hat{\alpha}_i) \\ &= W_{yy}\hat{\alpha}_i + \mu\hat{\Sigma}_{vv}\hat{\alpha}_i\end{aligned} \tag{4.4.63}$$

by virtue of the normalization condition (4.4.52). We can rewrite this equation as

$$\hat{\Sigma}_{vv}\hat{\alpha}_i = \frac{1}{1-\mu} W_{yy}\hat{\alpha}_i. \tag{4.4.64}$$

The last of our maximizing conditions can be expressed as

$$\begin{aligned}0 &= \hat{\Pi}_{yz}\hat{\lambda} = -(P_{yz} - \hat{\Sigma}_{vv}\hat{\alpha}_i\hat{\alpha}'_i P_{yz})(\hat{\alpha}'_i P_{yz} M_{zz})' \\ 0 &= P_{yz} M_{zz} P'_{yz}\hat{\alpha}_i - \hat{\Sigma}_{vv}\hat{\alpha}_i(\hat{\alpha}'_i P_{yz} M_{zz} P'_{yz}\hat{\alpha}_i) \\ 0 &= P_{yz} M_{zz} P'_{yz}\hat{\alpha}_i - \mu\hat{\Sigma}_{vv}\hat{\alpha}_i.\end{aligned} \tag{4.4.65}$$

We, therefore, have

$$\mu\hat{\Sigma}_{vv}\hat{\alpha}_i = P_{yz} M_{zz} P'_{yz}\hat{\alpha}_i = \frac{\mu}{1-\mu} W_{yy}\hat{\alpha}_i \tag{4.4.66}$$

or

$$\left(P_{yz} M_{zz} P'_{yz} - \frac{\mu}{1-\mu} W_{yy}\right)\hat{\alpha}_i = 0. \tag{4.4.67}$$

In order that a nontrivial $\hat{\alpha}_i$ satisfy this system of *linear·homogeneous* equations, we must have

$$\left| P_{yz} M_{zz} P'_{yz} - \frac{\mu}{1-\mu} W_{yy} \right| = 0; \tag{4.4.68}$$

this is a determinantal equation in

$$\nu = \frac{\mu}{1 - \mu}$$

with n_i roots. The smallest root will make the likelihood function, L, the largest. The characteristic vector $\hat{\alpha}_i$ corresponding to the smallest root $\hat{\nu}$ will give us estimates of the coefficients of $y_{1t}, \ldots, y_{n_it}$, in the structural equation being estimated. The coefficients of $x_{1t}, \ldots, x_{m_it}$ are obtained from

$$\hat{\beta}_i = \hat{\alpha}_i' \hat{\Pi}_{yx}.$$

Having the estimated equation

$$\sum_{i=1}^{n_i} \hat{\alpha}_{ij} y_{jt} + \sum_{j=1}^{m_i} \hat{\beta}_{ij} x_{jt} = (\text{res.})_{it}$$

we choose some variable, say y_{1t}, to have unit coefficient and express the equation as

$$y_{1t} = -\sum_{j=2}^{n_i} \frac{\hat{\alpha}_{ij}}{\hat{\alpha}_{i1}} y_{jt} - \sum_{j=1}^{m_i} \frac{\hat{\beta}_{ij}}{\hat{\alpha}_{i1}} x_{jt} + \frac{(\text{res})_{it}}{\hat{\alpha}_{i1}}.$$

If another variable were to be chosen as the one to have a unit coefficient, we would have used the same estimates of $\hat{\alpha}_i$, $\hat{\beta}_i$ and divided each element by the estimated coefficient of the variable selected to have a unit coefficient in the final expression.

From the residuals we can estimate $\text{var}(e_i)$ as

$$S_{e_i}^2 = \frac{1}{T - n_i - m_i + 1} \sum_{t=1}^{T} \left[\frac{(\text{res})_{it}}{\hat{\alpha}_{i1}} \right]^2. \tag{4.4.69}$$

The relationship of LIML estimates to k-class estimates can now be seen. The k-class estimates are, in the present notation

$$\begin{pmatrix} {}_{11}M_{yy} - k\,{}_{11}W_{yy} & {}_1M_{yx} \\ {}_1M'_{yx} & M_{xx} \end{pmatrix} \begin{pmatrix} a_i \\ b_i \end{pmatrix}_k = \begin{pmatrix} \Sigma y_{1t} y_t - k \Sigma y_{1t} \hat{v}_t \\ \Sigma y_{1t} x_t \end{pmatrix}. \tag{4.4.70}$$

In this notation, we write left subscripts to denote the deletion of y_{1t} from moment matrices involving y_{1t}, because that variable has the unit coefficient assigned in the determination of the k-class estimate. The notations

$$\Sigma y_{1t} y_t = \begin{pmatrix} \Sigma y_{1t} y_{2t} \\ \cdot \\ \cdot \\ \cdot \\ \Sigma y_{1t} y_{n_it} \end{pmatrix}; \quad \Sigma y_{1t} \hat{v}_t = \begin{pmatrix} \Sigma y_{1t} \hat{v}_{2t} \\ \cdot \\ \cdot \\ \cdot \\ \Sigma y_{1t} \hat{v}_{n_it} \end{pmatrix}$$

$$\Sigma y_{1t}x_t = \begin{pmatrix} \Sigma y_{1t}x_{1t} \\ \cdot \\ \cdot \\ \cdot \\ \Sigma y_{1t}x_{m_1t} \end{pmatrix}$$

are used in the right-hand side as column matrices.

From the second of the two sets of matrix equations we have

$$\begin{aligned} {}_1M'_{yx}a_{ik} + M_{xx}b_{ik} &= \Sigma y_{1t}x_t \\ b_{ik} &= -M_{xx}^{-1}\,{}_1M'_{yx}a_{ik} + M_{xx}^{-1}\Sigma y_{1t}x_t. \end{aligned} \tag{4.4.71}$$

On substituting this value for b_{ik} into the first set, we have

$$\begin{aligned} ({}_{11}M_{yy} - k\,{}_{11}W_{yy})a_{ik} - {}_1M_{yx}M_{xx}^{-1}\,{}_1M'_{yx}a_{ik} = &-{}_1M_{yx}M_{xx}^{-1}\Sigma y_{1t}x_t \\ &+\Sigma y_{1t}y_t - k\Sigma y_{1t}\hat{v}_t. \end{aligned} \tag{4.4.72}$$

This can be rewritten as

$$\begin{aligned} ({}_{11}M_{yy} - {}_1M_{yx}M_{xx}^{-1}\,{}_1M'_{yx} - {}_1M_{yz}M_{zz}^{-1}\,{}_1M'_{yz} + {}_1M_{yz}M_{zz}^{-1}\,{}_1M'_{yz})a_{ik} - k\,{}_{11}W_{yy}a_{ik} \\ = -{}_1M_{yx}M_{xx}^{-1}\Sigma y_{1t}x_t + \Sigma y_{1t}y_t - k\Sigma y_{1t}\hat{v}_t. \end{aligned} \tag{4.4.73}$$

The left-hand side is simply

$$({}_1M_{yz}M_{zz}^{-1}\,{}_1M'_{yz} + (1-k)\,{}_{11}W_{yy})a_{ik}.$$

Except for the assigning of a unit coefficient to y_{1t}, this is precisely the characteristic equation of the LIML method, where

$$1 - k = -\nu.$$

If $\hat{\alpha}_{i1}$ is made unity in advance, then the LIML estimates must satisfy

$$\begin{aligned} ({}_1M_{yz}M_{zz}^{-1}\,{}_1M'_{yz} - \nu\,{}_{11}W_{yy})\hat{\alpha}_i = &-{}_1M_{yx}M_{xx}^{-1}\Sigma y_{1t}x_t + \Sigma y_{1t}y_t \\ &-(1+\nu)\Sigma y_{1t}\hat{v}_t. \end{aligned} \tag{4.4.74}$$

The asymptotic sampling errors of k-class estimators are given by diagonal elements of the variance-covariance matrix

$$\text{est var } (e_i) \begin{pmatrix} {}_{11}M_{yy} - k\,{}_{11}W_{yy} & {}_1M_{yx} \\ {}_1M'_{yx} & M_{xx} \end{pmatrix}^{-1}; \tag{4.4.75}$$

therefore, the estimated variance-covariance of the LIML estimators is

$$S^2_{e_i} \begin{pmatrix} {}_{11}M_{yy} - (1+\hat{\nu})\,{}_{11}W_{yy} & {}_1M_{yx} \\ {}_1M'_{yx} & M_{xx} \end{pmatrix}^{-1}. \tag{4.4.76}$$

LIML estimates are computed by using the linear-type calculations of regression analysis (matrix multiplication and matrix inversion) in a particular way up to the final stage of obtaining the point estimates, $\hat{\alpha}_i$. At the final stage, a root of a characteristic equation must be extracted, but iterations of the usual linear type calculations are suitable for this stage. The vector $\hat{\beta}_i$ is obtained simply by matrix multiplication of $\hat{\alpha}_i$ and regression estimates of $\hat{\Pi}_{yx}$. As compared with FIML, it is therefore seen that LIML is much simpler computationally. Indeed, the method was first proposed as a computational simplification of FIML. By not using all the restrictions in the system simultaneously, we avoid the large systems of nonlinear estimation equations that typify FIML methods.

LIML is, however, a single equation method and therefore has a measure of flexibility. When all the single equation LIML estimates in a system are put together, they imply a reduced form. This reduced form, derived from the whole system of equations, may be different from the restricted reduced forms associated with the estimation of any of the single LIML estimates.

Because LIML estimates are maximum likelihood estimates of a kind, they enjoy some properties of maximum likelihood estimates generally. In particular, they are invariant under a choice of normalization in the sense that any variable in the equation can be singled out to have a unit coefficient and the essential results are unchanged. Among the alternative estimates that we are considering here, only FIML and LIML estimators possess this property. As we shall note below, however, LIML estimates are very sensitive. Poor identification, misspecification, and collinearity can cause great difficulty in obtaining LIML estimates and they often yield unreasonable results when conditions are unfavorable.

Questions and Problems

1. Is there a "natural" way to write the equations of economic systems with one variable dependent, having a unit coefficient, and explicit function of the others? Consider demand functions, production functions, consumption functions, etc.

2. How does your answer to 1 affect the choice of TSLS vs. LIML estimation for model building?

3. In equation (4.4.68)

$$\left| P_{yz}M_{zz}P'_{yz} - \frac{\mu}{1-\mu} W_{yy} \right| = 0$$

show that the smallest root leads to the highest point on the likelihood function.

4. Show that there is no loss of generality in assuming $x_{1t}, \ldots, x_{m_1 t}$ and $x_{m_1+1,t}, \ldots, x_{m_t}$ to be mutually orthogonal.

5. EQUATION SYSTEM ESTIMATORS

The preceding section dealt with the estimation of single equations containing two or more jointly dependent variables with unknown coefficients, and the estimate of a whole system can be obtained by the successive application of such methods to all equations in the model. We can, however, introduce more simultaneity into the process and use all the restrictions on the several equations at once. FIML estimates are, of course, equation system estimates that can determine all parameters simultaneously. They are not, however, easy to determine computationally. We now consider some simpler methods of extending the results of the previous section to simultaneous estimation of the whole system.

Three Stage Least Squares (3SLS)

Zellner and Theil have introduced this method of estimation based on the alternative (historically original) derivation of TSLS estimates and a further application of the Aitken theory of estimation.

Let us write the i-th equation of the system as

$$y_i = Y_i\alpha_i + X_i\beta_i + e_i, \tag{4.5.1}$$

where y_i is the column of observations $(1, 2, \ldots, T)$ on the endogenous variable with unit coefficient in the i-th equation, Y_i is a matrix of observations on the other endogenous variables $(T \times (n_i - 1))$; X_i is a matrix of observations on the included predetermined variables $(T \times m_i)$; α_i is a column of coefficients of endogenous variables; β_i is a column of coefficients of predetermined variables; and e_i is a T-element column of disturbances in the i-th equation. All identities are assumed to have been substituted in the equation.

The equations can be written more compactly as

$$y_i = Z_i\gamma_i + e_i \tag{4.5.2}$$

if we combine as follows:

$$Z_i = (Y_iX_i) \text{ and } \gamma_i = \begin{pmatrix} \alpha_i \\ \beta_i \end{pmatrix}.$$

We multiply each equation by X', the matrix of all predetermined variables in the entire system.

$$X'y_i = X'Z_i\gamma_i + X'e_i. \tag{4.5.3}$$

The whole system can be written as

$$\begin{pmatrix} X'y_1 \\ \cdot \\ \cdot \\ \cdot \\ X'y_n \end{pmatrix} = \begin{pmatrix} X'Z_1 & 0 & \cdots & 0 \\ 0 & X'Z_2 & \cdots & 0 \\ \vdots & \vdots & & \vdots \\ 0 & 0 & \cdots & X'Z_n \end{pmatrix} \begin{pmatrix} \gamma_1 \\ \gamma_2 \\ \vdots \\ \gamma_n \end{pmatrix} + \begin{pmatrix} X'e_1 \\ X'e_2 \\ \vdots \\ X'e_n \end{pmatrix}. \tag{4.5.4}$$

We now apply the generalized least squares theory to these equations. The covariance matrix of the vector of disturbances is

$$\begin{pmatrix} \sigma_{11}X'X & \sigma_{12}X'X & \cdots & \sigma_{1n}X'X \\ \sigma_{21}X'X & \sigma_{22}X'X & \cdots & \sigma_{2n}X'X \\ \vdots & & & \vdots \\ \sigma_{n1}X'X & \sigma_{n2}X'X & \cdots & \sigma_{nn}X'X \end{pmatrix}.$$

In this matrix, σ_{ij} is the covariance of e_i and e_j. The generalized least squares estimator of γ is

$$\text{est. } \gamma = \begin{pmatrix} \sigma^{11}Z_1'X(X'X)^{-1}X'Z_1 & \cdots & \sigma^{1n}Z_1'X(X'X)^{-1}X'Z_n \\ \vdots & & \vdots \\ \sigma^{n1}Z_n'X(X'X)^{-1}X'Z_1 & \cdots & \sigma^{nn}Z_n'X(X'X)^{-1}X'Z_n \end{pmatrix}^{-1} \times \begin{pmatrix} \Sigma\sigma^{1i}Z_1'X(X'X)^{-1}X'y_i \\ \vdots \\ \Sigma\sigma^{ni}Z_n'X(X'X)^{-1}X'y_i \end{pmatrix}. \tag{4.5.5}$$

As is usual in the application of the Aitken theory of estimation, we need to know the variance-covariance matrix of errors in order to compute the estimate. In this problem, the only elements needed for estimation of γ besides sample observations are values for σ^{ij}, elements of the inverse of $\|\sigma_{ij}\|$. If we denote estimates of σ_{ij} by s_{ij}, the sample covariances of e_i and e_j obtained from TSLS estimates in the first round, we have

$$\hat{\gamma} = \begin{pmatrix} s^{11}Z_1'X(X'X)^{-1}X'Z_1 & \cdots & s^{1n}Z_1'X(X'X)^{-1}X'Z_n \\ \vdots & & \vdots \\ s^{n1}Z_n'X(X'X)^{-1}X'Z_1 & \cdots & s^{nn}Z_n'X(X'X)^{-1}X'Z_n \end{pmatrix}^{-1} \times \begin{pmatrix} \Sigma s^{1i}Z_1'X(X'X)^{-1}X'y_i \\ \vdots \\ \Sigma s^{ni}Z_n'X(X'X)^{-1}X'y_i \end{pmatrix}. \tag{4.5.6}$$

These are 3SLS estimates of γ.

Let us summarize the procedures in this case. (1) In the usual way, we form TSLS estimates of each equation in the system and from the sample residuals associated with each equation we estimate the variance-covariance matrix of error $\|E(e_ie_j)\|$. (2) We then form an equation system for all the equations in moment form

$$X'y_i = X'Z_i\gamma_i + X'e_i.$$

This is a relation connecting the *moments* of the i-th equation. We apply the Aitken theory of generalized least squares to this *system.* (3) Because the variance-covariance matrix of the error vector is $\|EX'e_i(X'e_j)'\|$, or $\|\sigma_{ij}X'X\|$, we need to use the estimates of σ_{ij} obtained in step (1) in order to form the Aitken estimators of γ.

It is evident that if $\sigma_{ij} = 0$, $i \neq j$; that is, the covariances of e_i and e_j are zero, the above formulas for $\hat{\gamma}$ become precisely those of TSLS. The method of 3SLS is generally more efficient than TSLS because it uses more information on a priori restrictions in the model, but if the errors in each equation are independent of errors in other equations there is no gain in information by taking account of restrictions in other equations of the system.

In contrast with FIML and LIML estimation, it is seen that 3SLS estimation imposes an arbitrary normalization on the system, for the equations are written with some variable chosen in each equation to have a unit coefficient. *Essentially* different results are obtained if a different choice is made on normalization. One cannot change the normalization rule without recomputing all the estimates.

The method of 3SLS makes one extra type of calculation after the computation of TSLS estimates. But the process need not stop at that stage. A new estimated variance-covariance matrix of error $\|E(e_ie_j)\|$ can be determined from the 3SLS equations and the process continued iteratively until the estimates fail to change from iteration to iteration. The iterations, however, do not improve the asymptotic efficiency of the method.[8] Indeed, TSLS estimates can be iterated in this manner. After TSLS estimates are obtained in the usual way for each equation in a system, a complete set of estimated reduced forms, with all a priori restrictions,

$$\hat{y}_t = -\hat{A}^{-1}\hat{B}x_t \tag{4.5.7}$$

can be used to generate *computed* values of $y_{1t}, \ldots, y_{nt}$. The matrices $\hat{A}$, $\hat{B}$ are TSLS estimates obtained by applying the method to each single equation of a complete system. From this complete set of computed values, we may form subsets

$$\hat{Y}'_i\hat{Y}_i = \left\|\sum_{t=1}^{T}\hat{y}_{jt}\hat{y}_{kt}\right\| \qquad j, k = 2, 3, \ldots, n_i$$

to compute a second round of TSLS estimates. In this round, we do not assume (by analogy with the first round)

$$\hat{Y}'_iX_i = Y'_iX_i;$$

[8] This is proved by A. Madansky, "On the Efficiency of Three-Stage-Least-Squares Estimation," *Econometrica*, 32 (Jan.-April, 1964), 51–56.

otherwise we use the ordinary TSLS equations. After each equation is estimated this way in a second round of TSLS estimation, we determine

$$\hat{\hat{y}}_t = -\hat{\hat{A}}^{-1}\hat{\hat{B}}x_t \tag{4.5.8}$$

and continue as before, until the estimates fail to change from iteration to iteration. Although this method seems to be intuitively attractive and appears to be a natural extension of TSLS or 3SLS methods, it has not been found to work satisfactorily in practice.[9]

Other Methods

For a number of years, the methods of FIML, LIML, and IV developed by members of the Cowles Commission for Research in Economics dominated our thinking on the subject of estimation of equation systems in econometrics. Theil's introduction of TSLS and the k-class estimators, opened up the area of research again. In this reawakening, Theil himself, with Zellner, proposed the 3SLS method and considered iterative TSLS as well, but many new estimators have been recently introduced.

An interesting new proposal by H. Wold is called the method of Iterative Least Squares (ILS). This is an attractive method because of its simplicity, yet it is a full information method, in the sense that it takes into account all the economic restrictions imposed on a large complete system, although it makes no use of error covariance information.

To illustrate the principles of ILS, let us write our model as

$$y_t = Ay_t + Bx_t + e_t. \tag{4.5.9}$$

This differs from our usual way of writing the system as

$$Ay_t + Bx_t = e_t$$

in the specification that a single, *and different*, element of $(y_{1t}, y_{2t}, \ldots, y_{nt})$ is chosen to have a unit coefficient in each structural equation of the model.

The first step is to choose an initial set of values for y_t, say

$$y_t^{(0)} = 0.$$

Regress each element of y_t on $y_t^{(0)}$ and x_t to get $A^{(1)}(= 0)$ and $B^{(1)}$. From the estimated coefficients, compute

$$y_t^{(1)} = A^{(1)}y_t^{(0)} + B^{(1)}x_t = B^{(1)}x_t, \tag{4.5.10}$$

[9] It is mentioned in the first edition of H. Theil's *Economic Forecasts and Policy* (Amsterdam: North-Holland Publishing Co., 1958) p. 361, attributed to a remark by H. Houthakker. In a later edition (p. 355) it is remarked that it does not always converge. The use of $\hat{y}_t$, without further iteration, in an extension of TSLS regression methods is proposed by D. Jorgenson. See R. L. Cooper and D. W. Jorgenson, "The Predictive Performance of Quarterly Econometric Models of the U.S.," presented at the Bonn meetings at the Econometric Society, 1967.

and form the regressions of the elements of y_t on $y_t^{(1)}$ and x_t. We calculate $A^{(2)}$ and $B^{(2)}$ from these regressions and determine the values

$$y_t^{(2)} = A^{(2)} y_t^{(1)} + B^{(2)} x_t. \tag{4.5.11}$$

We regress each element of y_t on $y_t^{(2)}$ and x_t to get $A^{(3)}$ and $B^{(3)}$ and continue as before. We stop when the values of $y_t^{(r)}$ do not change from iteration to iteration. The r-th iteration regression is based on

$$y_t = A^{(r)} y_t^{(r-1)} + B^{(r)} x_t + e_t; \tag{4.5.12}$$

that is, we regress each y_{it} on $y_t^{(r-1)}$ and x_t, where

$$y_t^{(r-1)} = A^{(r-1)} y_t^{(r-2)} + B^{(r-1)} x_t \tag{4.5.13}$$

est. $A = \lim_{r\to\infty} A^{(r)}$ and est. $B = \lim_{r\to\infty} B^{(r)}$.

If we have

$$y_t^{(r)} = y_t^{(r-1)}$$

we have a fixed point; thus, the criterion for convergence of the iterative procedure is the existence of a *fixed point.*The existence and uniqueness of a fixed point is in doubt, however.

The attractiveness of this method is the simplicity of calculation on each iterative round. Nothing more than a least squares regression of modest size need be calculated on each iterative round because all the zero-type restrictions are built into each equation. Nonlinearities could be handled with comparative ease, provided they permit separation of one different element of y_t as the left-hand variable with unit coefficient in each equation. The method also assumes somewhat less in the specification of independence between elements of x_t and e_t. It does not assume that every element of x_t is independent of every element of e_t; it merely assumes

$$E x_t e_{it} = 0$$

for all those elements of x_t *appearing with nonzero coefficients in the i-th equation.* It also assumes

$$\lim_{r\to\infty} E y_t^{(r)} e_{it} = 0$$

for all those elements of y_t *appearing with nonzero coefficients in the right-hand side of the i-th equation.*

It is important to start the iterative process with a consistent estimator; therefore, if we choose $y_t^{(0)} = 0$, we simply regress the elements of y_t on the x_t variables appearing in each equation with nonzero coefficients. This will provide consistent estimates of $B^{(1)}$ and of $y_t^{(1)}$. These are similar to the first round estimates of TSLS, except that in those cases we use all elements of x_t in each regression and not simply those appearing with nonzero coefficients in each equation.

It is restrictive, however, to insist that the equations be specified as

$$y_t = Ay_t + Bx_t + e_t.$$

The results depend on the normalization rule, and the system cannot be estimated with the same variable being on the left-hand side with unit coefficient in more than one equation.

Other proposals concern the treatment of the estimation problem from the point of view of solution of a system—one in reduced form and one in "final" form. The methods of maximum likelihood, both FIML and LIML, are attractive in that their optimal properties are preserved under a wide class of transformations. Thus, maximum likelihood estimates of reduced forms are reduced forms of maximum likelihood estimates. This property of the likelihood function was used in deriving LIML estimates. The following two procedures, as indicated above (p. 164), are equivalent:

1. For the structural system

$$Ay_t + Bx_t = e_t,$$

form the likelihood function

$$\begin{aligned} L_e^* &= p(e_{11}, \ldots, e_{nT}) \left| \frac{\partial(e_{11} \cdot \ldots, e_{nT})}{\partial(y_{11}, \ldots, y_{nT})} \right| \\ &= p(\Sigma\alpha_{1j}y_{j1} + \Sigma\beta_{1j}x_{j1}, \ldots, \Sigma\alpha_{nj}y_{jT} + \Sigma\beta_{nj}x_{jT}) \, |A|^T \end{aligned}$$

and evaluate

$$\frac{\partial L_e^*}{\partial \alpha_{ij}} = 0; \quad \frac{\partial L_e^*}{\partial \beta_{kl}} = 0; \quad \frac{\partial L_e^*}{\partial \theta_p} = 0,$$

where θ_p are other parameters of the joint probability distribution of e_{it}.

2. For the reduced form system

$$y_t = -A^{-1}Bx_t + v_t,$$

form the likelihood function

$$\begin{aligned} L_v^* &= g(v_{11}, \ldots, v_{nT}) \left| \frac{\partial(v_{11}, \ldots, v_{nT})}{\partial(y_{11}, \ldots, y_{nT})} \right| \\ &= g(y_{11} + \Sigma\pi_{1j}x_{j1}, \ldots, y_{nT} + \Sigma\pi_{nj}x_{jT}) \end{aligned}$$

and evaluate

$$\frac{\partial L_v^*}{\partial \alpha_{ij}} = 0; \quad \frac{\partial L_v^*}{\partial \beta_{kl}} = 0; \quad \frac{\partial L_v^*}{\partial \varphi_p} = 0.$$

The π_{ij} are elements of $A^{-1}B$, and φ_p are other parameters of the joint probability distribution of the v_{it}. The parameter values in A and B, satisfying the maximization conditions for either of these two formulations, are the same. This is not generally the case with other methods.

In practice it is assumed that p and g are joint normal distributions and that θ_p and φ_p are variance-covariance parameters. A general distribution free method of estimation, proposed by T. M. Brown, had been to minimize the diagonal terms of the variance-covariance matrix of the (sample) v_{it}[10]. Form

$$S = \sum_{i=1}^{n} \sum_{t=1}^{T} v_{it}^2 = \sum_{i=1}^{n} \sum_{t=1}^{T} (y_{it} + \pi_{i1}x_{1t} + \cdots + \pi_{im}x_{mt})^2 \tag{4.5.14}$$

and evaluate

$$\frac{\partial S}{\partial \alpha_{ij}} = 0; \quad \frac{\partial S}{\partial \beta_{kl}} = 0;$$

where

$$\Pi = A^{-1}B.$$

All the restrictions in the system are assumed to be imposed on $A^{-1}B$ prior to optimization. This procedure minimizes the squared deviation between y_{it} and $\Sigma\pi_{ij}x_{jt}$. It is, in this sense, a minimum distance estimator. It chooses parameter values that give best one period predictions for the system as a whole. M. Nakamura has proved consistency of these estimates.[11]

These estimates are not especially easy to compute. Because $A^{-1}B$ is nonlinear in the original parameters, the estimation equations are not linear and computational effort something like that expended in the FIML case is required. This is, however, a full information method in the sense that restrictions in all the equations of the system are simultaneously taken into account. It does not, however, make use of information from the covariance matrix of disturbances.

A serious problem confronting this method of estimation is that the results are not invariant under simple (for example, scale) transformations. That is to say, if the criterion is

$$S = \sum_{i=1}^{n} \sum_{t=1}^{T} v_{it}^2 = \text{min.},$$

we get essentially different results from

$$S^* = \sum_{i=1}^{n} \sum_{t=1}^{T} k_i^2 v_{it}^2 = \text{min.},$$

[10] T. M. Brown, "Simultaneous Least Squares—A Distribution Free Method of Equation Structure Estimation," *International Economic Review*, I (Sept., 1960), 173–91.

[11] M. Nakamura, "A Note on the Consistency of Simultaneous Least Squares Estimation," *International Economic Review*, I (Sept., 1960), 192–97.

where the y_{it} (the dependent variables of the system) have been rescaled according to

$$y^*_{it} = k_i y_{it}.$$

If units of measurement are changed from billions to millions of dollars, from feet to yards, from pounds to tons, and so on, the results change. The results are invariant under orthogonal transformations of variables but not under general linear transformations of variables.

A way out of this difficulty would be to scale each y_{it} in the system by dividing by its own sample standard deviation, that is, to express the y_{it} in standard units. The equation

$$\Sigma\alpha_{ij}y_{jt} + \Sigma\beta_{ij}x_{jt} = e_t$$

would become

$$\begin{aligned} \Sigma(\alpha_{ij}S_{y_j})\frac{y_{jt}}{S_{y_j}} + \Sigma\beta_{ij}x_{jt} &= e_t \\ \Sigma\alpha'_{ij}y'_{jt} + \Sigma\beta_{ij}x_{jt} &= e_t. \end{aligned} \tag{4.5.15}$$

The reduced form of this system would be

$$y'_{it} = -\sum_{j=1}^{m}\pi'_{ij}x_{jt} + v'_{it} = -\frac{1}{S_{y_i}}\sum_{j=1}^{m}\pi_{ij}x_{jt} + \frac{v_{it}}{S_{y_i}}, \tag{4.5.16}$$

and the criterion would change to

$$S' = \sum_{i=1}^{n}\sum_{t=1}^{T}(v'_{it})^2 = \min.$$

This result would be invariant under a scale change. It amounts to weighting the squared errors in each reduced form by $\frac{1}{S^2_{y_i}}$, the reciprocal of the variance of the associated dependent variable.

If the system were not dynamic, the reduced form would be used to generate the whole time path of future values of y_t, given the future course of x_t. The reduced form would be the final form.

In dynamic models, reduced and final forms are not the same. The fundamental result of Mann and Wald, however, that lagged dependent variables may, in large samples, be treated like independent variables makes the formal treatment of reduced and final forms equivalent for one-period analysis—say one period prediction.[12] In multiperiod applications, though, lagged values are generated by the economic process—as in predicting variables for future period $T + j$ to be lagged input into equations for period $T + j + 1$—and the error structures of reduced and final forms are quite different.

[12] H. B. Mann and A. Wald, *op. cit.*

Let us consider the linear dynamic system

$$\sum_{i=0}^{p} A_i y_{t-i} + Bx_t = e_t. \tag{4.5.17}$$

As in the treatment above of lag distributions, we can write this as

$$A(L)y_t = -Bx_t + e_t, \tag{4.5.18}$$

where

$$A(L) = A_0 + A_1 L + A_2 L^2 + \cdots + A_p L^p.$$

Let $a(L)$ be the adjoint of $A(L)$ and $\Delta(L) = |A(L)|$ denote the determinant polynomial of $A(L)$. If we premultiply both sides of the structural equation system by $a(L)$, we obtain the *final form*

$$\|\Delta(L)\| y_t = -a(L)Bx_t + a(L)e_t, \tag{4.5.19}$$

where $\|\Delta(L)\|$ is a matrix with $\Delta(L)$ on the main diagonal and zeros everywhere else.[13]

There are two special features of the final form: (1) Each equation in the system has identical autoregressive structure.[14] Each element of y_t is expressed as the same linear function of its own lag structure (up to order of lag np) plus a separate linear function of independent variables and errors. (2) The error term of the final form is a linear function of current and lagged errors; therefore, it has an *induced* serial correlation structure.[15]

At various times, suggestions have been made that each dependent variable could be regressed on its own lags and independent variables. This would be suggested if it were to be desired to estimate final forms alone, without attempting to relate the estimates to structural parameters. A typical equation to be estimated would be

$$\sum_{j=0}^{np} a_{ij} y_{i,t-j} = \sum_{j=1}^{n} \sum_{k=1}^{(n-1)p} b_{ijk} x_{j,t-k} + \sum_{j=1}^{n} \sum_{k=1}^{(n-1)p} c_{ijk} e_{j,t-k}. \tag{4.5.20}$$

Not only would we lose structural information through this approach, but we would have the problem that the error terms being minimized, in the square, are not independent.

[13] This derivation follows that of E. P. Howrey, "Stochastic Properties of the Klein-Goldberger Model," *Econometrica*, 39 (January, 1971) 73–87, and G. H. Orcutt, "A Study of the Autoregressive Nature of the Time Series Used for Tinbergen's Model of the Economic System of the United States, 1919–1932," *Journal of the Royal Statistical Society*, X (1948), Ser. B, 1–53.

[14] Orcutt, (*op. cit.*), pointed this out at an early stage.

[15] See L. Hurwicz, "Stochastic Models of Economic Fluctuations," *Econometrica*, 12 (April, 1944) 114–24.

It is possible to minimize the squared errors

$$\sum_{t=1}^{T}[\sum_{j=1}^{n}\sum_{k=1}^{(n-1)p} c_{ijk}e_{j,t-k}]^2 \tag{4.5.21}$$

with respect to the original structural parameters, but the coefficients of the final form are complicated nonlinear functions of these parameters.

Closely allied to the concept of the final form is the *solution.* The finite difference equations

$$||\Delta(L)||\, y_t = -a(L)Bx_t + a(L)e_t$$

have the solution (complete)

$$y_t = K\lambda^t - \frac{a(L)}{\Delta(L)}Bx_t + \frac{a(L)}{\Delta(L)}e_t. \tag{4.5.22}$$

K is a matrix ($n \times np$) of constants determined by the initial conditions of the system and λ^t is an np-element vector of roots ($\lambda_1^t, \lambda_2^t, \ldots, \lambda_{np}^t$) of the characteristic polynomial associated with the autoregressive structure. If we were to minimize the trace of

$$\sum_{t=1}^{T} v_t v_t'; \quad v_t = \frac{a(L)}{\Delta(L)}e_t \tag{4.5.23}$$

or some normalized variant, to get round the problem of units of measurement, with respect to the original structural parameters in $a(L)$, $\Delta(L)$, B, λ we would be minimizing error along the solution path of the system. Instead of minimizing one-point prediction errors (by T. M. Brown's method), we would be minimizing dynamic simulation, or multipoint prediction, errors. As in Brown's method, we have a nonlinear estimation problem, but we also have a serial correlation problem since the elements of v_t are not mutually independent for different values of t.

In simplified systems it is possible to estimate the structural parameters by minimizing the squared error expression for the final form or the solution form and even to establish the sampling properties of such estimates, but in models of slight complexity or, in general, it appears that one can do little more than write down formal expressions for such estimates without being able to show clearly how such formal expressions can be solved for the parameter estimates. A "cut and try," or search, procedure can be used.[16]

A straightforward method, using mainly linear computations, can be devised by extending Jorgenson's adaptation of iterative TSLS, mentioned

[16] A nongeneral search procedure, applicable to a particular model, is used by K. J. Cohen, *Computer Models of the Shoe, Leather, Hide Sequence* (Englewood Cliffs, New Jersey: Prentice-Hall, Inc., 1960).

above. The main point concerned with minimization of the trace of

$$\sum_{t=1}^{T} v_t v_t'; \quad v_t = \frac{a(L)}{\Delta(L)} e_t \tag{4.5.23}$$

is that lagged dependent variables are not treated as predetermined. In the expression

$$y_t = K\lambda^t - \frac{a(L)}{\Delta(L)} Bx_t + \frac{a(L)}{\Delta(L)} e_t, \tag{4.5.22}$$

only the *initial conditions* (determining K) and the independent variables (x_t) are given. We, therefore, seek estimates of $A(L)$ and B that optimize solution paths of the system given the initial conditions and x_t. Suppose that we determine $\hat{y}_t$ in the first *full information* round of iterated TSLS from

$$\hat{y}_t = K\hat{\lambda}^t - \frac{\hat{a}(L)}{\hat{\Delta}(L)} \hat{B}x_t. \tag{4.5.24}$$

Let us now choose a typical equation in the system, say the i-th. It has the normalized form

$$y_{1t} = -\sum_{j=1}^{p} \alpha_{i1j} y_{1,t-j} - \sum_{k=2}^{n_i} \sum_{l=0}^{p} \alpha_{ikl} y_{k,t-l} - \sum_{k=1}^{m_i} \beta_{ik} x_{kt} + e_{it}. \tag{4.5.25}$$

In the final stage regressions, we regress y_{1t} on $\hat{y}_{1,t-j}$, $\hat{y}_{k,t-l}$, and x_{kt}. This differs from the usual treatment of TSLS, because $\hat{y}_{1,t-j}$ and $\hat{y}_{k,t-l}$ are used in the regression. For TSLS, $\hat{y}_{k,t}$ would be used as a regressor, but not $\hat{y}_{kt}$ or computed lag values. It also differs from the original suggestion by Jorgenson because $\hat{y}_t$ are computed from the dynamic solution and not from

$$\hat{y}_t = -\hat{A}_0^{-1}\left(\sum_{i=1}^{p} \hat{A}_i y_{t-i} + \hat{B}x_t\right). \tag{4.5.26}$$

In the final stage the coefficients are to be estimated on the basis of given initial conditions and given independent variables—not on the basis of given lagged dependent variables.

The values of $\hat{y}_{1,t-j}$ and $\hat{y}_{k,t-l}$ need not be taken from dynamic simulations over the whole sample period. Successive short-run dynamic simulations would seem to be useful for estimating systems that are going to be used for short-run extrapolations.

The estimation equations involve only the solution of linear systems except for the evaluation of $\hat{\lambda}$. These may be avoided in the computation of $\hat{y}_t$ by using iterative numerical methods for solving finite difference equation systems. These methods will be discussed in a later chapter, for both linear and nonlinear dynamic systems.

Questions and Problems

1. Show that 3SLS estimates become TSLS estimates if

$$Ee_{it}e_{jt} = 0, \quad i \neq j,$$

e_{it} is the disturbance variable of the i-th structural equation.

2. In the linear dynamic system with two equations

$$\alpha_{110}y_{1t} + \alpha_{120}y_{2t} + \alpha_{111}y_{1,t-1} + \alpha_{121}y_{2,t-1} + \beta_{11}x_{1t} = e_{1t}$$
$$\alpha_{210}y_{1t} + \alpha_{220}y_{t2} + \alpha_{211}y_{1,t-1} + \alpha_{221}y_{2,t-1} + \beta_{22}x_{2t} = e_{2t},$$

show explicitly that the error terms in the *solution* are, in general, serially dependent even though the e_{it} are serially independent.

3. Show the equivalence between *reduced form* and *solution* if the model is static.

4. If performance criteria of systems are for single-period error minimization (in the square), show that there is no distinction between procedures for dynamic or static systems.

6. SOME PROBLEMS IN ESTIMATING EQUATION SYSTEMS

Degrees of Freedom

In obtaining ordinary least squares (OLS) estimates for single equations

$$y_t = \sum_{j=1}^{n} \alpha_j x_{jt} + e_t, \quad t = 1, 2, \ldots, T,$$

it has long been recognized that we must have $T \geq n$; otherwise the estimation equations would be singular. In case $T = n$, we have no degrees of freedom in the sense that all sample points lie on the fitted hyperplanes and the coefficients are estimated so as to achieve this perfect fit.

If consistency were to be ignored and each equation fitted by OLS in the system

$$Ay_t + Bx_t = e_t,$$

we would say that the i-th equation had $T - (n_i - 1) - m_i$ degrees of freedom, if there were $n_i - 1$ elements of A and m_i elements of B in this equation. As long as $T \geq n_i - 1 + m_i$, we would say that there are enough degrees of freedom in the system to estimate all the equations. These would be *enough* in the sense of being able to calculate the estimates but not necessarily enough to bring large sample precision. For that, we would need to have T strongly larger than $(n_i - 1) + m_i$.

In any event, degrees of freedom are evaluated separately for each equation in this approach, counting T fresh degrees, against which to offset $(n_i - 1) + m_i$, because there are T fresh random elements associated with each stochastic equation.

But the methods of TSLS, LIML, 3SLS, and any member of the k-class, have another problem in degrees of freedom. They all require estimation of the reduced form regressions

$$y_{jt} = \sum_{k=1}^{m} \pi_{jk} x_{kt} + v_{jt} \tag{4.6.1}$$

where the estimates of elements of π for the i-th structural equation are

$$\text{est}\ \pi_i = p_i = (X'X)^{-1}X'Y_i. \tag{4.6.2}$$

The problem here is the conditioning of the moment matrix $X'X$. If there is a lack of degrees of freedom, this matrix will be singular and it will not be possible to calculate the p_i. In this case, the number of degrees of freedom are $T - m$. If m is large, as it will be in large systems of equations with many predetermined variables, there may be too few observations. Even though we may have

$$T \geq (n_i - 1) + m_i, \text{ for all } i,$$

we might find

$$T < m.$$

Thus, we have enough degrees of freedom for the individual structural equations but too few for the complete reduced forms.

There are several ways out of this difficulty. If the reduced forms are estimated from a subset of m, giving adequate degrees of freedom, the estimates may still retain their property of consistency. This is evident from the instrumental variable interpretation of k-class estimators, for all instruments need not be used at one time. A subset of x_t, say, $x_{1t}, \ldots, x_{m_i t}, x_{m_i+1,t}, \ldots, x_{m_s, t}$, where

$$m_s < m$$

may be used for estimating the i-th equation. In place of $(X'X)$ we would use $(X_s'X_s)$ in the reduced form estimation equations, where X_s has T rows and m_s columns. This approach, like the instrumental variable method, has a degree of arbitrariness about it.

A second approach is to evaluate principal components of X. These are mutually orthogonal, linear combinations of the elements of X,

$$\begin{aligned} p_{c1t} &= \sum_{j=1}^{m} \gamma_{1j} x_{jt} \\ &\vdots \\ p_{crt} &= \sum_{j=1}^{m} \gamma_{rj} x_{jt} \end{aligned} \tag{4.6.3}$$

such that p_{c1t} has maximum variance for $\gamma_1'\gamma_1 = 1$; p_{c2t} has maximum variance among all linear combinations uncorrelated with p_{c1t}; for $\gamma_2'\gamma_2 = 1$; and so on. The principal components are estimated as the set of characteristic vectors corresponding to the characteristic roots of

$$\left| \frac{1}{T} X'X - \lambda 1 \right| = 0. \tag{4.6.4}$$

In place of the moment matrix $X'X$, we may use a standardized form, the correlation matrix. The first (largest) r roots yielding components that account for a preassigned percentage of the variance of X can be selected as instruments. Instead of regressing y_{jt} on $x_{1t}, \ldots, x_{mt}$, we regress y_{jt} on $p_{c1t}, \ldots, p_{crt}$, where $T > r$, and there are adequate degrees of freedom in the reduced form equations. Instead of finding the inverse $(X'X)^{-1}$, we compute $(P_c'P_c)^{-1}$. This is a simpler problem, because the nondiagonal elements of this latter matrix are zero.[17] The TSLS estimate will become

$$\begin{pmatrix} a_i \\ b_i \end{pmatrix} = \begin{pmatrix} \tilde{Y}_i'Y_i & \tilde{Y}_i'X_i \\ X_i'Y_i & X_i'X_i \end{pmatrix}^{-1} \begin{pmatrix} \tilde{Y}_i'y \\ X_i'y \end{pmatrix} \tag{4.6.5}$$

where

$$\tilde{Y}_i = P_c(P_c'P_c)^{-1}P_c'Y_i.$$

The reader should note that we *cannot* assume

$$\tilde{Y}_iX_i = Y_iX_i$$

in analogy with our simplification of TSLS estimates in the usual case because elements of X are not necessarily orthogonal to residuals in

$$y_{jt} = \tilde{y}_{jt} + (\text{res.})_{jt}.$$

[17] This approach to TSLS estimation was first proposed by T. Kloek and L. B. M. Mennes, "Simultaneous Equations Estimation Based on Principal Components of Predetermined Variables," *Econometrica*, 28 (January, 1960), 45–61.

We can, however, make the moment matrix symmetrical by replacing $X_i'Y_i$ by $X_i'\tilde{Y}_c$ and $\tilde{Y}_i'Y_i$ by $\tilde{Y}_i'\tilde{Y}_i$. In this formulation, we regress on $\tilde{Y}_i$ and X_i instead of using them as instrumental variables. Care should be exercised, however, by using $x_{1t}, \ldots, x_{m_it}$ as separate first stage regressors together with p_{cit}.

The rationale for this use of principal components is that we use them as instruments in place of X because there are too many elements in X for the sample size, and the elements of P_c explain a given fraction of the variation in X. Thus, we choose as instruments, combinations of X that are closely related to the original X values. In terms of generalized correlation, we replace X by a set that optimizes the relationship to X.

The use of principal components for TSLS estimation is straightforward, as outlined above. It is not quite as obviously applied in the case of LIML estimation, but it can be used. The matrix

$$P_{yz}M_{zz}P'_{yz} = M_{yz}M_{zz}^{-1}M'_{yz} \tag{4.6.6}$$

that we developed in deriving LIML estimates should be positive definite. In this derivation, we have assumed that the z_t vector is orthogonal to the x_t vector. We generally would not have z_t and x_t orthogonal and usually do not extract residuals of the regression of $x_{m_i+1,t}, \ldots, x_{mt}$ on $x_{it}, \ldots, x_{m_it}$ in order to make them orthogonal. We form this matrix as

$$M_{yx}M_{xx}^{-1}M'_{yx} - M_{yx*}M_{x*x*}^{-1}M'_{yx*} \tag{4.6.7}$$

where $x_t^* = (x_{1t}, \ldots, x_{m_it})$ — the included x_t variables
$x_t = (x_{1t}, \ldots, x_{mt})$ — all the x_t variables.

Now, if we replace

$$M_{yx}M_{xx}^{-1}M'_{yx}$$

by

$$M_{yp_c}M_{p_cp_c}^{-1}M'_{yp_c},$$

where

$$p_{ct} = (p_{c1t}, \ldots, p_{crt}),$$

it is not absolutely certain that

$$M_{yp_c}M_{p_cp_c}^{-1}M'_{yp_c} - M_{yx*}M_{x*x*}^{-1}M'_{yx*} \tag{4.6.8}$$

will be positive definite. If we include enough components in p_c we can make this matrix positive definite, but it will not necessarily be positive for any choice of p_c. This matrix is the variance-covariance matrix of residuals obtained by regressing y on x^*, less that obtained by regressing y on p_c. Clearly, if the p_c explain almost as much of the variation in y as the x do, then the variance-covariance matrix of residuals from the regression on the p_c will be small relative to that from the regression on the x^*. If the elements of x^* are included with p_{cit} in obtaining an estimate of $M_{yx}M_{xx}^{-1}M'_{yx}$, we shall always have a positive definite matrix in (4.6.7).

Apart from caution in constructing this matrix, the use of principal components in LIML estimation will be straightforward. We shall obtain the W-matrix by regressing y on the p_c. Where regression on x^* are required, we shall use $x_{1t}, \ldots, x_{m_1 t}$ and not the principal components.

The concentrated likelihood function used in computing FIML estimates is written as

$$\log|A| - \tfrac{1}{2}\log|\Sigma|; \tag{4.6.9}$$

therefore, we must have

$$\text{est.}\,|\Sigma| \neq 0. \tag{4.6.10}$$

A shortage of degrees of freedom can, in various ways, cause our estimate of Σ to vanish. Let us consider, as we have been doing, a system with n unlagged dependent variables (endogenous) and m independent variables (exogenous). The sample has T observations. In order to ensure that the estimate of Σ is nonsingular and that the likelihood function be finite, we must have

$$\begin{aligned} &n < T, \\ &m < T, \\ &m + n < T. \end{aligned} \tag{4.6.11}$$

The first inequality states that the number of linear equations in the system must be less than the number of observations. The estimate of Σ is obtained from

$$\text{est}\,\Sigma = \left(\frac{1}{T}\sum_{t=1}^{T}(\text{res})_{it}(\text{res})_{jt}\right), \tag{4.6.12}$$

where res_{it} is the residual from the i-th equation in period t. The determinant of this matrix will be zero unless n (the number of rows and columns) is less than T. This will be true on every iteration or step of any approximate computational procedure.

The same matrix must be inverted for calculation of 3SLS estimates in order to obtain s^{ij} terms in (4.5.6); therefore, we must have $n < T$ for that method.

The second inequality is the same one that prevails for LIML, TSLS, and 3SLS in which the first step is the evaluation of the unrestricted reduced form regressions. We show that this same inequality must hold for FIML estimation.

$$\text{est}\,\Sigma = \frac{1}{T}\sum_{t=1}^{T}(Ay_t + Bx_t)(Ay_t + Bx_t)'. \tag{4.6.13}$$

Define

$$W = (YX) = \begin{pmatrix} y_{11} & \cdots & y_{n1} & x_{11} & \cdots & x_{m1} \\ \vdots & & \vdots & \vdots & & \vdots \\ y_{1T} & \cdots & y_{nT} & x_{1T} & \cdots & x_{mT} \end{pmatrix}$$

$$\Gamma = (AB) = \begin{pmatrix} \alpha_{11} & \cdots & \alpha_{1n} & \beta_{11} & \cdots & \beta_{1m} \\ \vdots & & \vdots & \vdots & & \vdots \\ \alpha_{n1} & \cdots & \alpha_{nn} & \beta_{n1} & \cdots & \beta_{nm} \end{pmatrix}.$$

We may also write

$$\text{est } \Sigma = \frac{1}{T}(\hat{\Gamma}\, W'W\, \hat{\Gamma}'). \tag{4.6.14}$$

For this matrix to be nonsingular, we require the moment matrix $W'W$ to be positive definite.[18] Because $Y'Y$ and $X'X$ are principal minors of $W'W$, they too must be positive definite. The definiteness of $X'X$ rules out the case $T \leq m$, as in the computation of unrestricted reduced forms.

The third inequality follows from the condition that $W'W$ be positive definite. The third, in combination with one of the other two, implies the remaining one.

Another inequality on degrees of freedom for FIML estimation is that the number of unknown coefficients R in a linear system be less than nT; otherwise we could fix R-nT coefficients at arbitrary values and find the remainder as solutions to the nT equations

$$Ay_t + Bx_t = 0 \quad t = 1, 2, \ldots, T.$$

This would give us sets of coefficients that satisfied the equation system with zero residuals and singular moment matrix Σ.

Multicollinearity

Until one begins serious econometric calculation on a frequent and large scale, he is apt to be unaware of the importance and significance of multicollinearity. It is a very serious problem in applied econometrics and arises in almost every substantial time series problem undertaken. There are basic trends and cycles that pervade many economic series in a similar way, thus giving rise to much interrelationship among independent variables. It is the essence of the structure and treatment of simultaneous equation systems that the dependent (endogen-

[18] We exclude the case of "perfect fit" when there are ample degrees of freedom, but all observations satisfy the equations precisely.

ous) variables be interrelated. If there is much collinearity among predetermined variables, we shall have trouble.

The trouble we have is that multicollinearity causes certain moment matrices to be singular; thus, we cannot evaluate reliable inverses. This is partly a computational problem and partly a problem in reliability of individual coefficients. In many respects, the problems are like those in having too few degrees of freedom, and one of the proposed solutions will be a similar use of principal components.

Consider first the methods of TSLS and LIML and all other k-class estimates (also, the first part of 3SLS). In these methods, we must evaluate reduced forms. Lack of degrees of freedom for estimating

$$y_{jt} = \sum_{k=1}^{m} \pi_{jk} x_{kt} + v_{jt}$$

was seen to give rise to singularity of $(X'X)$, and collinearity among elements of $(x_{1t}, \ldots, x_{mt})$ will also cause singularity of $X'X$. This is precisely the problem encountered with singularity in making OLS regression estimate of single equations in the preceding chapter. There is a *saving point* in the present context, however. Contrary to some opinions, we are not especially interested in the reliability of elements of

$$\text{est } \Pi_i = P_i = (X'X)^{-1}X'Y_i,$$

the OLS regression coefficients of the reduced forms. We are primarily interested in estimating the variance-covariance matrix of unrestricted reduced form residuals

$$\frac{1}{T}\hat{V}_i'\hat{V}_i = \frac{1}{T}\left\| \sum_{t=1}^{T} \hat{v}_{jt}\hat{v}_{kt} \right\|.$$

The general k-class estimator, of which TSLS and LIML are special cases, require

$$Y_i'Y_i - k\hat{V}_i'\hat{V}_i.$$

If elements of $x_{1t}, \ldots, x_{mt}$ are collinear, it will be difficult to evaluate $\hat{V}_i'\hat{V}_i$, but if an accurate computation can be made, we may have a good estimate of this matrix even though elements of P_i are estimated with large sampling error. In the limiting case, when there is perfect collinearity, say, unit correlation between x_{it} and x_{jt}, we find that $X'X$ is singular and cannot be inverted. If one of the two collinear variables is deleted, we would find that the reduced form could then be evaluated, assuming that no other strong collinearities are present, and we shall have an estimate of the variance-covariance matrix of error. Because the residuals are orthogonal to the excluded element of x_t, it could have had no independent effect on the estimation of the variance-covariance matrix of error. By continuity arguments, if collinearity is high but not perfect, the exclusion of one of two collinear variables should have small effect on the estimate of $\hat{V}_i'\hat{V}_i$. This argument is not completely general, but holds in the case in which the two highly related variables have the *same* correlation with the dependent variables. We can make the following kind of statement:

The multiple correlation, or residual variance, of the regression of y_{jt} on $x_{1t}, \ldots, x_{mt}$ has a definite limit that does not depend on one of two collinear variables, x_{kt} and x_{lt}, as long as x_{lt} approaches x_{kt} in such a way that the limit of

$$\frac{(x_{lt} - x_{kt})}{|x_{lt} - x_{kt}|} \tag{4.6.15}$$

exists.[19]

To carry the argument further, we observe that if we replace $x_{1t}, \ldots, x_{mt}$ by principal components, and if the components explain a high proportion of the variance of $x_{1t}, \ldots, x_{mt}$, we shall find that the estimate of $\hat{V}_i'\hat{V}_i$ computed from residuals of regressions on the principal components is hardly different from that based on residuals from the complete reduced form.

Collinearity among elements of $x_{1t}, \ldots, x_{mt}$ may occur in many ways. Some of these ways are

1. collinearity among $x_{1t}, \ldots, x_{m_it}$
2. collinearity among $x_{m_i+1,t}, \ldots, x_{mt}$
3. collinearity between elements of $x_{1t}, \ldots, x_{m_it}$ and $x_{m_i+1,t}, \ldots, x_{mt}$.

Each of these may give rise to specific problems of singularity. Collinearity among $x_{1t}, \ldots, x_{m_it}$, the included predetermined variables in the i-th equation, give rise to estimation and near-singularity problems in all methods of estimation alike. All the k-class methods will find rows and columns of

$$\begin{pmatrix} Y_i'Y_i - k\hat{V}_i'\hat{V}_i & Y_i'X_i \\ X_i'Y_i & X_i'X_i \end{pmatrix}$$

tending towards proportionality regardless of the value of k, because the source of collinearity occurs everywhere except in the N. W. block.

If there is collinearity among elements of $x_{m_i+1,t}, \ldots, x_{mt}$, this will not affect OLS estimates of the i-th equation (although it could affect such estimates of other equations in the system) because these variables have no bearing on anything in the matrix to be inverted, except on $\hat{V}_i$, and with $k = 0$ in the OLS case, these variables are excluded from the calculations.

Next we consider collinearity between included and excluded predetermined variables. It should be noted that the exclusion of predetermined variables from the i-th equation gives rise to the identifying restrictions that we use

[19] See L. R. Klein and M. Nakamura, "Singularity in the Equation System of Econometrics: Some Aspects of the Problem of Multicollinearity," *International Economic Review*, 3 (Sept., 1962), 274–99.

to ensure identification. If the excluded variables are related to included variables, it means that our conditions for identification are weak. In the Anderson-Rubin derivation of LIML estimators that we presented above, we eliminated the dependence of $x_{m_i+1,t}, \ldots, x_{mt}$ on $x_{1t}, \ldots, x_{m_it}$ by using only the residuals from the regressions of each of the former on the latter set. This automatically eliminated the possibility of collinearity between the two sets, but, of course, if they were strongly related to begin with we would find that the residuals were small and made little contribution to the explanation of the Y_i. A case of singularity arises, because the LIML estimates can be written in the general case where the $x_{m_i+1,t}, \ldots, x_{mt}$ are not first regressed on $x_{1t}, \ldots, x_{m_it}$, as the characteristic vector satisfying $\|(Y_i'X(X'X)^{-1}X'Y_i - Y_i'X_i(X_i'X_i)^{-1}X_i'Y_i) - \nu W_{yy}\|\hat{\alpha} = 0$. In this expression we have written the full matrix of observations of predetermined variables as X and the subset in the i-th equation as X_i.[20] We can transform the TSLS estimates from

$$\begin{pmatrix} Y_i'X(X'X)^{-1}X'Y_i & Y_i'X_i \\ X_i'Y_i & X_i'X_i \end{pmatrix}\begin{pmatrix} a_i \\ b_i \end{pmatrix} = \begin{pmatrix} Y_i'X(X'X)^{-1}X'y \\ X_i'y \end{pmatrix}$$

to

$$\begin{aligned}(Y_i'X(X'X)^{-1}X'Y_i - Y_i'X_i(X_i'X_i)^{-1}X_i'Y_i)a_i = {} & Y_i'X(X'X)^{-1}X'y \\ & - Y_i'X_i(X_i'X_i)^{-1}X_i'y\end{aligned} \tag{4.6.16}$$

by substituting

$$b_i = (X_i'X_i)^{-1}X_i'y - (X_i'X_i)^{-1}X_i'Y_ia \tag{4.6.17}$$

from the second row block of matrix equations into the first row block. Thus, except for the differences in normalization giving rise to a different treatment of one y-variable in TSLS, we have the same basic matrix involved in both TSLS and LIML for calculation of est α_i, namely

$$Y_i'X(X'X)^{-1}X'Y_i - Y_i'X_i(X_i'X_i)^{-1}X_i'Y_i. \tag{4.6.18}$$

This matrix could be singular, or ill-conditioned, if there were correlation between $x_{m_i+1,t} \ldots x_{mt}$ and $x_{1t} \ldots x_{m_it}$. If the former set of variables is highly dependent on the latter set, the first of the two matrices being subtracted will have elements similar to the second and their difference will be small. These two matrices are the variance-covariance matrices of sample residuals

$$Y_i'Y_i - Y_i'X_i(X_i'X_i)^{-1}X_i'Y_i \tag{4.6.19}$$

of the regression of the y's on the included x's in the i-th equation and of the

[20] In our prior notation we had $P_{yz}M_{zz}P_{yz}'$ instead of $Y_i'X(X'X)^{-1}X'Y_i - Y_i'X_i(X_i'X_i)^{-1}X_i'Y_i$.

sample residuals

$$Y_i'Y_i - Y_i'X(X'X)^{-1}X'Y_i \tag{4.6.20}$$

of the regression of the y's on all the x's in the system.[21]

There is yet another avenue of singularity or possible multicollinearity in the estimation of parameters by the TSLS or LIML methods. We have focused attention so far on interrelationships among the $x_{1t}, \ldots, x_{mt}$. We should also consider $y_{1t}, \ldots, y_{n_it}$. In the OLS method, collinearity among $y_{2t}, \ldots, y_{n_it}$, or between them and $x_{1t}, \ldots, x_{m_it}$, can be troublesome. In TSLS estimation we similarly are concerned with collinearity between $y_{2t}, \ldots, y_{n_it}$ and $x_{1t}, \ldots, x_{m_it}$. The matrices to be inverted are

$$\begin{matrix} \text{OLS} & & \text{TSLS} \\ \begin{pmatrix} Y_i'Y_i & Y_i'X_i \\ X_i'Y_i & X_i'X_i \end{pmatrix} & & \begin{pmatrix} \hat{Y}_i'\hat{Y}_i' & Y_i'X_i \\ X_i'Y_i & X_i'X_i \end{pmatrix}. \end{matrix}$$

It is clear that they differ only in the replacement of $Y_i'Y_i$ by $\hat{Y}_i'\hat{Y}_i$ as we shift from OLS to TSLS. In the limit as two variables y_{kt} and y_{lt} (in $y_{2t}, \ldots, y_{n_it}$) tend to have perfect correlation between them, it will also be true that $\hat{y}_{kt}$ and $\hat{y}_{lt}$ tend to be perfectly correlated. As y_{kt} and y_{lt} approach being linearly related, they approach having identical correlations on $x_{1t}, \ldots, x_{mt}$. Thus

if

$$r_{y_{kt}y_{lt}} \longrightarrow 1,$$

then

$$r_{\hat{y}_{kt}\hat{y}_{lt}} \longrightarrow 1. \tag{4.6.21}$$

But even though

$$r_{\hat{y}_{kt}\hat{y}_{lt}} \longrightarrow 1, \tag{4.6.22}$$

that is, the computed values approach perfect correlation between themselves, we need not have $r_{y_{kt}y_{lt}} \longrightarrow 1$. Also, even if y_{kt} and y_{lt} have zero correlation between themselves, $\hat{y}_{kt}$ and $\hat{y}_{lt}$ may have some nonzero correlation between themselves. On the basis of these arguments, we conclude that multicollinearity is more likely to occur and raise problems for TSLS estimation than for OLS estimation.

Similarly, we argue that LIML estimation is more sensitive to multicollinearity than is TSLS estimation. We have already seen that collinearity among elements of $x_{1t}, \ldots, x_{mt}$, the predetermined variables, gives rise to ill-conditioning of the matrix $X'X$ that must be inverted in order to determine $\hat{V}_i'\hat{V}_i$ for any k-class estimator, including both TSLS and LIML estimates. Similarly both

[21] The X-matrix could include observations on only a subset of $x_{1t}, \ldots, x_{mt}$ provided it included all $x_{1t}, \ldots, x_{m_it}$ in the i-th equation.

methods make use of

$$Y_i'X(X'X)^{-1}X'Y_i - Y_i'X_i(X_i'X_i)^{-1}X_i'Y_i$$

that may be ill-conditioned by virtue of collinearity between elements of x_{1t}, $\ldots, x_{m_it}$ and $x_{m_i+1,t}, \ldots, x_{mt}$. We also note that this matrix could be near singular even if the two sets of x-variables (included and excluded) are unrelated, provided that they are equally poorly associated with the elements of $y_{2t}, \ldots, y_{n_it}$.

There is, however, an additional route through which near singularity can manifest itself in the case of LIML estimation, namely through the stochastic nature of ν, the root of

$$|B - \nu W| = 0, \tag{4.6.23}$$

where B stands for the above matrix expressed as the difference of two covariance matrices. In the case of TSLS estimates, we have

$$k = 1$$

and there can be no problem of collinearity in the determination of k, but for LIML estimates, where

$$k = 1 + \nu$$

we must determine k from sample values. This may be an added source of near singularity. Multiplicity of roots of

$$|B - \nu W| = 0$$

is one condition leading to indeterminacy in the calculation of LIML estimates that does not arise in the TSLS case.

Full information estimates such as FIML or 3SLS use single equation estimators, probably, but not necessarily, LIML and TSLS, as initial values. In the one case they are used for starting iterations and in the other they are used for getting sample estimates of

$$\Sigma^{-1} = (\sigma^{ij}) = (Ee_{it}e_{jt})^{-1}. \tag{4.6.24}$$

We would, therefore, expect collinearity problems in single equation estimation to carry over in this way to FIML and 3SLS estimation. It is, however, possible to avoid some of the starting difficulties of multicollinearity among elements of $x_{1t}, \ldots, x_{mt}$ by using instrumental variable or other starting estimates.

A serious new problem of near singularity does arise, though. At each iteration of FIML algorithms, the inverse Σ-matrix noted above must be estimated.

In FIML estimation the concentrated likelihood function depends directly on $|\Sigma|$. The Σ-matrix must be evaluated directly from prior estimates, say TSLS, for the final round of 3SLS estimation. If two equations in a system are quite similar, or differ only by the presence of insignificant variables, or differ only by the individual presence of separate collinear variables, we shall find that estimates of $(E\, e_{it}e_{jt})$ tend to produce a singular matrix and a poorly computed inverse. The more poorly we specify each equation by using weak identifying criteria, the more sensitive will be the estimates to near singularity in the estimated Σ matrix. Collinearity is a major cause of this ill-conditioning, but not the only one.

Questions and Problems

1. Show that the matrix

$$\begin{pmatrix} \sum_{t=1}^{T} X_{1t}^2 & \cdots & \sum_{t=1}^{T} X_{1t}X_{nt} \\ \cdot & & \cdot \\ \cdot & & \cdot \\ \cdot & & \cdot \\ \sum_{t=1}^{T} X_{1t}X_{nt} & \cdots & \sum_{t=1}^{T} X_{nt}^2 \end{pmatrix}$$

is singular if $n > T$.

2. Show that the reduced forms

$$y_{it} = \sum_{j=1}^{m} \pi_{ij}X_{jt} + v_{it}$$

can be fit perfectly to a T-element data sample with an infinity of estimates of π_{ij} if $m > T$.

3. Sketch the geometry of the likelihood function of a system that has collinearity among two or more predetermined variables.

4. Give economic reasons why collinearity might occur in multivariate models of simultaneous equations.

SUGGESTED READINGS

GENERAL TEXTBOOKS ON EQUATION SYSTEM ESTIMATION

Christ, C., *Econometric Models and Methods*, New York: John Wiley & Sons, 1966.

Dhrymes, P. J., *Econometrics*, New York: Harper and Row, 1970.

Goldberger, A. S., *Econometric Theory*, New York: John Wiley & Sons, 1964.

Johnston, J., *Econometric Methods*, New York: McGraw-Hill, 1972, 2nd ed.

Malinvaud, E., *Statistical Methods of Econometrics*, Chicago: Rand McNally, 1966.

Theil, H., *Principles of Econometrics*, New York: John Wiley & Sons, 1971.

Tintner, G., *Econometrics*, New York: John Wiley & Sons, 1952.

ARTICLES AND CHAPTERS

Anderson, T. W., Jr., and H. Rubin, "Estimation of the Parameters of a Single Equation in a Complete System of Stochastic Equations," *Annals of Mathematical Statistics*, 20, (March, 1949), 46–63. The basic paper on the development of the limited-information-maximum-likelihood method of estimation.

Brown, T. M., "Simultaneous Least Squares: A Distribution Free Method of Equation Structure Estimation," *International Economic Review*, 1 (September, 1960), 173–91. The paper first proposing the simultaneous least squares method of estimation.

Chernoff, H. and H. Rubin, "Asymptotic Properties of Limited Information Estimates Under Generalized Conditions," *Studies in Econometric Method*, ed. W. C. Hood and T. C. Koopmans, New York: John Wiley & Sons, 1953, 200–12. Develops the important properties of estimators in incomplete systems, which becomes a key to the understanding of many special problems.

Chow, G., "A Comparison of Alternative Estimators for Simultaneous Equations," *Econometrica*, 32, (October, 1964), 532–53. A perceptive comparison of various estimators of equation systems.

Fisher, F. M., *The Identification Problem in Econometrics*, New York: McGraw-Hill, 1966. A basic treatise on the whole question of identification, containing the extension of many standard results to more general situations.

Klein, L. R. and M. Nakamura, "Singularity in the Equation Systems of Econometrics: Some Aspects of the Problem of Multicollinearity," *International Economic Review*, 3, (September, 1963), 274–99. Compares the sensitivity of alternative estimators to the presence of multicollinearity.

Kloek, T. and L. B. M. Mennes, "Simultaneous Equations Estimation Based on Principal Components of Predetermined Variables," *Econometrica*, 28, (January, 1960), 45–61. Introduced the use of principal components of predetermined variables to conserve degrees of freedom.

Koopmans, T. C., "Identification Problems in Economic Model Construction," *Studies in Econometric Method*, ed. W. C. Hood and T. C. Koopmans, New York: John Wiley & Sons, 1953, 27–48. An expository treatment of identification.

Koopmans, T. C. and W. C. Hood, "The Estimation of Simultaneous Linear Economic Relationships," *Studies in Econometric Method*, ed. W. C. Hood and T. C. Koopmans, New York: John Wiley & Sons, 1953, 112–99. Contains many basic results in equation system estimation.

Koopmans, T. C., H. Rubin, and R. B. Leipnik, "Measuring the Equation Systems of Dynamic Economics," *Statistical Inference in Dynamic Economic Models*, ed. T. C. Koopmans, New York: John Wiley & Sons, 1950, 53–237. An early and comprehensive discussion of equation system estimation, covering maximum likelihood methods in detail.

Mann, H. B. and A. Wald, "On the Statistical Treatment of Linear Stochastic Difference Equations," *Econometrica*, 11 (July-October, 1943), 173–220. Path-breaking article on maximum likelihood estimation of equations with lagged variables.

Wold, H., "A Fix-point Theorem with Econometric Background," *Arkiv för Matematik* 6, (1966), 209–40. A mathematical discussion of iterated least squares methods applied to econometric systems.

Zellner, A. and H. Theil, "Three-Stage Least Squares: Simultaneous Estimation of Simultaneous Equations," *Econometrica*, 30, (January, 1962), 54–78. The original development of the 3SLS estimator.

5

Special Cases and Extensions: Systems of Simultaneous Equations

1. RECURSIVE SYSTEMS

The problems of dealing with systems of simultaneous equations, even if we restrict ourselves to the linear case, are formidable, and we are inevitably drawn towards formulations of models that simplify things. At one extreme we have treatments of single equations, one by one, without regard to their position in a whole system. We then have single equation methods that take account of the position of such individual equations in a larger system. These include the whole k-class estimators, especially TSLS and LIML. Finally, we have full information methods such as FIML, 3SLS, and some of the other techniques mentioned at the end of the previous chapter. These present substantial, but not overwhelming, problems in applied work. We are led to inquire whether simplifications can be introduced that would make our work easier. At the time of early discussion and application of equation system methods in econometrics, Wold and Bentzel immediately pointed out an enormously simplifying approach in the structure of recursive systems.[1]

A fully recursive linear system will be defined here in terms of two characteristics, the Jacobian and the variance-covariance matrices. *If, in the linear model*

$$Ay_t + Bx_t = e_t, \tag{5.1.1}$$

we have

$$\begin{aligned} Ee_{it}^2 &= \sigma_i^2 < \infty && i = 1, 2, \ldots, n \\ Ee_{it}e_{jt'} &= 0 && \text{for } i \neq j \text{ and } t \neq t' \\ \alpha_{ij} &= 0 && \text{for } i < j \end{aligned}$$

[1] R. Bentzel and H. Wold, "On Statistical Demand Analysis from the Viewpoint of Simultaneous Equations," *Skandinavisk Aktuarietidskrift*, 29 (1946), 95–114.

we say that the model is fully recursive and that FIML estimates can be obtained by forming OLS estimates of each individual equation.

By the independence and triangularity assumptions made here, we can write the joint likelihood function as

$$e^L = |A|^T\left(\frac{1}{\sqrt{2\pi}}\right)^{Tn}\left(\frac{1}{\sigma_1^2 \cdots \sigma_n^2}\right)^{T/2} \exp\left\{-\sum_{i=1}^{n}\frac{1}{2\sigma_i^2}\sum_{t=1}^{T}\left(\sum_{j=1}^{i}\alpha_{ij}y_{jt} + \sum_{j=1}^{m}\beta_{ij}x_{jt}\right)^2\right\}. \tag{5.1.2}$$

The diagonality of the $\sum$-matrix is already built into the structure of the likelihood function by exclusion of all covariance terms involving σ_{ij} or σ^{ij}. The coefficient matrix, A, is the Jacobian in this system and has the form

$$A = \begin{pmatrix} \alpha_{11} & 0 & 0 & \cdots & 0 \\ \alpha_{21} & \alpha_{22} & 0 & \cdots & 0 \\ \alpha_{31} & \alpha_{32} & \alpha_{33} & \cdots & 0 \\ \cdot & \cdot & \cdot & & \cdot \\ \cdot & \cdot & \cdot & & \cdot \\ \cdot & \cdot & \cdot & & \cdot \\ \alpha_{n1} & \alpha_{n2} & \alpha_{n3} & \cdots & \alpha_{nn} \end{pmatrix}. \tag{5.1.3}$$

Its determinantal value is

$$\text{det. } A = |A| = \prod_{i=1}^{n} a_{ii}. \tag{5.1.4}$$

If we order the equations in such a way that the single variable with unit coefficient always appears in the diagonal position, we have further

$$|A| = 1. \tag{5.1.5}$$

This means that the structure of the system is not arbitrary, but that an ordering exists that will give us a unit valued determinant of the Jacobian. This means that although not every set of OLS estimates will be FIML estimates, that a particular set will be.

If we have an ordering with $a_{ii} = 1.0$, we shall find

$$L = \max.$$

when we find OLS regression values for the parameters by regressing

$$\begin{aligned} &y_{1t} \text{ on } x_{1t}, \ldots, x_{mt} \\ &y_{2t} \text{ on } y_{1t}, x_{1t}, \ldots, x_{mt} \\ &y_{3t} \text{ on } y_{1t}, y_{2t}, x_{1t}, \ldots, x_{mt} \\ &\quad\cdot \\ &\quad\cdot \\ &\quad\cdot \\ &y_{nt} \text{ on } y_{1t}, y_{2t}, \ldots, y_{n-1,t}, x_{1t}, \ldots, x_{mt}. \end{aligned}$$

Identifying restrictions on some of the $\alpha_{ij}(i < j)$ may be imposed. That would mean that some values of y_{kt} may be omitted from the ith regression $(k < i)$ or have their coefficients otherwise restrained. Similarly, there will be restrictions on some of the β_{ij}; therefore, all x_{jt} will not appear in each equation or have unrestricted coefficients in each equation.

If the A-matrix is triangular without the diagonality restriction imposed on Σ, the likelihood function is more complicated. From the concentrated likelihood function, we would have

$$\begin{aligned} \frac{\partial|\Sigma|}{\partial\alpha_{ij}} &= 0 \\ \frac{\partial|\Sigma|}{\partial\beta_{ij}} &= 0 \end{aligned} \tag{5.1.6}$$

as estimation equations to be solved for the coefficients. These are not easy to solve in spite of the simplifications assumed, but we can obtain some consistent estimates that are *not* maximum likelihood estimates by regressing

$$\begin{aligned} &y_{1t} \text{ on } x_{1t}, \ldots, x_{mt} \\ &y_{2t} \text{ on } \hat{y}_{1t}, x_{1t}, \ldots, x_{mt} \\ &y_{3t} \text{ on } \hat{y}_{1t}, \hat{y}_{2t}, x_{1t}, \ldots, x_{mt} \qquad \text{etc.} \end{aligned}$$

The computed values used in the regression equations for $\hat{y}_{1t}, \hat{y}_{2t}, \ldots$ are the computed endogenous variables obtained from the regression equations of the previous recursive step for values of variables used in the regressions. This is a modification of the method of two stage least squares.

The familiar cobweb model applied in many agricultural markets provides a useful example of a recursive system. This model often deals with the case of a perishable agricultural commodity requiring time for maturation, as a crop season. Supply depends on the prior season's price, and the current season's price is obtained through clearing of the market. If the commodity is storable or can be obtained through importation, the model becomes more complicated.

$$\begin{aligned} q_t &= \beta_{s0} + \beta_{s1}p_{t-1} + e_{st} \\ p_t &= \beta_{d0} + \alpha_{d1}q_t + e_{dt}, \qquad t = 1, 2, \ldots, T. \\ q_t &= \text{quantity produced and consumed during period } t. \\ p_t &= \text{price during period } t. \end{aligned} \tag{5.1.7}$$

The matrix expression for this system is

$$\begin{pmatrix} 1 & 0 \\ -\alpha_{d1} & 1 \end{pmatrix}\begin{pmatrix} q_t \\ p_t \end{pmatrix} + \begin{pmatrix} -\beta_{s0} & -\beta_{s1} \\ -\beta_{d0} & 0 \end{pmatrix}\begin{pmatrix} 1 \\ p_{t-1} \end{pmatrix} = \begin{pmatrix} e_{st} \\ e_{dt} \end{pmatrix}. \tag{5.1.8}$$

The zero coefficient in each equation makes the system identified. If we impose the additional restriction

$$E(e_{st}e_{dt}) = 0, \tag{5.1.9}$$

we can write the likelihood function as

$$\begin{aligned} e^L = \left(\frac{1}{2\pi}\right)^T \left(\frac{1}{\sigma_s\sigma_d}\right)^T \exp\Big\{ & -\frac{1}{2\sigma_s^2}\sum_{t=1}^T (q_t - \beta_{s0} - \beta_{s1}p_{t-1})^2 \\ & -\frac{1}{2\sigma_d^2}\sum_{t=1}^T (p_t - \beta_{d0} - \alpha_{d1}q_t)^2\Big\}. \end{aligned} \tag{5.1.10}$$

We observe that the Jacobian has a unit valued determinant

$$\begin{vmatrix} 1 & 0 \\ -\alpha_{d1} & 1 \end{vmatrix} = 1. \tag{5.1.11}$$

The maximum likelihood equations are

$$\begin{aligned} \frac{\partial L}{\partial \beta_{s0}} &= 0 = \frac{1}{\sigma_s^2}\sum_{t=1}^T (q_t - \beta_{s0} - \beta_{s1}p_{t-1}) \\ \frac{\partial L}{\partial \beta_{s1}} &= 0 = \frac{1}{\sigma_s^2}\sum_{t=1}^T (q_t - \beta_{s0} - \beta_{s1}p_{t-1})p_{t-1} \\ \frac{\partial L}{\partial \sigma_s} &= 0 = -\frac{T}{\sigma_s} + \frac{1}{\sigma_s^3}\sum_{t=1}^T (q_t - \beta_{s0} - \beta_{s1}p_{t-1})^2 \\ \frac{\partial L}{\partial \beta_{d0}} &= 0 = \frac{1}{\sigma_d^2}\sum_{t=1}^T (p_t - \beta_{d0} - \alpha_{d1}q_t) \\ \frac{\partial L}{\partial \alpha_{d1}} &= 0 = \frac{1}{\sigma_d^2}\sum_{t=1}^T (p_t - \beta_{d0} - \alpha_{d1}q_t)q_t \\ \frac{\partial L}{\partial \sigma_d} &= 0 = -\frac{T}{\sigma_d} + \frac{1}{\sigma_d^3}\sum_{t=1}^T (p_t - \beta_{d0} - \alpha_{d1}q_t)^2 \end{aligned} \tag{5.1.12}$$

These contain the normal equations for OLS estimation of β_{s0}, β_{s1}, β_{d0}, α_{d1}, obtained by regressing q_t on p_{t-1} and p_t on q_t. It is, of course, natural to regress q_t on p_{t-1}, but the theory requires that p_t be regressed on q_t and not vice versa. This would not be obvious unless the causal structure were brought to bear on the procedure of estimation.

A generalization of the notion of recursive systems, as we have developed them here, would be to assume that the matrix A is not triangular row by row but block by block.[2] In a triangular system with p diagonal blocks, we would

[2] The systematic development of this approach is due to F. Fisher, "Dynamic Structure and Estimation in Economy-Wide Econometric Models," in *The Brookings Quarterly Econometric Model of the United States*, ed. J. Duesenberry et al. (Chicago: Rand McNally, 1965), pp. 588–635.

have

$$A = \begin{pmatrix} A_{11} & 0 & 0 & \cdots & 0 \\ A_{21} & A_{22} & 0 & \cdots & 0 \\ A_{31} & A_{32} & A_{33} & \cdots & 0 \\ \cdot & \cdot & \cdot & & \cdot \\ \cdot & \cdot & \cdot & & \cdot \\ \cdot & \cdot & \cdot & & \cdot \\ A_{p1} & A_{p2} & A_{p3} & \cdots & A_{pp} \end{pmatrix}. \tag{5.1.13}$$

The block elements of A are submatrices whose elements are the parameters of the system. Diagonal blocks are square, and off-diagonal blocks are rectangular. In the treatment of such systems we begin by regarding A_{11} as the matrix of a self-contained subsystem

$$A_{11}y_{1t} + B_1x_t = e_{1t}. \tag{5.1.14}$$

In this system of equations, all the dependent variables occurring with nonzero coefficients in the first block of equations are in the column vector y_{1t}. We would treat this subsystem in estimation just as we treat any linear open model with exogenous variation; that is, we would estimate A_{11} and B_1 by TSLS, LIML, FIML, 3SLS or similar methods. We would apply these methods as though this block of equations formed a complete system. If A_{11} were triangular and the block covariance of error diagonal, we could use OLS methods at this stage.

Next consider

$$A_{21}y_{1t} + A_{22}y_{2t} + B_2x_t = e_{2t}. \tag{5.1.15}$$

If the covariances between elements of e_{1t} and e_{2t} vanish

$$Ee_{1it}e_{2jt} = 0 \tag{5.1.16}$$

for all i in block 1 and all j in block 2, we can treat y_{1t} as a vector of predetermined variables. Together with the elements of x_t that have nonvanishing coefficients, they constitute the set of predetermined variables in the second block. The square matrix of coefficients in A_{22} are associated with dependent variables of the subsystem and y_{1t} and x_t are predetermined. If the system is identified but if the covariances of error do not vanish, we can use computed values of y_{1t} from the first block equations as predetermined variables for block 2. Given these extra predetermined variables in block 2 and assuming that identification criteria are met, we can use any of the standard methods for estimating the square matrix of coefficients of dependent variables A_{22} and the rectangular matrices of coefficients of predetermined variables A_{21} and B_2. It should be noted that the magnitude of the estimating effort involved is much smaller if the blocks are estimated separately than if the whole system is estimated simultaneously.

We continue in an obvious way. Variables from blocks 1 and 2 (either y_{1t} and y_{2t} or computed values of the same) are used as predetermined variables in block 3

$$A_{31}y_{1t} + A_{32}y_{2t} + A_{33}y_{3t} + B_3 x_t = e_{3t}. \tag{5.1.17}$$

Variables from lower numbered blocks are successively used as predetermined variables in higher numbered blocks until all blocks have been estimated. This is a direct analogue, by block systems, of the equation by equation approach in cobweb models and similar recursive systems. It may serve to avoid some problems of paucity of degrees of freedom by considering small block subsystems separately rather than the whole model simultaneously. It is perhaps the only practical method for using FIML techniques in large systems.

Questions and Problems

1. Construct a cobweb (recursive) model that is not based on the conditions for agricultural supply and demand for perishables.

2. Discuss the plausibility of having a diagonal covariance matrix in the recursive model of question 1.

3. Construct the likelihood function for the recursive model in (5.1.7) without the restriction in (5.1.9); that is, assume

$$E(e_{st}e_{dt}) \neq 0.$$

Derive the maximum likelihood estimation equations in this case.

2. NONLINEAR SYSTEMS

We have already dealt with the problem of estimating nonlinear, single equation regressions. We have also been confronted with the general problem of solving maximum likelihood equations that are nonlinear in the parameters to be estimated. These are nonlinear even though the original system of equations is linear. Thus, we have met with the question of the uses of nonlinear methods. We now apply these methods in a general way to the estimation of nonlinear models.

As we saw in the case of single regression equations, nonlinearities may arise in the parameters or the variables. Equations that are linear in parameters but nonlinear in variables are easy to deal with on a single equation basis. That remains true for equation systems methods of estimation but not for all methods. TSLS and LIML methods can easily be adapted to the treatment of single equations that are linear in parameters but nonlinear in variables.

Let

$$f_{jt} = f_j(y_{1t}, \ldots, y_{n_1t}, x_{1t}, \ldots, x_{m_1t}) \tag{5.2.1}$$

be *nonparametric* nonlinear functions of some or all variables in a system. We might have

$$
\begin{aligned}
f_{jt} = {} & \log y_{kt} \\
& \text{or } y_{kt} y_{lt} \\
& \text{or } x_t \sin y_{lt} \\
& \text{or other functions of variables.}
\end{aligned}
$$

If the ith equation in the system takes the form

$$y_{it} = \sum_{j=1}^{M} \alpha_{ij} f_{jt} + \sum_{j=1}^{m_i} \beta_{ij} x_{jt} + e_{it}, \tag{5.2.2}$$

we can estimate this equation by TSLS and LIML methods through the device of redefining endogenous variables as

$$y_{jt}^* = f_{jt} \tag{5.2.3}$$

and treating the y_{jt}^* as new endogenous variables in an *incomplete* system. The system is incomplete in this form because there are new endogenous variables without new equations. We assume that other equations in the system will contain $y_{1t}, \ldots, y_{nt}$ in their original linear form. If the nonlinear functions f_{jt} depend solely on predetermined variables, we simply redefine these as new predetermined variables and lengthen the list $x_{1t}, \ldots, x_{mt}, x_{m+1,t}, \ldots$ without affecting the completeness of the system. If the nonlinear functions contain any dependent variables (are not *wholly* predetermined), we treat them as dependent variables.

Rubin and Chernoff have shown that the consistency properties of LIML (and TSLS) carry over to incomplete systems; therefore, we derive reduced forms for

$$
\begin{aligned}
y_{it} &= \sum_{k=1}^{m} \pi_{ik} x_{kt} + v_{it} \\
y_{1t}^* &= \sum_{k=1}^{m} \pi_{1k}^* x_{kt} + v_{it}^* \\
y_{Mt}^* &= \sum_{k=1}^{m} \pi_{Mk}^* x_{kt} + v_{Mt}^*
\end{aligned}
\tag{5.2.4}
$$

and continue as before with the usual calculations by these methods.[3]

Such simplified methods cannot be extended to FIML estimation because we want the joint probability distribution of all the variables in the system, and we must deal with a complete system. In deriving the joint probability distribution of a complete system that is nonlinear in variables, even if it is linear in

[3] H. Chernoff and H. Rubin, "Asymptotic Properties of Limited-Information Estimates under Generalized Conditions," in *Studies in Econometric Method*, ed. Wm. C. Hood and T. C. Koopmans (New York: John Wiley & Sons, 1952), pp. 200–12.

parameters, we shall have a *variable* Jacobian determinant, and this is different from the case we have considered so far. That is to say, the ith row of the Jacobian for a truly linear system whose i^{th} equation is

$$y_{it} = \sum_{j=1}^{n_i}{}' \alpha_{ij} y_{jt} + \sum_{j=1}^{m_i} \beta_{ij} x_{jt} + e_{it}, \tag{5.2.5}$$

where Σ' deletes the running subscript $j = i$, is

$$-\alpha_{i1} \; -\alpha_{i2} \; \cdots \; 1 \; \cdots \; -\alpha_{in_i} \; 0 \; \cdots \; 0.$$

In the nonlinear formulation (5.2.2), it is

$$-\sum_{j=1}^{M} \alpha_{ij} \frac{\partial f_j}{\partial y_{1t}} - \sum_{j=1}^{M} \alpha_{ij} \frac{\partial f_j}{\partial y_{2t}} \cdots 1 - \sum_{j=1}^{M} \alpha_{ij} \frac{\partial f_j}{\partial y_{it}} \cdots - \sum_{j=1}^{M} \alpha_{ij} \frac{\partial f_j}{\partial y_{n_i t}} \cdots 0.$$

In general, these terms will vary with the sample observations. Because there are no great simplifications in dealing with cases that are linear in parameters but nonlinear in variables for FIML estimation, we may as well turn immediately to nonlinear problems where both parameters and variables enter nonlinearly. The approximation procedures will be the same for this general case as well as the case where nonlinearity is confined to variables.

In the preceding chapter, we developed the concentrated likelihood function for a general set of nonlinear relationships

$$f_i(y_{1t}, \ldots, y_{nt}; x_{1t}, \ldots, x_{mt}) = e_{it} \quad i = 1, 2, \ldots, n \tag{5.2.6}$$

as

$$L = \sum_{t=1}^{T} \log |J_t| - \frac{T}{2} \log |\Sigma|, \tag{5.2.7}$$

where

$$J_t = \frac{\partial(f_1, \ldots, f_n)}{\partial(y_{1t}, \ldots, y_{nt})}$$

$$\Sigma = \left\| \frac{1}{T} \sum_{t=1}^{T} f_i f_j \right\|.$$

This differs from the purely linear case in that Σ is not necessarily a quadratic function of the unknown parameters and $|J_t|$ is not a constant (unknown or known). To determine the maximum of L as a function of r unknown parameters, we could use Newton's method or some variant of it. We first express the maximization conditions as

$$\frac{\partial L}{\partial \theta_i} = \sum_{tjk} \frac{\partial L}{\partial J_{tjk}} \frac{\partial L_{tjk}}{\partial \theta_i} + \sum_{jk} \frac{\partial L}{\partial \sigma_{jk}} \frac{\partial \sigma_{jk}}{\partial \theta_i} = 0. \tag{5.2.8}$$

We denote the jk element of J_t by J_{tjk} and the jk element of Σ by σ_{jk}. In the present context, J varies with t, but Σ does not. Corresponding elements of the inverse will be denoted by jk superscripts,

$$\frac{\partial L}{\partial J_{tjk}} J_t^{kj}; \frac{\partial L}{\partial \sigma_{jk}} = -\frac{T}{2}\sigma^{jk}. \tag{5.2.9}$$

Also,

$$\frac{\partial J_{tjk}}{\partial \theta_i} = \frac{\partial^2 f_j}{\partial \theta_i \partial y_{kt}} \text{ and } \frac{\partial \sigma_{jk}}{\partial \theta_i} = \frac{1}{T}\sum_t \left(\frac{\partial f_j}{\partial \theta_i} f_k + \frac{\partial f_k}{\partial \theta_i} f_j\right). \tag{5.2.10}$$

We can also express our maximization condition as

$$\sum_{tjk} J_t^{kj} \frac{\partial^2 f_j}{\partial \theta_i \partial y_{kt}} - \frac{1}{2}\sum_{jk} \sigma^{jk} \sum_t \left(\frac{\partial f_j}{\partial \theta_i} f_k + \frac{\partial f_k}{\partial \theta_i} f_j\right) = 0. \tag{5.2.11}$$

We now express this as a set of nonlinear equations in θ_j

$$g_i(\theta_1 \cdots \theta_r) = 0 \tag{5.2.12}$$

and use Newton's method to solve them from the expansions

$$g_i(\theta_1^0, \ldots, \theta_r^0) + \sum_j \frac{\partial g_i}{\partial \theta_j}\bigg|_{\theta=\theta^0} (\theta_j - \theta_j^0) = 0. \tag{5.2.13}$$

Solution of this system of linear approximation equations starting from

$$\theta_1 = \theta_1^0$$
$$\vdots$$
$$\theta_r = \theta_r^0$$

gives us $\theta_1^{(1)}, \ldots, \theta_r^{(1)}$ as a first iteration solution. We expand g_i linearly about $\theta^{(1)}$ and proceed as before. Successive iterations give us $\theta_1^{(s)}, \ldots, \theta_r^{(s)}$, and we stop when

$$\left|\frac{\theta_j^{(s+1)} - \theta_j^{(s)}}{\theta_j^{(s)}}\right| < \epsilon, \tag{5.2.14}$$

for an assumed level of ϵ, say 0.0001. It is evident that $\frac{\partial g_i}{\partial \theta_j}$ involves higher derivatives of f_i such as

$$\frac{\partial^2 f_i}{\partial \theta_j \partial \theta_k} \text{ and } \frac{\partial^3 f_i}{\partial \theta_j \partial \theta_k \partial y_{lt}}.$$

A pure application of Newton's method, as suggested here, may not bring rapid convergence to a maximum; therefore, modifications to the iterative steps may be required as shown by Eisenpress and Greenstadt.[4]

Nonlinear methods are basic in econometrics because many problems that are slight variations on standard linear formulations are readily seen to be nonlinear problems.

In Chap. 3, we have already shown how the problems of serially correlated disturbances and lag distributions in otherwise linear models reduce to problems of nonlinear estimation of single equations. Also some problems that are linear in single equation formulations become nonlinear estimation problems in the context of equation systems.[5]

The Cobb-Douglas production function has been thought to be free of nonlinear complications because it can be made into a linear form by a logarithmic transformation; however, the simplest model involving both a Cobb-Douglas production function and a marginal condition for cost minimization is not a linear estimation problem. We have

$$\begin{aligned} \log X &= \log A + \alpha \log E + \beta \log K + e_t \\ \log \frac{w}{q} &= \log \frac{\alpha}{\beta} + \log \frac{K}{E} + u_t. \end{aligned} \tag{5.2.15}$$

$X =$ output; $E =$ employment; $K =$ capital; $w =$ wage rate; $q =$ capital rental. The joint probability distribution of e_t and u_t, treating X and $\frac{w}{q}$ as exogenous, does not lead to maximum likelihood estimators from a system that is linear in α and β. The likelihood function has jointly α, β, and $\log \frac{\alpha}{\beta}$ as arguments. This is the inherent cause of the nonlinearity.

Macroeconometric systems that are linear in parameters may have variable Jacobians if all accounting identities are expressed in current money values, as they must be, but associated behavior equations depend on relative prices and price deflated magnitudes. For these systems, we see that we cannot really express the economy as

$$Ay_t + Bx_t = e_t,$$

where A and B are matrices with constant elements. There are inherent nonlinearities in the system involving the accounting identities and behavioral equations. If, in addition, technological relations, such as the Cobb-Douglas are in logarithmic or other curvilinear form, the system may have even stronger nonlinearities.[6]

[4] H. Eisenpress and J. Greenstadt, "The Estimation of Non-Linear Econometric Systems," *Econometrica*, 34 (October, 1966), 851–61.

[5] See Chap. 8.

[6] See D. W. Katzner and L. R. Klein, "On the Possibility of the General Linear Economic Model," in *Economic Models, Estimation and Risk Programming*, ed. K. A. Fox et al. (Berlin: Springer-Verlag, 1969).

3. SERIAL CORRELATION

The single equation regression with serially correlated disturbances has been shown to be a problem in nonlinear estimation if the autoregressive parameter is unknown. The estimation problem, for both autoregressive parameter and equation coefficients can be completely solved by using either an iterative or a search procedure. The generalization from a single equation to a system of equations brings new complications. The complete system is

$$Ay_t + Bx_t = u_t \tag{5.3.1}$$

$$u_t = Pu_{t-1} + e_t. \tag{5.3.2}$$

By substitution, we can transform this to

$$(Ay_t - PAy_{t-1}) + (Bx_t - PBx_{t-1}) = e_t. \tag{5.3.3}$$

We cannot, as in the single equation case, write this as a system of linear equations in transformed variables because the transformation is different for each equation of the system. The complexity of the problem is shown by writing out, in full, the transformation of a two equation system.

$$\begin{aligned}
\alpha_{11}y_{1t} + \alpha_{12}y_{2t} + \beta_{11}x_{1t} + \beta_{12}x_{2t} &= u_{1t} \\
\alpha_{21}y_{1t} + \alpha_{22}y_{2t} + \beta_{21}x_{1t} + \beta_{22}x_{2t} &= u_{2t} \\
u_{1t} &= \rho_{11}u_{1,t-1} + \rho_{12}u_{2,t-1} + e_{1t} \\
u_{2t} &= \rho_{21}u_{1,t-1} + \rho_{22}u_{2,t-1} + e_{2t}.
\end{aligned} \tag{5.3.4}$$

The transformed equations are

$$\begin{aligned}
&\alpha_{11}y_{1t} + \alpha_{12}y_{2t} - (\rho_{11}\alpha_{11} + \rho_{12}\alpha_{21})y_{1,t-1} - (\rho_{11}\alpha_{12} + \rho_{12}\alpha_{22})y_{2,t-1} \\
&\qquad + \beta_{11}x_{1t} + \beta_{12}x_{2t} - (\rho_{11}\beta_{11} + \rho_{12}\beta_{21})x_{1,t-1} \\
&\qquad - (\rho_{11}\beta_{12} + \rho_{12}\beta_{22})x_{2,t-1} = e_{1t} \\
&\alpha_{21}y_{1t} + \alpha_{22}y_{2t} - (\rho_{21}\alpha_{11} + \rho_{22}\alpha_{21})y_{1,t-1} - (\rho_{21}\alpha_{12} + \rho_{22}\alpha_{22})y_{2,t-1} \\
&\qquad + \beta_{21}x_{1t} + \beta_{22}x_{2t} - (\rho_{21}\beta_{11} + \rho_{22}\beta_{21})x_{1,t-1} \\
&\qquad - (\rho_{21}\beta_{12} + \rho_{22}\beta_{22})x_{2,t-1} = e_{2t}.
\end{aligned} \tag{5.3.5}$$

It is evident from the structure of Eq. (5.3.5) that they are nonlinear, that they contain common parameters, and that parameters of the second (first) structural equation enter the transformed version of the first (second). It would be possible to try to use nonlinear estimation methods in a straightforward way for the estimation of these equations, taking all the restrictions into account, but this would be very complicated.

A way of simplifying the problem but still retaining much of the equation system aspect of the formulation is to assume that P is diagonal. Then the autoregressive error structure has the form

$$u_{it} = \rho_i u_{it-1} + e_{it}.$$

Each equation may be written in the simplified form

$$\sum \alpha_{ij}(y_{jt} - \rho_i y_{j,t-1}) + \sum \beta_{ij}(x_{jt} - \rho_i x_{j,t-1}) = e_{it}$$

and is linear in the α's and β's if P is known. It should be observed, though, that the autoregressive transformation is different for each equation. All the separate diagonal elements of P must be known, not simply a single autoregressive parameter.

There are some equation system complications in this case because there are no explicit reduced form equations for the transformed variables.

The reduced form equations could be written as

$$\begin{aligned} y_t &= -A^{-1}Bx_t + A^{-1}u_t \\ A^{-1}u_t &= A^{-1}Pu_{t-1} + A^{-1}e_t \end{aligned} \tag{5.3.6}$$

or as

$$y_t = A^{-1}PAy_{t-1} - A^{-1}Bx_t + A^{-1}PBx_{t-1} + A^{-1}e_t. \tag{5.3.7}$$

Two procedures are open for an application of TSLS methods. (1) Using (5.3.7) as an unrestricted reduced form, we may regress each element of y_t on all elements of y_{t-1}, x_t, and x_{t-1}. This enlarges the vector of reduced form regressors considerably because it augments x_t by x_{t-1} and y_{t-1}. It adds $m + n$ regressors to the reduced form equations and therefore taxes the degrees of freedom in the system heavily. In addition, it raises the possibility of strong multicollinearity by using both x_t and x_{t-1} as regressors. (2) If we estimate the reduced form (5.3.6) directly, using only the elements of x_t as regressors, we should also make use of the information that the elements of $A^{-1}u_t$ satisfy an autoregressive scheme. For the ith reduced form, the autoregressive relationship is

$$\sum_{j=1}^{n} \alpha^{ij}u_{jt} = \sum_{j=1}^{n} \alpha^{ij}\rho_j u_{jt-1} + \sum_{j=1}^{n} \alpha^{ij}e_{jt}. \tag{5.3.8}$$

This implies that the reduced form errors will not in general be uncorrelated. An estimation procedure that takes account of the serial correlation that is generated by the relationship in (5.3.8) is an iterative scheme using generalized least squares methods.

In the first instance an element of y_t will be regressed on all the elements of x_t if there are adequate degrees of freedom for the first stage regressions. Let the residuals be denoted as

$$\text{est.} \sum_{j=1}^{n} \alpha^{ij}u_{jt} = v_{it}^{(0)},$$

and compute the covariance matrix

$$\Omega_i^{(0)} = \begin{pmatrix} v_{i1}^{(0)} \\ v_{i2}^{(0)} \\ \cdot \\ \cdot \\ \cdot \\ v_{iT}^{(0)} \end{pmatrix} (v_{i1}^{(0)} \quad v_{i2}^{(0)} \quad \cdots \quad v_{iT}^{(0)})$$

$$= \begin{pmatrix} (v_{i1}^{(0)})^2 & v_{i1}^{(0)}v_{i2}^{(0)} & \cdots & v_{i1}^{(0)}v_{iT}^{(0)} \\ \cdot & \cdot & & \cdot \\ \cdot & \cdot & & \cdot \\ \cdot & \cdot & & \cdot \\ v_{iT}^{(0)}v_{i1}^{(0)} & v_{iT}^{(0)}v_{i2}^{(0)} & \cdots & (v_{iT}^{(0)})^2 \end{pmatrix}.$$

Writing (5.3.6) as

$$y_i = X\pi_i + v_i,$$

we obtain the generalized (Aitken) least squares estimate of π_i as

$$\text{est. } \pi_i = (X'\Omega_i^{-1}X)^{-1}(X'\Omega_i^{-1}y_i).$$

Having an estimate $\Omega_i^{(0)}$ of Ω_i, we can write

$$\pi_i^{(1)} = (X'(\Omega_i^{(0)})^{-1}X)^{-1}(X'(\Omega_i^{(0)})^{-1}y_i). \tag{5.3.9}$$

From the reduced form coefficient estimated in (5.3.9), we can compute new residuals $v_{it}^{(1)}$ and form a new estimate $\Omega_i^{(1)}$. This estimated covariance matrix can be used to obtain generalized least squares regression estimates $\pi_i^{(2)}$, and so on. The iteration formula will be

$$\pi_i^{(r)} = (X'(\Omega_i^{(r-1)})^{-1}X)^{-1}(X'(\Omega_i^{(r-1)})^{-1}y_i) \tag{5.3.10}$$

and when the elements of $\pi_i^{(r)}$ are stable to a preassigned level of approximation, the iteration process stops.

If each reduced form equation in (5.3.6) is so estimated, we should have more efficient estimates of the reduced forms. The final step is to obtain iterated estimates of the separate transformed structural equation

$$\sum \alpha_{ij}(y_{jt} - \rho_i y_{j,t-1}) + \sum \beta_{ij}(x_{jt} - \rho_i x_{j,t-1}) = e_{it}.$$

For this stage of the calculations, one of the transformed variables is chosen to have unit coefficient, say $\alpha_{ii} = 1.0$. The ith dependent variable $y_{it} - \rho_i y_{i,t-1}$ is regressed on the $\hat{y}_{jt} - \rho_i \hat{y}_{j,t-1}$ and the $x_{jt} - \rho_i x_{j,t-1}$, where the $\hat{y}_{j,t} - \rho_i \hat{y}_{j,t-1}$ for $j \neq i$ are computed from the final iterated version of the reduced form coefficients in (5.3.10). For the iterations of the structural equation regressions a value is assumed for ρ_i (often $\rho_i^{(0)} = 0$) and estimates $\alpha_{ij}^{(0)}$, $\beta_{ij}^{(0)}$ are obtained from second stage regressions. Residuals are computed from

$$\sum \alpha_{ij}^{(0)} y_{jt} + \sum \beta_{ij}^{(0)} x_{jt} = u_{it}^{(0)}.$$

The first order autoregression coefficient

$$\rho_i(1) = \frac{\frac{1}{T-1} \sum u_{it}^{(0)} u_{i,t-1}^{(0)}}{\frac{1}{T-1} \sum (u_{i,t-1}^{(0)})^2}$$

is used to transform the variables for an iterated second stage regression of $y_{it} - \rho_i^{(1)} y_{i,t-1}$ on $\hat{y}_{jt} - \rho_i^{(1)} \hat{y}_{j,t-1}$ and $x_{jt} - \rho_i^{(1)} x_{j,t-1}$ etc. until convergence is obtained.

This method requires iteration at both the first and second stages of TSLS regressions, but it is more economical than are other approaches in its use of first stage regressors.

4. SPECIFICATION PROBLEMS

Relationships included in a model of the economy, or its subsectors, may be loosely or generally stated as

y_t depends on x_t, lagged values of x_t, and error.

This may be stated in terms of a single y_t and a single x_t or in terms of vectors. If we are more *specific* and say that the relationship is linear or some other well defined parametric form, we have enormously narrowed the possible statistical estimates. A first step in specification is to give the parametric form of the relationships being studied: linear, semi-log, log-linear, sinusoidal, exponential, and so on. We have little guidance at this stage of analysis. We may know that asymptotic floors or ceilings exist; we may also know that points of inflection occur, but there are limitless possible parametric specifications that meet these pieces of a priori information. To a large extent, we use empirical guidance in choosing a linear or some definite nonlinear form of the relationship. When we find empirical evidence against some particular parametric relationship, say that y_t and x_t are not significantly correlated in a linear pattern

$$y_t = a + bx_t + (\text{residual})_t, \tag{5.4.1}$$

we have not disproved the existence of a relationship. We may have given very strong empirical evidence against the existence of a linear relationship, but not against an infinite number of other specifications in nonlinear form such as

$$\log y_t = \alpha + \beta \log x_t + e_t \tag{5.4.2}$$

or

$$y_t = \gamma \sin \delta x_t + e_t \tag{5.4.3}$$

or others.

Particular specifications are highly restrictive, and results of sample investigations may be extremely sensitive to the specification used. Of all the possible sources of gain in improved accuracy of econometric analysis, the reduction of specification error admits of some of the greatest potentialities.

If we follow tradition and assume that we have a linear model, even though such an assumption cannot be justified in pure theory,

$$Ay_t + Bx_t = e_t, \tag{5.4.4}$$

we still have problems in specification. The identifying restrictions give us specifications of the models. They tell which variables enter which equations and even the restricted way they enter in a linear fashion. The zero-nonzero properties of the variance-covariance error matrix are also part of the specification. All these parameter restrictions are identifying restrictions, but within the wide range of *overidentification* of a model, we can find many different specifications that may have a priori plausibility.

In the context of linear models, we might try to summarize what we know about the different estimators as regards specification error. We cannot be as precise in the case of sensitivity to specification error as we were in the case of multicollinearity in ranking the different estimators. We can, however, say something about the polar situations. Consider the OLS estimator of the ith equation of the general linear model

$$y_{1t} = \sum_{j=2}^{n_i} \alpha_{ij} y_{jt} + \sum_{j=1}^{m_i} \beta_{ij} x_{jt} + e_{it}. \tag{5.4.5}$$

The OLS estimates of α_{ij}, β_{ij}, and σ_i^2 will be sensitive to specifications of the ith equation, but they will be completely insensitive to alterations of the specifications of the other equations in the system. OLS estimates may be distributed about biased or poorly chosen values of the parameters and this may make them undesirable, but they will not show any sensitivity to changes in the zero-type or general linear homogenous restrictions on other equations in the system. They show a *stability* that may or may not be regarded as a virtue. In *partial* investigations, this form of insensitivity to specification error may be desirable in the sense that the investigator may not be able to give good specification to any part of the economy outside the partial sector being investigated.

At the other extreme, we have full information methods such as 3SLS or FIML. These methods take account of restrictions in the whole system when estimating any part of it. They are most sensitive to specification error. Special cases, such as the fully recursive models, leave the estimation of each individual equation independent of all others, provided we accept the fully recursive specification that, in itself, is not very general.

Poor specification of a system may make the likelihood function very flat in critical areas, thus making it difficult even to locate a set of FIML estimates for a given equation. If the function has a well defined maximum, this point can be altered by changed specifications almost anywhere in the system and not necessarily in close linkage with any subsystem being studied. It is, therefore, essential to build a good model of the economy as a whole when estimating any part of it by FIML methods.

There are no established relationships between the relative sensitivities of FIML and 3SLS estimates to specification error. We would also expect the newer method of iterative least squares (ILS) to have broadly similar sensitivity to specification error in the system as a whole because it too makes use of restrictions in all equations of the system.

LIML and TSLS estimates would seem to occupy an intermediate position between the two poles, but their own relative sensitivities are not established. Clearly, they are more sensitive to specification error than is the OLS method, for these two single equation methods depend on the *specification* of the list of predetermined variables in the entire system. The first step for all k-class estimation methods is to evaluate

$$Y_i'Y_i - k\hat{V}_i'\hat{V}_i,$$

and this calculation changes as the list of predetermined variables changes. If changes in this list involves changes in $x_{1t}, \ldots, x_{m_it}$—the list of predetermined variables included in the ith equation—then all methods will be affected, including OLS. The k-class estimators need not be affected at the point of evaluation of

$$Y_i'Y_i - k\hat{V}_i'\hat{V}_i$$

if it merely means the shifting of a variable from the list of included to excluded (in the ith equation) predetermined variables, but they will be affected at a later stage of parameter estimation. If, however, the altered specification moves an excluded predetermined variable into or out of the whole system, then there is a differential affect on k-class and on OLS estimators.

Two single equation (or limited information) methods, TSLS and LIML, are not strictly comparable between themselves, but they should be less sensitive to specification error than are the full information methods, FIML or 3SLS. The full information methods require that the econometrician specify all the equations of the system in order to estimate just one. The single equation consistent methods require only the specification of the listing of predetermined variables in the system outside the one being estimated and do not require the parametric specification of the other equations of the system. It is in this sense that they are less sensitive than FIML or 3SLS to general specification error.

An error of aggregation may appear as a specification error. If it is desired to use a full information method in the estimation of a single equation or subgroup of equations, the complete system may be rounded out in a highly aggregative manner. It is the step of aggregation in using a rough, consolidated set of equations for completion of the system that leads to specification error.

Questions and Problems

1. Construct a model of two or more simultaneous equations that is nonlinear in variables and parameters. Justify the choice on specification of each nonlinear relationship in the system; discuss identification criteria; show how estimation will be carried out.

2. In the linear model

$$Ay_t + Bx_t = u_t,$$

assume that the first order serial correlation matrix P of the error process is known

$$u_t = Pu_{t-1} + e_t.$$

Show why estimation of A and B cannot be calculated simply from a linear model with transformed variables and new lags as compared with the original system.

3. Discuss the problem of serial dependence of error in an equation system as a problem of specification.

5. SAMPLING EXPERIMENTS

The concept of specification has been generally discussed in the preceding section. There are unlimited ways in which a model can be misspecified. A convenient way to study particular cases of misspecification is in sampling experiments. These experiments, sometimes called Monte Carlo studies, have wider use than the investigation of specification error. They are generally useful in gaining insight into a number of problems that appear to be intractable to a complete mathematical analysis. These problems might be outlined as follows:

1. Specification error, such as zero restrictions on coefficients that are not valid, other homogeneous linear restrictions on coefficients that are not valid, assumed absence of autocorrelation in errors when it is present, other restrictions on error covariance matrix that are not valid, assumptions of recursive structure when the system is interdependent, assumptions of normality for nonnormal disturbances, misclassification between endogenous and exogenous groupings, and so on.
2. Small sample properties of distributions of estimates.
3. Sampling properties of estimates in nonlinear systems.

This is not an exhaustive list of problems that may be investigated by Monte Carlo methods, but it covers a number of questions that have been taken up in recent studies.[7] Monte Carlo results, by their nature, deal only with limited questions and provide answers that can be applied only to the particular model treated. The inability to generalize is one of the drawbacks, yet they do provide enormous insight and are important tools of analysis in the computer age.

The general procedure can best be explained in terms of our standard linear model,

$$Ay_t + Bx_t = e_t. \tag{5.5.1}$$

A sample length is chosen, $t = 1, 2, \ldots, T$. For practical purposes of studying small sample properties, we should choose $T \leq 50$. This is a realistic bound for most samples dealing with annual time series or grouped cross-section data. Monthly and quarterly time series samples are frequently much larger, although they show evidence of strong serial correlation, thus cutting down the *effective* sample size. Cross-section samples of individual households may well be large, say $T \geq 1000$. Small sample investigations are not relevant in these instances.

The first step is to fix elements of A, B, and x_t at specified numerical values for the whole experiment. In a linear system A and B are constant matrices, and $x_1, x_2, \ldots, x_T$ is a sequence of vectors of exogenous variables that are to remain fixed in repeated samples. The exogenous variables may be arbitrarily chosen or they may be realistically selected from values of exogenous variables that have been used in actual models.

The next step is to choose vectors of random variables $e_1, e_2, \ldots, e_T$. These are independent random variables drawn from some specified probability distribution and having a given variance-covariance matrix.

With known A, B matrices, selected values of x_t and selected disturbances e_t, we can solve for y_t

$$y_t = -A^{-1}Bx_t + A^{-1}e_t. \tag{5.5.2}$$

[7] J. G. Cragg, "On the Relative Small-Sample Properties of Several Structural Equation Estimators: The Results of Some Monte Carlo Experiments," *Econometrica*, 35 (January, 1967) 89–110. "Some Effects of Incorrect Specification on the Small Sample Properties of Several Simultaneous-Equation Estimators," *International Economic Review*, 9 (February, 1968), 63–68. G. W. Ladd, "Effects of Shocks and Errors in Estimation: An Empirical Comparison," *Journal of Farm Economics*, 38 (May, 1956), 485–95; E. Malinvaud, "Estimation et Prévision dans les Modèles Économiques Autorégressifs," *Review of the International Institute of Statistics*, 29: 2 (1961), 1–32; A. L. Nagar, *Statistical Estimation of Simultaneous Economic Relationships*, (Rotterdam: Netherlands, School of Economics, 1959); W. A. Neiswanger and T. A. Yancey, "Parameter Estimates and Autonomous Growth," *Journal of the American Statistical Association*, 54 (June, 1959), 389–402; R. E. Quandt, "On Certain Small Sample Properties of *k*-Class Estimators," *International Economic Review*, 6 (January, 1965), 92–104; S. M. Goldfeld and R. E. Quandt, "Nonlinear Simultaneous Equations: Estimation and Prediction," *International Economic Review*, 9 (February, 1968), 113–36; R. Summers, "A Capital Intensive Approach to the Small Sample Properties of Various Simultaneous Equation Estimators," *Econometrica*, 33 (January, 1965), 1–41; H. M. Wagner, "A Monte Carlo Study of Estimates of Simultaneous Linear Structural Equations," *Econometrica*, 27 (January, 1958), 117–33.

This gives us a sample vector $y_1, y_2, \ldots, y_T$. The Monte Carlo practitioner now has a sample

$$\begin{matrix} y_{11} & \cdots & y_{n1} & x_{11} & \cdots & x_{m1} \\ y_{12} & & y_{n2} & x_{12} & & x_{m2} \\ \vdots & & \vdots & \vdots & & \vdots \\ y_{1T} & & y_{nT} & x_{1T} & & x_{mT}. \end{matrix}$$

He assumes that he does not know A, B (though he really does) and that he does not know e_t (though he really does). He is thus in the same position as the statistician in the usual case, who has samples of data for y_t, x_t and wants to estimate a set of unknown linear relationships associating them

$$Ay_t + Bx_t = e_t. \tag{5.5.1}$$

Let us denote the first such sample as $y_t^{(1)}$, $x_t^{(1)}$ and the associated estimates as $A^{(1)}, B^{(1)}$. This procedure can be repeated many times. On each repetition, x_t is kept fixed, but a fresh set of random errors is drawn from the same population—same distribution function and same variance-covariance matrix.

If this procedure is repeated r times, we have $A^{(1)}, A^{(2)}, \ldots, A^{(r)}$; $B^{(1)}, B^{(2)}, \ldots, B^{(r)}$ to compare with the true values A, B. Although these true values were known to the Monte Carlo statistician, he acted as though they were unknown. He thus *simulated* the role of the statistician in the usual situation, but because he really knows the true values he has a standard of comparison. The distribution of $A^{(j)}$ and $B^{(j)}$ with reference to the true values A and B give us analogues of sampling distributions from which we can measure bias or lack of precision in the estimates.

The theoretical model used by the mathematical statistician in developing formulas for

$$\begin{array}{l} E(\text{est. } A),\ E(\text{est. } B),\ \text{plim est. } A,\ \text{plim est. } B \\ \text{var (est. } A),\ \text{var (est. } B) \end{array}$$

are duplicated by the sampling experiment. The theoretical statistician *imagines* an indefinite repetition of the sampling process in which a whole distribution of est.A and est.B are constructed. In the theoretical model, the exogenous variables are fixed from sample to sample, and the errors are independently drawn anew.

In practice we cannot draw repeated samples, for we deal in almost all cases with nonexperimental data and have no opportunity to sample again and again. The computer, however, has permitted us to *simulate* this process and play a make-believe game. Because the e_t can be quickly generated, and from them the repeated samples

$$y_t = -A^{-1}Bx_t + A^{-1}e_t \tag{5.5.2}$$

can also be quickly generated, we can play this game in a short period of time. Without much difficulty, 100 or more samples can be generated ($r = 100$), and the distributions $A^{(1)}, A^{(2)}, \ldots, A^{(100)}; B^{(1)}, B^{(2)}, \ldots, B^{(100)}$ can be analyzed.

Let us consider the study by R. Summers.[8] This is one of the most comprehensive Monte Carlo studies and interests us for the light it throws on specification error as well as on small sample properties. His model, in his notation, is

$$\begin{aligned} \beta_{11}y_{1t} + \beta_{12}y_{2t} + \gamma_{11}z_{1t} + \gamma_{12}z_{2t} + \gamma_{10} &= u_{1t} \\ \beta_{21}y_{1t} + \beta_{22}y_{2t} + \gamma_{23}z_{3t} + \gamma_{24}z_{4t} + \gamma_{20} &= u_{2t}. \end{aligned} \tag{5.5.3}$$

Normalization fixes $\beta_{11} = 1$ and $\beta_{21} = 1$. In both equations, therefore, we have y_1 dependent on y_2 and some exogenous variables. Two points deserve comment at this stage. (1) There are two zero coefficients (of exogenous variables) in each equation. We therefore have necessary conditions for overidentification in this model. (2) With the coefficient of y_{1t} made unity, by normalization in each equation we rule out such methods as Wold's iterative least squares procedure, for that method requires that the unit coefficient be associated with a different variable in each equation.[9]

This model could be a supply-demand model or a savings-investment model (among others). It could, for example, be considered as a representation of the process

$$\begin{aligned} \text{Demand} &= f(\text{price, exogenous variables}) + u_1 \\ \text{Supply} &= g(\text{price, exogenous variables}) + u_2 \\ \text{Supply} &= \text{Demand}. \end{aligned} \tag{5.5.4}$$

The actual signs chosen for β_{12} and β_{22} make it like a supply-demand model instead of a savings-investment model.

The sampling statistician in an experiment can "play God;" that is, he can fix the true values of the parameters.

In the standard experiment, Summers fixed

$$\begin{aligned} \beta_{12} &= -7; \gamma_{11} = .8; \gamma_{12} = .7; \gamma_{10} = -149.5 \\ \beta_{22} &= .4; \gamma_{23} = .6; \gamma_{24} = -.4; \gamma_{20} = -149.6. \end{aligned}$$

In variations of this standard experiment, β_{12} was raised and lowered to -0.1 and -1.3 respectively; otherwise, these parameter values were used throughout.

The identifying restrictions are

$$\begin{aligned} \gamma_{13} &= 0; \gamma_{14} = 0 \\ \gamma_{21} &= 0; \gamma_{22} = 0. \end{aligned}$$

[8] Summers, "Small Sample Properties of ... Estimators," *Econometrica*, (1965).

[9] Summers' study was formulated before Wold's method was developed.

The misspecification experiments change γ_{21} to 0.5 and -0.5. These are the true experimental values, but the statistician then proceeds as though they were zero. This is the extent of the misspecification.

In one group of experiments, z_1, z_2, z_3, z_4 were chosen as realistic time series of exogenous variables from an econometric study, and in another group, these variables were scrambled but their means and variances were kept constant. The resulting scrambled series had no special economic meaning, but they were nearly mutually orthogonal. In the set of experiments using realistic z-series with significant trends, the intercorrelations among z_i and z_j were non-negligible. The effect of such multicollinearity is a phenomenon well worth investigating.

The remaining model specifications were the choice of random disturbances. These were chosen so as to have given variances and covariances

$$\sigma_{u_1}^2 = 400; \; \sigma_{u_2}^2 = 400; \; \sigma_{u_1u_2} = 200.$$

If the errors are chosen from a unit normal distribution, we can scale them to have a given variance by multiplying each sample element by a constant. If

$$\sigma^2 = 1$$

for each unit normal $e_{11}, e_{12}, \ldots, e_{1T}$, then

$$\sigma_{u_1}^2 = 400$$

for

$$u_{1t} = 20\, e_{1t}.$$

If we were to choose independently another run of T unit normal variables with variance = 400 by the same method, we would not have

$$\sigma_{u_1u_2} = 200;$$

it would be

$$\sigma_{u_1u_2} = 0.$$

Our problem, therefore, is the following: Find a and b such that

$$\begin{aligned} \text{var}(ae_{1t} + be_{2t}) &= 400 \\ \text{cov}[20e_{1t}(ae_{1t} + be_{2t})] &= 200. \end{aligned} \tag{5.5.5}$$

This gives us

$$\begin{aligned} a^2 + b^2 &= 400 \\ 20a &= 200 \end{aligned} \tag{5.5.6}$$

or

$$a = 10; b = 10\sqrt{3}. \tag{5.5.7}$$

This method can easily be generalized to the selection of a variance-covariance matrix of any size with specified entries for the diagonal and off-diagonal elements.[10] To avoid singularity problems, we should have $T > n$, where n is the number of stochastic equations.

The sampling characteristics of the Monte Carlo model require the choice of a sample size and the number of sampling repetitions. In order to have a reliable sampling distribution of estimates, the sample drawings should be repeated many times. Summers had fifty replications, and this is surely a minimal number. Sample size for any given replication should be representative of small sample studies in econometrics. In time series analysis of advanced countries, we used to deal frequently with twenty annual observations between World Wars I and II. Now we deal with eighty quarterly observations, postwar, or one hundred to two hundred monthly observations. Our annual samples are frequently as large as thirty. In building models for less developed countries, we often have to try to make inferences from samples of ten to fifteen postwar annual observations. Summers' samples were twenty and forty. These are representative of much small sample time series work, although in many cases we are dealing with samples in the range fifty to one hundred.

There are essentially three kinds of statistical studies of estimates from alternative methods made in the Summers study. These are (1) normality of the distributions of coefficients, (2) prediction tests of the estimated models, (3) comparison of means and standard deviations of coefficient estimates. The methods compared are

OLS	ordinary least squares
LSNR	least squares (reduced forms) no restrictions
TSLS	two stage least squares
LISE	limited information single equation (LIML)
FIML	full information maximum likelihood.

Summers found that LISE and TSLS estimates were, in almost all cases, acceptable normal variates, but OLS estimates generally were not. Tests for normality were not made for FIML estimates and the LSNR estimates were made only for reduced forms.

Although we find an undoubtedly superior performance of LISE and TSLS estimates over OLS estimates in tests of normality of distributions of coefficients, there are two notable characteristics of situations in which the two consistent estimators depart from normality. (1) In the misspecification experiments, the coefficients in the misspecified equation show decided departures from normality. (2) In the experiments with high collinearity among predetermined variables,

[10] A. L. Nagar, "Stochastic Simulation of the Brookings Econometric Model," *The Brookings Model: Some Further Results*, ed. J. Duesenberry et al., (Chicago: Rand McNally, 1969). See Chap. VII for another method of drawing random disturbances that avoids the restriction $T > n$.

all methods perform *worse* than in the experiments with more nearly orthogonal predetermined variables.

The upshot of this part of the testing is that we must be extremely cautious in making probability statements about results based on OLS estimates in situations where we do not have

$$E(z_t u_t) = 0,$$

for the exogenous variables, z_t, and random errors, u_t. The point estimates may look reasonable and the computed sampling errors may look relatively small, but if they are not normally distributed we are not in a position to say how good these estimates are in a probability sense nor to test the point *values* against alternatives.

It is difficult to summarize the performance of a whole system that contains many parameters. A significant summary picture is given, however, by a comparison among methods of prediction performance. In a big system with many endogenous variables, forecast performance is not unambiguous because the results may change from variable to variable, but in Summers' model it is relatively easy to summarize performance characteristics of the whole set of parameter estimates by looking at prediction accuracy. In paired comparisons, it is clear that the OLS method yields poorer predictions than do the others. The relative performance of FIML is mixed, sometimes showing better performance than TSLS or LISE, and sometimes worse. These latter two methods are also mixed in their relative performance. On a pure count of superior performances measured by *root mean square error*, we might be inclined to rank methods in this order:

Preferred FIML
TSLS
LISE
LSNR
OLS.

The evidence, however, is far from being conclusive. A point to be stressed is that FIML estimates were not sensitive enough to the specification errors introduced to throw off predictions of y_{1t} and y_{2t}. It performed as well in the misspecification experiments as in the others. Its stability of performance in terms of prediction was stronger than its stability in terms of individual coefficient estimation.[11]

The minimum variance property of OLS estimators showed up clearly in Summers' estimates of distributions of individual coefficients. If we denote the

[11] In the misspecification experiments of Cragg, "... Effects of Incorrect Specification," *International Economic Review*, (1968), he found greatest sensitivity in the estimates of the misspecified equations and greater sensitivity for FIML than for single equation estimators. He found substantial effects on reduced form parameters.

OLS estimate of β_{ij} by b_{ij}, we find

$$\frac{1}{R}\sum_{r=1}^{R}(b_{ij}^{(r)} - \bar{b}_{ij})^2 = \text{min},$$

where there are R replications, $r = 1, 2, \ldots, R$. But the root mean square error statistic does not have this property if the squared deviations are computed about the true values of the coefficients.

$$\frac{1}{R}\sum_{r=1}^{R}(b_{ij}^{(r)} - \beta_{ij})^2 \neq \text{min}.$$

The two measures are related in the identity

$$\frac{1}{R}\sum_{r=1}^{R}(b_{ij}^{(r)} - \bar{b}_{ij})^2 = \frac{1}{R}\sum_{r=1}^{R}(b_{ij}^{(r)} - \beta_{ij})^2 - (\beta_{ij} - \bar{b}_{ij})^2. \qquad (5.5.8)$$

They differ by a measure of bias

$$(\beta_{ij} - \bar{b}_{ij})^2;$$

thus, the RMSE statistic is one that combines both efficiency and bias. If the variance of OLS estimators is sufficiently small to compensate for its bias, this fact should show up in a RMSE. In fact, however, its RMSE is generally large in Summers' tabulations. This indicates that in spite of its minimal variance property, it is so strongly biased that its RMSE about the true values is larger than the RMSE of consistent methods. All the methods are biased in small samples, but the bias of OLS estimate are the largest, and so much larger that they cause the RMSE of OLS estimates to be the largest of the group considered.

The Monte Carlo study by Summers deals with the small sample properties of a linear system. It, together with the other Monte Carlo studies cited, deals with some cases of specification error and multicollinearity. The major reason for using the Monte Carlo method in these studies was to reduce otherwise intractable problems to manageable proportions. We know very little about the properties of nonlinear systems, especially small sample properties; therefore, the sampling experiments of Goldfeld and Quandt are particularly interesting.[12] It is difficult to obtain point estimates for some nonlinear models in single samples. It is particularly welcome to have a look at properties of a nonlinear model in repeated samples. Goldfeld and Quandt consider two models:

$$\text{(I)} \quad \beta_{11}\log y_{1t} + \beta_{12}\log y_{2t} + \gamma_{11}z_t + \gamma_{10} = u_{1t}$$
$$\beta_{21}y_{1t} + \beta_{22}y_{2t} + \gamma_{21}z_t = u_{2t}$$

[12] Goldfeld and Quandt, "Nonlinear Simultaneous Equations . . . ," *International Economic Review*, (1968).

and

$$\text{(II)}\quad \beta_{11}y_{1t} + \beta_{12}y_{2t}^2 + \gamma_{11}z_t + \gamma_{10} = u_{1t}$$
$$\beta_{21}y_{1t}z_t + \beta_{22}y_{2t} + \gamma_{20} = u_{2t}.$$

The nonlinearities are special in these two models because they are linear in the parameters. It is obvious how OLS estimates could be made. With normalization, $\beta_{11} = \beta_{22} = 1$, in both models, we would regress:

$\log y_{1t}$ on $\log y_{2t}$ and z_t
y_{2t} on y_{1t} and z_t (constant term zero)
y_{1t} on y_{2t}^2 and z_t
y_{2t} on $y_{1t}z_t$.

We could form FIML estimates from the joint density function of u_{1t} and u_{2t}, taking into account dependence on the sample values of the data.

$$\text{(I)}\quad \left|\frac{\partial(u_{1t}, u_{2t})}{\partial(y_{1t}, y_{2t})}\right| = \begin{vmatrix} \dfrac{1}{y_{1t}} & \dfrac{\beta_{12}}{y_{2t}} \\ \beta_{21} & 1 \end{vmatrix}$$

$$\text{(II)}\quad \left|\frac{\partial(u_{1t}, u_{2t})}{\partial(y_{1t}, y_{2t})}\right| = \begin{vmatrix} 1 & 2\beta_{12}y_{2t} \\ \beta_{21}z_t & 1 \end{vmatrix}.$$

The concept of TSLS or LISE estimation in a nonlinear model is more complicated. A central concept for these methods is the reduced form. In a linear system, we have an explicit expression

$$y_t = -B^{-1}\Gamma z_t + B^{-1}u_t \tag{5.5.9}$$

or

$$y_t = \prod z_t + v_t. \tag{5.5.10}$$

For given z_t and u_t, we can compute explicit values of y_t if B^{-1} exists. This was Summers' procedure in his Monte Carlo experiment. In a nonlinear system, though, it is generally necessary to obtain approximate values of y_t, given z_t and u_t. In nonlinear models, there may be no solution in closed form. This is the case in model (I) of Goldfeld and Quandt.

The difficulty here, from a statistical viewpoint, even if close numerical values can be obtained, is that we cannot assume that y_t is made up of two parts, a nonstochastic value

$$-B^{-1}\Gamma z_t$$

and a random part

$$B^{-1}u_t.$$

The technique of TSLS, we have seen, is to replace values of y_t in a regression by estimates of their nonstochastic component, say

$$\hat{y}_t = Pz_t, \tag{5.5.11}$$

where P is a matrix of reduced form regression coefficients. In the process of solution of a set of nonlinear equations for computed values of y_t, the error terms get scrambled into the final result in what may be a complicated form. We cannot generally interpret solutions of reduced forms in nonlinear systems as $\hat{y}_t$, purged of random error.

If a closed form expression existed for dependent variables as functions of independent variables, these reduced forms may be nonlinear in both parameters and variables. Goldfeld and Quandt treat them as nonlinear functions of the independent variables and make polynomial approximations as functions of the powers of the independent variables. They use first and second degree polynomials, corresponding to a first order and a second order Taylor's Series expansion. These are denoted as TSLS1 and TSLS2. The second stage of the TSLS procedure is carried out in the usual way. One dependent variable is regressed on the computed values of the other dependent variables and the independent variables of that equation.

As we noted previously, Chernoff and Rubin suggest another procedure for systems that are linear in parameters but nonlinear in variables.[13] They redefine nonlinear functions of variables as new endogenous variables if they contain any endogenous arguments and proceed to use single equation methods of estimation applicable to incomplete systems. For system (I), they would define

$$\log y_{1t} = y^*_{1t}; \log y_{2t} = y^*_{2t}$$

and rewrite the equations as

$$\begin{aligned} \beta_{11}y^*_{1t} + \beta_{12}y^*_{2t} + \gamma_{11}z_t + \gamma_{10} &= u_{1t} \\ \beta_{21}y_{1t} + \beta_{22}y_{2t} + \gamma_{21}z_t &= u_{2t}. \end{aligned} \tag{5.5.12}$$

Correspondingly, their transformation of (II) would be

$$\begin{aligned} \beta_{11}y_{1t} + \beta_{12}y^*_{2t} + \gamma_{11}z_t + \gamma_{10} &= u_{1t} \\ \beta_{21}y^*_{1t} + \beta_{22}y_{2t} + \gamma_{20} &= u_t \end{aligned} \tag{5.5.13}$$

where

$$y_{1t}z_t = y^*_{1t}; y^2_{2t} = y^*_{2t}.$$

If there were no other predetermined variables, the pseudo reduced forms

[13] Chernoff and Rubin, "Asymptotic Properties of Limited-Information Estimates . . . ," in *Studies in Econometric Method.*

for either system could be expressed as

$$\begin{aligned} y_{1t} &= \pi_1 z_t + \pi_{10} + v_{1t} \\ y_{2t} &= \pi_2 z_t + \pi_{20} + v_{2t} \\ y^*_{1t} &= \pi^*_1 z_t + \pi^*_{10} + v^*_{1t} \\ y^*_{2t} &= \pi^*_2 z_t + \pi^*_{20} + v^*_{2t}. \end{aligned} \tag{5.5.14}$$

The structure of the Goldfeld-Quandt model is such that the Chernoff-Rubin methods can be used only for the second equation in each model. In the first equation of model (I) (5.5.12), a second stage regression of y^*_{1t} on $\hat{y}^*_{2t}$ and z_t would be indeterminate because $\hat{y}^*_{2t}$ is, by construction, a linear function of z_t. There is an added restriction in the second equation of (I) (5.5.12), namely, a specification that the constant term is zero. This would permit regression of y_{2t} on $\hat{y}_{1t}$ and z_t as long as the estimate of π_{10} does not vanish.

We have a similar problem in (II) (5.5.13). A regression of y_{1t} on $\hat{y}^*_{2t}$ and z_t in the second stage estimation of the first equation involves us in collinearity between a linear function of $z_t(\hat{y}^*_{2t})$ and z_t. In the second equation of (5.5.13), we would regress y_{2t} on $\hat{y}^*_{1t}$. This involves no singularity or indeterminancy. If there were sufficient predetermined variables in the whole system and enough restrictions on each equation, the Chernoff-Rubin methods could be used, provided the system were linear in parameters.

The sampling experiments of Goldfeld and Quandt yield the following rankings:

Model I (parameter estimation)[14]		Model II (parameter estimation and prediction)	
preferred	TSLS1	preferred	FIML
	FIML		TSLS2
	TSLS2		OLS.
	OLS		

For model (I), they do not present prediction tests, and for model (II) they use only second order approximation for the reduced forms. They encountered computational difficulties with the first order approximations. Indeed, these are the same difficulties that give rise to singularities in the application of the Chernoff-Rubin methods.

Their test statistics and method of testing was much like that of Summers. In view of the difficulty in interpreting reduced form calculations in nonlinear systems, we might pay less attention to the variants of TSLS methods and focus on the aspect of their results that show the superiority of FIML over OLS

[14] The authors present numerical results for TSLS1 in Model I, but according to their description of this method they should have had collinearity (except for rounding error) in the second stage of TSLS calculations.

estimation in this type of nonlinear situation. If we are fairly confident about model specification, the FIML method seems to be more straightforward in nonlinear systems.

There is no end to sampling experimentation. Ingenuity of individual investigators will inject new procedures into future studies of this type. Many more questions will be tackled by this method. We might sum up this approach by saying that small sample procedures, by and large, should follow the lead that can be analytically established for large samples.

Malinvaud has shown that lagged endogenous variables in regression equations may seriously bias the tests for serial correlation of residuals.[15] This is a useful negative result to have from a Monte Carlo study. On the other hand, Ladd's results suggest that relative rankings of estimation methods may not be changed if exogenous variables are subject to error.[16] For the most part, the results of sampling experiments are comforting. In simulation studies, to be taken up in a later chapter, they may make more positive contributions to econometric practice.

Questions and Problems

1. List additional specification errors whose effects can be studied by Monte Carlo Methods and describe the sampling experiments that you would devise for making such studies.

2. In a sampling experiment, we have replication of the matrices

$$A^{(r)} = (\alpha_{ij}^{(r)}); \; B^{(r)} = (\beta_{ij}(r))$$

from which frequency distributions of individual parameter estimates are constructed. What would be relevant *joint* frequency distributions and statistics from such *joint* distributions that would be useful in judging the results of the experiments?

3. Explain how sampling experiments could be used to study the validity of asymptotic estimates of sampling error calculations for different methods of econometric estimation.

SUGGESTED READINGS

Bentzel, R. and H. Wold, "On Statistical Demand Analysis from the Viewpoint of Simultaneous Equations," *Skandinavisk Aktuarietidskrift*, 29 (1946), 95–114. The original discussion of the recursive case in econometric systems.

[15] Malinvaud, "Estimation et Prévision dans les Modèles Économiques . . . ," *Review of . . . Statistics.*

[16] Ladd, ". . . Errors in Estimation . . . ," *Farm Economics.*

Cragg, J., "On the Relative Small Sample Properties of Several Structural Equation Estimators: The Results of Some Monte Carlo Experiments," *Econometrica*, 35 (January, 1967), 89–110. Studies sensitivity of rankings among estimators to design of sampling experiments.

Eisenpress, H. and J. Greenstadt, "The Estimation of Nonlinear Econometric Systems," *Econometrica*, 34, (October, 1966), 851–61. Designs computation procedures for FIML estimation of nonlinear econometric systems.

Fisher, F. M., "Dynamic Structure and Estimation in Economy-Wide Econometric Models," *The Brookings Quarterly Econometric Model of the United States*, ed. J. Duesenberry et. al., Chicago: Rand McNally, (1965). Generalizes estimation methods for recursive systems to block-recursive systems.

Ladd, G. W., "Effects of Shocks and Errors in Estimation: An Empirical Comparison," *Journal of Farm Economics*, 38 (May, 1956), 485–95. Constructs a sampling experiment for estimation in the case where variables are subject to measurement error.

Summers, R., "A Capital Intensive Approach to the Small Sample Properties of Various Simultaneous Equation Estimators," *Econometrica*, 33 (January, 1965), 1–41. An extraordinarily well designed sampling experiment that is comprehensive and deep.

6

Applications in Macroeconomics

The preceding chapters have dealt at length with statistical inference and methods of estimating economic relationships. At this stage, we shall pause in our discussion of econometric methodology and look at some realistic applications of the ideas taken up in the preceding chapters. Econometric techniques can be applied in a transparent way to very small models, but these are hardly realistic or useful in a wide range of applications. At the other extreme, we have large systems of equations that try to explain macroeconomic activity with a hundred or more relationships. These large detailed models require a whole volume to explain and, for this reason, are not well suited for explaining the use of the techniques that we desire to demonstrate. We, therefore, turn to a model of moderate size, based on annual time series. The macroeconomic system that will serve here as a demonstration model is an updated and slightly extended version of the Klein-Goldberger model—a system that has undergone extensive trials in forecasting, simulating business cycles, and multiplier analysis. It is a well-understood and well-documented system in this sense.

1. ESTIMATES OF THE KLEIN-GOLDBERGER (REVISED) MODEL

The model contains sixteen stochastic equations. These are equations with unknown coefficients, to be estimated from sample data, and subject to shock by an additive random error. In addition, there are four identities. These are social accounting relationships that must balance as a result of our national bookkeeping system. Taxes, transfers, and social insurance contributions are treated as exogenous variables in estimation of the model. Over the course of the sample period, 1929–41 and 1947–64, legislative and administrative policies of public authorities have changed markedly. Although each of these variables has a systematic relationship with overall measures of economic activity that are included among the endogenous variables of the model as long as a given policy is in effect, they have no such stable relationship to endogenous variables of the model over a longer period that spans many eras of policy decision. In estimation, therefore, we have treated these variables as being under exogenous influence, but in application of the estimated model we shall take into account the relationships governing these variables, as though they were endogenous, for groups of years within which relationships remained stable.

The economic rationale of this model is explained in other books; so attention will be focused here on the mathematical, rather than the economic, structure.[1] First, it should be noted that the model is nonlinear. Some of the relationships have been modified so as to eliminate nonlinearities where this is convenient. For example, price differences rather than price ratios have been used, and the production function of the model has been stated in linear form. Given that the accounting identities are in current prices (as they should be) and that the main relationships of the model are in constant prices, the system as a whole is not linear in all the variables involved. Each individual stochastic equation is linear in the unknown parameters. In single equation methods, the estimation problem is one that is applicable to linear models, but for FIML estimation the nonlinearity in variables, even in the presence of linearity of parameters, equation by equation, gives rise to complications in estimation. The Jacobian determinant associating the space of disturbances with the space of dependent variables is not constant.[2] FIML estimation equations are nonlinear even if the underlying model is linear, but they are somewhat more difficult to solve if they are determined for a system that is nonlinear.

The estimation theory of Chaps. 4 and 5 are basically developed for the general linear model

$$Ay_t + Bx_t = e_t,$$

where A and B are matrices of constant coefficients. In general, this is not a suitable model for the whole economy, as there are fundamental nonlinearities involved in any realistic macro model. The simplest of these are present in the formulation of the Klein-Goldberger model treated here. Additional nonlinearities would arise from price ratios, saturation levels of some variables, and production functions with diminishing marginal productivity.

[1] The original model is explained in L. R. Klein and A. S. Goldberger, *An Econometric Model of the United States, 1929–1952* (Amsterdam: North-Holland Publishing Co., 1955). The updated and extended version is explained in L. R. Klein, *The Keynesian Revolution*, 2nd ed. (New York: Macmillan, 1965), Chap. 8. See also L. R. Klein, "Problems in the Estimation of Interdependent Systems," in *Model Building in the Human Sciences*, ed. H. Wold (Monaco: Union Européenne d'Éditions, 1967).

[2] This property of the system is like that in the small model of Goldfeld and Quandt studied in the preceding chapter.

The model has been estimated by several methods, three of which are presented here—OLS, TSLS(4), and FIML. The notation TSLS(4) denotes *two stage least squares based on four principal components.*[3] Other numbers of principal components were also used for TSLS estimation. Our analysis here will be concentrated on TSLS(4) because they seem to simulate the model better than TSLS based on larger numbers of principal components.

The equation system estimated by these three methods is given below, followed by a list of variables with their definition. The first thirteen equations have been estimated by all three methods, which are separately listed, but the next three are already in a reduced form, containing only one dependent variable; therefore they have been estimated as single equation least squares regressions. The coefficients by each method are listed in fixed order in front of each associated coefficient. The estimated t-ratio is given in parentheses below each coefficient.

REVISED KLEIN-GOLDBERGER MODEL
(*Annual Observations; 1929–41, 1947–64*)[4]

(6.1.1) Consumption function (durables)

$$C_d - .7(C_d)_{-1} = \begin{bmatrix} .239 \\ (6.6) \\ .231 \\ (4.5) \\ .094 \\ (1.5) \end{bmatrix} (Y - .7Y_{-1}) - \begin{bmatrix} .121 \\ (1.6) \\ .104 \\ (1.0) \\ -.182 \\ (1.5) \end{bmatrix} (C_d)_{-1} - \begin{bmatrix} .475 \\ (4.7) \\ .462 \\ (3.7) \\ .228 \\ (1.5) \end{bmatrix} \qquad \begin{matrix} \text{Se} \\ .178 \\ \\ .178 \\ \\ .225 \\ \end{matrix}$$

(6.1.2) Consumption function (nondurables)

$$C_n = \begin{bmatrix} .332 \\ (6.5) \\ .250 \\ (4.0) \\ .232 \\ (5.9) \end{bmatrix} Y + \begin{bmatrix} .616 \\ (9.2) \\ .723 \\ (8.9) \\ .740 \\ (14.2) \end{bmatrix} (C_n)_{-1} - \begin{bmatrix} .378 \\ (0.3) \\ 1.17 \\ (0.8) \\ .296 \\ (0.2) \end{bmatrix} \qquad \begin{matrix} 2.44 \\ \\ 2.55 \\ \\ 2.62 \\ \\ \end{matrix}$$

(6.1.3) Investment function (residential)

$$R = \begin{bmatrix} .059 \\ (7.0) \\ .047 \\ (5.6) \\ .056 \\ (7.3) \end{bmatrix} Y - \begin{bmatrix} .035 \\ (1.7) \\ .046 \\ (2.1) \\ .005 \\ (0.2) \end{bmatrix} r_{-1} + \begin{bmatrix} .252 \\ (2.4) \\ .398 \\ (3.8) \\ .314 \\ (3.0) \end{bmatrix} R_{-1} - \begin{bmatrix} 2.640 \\ (1.9) \\ 1.228 \\ (0.9) \\ 3.975 \\ (3.6) \end{bmatrix} \qquad \begin{matrix} 1.07 \\ \\ 1.11 \\ \\ 1.13 \\ \\ \end{matrix}$$

[3] The FIML estimation was done by Mr. H. Eisenpress of the IBM Corporation, based on a computer program for nonlinear equation systems. The TSLS (4) estimation was done by Dr. M. Norman, then of the University of Pennsylvania.

[4] The data on which these estimates are based are largely the official national accounting series of the U.S. Department of Commerce, prior to the revisions of August, 1965.

(6.1.4) Investment function (inventories)

$$H = \begin{bmatrix} .130 \\ (6.5) \\ .134 \\ (6.1) \\ .191 \\ (9.1) \end{bmatrix} (X - \Delta H) + \begin{bmatrix} .426 \\ (4.5) \\ .405 \\ (3.9) \\ .147 \\ (1.5) \end{bmatrix} H_{-1} - \begin{bmatrix} 23.5 \\ (6.2) \\ 24.3 \\ (5.7) \\ 35.2 \\ (8.8) \end{bmatrix} \qquad \begin{matrix} \text{Se} \\ 2.39 \\ \\ 2.39 \\ \\ 2.76 \end{matrix}$$

(6.1.5) Import demand function

$$I_m = \begin{bmatrix} .027 \\ (4.7) \\ .033 \\ (4.4) \\ .023 \\ (3.3) \end{bmatrix} X - \begin{bmatrix} .087 \\ (2.7) \\ .166 \\ (3.5) \\ .061 \\ (2.2) \end{bmatrix} (p_m - p) + \begin{bmatrix} .480 \\ (3.8) \\ .348 \\ (2.1) \\ .583 \\ (3.9) \end{bmatrix} (I_m)_{-1} - \begin{bmatrix} .901 \\ (2.0) \\ 1.21 \\ (2.3) \\ .800 \\ (1.8) \end{bmatrix} \qquad \begin{matrix} .914 \\ \\ 1.02 \\ \\ .918 \end{matrix}$$

(6.1.6) Production function

$$X - W_g - .95(X - W_g)_{-1} = \begin{bmatrix} .269 \\ (3.6) \\ .334 \\ (2.9) \\ .199 \\ (1.8) \end{bmatrix} (I + R)$$

$$+ \begin{bmatrix} 5.05 \\ (5.7) \\ 2.24 \\ (0.8) \\ 5.47 \\ (2.9) \end{bmatrix} [(N_w - N_g + N_s) - .95(N_w - N_g + N_s)_{-1}]$$

$$+ \begin{bmatrix} .929 \\ (2.5) \\ 1.88 \\ (1.9) \\ 1.65 \\ (2.4) \end{bmatrix} (h - .95h_{-1}) - \begin{bmatrix} 6.81 \\ (2.3) \\ 5.86 \\ (1.5) \\ 8.97 \\ (1.9) \end{bmatrix} \qquad \begin{matrix} 6.62 \\ \\ 7.90 \\ \\ 7.15 \end{matrix}$$

(6.1.7) Hours worked function

$$h = \begin{bmatrix} .331 \\ (6.2) \\ .405 \\ (2.5) \\ 1.61 \\ (0.7) \end{bmatrix} (w - w_{-1}) - \begin{bmatrix} 1.75 \\ (11.2) \\ 1.83 \\ (4.0) \\ 4.72 \\ (0.8) \end{bmatrix} (N_L - N_W - N_S) + \begin{bmatrix} 1.13 \\ (82.0) \\ 1.14 \\ (27.3) \\ 1.43 \\ (2.5) \end{bmatrix} \qquad \begin{matrix} .020 \\ \\ .021 \\ \\ .043 \end{matrix}$$

(6.1.8) Labor demand function (wage share)

$$W - W_g = \begin{bmatrix} .422 \\ (18.4) \\ .496 \\ (11.9) \\ .351 \\ (11.3) \end{bmatrix} (X - W_g) + \begin{bmatrix} .266 \\ (6.3) \\ .131 \\ (11.7) \\ .394 \\ (7.0) \end{bmatrix} (W - W_g)_{-1} - \begin{bmatrix} 10.8 \\ (10.6) \\ 12.5 \\ (8.7) \\ 8.88 \\ (7.3) \end{bmatrix} \qquad \begin{matrix} 1.86 \\ \\ 2.17 \\ \\ 2.15 \end{matrix}$$

(6.1.9) Wage rate determination equation

$$w - w_{-1} = -\begin{bmatrix} 1.42 \\ (3.3) \\ 2.18 \\ (3.5) \\ 2.16 \\ (5.2) \end{bmatrix}(N_L - N_W - N_S) + \begin{bmatrix} 1.32 \\ (2.6) \\ .679 \\ (1.1) \\ .252 \\ (0.6) \end{bmatrix}(p - p_{-1}) + \begin{bmatrix} 1.66 \\ (5.4) \\ 2.16 \\ (5.1) \\ .221 \\ (7.9) \end{bmatrix} \qquad \begin{matrix} \text{Se} \\ .063 \\ .066 \\ .068 \end{matrix}$$

(6.1.10) Interest rate structure equation

$$r = \begin{bmatrix} .172 \\ (3.4) \\ .169 \\ (3.0) \\ .129 \\ (3.6) \end{bmatrix} r_s + \begin{bmatrix} .830 \\ (12.7) \\ .812 \\ (12.0) \\ .810 \\ (15.3) \end{bmatrix} r_{-1} + \begin{bmatrix} .320 \\ (1.2) \\ .402 \\ (1.5) \\ .498 \\ (2.7) \end{bmatrix} \qquad \begin{matrix} .356 \\ .357 \\ .362 \end{matrix}$$

(6.1.11) Corporate savings function

$$pS_c = \begin{bmatrix} .880 \\ (28.7) \\ .901 \\ (25.1) \\ .765^* \\ (13.0) \end{bmatrix}(pP_c - T_c) - \begin{bmatrix} .855 \\ (13.3) \\ .889 \\ (12.1) \\ .592^* \\ (5.0) \end{bmatrix}(pP_c - T_c - pS_c)_{-1} + \begin{bmatrix} .020 \\ (0.1) \\ .024 \\ (0.1) \\ -.407^* \\ (0.7) \end{bmatrix} \qquad \begin{matrix} .630 \\ .636 \\ 1.83^* \end{matrix}$$

(6.1.12) Noncorporate income equation

$$p(\Pi - P_c) = \begin{bmatrix} .013 \\ (1.7) \\ .010 \\ (1.3) \\ .001 \\ (0.1) \end{bmatrix} pX + \begin{bmatrix} .878 \\ (10.8) \\ .909 \\ (11.3) \\ .998 \\ (9.07) \end{bmatrix}[p(\Pi - P_c)]_{-1} + \begin{bmatrix} .744 \\ (0.9) \\ .627 \\ (0.7) \\ .354 \\ (0.4) \end{bmatrix} \qquad \begin{matrix} 2.22 \\ 2.22 \\ 2.31 \end{matrix}$$

(6.1.13) Rent income equation

$$p\Pi_r = \begin{bmatrix} .062 \\ (6.8) \\ .075 \\ (5.5) \\ -.026 \\ (1.4) \end{bmatrix} p(I + R) + \begin{bmatrix} -.024 \\ (1.1) \\ -.108 \\ (1.9) \\ .377 \\ (3.1) \end{bmatrix}(r - r_{-1}) + \begin{bmatrix} .937 \\ (38.2) \\ .913 \\ (26.9) \\ 1.11 \\ (25.4) \end{bmatrix}(p\Pi_r)_{-1} - \begin{bmatrix} .387 \\ (2.1) \\ .472 \\ (2.0) \\ -.102 \\ (0.3) \end{bmatrix} \qquad \begin{matrix} .488 \\ .615 \\ 1.92 \end{matrix}$$

(6.1.14) Investment function (nonresidential)

$$I - .95I_{-1} = \underset{(4.2)}{.066}\,(X - W_g)_{-1} - \underset{(3.8)}{2.11}r_{-1} - .590I_{-1} + \underset{(3.1)}{9.329} \qquad 2.54$$

(6.1.15) Depreciation equation

$$D = \underset{(39.4)}{.049} \sum_{i=1}^{20} [p(I + R)]_{-i} + \underset{(13.5)}{8.56}\, Du - 1.411 \qquad 1.32$$

(6.1.16) Interest rate determination equation

$$r_s = \underset{(13.9)}{1.145}r_d - \underset{(2.4)}{.815}(R_e)_{-1} + \underset{(2.9)}{.533}Du - \underset{(1.7)}{.511} \qquad .370$$

* In the data preparation for FIML estimation, inventory valuation adjustment was not included in the calculation of corporate savings.

(6.1.17) Definition of real GNP

$$X = C_d + C_n + I + R + (H - H_{-1}) + G + E - Im$$

(6.1.18) National income and product identity

$$pY = pX - D - T_i - pS_c - T_c - T$$

(6.1.19) Definition of profit

$$p\Pi = pX - D = T_i - pW - p\Pi_r$$

(6.1.20) Wage identity

$$pW = whN_w$$

Variables

$^*C_d$	Consumption of durables, billions of 1954 dollars.
$^*Y$	Personal disposable income, billions of 1954 dollars.
$^*C_n$	Consumption of nondurables and services, billions of 1954 dollars.
$^*I$	Investment in plant and equipment, billions of 1954 dollars.
$^*X$	Gross national product, billions of 1954 dollars.
W_g	Government wages and salaries, billions of 1954 dollars.
$^*r$	Average yield on corporate bonds (Moody's), percent.
$^*R$	Residential construction, billions of 1954 dollars.
$^*r_s$	Yield on prime commercial paper, 4-6 months, percent.
$^*H$	Stock of inventories, billions of 1954 dollars.
$^*I_m$	Imports, billions of 1954 dollars.
p_m	Implicit price deflator for imports, 1954 = 1.00.
$^*N_w$	Wage and salary workers, millions.
N_g	Government employees, millions.
N_s	Self-employed workers, millions.
$^*h$	Index of hours worked per week, 1954 = 1.00.
$^*W$	Wages and salaries and supplements to wages and salaries, billions of 1954 dollars.
$^*w$	Annual earnings, thousands of dollars.
N_L	Total labor force, millions.
$^*p$	Implicit price deflator for GNP, 1954 = 1.00.
$^*S_c$	Corporate savings including inventory valuation adjustment, billions of 1954 dollars.
$^*P_c$	Corporate profits including inventory valuation adjustment, billions of 1954 dollars.
T_c	Corporate profits taxes, billions of current dollars.
$^*\Pi - P_c$	Proprietors' income, billions of 1954 dollars.
$^*\Pi_r$	Rental income and net interest, billions of 1954 dollars.
$^*D$	Capital consumption allowances, billions of current dollars.
D_u	Dummy variable, 0 for 1929–1941, 1 for 1947–1964.
r_d	Average discount rate at all Federal Reserve Banks, percent.
R_e	Year-end ratio of member banks' excess to required reserves.

* Denotes endogenous or dependent variable.

G Government expenditures, billions of 1954 dollars.
E Exports, billions of 1954 dollars.
T_i Reconciling item between net national product and national income, billions of current dollars.
T Personal taxes + Contributions for social insurance − Government and business transfer payments − Interest on government debt, billions of current dollars.

From the viewpoint of econometric method, it will be worthwhile to examine these alternative estimates of parameters in a system of simultaneous econometric relationships. First, let us comment on the separate treatment of the three single equation regressions in Eqs. (6.1.14)–(6.1.16). After substitution of identities, this is a sixteen equation system with errors $e_1, e_2, \ldots, e_{16}$. Let us write

$$p(e_1, e_2, \ldots, e_{16}) = f(e_1, e_2, \ldots, e_{13})\, g(e_{14}, e_{15}, e_{16}). \tag{6.1.21}$$

This assumes that the joint density function of $e_1, e_2, \ldots, e_{16}$ can be factored as a result of independence between each element of $e_1, e_2, \ldots, e_{13}$ on the one hand, and e_{14}, e_{15}, e_{16} on the other. We thus assume that the covariance matrix Σ is block-diagonal

$$\Sigma = \begin{bmatrix} \sigma_{11} & \cdots & \sigma_{1,13} & 0 & 0 & 0 \\ \vdots & & \vdots & & & \\ \sigma_{1,13} & \cdots & \sigma_{13,13} & 0 & 0 & 0 \\ 0 & \cdots & 0 & \sigma_{14,14} & 0 & 0 \\ 0 & \cdots & 0 & 0 & \sigma_{15,15} & 0 \\ 0 & \cdots & 0 & 0 & 0 & \sigma_{16,16} \end{bmatrix}. \tag{6.1.22}$$

We further assume that the parameters occuring in the first thirteen equations are not included among those in the next three and vice versa. We then see that

$$\max\, [p(e_1, e_2, \ldots, e_{16})]^T$$

is given by

$$\max\, [f(e_1, e_2, \ldots, e_{13})]^T$$

and

$$\max\, [g(e_{14}, e_{15}, e_{16})]^T.$$

The latter maximum is secured by computing OLS regressions, as in Eqs. (6.1.14)–(6.1.16). With fewer zero-covariance assumptions in Σ, these OLS regressions would not yield FIML estimates.

It is difficult to make any general statement about the three sets of estimates of Eqs. (6.1.1)–(6.1.13) other than to observe that they are quite different.

Possibly, the TSLS and OLS estimates are more alike than any other paired comparison. As to the direction of effect shown by the signs of coefficients, there are only two cases of contradiction. In the first equation (consumer durables), the coefficient of $(C_d)_{-1}$ is positive for the FIML estimate and this seems to contradict a priori theory.

In the equation for rentier income (6.1.13), the coefficients of both $p(I + R)$ and Δr ought to be positive. FIML is opposite to the results of OLS and TSLS, but each method contains one perverse sign. One comforting thought about all these contradictions of a priori knowledge on qualitative effects is that they are not significant in the sense that the estimated coefficients in question are all subject to large sampling error.

Equation by equation, these differently estimated systems can be compared for goodness of fit, sharpness of coefficient estimates, or a priori plausibility. We shall, however, try to add a new comparative dimension by showing how the equations function *as a system* by the different methods of estimation. This method of testing alternative estimates brings us to the areas of applied econometrics known as *simulation* and *forecasting*.

Questions and Problems

1. Explain in detail why the years of World War II should or should not be deleted from the sample for parameter estimation.

If they are not to be deleted, show how these sample observations may be included without distorting estimates of parameters.

2. Calculate the long and short run marginal propensities to consume in the estimated model for any one method of estimation.

3. Show how more nonlinearities may be introduced into the equation system and indicate how to deal with the nonlinearities in estimation.

2. SIMULATION

Given the dynamic system

$$f_i(y_{1t}, \ldots, y_{nt}, \ldots, y_{1,t-p}, \ldots, y_{n,t-p}, x_{1t}, \ldots, x_{mt}) = e_{it}, \tag{6.2.1}$$

we define a simulation as the solution of the (nonstochastic) dynamic system

$$y_{i,t_1}, y_{i,t_1+1}, y_{i,t_1+2}, \ldots, y_{i,t_1+s}, \qquad i = 1, 2, \ldots, n,$$

given

$$y_{i,t_1-1}, y_{i,t_1-2}, y_{i,t_1-3}, \ldots, y_{i,t_1-p}, \qquad i = 1, 2, \ldots, n,$$

and

$$x_{i,t_1}, x_{i,t_1+1}, x_{i,t_1+2}, \ldots, x_{i,t_1+s}, \qquad i = 1, 2, \ldots, m.$$

We start with given values of lagged variables $y_{i,t_1-1}, \ldots, y_{i,t_1-p}$ at t_1 and with given values of exogenous variables x_{i,t_1}. We then compute y_{i,t_1}. In the next period $t_1 + 1$, we use previously computed values of y_{i,t_1} and given lagged values, together with exogenous variables x_{i,t_1+1}, to get computed values of y_{i,t_1+1} and continue in this way until $t_1 + s$ is reached.

This step by step solution to the dynamic finite difference equation is convenient with computer facilities and is essential to the treatment of general nonlinear systems such as we have in the present case. For the linear case, however, a complete analysis of the problem can be given in terms of the coefficients of the model. A linear difference equation can generally be reduced by elimination methods to a single equation of higher order lag than the original. As an example, the general linear system of first order lags

$$\begin{aligned} \alpha_{110}y_{1t} + \alpha_{120}y_{2t} + \alpha_{111}y_{1,t-1} + \alpha_{121}y_{2,t-1} + \beta_{11}x_{1t} &= e_{1t} \\ \alpha_{210}y_{1t} + \alpha_{220}y_{2t} + \alpha_{211}y_{1,t-1} + \alpha_{221}y_{2,t-1} + \beta_{21}x_{1t} &= e_{2t} \end{aligned} \tag{6.2.2}$$

can be reduced to

$$\begin{aligned} &\left(\alpha_{110} - \frac{\alpha_{120}\alpha_{210}}{\alpha_{220}}\right)y_{1t} + \left(\alpha_{111} + \frac{\alpha_{110}\alpha_{221} - \alpha_{120}\alpha_{211} - \alpha_{121}\alpha_{210}}{\alpha_{220}}\right)y_{1,t-1} \\ &\quad \frac{\alpha_{111}\alpha_{221} - \alpha_{121}\alpha_{211}}{\alpha_{220}}y_{1,t-2} + \left(\beta_{11} - \frac{\beta_{21}\alpha_{120}}{\alpha_{220}}\right)x_{1t} \\ &\quad \left(\frac{\beta_{11}\alpha_{221} - \alpha_{121}\beta_{21}}{\alpha_{220}}\right)x_{1,t-1} = e_{1t} + \frac{\alpha_{221}}{\alpha_{220}}e_{1,t-1} - \frac{\alpha_{120}}{\alpha_{220}}e_{2t} - \frac{\alpha_{121}}{\alpha_{220}}e_{2,t-1}. \end{aligned} \tag{6.2.3}$$

This is derived, in a straightforward manner, by augmenting the original system of two equations with the two delayed value equations

$$\begin{aligned} \alpha_{110}y_{1,t-1} + \alpha_{120}y_{2,t-1} + \alpha_{111}y_{1,t-2} + \alpha_{121}y_{2,t-2} + \beta_{11}x_{1,t-1} &= e_{1,t-1} \\ \alpha_{210}y_{1,t-1} + \alpha_{220}y_{2,t-1} + \alpha_{211}y_{1,t-2} + \alpha_{221}y_{2,t-2} + \beta_{21}x_{1,t-1} &= e_{2,t-1} \end{aligned} \tag{6.2.4}$$

and observing that we have four equations in y_{1t}, y_{2t}, $y_{2,t-1}$, and $y_{2,t-2}$, in terms of linear expressions in $y_{1,t-1}$, $y_{1,t-2}$, $x_{1,t}$, $x_{1,t-1}$, e_{1t}, e_{2t}, $e_{1,t-1}$ and $e_{2,t-1}$. The *final equation* is derived by solving the four equation system for y_{1t}.

It should be noted that the *final equation* is of second order. Two first order equations reduce to a second order final equation. In general, n equations of the pth order reduce to a *final equation* of the np^{th} order. Another point to note is that if we had solved for y_{2t} instead of y_{1t}, we would have had *exactly* the same coefficients of y_{2t}, $y_{2,t-1}$, $y_{2,t-2}$. This part of the *final equation*, the homogeneous equation part, is the same for every variable in a linear system.[5] Finally, it should be remarked that the final equation contains lag functions of x_{1t}, e_{1t}

[5] G. H. Orcutt, "A Study of the Autoregressive Nature of the Time Series Used for Tinbergen's Model of the Economic System of the United States, 1919–1932," *Journal of the Royal Statistical Society*, X, (1948), Series B, 1–53.

and e_{2t}. Coefficients of these variables are not the same for both y_{1t} and y_{2t}.

A general expression for the final form was derived in Chap. 4 for the whole system

$$\sum_{i=0}^{p} A_i y_{t-i} + Bx_t = e_t. \tag{6.2.5}$$

Using matrix and lag operator notation

$$A(L) = A_0 + A_1 L + A_2 L^2 + \cdots A_p L^p, \tag{6.2.6}$$

we may write the system as

$$A(L)y_t = -Bx_t + e_t. \tag{6.2.7}$$

Let $a(L)$ denote the adjoint of $A(L)$ and $\Delta(L) = |A(L)|$. The final equation is

$$||\Delta(L)||\, y_t = -a(L)BX_t + a(L)e_t, \tag{6.2.8}$$

where $||\Delta(L)||$ is a matrix with $\Delta(L)$ on the main diagonal and zeros everywhere else. This equation expresses the fact that the final equation for each variable in y_t has the same autoregressive structure; that is, the left-hand side is identical for each variable. On the other hand, $a(L)BX_t$ and $a(L)e_t$ are different for each final equation.

We now consider the solution of the final equation. As an example, the general p^{th} order equation has, as solution of its homogeneous part,

$$\begin{aligned} \alpha_0 y_t + \alpha_1 y_{t-1} + \cdots + \alpha_p y_{t-p} &= 0 \\ y_t &= C\lambda^t. \end{aligned} \tag{6.2.9}$$

We determine λ on substitution

$$\alpha_0 C\lambda^t + \alpha_1 C\lambda^{t-1} + \cdots + \alpha_p C\lambda^{t-p} = 0$$

or

$$\alpha_0 \lambda^p + \alpha_1 \lambda^{p-1} + \cdots + \alpha_p = 0. \tag{6.2.10}$$

There are generally p roots to this characteristic equation, and the most general solution (distinct roots case) is

$$y_t = \sum_{i=1}^{p} C_i \lambda_i^t. \tag{6.2.11}$$

The values of λ obtained as roots depend on the α's; thus, the parameters of the model determine the dynamic path. The complete solution would be given by adding a particular solution to $\sum C_i \lambda_i^t$, based on the time function governing the movement of x_{it} and e_{it}. In the iterative build up of a numerical solution, we specify exogenous values of x_{it} over the whole nonstochastic ($e_{it} = 0$) time path of the solution; therefore, we, in effect, have a complete solution.

In a more general linear formulation of the homogeneous equations, let us write, in the first order case

$$\sum_{j=1}^{n} \alpha_{ij0} y_{jt} + \sum_{j=1}^{n} \alpha_{ij1} y_{j,t-1} = 0, \qquad i = 1, 2, \ldots, n. \tag{6.2.12}$$

Let us express the solution for the jth variable, noting that they all satisfy the same *final equation*

$$y_{jt} = C_j \lambda^t,$$

and substitute to obtain

$$\sum_{j=1}^{n} \alpha_{ij0} C_j \lambda^t + \sum_{j=1}^{n} \alpha_{ij1} C_j \lambda^{t-1} = 0.$$

This reduces to

$$\sum_{j=1}^{n} (\alpha_{ij1} + \alpha_{ij0}\lambda) C_j = 0, \qquad i = 1, 2, \ldots, n. \tag{6.2.13}$$

A nontrivial solution, $C_1, C_2, \ldots, C_n$, exists if

$$|(\alpha_{ij1} + \alpha_{ij0}\lambda)| = 0. \tag{6.2.14}$$

This is an nth order characteristic equation in λ, with roots $\lambda_1, \lambda_2, \ldots, \lambda_n$.

The analysis of the roots of the characteristic equation can tell much about the nature of dynamic movement in the system. For stability, we require

$$|\lambda_i| < 1.$$

This is a necessary condition and would also be sufficient if we were considering the homogeneous equation alone. The time path of exogenous variables x_{it} over the period of solution defines a particular solution that must be added to the general solution of the homogeneous equation in the linear case. This particular solution could impose instability on an otherwise stable system.

The stochastic error, however, introduces another element of extreme importance. One of the most fertile ideas in dynamic economics was that of Slutsky, who showed that moving averages of random series tend to show cyclic properties.[6] In the reduction of a linear system to a final autoregressive equation, serial correlation may be introduced in the error term. We find this in our simple two equation model, where the composite error in the final equation is[7]

[6] E. Slutsky, "The Summation of Random Causes as the Source of Cyclic Processes," *Econometrica*, 5 (April, 1937), 105–46.

[7] Cf. L. Hurwicz, "Stochastic Models of Economic Fluctuations," *Econometrica*, 12 (April, 1944), 114–24.

$$u_{1t} = e_{1t} + \frac{\alpha_{221}}{\alpha_{220}} e_{1,t-1} - \frac{\alpha_{120}}{\alpha_{220}} e_{2t} - \frac{\alpha_{121}}{\alpha_{220}} e_{2,t-1}.$$

If we write the general second order linear difference equation as

$$y_t + \lambda_1 y_{t-1} + \lambda_2 y_{t-2} = f(t) \tag{6.2.15}$$

where

$$f(t) = \mu_0 x_t + \mu_1 x_{t-1} + u_t,$$

we can express the solution as

$$y_t = C_1 \rho_1^t + C_2 \rho_2^t + \sum_{i=0}^{t-2} \frac{\rho_1^{i+1} - \rho_2^{i+1}}{\rho_1 - \rho_2} f(t-i). \tag{6.2.16}$$

In this formulation, ρ_1 and ρ_2 are roots of the characteristic equation

$$\rho^2 + \lambda_1 \rho + \lambda_2 = 0 \tag{6.2.17}$$

$$\rho_1 = \frac{-\lambda_1 + \sqrt{\lambda_1^2 - 4\lambda_2}}{2}, \qquad \rho_2 = \frac{-\lambda_1 - \sqrt{\lambda_1^2 - 4\lambda_2}}{2}. \tag{6.2.18}$$

The particular solution

$$\sum_{i=0}^{t-2} \frac{\rho_1^{i+1} - \rho_2^{i+1}}{\rho_1 - \rho_2} f(t-i)$$

is thus a moving summation of $f(t)$, that, in turn, includes a moving summation of e_{it}. Moving summations like these may closely approximate the kinds of moving averages that Slutsky showed to create cyclic processes; thus, we have a possibility of added dynamic movement in cyclical form if stochastic solutions are used instead of nonstochastic. It is transparent in the simple case of second order lags that the solution to the homogeneous equation will be sinusoidal though not necessarily maintained or stable, if ρ_1 and ρ_2 are (conjugate) complex, that is if

$$\lambda_1^2 - 4\lambda_2 < 0.$$

Thus, the parameters of the model (α_{ijk}) combine, as in (6.2.3), into the λ_i, and these, in turn, characterize part of the complete solution. This is, in Frisch's attractive terminology, the *propagation* aspect of the system that may give rise to cycles and either stable or unstable dynamic motion.[8] The other aspect of the system, again in Frisch's terminology, is the impulse part. The impulses, $f(t)$,

[8] R. Frisch, "Propagation Problems and Impulse Problems in Dynamic Economics," in *Readings in Business Cycles*, ed. R. A. Gordon and L. R. Klein (Homewood, Ill.: Irwin & Sons, 1965).

are propagated through the system by their combination with the roots in the expression

$$\sum_{i=0}^{t-2} \frac{\rho_1^{i+1} - \rho_2^{i+1}}{\rho_1 - \rho_2} f(t - i)$$

and may, according to Slutsky's theories, give rise to motion described in his "Law of the Sinusoidal Limit."

The linear model can thus be completely analyzed, a priori, except for specification of the values of $f(t)$, the exogenous and random components. The solution has the convenient property of combining two solutions additively, the general solution to the homogeneous equation and a particular solution of the complete equation. The latter can also be decomposed into two additive parts: the nonstochastic part, depending on the exogenous variables, and the stochastic part, dependent on the random errors.

The general solution to the final equation of the complete linear system in matrix form was shown to be

$$y_t = K\lambda^t - \frac{a(L)}{\Delta(L)} BX_t + \frac{a(L)}{\Delta(L)} e_t. \tag{6.2.19}$$

K is a matrix ($n \times np$) of constants determined by the initial conditions of the system, and λ is an np element vector of roots of the characteristic polynomial associated with the autoregressive structure $(\lambda_1^t, \lambda_2^t, \ldots, \lambda_{np}^t)'$. The particular solution is

$$y_t = -\frac{a(L)}{\Delta(L)} BX_t + \frac{a(L)}{\Delta(L)} e_t.$$

It should be pointed out that $\frac{a(L)}{\Delta(L)}$ is the rational function lag distribution that we studied earlier from the point of view of estimation theory. The vector λ depends on the parameters of the original system and shows the internal dynamics. The particular solution shows the separate contributions of the time path of the exogenous variables and the stochastic error accumulation.

We cannot superimpose solutions this way, in general, for nonlinear systems. Numerical and approximate methods for working out digital values of solutions at successive discrete periods provide a natural method that we shall apply to the case at hand. There are many approximate numerical methods for solving systems of nonlinear dynamic equations. One that is easy to execute and quite efficient is the Gauss-Seidel method. Suppose that the general nonlinear model can be written as

$$y_{it} = g_i(y_{1t}, \ldots, y_{nt}, y_{1,t-1}, \ldots, y_{n,t-p}, x_{1t}, \ldots, x_{mt}) + u_{it}. \tag{6.2.20}$$

It is usually possible to transform nonlinear models from the implicit form stated in (6.2.1) to this form, in which some one dependent variable in each equation is expressed as a function of all the variables of the system plus a random error. Using the estimated parameter values and zero (mean) values for the additive random error, we obtain nonstochastic solutions of the dynamic system from the algorithm

$$y_{it}^{(r)} = g_i(y_{1t}^{(r)}, \ldots, y_{i-1,t}^{(r)}, y_{it}^{(r-1)}, \ldots, y_{nt}^{(r-1)}, y_{1,t-1}, \ldots, y_{n,t-p}, x_{1t}, \ldots, x_{mt}) \tag{6.2.21}$$

$$\left| \frac{y_{it}^{(r)} - y_{it}^{(r-1)}}{y_{it}^{(r-1)}} \right| < \epsilon.$$

Given initial approximations, we use these equations for passing from the $(r - 1)^{st}$ iterative values to the rth, and stop the iterations when the absolute percentage change in each dependent variable is less than ϵ, a preassigned accuracy level. For the whole time period of solution, x_{it} are specified. The lagged values of y_{it} are taken as initial conditions at the start and are developed as successive inputs as the solution progresses through time. Unlagged values change from iteration to iteration at a given time point. If numerical values of random errors were read into the input, as in Monte Carlo studies, we could then obtain stochastic solutions that implicitly cumulate the effects of such errors.

Solutions of nonlinear equations may not be unique, although they appear to be in most applied problems. By varying initial conditions and testing whether solutions converge to different values, we can often determine whether there are multiple solutions. Also, it must be pointed out that iterations by the Gauss-Seidel method do not always converge. Convergence depends on both the ordering of equations in the solution steps and the choice of the dependent variable to be placed on the left of the equation[9]

$$y_{it} = g_i + u_{it}.$$

Other numerical methods may be used to solve the nonlinear equation system. The original implicit form

$$f_i(y_{1t}, \ldots, y_{nt}, y_{1,t-p}, \ldots, y_{n,t-p}, x_{1t}, \ldots, x_{mt}) = e_{it} \tag{6.2.1}$$

can be approximated by a linear Taylor's expansion. The solution algorithm can be written as

$$\begin{aligned} & f_i(y_{1t}^{(r-1)}, \ldots, y_{nt}^{(r-1)}, y_{1,t-1}, \ldots, y_{n,t-p}, x_{1t}, \ldots, x_{mt}) \\ & \quad + \sum_{j=1}^{n} \frac{\partial f_i}{\partial y_{jt}} \bigg|_{y_t = y_t^{(r-1)}} (y_{jt}^{(r)} - y_{jt}^{(r-1)}) = 0. \end{aligned} \tag{6.2.22}$$

[9] A discussion of convergence problems and application of the method to the solution of the large-scale Brookings Model is given in G. Fromm and L. R. Klein, "Solutions of the Complete System," *The Brookings Model: Some Further Results*, ed. J. Duesenberry, et al. (Chicago: Rand McNally, 1969).

This is a linear equation system in $y_{it}^{(r)}$, given $y_{it}^{(r-1)}$, $y_{i,t-1}, \ldots, y_{i,t-p}$ and x_{it}. This equation system can be solved on each iteration for $y_{it}^{(r)}$ and the steps terminated when

$$\left| \frac{y_{it}^{(r)} - y_{it}^{(r-1)}}{y_i^{(r-1)}} \right| < \epsilon.$$

Because the process of solving linear equations is much more time consuming than the straightforward evaluation of nonlinear functions as in the Gauss-Seidel method, this method, known as the Newton-Raphson method, must be slower to execute in numerical work. The Newton-Raphson method may be economical in the number of iterations used, but may use much arithmetic on each iteration; therefore the Gauss-Seidel method appears to be a very practical system for modern computation.

Questions and Problems

1. Suppose that two roots of the characteristic equation of a dynamic system are conjugate complex

$$\lambda_1 = a + ib$$
$$\lambda_2 = a - ib.$$

Transform these to trigonometric expressions and show how periodicity and stability may be expressed in terms of a and b.

2. Show the conditions for convergence of the Gauss-Seidel algorithm in the linear system

$$y_{1t} = \alpha y_{2t} + \beta$$
$$y_{2t} = \gamma y_{1t} + \delta$$

3. Show that the variance of the solution of the second order linear difference equation in the stochastic case is unbounded if either root is greater than unity in absolute value.

$$|\rho_i| > 1.$$

In any case, numerical paths for solutions to nonlinear dynamic systems can be obtained. These are the values needed for simulation studies.

Two kinds of simulation will be discussed. First, we shall simulate over the sample period. We start the model at the beginning of the sample in 1929, using 1927 and 1928 values where necessary for initial conditions, and let the model develop its own path of endogenous variables until 1941, when a break in the time span occurs because of World War II. We could also make a series of shorter simulations of one to twelve years. In short simulations, we start up anew using *actual* instead of *computed* values of lagged endogenous variables. After the interval spanning World War II, we repeat our simulation methods, using either computed or actual lag values from 1947–1964. These are all within-sample simulations, to see how the model as a whole works in the sample period. The special feature of this period is that the parameters are chosen, in some sense, so that the equations lie close to sample observations. Hypothetical simulations may be made for nonsample periods to study various cyclical or growth properties of systems.[10] In the sample period, if we are checking on the accuracy of the model as a whole, it would seem sensible to choose observed values of exogenous variables. In hypothetical simulations to arbitrary periods we can fix the exogenous variables in a variety of ways.

Simulation by extrapolation beyond the bounds of the sample, either to antecedent or succedent time, can be viewed as an application in back casting or forecasting. The forecasting may be genuine, before the event, in which case we call it *ex ante* forecasting, or prediction. If it comes after the event, so that we have a means of checking on the accuracy of the values of the endogenous variables, we call it *ex post* forecasting. The main point, however, is that calculations are made for values of the variables that were not in the sample and that did not have a direct bearing on the determination of parameter values.

In order to study economic policy or the application of *multiplier* analysis in economics, we shall make another kind of simulation, either inside or outside the sample confines. First, we shall establish a *control* solution by the methods just described using actual values of exogenous variables in the sample for past periods. In future periods, we use best judgment on values of exogenous variables. The use of actual values for past periods is not absolutely necessary because our control solution simply establishes a reference point, but it seems to be the natural thing to do, because realism and accuracy checks are usually involved. We then make a new simulation corresponding to different specific values of exogenous variables (or parameter estimates) to see how much influence on the system, measured by departure from the control solution, they have. We compare the control solution,

$$y_{i,t_1}, \ldots, y_{i,t_1+1}, \ldots, y_{i,t_1+2}, \ldots, y_{i,t_1+s}$$

corresponding to exogenous variables

$$x_{i,t_1}, \ldots, x_{i,t_1+1}, \ldots, x_{i,t_1+2}, \ldots, x_{i,t_1+s}$$

with the disturbed solution,

$$y^*_{i,t_1}, \ldots, y^*_{i,t_1+1}, \ldots, y^*_{i,\ 1+2}, \ldots, y^*_{i,t_1+s}$$

corresponding to exogenous variables

$$x^*_{i\ t_1}, \ldots, x^*_{i,t_1+1}, \ldots, x^*_{i,t_1+2}, \ldots, x^*_{i,t_1+s}.$$

[10] F. and I. Adelman, "The Dynamic Properties of the Klein-Goldberger Model," *Econometrica*, 27 (October, 1959), 596–625.

Some measure of the relative distances between y^*_{i,t_1+s} and y_{i,t_1+s}, on the one hand, and x^*_{i,t_1+s} and x_{i,t_1+s} on the other, shows us the multiplier effect after s periods of dynamic simulation. Dynamic multipliers in economics can be estimated in this way.

Changes in exogenous variables can be simple, as in the conventional multiplier analysis where a single variable is changed by a constant amount, or changes can be varied over time and extended to simultaneous variations in a wide variety of related variables. We thus have a generalization of the multiplier concept to dynamic policy variations. We may also vary parameters as well as variables, and we can carry out the whole set of calculations for nonlinear systems. The most general way of looking at multiplier analysis is through the comparison of alternative time paths of an economy.

To compare the different methods of estimation, we place, side by side, their sample period performance in simulation from fixed initial conditions—1929–1941 and 1947–1964. As a summary measure of goodness of fit, we tabulate *mean absolute percentage error*

$$MAPE = \frac{1}{T}\sum_{t=1}^{T}\frac{|\hat{y}_t - y_t|}{y_t}.$$

Other plausible error measures are *mean square percentage error*

$$MSPE = \left(\frac{1}{T}\sum_{t=1}^{T}\frac{(\hat{y}_t - y_t)^2}{y_t^2}\right)^{1/2};$$

the same measures in absolute units

$$MAE = \frac{1}{T}\sum_{t=1}^{T}|\hat{y}_t - y_t|$$

$$MSE = \left(\frac{1}{T}\sum_{t=1}^{T}(\hat{y}_t - y_t)^2\right)^{1/2};$$

ratios of the latter to *standard deviations*

$$\frac{MAE}{SD} = \frac{\sum|\hat{y}_t - y_t|}{\left[\sum_{t=1}^{T}(y_t - \bar{y}_t)^2\right]^{1/2}}$$

$$\frac{MSE}{SD} = \left[\frac{\sum_{t=1}^{T}(\hat{y}_t - y_t)^2}{\sum_{t=1}^{T}(y_t - \bar{y}_t)^2}\right]^{1/2};$$

or linear correlation between actual and computed values

$$\hat{y}_t = a + by_t$$

$$b = \frac{\sum_{t=1}^{T} (y_t - \bar{y}_t)(\hat{y}_t - \bar{\hat{y}}_t)}{\sum_{t=1}^{T} (y_t - \bar{y}_t)^2}, \qquad a = \bar{\hat{y}} - b\bar{y}.$$

For the last measure, perfect fit corresponds to the parameter values, $a = 0$, $b = 1$.

These are all sample period values; therefore, the standard deviations in the denominators of MAE/SD or MSE/SD are evaluated over the same period as the measures of MAE or MSE. If the system were linear, we would have $\bar{\hat{y}} = \bar{y}$. The nonlinearity of the present model leads to a difference between $\bar{\hat{y}}$ and $\bar{y}$, because it is only in a linear system that we can be sure that the solution is made up of a nonstochastic part plus a stochastic part that is a linear combination of past errors.

In *ex post* extrapolation beyond the sample values we would have MAE or MSE evaluated outside the sample span and SD evaluated within the sample span. Similarly, the regression relationship between $\hat{y}_t$ and y_t is computed from nonsample values.

The reasons for using percentage error in MAPE or MSPE or for dividing MAE and MSE by SD are obvious. They are to make the accuracy measures of forecasting independent of units of measurement. The different components of the vector $y_t = (y_{1t}, y_{2t}, \ldots, y_{nt})$ are all in distinctive units—current dollars, constant dollars, other monetary units, persons, acres, index points, hours, and so on. Percentage errors or standard unit errors avoid the problem of having the accuracy measures depend on units.

Only some of the more popular accuracy measures are listed here. It is essentially an arbitrary matter of description and exposition choosing one or another of these measures. If a particular measure were more tractable, from a mathematical point of view, for deriving a sampling distribution, it would be desirable for testing hypotheses about model structure in forecast and sample periods; otherwise, the pure description of forecast accuracy is equally well presented by several of these measures. The main point is to use a consistent, unit free method when comparing different model estimates over a forecast period.

The performance characteristics of the three sets of estimates are clearly different, as regards simulation path. The TSLS(4) estimates are consistently superior. OLS estimates break down completely after 1962 and this increases the average errors, especially in aggregate output. The error cumulation becomes so great that the OLS simulation ultimately leaves the general path of the system. This is a manifestation of least squares bias in simultaneous equation estimation.

Alternative TSLS estimators based on different numbers of principal components do not do as well as TSLS(4) in simulating the actual movements of the economy. This suggests that there are optimal choices in the selection of principal components for TSLS estimation.

There are many dimensions to the comparisons revealed in Table 6.2.1; therefore, it is instructive to examine in detail the simulation path for the central variable of the system, namely real GNP($=X$). For each year 1929–41 and 1947–64, we present the actual values of X and the simulated values computed from each of the three estimated models.

TABLE 6.2.1

Simulation Error, 1929–41 and 1947–64.
(*MAPE*)

Variable	*OLS*	*TSLS*(4)	*FIML*
C_d	13.6	11.2	13.2
C_n	5.4	2.3	4.5
R	19.5	14.6	20.4
H	84.8	19.4	75.3
I_m	18.9	23.2	22.6
h	2.5	2.3	2.2
w	21.6	13.3	28.7
W	6.1	3.7	4.6
N_w	5.0	3.0	4.6
S_c	158.7	322.5	174.6
P_c	157.2	90.6	229.6
Π_r	9.9	10.0	22.5
X	6.5	3.8	4.9
Y	6.6	4.6	5.1
Π	29.1	22.3	29.6
p	25.9	16.8	33.6
I	13.8	14.2	16.5
r_s	18.2	18.2	18.2
D	5.8	5.8	5.8
r	6.9	7.3	7.0

The FIML estimates show only a modest dip from 1929–33, but the OLS and TSLS(4) estimated values show definite declines. FIML performs better during 1947–64 than during the 1930's and shows pauses during the 1953–54, 1957–58 recessions, if not actual downturns. It does not fall apart during 1961–64, as does OLS.

These calculations are made for exogenous treatment of taxes, social insurance contributions, and transfer payments. These variables were treated as exogenous variables in the stage of parameter estimation. Simulations have also been made using different functional relationships for each of these variables, changing the relationship in an appropriate way as tax-transfer laws changed over the whole period since 1929.[11] For both endogenous and exogenous treat-

[11] M. Norman, "The Great Depression and What Might Have Been: An Econometric Model Simulation Study," (Ph.D. Dissertation, University of Pennsylvania, 1969).

TABLE 6.2.2

Simulation of Real GNP, *X*, 1929–41; 1947–64.

Year	*Actual X*	Computed *OLS*	*TSLS(4)*	*FIML*
1929	\$181.8	\$161.1	\$155.8	\$162.8
1930	164.5	156.7	144.4	159.7
1931	153.0	154.7	139.2	158.2
1932	130.1	148.4	135.9	154.3
1933	126.6	140.5	136.0	154.4
1934	138.5	139.3	144.0	157.0
1935	152.9	137.7	152.1	157.9
1936	173.3	145.8	167.9	166.7
1937	183.5	149.0	175.8	168.7
1938	175.1	159.2	187.9	174.9
1939	189.3	170.8	198.8	183.7
1940	205.8	185.4	210.6	193.3
1941	238.1	220.4	238.4	224.9
1947	282.3	281.6	283.2	283.7
1948	293.1	290.0	294.6	292.0
1949	292.7	309.1	313.2	307.6
1950	318.1	314.4	320.2	316.4
1951	341.8	338.4	348.2	347.0
1952	353.5	360.0	369.9	369.7
1953	369.0	375.1	383.4	385.6
1954	363.1	376.9	385.3	387.0
1955	392.7	382.2	394.2	396.0
1956	400.9	387.9	404.7	407.7
1957	408.6	398.0	419.3	422.2
1958	401.3	408.9	432.4	434.0
1959	428.6	411.1	441.5	443.8
1960	439.9	409.9	451.4	454.0
1961	447.9	414.2	467.1	469.3
1962	476.4	410.0	481.4	484.5
1963	492.6	388.4	491.4	496.1
1964	516.0	350.0	507.3	511.8

ment of taxes, these simulations follow the broad features of the economic dynamics in this period. During the Great Depression, 1929–34, they show a wide swing, as did actual activity, although the model may be off a year in timing at the trough and shows less amplitude than did the actual economy. The model misses minor short cycles in 1937–38, 1948–49, 1953–54, 1957–58, 1960–61, although it does show pauses if not downturns in some of those periods. The trend variables of the model carry it through the positive expansion phase of 1947–64 well, but OLS estimates break down towards the end of the simulation run. The models do better in terms of average residual error in simulating the postwar than in simulating the prewar period. Considering the whole period, the equation systems methods simulate the main output and employment variables better than do the OLS methods. This is what the theoretical exposition of the preceding chapters would suggest.

In many respects the TSLS(4) simulation pattern of real GNP is better than either the OLS or FIML simulations, confirming the previous results on summary measures of error in the preceding Table. It is worthwhile looking at another type of sample period simulation in order to throw some light on the comparatively poor performance of FIML estimates. Theoretically, these should be superior to the other two estimates in large samples, provided there has been no strong error of specification. The poor showing could, of course, be due to the smallness of the sample or the influence of specification error, but another set of calculations suggests an alternative explanation for the relatively poor performance of FIML in this situation.

One-period simulations are solutions of the whole system from periodic revisions of initial conditions (reinitializing each period); thus, instead of fixing lag values of dependent variables at the pre-1929 and pre-1947 levels and using *computed* lags for subsequent periods, we may change our procedure and use *observed* values of lags (together with observed values of independent variables) over the *ex post* solution period. When estimating stochastic relationships in econometrics, we conventionally treat lagged dependent (endogenous) variables

TABLE 6.2.3

Mean Absolute Percentage Errors in One-Period Simulations

	OLS	*TSLS(4)*	*FIML*
C_d	10.4	9.4	9.7
C_n	2.5	2.3	2.2
R	11.9	11.9	12.2
H	36.0	39.1	53.1
I_m	6.3	6.4	6.4
h	2.3	2.0	1.9
w	2.6	3.0	3.2
W	3.3	3.1	3.0
N_w	2.4	2.6	2.2
S_c	72.7	112.2	143.6
P_c	75.2	72.1	67.1
Π_r	3.9	4.3	4.2
X	3.5	3.2	2.8
Y	4.0	3.5	3.3
Π	12.5	12.7	9.4
p	2.7	3.7	3.5
I	9.5	9.5	9.5
r_s	18.2	18.2	18.2
D	5.8	5.8	5.8
r	5.3	5.2	5.0

like independent (exogenous) variables and place them all in the predetermined category. FIML provides optimal estimates (in the large sample sense) for parameters and for computed values of dependent variables, given the predetermined variables. If, in each period's solution, we duplicate the assumption that all predetermined variables are given, we ought to get relatively good results from the FIML estimates. The summary values of simulation error for one-period solutions show this in Table 6.2.3.

Although it does not have smaller error for every variable, FIML produces a smaller error for many of the most important variables of the system, notably real GNP (X). Were it not for the inconsistency in the treatment of inventory valuation adjustment, noted above, FIML would have produced better estimates of S_c and P_c in one-period simulations. Not only is its performance relatively strong in terms of average measures, but it produces a better time path. In particular, computed real output falls from a peak value of $162.8 billion to $124.8 billion in 1933.

The applications of the model have all been within the sample period. We now consider a one-period solution that extrapolates beyond the period of fit, to 1965. This is an exercise in *ex post* forecasting.

TABLE 6.2.4

Ex Post Forecasts, 1965.

		Computed		
	Actual values	*OLS*	*TSLS(4)*	*FIML*
C_d	59.6	55.2	55.1	57.0
C_n	308.1	303.0	303.2	303.4
R	20.6	22.8	22.4	23.3
H	76.5	75.6	75.4	76.5
I_m	32.7	29.7	30.3	29.9
h	1.038	1.016	1.015	1.026
w	5.492	5.502	5.515	5.522
W	315.1	311.3	310.5	312.3
N_w	68.0	67.5	67.8	68.3
S_c	12.9	1.3	1.32	4.60
P_c	51.5	40.0	41.6	46.5
Π_r	33.6	34.2	33.8	34.0
X	539.2	530.8	529.6	534.1
Y	371.2	369.7	369.0	372.8
Π	95.3	85.0	85.6	89.4
p	1.23	1.21	1.22	1.24
I	50.0	46.7	46.7	46.7
r_s	4.38	4.63	4.63	4.63
D	55.7	59.1	59.1	59.1
r	4.64	4.91	4.90	4.80

The national income and product accounts on which these estimates were based were drastically revised in August, 1965. We have tried to reconstruct, on the basis of estimates for the first six months of 1965 and regressions between the new and old data, what the values of the variables of the model would have been in 1965 had the old accounting system been continued. In principle, many ex post forecasts could be made, but it is difficult to extrapolate the observed data beyond 1965 as a result of the revisions of the accounts.

In this calculation, FIML provides, in many respects, the outstanding set of estimates. Because this is a one-period calculation with all lag values assumed to be given at observed levels, the conditions for strong performance of FIML methods are favorable, and they do perform well. The competition between OLS and TSLS(4) in the 1965 extrapolation is very close. For all practical purposes, we should call these two sets of estimates equivalent in this application.

Questions and Problems

1. Outline the simulation calculations that would be needed to evaluate a balanced budget multiplier from an econometric model.

2. How can dynamic multipliers be calculated from single unit—as distinct from sustained—impulses on equations of a model. One equation is to be disturbed or one exogenous variable is to be changed for only one period in a dynamic system.

3. Appraise the different features of alternative measures of prediction error associated with performance of a particular model.

3. ANALYSIS OF ECONOMIC POLICY

The types of economic policy alternatives or multiplier calculations that can be made with an estimated model are largely governed by the detail included in the vector of exogenous variables and the parameters of the system. The main variables that may be altered in the particular model being used as an example in this chapter are government expenditures and taxes (fiscal policy), discount rate and bank reserves (monetary policy), and exports (trade policy). By modern standards, this is not a large model and is therefore not as readily applicable to the analysis of a broad variety of problems in economic policy as are systems of fifty to one hundred or more equations.

Nevertheless, useful and revealing policy questions can be studied within the framework of the present model. First, in order to get the full benefit of fiscal policy calculations, we must introduce tax and transfer payment equations. These are aggregative approximations to the tax, social insurance, and welfare laws that apply to individuals and businesses. We introduce equations for:

Personal Income Taxes

$$T_p = a + b(pY + T_p) \tag{6.3.1}$$

Constant	Slope	Period	Constant	Slope	Period
−0.175	0.033	1929–32	−14.6	0.039	1939–41
−0.400	0.040	1933	−11.5	0.0172	1947
−0.460	0.039	1934–36	−10.0	0.149	1948
−0.460	0.045	1937	−12.0	0.146	1949
−0.460	0.048	1938	−13.0	0.152	1950

Constant	Slope	Period
−16.0	0.176	1951
−16.0	0.187	1952
−17.0	0.182	1953
−15.6	0.165	1954–64

Corporate Income Taxes

$$T_c = a + b\,pP_c \tag{6.3.2}$$

Constant	Slope	Period	Constant	Slope	Period
0.591	0.0807	1929–32	1.96	0.319	1947–50
0.469	0.1590	1933–39	0.173	0.525	1951–53
0.0	0.3000	1940	0.0	0.475	1954–64
0.0	0.4500	1941			

Indirect Business Taxes

$$T_i = a + b\,pX \tag{6.3.3}$$

Constant	Slope	Period
6.47	0.0006	1929–32
3.86	0.0600	1933–41
−5.00	0.1010	1947–50
−13.00	0.1170	1951–64

Transfer Payments

(a) Government

$$\begin{aligned} T_{rg} &= 0.788 + 0.0517(N_L - N_w - N_s) && 1929\text{–}33 \\ &= 0.184^* + 0.1190(N_L - N_w - N_s) + 0.025t && 1934\text{–}41 \\ &= -1.88 + 1.244(N_L - N_w - N_s) + 0.1295B_w && 1947\text{–}64 \end{aligned} \tag{6.3.4}$$

* The constant is raised to 1.48 in 1936 to account for a special bonus payment.

(b) Business

$$T_{rb} = 0.066 + 0.0017\,pX + 0.6149(T_{rb})_{-1} \tag{6.3.5}$$

(c) Social Insurance Contributions

$$T_{si} = a + b(pY + T_p) \tag{6.3.6}$$

Constant	*Slope*	*Period*	*Constant*	*Slope*	*Period*
0.2	0.0	1929	0.0	0.030	1947
0.3	0.0	1930–35	−1.0	0.030	1948
0.6	0.0	1936	−0.5	0.030	1949
0.3	0.02	1937	−1.56	0.0373	1950–54
−0.011	0.0292	1938–41	−15.30	0.0844	1955–57
			−23.10	0.1070	1958–64

The following new variables are introduced:

T_p = personal income tax receipts, billions of current dollars.
T_{rg} = government transfer payments, billions of current dollars.
T_{rb} = business transfer payments, billions of current dollars.
B_w = average weekly benefit, current dollars.
T_{si} = social insurance contributions, billions of current dollars.
IVA = inventory valuation adjustment, billions of current dollars.
I_{gd} = interest on government debt, billions of current dollars.
S_u = subsidies less surplus of government enterprises, billions of current dollars.
S_d = statistical discrepancy, billions of current dollars.

Some identities must be added:

$$T = T_p + T_{si} - T_{rg} - T_{rb} - I_{gd}$$
$$T_i = T_c + T_{rb} - S_u - S_d$$

I_{gd}, S_u, and S_d are treated as exogenous variables. The endogenous treatment of the other tax and transfer variables is noteworthy. It is evident that tax laws change frequently; that is the basis of our treating them as exogenous variables in estimation. Actually, it is a better assumption to treat the rates and other coefficients of the tax transfer functions as exogenously determined by law, but it is a simpler estimation problem if total tax collections are treated as exogenous so that target levels of tax yield or transfer payments are realized, in the short run. For a given set of laws, however, we would not find the appropriate multiplier response and we would find it difficult to predict ahead unless we treated taxes and transfers as endogenous variables restricted by the estimated functional relationships. These relationships are estimated from a very small number of data points and knowledge of the underlying laws. We use, in historical analysis of the system, the tax or transfer law that is appropriate to each period.

To illustrate multiplier analysis and policy simulation, let us examine the historical episode of the Great Depression, 1929–34. In Table 6.3.1 there are four columns of calculations: (1) A simulation solution using initial conditions, observed exogenous variables, and the appropriate tax transfer functions for each period, 1929–34.[12] This is called the *control* solution. (2) A policy simulation in which government expenditures plus exports are increased by 10 percent, r_d is set at 2.3 percent, and R_e is fixed at 0.75. These changes are for 1930–34. (3) A policy simulation in which C_n, C_d, R, I are increased by 5 percent, 1930–34. (4) A policy simulation in which r is fixed at 4 percent for 1930 and at 3 percent for 1931–34.

TABLE 6.3.1

Alternative Policy Simulations, 1929–34.
(*GNP, Billions of 1954 Dollars*)

	Observed	*Control*	*G + E up 10%* $r_d = 2.3$ $R_e = 0.75$	C_n, C_d, R, I *up 5%*	$r = 4.0$ *1930* $r = 3.0$ *1931–34*
1929	181.8	158.1	158.1	158.1	158.1
1930	164.5	146.6	149.3	155.3	148.5
1931	153.0	140.6	147.4	154.6	147.7
1932	130.1	136.4	150.1	153.3	148.7
1933	126.6	135.8	154.3	154.1	150.9
1934	138.5	143.6	162.0	162.3	160.3

For this cyclical experience, the control solution has the right peak and trough date, but the amplitude is far too low. For purposes of multiplier and policy analysis, we compare deviant solutions, however, with the control solution, and the deviant solutions have the same biased amplitude movement. The first policy simulation combines fiscal (expenditure) policy and monetary policy. The discount rate was lowered, raised, and then lowered in this period, but the reserve ratio was increased, lowered, and then increased. Our combinations ($r_d = 2.3\%$, $R_e = 0.75$) are approximately the most favorable values for the whole period. We thus have both fiscal and monetary stimuli. Since $G + E$ is close to \$30 billion for this whole period, the fiscal stimulus amounts to about \$3.0 billion. The data suggest that real GNP would, in five years, be increased by \$18 billion as a result of these policies.

[12] This control solution is computed from TSLS (4), but differs from that in Table 6.2.2 above, in that taxes and transfers are here computed from formulas listed above. In the previous simulation they were exogenous.

The next column shows the path that the economy would have been expected to follow if the main components of private spending could each have been autonomously raised by 5 percent. Because these expenditures totalled \$160.2 billion at the start of the calculation, this represents a starting increase of approximately \$8 billion. This works out to an eventual multiplier calculation in excess of 2.0, but in the first period it is close to 1.0.

Finally, we have a simulation of a pure monetary policy in which the final result is to maintain r at low values for the whole period. Interest rates fell, rose, and then fell in this period but were never as low as 4.0 percent at long term. This particular monetary policy gives less stimulus than the other two types of policy considered.

Questions and Problems

1. How are empirical tax functions changed, parametrically, if exemption levels are changed? If marginal tax rates are changed?

2. Can tax reductions result in increased tax collections? Indicate your answer in terms of policy simulation of a model.

4. STOCHASTIC SIMULATION AND THE ANALYSIS OF BUSINESS CYCLES

An explicit solution of this system has never been determined.[13] The nonlinearity is a difficulty in obtaining such a solution, but it has never been obtained as a complete system solution for a linear approximation. Numerical methods have, however, been used to study the cyclical properties of the system. Actually, the calculations were made for the original Klein-Goldberger model that served as the parent of this system.

The dynamic solution of the model over the sample period would be given by nonstochastic simulation for the study of business cycles by numerical methods. These solutions could be extended for much longer time periods if some reasonable assumptions can be made about the time paths of the exogenous variables. For example, these variables may be projected along historically established trend lines.

For the given exogenous variables, the nonstochastic (system) does exhibit the 1929–33 depression and the subsequent recovery. It does not, however, show declines in 1937–38, 1948–49, 1953–54, 1957–58, that were all periods of

[13] A. S. Goldberger has obtained solutions for truncated versions of the system. See A. S. Goldberger, *Impact Multipliers and Dynamic Properties of the Klein-Goldberger Model* (Amsterdam: North-Holland Publishing Co., 1959) Chap. 6.

minor recessions. In some cases, the solution shows a slow growth rate during these recessions, but it does not actually decline. If the system were to be solved for many periods in the future, it is not clear that the solution would indicate the persistence of business cycles. Indeed, the study of Adelman and Adelman, referred to above, suggests that the predecessor model shows a strong tendency to follow its trend growth path. If the system is seriously shocked, it shows an oscillation that rapidly dies out, and the model returns to its growth path. It, therefore, appears desirable to consider the properties of a stochastic simulation.

The fundamental contribution of Slutsky referred to above shows that moving averages of random time series are capable of exhibiting cyclical movement; we noted that the general solution of the dynamic, linear, stochastic model does contain a weighted cumulation of random errors; therefore, we should look to stochastic simulation of the model to find the persistence of business cycles. The weighted cumulations of error that occur in the solution of stochastic linear difference equations are not the same as Slutsky's iterated moving averages of error, yet they are similar in appearance.

The procedure of Adelman and Adelman is to solve the system with error shocks added to each equation and exogenous variables extrapolated along historical growth paths.[14] The shocks can be selected so that the random variables chosen have the same variance-covariance matrix as that given by the sample estimates of variances and covariances of residuals. The problem of choosing random errors for these simulation experiments is very much like that in choosing errors for the study of parameter estimates in sampling experiments referred to in the preceding chapter. The Adelmans, however, chose a diagonal variance-covariance matrix of error. They made their shocks agree only with the sample variances and neglected covariances, both lagged and unlagged.

The Adelmans' findings show that the simulation of a stochastic version of the Klein-Goldberger over a long hypothetical period (100 years) produces cycles that average four years in duration. These cycles have many properties that are commonly attributed to U.S. business cycles on the basis of independent quantitative study. The mean duration of cycle upswing and downswing, and the percentages of leading and lagging series agree closely with historical findings on U.S. business cycles. It is interesting that the stochastic simulation of the model has these documented cyclical properties but the nonstochastic simulation does not.

There is yet another approach to stochastic simulation, through spectral analysis. Consider a random variable v_t, which is a time process.[15] Its spectrum representation is

$$v_t = \int_{-\pi}^{\pi} e^{i\omega t}\, dV(\omega) \tag{6.4.1}$$

[14] Adelman, "Dynamic Properties of Klein-Goldberger Model, (1959).

[15] Because we shall be using the natural logarithm base $e = 2.71828\ldots$, we shall change our usual notation of random error from e_t to v_t in order not to confuse uses of e and e_t.

It is assumed that v_t is a stationary time series in the sense that its means, variances, and lag covariances do not depend on t. We define $V(\omega)$ by

$$dV(\omega) = \frac{1}{2\pi} \sum_{s=-\infty}^{\infty} e^{-i\omega s} v_s. \tag{6.4.2}$$

The spectrum matrix of the disturbance process is

$$f(\omega) = E[dV(\omega)\, dV^*(\omega)] = \frac{1}{2\pi} \sum_{s=-\infty}^{\infty} e^{-i\omega s} E(V_t V^*_{t-s}). \tag{6.4.3}$$

The asterisk represents the conjugate transpose operation.

The problem now is to derive an expression for the spectrum matrix of a linear economic system from the spectrum matrix of its disturbance process. The *final form* of the general linear dynamic model was previously derived as

$$y_t = -\frac{a(L)}{\Delta(L)} Bx_t + \frac{a(L)}{\Delta(L)} v_t;$$

therefore, we have, *neglecting the influence of exogenous variables*, x_t,

$$\frac{a(L)}{\Delta(L)} \int_{-\pi}^{\pi} e^{i\omega t}\, dV(\omega) = \int_{-\pi}^{\pi} e^{i\omega t}\, T(\omega)\, dV(\omega). \tag{6.4.4}$$

The *transfer matrix* $T(\omega)$ is defined as the matrix of rational functions in ω obtained by operating on $e^{i\omega t}$ by $a(L)/\Delta(L)$. The interchange of the order of operations $\left(\text{integration and } \frac{a(L)}{\Delta(L)}\right)$ is permissible for stable systems. The spectrum representation of the stochastic response of the system is

$$dY(\omega) = T(\omega)\, dV(\omega);$$

hence, the spectrum matrix of the system is

$$E[T(\omega)\, dV(\omega)\, dV^*(\omega)\, T^*(\omega)] = T(\omega)\, f(\omega)\, T^*(\omega). \tag{6.4.5}$$

The Klein-Goldberger model is not linear, but E. P. Howrey has made a linear approximation of the system and evaluated the spectrum matrix from the above formulas.[16] He finds that most of the endogenous variables in first difference form show relative peaks in the computed power spectra at a point between four and six years in the endogenous tax yield case. This agrees with the four year cycle found by Adelman and Adelman using numerical methods.

If taxes are treated as exogenous variables, only long cycles appear in the

[16] E. P. Howrey, "Stochastic Properties of the Klein-Goldberger Model," *Econometrica*, 39 (January, 1971), 73–87.

power spectra. For simulation of the system, as opposed to parameter estimation, we would treat taxes as endogenous variables.

Not only did Howrey find the same estimate of periodicity using spectral methods, as did Adelman and Adelman using numerical methods, but he found almost the same phase difference among series.

The two approaches should be expected to give consistent and similar results, but the numerical-experimental method is subject to a sampling error. Its results depend on the particular sample of random errors that are chosen. Although the spectral technique may appear to be theoretically superior, it should be pointed out that it, too, is not free of sampling error. The estimated power spectra depend on the estimated parameter values of the whole system and are subject to error. We do not have the true power spectra—only estimates of them. Moreover, it should be pointed out that numerical methods are often simpler to apply in nonlinear models.

The application of spectral analysis described above is for linear models or linear approximations of nonlinear models. A way of getting around the restrictions of linearity is to form numerical simulations of nonlinear models and calculate the spectra of variables from such dynamic solutions. This is a combination of the Adelman and Howrey procedures.

The particular model simulated for the purposes of spectral analysis is the Wharton Econometric Forecasting Model.[17] It was solved for one hundred future quarters from the third quarter of 1968. Exogenous variables were projected along their historical trend paths or fixed at policy levels to assure a smooth growth solution with approximately 4 percent unemployment. The numerical analysis was somewhat more general than that of Adelman and Adelman in their simulation of the Klein-Goldberger Model:

(i) The Wharton Model is simulated quarterly; the Klein-Goldberger Model is simulated annually. This is, of course, a difference in the structure of the two models.

(ii) For the Wharton Model simulation, the covariance matrix of error allowed for nonzero off-diagonal terms; the Adelman study of the Klein-Goldberger Model used a diagonal covariance matrix of error.

(iii) Nonzero serial correlation of error was permitted in the Wharton Model simulation; the errors for the simulation of the Klein-Goldberger model were serially uncorrelated.

(iv) The Wharton Model simulations were replicated fifty times; the Klein-Goldberger Model simulation was made once.

Fifty spectral diagrams were made for each of several variables in the model from the formula

$$f(\omega_j) = \frac{1}{2}\lambda_0 r_0 + \sum_{k=1}^{m} \lambda_k r_k \cos(\omega_j k) \tag{6.4.6}$$

[17] M. K. Evans, L. R. Klein, and M. Saito, "Short Run Prediction and Long Run Simulation of the Wharton Model," *Econometric Models of Cyclical Behavior*, ed. B. Hickman, N. Y.: Columbia Univ. Press, (1972), 139–85.

where

$$\omega_j = \frac{\pi j}{n} \qquad j = 0, 1, 2, \ldots, n$$

r_k = autocorrelation coefficient of lag k

λ_k = weight of a filter

$$\lambda_k = \begin{cases} 1 - \frac{6k^2}{m^2}\left(1 - \frac{k}{m}\right), & 0 \leq k \leq \frac{m}{2} \\ 2\left(1 - \frac{k}{m}\right)^3 & \frac{m}{2} \leq k \leq m \end{cases}$$

m = number of lags used (80)

n = number of points at which the spectrum is evaluated (40).

In Fig. (6.4.1), the average spectrum of real GNP is graphed. The ordinates are averaged over the fifty replications at each of the forty frequency points at which the spectrum is evaluated. The long run simulations of GNP all exhibited strong upward growth trends and needed to be de-trended for spectral analysis. Deviations of each stochastic simulation from the mean value of each time point (approximately the same as the corresponding nonstochastic simulation) gave appropriate trendless series of cyclic variation.

Evidence of a cycle is indicated by distinct peaks in the spectral diagram. In this case there is a distinct peak at a frequency of sixteen quarters (four years). We neglect the peak at eighty quarters, for the simulation is not long enough to provide evidence of a fluctuation of this length. Many of the individual simulations among the fifty replications showed different periodicities but the average spectrum gives a good estimate of a dominant prevailing cycle length. It is interesting that the finding from this analysis of a large quarterly model is close to the result found by the Adelmans and Howrey, using another, smaller model and different methods of analysis.

There is yet another way to measure cyclic variation. Slutsky noted, in his celebrated paper, that a tendency towards sinusoidal fluctuation will be revealed in proportionality between a series x_t and the negative of its second difference.

$$\Delta^2 x_t = x_{t+2} - 2x_{t+1} + x_t = -\lambda x_{t+1}. \tag{6.4.7}$$

Points on a sine curve would satisfy this relationship provided

$$(2 - \lambda)^2 < 4. \tag{6.4.8}$$

The solution to the finite difference equation in (6.4.7) restricted by (6.4.8) is an undamped sine curve because the characteristic equation is

$$\rho^2 - (2 - \lambda)\rho + 1 = 0 \tag{6.4.9}$$

with roots

$$\rho = \frac{(2 - \lambda) \pm \sqrt{(2 - \lambda)^2 - 4}}{2}. \tag{6.4.10}$$

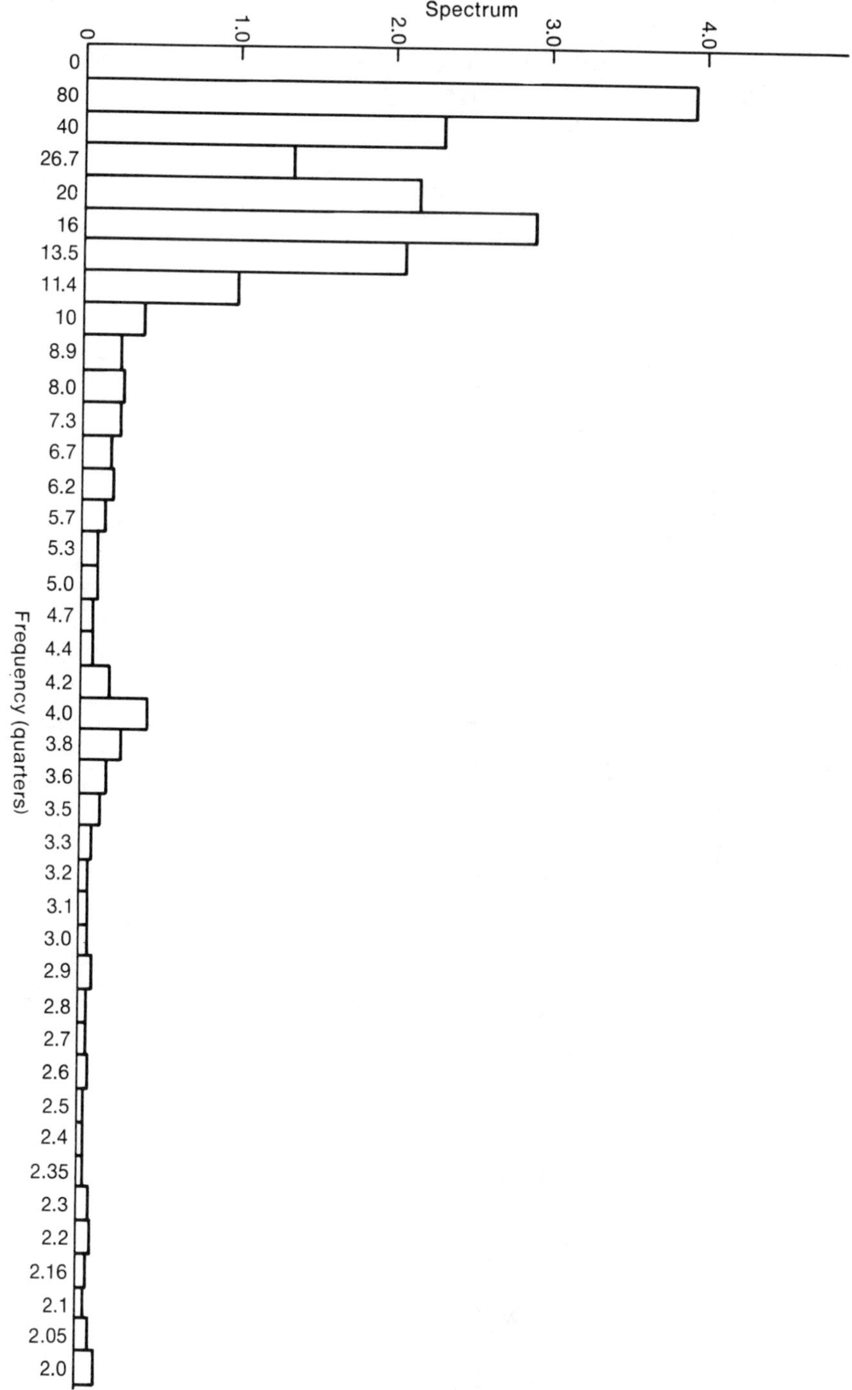

Figure 6.4.1 Average Spectrum of Simulated GNP (1958 dollars)

The roots are imaginary if (6.4.8) holds and the modulus is unity. The fact that the coefficient of x_t is unity guarantees that

$$|\rho| = 1$$

in this case.

An intuitive reason why the finite difference relation suggested by Slutsky should hold is that for

$$x = \mu \sin \sqrt{\lambda}\, t$$

we have

$$\frac{dx}{dt} = \mu\sqrt{\lambda} \cos \sqrt{\lambda}\, t$$

$$\frac{d^2x}{dt} = -\mu\lambda \sin \sqrt{\lambda}\, t = -\lambda x.$$

Given the experimental time series (replicated) for real GNP, expressed as deviations from the nonstochastic trend path, we can fit relations such as (6.4.7) by least squares methods to estimate λ. With an estimate of this parameter, we can determine the periodicity of the solution in the form of a sine function. This approach finds the best fitting undamped sine function. Its periodicity is an estimate of the periodicity of GNP in the simulated models. *Best-fitting* is understood to be defined in terms of the corresponding finite difference equation expressed in (6.4.7). It is appropriate in this connection to regress $\Delta^2 x_t$ on x_{t+1} because the latter is predetermined with respect to the former. This can be seen by writing

$$x_{t+2} + x_t = (2 - \lambda)x_{t+1}.$$

The dependent variable for regression purposes may be $x_{t+2} + x_t$. This restricts the coefficient of x_t and guarantees that the roots have unit modulus. If the regression coefficient of x_t is fixed, then the right-hand side is predetermined with respect to the left.

The mean value of the estimate of $2 - \lambda$ from fifty regressions is

$$\text{mean est. } (2 - \lambda) = 1.7945.$$

Each of the fifty separate regressions is highly significant.

Because

$$(1.7945)^2 < 4,$$

the characteristic roots are conjugate complex (6.4.10). In trigonometric form, we have

$$\text{Cos } \theta = \frac{1.7945}{2} = 0.89725$$

$$\theta = 26.17$$

$$\text{period} = \frac{360}{26.17} = 13.8 \text{ quarters,}$$

that is only slightly less than the spectral estimate.

The analysis is simple and unambiguous in the second-order case, but there is no reason why we should not fit higher order difference equations with more than one pair of conjugate complex roots and unit modulus. The observed fluctuations in GNP may be the result of combinations of sine curves. We could fit[18]

$$x_{t+4} + x_t = \lambda_3 x_{t+3} + \lambda_2 x_{t+2} + \lambda_1 x_{t+1} \tag{6.4.11}$$

and find the roots of

$$\rho^4 - \lambda_3 \rho^3 - \lambda_2 \rho^2 - \lambda_1 \rho + 1 = 0. \tag{6.4.12}$$

The solution for this and higher order cases cannot be written in closed form expressions, but the roots could be determined by numerical methods.

The choice between (6.4.11) and (6.4.7) would depend on whether the addition of higher order lags significantly improved the goodness of fit. Because the dependent variable in the regression changes from $x_{t+2} + x_t$ to $x_{t+4} + x_t$, the correlation coefficient is not a satisfactory measure of goodness of fit. A more appropriate measure would be the estimate of residual variance that shows how closely the time series of x is being fitted under the restriction that all the roots have unit modulus. In the case at hand, the residual variance decreases markedly as we move from specification (6.4.7) to (6.4.11); we therefore accept the latter.

Questions and Problems

1. Devise a test for an answer to the question whether business cycles are endogenous or exogenous.

2. Contrast the methods of cyclical analysis discussed in the text with the straight forward fitting of trigonometric functions to the observed or computed time series of dependent variables, y_{it}.

3. Is spectral analysis of cyclical characteristics implied by an econometric model free of sampling error? How does sampling error affect the conclusions of numerical stochastic simulation?

[18] If we impose the restriction $\lambda_3 = \lambda_1$, we shall find that the roots are, in pairs, all conjugate complex. The fact that the coefficient of x_t is unity guarantees that the roots have unit modulus. The added restriction may be simply taken into account by using $x_{t+3} + x_{t+1}$ as a single independent variable in the regression calculation for λ's.

5. STANDARD ERROR OF FORECAST

The applications of macroeconometric models discussed so far in this chapter have been entirely in terms of point estimates, that is, the numerically estimated values of parameters have been used as though they were the correct values, and computations have been made from them. No attention has been paid yet to the reliability of simulation, predictions, or quantitative cyclical characteristics.

First, we shall consider the linear, static model. Dynamics and nonlinearities will introduce complications that we shall deal with later. The simplest case of the linear dynamic model is the single equation of the form

$$y_t = \sum_{i=1}^{m} \beta_i x_{it} + e_t.$$

The typical problem of prediction is usually posed as the second step of a two-step problem. In the first step, we use the sample observations ($y_1, y_2, \ldots, y_T$; $x_1, x_2, \ldots, x_T$) to estimate the β_i and $var(e_t)$. In the second step, we use the estimated relation to predict y_{T+1} from

$$y^f_{T+1} = \sum_{i=1}^{m} b_i x_{i,T+1}, \tag{6.5.1}$$

where $b_i = est.\ \beta_i$. It is the reliability of this prediction that we want to judge on the basis of evaluation of standard error of forecast.

It should be observed that this formulation of the problem generalizes to any statement outside the sample, $t \neq 1, 2, \ldots, T$; and applications can also be made to within-sample simulations. Because the model is static, what we say about $t = T + 1$ could also be said about $T + j$, $j = 2, 3, 4, \ldots$.

The well-known formula for the variance of y^f_{T+1} is

$$S^2_{y^f_{T+1}} = \sum_{i,j} S_{ij} x_{i,T+1} x_{j,T+1} + S^2_e \tag{6.5.2}$$

where

S_{ij} = estimated covariance between b_i and b_j
S_e = estimated variance of e_t.

This is derived from the two expressions

$$y^f_{T+1} = \sum_{i=1}^{m} b_i x_{i,T+1} \tag{6.5.1}$$

$$y_{T+1} = \sum_{i=1}^{m} \beta_i x_{i,T+1} + e_{T+1}. \tag{6.5.3}$$

We subtract to form

$$(y^f_{T+1} - y_{T+1}) = \sum_{i=1}^{m} (b_i - \beta_i) x_{i,T+1} - e_{T+1}. \tag{6.5.4}$$

We obtain

$$E(y^f_{T+1} - y_{T+1})^2 = var\, y^f_{T+1}$$
$$= \sum_{i,j} E(b_i - \beta_i)(b_j - \beta_j)x_{i,T+1}x_{j,T+1} + var\,(e_{T+1}). \quad (6.5.5)$$

We note that e_{T+1} is independent of $(b_i - \beta_i)$. The latter is a linear function of $e_1, e_2, \ldots, e_T$ and if the e_t are mutually independent, we have zero covariance between e_{T+1} and any element of $(b_i - \beta_i)$. In the formula for $S^2_{y^f_{T+1}}$, we replace expected values of variances and covariances by their sample estimates.

The estimates S_{ij} are computed from

$$(S_{ij}) = S^2_e\left(\sum_{t=1}^{T} x_{it}x_{jt}\right)^{-1}$$
$$S^2_e = \frac{1}{T-m}\sum_{t=1}^{T}\left(y_t - \sum_{i=1}^{m} b_i x_{it}\right)^2.$$

This formula shows that the standard error of forecast depends on the reliability of the regression coefficients b_i, and on the size of the residual error variance S^2_e. It also depends on the values of the exogenous variables $x_{i,T+1}$ in the prediction period. This expression is a positive definite quadratic form in $x_{i,T+1}$; therefore, as values of $x_{i,T+1}$ become large, the forecast error increases. In a bivariate relationship, the picture is

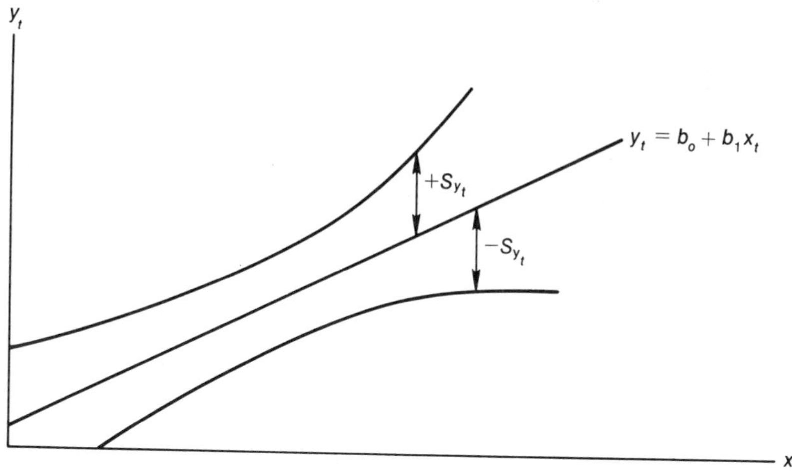

Figure 6.5.1 Standard Error of Forecast

For values of x_t near the sample mean, the width between the two error bands is minimal, and, as applications are made at points more distant from average experience, the band width grows.

The interval $y^f_{T+1} \pm k\,S_e$, where k depends on $S_{ij}x_{i,T+1}\,x_{j,T+1}$, and e_t is normally distributed, defines a range within which at least p percent of such future observations are expected to lie with probability γ, for suitably chosen k. The value selected for k depends on p, γ, $x_{i,T+1}$, and sample size. Wallis has shown how to calculate k.[19] He estimates the *effective* sample size, that is, the number of observations on y_{T+1} at the given values of $x_{i,T+1}$ needed to give the same degree of precision as would be obtained by estimating y_{T+1} from

$$y^f_{T+1} = \sum_{i=1}^{m} b_i x_{i,T+1}.$$

The variance of the computed value, y^f_{T+1}, for given values $x_{i,T+1}$, apart from the contribution of *var* e_{T+1}, is given by,

$$var\,(y^f_{T+1}) = var\,(e) \sum_{i,\,j} m^{ij} x_{i,T+1} x_{j,T+1}$$

$$(m^{ij}) = \left(\sum_{t=1}^{T} x_{it} x_{jt}\right)^{-1}.$$

The *effective* number of observations is, therefore,

$$T' = \frac{1}{\sum_{i,\,j} m^{ij} x_{i,T+1} x_{j,T+1}}. \tag{6.5.6}$$

The value of k is computed from

$$\chi^2_\gamma(T - m) = \frac{(T - m)r^2}{k^2} \tag{6.5.7}$$

where $\chi^2_\gamma(T - m)$ is the *chi*-square distribution value for $T - m$ degrees of freedom and probability γ that χ^2 exceeds $\chi^2_\gamma(T - m)$. The quantity r is determined from tables of the normal distribution so that the following probability expression is satisfied:

$$p = \frac{1}{\sqrt{2\pi}} \int_{(1/\sqrt{T'})-r}^{(1/\sqrt{T'})+r} e^{-u^2/2}\, du. \tag{6.5.8}$$

Given r from normal tables and $\chi^2_\gamma(T - m)$ from *chi*-square tables, we can determine k. The sample estimate of *var*(e) is then used to form the interval

$$y^f_{T+1} \pm kS_e,$$

that has probability γ of including proportion p of population values of y. The interval may be used to judge the precision of forecasting or to test whether

[19] W. Allen Wallis, "Tolerance Intervals for Linear Regressions," *Proceedings of the Second Berkeley Symposium on Mathematical Statistics and Probability*, ed. J. Neyman (Berkeley and Los Angeles: University of California Press, 1951), pp. 43–51.

nonsample observations on y_t come from the same universe (relationship and error distribution) as the sample values.

A strong assumption made in the derivation of the formula for $S_{y^f_{T+1}}$ is that $x_{i,T+1}$ are known without error. If the $x_{i,T+1}$ are generated by a stochastic mechanism, even if it is independent of e_{T+1}, we must still account for the terms

$$\sum_{i,j} b_i b_j \operatorname{cov} x_{i,T+1} x_{j,T+1}$$

in the complete formula. This is a realistic correction to the formula for $S_{y^f_{T+1}}$ because in applied econometrics we frequently have very uncertain knowledge about the values of exogenous variables.

The situation is even clearer if the prediction formula is dynamic and contains lagged dependent variables. These are given as initial conditions in one-period predictions, that is, we know y_T as a lagged variable for input in the calculation of y_{T+1}, but if we go ahead by two or more time periods, we must generate lagged values of dependent variables to be used as future inputs. These generated values have error. This accounts for the known result that error accumulates, and precision declines as we predict further and further into the future.

In the linear dynamic single equation

$$y_t = \sum_{i=1}^{p} \alpha_i y_{t-i} + \sum_{l=1}^{m} \beta_l x_{lt} + e_t, \tag{6.5.9}$$

the prediction formula is

$$y_{T+j} = \sum_{i=1}^{p} \lambda_i^j C_{iT} + \sum_{k=1}^{j} w_k z_{T+k} \tag{6.5.10}$$

$$z_{T+k} = \sum_{l=1}^{m} \beta_l x_{l,T+k} + e_{T+k}. \tag{6.5.11}$$

The λ_i are roots of the characteristic polynomial

$$\lambda^p - \sum_{i=1}^{p} \alpha_i \lambda^{p-i} = 0; \tag{6.5.12}$$

the C_{iT} are functions of the initial conditions at $t = T$; the w_k are weights that depend on the structural coefficients. Similarly, the roots λ_i depend on the α_i. Variances and covariances of the terms defining y_{T+j} could be approximated as functions of the variances and covariances of the parameter estimates, but these would be complicated expressions, and it seems best to estimate $S_{y^f_{T+1}}$ for this case by numerical methods that we shall outline below. It should be noted, though, that the terms

$$\sum_{k=1}^{j} w_k e_{T+k}$$

in the above expression have a variance component

$$\sum_{k=1}^{j} w_k^2 \, var\,(e)$$

that grows with j. In a stable system, that is, with roots $|\lambda_i| < 1$, this variance converges to a finite limit.

Before considering a numerical approach to the evaluation of $S_{y^f_{T+1}}$ for dynamic systems, let us generalize the single equation results for the static case to equation systems.

The static system of equations will be

$$A\, y_t + B\, x_t = e_t$$

with reduced form

$$\begin{aligned} y_t &= \Pi x_t + v_t \\ \Pi &= -A^{-1}B \\ v_t &= A^{-1}e_t. \end{aligned}$$

The covariance matrix of forecast error, for given elements in x_t, is[20]

$$S^2_{y^f_{T+1}} = F_{T+1}\Omega_\pi F'_{T+1} + \Sigma_v \tag{6.5.13}$$

$$F_{T+1} = \begin{bmatrix} x_{1,T+1} & \cdots & x_{m,T+1} & 0 & \cdots & 0 & \cdots & 0 & \cdots & 0 \\ 0 & \cdots & 0 & x_{1,T+1} & \cdots & x_{m,T+1} & \cdots & 0 & \cdots & 0 \\ \cdot & & \cdot & \cdot & & \cdot & & & & \cdot \\ \cdot & & \cdot & \cdot & & \cdot & & & & \cdot \\ \cdot & & \cdot & \cdot & & \cdot & & & & \cdot \\ 0 & \cdots & 0 & 0 & \cdots & 0 & \cdots & x_{1,T+1} & \cdots & x_{m,T+1} \end{bmatrix}$$

$$\Omega_\pi = \begin{bmatrix} \Omega_{11} & \cdots & \Omega_{1n} \\ \cdot & & \cdot \\ \cdot & \Omega_{ij} & \cdot \\ \cdot & & \cdot \\ \Omega_{n1} & \cdots & \Omega_{nn} \end{bmatrix}$$

$$\Sigma_v = \begin{bmatrix} Ev_{1t}^2 & \cdots & Ev_{1t}v_{nt} \\ \cdot & & \cdot \\ \cdot & & \cdot \\ \cdot & & \cdot \\ Ev_{nt}v_{1t} & \cdots & Ev_{nt}^2. \end{bmatrix}$$

F_{T+1} is an $n \times nm$ matrix display of the exogenous variables at forecast period

[20] See A. S. Goldberger, A. L. Nagar, and H. S. Odeh, "The Covariance Matrices of Reduced Form Coefficients and of Forecasts for a Structural Econometric Model," *Econometrica*, 29 (October, 1961), 556–73. See also T. M. Brown, "Standard Errors of Forecast of a Complete Econometric Model," *Econometrica*, 22 (April, 1954), 178–92.

$T+1$; Ω_π is an $mn \times mn$ covariance matrix of reduced form coefficients. Each element of $\Omega_\pi(\Omega_{ij})$ is an $m \times m$ covariance matrix associating variation of parameter estimates in the ith with variation of parameter estimates in the jth reduced form. Σ_v is an $n \times n$ covariance matrix of reduced form disturbances.

From unrestricted reduced form regressions it would be simple enough to evaluate estimates of expressions for Ω_π and Σ_v. If there are identifying restrictions on A and B, it is more difficult to derive the appropriate expressions and execute the necessary calculations.

First, let us consider Σ_v. The estimation of this matrix presents fewer problems. If there are (restricted) structural estimates of A and B ($\hat{A}$ and $\hat{B}$), we could compute (restricted) reduced form residuals from

$$y_t + \hat{A}^{-1}\hat{B}x_t = (\text{res.})_t. \tag{6.5.14}$$

The sample covariance matrix of these residuals provides an estimate $\hat{\Sigma}_v$. From the structural equation residuals, it is also possible to compute directly $\hat{\Sigma}_e$ and therefore to evaluate

$$\hat{\Sigma}_v = \hat{A}^{-1}\hat{\Sigma}_e(\hat{A}^{-1})'. \tag{6.5.15}$$

It is more of a problem to express Ω_π in terms of Ω_{AB}, the covariance matrix of the estimated parameters in A and B. Goldberger, Nagar, and Odeh make use of the asymptotic formulas for expressing the covariance matrix of one set of random variables in terms of the covariance matrix of a functionally related set.

Let the functional relationships be

$$z_i = f_i(w_1, \ldots, w_m) \qquad i = 1, 2, \ldots, n$$

and

$$\lim_{T\to\infty} E\, w_i = r_i; \;\; \lim_{T\to\infty} TE\,[(w-r)(w-r)'] = \Sigma_w.$$

Then

$$\lim_{T\to\infty} TE\,[(z - f(r_1, \ldots, r_m))(z - f(r_1, \ldots, r_m))'] = D\Sigma_w D' \tag{6.5.16}$$

where

$$D = \left| \frac{\partial f_i}{\partial w_j} \right|_{w=r}.$$

If this result is applied to the problem of relating the covariance matrix of reduced form coefficients to that of structural coefficients, we have

$$\Omega_\pi = G\Omega_{AB}G' \tag{6.5.17}$$

$$G = A^{-1} \otimes (\Pi I) = \begin{pmatrix} \alpha^{11}(\Pi I) & \cdots & \alpha^{1n}(\Pi I) \\ \cdot & & \cdot \\ \cdot & & \cdot \\ \cdot & & \cdot \\ \alpha^{n1}(\Pi I) & \cdots & \alpha^{nn}(\Pi I) \end{pmatrix}. \tag{6.5.18}$$

$\otimes$ is the Kronecker product symbol, and I is the $m \times m$ identity matrix. An estimate of G is obtained by substituting $\hat{A}$ and $\hat{\Pi}$ to obtain

$$\hat{G} = \hat{A}^{-1} \otimes (\hat{\Pi} I).$$

We, therefore, have

$$\hat{\Omega}_\pi = \hat{G}\hat{\Omega}_{AB}\hat{G}'. \tag{6.5.19}$$

The structural parameter estimates, together with their covariance estimates, give us enough information to evaluate $\hat{\Omega}_\pi$ and $\hat{\Sigma}_v$, and we can estimate $S^2_{y^f_{T+1}}$.

Full information maximum likelihood methods for estimating A, B, Σ_e provide us with direct, asymptotic estimates of the covariance matrix Ω_{AB} for all coefficients in the system, whether in the same or different equations. If we use a single equation method of estimation, however, it is not obvious how covariance between coefficients in different equations should be estimated. This would be relevant for TSLS or LIML methods. Theil gives the following result for the covariance estimates of coefficients in the ith and j^{th} equations of a system computed by TSLS methods.[21]

$$\hat{\sigma}_{e_{ij}} \lim_{T\to\infty} TE\left[\begin{pmatrix} \hat{Y}_i'\hat{Y}_i & Y_i'X_i \\ X_i'Y_i & X_i'X_i \end{pmatrix}^{-1} \begin{pmatrix} \hat{Y}_i'\hat{Y}_j & Y_i'X_j \\ X_i'Y_j & X_i'X_j \end{pmatrix} \begin{pmatrix} \hat{Y}_j'\hat{Y}_j & Y_j'X_j \\ X_j'Y_j & X_j'X_j \end{pmatrix}^{-1}\right]. \tag{6.5.20}$$

$\hat{\sigma}_{e_{ij}}$ is the estimated covariance between e_i and e_j. It can be computed from sample residuals. Y_i is a submatrix of

$$\begin{pmatrix} y_{11} & \cdots & y_{n1} \\ \cdot & & \cdot \\ \cdot & & \cdot \\ \cdot & & \cdot \\ y_{1T} & \cdots & y_{nT} \end{pmatrix},$$

and X_i is a submatrix of

$$\begin{pmatrix} x_{11} & \cdots & x_{m1} \\ \cdot & & \cdot \\ \cdot & & \cdot \\ \cdot & & \cdot \\ x_{1T} & \cdots & x_{mT} \end{pmatrix}.$$

In each case, the submatrices include only the variables with nonzero coefficients in the ith equation. $\hat{Y}_i$ are values of Y_i computed from unrestricted reduced forms.

Treating lag values as though they were exogenous variables in a small six-equation dynamic model (three stochastic equations plus three definitions)

[21] H. Theil, *Economic Forecasts and Policy* (Amsterdam: North-Holland, 1958), p. 341.

fitted to data of the interwar period, Goldberger, Nagar, and Odeh computed the standard error of forecast in conjunction with an extrapolation of the model to a postwar year—1948.[22] In Table 6.5.1, the actual values, point prediction, and estimates of Sy^f_{1948} are given.

TABLE 6.5.1

Forecasts and Error, 1948
(*1934 Prices*)

	Observation	*Prediction*	Sy^f_{1948}
Consumption	82.8	78.2	7.6
Investment	6.4	9.3	5.8
Wage bill	60.7	59.9	7.1
Profits	27.9	27.2	7.2
National income	97.4	95.7	12.6
Capital stock	204.1	207.0	5.8

Some comments appear to be called for in connection with this table:

1) The model seems to perform reasonably well. Although it is a small system, its extrapolation from the end of the sample period, 1941, to a postwar year, 1948, is reasonably close. This is noteworthy because the economy underwent such unusual stress during the intervening period, 1942–47.

2) The goodness of the extrapolation may be measured by the size of error (observed-predicted value) relative to the estimated standard error of forecast. In all cases, the error is much smaller, in absolute value, than the standard error of forecast.

3) The standard error of forecast, by itself, defines a wide interval, one that is too wide for practical application. On modern standards for economic analysis, we require total output (GNP or national income) to be estimated within \$5 billion for production levels that are considerably larger than those of 1948.

In practice, we do much better in accuracy of prediction than would be suggested by calculation of standard error of forecast. Of course, we have not taken up the issue of how large to make the present error band for given probability levels of protection against mistakes. If the appropriate error band exceeds one standard error of forecast, as seems reasonable, the interval will be even more useless for economic analysis.

The lack of precision may be a result of the smallness of the system, the failure to deal appropriately with problems of lags and serial correlation, or the linear approximation formulas in (6.5.16).[23] Also, the system is purely linear;

[22] The model used is Model I from L. R. Klein, *Economic Fluctuations in the United States, 1921–1941* (New York: John Wiley & Sons, 1950).

[23] The numerical methods of estimating standard error of forecast, described below, suggest that the errors for the same six-equation model used for illustrative purposes are much smaller. The numerical methods do not make linear approximations.

whereas nonlinear systems are more appropriate for general models of the economy as a whole. Nonlinearity may be a necessary part of correct specification in economic models and may not contribute to the largeness of the forecast intervals in this instance. Judging by the closeness between predicted and actual values, nonlinearity does not seem to have been a problem in the extrapolation of this model over a long distorted stretch of time.

In single period point forecasting, lag variables are no problem. They are treated like exogenous variables, both in the sample estimation period and in the forecast application period. In general, however, lag values are not known without error in applications. Even in single period predictions, the lag values are often assigned imprecise preliminary values. But in multiperiod prediction, lags must be generated by the solution of the dynamic system from fixed initial conditions; thus they are not assumed to be known values, as are exogenous variables.

We remarked above that some exogenous variables are known only imprecisely in some applications; therefore, the formula for standard error of forecast must take into account the variability of such magnitudes. Similarly, they must allow for variability in lag variables if they have been generated, with accumulated error, by solution of the system.

In the single equation, with lag variables

$$y_t = \sum_{i=1}^{p} \alpha_i y_{t-i} + \sum_{i=1}^{m} \beta_i x_{it} + e_t,$$

the prediction of y_{T+2} would be from the formula

$$y^f_{T+2} = \hat{\alpha}_1 y^f_{T+1} + \sum_{i=2}^{p} \hat{\alpha}_i y_{T+2-i} + \sum_{i=1}^{m} \hat{\beta}_i x_{i,T+2},$$

where

$$y^f_{T+1} = \sum_{i=1}^{p} \hat{\alpha}_i y_{T+1-i} + \sum_{i=1}^{m} \hat{\beta}_i x_{i,T+1}.$$

In addition to the usual allowances for sampling variability in $\hat{\alpha}_i$ and $\hat{\beta}_i$ for given lags and exogenous variables, we must allow for variability in y^f_{T+1}, including covariation between y^f_{T+1} and $\hat{\alpha}_i$, $\hat{\beta}_i$. In the limit as $\hat{\alpha}_i$ and $\hat{\beta}_i$ approach α_i and β_i, we would have the stochastic part of y^f_{T+1} dependent only on e_{T+1}; it would thus be independent of $\hat{\alpha}_i$, $\hat{\beta}_i$, that depend on $e_1, \ldots, e_T$, in the serially uncorrelated case. For finite samples, however, we must add the following terms to the formula for standard error of forecast:

$$\hat{\alpha}_1^2 S^2_{y^f_{T+1}} + \sum_{i=2}^{p} S_{\hat{\alpha}_i y^f_{T+1}}(\hat{\alpha}_1 y_{T+2-i}) + \sum_{i=1}^{m} S_{\hat{\beta}_i y^f_{T+1}}(\hat{\alpha}_1 x_{i,T+2}).$$

As we generate more lagged input for more distant prediction, we have more terms like these to add to the formula for standard error of forecast.

For the large system, the nonlinear system, and the dynamic system, the formulas for standard error of forecast would become quite complicated; therefore a numerical method is suggested for dealing with the general situation. Let us assume that the parameters of the system,

$$f_i(y_{1t}, \ldots, y_{nt}, y_{1,t-1}, \ldots, y_{n,t-p}, x_{1t}, \ldots, x_{mt}) = e_{it}$$

have been estimated by some consistent method, using nonlinear techniques of estimation theory as discussed above.

Among the parameter estimates of this model, we shall have an estimate of the elements of Σ_e, the variance-covariance matrix of error. We may draw fresh sets of random errors, say from a normal distribution, having the same covariance matrix as this sample estimate.[24] For the sample observations on exogenous variables,

$$x_{i1}, x_{i2}, \ldots, x_{iT} \qquad i = 1, 2, \ldots, m,$$

the sample parameter estimates, and the random error drawings, we can solve the equation system for a pseudo sample

$$y_{i1}^{(s)}, y_{i2}^{(s)}, \ldots, y_{iT}^{(s)}, \qquad i = 1, 2, \ldots, n$$

of dependent variables. If the system is nonlinear, the algorithm discussed on pp. 240–241 may be used to generate the pseudo sample. The solution can be obtained in the following ways:

(a) From fixed initial conditions

$$y_{i,-1}, y_{i,-2}, \ldots, y_{i,-p} \qquad i = 1, 2, \ldots, n$$

the system can be solved over the whole sample period to give all current and lagged values of dependent variables.

(b) The initial values can be reset every period so that observed lag values are used. This solution corresponds to the calculations for one-period predictions and the treatment of lag variables *as though they were exogenous variables.*

(c) The initial values can be reset periodically to cover spans as long as typical forecasts.

Using one of these methods, preferably (a) or (c), we can generate $S(s = 1, 2, \ldots, S)$ pseudo samples of y_{it} and the corresponding lag values. Each pseudo sample and the observed values $x_{i1}, \ldots, x_{iT}$ can be used as a new sample

[24] A. L. Nagar has shown how to draw random variables with a given covariance matrix. See his paper on "Stochastic Simulation of the Brookings Econometric Model," *The Brookings Model: Some Further Results*, ed. J. Duesenberry et al. (Chicago: Rand-McNally, 1969). An alternative and simpler technique has been suggested by M. D. McCarthy, "Some Notes on the Generation of Pseudo Structural Errors for Use in Stochastic Simulation Studies," *Econometric Models of Cyclical Behavior*, ed. B. Hickman, N.Y.: Columbia Univ. Press, 1972, 185–91.

from which to estimate new coefficients. We shall then have S numerical systems

$$f_i^{(s)}(y_{1t}, \ldots, y_{nt}, y_{1,t-1}, \ldots, y_{n,t-p}, x_{1t}, \ldots, x_{mt}) = 0. \tag{6.5.21}$$

These systems will each be projected into a forecast period $T+1, T+2, \ldots, T+k$, all using the same exogenous variables, $x_{i,T+1}, \ldots, x_{i,T+k}$. Each period's forecast should be computed from disturbed equations, the disturbances being drawn for the forecast period from a normal population with covariance matrix, $\hat{\Sigma}_e$. This will provide S forecasts of length k. The standard error of forecast for any particular variable will be

$$Sy_{i,T+j}^f = \sqrt{\frac{1}{S}\sum_{s=1}^{S}(y_{i,T+j}^{(s)f} - y_{i,T+j}^f)^2}. \tag{6.5.22}$$

The reference values $y_{j,T+j}^f$ will be taken from projections of the sample estimates of the system, or from observations if they are available ex post.

The computation of standard error of forecast by this method jointly takes into account nonlinearity, small sample variability of coefficients, superimposed random error, and cumulation of error through sequential solution of a dynamic system. The calculation is specific to the actual numerical experiment, but it should give a good indication of error in a general model containing many complications.[25]

Thus far, we have been treating the prediction problem as though the errors are mutually independent. In the derivation of the general formulas for standard error of forecast, it has been assumed that the errors at different time points are mutually independent. Independence was not specified in the numerical method just outlined for calculating the standard error of forecast on an experimental basis; it could, if so desired, be built into the solution process for generating the random errors.

The essential problem is the use of whatever information is available about the prediction of specific values for e_{T+j}, $j = 1, 2, \ldots, k$, in the application of a model. A standard procedure would be to assign zero to each value of e_{T+j} since

$$E\,e_t = 0,$$

and attach a measure of precision to this estimate on the basis of S_e^2. Two possibilities exist for the assignment of particular nonzero values to e_{T+j}. A priori information about some components of e_{T+j} may enable us to assign values $\hat{e}_{T+j}$. A more statistical approach would be to estimate e_{T+j} on the basis of lag correla-

[25] See George Schink, "Estimation of Forecast Error in a Dynamic and/or Non-linear Econometric Model," paper presented at the Evanston Meetings of the Econometric Society, December, 1968, (Ph.D. dissertation, University of Pennsylvania, 1971).

tions. If the original structure of a linear system is

$$\sum_{i=0}^{p} A_i y_{t-i} + Bx_t = e_t, \tag{6.5.23}$$

$$e_t = \sum_{i=1}^{q} P_i e_{t-i} + v_t, \tag{6.5.24}$$

we can transform the system to

$$\sum_{i=0}^{p} A_i y_{t-i} - \sum_{i=1}^{q} \sum_{j=0}^{p} P_i A_j y_{t-i-j} + Bx_t - \sum_{i=1}^{q} P_i B x_{t-i} = v_t. \tag{6.5.25}$$

In the absence of special knowledge about v_{T+j}, we can assign zero values to this transformed error term and use the transformed system with longer lag structure for prediction application.

The methods of estimation of parameters in A_i, P_i, and B for the autoregressive case, as discussed above, can be used to determine $\hat{A}_i$, $\hat{P}_i$ and $\hat{B}$. Either, we can predict from the above transformed equation system (6.5.25) using these parameter estimates, or we can predict from

$$\sum_{i=0}^{p} \hat{A}_i y_{t-i} + \hat{B}x_t = \hat{e}_t; \qquad t = T+1, \ldots, T+k, \tag{6.5.26}$$

where $\hat{e}_{T+j}$ are estimated from the sample autoregression of residuals. The last sample estimates $\hat{e}_T, \hat{e}_{T-1}, \ldots, \hat{e}_{T-(q-1)}$ are used as known initial values to start the autoregressive calculation. These two approaches are equivalent.

If we consider the prediction problem from the point of view of the transformed equation, (6.5.25), in estimation form,

$$\sum_{i=0}^{p} \hat{A}_i y_{t-i} - \sum_{i=1}^{q} \sum_{j=0}^{p} \hat{P}_i \hat{A}_j y_{t-i-j} + \hat{B}x_t - \sum_{i=1}^{q} \hat{P}_i \hat{B} x_{t-i} = 0,$$

we see that prediction involves using a formula with longer lags than in the serially uncorrelated case. As we have already argued, there may be error cumulation in multiperiod prediction from lag schemes and it is not obvious that this prediction formula is going to perform better than

$$\sum_{i=0}^{p} \hat{A}_i y_{t-i} + \hat{B}x_t = 0; \qquad t = T+1, \ldots, T+k$$

or even

$$\sum_{i=0}^{p} \tilde{A}_i y_{t-i} + \tilde{B}x_t = 0; \qquad t = T+1, \ldots, T+k,$$

where $\tilde{A}$ and $\tilde{B}$ are estimates that disregard the presence of serial correlation in the error structure.

In applied econometric forecasting from estimated models, it appears that a combination of use of a priori information about some components of $\hat{e}_{T+j}$ and use of estimated autoregressive properties provide the best predictions. For approximately the last six values before each prediction period, mean values of $(res.)_T$, $(res.)_{T-1}$, $(res.)_{T-2}$, $(res.)_{T-3}$, $(res.)_{T-4}$, $(res.)_{T-5}$ are computed. Where there is a priori information about the reasons for nonzero values of $(res)_t$ in the recent past and serial reasons for corresponding nonzero values into the future, we assign particular values to $(res.)_{T+j}$. The system is started on a prediction period with approximate equality between actual and computed values for each variable. This has proved to be a workable and efficient method for economic prediction.[26]

Questions and Problems

1. What are the sources of error in econometric forecasting?
2. What suggestions do you have for the reduction of forecast error in econometrics?
3. How does serial correlation of error affect forecast accuracy?

6. ESTIMATION AND PREDICTION

The applications of econometric models to policy questions, tests of economic hypotheses, and prediction are made as the second step of a two-step procedure. In the first instance, the parameters of a model are estimated from sample data according to criteria such as goodness of fit or optimal probability characteristics. In the next step, the estimated models are applied to nonsample situations. This two-step procedure is intuitively attractive and, in some sense, optimal for applications if there are no lag values. The presence of lags and other dynamic properties makes the two-step procedure, in the usual case, inconsistent between the sample and application situation. The problem is that in prediction, simulation, and other nonsample applications of a model, we customarily make different assumptions about lag values in the estimation stage and in the application stage. For purposes of estimation, we assume that lag values should be treated like exogenous variables. If the error terms are serially correlated, this procedure leads to an inconsistency in estimation, but in the serially uncorrelated case, Mann and Wald, as we pointed out previously, demonstrated the propriety of treating lag variables as though they were exogenous variables.[27] In

[26] See M. K. Evans and L. R. Klein, *The Wharton Econometric Forecasting Model*, 2nd ed. (Philadelphia: Economic Research Unit, University of Pennsylvania, 1968), especially Appendix A.

[27] H. B. Mann and A. Wald, "On the Statistical Treatment of Linear Stochastic Difference Equations," *Econometrica* 11 (July-Oct., 1943), 173–220.

one-period predictions or applications, as in the static case, there is no problem because lag values are, in fact, initially given. But for multiperiod applications, *the lag values must be generated for periods after the first*. The generated lag values are not error free and cannot be assumed to be given.

The problem we now consider is how to estimate parameters so that we make the same assumptions about lag values in both the sample and application periods. We shall seek estimates that optimize in the sample period with respect to criteria that are analogues of those we use in the prediction period. If the linear system

$$\sum_{i=0}^{p} A_i y_{t-i} + Bx_t = e_t$$

has a solution

$$y_t = K\lambda^t - \frac{a(L)}{\Delta(L)} Bx_t + \frac{a(L)}{\Delta(L)} e_t,$$

we already suggested minimization of the trace of

$$\sum_{t=1}^{T} v_t v_t', \qquad v_t = \frac{a(L)}{\Delta(L)} e_t.$$

In order to avoid the problem of diversity of units of measurement, we might normalize by dividing each trace element by $\sum_{t=1}^{T} (y_{it} - \bar{y}_i)^2$.

This criterion looks for parameter estimates that minimize squared error along the solution path from the start to the end of the sample. Lag values are not assumed to be given; *only the initial conditions and exogenous variables are given*. This is the same assumption that is made in application periods.

If the sample is of T-period length, it is not necessarily true that applications will also be of T period length. If the applications are to be for F periods, $F < T$, we seek parameter estimates such that all F period solutions from fixed initial conditions in the sample period have minimal squared error along the path. It should be emphasized that structural estimates are sought in terms of criteria regarding the solution path. Best unrestricted estimates of solution path parameters or parameters of the final form are not the objective, for these would not enable us to study structural change or many alternative economic policies.

Minimization of $\sum_{t=1}^{T} v_t v_t'$ *w.r.t.* elements of the operator polynomial $A(L)$ and B is a complicated nonlinear estimation problem. An approach that involves nothing more than linear type calculations for linear systems was outlined in a previous chapter as an extension of Jorgenson's method of iterating (one step) two stage least squares estimates. For the case in which the forecast period is short, $F < T$, the calculations may be detailed as follows: Solutions of the system based on initial estimates have to be obtained every sample period for the subsequent F periods. These are

$$\hat{y}_{1,t}, \hat{y}_{2,t}, \ldots, \hat{y}_{F,t} \text{ given } y_{t-1}, y_{t-2}, \ldots, y_{t-p}.$$

The two subscripts on solution values denote respectively how far ahead the solution is to be made and from what initial point it is made. The original system may be rewritten as

$$y_t = -A_0^* y_t - \sum_{i=1}^{p} A_i y_{t-i} - Bx_t + e_t \qquad \alpha_{0_{ii}}^* = 0. \tag{6.6.1}$$

Each element of y_t is a linear function of other elements in y_t, lagged values of y_{t-i} $(i = 1, 2, \ldots, p)$ and independent variables in x_t. In the final regressions, we replace elements of y_t by $\hat{y}_t$ and appropriate elements in y_{t-i} by $\hat{y}_{t-i}$, as follows: We form one single regression for each element of y_t

on

$\hat{y}_{1t}, y_{t-i}$ $(i = 1, 2, \ldots, p)$, and x_t; $\qquad t = 1, 2, \ldots, T$

on

$\hat{y}_{2,t-1}, \hat{y}_{1,t-1}, y_{t-i}$ $(i = 2, 3, \ldots, p)$ and x_t; $\qquad t = 2, 3, \ldots, T$

on

$\hat{y}_{3,t-2}, \hat{y}_{2,t-2}, \hat{y}_{1,t-2}, y_{t-i}$ $(i = 3, \ldots, p)$ and x_t; $\qquad t = 3, 4, \ldots, T$

.
.
.

on

$\hat{y}_{F,t-F+1}, \hat{y}_{F-1,t-F+1}, \hat{y}_{F-2,t-F+1}, \ldots,$ and x_t; $\qquad t = F, F+1, \ldots, T.$

This could be done as one unweighted regression or as weighted regressions in which we attach some a priori significance to predictions of particular length.

In a linear system, values of $\hat{y}_t$ computed for standard applications of TSLS methods of estimation are *instrumental variables* because they are linear functions of predetermined variables. In linear systems, the reduced forms split into a part that is dependent (linearly) on predetermined variables and an independent part that is a linear combination of random errors from the structural equations. The same is true of $\hat{y}_{j,t}$, used in the above method. They are linear functions of exogenous variables and random errors for given initial conditions. This can be seen from the expression

$$y_t = K\lambda^t - \frac{a(L)}{\Delta(L)} Bx_t + \frac{a(L)}{\Delta(L)} e_t.$$

The computed values from this expression are also instrumental variables and are so used in the method of estimation that corresponds to optimal prediction.

This is not true for nonlinear systems. Closed form expressions for dynamic solutions or reduced form equations may not exist.[28] It is not generally possible to express each $\hat{y}_t$ or $\hat{\hat{y}}_{j,t}$ as linear functions of predetermined variables; therefore these magnitudes are not proper instruments for estimation in nonlinear systems. This holds true for systems that are linear in parameters but nonlinear in economic variables. This covers a large number of macroeconometric models now in use.

It is possible, however, to make analogous calculations for nonlinear systems. If such systems are linear in parameters, we can use incomplete systems and estimate coefficients by the methods of TSLS.[29] Having TSLS estimates of a nonlinear system

$$y_{it} = g_i(y_{1t}, \ldots, y_{nt}, y_{1,t-1}, \ldots, y_{n,t-p}, x_{1t}, \ldots, x_{mt}) + e_{it},$$

we can make nonstochastic simulations forward for periods of length F, using the Gauss-Seidel algorithm for solving dynamic, nonlinear, simultaneous equations. This will provide us with estimates $\hat{\hat{y}}_{j,t}$, but they may not be proper instruments. It would seem sensible to use the $\hat{\hat{y}}_{j,t}$ as though they were instruments and proceed, as in the linear case, to make a final stage estimate by regressing elements of y_t on $\hat{\hat{y}}_{j,t}$, y_{t-i}, and x_t laid out in the same manner as for the linear case.

Accuracy of Prediction

The standard error of forecast defines properties of the distribution of forecast values and suggests that a measure of prediction accuracy might be root mean square error

$$\sqrt{\frac{1}{N}\sum_{T=0}^{N-1}(y^f_{T+j} - y_{T+j})^2}. \tag{6.6.2}$$

In this case, a variable is being predicted N times from points $T, T+1, \ldots, T+N-1$ into the future for j periods and then compared with the actual values for y_{T+j} that are eventually observed. The averaging of squared error may be over different starting values for the forecast, over forecasts of different variables (all in homogeneous units), or over forecasts of different length. The usual situation is the first.

We can similarly measure errors by formulas for MAPE, MSPE, MAE, MSE, MAE/SD, MSE/SD, as we developed them above (pp. 242–243) for sample period simulations to compare alternative estimators.

It may be useful to consider further the linear correlation between pre-

[28] Cf. Goldfeld and Quandt, "Nonlinear Simultaneous Equations," *International Economic Review*, (1968).

[29] See Chernoff and Rubin, "Asymptotic Properties of Limited-Information Estimates . . . ," in *Studies in Econometric Method.*

dicted and actual values, also defined above,

$$y^f_{T+j} = a + by_{T+j} + (res.)_{T+j}. \tag{6.6.3}$$

This regression relationship could be computed for different values of T, keeping the length of prediction interval fixed, or for different length predictions, letting j vary, or for a combination of variation in both subscripts. Perfect prediction would be attained when the regression coefficient $a = 0$ and $b = 1$, and all residuals are zero. Then the points (y^f_{T+j}, y_{T+j}) would lie along the 45° line in the prediction-realization diagram. If there is a predominance of points in region

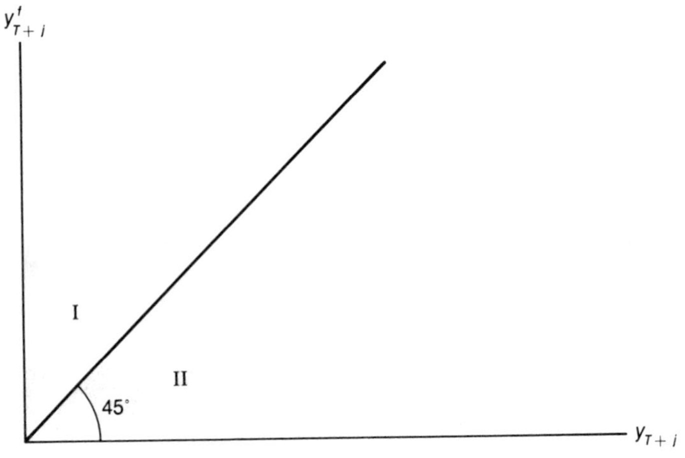

Figure 6.6.1 Prediction-Realization Diagram

I, predicted values tend to be high relative to actual values. There is an upward prediction bias. Conversely, II is a region of concentration where there is a downward prediction bias.

Finally, Theil has proposed the U-statistic[30]

$$U = \sqrt{\frac{\sum_{T=0}^{N-1} (\Delta y^f_{T+j} - \Delta y_{T+j})^2}{\sum_{T=0}^{N-1} (\Delta y_{T+j})^2}}. \tag{6.6.4}$$

This measure is zero when prediction is perfect and unity when the predicted change has the same root mean square error as no change extrapolation. This measure could be stated in terms of differences or levels of the variable being investigated.

[30] H. Theil, *Applied Economic Forecasting* (Amsterdam: North-Holland Publishing Co., 1966), p. 28.

The alternative accuracy measures are simply descriptive statistics and are thus largely arbitrary. The choice among them is mainly a matter of selecting the measure that conveys the best expository information for the particular problem at hand. When it is a matter of statistical inference and the degree of accuracy, it would appear that use of the standard error of forecast as suggested by Wallis to construct tolerance intervals would be the best choice.[31]

Descriptive measures of forecast error, such as average absolute error, when applied to actual *ex ante* forecasts made with the help of a macroeconometric model, appear to produce much smaller errors in repeated applications than would be suggested by the appropriate calculation of a confidence region.[32] In realistic *ex ante* forecasting, a formal dynamic model is used, but two sources of additional a priori information are used in order to improve forecast accuracy.

1. Prior to every forecast period, the residuals from each individual estimated equation are examined for the recent past. This point has already been discussed in connection with serial properties of error. In quarterly prediction, eight periods ahead, the approximately six previous residuals are examined. Where there is a priori information that residual variation is one sided (positive or negative serial dependence), and where there is a priori information that the deviation from formula computation is not just temporary, adjustments are made to the estimated parameters so that the system will correct for these recent errors when projected into the future. The principal adjustments are made to constant terms of equations that are linear in parameters.

One of the main causes for such adjustments is the continual revision of data. The sample series underlying coefficient estimation are continuously being revised by data collection agencies, so that the corresponding series in the prediction period come from a different base. From time to time, reestimation of systems can objectively correct for these revisions, but in exercises of repeated short term prediction, it is not feasible to reestimate as often as series are revised.

Another cause for equation adjustment is that behavioral patterns may gradually drift from their sample structure. This drift is often gradual and serial; therefore it can be recognized and allowed for in equation adjustment in the application period.

2. Nonstatistical, nonsample information is often available about the functioning of the economy or parts of it, with high degrees of reliability, into the future. This kind of information may be on the likelihood of a strike (incidence and duration), an economic edict by public authorities, or existence of a production bottleneck. Quantitative estimates of the impact of such events on structural equations can often be made, and such revisions of statistically estimated equations should be carried out before they are used in situations where the a priori information is relevant.

Mechanical application of estimated models in ex ante prediction is almost

[31] See Wallis, "Tolerance Intervals," Berkeley Symposium (1951).

[32] F. G. Adams and M. K. Evans, "Econometric Forecasting with the Wharton Model," *Business Economics*, III (Spring, 1968), 52–56.

sure to produce poor results. Combinations of a priori information and discernible bias corrections together with an estimated model can lead to much improved results—results that apparently suit the needs of public authorities and large producers. It is a fact of life that purely numerical methods cannot be used, but must be supplemented by special information and personal judgment. On the other hand, personal judgment alone is not suitable for prediction of a wide range of variables in a complicated industrial economy. The two must be used together. The objectively estimated model is needed as a framework in which to interpret special and subjective information. In forecasting magnitudes like aggregate production (GNP), average absolute prediction error may be cut by as much as 50 percent if adjustments and a priori information are used together with a model instead of following through with the pure arithmetic of solving models estimated from an historical sample period.

In *ex ante* forecasting, uncertainty about independent variables, the use of data that are subject to subsequent revision, and the uncertainty about future equation residuals all serve to make predictions err from the correct values. In *ex post* predictions, these alternative sources of error can be assessed. It is always easier to predict with hindsight, and *ex post* predictions are not really of substantive interest to makers of economic policy. They are, however, extremely useful in diagnosing the faults in model construction.

It would seem reasonable to insist that a model should perform well, in some sense, if correct lags and correct independent variables are used for the period $T + 1, T + 2, \ldots$; where the model has been fit to a sample of (correctly revised) data for $1, 2, \ldots, T$. This is not a test of the *ex ante* forecasting power of the model; it is a test of the validity or explanatory power of the model. The test should be an examination whether the postsample data come from the same universe as the sample data, or whether the estimated model performs as well in the postsample period as it did in the sample period, assuming that its performance was deemed acceptable in the sample period. For given tolerance or confidence coefficients, the issue is whether intervals (or more generally, regions)

$$\hat{y}_{T+j} \pm kSy^f_{T+j}$$

include a specified percentage of actual post sample values.

The test of the predictive power of a model is, however, different. In that case, we want to know ex post *what would have been the ex ante forecast with the model, given what we subsequently know about revised values of lag variables and correct values of independent variables.* This is much different from making arithmetic forecasts in a mechanistic way; that is, it does not simply involve computing $\hat{y}_{T+j}$ from

$$\hat{y}_{T+j} = K\hat{\lambda}^t - \frac{\hat{a}(L)}{\hat{\Delta}(L)}\hat{B}x_t$$

in a linear system where K is determined from revised initial conditions. It involves the use of adjustments for $[\hat{a}(L)/\hat{\Delta}(L)]\hat{e}_{T+j}$ in the prediction period, as well as the adjustment of parameter values in $a(L)$ or $\Delta(L)$ on the basis of a priori information. It is somewhat subjective to inquire what would have been the *ex ante* prediction at some prior time if present information about data input had been available earlier. *Ex post* prediction tests have not tried to answer this question, although they should have done so.

Another criterion for the success of *ex ante* prediction is whether an estimated model can generate useful information in comparison with other types of forecasts that were then available. This, too, is a somewhat subjective matter. The use of econometric results should be as quantitative and objective as possible, but attempts at pure push button mechanistic uses are sure to fail and prove to be inferior to methods that combine formal estimated models with a priori information (qualitative as well as quantitative) and judgment. Economic prediction has been rendered less of an art and more of a science by the use of econometric methods, but it has not been reduced to a pure scientific exercise.

Questions and Problems

1. How can structural change of an estimated econometric model be detected?
2. How should one test forecast accuracy?

SUGGESTED READINGS

Adelman F. and I. Adelman, "The Dynamic Properties of the Klein-Goldberger Model," *Econometrica*, 27 (October, 1959), 596–625. A path-breaking paper on stochastic simulation and cyclical analysis.

Frisch, R., "Propagation Problems and Impulse Problems in Dynamic Economics," in *Readings in Business Cycles*, ed. R. A. Gordon and L. R. Klein (Homewood: Irwin & Sons, 1965). One of the earliest papers on mathematical models of the business cycle, with discussion of stochastic influence.

Fromm, G. and L. R. Klein, "Solutions of the Complete System," *The Brookings Model: Some Further Results*, ed. J. Duesenberry et. al. (Chicago: Rand McNally, 1969). Shows how to solve nonlinear dynamic systems with the Gauss-Seidel Algorithm and integrates input-output with an aggregative final demand model.

Fromm, G., and Taubman, P., *Policy Simulations With an Econometric Model*, (Amsterdam: North-Holland Publishing Co., 1967). Shows how to simulate fiscal and monetary policies with the large scale Brookings Econometric Model.

Goldberger, A. S., *Impact Multipliers and Dynamic Properties of the Klein-Goldberger Model*, (Amsterdam: North-Holland Publishing Co., 1959). Calculates multipliers and dynamic properties from derived reduced forms of a model.

Hickman, B., ed., *Econometric Models of Cyclical Behavior*, (N.Y.: Columbia University Press, 1972). Contains several studies of simulation, prediction, and cyclical properties of U.S. models.

Howrey, E. P., "Stochastic Properties of the Klein-Goldberger Model," *Econometrica* 39 (January, 1971), 73–87. Analyzes frequency response characteristics of the Klein-Goldberger model by spectral methods.

Howrey, E. P. and L. R. Klein, "Dynamic Analysis of Nonlinear Econometric Models," *International Economic Review*, 13 (October, 1972), 599–618. Applies spectral and autoregressive techniques to cyclical measurement in nonlinear models.

Klein, L. R., "Econometric Analysis of the Tax Cut of 1964," *The Brookings Model: Some Further Results*, ed. J. Duesenberry et. al., (Chicago: Rand McNally, 1969). Simulates the Brookings and Wharton Models for 1964–65 to study, ex-post, the effects of the income tax cut of 1964.

Klein, L. R., *An Essay on the Theory of Economic Prediction*, (Chicago: Markham, 1971). Analyzes the prediction problem in economics from an econometric point of view, with a description of actual forecast procedures from the Wharton Model.

Klein, L. R. and A. S. Goldberger, *An Econometric Model of the United States, 1929–1952*, (Amsterdam: North-Holland Publishing Co., 1955). The original presentation of the Klein-Goldberger Model.

McCarthy, M. D., *The Wharton Quarterly Econometric Forecasting Model:* Mark III, (Philadelphia, Economic Research Unit, University of Pennsylvania, 1972). Presents an updated, extended, and revised version of the Wharton Model, together with a description of forecasting procedures in a particular case.

Nagar, A. L., "Stochastic Simulation of the Brookings Econometric Model," *The Brookings Model: Some Further Results*, ed. J. Duesenberry et. al, (Chicago: Rand McNally, 1969). Simulates the Brookings Model under stochastic conditions and shows how to construct random errors for dynamic simulation.

Otsuki, M. "Oscillations in Stochastic Simulation of Linear Systems," *Economic Studies Quarterly*, XXII, (December, 1971), 54–71. Derives a sinusoidal limit theorem for solutions to linear stochastic models and develops new method of cyclical analysis in the time domain.

Slutsky, E., "The Summation of Random Causes as the Source of Cyclical Processes," *Econometrica*, 5, (April, 1937), 105–46. One of the great classics of economic theory showing how iterated moving averages of random series tend toward a sinusoidal limit.

Theil, H., *Applied Economic Forecasting*, (Amsterdam: North-Holland Publishing Co., 1966). Develops interesting error measures for accuracy analysis of economic forecasts.

7

Econometric Computation

1. INTRODUCTION

Econometrics is a relatively young subject, having its earliest roots at the beginning of this century but real development only since the 1920s or 1930s; therefore, many early practitioners are still active and they can fully appreciate the enormous technological revolution that has been introduced into the subject by the computer. Seemingly intractable problems are now solved with comparative ease; techniques are no longer distorted by being reduced to manageable hand calculations; the whole process of empirical experimentation has been radically changed. It is difficult to write about computation procedures in econometrics now because there is no single approach. The issue is to evaluate the standard formulas by using the best machine facilities at hand, and these vary from case to case with different machine languages and capacities. A proper approach to econometric computation actually involves a whole treatise on computer programming.

Given the diversity of machines and programs available, I shall attempt in this chapter only to set out some general principles that will be useful to follow in applied econometrics. Partly as a throwback to earlier training and partly because of pedagogical fundamentals, I shall try to illustrate some of the most basic hand calculations. These are not introduced with the idea that the student will suddenly find himself stranded without access to a computer and forced to make hand calculations, but with the idea that the calculations will be better understood if one works through basic cases by hand. There is a detachment of the modern econometrician from his data by the intervention of the powerful complicated machine. A certain amount of elementary data manipulation is useful in keeping the econometrician in touch with his materials.

The most basic set of calculations in the entire field of econometrics are those associated with the estimation of the single equation regression by the method of ordinary least squares (OLS). The related calculations of TSLS, 3SLS, LIML, FIML, ILS will be discussed after a full treatment is given to OLS methods. Special calculations required for principal component analysis, simulation, and stochastic application will also be taken up.

In preparing OLS estimates of

$$y_t = \sum_{i=1}^{n} \alpha_i x_{it} + e_t$$

from a sample of observations $y_1, \ldots, y_T; x_{i1}, \ldots, x_{iT}$ $(i = 1, 2, \ldots, n)$, many of the underlying calculations for other methods are actually made or exemplified. In terms of computer programming, once the basic calculations have been programmed for this method, it is simple to repeat and extend these same kinds of calculations for the other methods with some added features. The OLS calculations are, however, basic. They involve the calculation of moments and the solution of simultaneous linear equations. In a final stage, there are numerous descriptive statistics needed from the estimated linear equation or from the relevant moment matrices. These are all called *linear* computations because they are associated with the solution of linear equations and the estimation of a linear equation. If the equations are not linear, iterated solutions of linear equations are used; therefore, the programming problem becomes one of repeating the calculations done for the standard linear case.

2. THE OLS REGRESSION CALCULATIONS

The time-honored procedure for linear regression calculation is called the Gauss-Doolittle method. An efficient outline and explanation of this technique is presented in this section on the assumption that the investigator is using an ordinary electric desk calculating machine. Some of the calculations may be done differently on an electronic computer, but the Gauss-Doolittle method is in fact quite versatile.

The first computational step for any method is to calculate the moments of variables being analyzed. For an equation of the form

$$y = \alpha_0 + \sum_{i=1}^{n} \alpha_i x_i + e, \tag{7.2.1}$$

the relevant moments are

$$m_{yy} = \sum_{t=1}^{T} (y_t - \bar{y})^2,$$

$$m_{yx_i} = \sum_{t=1}^{T} (y_t - \bar{y})(x_{it} - \bar{x}_i), \quad i = 1, 2, \ldots, n, \tag{7.2.2}$$

$$m_{x_ix_j} = \sum_{t=1}^{T} (x_{it} - \bar{x}_i)(x_{jt} - \bar{x}_j), \; i, j = 1, 2, \ldots, n, \tag{7.2.2}$$

$$\bar{y} = \frac{1}{T} \sum_{t=1}^{T} y_t,$$

$$\bar{x}_i = \frac{1}{T} \sum_{t=1}^{T} x_{it}.$$

The sums of products and squares are calculated in terms of deviations from sample means, but we use the formulas

$$\begin{aligned} \sum_{t=1}^{T} (y_t - \bar{y})^2 &= \sum_{t=1}^{T} y_t^2 - T\bar{y}^2 \\ \sum_{t=1}^{T} (y_t - \bar{y})(x_{it} - \bar{x}_i) &= \sum_{t=1}^{T} y_t x_{it} - T\bar{y}\bar{x}_i, \\ \sum_{t=1}^{T} (x_{it} - \bar{x}_i)(x_{jt} - \bar{x}_j) &= \sum_{t=1}^{T} x_{it}x_{jt} - T\bar{x}_i\bar{x}_j, \end{aligned} \tag{7.2.3}$$

to enable us to develop moments about the means by calculating only the ordinary moments about a zero origin and the means. This is a much simpler procedure than subtracting each observation from the sample mean and then evaluating the sums of squares and cross products. It is not essential, except for the evaluation of some descriptive statistics, to compute moments about the mean for electronic computation. The formulation here is specific to hand calculation.

The estimation equations for all methods discussed here are written in terms of moments. These are the known coefficients in the estimation equations. The unknown parameters that it is desired to estimate are the variables in the equations. The estimation equations can be expressed in terms of moments as given in (7.2.2) or in terms of these same moments divided or multiplied by T, the number of observations. For example we could use either

$$\frac{m_{yy}}{T}, \quad \frac{m_{yx_i}}{T}, \quad \frac{m_{x_ix_j}}{T}$$

or

$$Tm_{yy}, \quad Tm_{yx_i}, \quad Tm_{x_ix_j}$$

instead of the moments in (7.2.2). There is little to choose between m_{yy}, m_{yx_i}, $m_{x_ix_j}$ on the one hand, and the same values divided by T on the other; however, there is a situation in which it does become desirable to multiply the basic moments by the number of observations. When $\sum (y_t^2)$, $\sum y_t x_{it}$, $\sum x_{it}x_{jt}$, $\sum y_t$, $\sum x_{it}$ are not exactly divisible by T, some rounding is necessarily involved in the computation of moments m_{yy}, m_{yx_i}, $m_{x_ix_j}$, or $\frac{1}{T}m_{yy}$, $\frac{1}{T}m_{yx_i}$, $\frac{1}{T}m_{x_ix_j}$. Superfluous accuracy is never an objective in econometrics, but solution of the estimation equations, often in large systems, involves a considerable loss of accuracy at each step of the computation procedure, and even the modest requirement that the ultimate parameters be estimated to one or two significant figures will not be met unless the original moments are written as accurately as possible. The *augmented moments*—Tm_{yy}, Tm_{yx_i}, $Tm_{x_ix_j}$—require no rounding and are most accurately given in terms of the observations.

Any reasonable method of statistical estimation possesses the property that there is no essential effect on the results following from a simple scale change in the units of the observed variables. Concretely, it should not matter whether aggregate wage payments are recorded for a certain year as

$65,347.0 millions,
$6,534.7 tens of millions,
$653.47 hundreds of millions, or
$65.347 billions.

In a linear equation, the only alteration required is that the estimated term

$$\hat{\alpha} W$$

be adjusted so that $\hat{\alpha}$ is multiplied by a power of 10 according as W is divided by a power of 10, or vice versa. If the square moments m_{yy} or $m_{x_ix_j}$ turn out to be one hundred, one thousand, or more times as large for some variables than for others, this makes for rapid loss of accuracy in the ensuing computations; therefore it is recommended that all variables be divided or multiplied by appropriate powers of 10 until the final set of square moments are nearly all of the same order of magnitude.

The original observations should be listed in columns.

Observation	y	x_1	x_2	$\cdots$	x_n	S
1						
2						
3						
⋮						

The column headed S contains the row sums of each of the variables and is used for checking purposes. The tth value, S_t, is

$$S_t = y_t + x_{1t} + x_{2t} + \cdots + x_{nt}. \tag{7.2.4}$$

The first step is to compute column totals $\sum y_t$, $\sum x_{it}$ and $\sum S_t$. The check is provided by

$$\sum_{t=1}^{T} S_t = \sum_{t=1}^{T} y_t + \sum_{t=1}^{T} x_{1t} + \cdots + \sum_{t=1}^{T} x_{nt}; \tag{7.2.5}$$

the column total for the check column must equal the sum of the column totals for the other columns.

The next step is to calculate the sums of squares and cross products of all variables, or the elements of the matrix of moments in terms of deviations from a zero origin. We fill in the cells of the table

	y	x_1	x_2	$\cdots$	x_n	S
y	$\sum y_t^2$	$\sum y_t x_{1t}$	$\sum y_t x_{2t}$		$\sum y_t x_{nt}$	$\sum y_t S_t$
x_1	$\sum y_t x_{1t}$	$\sum x_{1t}^2$	$\sum x_{1t} x_{2t}$		$\sum x_{1t} x_{nt}$	$\sum x_{1t} S_t$
x_2	$\sum y_t x_{2t}$	$\sum x_{1t} x_{2t}$	$\sum x_{2t}^2$		$\sum x_{2t} x_{nt}$	$\sum x_{2t} S_t$
		$\vdots$				$\vdots$
x_n	$\sum y_t x_{nt}$	$\sum x_{1t} x_{nt}$	$\sum x_{2t} x_{nt}$	$\cdots$	$\sum x_{nt}^2$	$\sum x_{nt} S_t$
S	$\sum y_t S_t$	$\sum x_{1t} S_t$	$\sum x_{2t} S_t$		$\sum x_{nt} S_t$	$\sum S_t^2$

The reader will notice immediately that every entry below the main diagonal has an equal counterpart above the main diagonal; thus, the elements below the main diagonal need not actually be completed or written into the table. The first n entries in the column headed by S should equal the sum of the entries in the same row, because by (7.2.4)

$$S_t = y_t + x_{1t} + \cdots + x_{nt},$$

and

$$x_{it} S_t = y_t x_{it} + x_{1t} x_{it} + \cdots + x_{it} x_{nt}, \tag{7.2.6}$$

$$\sum_{t=1}^{T} x_{it} S_t = \sum_{t=1}^{T} y_t x_{it} + \sum_{t=1}^{T} x_{1t} x_{it} + \cdots + \sum_{t=1}^{T} x_{it} x_{nt}.$$

The final entry in the S column satisfies the equation

$$\begin{aligned}\sum_{t=1}^{T} S_t^2 &= \sum_{t=1}^{T} y_t^2 + \sum_{t=1}^{T} x_{1t}^2 + \cdots + \sum_{t=1}^{T} x_{nt}^2 \\ &+ 2\left(\sum_{t=1}^{T} y_t x_{1t} + \cdots + \sum_{t=1}^{T} y_t x_{nt}\right) \\ &+ 2\left(\sum_{t=1}^{T} x_{1t} x_{2t} + \cdots + \sum_{t=1}^{T} x_{1t} x_{nt}\right) + \cdots + 2\sum_{t=1}^{T} x_{n-1,t} x_{nt}.\end{aligned} \tag{7.2.7}$$

Equation (7.2.7) states that $\sum S_t^2$ equals the sum of the diagonal entries and twice the sum of all entries above the diagonal covering columns $y, x_1, x_2, \ldots, x_n$. The check given by equation (7.2.6) may be applied successively at each stage of the moment calculations; or, alternatively, one may wait until the final stage and use the single check, in (7.2.7). An individual investigator must balance the cost of step by step checks against the advantage of being able to locate mistakes more quickly in choosing between the two procedures.

The final step in obtaining the moment matrix to be used for estimation of parameters is to convert the sums of squares and cross products in terms of deviations from a zero origin to the same set of sums in terms of deviations from the sample means. Items that are already calculated from the previous steps can be substituted into (7.2.3) to get the desired quantities m_{yy}, m_{yx_i}, and $m_{x_ix_j}$. In addition, for checking purposes, we calculate m_{yS}, m_{x_iS}, and m_{SS}. The same check conditions as those in (7.2.6)-(7.2.7) hold for the moments in terms of mean deviations. The final results are arranged as

	y	x_1	x_2	$\cdots$	x_n	S
y	m_{yy}	m_{yx_1}	m_{yx_2}		m_{yx_n}	m_{yS}
x_1	m_{yx_1}	$m_{x_1x_1}$	$m_{x_1x_2}$		$m_{x_1x_n}$	m_{x_1S}
x_2	m_{yx_2}	$m_{x_1x_2}$	$m_{x_2x_2}$		$m_{x_2x_n}$	m_{x_2S}
$\vdots$						
x_n	m_{yx_n}	$m_{x_1x_n}$	$m_{x_2x_n}$		$m_{x_nx_n}$	m_{x_nS}
S	m_{yS}	m_{x_1S}	m_{x_2S}		m_{x_nS}	m_{SS}

The matrix is also symmetrical, the terms below the diagonal each having an equal counterpart above the diagonal.

Having the moment matrix fully checked we turn to the next step, solving the system of simultaneous linear estimating equations. We illustrate this procedure for a problem having one dependent and four independent variables.

The details of the computing outline follow on pages 290 and 291. The first four rows and columns contain the coefficients of the least squares estimating equations, the sums of squares and cross products of x_1, x_2, x_3, x_4. Because this matrix is symmetrical, we do not bother to fill in the terms below the main diagonal. Along each row between the fourth and fifth columns, it is understood that an equals sign, $=$, belongs there because we are at all times dealing with equations in this outline. The first of such equations is

$$m_{x_1x_1}\alpha_1 + m_{x_1x_2}\alpha_2 + m_{x_1x_3}\alpha_3 + m_{x_1x_4}\alpha_4 = m_{x_1y}.$$

We put it as

$$m_{x_1x_1} \quad m_{x_1x_2} \quad m_{x_1x_3} \quad m_{x_1x_4} \quad m_{x_1y}$$

in the first row and first five columns of our outline form. The same meaning is attached to the next three rows. After the first five columns, the diagonal matrix appears

$$\begin{matrix} 1 & 0 & 0 & 0 \\ 0 & 1 & 0 & 0 \\ 0 & 0 & 1 & 0 \\ 0 & 0 & 0 & 1 \end{matrix}$$

in the next four columns and in the first four rows. These numbers are introduced for the purpose of obtaining the inverse moment matrix that will satisfy

$$\begin{Vmatrix} m_{x_1x_1} & m_{x_1x_2} & m_{x_1x_3} & m_{x_1x_4} \\ m_{x_1x_2} & m_{x_2x_2} & m_{x_2x_3} & m_{x_2x_4} \\ m_{x_1x_3} & m_{x_2x_3} & m_{x_3x_3} & m_{x_3x_4} \\ m_{x_1x_4} & m_{x_2x_4} & m_{x_3x_4} & m_{x_4x_4} \end{Vmatrix} \begin{Vmatrix} m^{11} & m^{12} & m^{13} & m^{14} \\ m^{12} & m^{22} & m^{23} & m^{24} \\ m^{13} & m^{23} & m^{33} & m^{34} \\ m^{14} & m^{24} & m^{34} & m^{44} \end{Vmatrix} = \begin{Vmatrix} 1 & 0 & 0 & 0 \\ 0 & 1 & 0 & 0 \\ 0 & 0 & 1 & 0 \\ 0 & 0 & 0 & 1 \end{Vmatrix}.$$

In the outline form, we understand that the elements of each column after the fifth are successively put equal to the expression implied by the first four columns. Thus we imply the equations

$$m_{x_1x_1}m^{11} + m_{x_1x_2}m^{12} + m_{x_1x_3}m^{13} + m_{x_1x_4}m^{14} = 1,$$

then

$$m_{x_1x_1}m^{12} + m_{x_1x_2}m^{22} + m_{x_1x_3}m^{23} + m_{x_1x_4}m^{24} = 0,$$

$$m_{x_1x_1}m^{13} + m_{x_1x_2}m^{23} + m_{x_1x_3}m^{33} + m_{x_1x_4}m^{34} = 0,$$

$$m_{x_1x_1}m^{14} + m_{x_1x_2}m^{24} + m_{x_1x_3}m^{34} + m_{x_1x_4}m^{44} = 0.$$

Similar equations follow, involving the other rows of the moment matrix and the same set of unknowns, the elements of the inverse matrix. The student will recognize that the set of equations implied by the layout of the Doolittle calculations are identical with those implied by the matrix product written above

$$M_{xx}M_{xx}^{-1} = 1.$$

The check column headed by S stands by itself. The elements of the S column are row sums. Where an element is omitted from the first four rows of the symmetric moment matrix, the missing element must be supplied in getting the check items S_i.

The fifth row merely copies the first row. In row (6), we divide each element of (5) by the leading term (l.t.) of (5). This is an operation which is repeated at each stage of the procedure. The instructions for row (7) read

Outline of Doolittle Method for Solving Systems of Symmetric Linear Equations

	x_1	x_2	x_3	x_4	y					S
(1)	$m_{x_1x_1}$	$m_{x_1x_2}$	$m_{x_1x_3}$	$m_{x_1x_4}$	m_{x_1y}	1	0	0	0	S_1
(2)		$m_{x_2x_2}$	$m_{x_2x_3}$	$m_{x_2x_4}$	m_{x_2y}	0	1	0	0	S_2
(3)			$m_{x_3x_3}$	$m_{x_3x_4}$	m_{x_3y}	0	0	1	0	S_3
(4)				$m_{x_4x_4}$	m_{x_4y}	0	0	0	1	S_4
(5) Copy (1)	$m_{x_1x_1}$	$m_{x_1x_2}$	$m_{x_1x_3}$	$m_{x_1x_4}$	m_{x_1y}	1	0	0	0	S_1
(6) Divide by leading term	1.0	(A) $\frac{m_{x_1x_2}}{m_{x_1x_1}}$	(B) $\frac{m_{x_1x_3}}{m_{x_1x_1}}$	(D) $\frac{m_{x_1x_4}}{m_{x_1x_1}}$	$\frac{m_{x_1y}}{m_{x_1x_1}}$	$\frac{1}{m_{x_1x_1}}$	0	0	0	$\frac{S_1}{m_{x_1x_1}}$
(7) (2) − A(5)		$m_{x_2x_2} - Am_{x_1x_2}$	$m_{x_2x_3} - Am_{x_1x_3}$	$m_{x_2x_4} - Am_{x_1x_4}$	$m_{x_2y} - Am_{x_1y}$	$-A$	1	0	0	$S_2 - AS_1$
(8) Divide by l.t.		1.0	(C)	(E)						
(9) (3) − B(5) − C(7)										
(10) Divide by l.t.			1.0	(F)						
(11) (4) − D(5) − E(7) − F(9)										

(12) Divide by l.t.				1.0	$\hat{\alpha}_4$	m^{14}	m^{24}	m^{34}	m^{44}
(13) Back solution, $\hat{\alpha}_i$	$\hat{\alpha}_1$	$\hat{\alpha}_2$	$\hat{\alpha}_3$	$\hat{\alpha}_4$					
(14) Back solution	m^{11}	m^{12}	m^{13}	m^{14}					
(15) Back solution	m^{12}	m^{22}	m^{23}	m^{24}					
(16) Back solution		m^{23}	m^{33}	m^{34}					
(17) Back solution			m^{34}	m^{44}					

$$R^2 = \frac{\sum_{i=1}^{4} \hat{\alpha}_i m_{x_i y}}{m_{yy}}$$

$$\bar{R}^2 = 1 - (1 - R^2)\frac{T-1}{T-5}$$

$$\bar{S}^2 = \frac{m_{yy}}{T-1}(1 - \bar{R}^2)$$

$$S^2_{\hat{\alpha}_i} = m^{ii}\bar{S}^2$$

$$\hat{\alpha}_0 = \bar{y} - \sum_{i=1}^{4} \hat{\alpha}_i \bar{x}_i$$

"(2) − A(5)." By this we mean that we select an element in the second row and subtract A times an element of the fifth row from it. *The elements from the second and fifth rows always refer to the same column.* This operation is repeated for each column including the check column. The row sum of all but the final element in (7) should be the same as the final checking element. The correct entry in the first column of row (7) is exactly zero; therefore it is omitted. This is true of all entries below and to the left of the unit entries in rows (6)–(12). In row (8) we write the quotients of the values of (7) divided by the leading nonzero term. The instructions for (9) are to select an element of row (3) and subtract from it B times an element of row (5), same column, and subtract again C times an element of row (7), same column. The entry in the check column should agree with the sum of the other entries in the ninth row. In (10), we divide the elements of (9) by the leading term and in (11) repeat operations analogous to those of (7) and (9). After having divided by the leading term in (12), we read according to our understanding about the equals sign

$$1.0\,\alpha_4 = \text{entry in column 5 row (12);}$$

therefore, this entry is our estimate of $\alpha_4 = \hat{\alpha}_4$. The next four entries in row (12) are the elements of the fourth column of the inverse moment matrix.

Row (10) enables us to read

$$1.0\,\alpha_3 + F\hat{\alpha}_4 = \text{entry in column 5 row (10)}$$

that gives us $\hat{\alpha}_3$, the value of the only unknown quantity in this equation. This step is part of the *back solution.* The remaining steps of the back solution are obvious from row (8) and row (6). We use $\hat{\alpha}_3$ and $\hat{\alpha}_4$ to get $\hat{\alpha}_2$ in (8) and then use all three to get $\hat{\alpha}_1$ in (6). The values of the estimated parameters obtained in the back solution should be checked by insertion into the original equations to see that *all four are simultaneously satisfied by* $\hat{\alpha}_1, \hat{\alpha}_2, \hat{\alpha}_3, \hat{\alpha}_4$.

The elements of the inverse moment matrix m^{ij} are obtained by repetitions of the back solution. The entries in row (12), columns 6–9, are the elements of the last column (or last row) of the inverse moment matrix. To get the other elements of the first row we solve successively

$$1.0\,m^{13} + F\,m^{14} = \text{entry in column 6 row (10),}$$

$$1.0\,m^{12} + C\,m^{13} + E\,m^{14} = \text{entry in column 6 row (8),}$$

$$1.0\,m^{11} + A\,m^{12} + B\,m^{13} + D\,m^{14} = \text{entry in column 6 row (6).}$$

We next use columns 7, 8, and 9 in place of 6 to determine the second, third, and fourth rows of the inverse matrix. If the original moment matrix is symmetrical, then the inverse matrix is symmetrical; hence we need not calculate all the elements of the inverse. In each row after the first, the elements are to be calculated to one position to the left of the diagonal term. The left element is then compared with its equal on the other side of the diagonal, and a complete check of the inverse calculations is provided in this way except for m^{11} that should be checked by recomputation. Another and more laborious check would be to multiply the moment matrix by its inverse. The matrix product, if correct, will give the unit matrix.

Formulas for the correlation coefficient R and the estimate of $\sigma_e (= S)$ are given below the Doolittle solution. $\bar{R}$ and $\bar{S}$ are statistics that have been corrected, as indicated, for the degrees of freedom used up in calculating $\hat{\alpha}_i$. The standard errors of the estimated coefficients are denoted by the symbol $S_{\hat{\alpha}_i}$.

A numerical example estimating parameters of an investment equation

$$I = \alpha_0 + \alpha_1 P_{-3/2} + \alpha_2 P_{-7/2} + \alpha_3 P_{-11/2} + \alpha_4 K_{-1} + e$$

shows how the previously described procedure works in actual practice. The data used in estimating the parameters of this equation are quarterly series, 1923–1940, seasonally adjusted, and deflated to 1939 prices. The fractional lags for P, nonwage income, are merely indicative of averages of integer lags as in

$$\begin{aligned} P_{-3/2} &= \tfrac{1}{2}(P_{-1} + P_{-2}), \\ P_{-7/2} &= \tfrac{1}{2}(P_{-3} + P_{-4}), \\ P_{-11/2} &= \tfrac{1}{2}(P_{-5} + P_{-6}). \end{aligned}$$

In the numerical example, the columns and rows contain exactly the same operations as the corresponding columns and rows of the general scheme outlined above, because both cases have four independent variables and one dependent variable. In addition, the moment matrix M_{xx} in the first four rows and columns has been multiplied by the inverse matrix M_{xx}^{-1} in rows (14)–(17), columns 1–4, to check the accuracy of the inversion. It is seen that the matrix product gives the unit matrix to two decimal places.

In most time series problems, the next important step is to calculate the estimates of the unexplained disturbance e, often called residuals. The most convenient way to arrange this calculation is to prepare, for each variable, a column with the product of the estimated coefficient and t^{th} observation entered in the tth row.

Observation	$\hat{\alpha}_1 x_1$	$\hat{\alpha}_2 x_2$	$\hat{\alpha}_3 x_3$	$\hat{\alpha}_4 x_4$	$\hat{y}$	y	$\hat{e} = y - \hat{y}$
1	$\hat{\alpha}_1 (x_1)_1$	$\hat{\alpha}_2 (x_2)_1$	$\hat{\alpha}_3 (x_3)_1$	$\hat{\alpha}_4 (x_4)_1$	$\hat{y}_1$	y_1	$y_1 - \hat{y}_1$
2	$\hat{\alpha}_1 (x_1)_2$	$\hat{\alpha}_2 (x_2)_2$	$\hat{\alpha}_3 (x_3)_2$	$\hat{\alpha}_4 (x_4)_2$	$\hat{y}_2$	y_2	$y_2 - \hat{y}_2$
3	$\hat{\alpha}_1 (x_1)_3$	$\hat{\alpha}_2 (x_2)_3$	$\hat{\alpha}_3 (x_3)_3$	$\hat{\alpha}_4 (x_4)_3$	$\hat{y}_3$	y_3	$y_3 - \hat{y}_3$
	⋮						
T	$\hat{\alpha}_1 (x_1)_T$	$\hat{\alpha}_2 (x_2)_T$	$\hat{\alpha}_3 (x_3)_T$	$\hat{\alpha}_4 (x_4)_T$	$\hat{y}_T$	y_T	$y_T - \hat{y}_T$

Calculation of Estimated Linear Equation by Doolittle Method

	$P_{-3/2}$	$P_{-7/2}$	$P_{-11/2}$	K_{-1}	I					Check sum S	Sum Cols. 1–9
(1)	70.59	60.33	50.57	8.11	61.36	1.0	0.0	0.0	0.0	251.96	
(2)		66.56	59.33	145.72	48.69	0.0	1.0	0.0	0.0	381.63	
(3)			68.16	283.67	30.25	0.0	0.0	1.0	0.0	492.98	
(4)				6479.37	−271.38	0.0	0.0	0.0	1.0	6646.49	
(5)	70.59	60.33	50.57	8.11	61.36	1.0	0.0	0.0	0.0	251.96	
		A	*B*	*D*							
(6)	1.0	0.854654	0.716390	0.114889	0.869245	0.014166	0.0	0.0	0.0	3.569344	3.569344
(7)		14.998724	16.110147	138.788756	−3.751569	−0.854654	1.0	0.0	0.0	166.291378	166.291404
			C	*E*							
(8)		1.0	1.074101	9.253371	−0.250126	−0.056982	0.066672	0.0	0.0	11.087035	11.087036
(9)			14.628233	128.786935	−9.678126	0.201595	−1.074101	1.0	0.0	133.864640	133.864536
				F							
(10)			1.0	8.803998	−0.661606	0.013781	−0.073427	0.068361	0.0	9.151115	9.151107
(11)				4060.334482	−158.508727	6.018700	0.203012	−8.803998	1.0	3900.242730	3900.243469
(12)				1.0	−0.039038	0.001482	0.000050	−0.002168	0.000246	0.960572	0.960572
(13)	0.714682	0.452581	−0.317916	−0.039038							
(14)	0.074564	−0.071483	0.000733	0.001482		$R^2 = \frac{66.866230}{91.12}$		0.999990	−0.000016	−0.000025	−0.001432
(15)	−0.071483	0.145550	−0.073867	0.000050		$= 0.733826$			0.999996	−0.000005	−0.000065
(16)		−0.073867	0.087448	−0.002168		$\bar{R}^2 = 1 - 0.282065$	$M_{xx}M_{xx}^{-1}$			1.000565	0.001145
(17)			−0.002166	0.000246		$= 0.717935$					0.998233
$S^2_{\hat{\alpha}}$	0.026992	0.052689	0.031656	0.000089							
$S_{\hat{\alpha}}$	0.164292	0.229541	0.177921	0.009434		$\bar{S}^2 = 0.361997$					

Constant = −2.350836

$I = -2.35 + 0.71\,P_{-3/2} + 0.45\,P_{-7/2} - 0.32\,P_{-11/2} - 0.04\,K_{-1}$

The added subscripts for each of the x, y and $\hat{y}$ variables denote the observation period. As a check upon the work, we must have

$$\sum_{t=1}^{T} \hat{e}_t = 0,$$

$$\sum_{t=1}^{T} \hat{\alpha}_i(x_i)_t = \hat{\alpha}_i \sum_{t=1}^{T} (x_i)_t,$$

$$\sum_{t=1}^{T} \hat{y}_t = \sum_{t=1}^{T} \hat{\alpha}_1(x_1)_t + \cdots + \sum_{t=1}^{T} \hat{\alpha}_4(x_4)_t.$$

The sums running from $t = 1$ to $t = T$ are column totals in the above table, but $\sum_{t=1}^{T} (x_i)_t$ are taken from the original moment calculations. As a final check on the work we should see whether

$$\bar{S}^2 = \frac{\sum_{t=1}^{T} \hat{e}_t^2}{T - 5}$$

is satisfied, $\bar{S}^2$ having been calculated by another method previously.

The simultaneous equations solved in this section are originally derived by making use of the assumption that the e_t are mutually independent. In the analysis of economic time series, it is important to test, at least, the assumption that

$$E(e_t e_{t-1}) = 0.$$

The statistic

$$\frac{\delta^2}{S^2} = \frac{\sum_{t=1}^{T} (e_t - e_{t-1})^2}{\sum_{t=1}^{T} e_t^2} \frac{T}{T - 1}$$

is used by substituting the residuals, $\hat{e}_t$ for e_t in this expression.

The Doolittle method, that might also be called the Gauss-Doolittle method, takes advantage of the symmetry of the moment matrix of the regressor variables in reducing the system of normal equations to a triangular system, as in rows (6)–(12) of the outline above. Having a triangular matrix, one variable may be solved for and the others obtained recursively in the steps of the back solution.

Another method that is applicable to nonsymmetrical matrices is called the Gauss-Jordan elimination method. It reduces a matrix

$$\begin{bmatrix} r_{11} & r_{12} & \cdots & r_{1m} \\ r_{21} & r_{22} & \cdots & r_{2m} \\ \cdot & \cdot & & \cdot \\ \cdot & \cdot & & \cdot \\ \cdot & \cdot & & \cdot \\ r_{m1} & r_{m2} & \cdots & r_{mm} \end{bmatrix}$$

to diagonal form

$$\begin{bmatrix} r_{11}^* & 0 & \cdots & 0 \\ 0 & r_{22}^* & \cdots & 0 \\ \cdot & & & \cdot \\ \cdot & & & \cdot \\ \cdot & & & \cdot \\ 0 & 0 & \cdots & r_{mm}^* \end{bmatrix}.$$

From the diagonal form, each variable may be obtained individually without going through the process of a back solution. A pivot element is selected, say in the kth row. The coefficient r_{kk} is used to eliminate the coefficients in the kth column except the pivot element itself. In a simple 2×2 system,

$$\begin{aligned} r_{11}b_1 + r_{12}b_2 &= r_{1y} \\ r_{21}b_1 + r_{22}b_2 &= r_{2y}, \end{aligned}$$

this method uses r_{11} as the pivot element and eliminates the other coefficient in the first column by forming

$$r_{11} \text{ row } 2 - r_{21} \text{ row } 1$$

for the second row.
The reduced system is:

$$\begin{aligned} r_{11}b_1 + r_{12}b_2 &= r_{1y} \\ 0\, b_1 + (r_{11}r_{22} - r_{21}r_{12})b_2 &= r_{11}r_{2y} - r_{21}r_{1y}. \end{aligned}$$

In the next elimination step, $(r_{11}r_{22} - r_{21}r_{12})$ is the new pivot element, and we form

$$(r_{11}r_{22} - r_{21}r_{12}) \text{ row } 1 - r_{12} \text{ row } 2.$$

The further reduction of the system is

$$\begin{aligned} r_{11}(r_{11}r_{22} - r_{21}r_{12})b_1 + 0\, b_2 &= r_{1y}(r_{11}r_{22} - r_{21}r_{12}) \\ &\quad - r_{12}(r_{11}r_{2y} - r_{21}r_{1y}) \\ 0\, b_1 + (r_{11}r_{22} - r_{21}r_{12})b_2 &= r_{11}r_{2y} - r_{21}r_{1y}. \end{aligned}$$

This diagonalized system may be solved directly for b_1 from the first equation and for b_2 from the second. This method can be readily generalized and extended so that an m-equation system can be made diagonal for any m. This is a good general method for solution of any type of linear equation system by computer.

Questions and Problems

1. For the symmetrical 3×3 equation system

$$\begin{aligned} m_{11}a_1 + m_{12}a_2 + m_{13}a_3 &= p_1 \\ m_{12}a_1 + m_{22}a_2 + m_{23}a_3 &= p_2 \\ m_{13}a_1 + m_{23}a_2 + m_{33}a_3 &= p_3 \end{aligned}$$

show that the Doolittle method gives the correct solution for the unknown coefficients a_1, a_2, a_3 in terms of the m_{ij} and p_i.

2. Instead of using moments (sums of squares and cross products) about the mean, one can use moments about zero in constructing the system of simultaneous equations to be solved for estimates of the coefficients in a single linear equation. In the example above, moments about the mean were used, and the constant term was estimated by the condition that the equation be satisfied by the mean values of all variables. Outline the alternative computational procedure to be used if moments about zero are used. How is the constant term estimated in this case? What are the relative merits of the two procedures? Is there any advantage to some particular ordering of the moments in the design of the forward Doolittle solution?

3. After having estimated the parameters of an equation by the method of least squares, it may be decided that another variable needs to be added. How much of the first set of calculating can be retained in estimating the new equation with an added variable? Outline an efficient procedure for dropping a variable in least squares estimation of a single equation. How is this procedure dependent on the ordering of the moments in the forward Doolittle solution (see question 2)?

For efficient calculation of the standard multiple regression problem, it would be preferable to list y_t, x_{it} on cards, tape, or disk in the form of matrices

$$y = \begin{bmatrix} y_1 \\ y_2 \\ \cdot \\ \cdot \\ \cdot \\ y_T \end{bmatrix}, \qquad X = \begin{bmatrix} x_{11} & \cdots & x_{n1} \\ \cdot & & \cdot \\ \cdot & & \cdot \\ \cdot & & \cdot \\ x_{1T} & \cdots & x_{nT} \end{bmatrix}$$

and to form the moment matrices by using standard routines for matrix multiplication in machine language.

$$X'y = \begin{bmatrix} \sum y_t x_{1t} \\ \sum y_t x_{2t} \\ \cdot \\ \cdot \\ \cdot \\ \sum y_t x_{nt} \end{bmatrix}, \qquad X'X = \begin{bmatrix} \sum x_{1t}^2 & \cdots & \sum x_{1t}x_{nt} \\ \cdot & & \cdot \\ \cdot & & \cdot \\ \cdot & & \cdot \\ \sum x_{nt}x_{1t} & \cdots & \sum x_{nt}^2 \end{bmatrix}.$$

FORTRAN programming for calculation of moments would be carried out by calling a subprogram MATMPY for matrix multiplication. The augmented matrix

$$Z = [y, X]$$

would be formed and the moments would be taken from

$$R = Z'Z.$$

```
      SUBROUTINE MATMPY (Z, NO, NV, R)
      DIMENSION Z(100,31), R(31, 31)
      DO 5 I = 1, NV
      DO 5 J = I, NV
      RS = 0.0
      DO 6 K = 1, NO
    6 RS = RS + Z(K, I) * Z(K, J)
      R (I, J) = RS
    5 R (J, I) = RS
      RETURN
      END
```

In this series of programming statements, the number of variables in Z is NV and the number of observations is NO. The dimension statement says that there are one hundred observations ($NO = 100$, the same as T in matrix notation) and thirty-one variables ($NV = 31$, standing for $n = 30$ and one dependent variable y).

The calculations are designed to take advantage of symmetry because I runs from 1 to NV and J from I to NV. This cuts the amount of work considerably, and checking that would be relevant in hand computation is not necessary in machine computation.

Matrix multiplication is carried out in statement 6 through cumulation of products. It is not necessary to form the transpose explicitly by computer, it is only necessary to designate the appropriate elements to be multiplied. In this case, the common subscript for multiplication is the first, K, and explicit transposition of the data matrix is not done.

The moment matrix formed from the cumulated products is 31×31 and contains all sums of squares and cross products of $y_t, x_{1t}, x_{2t}, \ldots x_{30,t}$.

In the hand calculations just presented, it was found that for solving the simultaneous linear estimating equations, it helps substantially to reduce the number of equations by one, and moments about the mean are recommended. In the case of electronic calculation, however, this is not a consideration; therefore, $X'y$ and $X'X$ should be used directly in estimating the regression coefficients without adjustment for deviation about the mean.

A computer program to calculate regression coefficients

$$a = (X'X)^{-1}X'y \tag{7.2.8}$$

and the associated test or goodness of fit statistics will be tailored to a particular machine and installation. Also, programs can be varied to fit the needs of different users. There is no single program for any standard econometric application, yet the nature of a typical program that produces essentially the same results as the above hand calculation can be described in terms of the card deck used for execution. The program described here is typical. It is not the most complete version with all the options, but it illustrates the flexibility of the program design for a variety of estimators and descriptive statistics associated with those estimators.

First, there will be job or computer readable statements identifying the user, allowing for fixed maximum stretch of computer time, and so on. These cards will be different for each installation. For many installations a frequently used program will be stored on disk and an EXEC card will simply withdraw the program from the disk for use. If disk storage is not used, the next set of cards will consist of the *main program* in the form of compiled binary decks. These decks will be programmed to do the necessary mathematical calculations such as

$$X'X,\ X'y,$$

or

$$(X'X)^{-1}\ X'y.$$

If so directed, they will be programmed to compute descriptive statistics, make diagrams, summarize results, use different forms of estimation, or do whatever analytical task the programmer has decided to build into the deck.

The binary main program decks are general. They are built to handle a wide variety of problems that do not exceed predetermined capacity limits. The specific cards for a given problem are *input cards*. The first input card is a *parameter card* giving information about the data. The input cards used for the ECON program written by Morris Norman at the University of Pennsylvania will form the basis for this discussion. The basic parameter card may be made up as follows:

Cols. 1–4 Number of observations. The program will be set up to deal with a maximum number in the hundreds or thousands. If more than 9,999 observations are to be used, this field must be made larger.

Cols. 5–8 The number of variables to be read from cards, tape, or disk.

Cols. 9–12 The number of predetermined variables. In OLS calculations, this field is left blank but would be used for TSLS or LIML estimation.

Col. 16 An option to compute the variance-covariance matrix and correlation matrix of all the variables. To exercise the option, punch 1 in this column, otherwise, leave this column blank.

Col. 20 If the series are to be transformed (lagged, divided, multiplied, formed into logarithms, and so on, punch 1 to place the appropriate cards in subroutine TRAN. Leave blank if no transformations are required.

Col. 24 Punch 1 if variables are to be ordered (first predetermined, then dependent) for TSLS or LIML estimation; otherwise, leave this column blank. For OLS estimation, this column should be left blank.

Cols. 25–80 Messages to describe the title and date of calculations can be punched here.

After the parameter card, we have the data cards. The variables are to be punched in 5-column fields with no decimal. There are sixteen variables on the first data card, variables seventeen through thirty-two are punched on the second data card, thirty-three through forty-eight on the third data card, and variables forty-nine through fifty on the fourth data card. The maximum capacity is fifty variables and two hundred observations per variable. A smaller number of variables and observations may be punched. One set of data cards, covering all variables, is punched for each observation (time point, locale, household, or firm). Data should be scaled so that all input variables are of the same order of magnitude.

Label cards. These follow the data cards and assign variable names in fields of 5 columns. Sixteen variables can be labeled on the first card, the next sixteen appear on the next card, and so on.

Location card. If 1 is punched in col. 24 of the *parameter card*, this card is needed for punching the fields of the variables—predetermined or dependent. The number of the field of each predetermined and dependent variable is punched in fields of 2 on the *location card*. The location of the constant term of the equation (total number of variables in the equation plus one) is the field just after the locations of the predetermined variables.

Control Cards. One card is constructed for each equation estimated. It gives the number of variables, their locations, and the method of estimation used.

Col. 1 Blank for OLS
Punch 1 for TSLS
Punch 2 for TSLS and LIML

Col. 2 If more equations are to be estimated, leave blank for reading of another control card. Punch 1 for reading of new parameter card. This punch also provides for the printing of a summary table of all the regressions estimated with one parameter card.

Cols. 3–4 Punch number of dependent variables minus 1. This is used only for TSLS or LIML. These columns are left blank for OLS.

Cols. 5–6 Punch number of variables in the equation being estimated.

Cols. 7–8, *etc.* to Col. *x*.
In fields of 2, punch the field number of the data matrix correspond-

ing to the variables used in the equation being estimated. The order for OLS is location of independent variables followed by the location of the dependent variables. For TSLS and LIML, the order is dependent explanatory variables, predetermined variables, the single dependent variable with normalized unit coefficient.

Cols. $x + 1, x + 2$

In this two-column field (following the location numbers) punch
01 for graph of actual and computed values from the regression
02 for the Durbin-Watson statistic
03 for scatter diagram of residuals against other variables (up to a maximum of 10)

Cols. $x + 3, x + 4$

01 for suppression of the constant term in the regression, otherwise 00

Cols. $x + 5, x + 6$

If 03 was punched in cols $x + 1, x + 2$, punch location numbers of variables to be plotted against residuals.

These instructions (cards and fields with coded punches) show the kind of computed information that can be programmed and produced in computer output for OLS regressions, and TSLS or LIML as well. The original data are read in according to the format of the data cards. If necessary, a subroutine for transformation of the original data can be called from the main deck to perform transformations of the original data. The transformed series can then be used in the regressions. As a matter of course, estimated coefficients, sampling errors, t-ratios, residual variance (corrected for degrees of freedom), and multiple correlation coefficient (corrected for degrees of freedom) are all printed out in a standardized form. Optional information can be withdrawn as indicated by the description on the *control card*.

The main program consists of twelve binary decks:

ECON	to make OLS regressions
LISE	to make limited information single equation calculations (LIML)
VERT	to perform matrix inversions
CLOCK	to time computer operations
INPUT	to control the input of data
GRAPH	to plot graphs of actual and computed regression values of the normalized dependent variables
RESULT	to organize a table of results in equation form
CORR	to compute correlation matrix of variables
MATOUT	to print out matrices in standard form
SCALE	to scale the data
MAT	to print matrices
SCAT	to plot scatter diagrams of residuals and different variables.

This is a basic regression program. It could be extended to deal with FIML,

3SLS, and other estimation methods, although these techniques tax the capacity of a computer and possibly should be dealt with in separate programs. In the case of 3SLS, however, TSLS estimates would be needed at an early stage; therefore a program for 3SLS should include one for TSLS.

A basic program for single equation regression (OLS, TSLS, or LIML) can be extended in various ways. Data can be autoregressively transformed and regression estimates made with the transformed variables. This would permit an extension to estimation of

$$y_t = \sum_{i=1}^{n} \alpha_i x_{it} + e_t; \quad e_t = \sum_{i=1}^{r} \rho_i e_{t-i} + u_t. \tag{7.2.9}$$

Iteration of regression or repeated regression in a search could be programmed. Also, different systems of distributed lag estimation can be programmed.

Principal components of predetermined variables can be estimated and TSLS or LIML carried out with principal components. This program does the equivalent of computing principal components of all predetermined variables that are then read in as additional predetermined variables in the data matrix. Short cuts, as indicated below, do this in principle without taking all the explicit steps in obtaining the principal components.

To compute the principal components of $x_{1t}, \ldots, x_{mt}$ we form linear functions of the x_{jt}

$$p_{cit} = \sum_{j=1}^{m} \gamma_{ij} x_{jt} \qquad i = 1, 2, \ldots r \tag{7.2.10}$$

where the γ_{ij} satisfy

$$\begin{aligned}
(r_{11} - \lambda_i)\gamma_{i1} + r_{12}\gamma_{i2} + \cdots + r_{1m}\gamma_{im} &= 0 \\
r_{12}\gamma_{i1} + (r_{22} - \lambda_i)\gamma_{i2} + \cdots + r_{2m}\gamma_{im} &= 0 \\
&\ \vdots \\
r_{1m}\gamma_{i1} + r_{2m}\gamma_{i2} + \cdots + (r_{mm} - \lambda_i)\gamma_{im} &= 0.
\end{aligned} \tag{7.2.11}$$

The coefficients in this equation system, r_{ij}, are the sample correlations between x_{it} and x_{jt}.

$$r_{ij} = \frac{\sum_{t=1}^{T} (x_{it} - \bar{x}_i)(x_{jt} - \bar{x}_j)}{\left[\sum_{t=1}^{T} (x_{it} - \bar{x}_i)^2 \sum_{t=1}^{T} (x_{jt} - \bar{x}_j)^2\right]^{1/2}}$$

The solutions γ_{ij} are characteristic vectors corresponding to the ith characteristic root λ_i. Provision is made for the extraction of the first r roots, giving r principal components. The program is written to produce either the first r components or to terminate when enough components have been computed to account for a preset fraction of the generalized variance.

The computations are designed to find the roots

$$R\gamma = \lambda\gamma \tag{7.2.12}$$

where R is a correlation matrix, γ is a vector of m elements, and λ is a scalar. For an initial vector $\gamma^{(0)}$, the program computes

$$R\gamma^{(0)} = \gamma^{(1)}.$$

This is simply matrix multiplication. The iteration calculations then proceed

$$\begin{aligned} R\gamma^{(1)} &= \gamma^{(2)} \\ &\vdots \\ R\gamma^{(s-1)} &= \gamma^{(s)} \end{aligned}$$

When the ratios of each component of the vector $\gamma^{(s+1)}$ satisfy

$$\left| \frac{\gamma_j^{(s+1)}}{\gamma_j^{(s)}} - \hat{\lambda} \right| < \epsilon$$

for an arbitrarily small ϵ, we say that $\gamma^{(s+1)}$ is an approximate solution to the equation system. This enables us to evaluate the principal components corresponding to the first (largest) characteristic root of the equation

$$|R - \lambda I| = 0. \tag{7.2.13}$$

The second root is the largest solution of

$$\begin{aligned} |R_2 - \lambda I| &= 0 \\ R_2 &= R - \hat{\lambda}_1 \hat{\gamma}_1 \hat{\gamma}_1'. \end{aligned}$$

The same iterations are made with R_2 replacing R, and the appropriate solution gives $\hat{\lambda}_2$ and $\hat{\gamma}_2$. The third root is

$$\begin{aligned} |R_3 - \lambda I| &= 0 \\ R_3 &= R_2 - \hat{\lambda}_2 \hat{\gamma}_2 \hat{\gamma}_2' \end{aligned}$$

and so on.

Each computed root provides an estimate of the variance of the associated component. The ratio of $\hat{\lambda}_i$ to the sum of the diagonal elements of R that are normalized to be unity in each case, gives the percentage of variance explained by the ith component. The cumulative total $\sum_{i=1}^{r} \hat{\lambda}_i/m$ gives the percentage of variance accounted for by the first r principal components. The linear combinations of the x_{jt} defined by the principal components p_{cit} can be read into the TSLS or LIML parts of the program together with the whole set of predetermined variables and used by themselves in the first stage regressions. Because the p_{cit} are linear functions of the x_{jt}, it is not necessary to evaluate the principal components as such and store them, for all moment calculations with linear combinations of variables can be expressed as linear combinations of moments of the original variables. Storage space is saved if the principal components are not explicitly evaluated and appropriate linear functions of moments are used instead.

The data matrix of principal components will be written as

$$P = \begin{pmatrix} P_{c11} & \cdots & P_{cr1} \\ \cdot & & \cdot \\ \cdot & & \cdot \\ \cdot & & \cdot \\ P_{c1T} & \cdots & P_{crT} \end{pmatrix}.$$

In terms of the data matrix of exogenous variables, the P matrix is

$$P = X\Gamma'. \tag{7.2.14}$$

The moment matrix of the principal components, therefore, is

$$P'P = \Gamma\, X'X\,\Gamma'. \tag{7.2.15}$$

The program, then, evaluates Γ and together with the original moment matrix forms the right-hand side expression in (7.2.15) without ever computing the individual observations of the principal components.

Because the principal components are mutually orthogonal (uncorrelated), the matrix in (7.2.15) will be diagonal

$$\Gamma X'X\Gamma' = \begin{pmatrix} \sum P_{c1t}^2 & 0 & \cdots & 0 \\ 0 & \sum P_{c2t}^2 & \cdots & 0 \\ \cdot & & & \cdot \\ \cdot & & & \cdot \\ \cdot & & & \cdot \\ 0 & & \cdots & \sum P_{crt}^2 \end{pmatrix},$$

therefore, the corresponding inverse that will be needed for the reduced form regressions is very simple to evaluate. It is

$$(\Gamma X'X\Gamma')^{-1} = \begin{pmatrix} \frac{1}{\sum P_{c1t}^2} & 0 & \cdots & 0 \\ 0 & \frac{1}{\sum P_{c2t}^2} & \cdots & 0 \\ \vdots & & \ddots & \vdots \\ 0 & \cdots & & \frac{1}{\sum P_{crt}^2} \end{pmatrix}.$$

If the first stage reduced form regressions use included predetermined variables together with principal components, the complete moment matrix for the regression calculation will not be diagonal, but it can be readily constructed from moments of the original data series.

3. TWO STAGE LEAST SQUARES

In referring to the various options available in a widely used regression program, we see that TSLS calculations can be obtained because they are simply variants of the standard OLS regression calculations. We shall now show how TSLS calculations can be designed as a straightforward application of OLS methods.

A literal interpretation of TSLS is that it is a replication of least squares—twice, instead of once. By this interpretation, we first make reduced form regression calculations

$$p_i = (X'X)^{-1}X'Y_i. \tag{7.3.1}$$

These give the reduced form regression coefficients and can be programmed as any OLS calculations provided an allowance is made for the dimensions that are likely to be involved, because X is a data matrix for all the predetermined variables in the system.

The computed values of dependent variables are obtained from

$$\hat{Y}_i = Xp_i = X(X'X)^{-1}X'Y_i. \tag{7.3.2}$$

This is only matrix multiplication, given the calculations for p_i, and can be programmed after the latter are obtained.

The second stage of TSLS computation simply makes another OLS regression—y_{1t} on $\hat{y}_{2t}, \hat{y}_{3t}, \ldots, \hat{y}_{nt}, x_{1t}, x_{2t}, \ldots, x_{mt}$. In practice, it would not be efficient to compute p_i, then $\hat{Y}_i$, and then the final regression. It would be more efficient to compute

$$\begin{pmatrix} Y_i'X(X'X)^{-1}X'Y_i & Y_i'X_i \\ X_i'Y_i & X_i'X_i \end{pmatrix}^{-1} \begin{pmatrix} Y_i'X(X'X)^{-1}X'y \\ X_i'y \end{pmatrix} \tag{7.3.3}$$

directly. Basically it is the same calculation as OLS, moment matrix inversion and multiplication. The only difference is in the ordering and arranging of special matrix multiplications to form the moment matrices that are peculiar to TSLS methods.

Essentially, the programming of TSLS involves arranging, sequencing, and tying together the same calculations that are made for OLS estimation. That is why the OLS regression calculation is the most important single calculation for programming in econometrics.

The above calculations provide the coefficient estimates for TSLS. From these and the sample data, residuals can be computed

$$(res)_t = y_{1t} - \sum_{j=2}^{n_i} a_{ij} y_{jt} - \sum_{j=1}^{m_i} b_{ij} x_{jt}. \tag{7.3.4}$$

The variance of residuals, adjusted for degrees of freedom, can be evaluated. Call the estimate $S^2_{e_i}$. The variance-covariance matrix of coefficient estimates is given by

$$S^2_{e_i} \begin{pmatrix} Y_i'X(X'X)^{-1}X'Y_i & Y_i'X_i \\ X_i'Y_i & X_i'X_i \end{pmatrix}^{-1}. \tag{7.3.5}$$

This, too, is a complete analogue of corresponding calculations for OLS estimation, except for the fact that the submoment matrix

$$Y_i'Y_i$$

is replaced by

$$Y_i'X(X'X)^{-1}X'Y_i.$$

4. LIMITED INFORMATION MAXIMUM LIKELIHOOD

Again, the OLS program is used together with other matrix operations to obtain LIML estimates. The first stage is precisely the same as in TSLS estimation. The unrestricted reduced forms are evaluated as

$$p_i = (X'X)^{-1}XY_i. \tag{7.4.1}$$

In this case, all dependent variables in the ith equation are contained in Y_i, including the dependent variable with normalized coefficient. The actual regression coefficients and computed values of $y_{1t}, \ldots, y_{n_i t}$ are not needed. The covariance matrix of reduced form residuals is needed. These can be written as

$$W = Y_i'Y_i - Y_i'X(X'X)^{-1}X'Y_i. \tag{7.4.2}$$

The next step is the evaluation of

$$B = Y_i'X(X'X)^{-1}X'Y_i - Y_i'X_i(X_i'X_i)^{-1}X_i'Y_i. \tag{7.4.3}$$

This is the difference between two residual covariance matrices. The first term on the right-hand side of (7.4.3) is determined from the regression of $y_{1t}, \ldots, y_{n_it}$ on $x_{1t}, \ldots, x_{mt}$ (all the predetermined variables of the system). The second term is determined from the regressions of $y_{1t}, \ldots, y_{n_it}$ on $x_{1t}, \ldots, x_{m_it}$ (the *included* predetermined variables).

Because W is a covariance matrix, it is symmetrical and positive definite. The same is true of B because the regressions on all the predetermined variables must dominate those determined from regressions on a subset of the predetermined variables.

The main departure from OLS type calculations is the extraction of the largest root of

$$|B^{-1}W - \lambda I| = 0. \tag{7.4.4}$$

This involves the same kind of calculation as in estimating principal components above. This is a polynomial in λ and appears to be a nonlinear type calculation. The computing algorithm, as we have already seen, is simply an iteration of successive linear type calculations. The characteristic vector a associated with the largest characteristic root λ of the determinantal polynomial satisfies

$$Aa = \lambda a,$$

where

$$A = B^{-1}W,$$

and a is a column vector with n_i elements. The algorithm for estimating characteristic vectors demonstrated above in connection with principal component calculation is a fast iterative procedure in this case; n_i is usually small—certainly less than ten.

The characteristic vector computed from the above algorithm $a_1, a_2, \ldots, a_{n_i}$, is an estimate of $1, -\alpha_{i2}, -\alpha_{i3}, \ldots, -\alpha_{in_i}$ after units normalization. We would write

$$1, \frac{a_2}{a_1}, \frac{a_3}{a_1}, \ldots, \frac{a_{n_i}}{a_1}$$

as the normalized estimate. If a different dependent variable were to be associated with the unit coefficient, we would simply renormalize the same estimated characteristic vector, that is,

$$\frac{a_1}{a_2}, \frac{a_3}{a_2}, \ldots, \frac{a_{n_i}}{a_2}$$

would be estimates of the coefficients of dependent variables

$$-\alpha_{i1}, 1, -\alpha_{i3}, \ldots, -\alpha_{in_i}$$

in

$$y_{2t} = \alpha_{i1} y_{1t} + \sum_{j=3}^{n_i} \alpha_{ij} y_{jt} + \sum_{j=1}^{m_i} \beta_{ij} x_{jt} + e_{it}. \tag{7.4.5}$$

The same characteristic vector is used for every choice of normalized dependent variable. This is an important invariance feature of LIML.

The estimates of $\beta_{i1}, \ldots, \beta_{im_i}$ are obtained from

$$b = -(X_i'X_i)^{-1}X_i'Y_i a. \tag{7.4.6}$$

First α_i is estimated by a; then β_i is estimated by b by using a.

To estimate the asymptotic standard errors of a and b in the LIML case, we refer to the matrix expression (4.4.76) of Chap. 4, where the correspondence between LIML and k-class estimators was explicitly developed. In the notation of the present chapter, that expression becomes

$$S_{ei}^2 \begin{pmatrix} (1+\hat{\lambda})Y_i'X(X'X)^{-1}X'Y_i - \hat{\lambda}Y_i'Y_i & Y_i'X_i \\ X_i'Y_i & X_i'X_i \end{pmatrix}^{-1}.$$

It is understood that Y_i in the present formula excludes the column corresponding to the series for the dependent variable that has unit (normalized) coefficient. The largest characteristic root from (7.4.4) gives $\hat{\lambda}$. All the other terms in the matrix are sample moments of observed variables. We are simply inverting the moment matrix for the k-class estimator, where

$$k = 1 + \hat{\lambda}$$

in this case and multiplying the inverse by the variance of residuals, adjusted for degrees of freedom.

5. FULL INFORMATION MAXIMUM LIKELIHOOD

The concentrated form of the likelihood function in the linear case has been written as

$$L_c = T \log |A| - \frac{T}{2} \log |\Sigma|. \tag{7.5.1}$$

The maximization of this function is obtained as the maximization of the ratio

$$\frac{|A|}{\left|\frac{1}{T}\sum (Ay_t + Bx_t)(Ay_t + Bx_t)'\right|^{1/2}}.$$

This is equivalent to maximization of

$$\frac{\left|\frac{1}{T}\sum(Ay_t)(Ay_t)'\right|}{\left|\frac{1}{T}\sum(Ay_t+Bx_t)(Ay_t+Bx_t)'\right|}$$

because the numerator can be written as

$$|A|^2\left|\frac{1}{T}Y'Y\right|$$

and $\left|\frac{1}{T}Y'Y\right|$ is a sample constant in this maximization problem.[1]

It is therefore possible to write a concentrated likelihood function as

$$L_c=\frac{T}{2}\log\left|\frac{1}{T}\sum(Ay_t)(Ay_t)'\right|-\frac{T}{2}\log\left|\frac{1}{T}\sum(Ay_t+Bx_t)(Ay_t+Bx_t)'\right| \tag{7.5.2}$$

or, in different notation, as

$$L_c=\frac{T}{2}\log\left|\frac{1}{T}AY'YA'\right|-\frac{T}{2}\log\left|\frac{1}{T}(AY'+BX')(YA'+XB')\right|. \tag{7.5.3}$$

We assume that the matrices A and B are restricted; that is, they contain zero elements or linear restrictions on elements that serve to identify the equations of the system.

The g, h-element of the first matrix will be denoted as

$$w_{gh}=\frac{1}{T}(\alpha_g Y')(Y\alpha_h'), \tag{7.5.4}$$

where α_g is the gth *row* of A. Similarly,

$$s_{gh}=\frac{1}{T}(\alpha_g Y'+\beta_g X')(Y\alpha_h'+X\beta_h'), \tag{7.5.5}$$

where β_g is the gth *row* of B.

$$W \doteq \|w_{gh}\|=\frac{1}{T}AY'YA'; \quad S=\|s_{gh}\|=\frac{1}{T}(AY'+BX')(YA'+XB').$$

[1] This formulation of FIML computation is due to Gregory C. Chow, "Two Methods of Computing Full-Information Maximum Likelihood Estimates in Simultaneous Stochastic Equations," *International Economic Review*, 9 (February, 1968), 100–112.

The conditions for a maximum of the concentrated likelihood function are:

$$\begin{aligned}\frac{\partial L_c}{\partial \alpha_i'} &= \frac{T}{2}\sum_{g,h} w^{hg}\frac{\partial w_{gh}}{\partial \alpha_i'} - \frac{T}{2}\sum_{g,h} s^{hg}\frac{\partial s_{gh}}{\partial \alpha_i'} = 0 \\ \frac{\partial L_c}{\partial \beta_i'} &= -\frac{T}{2}\sum_{g,h} s^{hg}\frac{\partial s_{gh}}{\partial \beta_i'} = 0.\end{aligned} \tag{7.5.6}$$

In these expressions, we have used the proposition that the derivative of the logarithm of a determinant with respect to an element is given by the transposed element of the inverse, that is,

$$\begin{aligned}\frac{\partial \log|S|}{\partial s_{gh}} &= s^{hg} \\ \frac{\partial \log|W|}{\partial w_{gh}} &= w^{hg}.\end{aligned} \tag{7.5.7}$$

It is now possible to express the maximization conditions in terms of moments of the observed variables and thus obtain normal equations that are analogues of those used in standard least squares theory for single equations.

If the identifying restrictions do not require that the same parameter appear in more than one equation, we can simplify the expressions for $\frac{\partial L_c}{\partial \alpha_i'}$ and $\frac{\partial L_c}{\partial \beta_i'}$ by noting

$$\begin{aligned}\frac{\partial s_{gh}}{\partial \alpha_i'} &= 0 \text{ for } i \neq g, h \\ \frac{\partial w_{gh}}{\partial \alpha_i'} &= 0 \text{ for } i \neq g, h \\ \frac{\partial s_{gh}}{\partial \beta_i'} &= 0 \text{ for } i \neq g, h.\end{aligned} \tag{7.5.8}$$

We, therefore, have

$$\begin{aligned}\frac{\partial s_{gh}}{\partial \alpha_i'} &= \frac{1}{T} Y_i'(Y_h\alpha_h' + X_h\beta_h') \text{ for } i = g \\ \frac{\partial w_{gh}}{\partial \alpha_i'} &= \frac{1}{T} Y_i'(Y_h\alpha_h') \qquad\qquad \text{for } i = g \\ \frac{\partial s_{gh}}{\partial \beta_i'} &= \frac{1}{T} X_i'(Y_h\alpha_h' + X_h\beta_h') \text{ for } i = g.\end{aligned} \tag{7.5.9}$$

The notation is the same as in the case of TSLS estimates; X_i and Y_i are data matrices for variables appearing with nonzero coefficients in the ith equation. When these expressions are substituted into (7.5.6), we obtain the normal equations

$$\begin{bmatrix} q^{11}Y_1'Y_1 & \cdots & q^{n1}Y_1'Y_n & s^{11}Y_1'X_1 & \cdots & s^{n1}Y_1'X_n \\ \cdot & & \cdot & & & \\ \cdot & & \cdot & & & \\ \cdot & & \cdot & & & \\ q^{1n}Y_n'Y_1 & \cdots & q^{nn}Y_n'Y_n & s^{1n}Y_n'X_1 & \cdots & s^{nn}Y_n'X_n \\ s^{11}X_1'Y_1 & \cdots & s^{n1}X_1'Y_n & s^{11}X_1'X_1 & \cdots & s^{n1}X_1'X_n \\ \cdot & & \cdot & & & \\ \cdot & & \cdot & & & \\ \cdot & & \cdot & & & \\ s^{1n}X_n'Y_1 & \cdots & s^{nn}X_n'Y_n & s^{1n}X_n'X_1 & \cdots & s^{nn}X_n'X_n \end{bmatrix} \begin{bmatrix} \hat{\alpha}_1' \\ \cdot \\ \cdot \\ \cdot \\ \hat{\alpha}_n' \\ \hat{\beta}_1' \\ \cdot \\ \cdot \\ \cdot \\ \hat{\beta}_n' \end{bmatrix} = \begin{bmatrix} Y_1' \sum_h q^{h1} y_h \\ \cdot \\ \cdot \\ \cdot \\ Y_n' \sum_h q^{hn} y_h \\ X_1' \sum_h s^{h1} y_h \\ \cdot \\ \cdot \\ \cdot \\ X_n' \sum_h s^{hn} y_h \end{bmatrix}. \tag{7.5.10}$$

Two simplifications of notation have been introduced in the writing of these normal equations:

$$q^{hi} = s^{hi} - w^{hi},$$

and

$$(-\hat{\alpha}_{g1}, - \ldots, 1, \ldots, -\hat{\alpha}_{gn_g}, -\hat{\beta}_{g1}, \ldots, -\hat{\beta}_{gm_g}) = (\alpha_{g1}, \ldots, \alpha_{gn_g}, \beta_{g1}, \ldots, \beta_{gm_g}).$$

The vector of nonzero coefficients in the gth equation is written so that one variable (y_g) has a unit coefficient and all the others have a sign change. This is the usual normalized way of writing a linear economic equation system in *explicit* form.

The normal equations are seemingly linear, but the elements q^{gh} and s^{gh} depend on α and β; therefore we must use nonlinear methods of solution. A straightforward algorithm is to form preliminary estimates of A, B. From these it is possible to evaluate

$$W = \frac{1}{T} AY'YA'$$

$$S = \frac{1}{T}(AY' + BX')(YA' + XB').$$

The elements of S^{-1} and W^{-1} are the weights in the normal equations. If values are substituted for these weights, the equations are linear, with weighted moments as coefficients. We can then solve for $\hat{\alpha}_g'$ and $\hat{\beta}_g'$. Iteration is straightforward. Given estimates of the parameters, new estimates of W^{-1} and S^{-1} can be formed, new solutions for $\hat{\alpha}_g'$ and $\hat{\beta}_g'$ obtained, and so on.

The computation involves the evaluation of equation residuals for computing S and other functions of the variables for computing W, inversion of these two symmetric matrices, and solution of linear symmetric normal equations. These are the same kinds of calculations that are made for ordinary regression estimates. They are repeated, specifically sequenced, and of large scale; otherwise, they are standard linear calculations. The normal equations are as large in number as the totality of coefficients in the whole system; therefore, the problem is much bigger than computation of single equation estimates.

The left-hand matrix of the normal equations can be condensed to the block matrix expression

$$\begin{bmatrix} (q^{ji}Y_i'Y_j) & (s^{ji}Y_i'X_j) \\ (s^{ji}X_i'Y_j) & (s^{ji}X_i'X_j) \end{bmatrix}.$$

In equilibrium, after iterations for A, B have converged, the evaluation of

$$\begin{bmatrix} (q^{ji}Y_i'Y_j) & (s^{ji}Y_i'X_j) \\ (s^{ji}X_i'Y_j) & (s^{ji}X_i'X_j) \end{bmatrix}^{-1}$$

provides estimates of the variance-covariance matrix of coefficients.

If this iterative technique is slow in reaching convergent estimates for A, B, it is possible to change the algorithm and speed the process. To show this, let us write the normal equations as

$$D\alpha = c, \tag{7.5.11}$$

where both D and c depend on α, a column vector. The standard algorithm is

$$\alpha_{r+1} = D_r^{-1}c_r \tag{7.5.12}$$

where D_r and c_r are computed from α_r. The step size can be varied by using

$$\alpha_{r+1} = hD_r^{-1}c_r + (1-h)\alpha_r. \tag{7.5.13}$$

When $h = 1$ (unit step size), we have the standard case. As long as the concentrated likelihood is increasing, determined by an examination of

$$\frac{|W_r|}{|S_r|}$$

after the rth iteration, the value of h should be kept large, possibly as great as 2.0. If the likelihood ceases to increase, the step size can be reduced.

Another approach is to use Newton's method for the iteration. If we write

$$c - D(\alpha) = F(\alpha) = 0. \tag{7.5.14}$$

Newton's method consists of the iteration

$$\begin{aligned} \alpha_{r+1} &= \alpha_r - [F(\alpha_r)]^{-1}f(\alpha_r) \\ F(\alpha) &= \left(\frac{\partial f_i}{\partial \alpha_j}\right). \end{aligned} \tag{7.5.15}$$

The matrix F is the matrix of second derivatives of the concentrated log-likelihood function. The equations can be written as

$$\begin{bmatrix} \left(\frac{\partial L_c}{\partial \alpha' \partial \alpha}\right) & \left(\frac{\partial L_c}{\partial \alpha' \partial \beta}\right) \\ \left(\frac{\partial L_c}{\partial \beta' \partial \alpha}\right) & \left(\frac{\partial L_c}{\partial \beta' \partial \beta}\right) \end{bmatrix} \begin{bmatrix} \alpha'_{r+1} - \alpha'_r \\ \beta'_{r+1} - \beta'_r \end{bmatrix} = \begin{bmatrix} \frac{\partial L_c}{\partial \alpha'} \\ \frac{\partial L_c}{\partial \beta'} \end{bmatrix}. \tag{7.5.16}$$

The vectors α and β are row vectors in this expression. Iterations with Newton's method may converge faster, but the computations are somewhat more complicated.

The normal equations of 3SLS estimation are quite similar to the above normal equations for FIML estimation. The 3SLS equations in Chap. 4 differ in two respects. The moments are of the form

$$Z_i'X(X'X)^{-1}X'Z_j; \qquad Z_i = (Y_i X_i)$$

instead of

$$Y_i'Y_j,\ Y_i'X_j, \text{ or } X_i'X_j,$$

and all the weighting factors are elements of S^{-1}. Those in the northwest corner of the FIML estimation matrix are elements of $S^{-1} - W^{-1}$.

The method of 3SLS could allow for iteration, but as was pointed out in Chap. 4, Madansky has shown that all the gains in asymptotic efficiency are realized without iteration. It is therefore a single solution of the normal equations instead of iterated solutions as in FIML estimation. Apart from the aspect of iteration, all the 3SLS computations are of the same general class as those for FIML outlined above. They involve moment matrix calculation, other matrix multiplication, and matrix inversion.

6. SOLUTION AND SIMULATION PROGRAMMING

The calculation procedures discussed so far are pertinent to the estimation problem, but having an estimated system we are faced with the problems of application, and this poses new types of computing problems. If the system were linear, we could compute values of y_t, for any time period t, from the reduced form

$$y_t = -\hat{A}_0^{-1}\left(\sum_{i=1}^{p} \hat{A}_i y_{t-i} + \hat{B}x_t\right), \tag{7.6.1}$$

where $\hat{A}_i$ and $\hat{B}$ are estimated coefficient matrices. To carry out the indicated calculations, we would need to read in values of the vectors $y_{t-1}, y_{t-2}, \ldots, y_{t-p}, x_t$ for period t and earlier periods. We would then invert $\hat{A}_0$ and multiply it into $\hat{A}_i$ and y_{t-i} and $\hat{B}$ and x_t. These are all standard programming problems of matrix inversion and multiplication that we use for moment calculation and parameter estimation in linear systems. In this case, however, $\hat{A}_0$ is not symmetric or positive definite. Similarly, all we can say in advance about $\hat{A}_i$ and $\hat{B}$ is that they are real.

In simulation, we advance one period at a time in the numerical solution of finite difference equations. We compute

$$y_{t+1} = -\hat{A}_0^{-1}\Big(\sum_{i=1}^{p} \hat{A}_i y_{t+1-i} + \hat{B}x_{t+1}\Big), \tag{7.6.2}$$

where y_{t+1-i} for $i = 1$ is carried forward from the previous step, unless it is a value from the initial conditions. The matrices $\hat{A}_0^{-1}\ \hat{A}_i$ and $\hat{A}_0^{-1}\hat{B}$ can be evaluated just once for the whole simulation run; $t, t+1, t+2, \ldots$. This is the real benefit of linear systems. An alternative approach with linear systems would be to extract the roots of the characteristic equation and express the *solution* numerically as

$$y_t = \hat{K}\hat{\lambda}^t - \frac{\hat{a}(L)}{\hat{\Delta}(L)}\hat{B}x_t. \tag{7.6.3}$$

The extraction of the roots in $\hat{\lambda}$ may require complicated nonlinear calculations; therefore, it is easier to work digitally, printing out the solution values for several periods; $y_t, y_{t+1}, y_{t+2}, y_{t+3}, \ldots,$. Standard matrix calculations, therefore, suffice.

A simplification can be introduced at an early stage if the maximum amount of recursion can be discovered and an entire recursive block set aside for advance calculation. At time point t, all values of y_{t+1-i}; $i = 1, 2, \ldots, p$ as well as x_t are assumed to be given. The expressions

$$\sum_{i=1}^{p} \hat{A}_i y_{t-i} \text{ and } \hat{B}x_t$$

can all be evaluated at once in the series of calculations. If, in addition, some part of $\hat{A}_0$ is triangular, we can devise a first recursive block of equations. For the part of $\hat{A}_0$ that is triangular, we can avoid matrix inversion

$$\begin{matrix} \hat{\alpha}_{110} & 0 & 0 & \cdots \\ \hat{\alpha}_{210} & \hat{\alpha}_{220} & 0 & \cdots \\ \hat{\alpha}_{310} & \hat{\alpha}_{320} & \hat{\alpha}_{330} & \cdots \\ \vdots & & & \end{matrix}$$

The first equation can be solved for y_{1t} by dividing $\hat{\alpha}_{110}$ into the (predetermined) right-hand side. Because y_{1t} has been evaluated in the previous step, we can solve for y_{2t} in the second equation by transposing $\hat{\alpha}_{210}y_{1t}$ to the right-hand side and dividing the new r.h.s. by $\hat{\alpha}_{220}$. In a similar way, we can solve for y_{3t} by using y_{1t} and y_{2t}, taken from the previous steps, together with the r.h.s. and $\hat{\alpha}_{330}$.

There is no simple procedure to find the maximum amount of recursiveness in a system. The equations with only one dependent variable can be located at once and placed at the top of the recursive block. Among all equations with two dependent variables, those that contain y_{1t} and any other dependent variable can be placed next (in natural order, depending on the single dependent variable in addition to y_{1t}) in the recursive block ordering. Next, all equations with three dependent variables are studied for recursive ordering, and so on.

After the recursive block of equations, there comes a simultaneous block. In linear form, this block has a matrix of coefficients that cannot be put into a triangular array. There may be a final recursive block at the end of the equation system, especially if it is concerned with making up variables from combinations of variables already determined in the *first recursive* or *simultaneous* block.

The equations in the simultaneous block are solved by the Gauss-Seidel iterative procedure explained in the preceding chapter. The beginning and ending recursive parts of the system require no iteration, the central simultaneous part does, and must be organized so as to form a convergent pattern. The steps in the solution are exemplified by the following two-dimensional diagram.

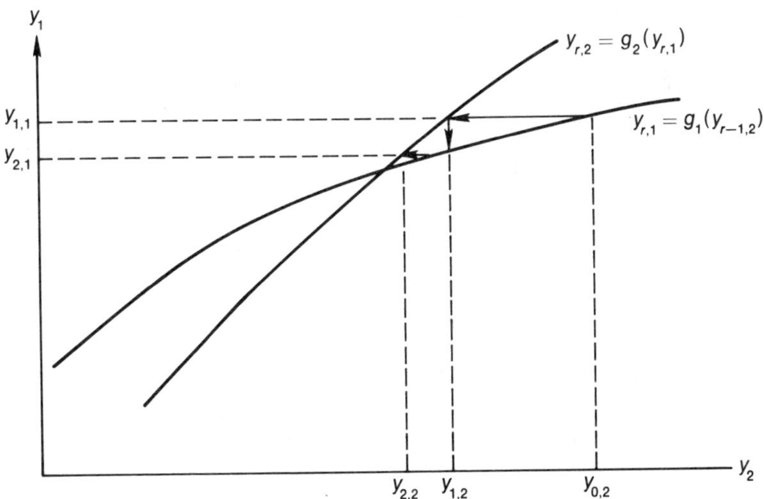

Figure 7.1 Convergent Iteration Solution

From an initial value $y_{0,2}$, we compute $y_{1,1}$ from g_1. This value of $y_{1,1}$ is substituted into g_2, and $y_{1,2}$ is computed. This new value is used to compute $y_{2,1}$ from g_1, and so on.

This convergent process normalizes the first equation on y_1 and the second on y_2. Had we used the opposite normalization

$$y_{r,1} = g_2^{-1}(y_{r-1,2})$$
$$y_{r,2} = g_1^{-1}(y_{r,1}),$$

the iteration process would have been divergent, as in Fig. 7.2. Corresponding

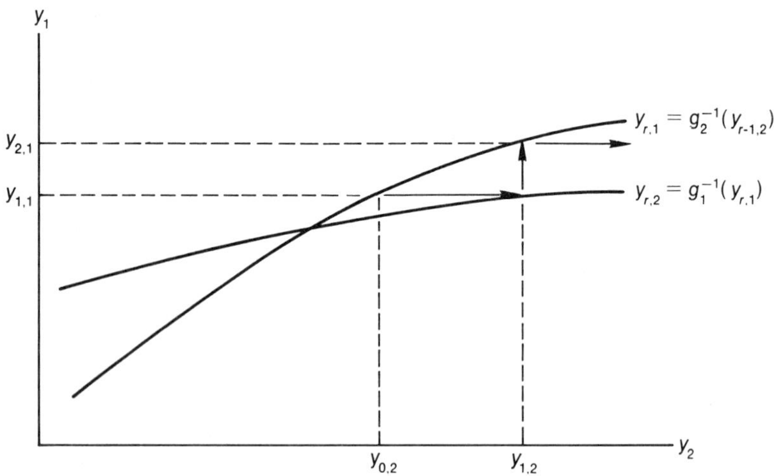

Figure 7.2 Divergent Iteration

to a convergent (divergent) normalization, there is a divergent (convergent) normalization. It is necessary to examine the logic and mathematical structure of a system in advance in order to secure convergence. A good rule to follow is to make the normalization follow the reasoning of the economic logic of construction.

In systems of more than two equations, it is not only the normalization rule, but also the ordering of equations in the iterative steps that affects convergence. Another way of affecting convergence is to change the step size. The diagrams above use a unit step size, but the speed and existence of convergence can be affected by step size. A system should be tried for convergence. If the results diverge, the equations should be renormalized, reordered, and varied in step size until convergence is attained. Generally speaking, convergence is fast. A solution should be reached in fewer than twenty iterations for most macro models.

The solution programs are general. Within dimensionality limits (number of equations and number of variables), any equation system can be written in computer language in the parts of the program where each equation fits. The first recursive equations are written in a subroutine REC1; the simultaneous equations are written in a subroutine SOLVE; and the final recursive equations are written in a subroutine REC2. In writing the equations, it should be noted that the variables are grouped into several different categories. First, there are the lag values. These are read in from cards or tape into their major groupings, that is, as lags of exogenous variables, as lags of recursive endogenous variables, or as lags of simultaneous endogenous variables. Next, exogenous variables are read in for the solution period. The whole time path of exogenous variables must be given for the period over which an equation system is to be solved. Also, the parameter estimates and initial approximations for simultaneous variables must be read in.

The exogenous values for a given period and the lag values relevant to that period are developed as numerical values of the right-hand side of an equation. The right-hand side values for an equation at a given time point will not change in successive iterations if these values can be isolated as lags or exogenous variables. In writing the equations and in evaluating the right-hand side, the parameter estimates (coefficients) must be called from a matrix or listing where each parameter value is stored in a given location.

In the first recursive block, a value is computed for each left-hand side variable once and for all for a given time period. The simultaneous variables are used in two forms—once from the initial approximations or values of the previous iteration that are substituted in the right-hand side of the simultaneous equations together with exogenous and lagged values, and again from the left-hand side of the simultaneous equations. As soon as a simultaneous variable is developed on the left-hand side, it is substituted into subsequent simultaneous equations in the same iteration. The program keeps iterating until the simultaneous variables change by less than a preassigned amount on successive iterations.

The equations in the second recursive block recombine, in programmed equation form, the variables developed for the given period in REC1, SOLVE, and in the input locations for exogenous or lagged variables. These variables are computed once and for all in a given period.

As needed, in the equation specifications, variables developed in the first solution period are read into equations as one-period lag values for the second period and the most distant lag values for each equation in the previous period are not used in the second period. The initial approximations for the simultaneous variables in the second period are the solution values from the first period. When all the periods called for in the solution have been completed, the RESULT subroutine is used to print out the final tabulations in a neat expository form. The final printout should contain all the exogenous assumptions and all the solution values from REC1, SOLVE, and REC2.

If the equations are written so that all or many important parameters can be changed, this enables the investigator to cope with policy changes, multiplier analysis, or data revision. If storage capacity is scarce, so that every estimated parameter cannot be written as

$$a_{ij} + \text{CONIJ}$$

where CONIJ stands for an increment or decrement to the (i, j)-parameter value, there should certainly be provision for adding CONI to the ith equation (a change in the constant term parameter) and other CON values to strategic coefficients, such as tax rates, transfer payment rates, and so on. The values of all CON adjustments are read into the program as data over the solution period together with the exogenous variables. Short of reestimation, it is a quick approximation to lower or raise individual equations by the amount of a CON adjustment to cope with the frequent data revision that prevails in the publication of economic statistics. Some kinds of multiplier calculations can be made by changing the input values for exogenous variables over the solution period, but others may be made by changing the values of CONI in the ith equation.

This program is very flexible. It can be run for as many or as few periods as the investigator likes, provided he supplies the appropriate input data. Impulses can be constant or variable over time, depending on the kind of analysis being made. This is done by specifying the values of exogenous variables or CON adjustments for each time period of the solution. By changing CONI randomly, according to the planned drawing of random variables, we can obtain stochastic simulation patterns over time. Also, final display can be in tables or graphs and can be in terms of solution values alone or in comparison with observed values.

The program input cards are known as a *Data Deck*. The listing of a typical data deck will show specifically what inputs are needed, the output form, and the flexibility of the program.[2]

I. *Message Card.*
In columns 1–72, the user may print any message desired in order to identify the solution by title (such as, POST VIET NAM DEMOBILIZATION).

II. *Master Control Card.*
In six fields of three digits each, there is program information explained below, while columns 19–30 give beginning and end period dates (such as, in year and quarter).

Cols.	*Name*	
1–3	NPER	Number of time periods in the solution (≥ 1)
4–6	IDATA	001 Read data from cards; do not store on disc file.
		002 Read data from cards; place initial approximations and matrix of lagged values on disc for future alternative solutions.
		003 Read initial approximations and matrix of lagged values from disc.
7–9	NTBLS	Number of copies of solution tables desired (≥ 1).

[2] The Data Deck listed is the one used in *Econometric Gaming: A Kit for Computer Analysis of Macroeconomic Models*, by L. R. Klein, M. K. Evans, and M. Hartley (New York: Macmillan, 1969). A complete listing of the program, together with solution results, is given in the *Kit*.

10–12	IPRNT	000 Print out *Message*, *Master Control Card*, and *Solution*.
		001 Print out the preceding values and *Initial Approximations*, *Lagged Variables*, *Coefficients*.
13–15	NGRAPH	Number of variables to be graphed ($0 \leq$ NGRAPH ≤ 20).
16–18	NNZCON	Number of nonzero CON adjustments.
19–30	SOLRNG	Time span of solution (six characters for year, decimal, quarter—beginning and ending).

III. *Graph Control Card.*
This is needed if NGRAPH > 0.

1–3	IACT	000 Actual values not graphed.
		001 Read in and graph actual values.
		002 Read and graph control values.
4–6		Location numbers of variables to be graphed;
7–9		variables numbered from 001 to 150.
.		
.		
.		
61–63.		

IV. *Constant Adjustment Numbers.*
If NNZCON > 0, the location numbers of the CON values must be punched in 3-column fields. More than one card must be used if NNZCON > 26.

V. *Coefficients*
Each parameter estimate is assigned a location number, and the corresponding parameter value is punched in 10-digit fields with decimal points. There will be eight parameter values per card.

VI. *Initial Approximations*
In 10-digit fields with decimal points, the starting approximations for all simultaneous variables are punched in the order of appearance. There will be eight values per card.

VII. *Nonzero Lagged Variables*
Lagged values, in 10-digit fields with decimal points, are punched, beginning with $t - 1$ and extending as far back as necessary. Each variable is punched on a separate card or cards.

VIII. *Solution Period Values of Exogenous Variables and Constant Adjustments*
For each solution period, values are punched in 10-digit fields with decimal points for exogenous variables and all CON values used. One card contains values up to eight solution periods. Added cards are used for longer solutions.

IX. *Actual and Control Values*
If IACT > 0 on the graph control card, and if actual or some control (base) solution values are to be plotted for comparison with present solution values, they must be punched in fields of 10 digits, with decimal points. There must be values punched for each solution period, and more than one card will be needed if NPER > 8.

This specification constitutes the Data Deck, that determines the characteristics of the solution to be obtained and its output presentation. This particular program gives much flexibility in designing a solution and in adapting it to different economic applications.

To compute stochastic simulations of a model, this program can readily be adapted for the task. Each of the intercept values, CONI, can be randomly impulsed; this is equivalent to adding disturbance values to each equation. If random numbers are drawn from a table listing or from an internal machine generator, each CONI can be raised or lowered by a random amount. These shock values are superimposed on whatever zero or nonzero CON adjustment values are being used for a nonstochastic simulation. The random values of CONI must be read in at the part of the program that calls for CON adjustment values to cover the whole solution period.

A simple way of choosing the random numbers so as to preserve the sample estimates of variances and covariances of disturbances is as follows:[3]

(a) List all sample period residuals in a data matrix

$$R = \begin{pmatrix} r_{11} & r_{21} & \cdots & r_{n1} \\ r_{12} & r_{22} & \cdots & r_{n2} \\ \cdot & \cdot & & \\ \cdot & \cdot & & \\ \cdot & \cdot & & \\ r_{1T} & r_{2T} & \cdots & r_{nT} \end{pmatrix}$$

(b) Draw mutually independent unit normal variables in series of length T (sample length) for each period to be simulated (N periods)

$$E = \begin{pmatrix} e_{11} & e_{12} & \cdots & e_{1T} \\ e_{21} & e_{22} & \cdots & e_{2T} \\ \cdot & \cdot & & \cdot \\ \cdot & \cdot & & \cdot \\ \cdot & \cdot & & \cdot \\ e_{N1} & e_{N2} & & e_{NT} \end{pmatrix}.$$

This is a matrix of random drawings. It need not be from a normal population, but it must have unit variance and zero mean.

(c) Form the matrix product, ER

$$\frac{1}{\sqrt{T}} ER = \frac{1}{\sqrt{T}} \begin{pmatrix} \sum e_{1t} r_{1t} & \cdots & \sum e_{1t} r_{nt} \\ \cdot & & \\ \cdot & & \\ \cdot & & \\ \sum e_{Nt} r_{1t} & \cdots & \sum e_{Nt} r_{nt} \end{pmatrix}$$

[3] This method is suggested by M. D. McCarthy, in Hickman, *Econometric Models of Cyclical Behavior*, *op. cit.*

$$\frac{1}{\sqrt{T}} ER = \begin{pmatrix} CON_{11} & \cdots & CON_{n1} \\ \cdot & & \\ \cdot & & \\ \cdot & & \\ CON_{1N} & & CON_{nN} \end{pmatrix}.$$

The expected value of the variance of any element in the jth column of $\frac{1}{\sqrt{T}} ER$ is $\frac{1}{T} \sum_{t=i}^{T} r_{jt}^2 = S_{jj}$, and the expected value of the covariance for any contemporaneous pair in the jth and k^{th} columns is $\frac{1}{T} \sum_{t=1}^{T} r_{jt} r_{kt} = S_{jk}$. The columns of $\frac{1}{\sqrt{T}} ER$ are the desired CON adjustment values to be added to each equation over the simulation period.

The advantage of this method is that it is so easy to execute within the solution program being discussed, and it avoids degrees of freedom problems that may arise in large systems where the number of equations, n, exceeds the number of samples values, T. This is a difficult problem in the application of Nagar's method.[4]

SUGGESTED READINGS

Chow, G. C., "Two Methods of Computing Full-Information Maximum Likelihood Estimates in Simultaneous Stochastic Equations," *International Economic Review*, 9 (February, 1968), 100–12. Derives "normal" equations for full information estimators of equation systems.

Dwyer, P. S., *Linear Computations*, (New York: John Wiley & Sons, 1951). An excellent account of pre-computer methods of solving systems of linear simultaneous equations.

Eisenpress, H. and J. Greenstadt, "The Estimation of Nonlinear Econometric Systems," *Econometrica*, 34 (October, 1966), 851–61. Develops equations for numerical methods in the estimation of linear or non-linear equation systems by maximum likelihood techniques.

Faddeeva, V. N., *Computational Methods of Linear Algebra*, trans. C. D. Benster, (New York: Dover, 1959). Summarizes methods of numerical solution of linear equation systems and associated matrix calculations.

Klein, L. R., M. K. Evans, and M. Hartley, *Econometric Gaming: A Kit for Computer Analysis of Macroeconometric Models*, (New York: Macmillan, 1969). Shows how

[4] A. L. Nagar, "Stochastic Simulation of the Brookings Econometric Model," *op. cit.*

to make multiplier and general simulation analyses with a large dynamic model, complete with computer program and operating instructions.

Shan, S. Kuo, *Numerical Methods and Computers*, (Reading, Mass.: Addison-Wesley, 1965). An instructive account of programming for computer calculations that arise in applied research.

8

Methods of Sector Analysis

1. TYPES OF DISAGGREGATION

The distinguishing characteristic of the examples discussed so far is that they deal with aggregative equations estimated or tested with time series information. In this chapter we introduce variations on this theme by considering the problems involved in the construction of models for sectors of the economy from either time series or *cross-section* data. By the latter, we mean observations at an instant of time on several microeconomic units.

Two different considerations are in order. By studying sectors of the economy, we disaggregate. Aggregation, however, occurs in two dimensions—over individuals (firms and households) and over commodities. A study of a particular industry may be carried out by aggregating data for all firms in that industry and estimating a model from time series observations on these aggregative data. The disaggregation has occurred by commodities, because the model concentrates attention on the outputs and inputs of a single industry. Further disaggregation may be carried out by using time series data for a particular firm as the sample of observations. In a cross-section sample for a single industry, we disaggregate at once over both firms and commodities, because our data refer to the outputs and inputs of individual firms in this industry during a fixed time period. The new consideration in this case, however, is that we do not use temporal variation for making statistical inferences; instead, we use spatial variation, that is, interfirm differences. Cross-section samples need not disaggregate over commodities, although they must, to some extent, over firms and individuals. From a survey of households we may tabulate such aggregative variables as total consumption expenditures, total savings, and total income for each individual household. The unit of observation is microeconomic, but the variables are macroeconomic—aggregated over types of consumer expenditures, types of saving, and types of income. Naturally, we may disaggregate the variables in such surveys provided the basic data are collected.

Time series and cross-section analyses are not mutually exclusive, for we may have a time sequence of cross-section samples. Then, we must go into the problem of pooling statistical information from the two sources.

2. ESTIMATION OF SECTOR MODELS

In Chap. 4 we saw from the discussion of the single equation estimation methods that one does not have to construct a complete model of the whole economic system in order to estimate some particular equation. All that is required in this respect is a knowledge of some or all of the predetermined variables in the equations other than the one being estimated. These estimation methods could then be used to determine the structural characteristics of some sector of the economy.

Let us consider the problem of estimating equations for industry i from a time series sample. Equations of interest for this industry are its production function, its demand for factors of production, and the demand for the industry's output. These together will determine either cost or supply equations. The model studied will consist of the following variables:

$$
\begin{aligned}
x_{it} &= \text{output} \\
n_{it} &= \text{employment} \\
c_{it} &= \text{use of raw materials} \\
d_{it} &= \text{use of capital services} \\
p_{it} &= \text{price of output} \\
w_{it} &= \text{wage rate} \\
q_{it} &= \text{price of raw materials} \\
r_{it} &= \text{price of capital services} \\
p_t &= \text{general price level} \\
Y_t &= \text{national income.}
\end{aligned}
$$

All variables refer to the tth time period, and all except the last two refer to the ith industry.

The production function is

$$x_{it} = f(n_{it}, c_{it}, d_{it}, u_{1t}). \tag{8.2.1}$$

u represents random disturbance. Assuming a competitive market, we get the stochastic marginal productivity or factor demand equations

$$\frac{\partial f}{\partial n_{it}} = g_1\left(\frac{w_{it}}{p_{it}}, u_{2t}\right) \tag{8.2.2}$$

$$\frac{\partial f}{\partial c_{it}} = g_2\left(\frac{q_{it}}{p_{it}}, u_{3t}\right) \tag{8.2.3}$$

$$\frac{\partial f}{\partial d_{it}} = g_3\left(\frac{r_{it}}{p_{it}}, u_{4t}\right) \tag{8.2.4}$$

If the assumption of a competitive market is dropped, these equations can be modified by introducing coefficients depending on elasticities of product demand and factor supply. For example, the marginal productivity of labor equation would become

$$\frac{\partial f}{\partial n_{it}} = g_1\left[\frac{w_{it}\left(1 + \frac{1}{\eta}\right)}{p_{it}\left(1 - \frac{1}{\epsilon}\right)}, u_{2t}\right] \tag{8.2.2a}$$

in which η = supply elasticity and ϵ = demand elasticity. Similar alterations would be made in (8.2.3) and (8.2.4).

The demand equation for the industry's product is

$$x_{it} = h\left(\frac{p_{it}}{p_t}, \frac{Y_t}{p_t}, u_{5t}\right). \tag{8.2.5}$$

It is best to think of this model as that of an industry supplying goods to ultimate consumers. In that case, (8.2.5) is reasonable as a demand equation, both relative prices and real income being explanatory demand variables. If the industry being studied supplies goods to other industries, perhaps national income (disposable or not) is not the proper variable in (8.2.5). Industrial profits, in general or particular, would be more appropriate.

If the industry deals in a competitive market, demand elasticity is infinite to the individual firm as assumed in (8.2.2)–(8.2.4) but not to the entire industry's output as in (8.2.5) [assuming a slope to the h function in the (x_i, p_i) plane]. If the market is imperfect, then demand elasticities from Eq. (8.2.5) are also parameters in (8.2.2)–(8.2.4).

We lack equations expressing the condition under which factors of production are supplied to the ith industry. The difficult thing in connection with such equations is that they tend to take us beyond the bounds of our chosen task, namely, to study the ith industrial sector of the economy without simultaneously studying every other sector. Materials are supplied to the ith industry by other industries whose production functions and marginal productivity functions are ruled out of our present analysis. In some cases, the interrelationships between industries are so strong that a single one cannot be isolated for individual study. These remarks apply with equal force to the supply of capital to the ith industry. Labor supply, on the other hand, comes from the household sector of the economy and can be treated in much the same way as we treated demand for output of the ith industry by the household sector.

The number of workers, or better, manhours, available to the ith industry will depend on at least two things—the general availability of workers and the relative attractiveness of wages in the ith industry. General availability is indicated by the labor force L_t assuming that all workers are mobile enough to be candidates for work in the ith industry. The ratio of w_{it} to w_t shows the relative attractiveness of wages. The supply equation is

$$n_{it} = k\left(L_t, \frac{w_{it}}{w_t}, u_{6t}\right). \tag{8.2.6}$$

We shall not write down specific structural equations for the supply of materials and capital to the ith industry. Instead, we make the two following assumptions:

1. Raw material prices paid by the ith industry fluctuate in accordance with the general level of raw material prices in the economy.
2. Prices paid for capital services in the ith industry fluctuate in accordance with the general level of capital prices in the economy.

More formally, we use the equations

$$q_{it} = l(q_t, u_{7t}) \tag{8.2.7}$$

$$r_{it} = m(r_t, u_{8t}). \tag{8.2.8}$$

These two equations are not structural relations showing behavior of some specific economic agents as in (8.2.2)–(8.2.6). They are used here merely for purposes of closing the system conveniently without going into the detailed workings of the industries supplying materials and capital.

We shall assume some particular types of equations in order to make the model amenable to statistical handling. Perhaps the most obvious form to assume is a linear approximation of each equation

$$x_{it} = \alpha_0 + \alpha_1 n_{it} + \alpha_2 c_{it} + \alpha_3 d_{it} + u_{1t}, \tag{8.2.9}$$

$$w_{it} + \beta p_{it} = \beta_0 + \beta_1 n_{it} + \beta_2 c_{it} + \beta_3 d_{it} + u_{2t}, \tag{8.2.10}$$

$$q_{it} + \gamma p_{it} = \gamma_0 + \gamma_1 n_{it} + \gamma_2 \dot{c}_{it} + \gamma_3 d_{it} + u_{3t}, \tag{8.2.11}$$

$$r_{it} + \delta p_{it} = \delta_0 + \delta_1 n_{it} + \delta_2 c_{it} + \delta_3 d_{it} + u_{4t}, \tag{8.2.12}$$

$$x_{it} = \epsilon_0 + \epsilon_1 p_{it} + \epsilon_2 p_t + \epsilon_3 Y_t + u_{5t}, \tag{8.2.13}$$

$$n_{it} = \eta_0 + \eta_1 w_{it} + \eta_2 w_t + \eta_3 L_t + u_{6t}, \tag{8.2.14}$$

$$q_{it} = \zeta_0 + \zeta_1 q_t + u_{7t}, \tag{8.2.15}$$

$$r_{it} = \theta_0 + \theta_1 r_t + u_{8t}. \tag{8.2.16}$$

Price ratios instead of absolute prices could be used in a variant of this model. The identifiability of Eqs. (8.2.9)–(8.2.16) depends on the nature of the more complete system in which it is embedded. The above equations contain fourteen variables, all of which may be endogenous. Analysis of particular circumstances are required in order to classify the variables as endogenous or exogenous. For example, in an industry that imports raw materials, the price paid for such materials may be exogenous as far as our model is concerned. The same may be true of industries purchasing small portions of aggregate raw materials being produced by a monopoly. We shall not, however, use the argument that national income is exogenous to this sector merely because the sector plays such a small role in the total economy. If the demand for the output of final commodities by each producing sector depends on national income, the bias in parameter estimation introduced by considering income to be exogenous, where it is really endogenous, for each individual sector may be small in each case; but, at the same time, the parameters will be small and percentage biases are not negligible.

For expository purposes of our sector analysis, we shall assume each of the fourteen variables in (8.2.9)–(8.2.16) to be endogenous. There are eight equations in our model; hence, we cannot close the model with less than an additional six. Our shortcut method for closing the system will be called *grafting*, that is, we shall graft our sector model to an overall aggregative model. The aggregative model, or the master model as we may name it, should be one that explains fluctuations in national income Y_t, labor force L_t, the general price level p_t, the general wage rate w_t, the general price of raw materials q_t, and the general price of capital r_t. The master model will have to be somewhat more general than the aggregative model we developed in Chap. 6. That system attempts to explain movements in national income, the general price level, and the general wage rate. In the present example we would have to expand this to cover raw material and capital prices. Such phenomena involve equations of aggregative inventory holdings broken down at least by raw materials and other inventories, and the intensity of use of fixed capital.

In the master model, there are a number of predetermined variables, such as government expenditures, taxes, exports, discount rate, bank reserves, lagged incomes, time trends, and others. Denote them by the symbols $z_1, z_2, z_3, \ldots$. A linear model can be solved for each of the endogenous variables in terms of predetermined variables alone. The six that interest us are

$$Y_t = \iota_0 + \sum \iota_i z_{it} + u_{9t}, \tag{8.2.17}$$

$$L_t = \kappa_0 + \sum \kappa_i z_{it} + u_{10t}, \tag{8.2.18}$$

$$p_t = \lambda_0 + \sum \lambda_i z_{it} + u_{11t}, \tag{8.2.19}$$

$$w_t = \mu_0 + \sum \mu_i z_{it} + u_{12t}, \tag{8.2.20}$$

$$q_t = \nu_0 + \sum \nu_i z_{it} + u_{13t}, \tag{8.2.21}$$

$$r_t = \xi_0 + \sum \xi_i z_{it} + u_{14t}. \tag{8.2.22}$$

One way of stating necessary conditions for identifiability is as follows: In order for a linear equation in a system to be identified, the number of predetermined variables in the system, but not in the particular equation, must be greater than or equal to the number of endogenous variables in the equation less one. Each of the equations in (8.2.9)–(8.2.16) contains five or fewer endogenous variables; therefore, as long as there are four or more z variables in (8.2.17)–(8.2.22), each equation of our sector model satisfies the necessary condition for identifiability.

One estimation procedure would be to use the z variables of (8.2.17)–(8.2.22), provided we have identification, with the single equation methods of Chap. 4 to estimate the parameters. The application of the notation used there to Eq. (8.2.9) of the present model yields the correspondences

$$\begin{aligned} x_{it} &= y_{1t}, \\ n_{it} &= y_{2t}, \\ c_{it} &= y_{3t}, \\ d_{it} &= y_{4t}. \end{aligned}$$

These are the endogenous variables in the first equation of the sector model. This equation contains no predetermined variables as written, so all the predetermined variables come from the list of z variables in (8.2.17)–(8.2.22).

Given the estimates of the structural parameters in the master model, we can derive Eqs. (8.2.17)–(8.2.22) with numerical coefficients that are combinations of the structural estimates. For each time point, values of z_{it} can be substituted in the estimated versions of (8.2.17)–(8.2.22) and estimated values of Y_t, L_t, p_t, w_t, q_t, and r_t can be obtained corresponding to each value of t. The u's are put at their mean values, 0. The estimates are written as Y_t^0, L_t^0, p_t^0, w_t^0, q_t^0, and r_t^0. A second procedure would then be to use Y_t^0, L_t^0, p_t^0, w_t^0, q_t^0, and r_t^0 as predetermined variables in (8.2.9)–(8.2.16) in place of their endogenous counterparts. In this way we may view the sector model as one of eight equations in eight endogenous variables x_{it}, n_{it}, c_{it}, d_{it}, p_{it}, w_{it}, q_{it}, r_{it}, and six predetermined variables Y_t^0, L_t^0, p_t^0, w_t^0, q_t^0, and r_t^0. The methods of two stage least squares or limited information may then be applied to this model and will not, in general, lead to the same estimation as the more conventional application of the methods.

Reduced form Eqs. (8.2.17)–(8.2.22) are written explicitly for a linear system. If the master model is nonlinear in the variables, as is the case for the aggregative system of Chap. 6, we cannot generally derive closed form expressions for the endogenous variables as in (8.2.17)–(8.2.22). In this case, a recommended procedure would be to approximate Y_t^0, L_t^0, p_t^0, w_t^0, q_t^0, r_t^0 by using the Gauss-Seidel or similar algorithms to solve for numerical values of the endogenous variables in the master model for each sample period. These solutions can use dynamically generated values of all variables from fixed initial conditions, or one-period solution values for which lags are treated as predetermined.

The single equation methods, following either of the two suggested approaches, are recommended because they enable us to study separately that part of the system referring explicitly to the ith industry. The master model breaks off as a self-contained system, and we want to use estimation methods that take advantage of that fact so that we do not have to estimate the parameters of both the master and sector models simultaneously.

The sector model presented serves only to illustrate a method of grafting, and there is no compelling reason to accept this exact form of sector model in any particular case. There may well be sector models in which predetermined variables other than those estimated from the master model occur explicitly. For example, productivity trends may appear in the production function and lags may appear in any number of the sector equations. Such predetermined variables affect the criteria for identification, but do not alter the nature of the statistical estimation problem in grafting identifiable equations.

Equations (8.2.1)–(8.2.4) establish a relationship between the parameters of the production function and each of the marginal productivity equations. This relationship is lost when linear approximations are used for each equation separately. Indeed, the partial derivatives of a linear production function are constants, and not the linear functions we assume in (8.2.10)–(8.2.12). A model that preserves the relationship among parameters in different equations and has many other features to recommend it is the well-known Cobb-Douglas production function and associated log-linear equations.

$$x_{it} = An_{it}^{\alpha_1}c_{it}^{\alpha_2}d_{it}^{\alpha_3}u_{1t}, \tag{8.2.23}$$

$$\frac{w_{it}n_{it}}{p_{it}x_{it}} = \alpha_1 u_{2t}, \tag{8.2.24}$$

$$\frac{q_{it}c_{it}}{p_{it}x_{it}} = \alpha_2 u_{3t}, \tag{8.2.25}$$

$$\frac{r_{it}d_{it}}{p_{it}x_{it}} = \alpha_3 u_{4t}, \tag{8.2.26}$$

$$x_{it} = E\left(\frac{p_{it}}{p_t}\right)^{-\epsilon_1}\left(\frac{Y_t}{p_t}\right)^{\epsilon_2} u_{5t}, \tag{8.2.27}$$

$$n_{it} = H\left(\frac{w_{it}}{w_t}\right)^{\eta_1} L_t^{\eta_2} u_{6t}, \tag{8.2.28}$$

$$q_{it} = z(q_t)^{\xi_1} u_{7t}, \tag{8.2.29}$$

$$r_{it} = \theta(r_t)^{\theta_1} u_{8t}. \tag{8.2.30}$$

The model also has the property of constant elasticity of demand and labor supply; hence, modification of the marginal productivity equations to permit the consideration of imperfectly competitive markets becomes a simpler problem. Moreover, it has been shown elsewhere that the aggregation of individual behavior equations to industry equations is well defined and relatively simple for the type of model we are using in (8.2.23)–(8.2.30).[1] Industry variables actually used in empirical work will be sums or arithmetic means; whereas a properly

[1] See L. R. Klein, "Macroeconomics and the Theory of Rational Behavior," *Econometrica*, 14 (1946), 93–108.

aggregated model derived from (8.2.23)–(8.2.30) should be in terms of geometric means; time series of the latter will show much the same period to period variation as time series of the former. Another reason for using the type of model in (8.2.23)–(8.2.30) is that the frequency distributions of estimated values of disturbances in the above type model fitted to data of individual companies appear to be closely approximated by the logarithmic normal distribution. An example of this phenomenon will be fully discussed below. Suffice it to say at the moment that the logarithmic normal distribution has a long history of application for the study of industry distributions[2] that form a pattern consistent with the model we are now discussing. In the lognormal case, there is a simple relationship between the arithmetic and the geometric mean

$$A.M. = G.M.e^{\sigma^2/2}$$

where σ^2 is the variance of the lognormal distribution.

The sector model in (8.2.23)–(8.2.30) contains exactly the same variables as (8.2.9)–(8.2.16). It appears that the two models differ in that the latter is linear but the former is not; however, it is immediately obvious that (8.2.23)–(8.2.30) is linear in the logarithms of all variables. Another difference between the two models is that prices occur in ratio form in the linear logarithmic model but they do not in the first model, although the first case can be recast in terms of price ratios instead of absolute prices. A more essential difference is that the α_i that appear as parameters in (8.2.23) also appear in (8.2.24)–(8.2.26). Moreover, when the model is written in terms of logarithmic variables, it is seen that α_i are constant coefficients in (8.2.23), but log α_i appear in the same role in (8.2.24)–(8.2.26). In general, restrictions among coefficients in different equations are complicated to handle by equation system methods of estimation, but the particular restrictions we have in the example can be handled by simple computations. Added restrictions of this type have the advantage of enhancing the possibility of identification. We add to the restrictions if we form a model of an imperfectly competitive market that requires that parameters of the demand equation for output and the supply equations of input also appear in the marginal productivity equations.

The basic idea underlying the methods of two stage least squares and limited information is that restrictions on equations other than the one being currently estimated are not utilized. For this reason, we do not apply those methods to the sector model in (8.2.23)–(8.2.30), for we want to permit the relations among parameters in different equations to be a central feature of the model.

Equations (8.2.24)–(8.2.26) are all of one special type,

$$\log x_{it} = \log \alpha + \log u_t, \qquad (8.2.31)$$

[2] See R. Gibrat, *Les Inégalités Économiques* (Paris: Recueil Sirey, 1931).

that involves only one endogenous variable and one unknown parameter. Log u_t is a random variable, marginally distributed according to the density function

$$p(\log u_t).$$

Assuming $\log u_t$ to have a zero mean (expected value), we have the problem simply of estimating the mean of

$$p(\log u_t) = p(\log x_{it} - \log \alpha)$$

from observations

$$\log x_{i1}, \log x_{i2}, \ldots, \log x_{iT} \text{ in a sample of } T.$$

The best linear unbiased estimate of $\log \alpha$ under fairly general mathematical assumptions is

$$\text{b.l.u.e. } \log \alpha = \frac{1}{T}\sum_{t=1}^{T} \log x_{it}.$$

Our estimate of α is given by the geometric mean of the x_{it}. If, in addition, we can say that $\log u_{it}$ is normally distributed, we have a maximum likelihood estimate. Using these considerations, we can estimate α_1, α_2, and α_3 in (8.2.24)–(8.2.26) from

$$\hat{\alpha}_1 = \prod_{t=1}^{T}\left(\frac{w_{it}n_{it}}{p_{it}x_{it}}\right)^{1/T}$$

$$\hat{\alpha}_2 = \prod_{t=1}^{T}\left(\frac{q_{it}c_{it}}{p_{it}x_{it}}\right)^{1/T}$$

$$\hat{\alpha}_3 = \prod_{t=1}^{T}\left(\frac{r_{it}d_{it}}{p_{it}x_{it}}\right)^{1/T}.$$

We substitute the estimated values in the production Eq. (8.2.23) and estimate the remaining parameter as

$$\hat{A} = \prod_{t=1}^{T}\left(\frac{x_{it}}{n_{it}^{\hat{\alpha}_1}c_{it}^{\hat{\alpha}_2}d_{it}^{\hat{\alpha}_3}}\right)^{1/T}$$

This follows because (8.2.23) with the estimated values can be written as

$$\log x_{it} - \hat{\alpha}_1 \log n_{it} - \hat{\alpha}_2 \log c_{it} - \hat{\alpha}_3 \log d_{it} = \log A + \log u_{1t}.$$

The entire left-hand side of this equation is treated merely as a new endogenous variable—a weighted combination of other endogenous variables with known or estimated weights.

Straightforward applications of single equation methods can be used for the linear-logarithmic versions of (8.2.27)–(8.2.28).

$$\log x_{it} = \log E - \epsilon_1(\log p_{it} - \log p_t) + \epsilon_2(\log Y_t - \log p_t) + \log u_{5t}$$
$$\log n_{it} = \log H + \eta_1(\log w_{it} - \log w_t) + \eta_2 \log L_t + \log u_{6t}.$$

Two possibilities are open here: (a) We may use z variables from the master model in (8.2.17)–(8.2.22) and follow conventional TSLS or LIML methods. (b) Because the system could be written as one having two different endogenous variables in each equation,

$$\log x_{it}, \log p_{it} - \log p_t$$

and

$$\log n_{it}, \log w_{it} - \log w_t,$$

respectively, we could use $\log Y_t^0 - \log p_t^0$ and $\log L_t^0$ as two instrumental variables and derive simple estimation equations, in terms of deviations from means, of the form

$$m_{y_1z_1} = -\epsilon_1 m_{y_2z_1} + \epsilon_2 m_{z_1z_1}$$
$$m_{y_1z_2} = -\epsilon_1 m_{y_2z_2} + \epsilon_2 m_{z_1z_2}$$

for estimating ϵ_i and

$$m_{y_3z_1} = \eta_1 m_{y_4z_1} + \eta_2 m_{z_1z_2}$$
$$m_{y_3z_2} = \eta_1 m_{y_4z_2} + \eta_2 m_{z_2z_2}$$

for estimating η_i.

$$\begin{aligned} y_1 &= \log x_i, & z_1 &= \log Y^0 - \log p^0, \\ y_2 &= \log p_i - \log p, & z_2 &= \log L^0. \\ y_3 &= \log n_i, & & \\ y_4 &= \log w_i - \log w, & & \end{aligned}$$

The student must realize that this particular situation is special because (8.2.27) and (8.2.28) are each written with two endogenous variables and one different predetermined variable in each equation. In genèral, we are faced with methods involving considerably more calculation than the solution of two sets of two linear equations.

An interesting application arises if we permit imperfectly competitive markets in the model. Consider the case in which the marginal productivity equations are

$$\frac{w_{it}n_{it}}{p_{it}x_{it}} = \alpha_1\left(1 - \frac{1}{\epsilon_1}\right)u_{2t}, \tag{8.2.32}$$

$$\frac{q_{it}c_{it}}{p_{it}x_{it}} = \alpha_2\left(1 - \frac{1}{\epsilon_1}\right)u_{3t}, \tag{8.2.33}$$

$$\frac{r_{it}d_{it}}{p_{it}x_{it}} = \alpha_3\left(1 - \frac{1}{\epsilon_1}\right)u_{4t}. \tag{8.2.34}$$

Geometric means of sample observations of the left-hand terms provide estimates of $\alpha_i\left(1 - \frac{1}{\epsilon_1}\right)$. We desire to decompose these estimates into separate estimates of α_i and ϵ_1. A method of doing this would be to form ratios of the estimates of $\alpha_i\left(1 - \frac{1}{\epsilon_1}\right)$ to get

$$\text{est. } \frac{\alpha_2}{\alpha_1} = \widehat{\left(\frac{\alpha_2}{\alpha_1}\right)},$$

$$\text{est. } \frac{\alpha_3}{\alpha_1} = \widehat{\left(\frac{\alpha_3}{\alpha_1}\right)}.$$

Equation (8.2.23) can be written as

$$\frac{1}{\alpha_1}\log x_{it} = \frac{\log A}{\alpha_1} + \log n_{it} + \frac{\alpha_2}{\alpha_1}\log c_{it} + \frac{\alpha_3}{\alpha_1}\log d_{it} + \frac{1}{\alpha_1}\log u_{1t}.$$

Treat $\log x_{it}$ as one endogenous variable and $\log n_{it} + \frac{\hat{\alpha}_2}{\alpha_1}\log c_{it} + \frac{\hat{\alpha}_3}{\alpha_1}\log d_{it}$ as another. The production function is then viewed as one equation of a system involving two endogenous variables. Using TSLS or LIML methods, we can estimate $\frac{1}{\alpha_1}$ and $\frac{1}{\alpha_1}\log A$ from which we can get $\hat{\alpha}_1$ and $\hat{A}_1$. This gives us enough information to estimate each of the α_i and ϵ_i separately. Finally, substitute $\hat{\epsilon}_1$ into (8.2.27)

$$\log x_{it} + \hat{\epsilon}_1(\log p_{it} - \log p_t) = \log E + \epsilon_2(\log Y_t - \log p_t) + \log u_{5t}.$$

In this equation, $\log x_{it} + \hat{\epsilon}_1(\log p_{it} - \log p_t)$ is one endogenous variable. Log $Y_t^0 - \log p_t^0$ is one predetermined variable, and the regression of the endogenous variable on it gives us an estimate of ϵ_2. The labor supply equation can be estimated by using TSLS or LIML methods already mentioned. These methods could also be used to get an estimate of ϵ_2.

A further generalization allowing imperfection in the supply markets can be handled by variations of the same type of procedure.

In place of industrial sectors, one might prepare a model of a geographical sector of an economy. For a region being studied we have equations involving variables of that region and variables of the whole economy. The model explaining fluctuations in the variables of the whole economy is the same master model used in the preceding analysis, and we graft a model of a regional sector to the master model in the same way we graft the industrial sector model to the master model.[3]

[3] See L. R. Klein, "The Specification of Regional Econometric Models," *Papers of the Regional Science Association*, XXIII, (1969), 105–15.

A more general approach to the problem of estimation of a sector model of production and factor demand is to use full information maximum likelihood methods that simultaneously take into account nonlinearities and restrictions on parameters between different equations. This is an alternative to the two-step procedure in which some parameters are estimated from the marginal productivity equations and the remaining parameters are estimated from the production function. The FIML methods have been applied in both the Cobb-Douglas and CES formulations of a truncated model that deletes product demand and factor suppply equations.[4] Although this particular application deals with the aggregate production function, it could readily be adapted to a model of an industry or market.

The Cobb-Douglas case:

$$x_t = A10^{\lambda t} n_t^{\alpha} d_t^{\beta} u_t \quad \text{(production function with technical change)} \tag{8.2.35}$$

$$\frac{r_t}{w_t} = \frac{\beta}{\alpha} \frac{n_t}{d_t} v_t \quad \text{(marginal condition of cost minimization)} \tag{8.2.36}$$

From the joint distribution of $\log u_t$ and $\log v_t$, we can derive the joint density of n_t and d_t, given x_t, w_t, r_t

$$P_r(n_t, d_t : x_t, w_t, r_t; \alpha, \beta, \lambda, A, \sigma_u^2, \sigma_v^2, \sigma_{uv}).$$

Maximization of this density over the whole sample set, gives nonlinear FIML estimates of the parameters.

The CES case:

$$x_t = A10^{\lambda t}[\delta d_t^{-\rho} + (1 - \delta)n_t^{-\rho}]^{-\mu/\rho} u_t \quad \text{(production function with technical change)} \tag{8.2.37}$$

$$\frac{r_t}{w_t} = \frac{\delta}{1 - \delta} \left(\frac{d_t}{n_t}\right)^{-(\rho+1)} v_t \quad \text{(marginal condition of cost minimization).} \tag{8.2.38}$$

Using aggregative time series data for the U.S.A., 1900–49, we estimated these systems with the following results:[5]

Cobb-Douglas estimates

$\log_{10} A$	α	β	λ	$\sigma_{\log u}$	$r_{\log u \log v}$
1.7947	0.960	0.496	0.00484	0.02234	−0.0101
(0.0044)	(0.061)	(0.032)	(0.00054)		

[4] R. G. Bodkin and L. R. Klein, "Nonlinear Estimation of Aggregate Production Functions"; H. Eisenpress and J. L. Greenstadt, "The Estimation of Nonlinear Econometric Systems."

[5] The data are those used by R. Solow, "Technical Change and the Aggregate Production Function," *Review of Economics and Statistics*, XXXIX (August, 1957), 312–30.

CES estimates

$\log_{10}A$	ρ	δ	μ	λ	$\sigma_{\log u}$	$r_{\log u \log v}$
1.7340	1.130	0.6037	1.238	0.00643	0.02186	−0.7524
(0.0252)	(0.4169)	(0.0958)	(0.058)	(0.00041)		

Estimated sampling errors are given in parentheses below corresponding coefficients.

Other types of sector models are those that study the demand for particular goods and services. In our industry model, we emphasized the equations of technology and demand for factors of production but found need for placing an equation of market demand for the industry's product in the model. If attention is focused on the demand equation for final output, there will be an incidental need for fitting equations of production or supply into the model. A statistical model of the demand for food by Girshick and Haavelmo illustrates many interesting points about sector analysis.[6] The variables of their model are

F = per capita food consumption in constant prices

$\frac{p_f}{p}$ = ratio of retail food price index to consumer price index

Y = deflated per capita disposable income

A = per capita food production in constant prices

$\frac{p_a}{p}$ = ratio of index of food prices received by farmers to consumer price index

I = per capita investment in constant prices

t = time.

Expenditures on food are deflated by an index of retail food prices, and the value of food production at the farm is deflated by an index of food prices received by farmers in order to obtain F and A, respectively. Data in current prices for disposable income and investment are deflated by the consumers' price index to get Y and I. Investment is here defined as the difference between disposable income and consumption. The model with numerical coefficients and all variables expressed as indexes on a 1935–39 base is

$$F = 97.677 - 0.246\frac{p_f}{p} + 0.247\ Y + 0.051\ Y_{-1} - 0.104\,t \tag{8.2.39}$$

$$F = 13.319 + 0.157\frac{p_f}{p} + 0.653\,A + 0.339\,t \tag{8.2.40}$$

$$Y = 40.731 + 0.203\,I + 0.367\,Y_{-1} \tag{8.2.41}$$

[6] M. A. Girshick and Trygve Haavelmo, "Statistical Analysis of the Demand for Food: Examples of Simultaneous Estimation of Structural Equations," *Econometrica*, 15 (1947), 79–110.

$$A = 81.250 + 0.556 \frac{p_a}{p} - 0.300 \left(\frac{p_a}{p}\right)_{-1} - 0.190\, t \tag{8.2.42}$$

$$\frac{p_a}{p} = -200.068 + 2.883 \frac{p_f}{p} + 0.656\, t. \tag{8.2.43}$$

The first equation is of central importance in the model. It is an equation of food demand at the retail level constructed along classical lines in that it makes demand a function of relative prices (between food and other products) and income. A lag in income and a time trend are also used in this equation. The next equation is one of retail food supply to final consumers. Supply depends on relative prices and on farm production. The latter variable carries behavior in the model a step farther back in the marketing chain from primary producer to final consumer. The third Eq. (8.2.41) is a *multiplier* equation and grafts the food sector to a very simple model of the whole economy. It does this by trying to explain fluctuations in the level of national disposable income, an important endogenous variable in the equation of food demand.

The multiplier equation can be considered as being derived from the simple two-equation model consisting of

$$C = \alpha_0 + \alpha_1 Y + \alpha_2 Y_{-1} + u,$$
$$Y = C + I,$$

an aggregate consumption equation and an accounting definition. The two equations together imply

$$Y = \frac{\alpha_0}{1 - \alpha_1} + \frac{1}{1 - \alpha_1} I + \frac{\alpha_2}{1 - \alpha_1} Y_{-1} + \frac{1}{1 - \alpha_1} u$$

that is the multiplier equation estimated in (8.2.41). The simple multiplier model is almost too simple to serve as an adequate explanation of income fluctuations, but it is a useful pedagogical device to show how equations for a sector of the economy are grafted to a macroeconomic model of the economy as a whole.

Equation (8.2.42) is the supply of food products by farmers to the commercial market. It expresses supply entirely in terms of current and lagged relative prices without going into more fundamental structural equations such as those of production and factor demand, the equation we considered previously in models of an industrial sector. The present emphasis is on food demand; therefore, the supply or production side of the market is not treated in full detail. The final equation is intended to represent demand by the commercial sector for farm food products. In a sense, it is a superficial *markup* equation showing how farm food prices are transformed into retail food prices.

The parameters of this model were estimated by the method of limited information for data in the period 1922–41. The endogenous variables are

$F, \frac{p_f}{p}, Y, A, \frac{p_a}{p}$. Exogenous variables are I and t, with Y_{-1} and $\left(\frac{p_a}{p}\right)_{-1}$ being classified as predetermined together with the exogenous variables.

In a study of the demand for consumer installment credit, Kisselgoff has similarly constructed a model illustrating the principles of grafting equations for a sector of the economy to a simple (multiplier) model of the economy as a whole.[7] His variables are

$G =$ deflated installment credit granted per consumer unit
$Y =$ deflated disposable income per consumer unit
$\frac{p_d}{p} =$ ratio of consumer durable goods price index to consumer price index
$m =$ index of average monthly duration of installment sales contracts
$C =$ consumer expenditures per consumer unit in constant prices
$I =$ investment per consumer unit in constant prices.

Deflated or constant price magnitudes are expressed in 1935–39 prices. Indexes are on a 1935–39 base. As in the Girshick-Haavelmo model, investment is defined as the difference between disposable income and consumption, with the latter two variables being deflated by the price index of consumer goods. The estimated model, in 1935–39 dollars per consuming unit, is

$$G = -1.223 + 0.094\,Y + 0.015\,Y_{-1} - 1.045\left(\frac{p_d}{pm}\right), \tag{8.2.44}$$

$$C = 450.499 + 0.608\,Y + 0.122\,Y_{-1} \tag{8.2.45}$$

$$Y = C + I \tag{8.2.46}$$

$$\frac{p_d}{p} = 29.285 + 0.714\left(\frac{p_d}{p}\right)_{-1}. \tag{8.2.47}$$

In (8.2.44), credit granted is made a function of current and lagged disposable income and the size of the monthly installment $\frac{p_d}{pm}$. This is interpreted as the demand equation for credit. Equations (8.2.45) and (8.2.46) are the multiplier model for explaining fluctuations of income in terms of investment and lagged income. The fourth equation of the model is a first order autoregressive equation in $\frac{p_d}{p}$ derived by the following reasoning: define

$H_d =$ end of period inventories of consumer durables in constant prices,

[7] A. Kisselgoff, *Factors Affecting the Demand for Consumer Installment Sales Credit* [National Bureau of Economic Research, Technical Paper 7 (New York, 1951)].

and

C_d = sales of consumer durables in constant prices.

The demand for inventories is given by

$$H_d = \alpha_0 + \alpha_1 C_d + \alpha_2 \frac{p_d}{p} + \alpha_3 \left(\frac{p_d}{p}\right)_{-1} + \alpha_4 (H_d)_{-1} + v_1.$$

Inventory demand is made a function of sales (the transactions motive), the level and rate of change of real prices (speculative motive), and inventories at the beginning of the period (inertia). Excess demand or supply of durables is defined as

$$H_d - \alpha_1 C_d - \alpha_4 (H_d)_{-1},$$

those inventories held for reasons other than transactions and inertia. The classical law of supply and demand is used to develop

$$\frac{p_d}{p} - \left(\frac{p_d}{p}\right)_{-1} = \beta_0 + \beta_1 [H_d - \alpha_1 C_d - \alpha_4 (H_d)_{-1}] + \beta_2 \left(\frac{p_d}{p}\right)_{-1} + v_2$$

or

$$\frac{p_d}{p} - \left(\frac{p_d}{p}\right)_{-1} = \beta_0 + \beta_1 \left[\alpha_0 + \alpha_2 \frac{p_d}{p} + \alpha_3 \left(\frac{p_d}{p}\right)_{-1} + v_1\right] + \beta_2 \left(\frac{p_d}{p}\right)_{-1} + v_2$$

that has the same statistical form as the autoregressive equation in (8.2.47).

Kisselgoff's estimation method is to determine first the least squares estimates of (8.2.47) and from this empirical relation to calculate $\left(\frac{p_d}{p}\right)^0$. He next substitutes the calculated values of the price ratio for the corresponding variable in (8.2.44) and considers the model (8.2.44)–(8.2.46) consisting of the endogenous variables G, C, Y, and the predetermined variables Y_{-1}, $\left(\frac{p_d}{p}\right)^0 \frac{1}{m}$, I. The three-equation model under these assumptions is exactly identified, and from least squares estimates of the parameters in

$$G = \pi_0 + \pi_1 Y_{-1} + \pi_2 \left[\left(\frac{p_d}{p}\right)^0 \frac{1}{m}\right] + \pi_3 I + w_1,$$

$$Y = \rho_0 + \rho_1 Y_{-1} + \rho_2 I + w_2,$$

he is able to obtain a unique set of estimates of the structural parameters in (8.2.44) and (8.2.45). His observations are annual data for 1929–41.

Questions and Problems

1. It is commonly said that prosperity or depression in United States agriculture follows prosperity or depression in the rest of the economy. On the other hand, agriculture is not an insignificant sector of the economy and makes its own contribution to the level of aggregate economic activity. Construct a model showing the interdependence between agriculture and the rest of the economy.

2. Show how an econometric model of agriculture can be grafted, for purposes of statistical estimation, to a model of the economy as a whole. Assuming the method of instrumental variables to be used for estimating a model of the agricultural sector, indicate the set of instrumental variables you would choose. Justify their classification as instrumental variables and their significance as variables for parameter estimation in the model constructed.

3. Canada's foreign trade is important in its economy and is largely concentrated in exchange with the United States and the United Kingdom. Show explicitly how aggregative models for the latter two economies can be used in preparing a model of Canada.

4. Discuss the identification properties of the Girshick-Haavelmo model of the demand for food.

5. For Kisselgoff's model of installment credit demand, derive the reduced form equations for G and Y in terms of the structural parameters in the theoretical model underlying (8.2.44)–(8.2.47). How are the parameters of the reduced forms estimated? How are estimates of these parameters transformed into estimates of the structural parameters?

Methods of sector analysis that we have described thus far can be labeled as those that go from the general to the particular. By this phrase is meant that a general master model is first prepared, and then a particular sector model is constructed by making use, in the grafting process, of the general model. These methods obviously have the virtue of relative simplicity compared with the enormous task of deriving a general model from all the particular sectors that make up the whole. Although we recognize the gain in simplicity, we must be fully aware of the interindustrial relationships that are left obscure. In a formal sense our sector models could be expanded to include the structural equations of the industries supplying materials and services to the sector being studied. If the expansion stopped with one or two additional industries, we could consider undertaking the computational load involved in estimating a larger system of equations; but, in general, all industries are related to all others in a comprehensive system that is not, in a practical sense, manageable with our present methods and knowledge. An attempt has been made to obtain quantitative estimates of the structure of a general equilibrium system by Leontief[8] using an

[8] A large literature on this subject exists. A basic reference is W. W. Leontief, *Structure of the American Economy, 1919–1929*, 2nd ed., enlarged (New York: Oxford University Press, 1951).

alternative method called input-output analysis. In this approach, we define

x_i = output of the ith industry or sector, and
x_{ji} = output of sector i used as input in j.

By definition, we have

$$x_i = \sum_{j=1}^{n} x_{ji}, \qquad i = 1, 2, \ldots, n, \qquad j \neq i. \tag{8.2.48}$$

Equation (8.2.48) states that the output of the ith sector is distributed to each of the other n–1 sectors in the economy. Households and foreign countries are classified as separate sectors. It is assumed that $x_{ii} = 0$, in other words, that the ith sector does not supply input to itself. This assumption could be relaxed without complication. It is partly a matter of the degree of fineness of sectorial classification. The inputs of the ith sector are denoted by x_{ik}, $k = 1, 2, \ldots, n$, $k \neq i$. The ratios

$$a_{ik} = \frac{x_{ik}}{x_i} \tag{8.2.49}$$

are defined as technical coefficients. In input-output analysis, they are treated as meaningful parameters. Regarding the *as* as constants, we interpret (8.2.49) as a production function showing how x_i is produced from input x_{ik}. Because k may take on several values, excluding $k = i$, we could equally well write the production function for the ith sector as

$$a_{ij} = \frac{x_{ij}}{x_i}, \qquad j \neq i, k.$$

These considerations reveal the basic assumption of the method: inputs are used in fixed proportions so that output can be expressed as a function of any single input. No substitutions among productive factors is allowed. This is Leontief's stated interpretation of his model, although an alternative view, to be discussed later, shows that the a's may be defined as constants even in the framework of a technology permitting substitution among inputs.

The technology of an economy with production technique of the strict input-output type considered here implies that production *isoquants* are right angular. An alternative to this view at the other end of the spectrum as regards elasticity of substitution is the *linear* production function

$$x_i = \sum_{j=1}^{n} \alpha_{ij} x_{ij}, \qquad i = 1, 2, \ldots, n.$$

This production function has linear isoquants with infinite elasticity of substitution. Between the right angular isoquants of the input-output system (zero substitution elasticity) and the linear isoquants of the linear production function system (infinite substitution elasticity) we have the Cobb-Douglas system with curved or log linear isoquants (unit substitution elasticity). These are all special cases of the CES function (8.2.37), when the elasticity of substitution is given by

$$\sigma = \frac{1}{1+\rho}.$$

A statistical test on the parametric specification of production functions can be made on the basis of estimation of ρ:

$\rho \longrightarrow \infty$	input-output specification
$\rho = 0$	Cobb-Douglas specification
$\rho = -1$	linear specification
$\rho = \text{const.} \neq 0, -1$	general CES specification.

The first statistical problem in input-output analysis is to compute the technical coefficients, the a's, for a given decomposition of the economy into sectors. In practice, each a_{ik} is estimated from a single pair of observations, in some year, on x_{ik} and x_i. The estimation method thus involves no complexity from the point of view of statistical inference. The main problem, an exceedingly difficult one, is to collect reliable data on x_{ik} and x_i.

Equations (8.2.48)–(8.2.49) together yield

$$x_i = \sum_{j=1}^{n} a_{ji} x_j, \qquad i = 1, 2, \ldots, n \qquad j \neq i, \tag{8.2.50}$$

a system of n homogeneous linear equations in the n variables $x_1, x_2, \ldots, x_n$. By the nature of the construction of the equations, the determinant of the coefficient matrix in (8.2.50) must vanish. Transposing the left-hand term of this equation to the right, we get for the determinant of the coefficient matrix

$$|A| = \begin{vmatrix} -1 & a_{21} & a_{31} & \cdots & a_{n1} \\ a_{12} & -1 & a_{32} & \cdots & a_{n2} \\ \vdots & & & & \vdots \\ a_{1n} & a_{2n} & a_{3n} & \cdots & -1 \end{vmatrix} = 0. \tag{8.2.51}$$

We know this condition must hold because the elements of the observed vector $(x_1, x_2, \ldots, x_n)$ from which the technical coefficients were computed are a solution to (8.2.50), and in order for a nontrivial solution, one in which the observed vector is not $(0, 0, \ldots, 0)$, to exist in a homogeneous linear equation system, the determinant of the coefficient matrix must vanish.

The analysis problem in connection with Leontief models is to fix some values of x_i or change them in a known way and study the transmission of resulting effects throughout the interrelated economic system. It would not be meaningful simply to fix some total output x_k^0, eliminate an equation from the system, and solve for the remaining values of x_i in terms of x_k^0. All such solutions must be proportional, element by element, to the original observed set of values because (8.2.50) is a linear homogeneous system with a matrix of coefficients whose determinant vanishes. Instead, the procedure is as follows:

1. Select some final output x_k.
2. Eliminate from the homogeneous equation system that equation in which x_k has a unit coefficient.
3. In the remaining $(n - 1)$ equations, substitute for $a_{ki}x_k$ a set of fixed values of x_{ki}.
4. Solve the nonhomogeneous system of $(n - 1)$ equations for each x_i in terms of the *bill of goods*, x_{ki}.

The *bill of goods* shows the distribution of output of each of $(n - 1)$ sectors to the kth, or the demand by the kth sector for the output of the rest of the economy. If the kth sector consists of households, government, the business *capital* sector, and foreign countries, the bill of goods can be interpreted as the final demand by consumers of the output of domestic industry. In order for a solution to exist for the nonhomogeneous system, the determinant of the coefficient matrix must not vanish.

Let us construct a simple example from an economy of $n = 3$ sectors. The homogeneous system is

$$\begin{aligned} -x_1 + a_{21}x_2 + a_{31}x_3 &= 0, \\ a_{12}x_1 - x_2 + a_{32}x_3 &= 0, \\ a_{13}x_1 + a_{23}x_2 - x_3 &= 0. \end{aligned}$$

Choose the third sector as the one whose final demand is to be fixed and eliminate the third equation, because x_3 has a unit coefficient in that relation. The nonhomogeneous system is

$$\begin{aligned} -x_1 + a_{21}x_2 &= -a_{31}x_3 \\ a_{12}x_1 - x_2 &= -a_{32}x_3. \end{aligned}$$

By virtue of (8.2.49), we shall substitute x_{31} and x_{32} for $a_{31}x_3$ and $a_{32}x_3$ respectively,

$$\begin{aligned} -x_1 + a_{21}x_2 &= -x_{31} \\ a_{12}x_1 - x_2 &= -x_{32}. \end{aligned}$$

If the determinant

$$\begin{vmatrix} -1 & a_{21} \\ a_{12} & -1 \end{vmatrix} = 1 - a_{12}a_{21}$$

does not vanish, we can solve for x_1 and x_2 in terms of x_{31} and x_{32}. The determinant will not, in general, vanish since

$$a_{12}a_{21} = \frac{x_{12}x_{21}}{x_1x_2} \leq 1,$$

with the equality signs holding simultaneously only if sector 2 sends all of its output to sector 1 and sector 1 sends all of its output to sector 2. The solution takes the form

$$x_1 = \frac{x_{31} + a_{21}x_{32}}{1 - a_{12}a_{21}},$$

$$x_2 = \frac{x_{32} + a_{12}x_{31}}{1 - a_{12}a_{21}}.$$

Thus for any given demand by sector 3 for the production of sectors 1 and 2, we can determine the output of the latter two sectors, assuming a_{12} and a_{21} to be known constants. Any level of x_{31} and x_{32} or rate of change in them will determine the resulting level and rate of change of x_1 and x_2.

For general systems involving n sectors, the solutions can be written as

$$x_j = -\sum_{i=1}^{n}{}' A_{ji}x_{ki} \tag{8.2.52}$$

to express the dependence of the jth output on the bill of goods showing demand by the kth sector. The symbol $\sum'$ indicates that the k subscript is omitted in summation. The coefficients A_{ji} depend on the original a_{ij}

$$A_{ji} = \frac{|A|_{kk.ji}}{|A|_{kk}}, \tag{8.2.53}$$

where $|A|_{kk}$ is the minor of the element in the kth row and column of $|A|$, and $|A|_{kk.ji}$ is a cofactor of a_{ji} in $|A|_{kk}$.

The technique is quite straightforward and can be generalized to include more than one bill of goods. However, the computational burden can be substantial because, in practice, the number of sectors is large. As many as 100 or even 500 equations may well be treated simultaneously, but an important economy is realized, because there are numerous holes in the A matrix, that is, many of the a_{ij} are zero.

Leontief's approach has the virtue of showing interindustrial relationships. Other methods of sector analysis fail to show these relationships as clearly. Yet from the econometric point of view there are disadvantages in input-output analysis of this type. The ease with which the structural parameters a_{ik} can be estimated, given the data on x_{ik} and x_i, is deceptive. The model is assumed to consist of a series of one-parameter production functions, and one observation is used to estimate the single parameter. In a statistical sense, there are no degrees of freedom. The model has no stochastic properties, and we have no idea about the reliability or probabilistic properties of the estimated parameters. In principle, there is no compelling reason for building an input-output model in an exact, nonstochastic formulation, although the amount of data needed to estimate the parameters in a probability model may be enormous.

The assumption of linearity in Leontief's models is no more serious than in many other cases where simple approximations are very useful. In fact, the linearity assumption may even be less restrictive in input-output analysis of many finely divided industrial subdivisions because nonlinear functions can be approximated as closely as desired by joining series of linear segments. In a sense, however, the fundamental assumption of other econometric methods, that the equations being studied are linear in parameters only, permits a wider class of functional relationships than the linear production functions with fixed proportions of factor inputs.

Do the equations of input-output analysis describe purely technological production functions? In a sense, we are faced with the problem of *identifying* the system. In theory, Leontief writes his model in terms of x_{ik} and x_i, physical quantities of inputs and outputs. In practice, he obtains data on these magnitudes in dollar amounts involving relative prices. The use of dollar amounts is not accidental, because the output of each sector consists of a variety of physical products as does each input flowing from another sector. Joint production is the rule and not an exceptional case. The assumed parameters of Leontief's models are thus of the form

$$a_{ik} = \frac{\sum_{s=1}^{t} p_k^s x_{ik}^s}{\sum_{r=1}^{u} p_i^r x_i^r}, \tag{8.2.54}$$

in which

x_{ik}^s = the sth output of sector k flowing to sector i, and
x_i^r = the rth output of sector i.

Interpreting the numerator and denominator of (8.2.54) in terms of indexes, we may write

$$a_{ik} = \frac{P_k X_{ik}}{P_i X_i}. \tag{8.2.55}$$

In a competitive market economy, profit maximization leads to (8.2.55) if the production functions are

$$X_i = A_i X_{i1}^{a_{i1}} \cdots X_{i,i-1}^{a_{i,i-1}} X_{i,i+1}^{a_{i,i+1}} \cdots X_{in}^{a_{in}}, \qquad i = 1, 2, \ldots, n. \tag{8.2.56}$$

Equations (8.2.56) may therefore be regarded as technological implications of a set of constant ratios of factor payments to value of output. Without the index formulation of (8.2.54), the production functions may be developed in terms of the individual x_{ik}^s and x_i^r from a somewhat more intricate analysis that we shall not take up here.[9] Also, (8.2.56) is not the most general form of a production function satisfying the requirements of Leontief's model. It is a useful empirical framework because of the widespread practical work with exponential production functions. These functions differ from those assumed by Leontief in that they permit substitution among factors of production. They have the advantage over Leontief's interpretation that they describe production in terms of physical variables and put relative prices in their proper place—in the equations of economic (maximizing) behavior.

Using the strictest assumptions of the Leontief system, economists have been able to derive rational behavior models in which the production functions are linear with fixed proportions among inputs; thus, there is some justification for attempting to identify the elements of an input-output table as technological parameters. The strict assumptions require that each sector produce only one type of output and that the entire system have only one original unproduced factor of production (labor, for example). The requirement of one output per sector is crucial because it enables one to measure physical input x_{ji} and physical output x_i. If we drop this restrictive assumption, we are faced with the problem of weighting different commodities, and if the customary technique, using relative prices, is adopted as in (8.2.54), the behavior models justifying linearity and fixed proportions are no longer valid. On the other hand, behavior models based on nonlinear production functions permitting factor substitution remain valid under either weak or strong assumptions concerning joint production.

Two questions are involved in the interpretation of Leontief's input-output models: (a) Under what conditions can we identify the coefficients of an input-output table as technological parameters? (b) If the coefficients of an input-output table are technological parameters, do they occur as parameters in linear production functions with fixed proportions among inputs, or as parameters in other types of production functions? We have already considered the second question, actually confining our treatment to conditions under which Leontief coefficients can be given a technological interpretation. Market competition was assumed throughout this development, and it is under this assumption that the technological interpretation is valid. If market imperfections are introduced in the behavior model, we find that the a_{ik} in (8.2.54) must be interpreted in terms of two types of parameters—those from production functions and those from demand or supply functions.

We can show this result quite simply. In an imperfectly competitive market economy with production function (8.2.56), profit maximization leads to

$$\frac{a_{ik}\left(1 - \dfrac{1}{\epsilon_i}\right)}{1 + \dfrac{1}{\eta_k}} = \frac{P_k X_{ik}}{P_i X_i}. \tag{8.2.57}$$

[9] See L. R. Klein, "On the Interpretation of Professor Leontief's System," *Review of Economic Studies*, XX (1952–53), 131–136.

If the right-hand side of (8.2.57) is the assumed constant observed by the input-output analyst, it may be decomposed into three types of structural parameters given on the left-hand side: a_{ik} (production elasticity), ϵ_i (demand elasticity), and η_k (supply elasticity). These three parameters may all be constants, in which case the input-output coefficients would be observed as constants. However, if people's tastes were to change with technology invariant, input-output coefficients cannot, in general, be identified as technological parameters. The demonstration given here is drastically simplified, but can readily be extended to joint production under imperfect competition.

It would indeed be surprising if it were not the case that Leontief coefficients are a mixture of technological and various behavioral parameters. The coefficients are estimated as the ratios of two market values observed as the result of a conglomerate economic process covering technological production, price speculation, wage bargaining, monetary policies, consumer choice, and a large variety of other phenomena.[10]

In developing a stochastic approach to input-output analysis, a prohibitively large amount of data seem to be required, but there are possibilities for reducing the amount of basic statistical materials. A feature of input-output analysis is its use of direct measurement. Direct measurements are made on x_{ik} and x_i to estimate the coefficients[11]

$$a_{ik} = \frac{x_{ik}}{x_i}.$$

The direct measurements and parameter estimates are made for one time period. Adequate data are available only for crucial census periods, and processing of data for a single period alone requires a large amount of human effort. It has not been easy to collect time series of repeated observations on x_{ik} and x_i for parameter estimation.

The main problem in data collection is the obtaining of measurement of x_{ik}, the output of the kth sector flowing to the ith sector. It is not difficult to collect repeated measurements on x_i, the output of the ith sector. In equation system (8.2.50), we find a system of linear equations in constant coefficients relating the several outputs of the economy. A stochastic version of (8.2.50) could be written as

$$x_i - \sum_{j=1}^{n} a_{ji} x_j = u_i, \; a_{ii} = 0. \tag{8.2.58}$$

Because there are only $n - 1$ unknown parameters in each equation, we have

[10] Research on input-output analysis has made advances that free some of its relations from anonymity within the multitude of structural equations. An attempt has been made to determine coefficients directly from engineering data. In simple, well-defined technical processes not producing joint outputs, it is possible to determine coefficients from engineering information, but it is hardly feasible to determine coefficients in an entire system in this way.

[11] We shall revert to the standard assumption of no joint production in this discussion.

automatically a rule of normalization. A difficulty arises in that the Jacobian of the transformation from the u's to the x's vanishes

$$\frac{\partial(u_1, \ldots, u_n)}{\partial(x_1, \ldots, x_n)} = |-A| = 0.$$

We could avoid this problem by choosing sector k for the final bill of goods and using for the stochastic model

$$x_i - \sum_{j=1}^{n}{}' a_{ji} x_j = x_{ki} + u_i, \qquad i = 1, 2, \ldots, k-1, k+1, \ldots, n. \tag{8.2.59}$$

The symbol $\sum'$ indicates that the k subscript is omitted in summation. The Jacobian of this system does not necessarily vanish.

Different techniques may be used for the statistical estimation of input-output coefficients as parameters in this equation system. A particularly simple technique would be recommended if we were to drop the restriction $a_{ii} = 0$ (assumption that a sector not use its own output as input) and were justified in regarding the x_{ki} as a set of predetermined variables. In that case, assuming no other restrictions on the A matrix, the system would be exactly identified, with one unique predetermined variable in each equation. The relatively simple methods of parameter estimation in exactly identified linear systems would then be applicable. Numerous other possibilities exist depending on the restrictions placed on the A matrix and the resulting identifiability of the model. The final bill of goods need not be regarded as predetermined.

Regardless of the method of statistical inference used to estimate input-output coefficients as parameters of the stochastic system (8.2.59), we must restrict estimates to values in the interval

$$0 \leq a_{ik} \leq 1$$

if the output data are measured in monetary values rather than physical quantities. Direct estimates of the coefficients, whether from a series of values or the value from a single period, will always lead to coefficients between the permissible limits, zero and unity, by definition of the quantities $p_k x_{ik}$ and $p_i x_i$. When the coefficients are estimated indirectly by methods of statistical inference, there is no assurance that the estimated coefficients will lie in the appropriate region. If the coefficients are estimated by some optimal criterion, maximization of likelihood or minimization of sums of squares, and all estimates are within the appropriate bounds, we can do no better. A trial and error method for finding an optimal solution subject to inequalities as side conditions would be to put estimated coefficients outside the boundaries at the boundary and estimate the remaining coefficients by the optimum criterion. The most straightforward practical approach would be to change negative coefficients to zero values and estimate the remainder. If any coefficient is made unity, all other coefficients in the same equation should vanish. Any coefficients known to be zero in advance of estimation are, of course, assumed to be assigned zero values. A priori information should also be used as much as possible to judge the reasonableness of the assignment of other zeros. No investigator, for example, would be satisfied with an input-output model assigning zero to the coefficient showing the fraction of the output of the iron ore producing sector used in the steel producing sector.

In statistical estimation of input-output coefficients, some parameter estimates may lie outside circumscribed bounds, but the boundary violations may be insignificant. Confidence intervals for the estimates may enclose both acceptable and unacceptable values. In such cases, we do not necessarily seek another set of estimates.

Direct estimation of input-output coefficients is generally preferable, but this method, in practice, has not been able to yield reliability measures of the estimated coefficients; moreover, there are cases in which data are not available for direct estimation. On these grounds, statistical inference from a stochastic model deserves application in input-output analysis.

In studying sectors of the economy, there is a danger that we may lose sight of the simultaneous interrelationships among all sectors. Input-output analysis as developed by Leontief treats the simultaneous interrelationships of all sectors of the economy explicitly, but in doing so is forced to give superficial treatment to each sector. Only the simplest equations connect the several sectors, and as we saw above there is a problem in interpreting these equations in terms of basic structural behavior. The alternative approach presented earlier in this section, is to estimate detailed equations of specific behavior in each sector but without giving an adequate account of interrelationship with other sectors. Gradually these two approaches can be brought closer together. Intensive studies can be expanded to include more sectors simultaneously, and extensive studies can be expanded to include more than superficial analysis of each sector. More attention to problems of identification and underlying stochastic structure will do much to render input-output analysis more comparable with other methods of econometrics.

A statistical model for combining input-output analysis with standard econometric methods of inference can be developed from the assumption that value ratios (8.2.54) are constant. The extended production function is

$$x_i = A_i e^{\lambda_i t} \prod_{j=1}^{n} x_{ij}^{a_{ij}} n_i^{\alpha_i} d_i^{\beta_i} u_i.$$

In this specification

n_i = employment in the ith sector
d_i = capital services in the ith sector
u_i = random error.

The x_{ij} are the usual input-output flows from the jth to the ith sector. In this production function, we have added the inputs of labor and capital, n_i and d_i. Equilibrium conditions are

$$\begin{aligned} a_{ij} &= \frac{p_j x_{ij}}{p_i x_i} \\ \alpha_i &= \frac{w_i n_i}{p_i x_i} \\ \beta_i &= \frac{r_i d_i}{p_i x_i}. \end{aligned} \tag{8.2.60}$$

The value ratios in the input-output table serve as estimates of a_{ij}, and α_i and β_i can be estimated from values of labor's share and capital's share, respectively. The two-step procedure discussed earlier in this chapter can be used to estimate A_i and λ_i after the value ratio estimates of the other parameters are first determined.

Total consumption and other parts of final demand are obtained by summing the results from each sector's equations

$$C_i = B_i Y^{\gamma_i} \left(\frac{p_i}{p}\right)^{\delta_i} v_i. \tag{8.2.61}$$

If the data are available on a time series basis for C_i, Y, $\frac{p_i}{p}$, we can use some form of regression to estimate B_i, γ_i and δ_i. Having these estimates, we can add to obtain estimates for aggregative magnitudes such as $\sum_{i=1}^{n} C_i = C$. The whole of final demand can be treated in this way, and the input-output system and its associated final demand functions can be used together with equations of price level determination, wage rate determination, unemployment, and related macro variables to complete the model. It appears to be a formidable task, but it has already been carried out for data on Japanese industry.[12]

Another approach toward combining input-output analysis with an overall macroeconometric time series model of the usual sort has been used in the construction of the Brookings Econometric Model of the United States.[13] The inhomogeneous or open form of the input-output system can be written in matrix terms as

$$-Ax_t = f_t, \tag{8.2.62}$$

[12] M. Saito, "An Interindustry Study of Price Formation," *The Review of Economics and Statistics*, LIII (February, 1971), 11–25.

[13] F. Fisher, L. R. Klein, and Y. Shinkai, "Price and Output Aggregation in the Brookings Econometric Model," *The Brookings Quarterly Econometric Model of the United States*, ed. J. Duesenberry, et al. (Chicago: Rand-McNally & Co., 1965). See also D. Kresge, "Price and Output Conversion," *The Brookings Model: Some Further Results*, ed. J. Duesenberry, et al. (Chicago: Rand-McNally & Co., 1969).

where x_t is a column vector of gross outputs for n sectors, and f_t is a column vector of final demands for these sectors. Given some reconciling items, R_t, the elements of f_t satisfy

$$\sum_{i=1}^{n} f_{it} = R_t + (\text{GNP})_t. \tag{8.2.63}$$

In an approximate sense, we can explain the elements of f_{it} from

$$f_{it} = g_i((\text{gnp})_{1t}, \ldots, (\text{gnp})_{rt}) + u_{it}. \tag{8.2.64}$$

If GNP components or similar endogenous variables from a macro model can explain f_{it}, then we have a linkage in (8.2.62)–(8.2.64) between endogenous variables $(\text{gnp})_{it}$ and x_{it} that make use of input-output coefficients. Within the framework of the Brookings Model, this approach has enabled us to determine simultaneously the overall level of production $(\text{GNP})_t$ and its separate industrial components x_{it}. The latter variables are gross outputs and can be converted to a value-added concept like GNP through some standard, stable proportions.

In order to make this type of combination between input-output analysis and macroeconometric analysis, the latter must be detailed enough to supply adequate endogenous variables as arguments of the functions in (8.2.64). With a system as large as the Brookings Model this can be done.

Investment is in final demand in the input-output models considered so far. In static input-output analysis, it is generally treated in this way. Dynamic versions of input-output analysis can be obtained through application of accelerator theory. Let

$$b_{ij} = \frac{k_{ij}}{x_i} \tag{8.2.65}$$

where k_{ij} = amount of capital goods produced (over historical time) by sector j for use in sector i. From this relation, we derive

$$I_{ij} = k_{ij} - (k_{ij})_{-1} = b_{ij}(x_i - x_{i-1}). \tag{8.2.66}$$

The sum of intermediate and capital flows from j to i is thus

$$x_i = \sum_{j=1}^{n}{}' a_{ji}x_j + \sum_{j=1}^{n}{}' b_{ji}(x_j - x_{j-1}) + f_i^*. \tag{8.2.67}$$

In this equation, f_i^* stands for all the final demand for the output of the ith sector, excluding capital formation. This is a set of linear dynamic equations and represents a significant improvement over the static input-output model. In matrix form it is written as

$$-A\,x - B\,\Delta x = f^*. \tag{8.2.68}$$

This is a system of finite difference equations showing sectorial movement of the economy over time.

Questions and Problems

1. As alternatives to input-output variables showing flows among industries, we may consider

x_{ij} = shipments from region (country) j to region (country) i, and
x_i = total shipments from region (country) i.

Discuss possible uses of interregional (international) analogues of interindustrial input-output analysis. Is there a reason for preferring either

$$a_{ij} = \frac{x_{ij}}{x_i} \qquad \text{or} \qquad b_{ij} = \frac{x_{ij}}{x_j}$$

for definitions of the technical coefficients?

2. Describe input-output analysis that simultaneously combines interindustrial and interregional (international) flows.

3. Let

h_i = stocks of commodities in the ith sector, and

$b_i = \dfrac{h_i}{x_i}$ = stock-output coefficient for the ith sector.

The output of a sector flows either to other sectors or to increments in its own stock. Similarly, a sector may send more than its current output to other sectors by drawing on its stocks. Derive a system of differential or difference equations in $x_1, x_2, \ldots, x_n$ with the a_{ij} (Leontief's technical coefficients) and the b_i as constant coefficients. Compare this version of a dynamic model with that in (8.2.67).

3. ESTIMATION FROM CROSS-SECTION DATA

Cross-section data are usually obtained from specially designed surveys that sample individual economic units (households or firms) or from published accounting reports. If the number of individual units is large, such as millions of households in the United States, a *relatively* small sample is imperative. Cross-section data for individual industries may very well consist of returns from each member firm.

A contrast between the time series and cross-section approaches can be seen from the following simple linear relation

$$x_{it} = \alpha_0 + \alpha_1 y_{it} + u_{it} \tag{8.3.1}$$

in which

$$\begin{aligned} x_{it} &= \text{observed variable } x \text{ for individual } i \text{ at time } t, \\ y_{it} &= \text{observed variable } y \text{ for individual } i \text{ at time } t, \text{ and} \\ u_{it} &= \text{disturbance for individual } i \text{ at time } t. \end{aligned}$$

A time series sample of T observations is

$$x_{i_01}, x_{i_02}, \ldots, x_{i_0T}; \quad y_{i_01}, y_{i_02}, \ldots, y_{i_0T}.^{14}$$

The parameters α_0, α_1, and σ_u^2 are estimated from the time variability of this set of observations. For example, as individual i_0 experiences a change in y from $y_{i_0t_j}$ to $y_{i_0t_k}$ the associated change in x from $x_{i_0t_j}$ to $x_{i_0t_k}$ is governed by the size of α_1.

For any particular value of t, a cross section sample consists of N observations

$$x_{1t_0}, x_{2t_0}, \ldots, x_{Nt_0}; \quad y_{1t_0}, y_{2t_0}, \ldots, y_{Nt_0}.$$

In estimating the parameters from this type of sample, we make the assumption that the jth individual associating x_{jt_0} with y_{jt_0} would behave like the kth individual in associating x_{kt_0} with y_{kt_0}, if the former's value of y were to change from y_{jt_0} to y_{kt_0}.

As far as the structural relation in (8.3.1) is concerned, we assume that two individuals have different x values only because they have different y values, apart from random disturbance. This assumption implies a basic homogeneity among individuals; whereas the underlying assumption in time series analysis implies a basic homogeneity among time periods. Trends, additional variables, and parameter shifts are used in time series analysis to account for temporal heterogeneity. The same devices can be used in cross-section analysis to account for spatial or interindividual heterogeneity. There is general feeling that attempts to get homogeneity are even more urgent in cross-section studies; therefore, we may be faced with the necessity of using more variables in such studies than in more familiar time series studies.

Serial correlation of disturbances was seen to be a complicating factor in the estimation of parameters from time series samples. The corresponding phenomenon in a cross-section sample would be a lack of independence between u_{jt_0} and u_{kt_0} $(j \neq k)$. This complication is perhaps not so important for observations drawn according to a random sampling scheme in which the individual units chosen are selected in a mutually independent fashion.

The concepts of equation systems, endogenous, exogenous, and predetermined variables are as important in cross-section as in time series samples.

[14] In practice we more frequently have aggregative observations,

$$\sum_{i=1}^{N} x_{it} \quad \text{and} \quad \sum_{i=1}^{N} y_{it} \; (t = 1, 2, \ldots, T).$$

Differences that may arise, however, are that prices and other endogenous market variables are, except for geographical differentials, held constant in a cross section at a particular time point, and that some variables that are endogenous to an entire group of units are taken as given for the individual units. In an equation of the form

$$x_{it_0} = \alpha_0' + \alpha_1' p_{t_0} + \alpha_1 y_{it_0} + u_{it_0} \quad i = 1, 2, \ldots, N, \tag{8.3.2}$$

each individual is confronted at time t_0 with the same price quotation, p_{t_0}, and the constant term estimated from the cross section sample is $\alpha_0 = \alpha_0' + \alpha_1' p_{t_0}$.

Writing the probability density function of each u_{it} as $p(u_{it})$, we have

$$p(u_{it})du_{it} = p(x_{it} - \alpha_0 - \alpha_1 y_{it})dx_{it} \tag{8.3.3}$$

as the conditional distribution of x_{it} given y_{it}. Let us write

$$p(x_{it} - \alpha_0 - \alpha_1 y_{it}) = f(x_{it} \mid y_{it}), \tag{8.3.4}$$

showing that we have the conditional probability of x_{it} given y_{it}. The joint probability of x_{it} and y_{it} is

$$h(x_{it}, y_{it}) = f(x_{it} \mid y_{it})g(y_{it}) \tag{8.3.5}$$

in which g is the marginal probability density function of y_{it}. This is a direct application of the definitions of joint, conditional, and marginal distributions described previously in Chap. 2.

Maximum likelihood estimation methods bring out clearly the concepts of endogenous and exogenous variables in this type of sample. The likelihood function is the joint probability of sample observations

$$h(x_{1t_0}, y_{1t_0}) \cdots h(x_{Nt_0}, y_{Nt_0}) = f(x_{1t_0} \mid y_{1t_0})g(y_{1t_0}) \cdots f(x_{Nt_0} \mid y_{Nt_0})g(y_{Nt_0}). \tag{8.3.6}$$

We see from (8.3.3) and (8.3.4) that the conditional probability density function f depends on the unknown parameters α_0 and α_1. By (8.3.6), the likelihood function similarly depends on these parameters. The question that arises is whether the marginal density of y, g, also depends on the same parameters. If g is independent of the unknown parameters, it is evident that maximization of the likelihood function with respect to α_0 and α_1 is the same thing as maximization of

$$f(x_{it_0} \mid y_{it_0}) \cdots f(x_{N_0} \mid y_{Nt_0})$$

with respect to α_0 and α_1. We may interpret this as implying that y is an exogenous variable in the model because f is the conditional density function of x given y. Maximizing conditional probability given certain variables means treating those variables as though they were exogenous. In fact, if

$$f(x_{it} \mid y_{it}) = \frac{1}{\sqrt{2\pi}\sigma} e^{-(1/2\sigma^2)}(x_{it} - \alpha_0 - \alpha_1 y_{it})^2,$$

that is, f assumed to be the formal density function, maximization of conditional probability leads to ordinary least squares regression of x_{it_0} on y_{it_0}.

On the other hand, if g depends on α_0 and α_1, both x and y must be regarded as endogenous variables, and at least one additional equation must be introduced to complete the system. An analogous interpretation holds for the distinction between endogenous and exogenous variables in time series analysis. In that case, the exogenous variables may be regarded as a set of variables having a joint marginal distribution independent of the structural parameters to be estimated. They may also be given a nonprobabilistic interpretation and regarded simply as a set of known numbers.

It seems unlikely that interindividual differences observed in a cross-section sample can be explained by simple two-variable relations of the type in (8.3.1). From a sample of N observations at time $t = t_0$, let us select two pairs for discussion $(x_{jt_0}, y_{jt_0})(x_{kt_0}, y_{kt_0})$. According to one interpretation, these two points lie on or near the single line. The line joining the two points that shows

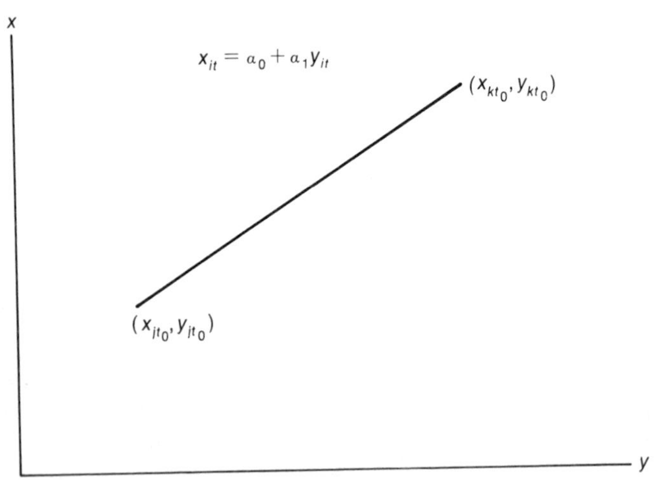

Figure 8.1

positions of two individuals in the xy-plane at $t = t_0$ is, in a rough sense, an estimate of the underlying structural equation. We say, "in a rough sense," because in practice we actually estimate an average relationships fitted to a scatter of many such points.

A second interpretation is that the underlying relation between x and y is

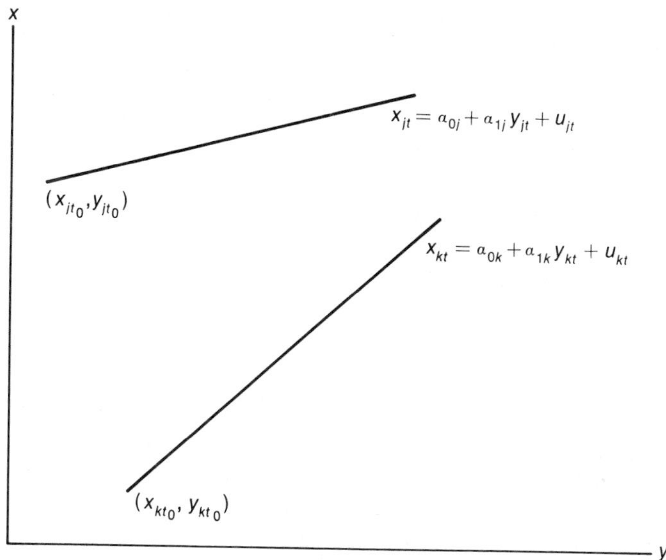

Figure 8.2

different for each individual. In this case, a line joining the two observations need not be a close approximation to either structural equation. If we ask why individual j acts according to one structural equation, yet k acts according to another, we find that the most plausible answer is that some important variables are missing. For example, if x is household saving and y is household income, it may happen that a *young* household adjusts its saving to its income along

$$x_{kt} = \alpha_{0k} + \alpha_{1k} y_{kt} + u_{kt},$$

but an *old* household adjusts its saving to its income along

$$x_{jt} = \alpha_{0j} + \alpha_{1j} y_{jt} + u_{jt}.$$

Age is a missing variable that accounts for the differences between the two equations connecting x and y. A trivariate equation connecting x, y and a = age may then have identical parameters for each individual. In studying cross-section samples of households, we must realize that age of head, number of persons, marital status, wealth holdings, income expectations, price expectations, and a number of other factors vary widely among individuals in the sample, and are likely to affect economic behavior; therefore, we must be prepared in such cases to use a large number of variables simultaneously. Average age, family size, marital status, and so on, do not change greatly over time for the whole community; hence, these variables may be properly neglected in time series analysis. This is the counterpart of the treatment of prices as variable over time but not over space at an instant of time. The same arguments hold for the treatment of cross-section samples of business firms.

Individuals differ greatly in behavior, and it may not be possible to obtain observations on a sufficiently large number of variables so that each unit may be considered to behave according to the same structural equation. We are then faced with the problem of interpreting a single estimated equation as representative in some sense of a large number of underlying equations. The main principles can be most easily demonstrated with reference to a single equation in two variables, one endogenous and one predetermined. The structural equation is

$$x_{it_0} = \alpha_{0i} + \alpha_{1i}y_{it_0} + u_{it_0}, \qquad i = 1, 2, \ldots, N. \tag{8.3.7}$$

In the customary form with fixed parameters, (8.3.1), we may consider the quantity $\alpha_0 + u_{it_0}$ as a random parameter with mean α_0. The constant parameter is a random variable but the slope is not. Equation (8.3.7) can be interpreted as a model in which both parameters, α_{0i} and α_{1i}, are treated as random variables. We choose as our objectives, if the structural equations are those of (8.3.7), the estimation of

$$E(\alpha_{0i} + u_{it_0}) = \alpha_0,$$
$$E\alpha_{1i} = \alpha_1.$$

The equation

$$x_{it} = \hat{\alpha}_0 + \hat{\alpha}_1 y_{it}$$

is interpreted as an average relation estimating the N equations in (8.3.7). This is known as the case of nonadditive disturbances or random parameters.

We shall consider two ways of estimating α_0 and α_1 in this model. A simple method is to prepare ordinary least squares estimates, assuming y_{it_0} to be a predetermined variable, and then to examine the conditions under which such estimates have specified properties, such as consistency. In general, least squares estimates will not be efficient. A second method is to prepare maximum likelihood estimates.[15]

The least squares estimate of α_1 is

$$\bar{\alpha}_1 = \frac{\sum_{i=1}^{N} (x_{it_0} - \bar{x}_{t_0})(y_{it_0} - \bar{y}_{t_0})}{\sum_{i=1}^{N} (y_{it_0} - \bar{y}_{t_0})^2}. \tag{8.3.8}$$

Barred variables are sample means. Substituting from (8.3.7) into (8.3.8) and

[15] Although maximum likelihood estimates are generally thought to be consistent and efficient, these properties are not always possessed by maximum likelihood estimates if the number of parameters grows with the number of observations. See J. Neyman and E. L. Scott, "Consistent Estimators Based on Partially Consistent Observations," *Econometrica*, 16 (January, 1948), 1–32.

rearranging terms, we get

$$\bar{\alpha}_1 = \alpha_1 + \frac{\sum_{i=1}^{N} (\alpha_{0i} + u_{it_0} - \bar{\alpha}_0 - \bar{u}_{t_0})(y_{it_0} - \bar{y}_{t_0})}{\sum_{i=1}^{N} (y_{it_0} - \bar{y}_{t_0})^2} + \frac{\sum_{i=1}^{N} (\alpha_{1i} - \alpha_1) y_{it_0}(y_{it_0} - \bar{y}_{t_0})}{\sum_{i=1}^{N} (y_{it_0} - \bar{y}_{t_0})^2}. \tag{8.3.9}$$

In order for $\bar{\alpha}_1$ to be a consistent estimate of α_1, we must have $\bar{\alpha}_1$ converge stochastically to α_1 or, in other words, the right-hand fraction in (8.3.9) must converge stochastically to zero. If $\alpha_{0i} + u_{it_0}$ is uncorrelated with y_{it_0} and if α_{1i} is uncorrelated with $y_{it_0}^2$ and $y_{it_0}\bar{y}_{t_0}$, then we have

$$\operatorname*{plim}_{N\to\infty} \sum_{i=1} (\alpha_{0i} + u_{it_0} - \bar{\alpha}_0 - \bar{u}_{t_0})(y_{it_0} - \bar{y}_{t_0}) = 0$$

$$\operatorname*{plim}_{N\to\infty} \sum_{i=1}^{N} (\alpha_{1i} - \alpha_1) y_{it_0}(y_{it_0} - \bar{y}_{t_0}) = 0,$$

$$\operatorname*{plim}_{N\to\infty} \bar{\alpha}_1 = \alpha_1,$$

and $\bar{\alpha}_1$ is a consistent estimate of α_1. These are sufficient conditions for consistency.

To obtain the maximum likelihood estimating equations, we form the variable

$$z_{it_0} = x_{it_0} - \alpha_0 - \alpha_1 y_{it_0} = (\alpha_{0i} + u_{it_0} - \alpha_0) + (\alpha_{1i} - \alpha_1) y_{it_0}.$$

z_{it_0} is assumed to be normally distributed. It has a zero mean and variance

$$\sigma_{z_{it_0}}^2 = \sigma_0^2 + \sigma_u^2 + y_{it_0}^2 \sigma_1^2.$$

We denote, in this expression, the variances of α_{0i}, u_{it_0}, and α_{1i} by σ_0^2, σ_u^2 and σ_1^2 respectively. The likelihood function is

$$e^L = \prod_{i=1}^{N} \left(\frac{1}{\sqrt{2\pi}\sigma_{z_{it_0}}} \right) \exp\left[-\frac{1}{2} \sum_{i=1}^{N} \frac{(x_{it_0} - \alpha_0 - \alpha_1 y_{it_0})^2}{\sigma_{z_{it_0}}^2} \right] \tag{8.3.10}$$

Maximizing with respect to α_0, α_1, $\sigma_0^2 + \sigma_u^2$, and σ_1^2 we get

$$\frac{\partial L}{\partial \alpha_0} = \sum_{i=1}^{N} \frac{(x_{it_0} - \alpha_0 - \alpha_1 y_{it_0})}{\sigma_{z_{it_0}}^2} = 0,$$

$$\frac{\partial L}{\partial \alpha_1} = \sum_{i=1}^{N} \frac{(x_{it_0} - \alpha_0 - \alpha_1 y_{it_0}) y_{it_0}}{\sigma_{z_{it_0}}^2} = 0,$$

$$\frac{\partial L}{\partial (\sigma_0^2 + \sigma_u^2)} = -\sum_{i=1}^{N} \frac{1}{\sigma_{z_{it_0}}^2} + \sum_{i=1}^{N} \frac{(x_{it_0} - \alpha_0 - \alpha_1 y_{it_0})^2}{\sigma_{z_{it_0}}^4} = 0, \tag{8.3.11}$$

$$\frac{\partial L}{\partial \sigma_1^2} = -\sum_{i=1}^{N} \frac{y_{it_0}^2}{\sigma_{z_{it_0}}^2} + \sum_{i=1}^{N} \frac{(x_{it_0} - \alpha_0 - \alpha_1 y_{it_0})^2 y_{it_0}^2}{\sigma_{z_{it_0}}^4} = 0.$$

Because σ_0^2 and σ_u^2 occur only as a sum, we treat $\sigma_0^2 + \sigma_u^2$ as a single unknown parameter. The four equations in (8.3.11) and the above definition of $\sigma_{z_{it_0}}^2$ form the system of estimating equations. They are nonlinear and not easily solved. In case there are a number of solutions, we choose that one that gives the highest point on the likelihood function and simultaneously only positive values as estimates of the unknown variances.

We have assumed that the variable parameters α_{0i} and α_{1i} do not change from one cross-section sample to another of identical individuals at a different time point. This assumption is of course not essential, because the entire argument thus far is unchanged if a subscript t_0 is attached to these parameters. Because it does seem reasonable to regard these parameters as unchanging over short time periods, we might construct another probability model in which α_{0i} and α_{1i} are not treated as random variables, but simply as a finite set of unknown numbers. We then pose the following question: what type of mean value of these numbers is estimated by some particular set of sample statistics, say the ordinary least squares equations? Assuming (8.3.7) as the equation we are trying to estimate, we define the probability structure entirely in terms of u_{it_0} as a normally distributed random variable with zero mean and constant variance σ^2. Instead of considering the α_{0i} and α_{1i} as random variables, we simply treat them as a set of numbers, each of which is associated with one individual in the population. If the population consists solely of an industry with not more than a few hundred firms, the idea of sampling to get estimates of the parameter coefficients is out of the question. A cross-section sample will contain observations on every firm in the industry. The disturbances u_{it_0} are more intractable and will vary in repeated sets of observations.

Define

$$\alpha_{0i} = \bar{\bar{\alpha}}_0 + \alpha_{0i}^*,$$
$$\alpha_{1i} = \bar{\bar{\alpha}}_1 + \alpha_{1i}^*.$$

The starred values are deviations of the α's about their average values to be defined. We minimize the sum of squares

$$\sum_{i=1}^{N} (x_{it_0} - \bar{\bar{\alpha}}_0 - \alpha_{0i}^* - \bar{\bar{\alpha}}_1 y_{it_0} - \alpha_{1i}^* y_{it_0})^2 = L \tag{8.3.12}$$

with respect to $\bar{\bar{\alpha}}_0$, $\bar{\bar{\alpha}}_1$, and σ, the parameters we are trying to estimate. Minimization equations with respect to $\bar{\bar{\alpha}}_0$ and $\bar{\bar{\alpha}}_1$ are

$$\frac{\partial L}{\partial \bar{\bar{\alpha}}_0} = \sum_{i=1}^{N} x_{it_0} - N\bar{\bar{\alpha}}_0 - \bar{\bar{\alpha}}_1 \sum_{i=1}^{N} y_{it_0} - \sum_{i=1}^{N} \alpha_{0i}^* - \sum_{i=1}^{N} \alpha_{1i}^* y_{it_0} = 0,$$
$$\frac{\partial L}{\partial \bar{\bar{\alpha}}_1} = \sum_{i=1}^{N} x_{it_0} y_{it_0} - \bar{\bar{\alpha}}_0 \sum_{i=1}^{N} y_{it_0} - \bar{\bar{\alpha}}_1 \sum_{i=1}^{N} y_{it_0}^2 \tag{8.3.13}$$
$$- \sum_{i=1}^{N} \alpha_{0i}^* y_{it_0} - \sum_{i=1}^{N} \alpha_{1i}^* y_{it_0}^2 = 0.$$

We notice that these two equations reduce to the familiar least squares estimation equations if

$$\sum_{i=1}^{N} \alpha_{0i}^* + \sum_{i=1}^{N} \alpha_{1i}^* y_{it_0} = \sum_{i=1}^{N} (\alpha_{0i} - \bar{\bar{\alpha}}_0) + \sum_{i=1}^{N} (\alpha_{1i} - \bar{\bar{\alpha}}_1) y_{it_0} = 0,$$
$$\sum_{i=1}^{N} \alpha_{0i}^* y_{it_0} + \sum_{i=1}^{N} \alpha_{1i}^* y_{it_0}^2 = \sum_{i=1}^{N} (\alpha_{0i} - \bar{\bar{\alpha}}_0) y_{it_0} + \sum_{i=1}^{N} (\alpha_{1i} - \bar{\bar{\alpha}}_1) y_{it_0}^2 = 0. \tag{8.3.14}$$

Equations (8.3.14) ensure that the estimating equations in (8.3.13) for $\bar{\bar{\alpha}}_0$ and $\bar{\bar{\alpha}}_1$ do not depend on the individual parameters α_{0i}^* and α_{1i}^*. Moreover, (8.3.14) enables us to interpret $\bar{\bar{\alpha}}_0$ and $\bar{\bar{\alpha}}_1$ as means of α_{0i} and α_{1i}. Solving (8.3.14) we get

$$\bar{\bar{\alpha}}_0 = \frac{\sum_{i=1}^{N} y_{it_0}^2 \left(\sum_{i=1}^{N} \alpha_{0i} + \sum_{i=1}^{N} \alpha_{1i} y_{it_0}\right) - \sum_{i=1}^{N} y_{it_0} \left(\sum_{i=1}^{N} \alpha_{0i} y_{it_0} + \sum_{i=1}^{N} \alpha_{1i} y_{it_0}^2\right)}{N \sum_{i=1}^{N} y_{it_0}^2 - \left(\sum_{i=1}^{N} y_{it_0}\right)^2},$$
$$\bar{\bar{\alpha}}_1 = \frac{N \left(\sum_{i=1}^{N} \alpha_{0i} y_{it_0} + \sum_{i=1}^{N} \alpha_{1i} y_{it_0}^2\right) - \sum_{i=1}^{N} y_{it_0} \left(\sum_{i=1}^{N} \alpha_{0i} + \sum_{i=1}^{N} \alpha_{1i} y_{it_0}\right)}{N \sum_{i=1}^{N} y_{it_0}^2 - \left(\sum_{i=1}^{N} y_{it_0}\right)^2}. \tag{8.3.15}$$

These equations express $\bar{\bar{\alpha}}_0$ and $\bar{\bar{\alpha}}_1$ as general weighted averages of the individual α_{0i} and α_{1i}. These averages do not have the simple property that $\bar{\bar{\alpha}}_0$ depends only on the α_{0i} and $\bar{\bar{\alpha}}_1$ on the α_{1i}. If the equation being estimated contained no constant term $\alpha_{0i} = 0$, the expression defining $\bar{\bar{\alpha}}_1$ in terms of the α_{1i} reduces to

$$\bar{\bar{\alpha}}_1 = \frac{\sum_{i=1}^{N} \alpha_{1i} y_{it_0}^2}{\sum_{i=1}^{N} y_{it_0}^2}, \tag{8.3.16}$$

in which we see clearly that $\bar{\bar{\alpha}}_1$ is a weighted arithmetic average of the α_{1i} with the $y_{it_0}^2$ as weights.

It is instructive to compare this particular result with the estimation of the corresponding parameter from time series aggregates. The basic equation is

$$x_{it} = \alpha_{1i} y_{it} + u_{it}. \tag{8.3.17}$$

The resulting aggregative equation is

$$\sum_{i=1}^{N} x_{it} = \frac{\sum_{i=1}^{N} \alpha_{1i} y_{it}}{\sum_{i=1}^{N} y_{it}} \sum_{i=1}^{N} y_{it} + \sum_{i=1}^{N} u_{it}, \tag{8.3.18}$$

we may write this as

$$x_t = \bar{\alpha}_1 y_t + u_t. \tag{8.3.19}$$

The parameter $\bar{\alpha}_1$ is a weighted arithmetic average of the α_{1i} with the weights being proportional to y_{it}. From a sample of time series observations $x_1, \ldots, x_T$; $y_1, \ldots, y_T$, we estimate $\bar{\alpha}_1$ in contrast to $\bar{\bar{\alpha}}_1$ that is estimated from a cross-section sample.[16] These are essentially the same parameters, but differ in the matter of weights used to combine the α_{1i} into an average.

If the parameters of a cross-section relationship are independent of time and if we have the special case in which the slope parameters do not vary among individuals, that is,

$$x_{it} = \alpha_{0i} + \alpha_1 y_{it} + u_{it}, \tag{8.3.7'}$$

it may be useful to eliminate the variable effect of α_{0i}, over individual observations, through time differencing.

$$\begin{aligned} x_{it} - x_{i,t-1} &= \alpha_1(y_{it} - y_{i,t-1}) + u_{it} - u_{i,t-1}, \\ \Delta x_{it} &= \alpha_1 \, \Delta y_{it} + \Delta u_{it}. \end{aligned} \tag{8.3.7''}$$

The estimation of (8.3.7″) from cross-section data would present no problem, provided data are available from two successive cross-section samples and provided Δu_{it} are mutually independent for different values of i. The process of differencing, in this case, does not necessarily induce mutual dependence among errors, as it might in a time series sample. The variability of α_{0i} over the index values of i represents *personality* effects (household sample) or *entrepreneurial* effects (business firm sample). Differencing for two successive cross sections can eliminate these effects.

Nonlinearity also accounts for differences between aggregative equations estimated from time series data and individual equations estimated from cross-section data. We have assumed linearity throughout this section, but have considered the case in which parameters vary among individuals. Interesting comparisons between cross-section and time series analysis result. We now consider nonlinear equations but will assume that parameters do not change from one individual to another.

[16] $x_t = \sum_{i=1}^{N} x_{it}$; $y_t = \sum_{i=1}^{N} y_{it}$.

Suppose that the nonlinear relation is a simple parabola

$$x_{it} = \alpha_0 + \alpha_1 y_{it} + \alpha_2 y_{it}^2 + u_{it}. \tag{8.3.20}$$

In a cross-section sample we estimate α_0, α_1, and α_2 from the sample $x_{1t_0}, \ldots, x_{Nt_0}; y_{1t_0}, \ldots, y_{Nt_0}$. Summing (8.3.20) over all individuals we get

$$\sum_{i=1}^{N} x_{it} = N\alpha_0 + \alpha_1 \sum_{i=1}^{N} y_{it} + \alpha_2 \sum_{i=1}^{N} y_{it}^2 + \sum_{i=1}^{N} u_{it}. \tag{8.3.21}$$

The variance of the distribution of y for any t is defined as

$$\sigma_{y_t}^2 = \frac{\sum_{i=1}^{N} y_{it}^2}{N} - \left(\frac{1}{N}\sum_{i=1}^{N} y_{it}\right)^2; \tag{8.3.22}$$

therefore, we can write (8.3.21) as

$$x_t = N\alpha_0 + \alpha_1 y_t + \alpha_2 N\left(\sigma_{y_t}^2 + \frac{1}{N^2} y_t^2\right) + u_t,$$

in which the omitted subscript on variables designates summation over all individuals. In terms of arithmetic means, we have

$$\bar{x}_t = \alpha_0 + \alpha_1 \bar{y}_t + \alpha_2(\sigma_{yt}^2 + \bar{y}_t^2) + \bar{u}_t.$$

This calculation shows that the time series equation, written in complete analogy to the individual equation, should include the variance of y over time as an additional variable. If the variance does not fluctuate much over time, $\alpha_2 \sigma_{y_t}^2$ can be combined with the constant term, and we get the same relation among aggregates as among individual variables.

Another way of aggregating is to form the equation

$$\bar{x}_t = \int_{-\infty}^{\infty}\int_{-\infty}^{\infty} (\alpha_0 + \alpha_1 y_{it} + \alpha_2 y_{it}^2 + u_{it}) p(y_{it}, u_{it}) dy_{it}\, du_{it}, \tag{8.3.23}$$

where p is the joint density function of y_{it} and u_{it}. The double integral in (8.3.23) is simply the definition of the mean of a bivariate distribution, the mean being the expected value of x_{it}, because x_{it} is the multiplicand of p in the integrand.

A example of a type of nonlinearity met with in practice is the savings relation

$$\frac{s_{it}}{y_{it}} = \alpha_0 + \alpha_1 \log y_{it} + u_{it} \qquad \alpha_1 > 0. \tag{8.3.24}$$

This equation gives a good empirical measure of the nonlinearity in the savings-income relation, savings growing at an increasing rate with income,

$$\frac{\partial^2 s_{it}}{\partial y_{it}^2} = \frac{\alpha_1}{y_{it}} > 0.$$

An advantage of the particular microeconomic equation in (8.3.24) is that $\sigma_{u_{it}}^2$ tends, empirically, to be constant for all y_{it}. A parabolic relation between s_{it} and y_{it} would not have disturbance with variance independent of y_{it}. We say that $\sigma_{u_{it}}^2$ is homoscedastic, a property that we implicitly use in our estimation methods.[17] To aggregate (8.3.24) we could define new variables

$$x_{it} = \frac{s_{it}}{y_{it}}$$

$$z_{it} = \log y_{it},$$

and derive

$$\bar{x}_t = \alpha_0 + \alpha_1 \bar{z}_t + \bar{u}_t.$$

This would not be a useful relation, however, because the customary aggregative data available would not be

$$\sum_{i=1}^{N} x_{it} = \sum_{i=1}^{N} \frac{s_{it}}{y_{it}}$$

$$\sum_{i=1}^{N} z_{it} = \sum_{i=1}^{N} \log y_{it}.$$

We nearly always have data only on

$$\sum_{i=1}^{N} s_{it} = s_t,$$

$$\sum_{i=1}^{N} y_{it} = y_t.$$

Our problem then is to aggregate (8.3.24) so that the resulting equation can be written in terms of $\bar{s}_t$ and $\bar{y}_t$.

The definition of $\bar{s}_t$ is

$$\bar{s}_t = \int_{-\infty}^{\infty} \int_{0}^{\infty} \left(\frac{s_{it}}{y_{it}}\right) y_{it} p(y_{it}, u_{it})\, dy_{it}\, du_{it}. \tag{8.3.25}$$

[17] Parabolic savings equations with disturbance variance proportional to income can, however, be transformed into a relation between the savings-income ratio, on the one hand, and the reciprocal and level of income, on the other, where the disturbance variance is independent of income. The importance of having homoscedasticity (disturbance variance independent of explanatory variables) can be seen directly from derivation of maximum likelihood estimates from a normal distribution, where the variance is treated as an *unknown constant* in the likelihood equation.

We confine $y =$ income to the range $(0, \infty)$. The integral can be transformed, using (8.3.24), to

$$\bar{s}_t = \int_{-\infty+\alpha_0+\alpha_1 \log y_{it}}^{\infty+\alpha_0+\alpha_1 \log y_{it}} \int_0^{\infty} \left(\frac{s_{it}}{y_{it}}\right) y_{it} p(y_{it}, u_{it})\, dy_{it}\, d\left(\frac{s_{it}}{y_{it}}\right). \tag{8.3.26}$$

A satisfactory empirical graduation of the income distribution is provided by the logarithmic normal curve, that is, the density

$$\frac{1}{\sqrt{2\pi}\sigma_t} e^{-(1/2\sigma^2_t)(\log y_{it}-\mu)^2}\, d\log y_{it},$$

or

$$\frac{1}{\sqrt{2\pi}\sigma_t y_{it}} e^{-(1/2\sigma^2_t)(\log y_{it}-\mu)^2}\, dy_{it}.$$

If we assume this distribution for y and an independent normal distribution for u_{it}, the integration of (8.3.26) becomes

$$\frac{\bar{s}_t}{\bar{y}_t} = \alpha_0 + \alpha_1\left(\frac{\sigma_t^2}{2} + \log \bar{y}_t\right) + \bar{u}_t. \tag{8.3.27}$$

In deriving (8.3.27) we make use of the relation between the arithmetic mean of $y(\bar{y}_t)$ and the geometric mean (antilog $\overline{\log y_t}$) under the logarithmic normal hypothesis.[18] Except for a variance parameter, we are able to aggregate the nonlinear relation into an analogous form involving only arithmetic means.

The examples of aggregating savings-income equations are only expository to demonstrate some underlying principles. As we remarked previously, individual households in a cross-section sample may save different amounts not only because their incomes are different, but also because of such variables as age, family size, liquid assets, and so on. Data gathered in the Surveys of Consumer Finances by the Survey Research Center suggest the following type of empirical savings equation, especially in the nonfarm, nonentrepreneurial sector of the economy:

$$\frac{s_{it}}{y_{it}} = \alpha_0 + \alpha_1 \log y_{it} + \alpha_2 \log n_{it} + \alpha_3 \frac{1_{i,t-1}}{y_{it}} + \alpha_4 1_{i,t-1} + \alpha_5 a_{it} + \alpha_6 h_{it} + u_{it} \tag{8.3.28}$$

in which

$n_{it} =$ number of persons in the household
$1_{i,t-1} =$ beginning of year liquid asset holdings
$a_{it} =$ age of household head

[18] $E(y_t) = e^{\mu} e^{\sigma_t^2/2}$. $E(y_t)$ is the expected value of y_t, or the arithmetic mean, and e^{μ} is the population geometric mean.

$$h_{it} = 1 \text{ if homeowner}$$
$$h_{it} = 0 \text{ if renter.}$$

Integrating over the joint distribution of $y_{it}, n_{it}, 1_{i,t-1}, a_{it}, h_{it}, u_{it}$, we get

$$\begin{aligned} \bar{s}_t = {} & \alpha_0 \bar{y}_t + \alpha_1 \overline{y_t \log y_t} + \alpha_2 \overline{y_t \log n_t} + \alpha_3 \overline{1_{t-1}} + \alpha_4 \overline{y_t 1_{t-1}} \\ & + \alpha_5 \overline{y_t a_t} + \alpha_6 \overline{y_t h_t} + \bar{y}_t \bar{u}_t. \end{aligned} \tag{8.3.29}$$

We assume independence between y and u. The notation $\overline{x_t z_t}$ is defined as

$$\overline{x_t z_t} = \frac{\sum_{i=1}^{N} x_{it} z_{it}}{N}.$$

Obviously, aggregative data are not in the form of sums of products of variables as in (8.3.29). If $\log y_{it}$ is normally distributed, we see by (8.3.26)–(8.3.27)

$$\overline{y_t \log y_t} = \bar{y}_t \left(\frac{\sigma_t^2}{2} + \log \bar{y}_t \right).$$

From the definition of the simple correlation coefficient we can write

$$\overline{x_t z_t} = \bar{x}_t \bar{z}_t + r_{x_t z_t} \sigma_{x_t} \sigma_{z_t};$$

thus, to express (8.3.29) in terms of time series aggregates we use the form

$$\begin{aligned} \bar{s}_t = {} & (\alpha_2 r_{y_t \log n_t} \sigma_{y_t} \sigma_{\log n_t} + \alpha_4 r_{y_t l_{t-1}} \sigma_{y_t} \sigma_{l_{t-1}} + \alpha_5 r_{y_t a_t} \sigma_{y_t} \sigma_{a_t} \\ & + \alpha_6 r_{y_t h_t} \sigma_{y_t} \sigma_{h_t}) + \left(\alpha_0 + \alpha_1 \frac{\sigma_t^2}{2} \right) \bar{y}_t + \alpha_1 \bar{y}_t \log \bar{y}_t \\ & + \alpha_2 \bar{y}_t \overline{\log n_t} + \alpha_3 \overline{l_{t-1}} + \alpha_4 \bar{y}_t \overline{l_{t-1}} + \alpha_5 \bar{y}_t \bar{a}_t + \alpha_6 \bar{y}_t \bar{h}_t + \bar{y}_t \bar{u}_t. \end{aligned} \tag{8.3.30}$$

The equation is now written as a function of time series means with the minor exception of $\overline{\log n_t}$, the log of the geometric mean of n_{it}. This is not difficult to compute, however. The time series equation corresponding to (8.3.28) is a complete analogue plus the addition of terms depending on correlations and variances. If the latter parameters were to remain constant over time, we would be able to estimate the corresponding time series equation by using a sample of means of the variables in (8.3.28). In general, however, many properties of the joint distribution of explanatory variables are relevant in bridging the gap between the micro- and macroeconomic equations.

In deriving an aggregative savings equation from (8.3.28), many approximations are used. The logarithmic normal distribution does not perfectly represent the income distribution; the correlations between income and other variables do not remain perfectly constant from one period to the next; the variances and means of the several variables assumed constant over time may not actually be so. For these reasons, the equation in (8.3.30) is not necessarily the best aggregative, time series analogue of (8.3.28), although it does serve well to illustrate the nature and difficulty of the aggregation problem in a practical case.

Questions and Problems

1. Let

e_i = expenditures on consumer durables by the ith household
y_i = income of the ith household.

In planning a consumer survey to collect data for estimating

$$e_i = f(y_i),$$

other things held constant, what variables would you include in the interview schedule besides e and y? How would you decide upon the a priori form of the f function? How would you expect variables other than income to be related to expenditures on durables?

2. Instead of using data for the individual economic units in a cross-section sample to estimate equations in an econometric model, one often groups the data into classes and studies the relationships among class means. For example, income may be arrayed in ten successive classes from $0–$1,000 to $15,000–$20,000. Within each class, mean savings and mean income are calculated. The relationship between the ten values of mean savings and the ten values of mean income is used to estimate the savings equation. Compare this approach with one in which the relationship is estimated directly from individual data without grouping. Suppose that many (more than two) variables are being simultaneously considered. How would you make the corresponding groupings? What are limitations on the number of variables and groups?

3. List types of variables not ordinarily available from time series records that could potentially be ascertained from individuals in a survey yielding a cross-section sample to be used for the estimation of econometric equations. Show how such variables could be used in particular equations.

4. A CROSS-SECTION MODEL OF PRODUCTION OF RAILWAY SERVICES

To give the reader a more concrete idea about the methods of this chapter, we turn to an example based on a cross-section study of the production of railway services in the United States, as these services used to be prior to World War II. This example studies an econometric model of a sector of the economy, the railway industry, and uses a cross-section sample of data on individual firms.

We shall not go thoroughly into all the details of this model that are necessary in presenting a completed scientific analysis, but will refer only to those points that enable us to illustrate the econometric method.

We consider the railroad industry as a regulated sector of the economy. Each road, being a common carrier, is required to accept traffic as offered. The industry follows neither the competitive nor the monopolistic model. Our model is further restricted to treatment only of current operations and decisions. This excludes capital items such as investment decisions, and uses observations only on variables appearing in operating or profit and loss statements.

The main functions of railroads are to carry goods (freight) and people (passengers). In performing these functions, carriers use up manpower, fuel, and physical capital. The variables of our model are

$$\begin{aligned} x_1 &= \text{net ton-miles of freight carried} \\ x_2 &= \text{net passenger miles} \\ n &= \text{man-hours of employment} \\ c &= \text{tons of fuel consumed (coal equivalents)} \\ d &= \text{train hours utilized} \\ w &= \text{average hourly earnings} \\ q &= \text{average cost of a ton of fuel} \\ r &= \text{average cost of capital services.} \end{aligned}$$

We are developing our model at the microeconomic level and will subsequently test it against observations on individual firms. A subscript i added to each variable denotes that the associated variable belongs to the ith firm in the industry.

The production function is assumed to have the form

$$x_{1i} = Ax_{2i}^{\delta}n_i^{\alpha}c_i^{\beta}d_i^{\gamma}u_i \tag{8.4.1}$$

that is linear in the logarithms of inputs and outputs. As in other places, u is a random disturbance. This type of function is not acceptable for a model of a firm in a purely competitive industry because the convexity in the (x_1, x_2) plane is such that the traditional marginal conditions do not lead to maximum profits.[19] This same problem does not arise in a model of a regulated industry, and the restrictions on the parameters of (8.4.1) are very mild in order to ensure the existence of second order maximization conditions. A more general function

$$f(x_{1i}, x_{2i}) = An_i^{\alpha}c_i^{\beta}d_i^{\gamma}u_i,$$

provided f is linear or concave to the origin in the (x_1, x_2) plane, is more appropriate for competitive models. We have found quite similar empirical results in the railroad industry using either (8.4.1) or a linear f function.

A main economic problem of common carriers is to meet the existing or given level of traffic at minimum cost. Mathematically this reduces to

$$wn_i + qc_i + rd_i = \text{min.}$$

[19] Cf. Marc Nerlove, *Estimation and Identification of Cobb-Douglas Production Functions* (Chicago: Rand McNally & Co., 1965), p. 82, fn. 3.

subject to

$$x_{1i} = Ax_{2i}^{\delta} n_i^{\alpha} c_i^{\beta} d_i^{\gamma} u_i.$$

The resulting marginal conditions can be written as

$$\frac{qc_i}{wn_i} = \frac{\beta}{\alpha} v_{1i} \tag{8.4.2}$$

$$\frac{rd_i}{wn_i} = \frac{\gamma}{\alpha} v_{2i}. \tag{8.4.3}$$

The v's are random disturbances, showing how actual factor and price ratios may differ from optimal values.

We shall carry on the discussion as though the structural parameters α, β, γ, δ, and A were the same for all roads although we could refer to the previous discussion on variable parameters to interpret the opposite assumption. No subscripts are attached to w, q, and r, implying that they are the same for all roads. Actually our only assumption is that each road accepts these market variables as given and adjusts its operations to them. Exactly the same techniques would be used even if the market variables differed among roads, provided that they are not influenced by the economic decisions of the individual roads.

Equations (8.4.2) and (8.4.3) when written in logarithmic form are seen to be of the special type discussed previously (8.2.31), involving only one endogenous variable and one unknown parameter.

$$\log \frac{qc_i}{wn_i} - \log \frac{\beta}{\alpha} = \log v_{1i},$$

$$\log \frac{rd_i}{wn_i} - \log \frac{\gamma}{\alpha} = \log v_{2i}.$$

If $\log v_{1i}$ and $\log v_{2i}$ are independent of each other and normally distributed, maximum likelihood estimates of $\log \frac{\beta}{\alpha}$ and $\log \frac{\gamma}{\alpha}$ are

$$\log \frac{\hat{\beta}}{\alpha} = \frac{1}{N} \sum_{i=1}^{N} \log \frac{qc_i}{wn_i}, \tag{8.4.4}$$

$$\log \frac{\hat{\gamma}}{\alpha} = \frac{1}{N} \sum_{i=1}^{N} \log \frac{rd_i}{wn_i}. \tag{8.4.5}$$

Even if the distributions are not normal, (8.4.4) and (8.4.5) give best linear unbiased estimates of the logarithmic parameters. From antilogs of the values in (8.4.4) and (8.4.5) or (what is the same thing) from geometric means of the sample observations of $\frac{qc_i}{wn_i}$ and $\frac{rd_i}{wn_i}$, we get estimates of $\frac{\beta}{\alpha}$ and $\frac{\gamma}{\alpha}$.

We write (8.4.1) in logarithms as

$$\frac{1}{\alpha}\log x_{1i} - \frac{\delta}{\alpha}\log x_{2i} - \frac{1}{\alpha}\log A - \frac{1}{\alpha}\log u_i = \log n_i + \frac{\beta}{\alpha}\log c_i + \frac{\gamma}{\alpha}\log d_i.$$

We substitute the estimates of $\frac{\beta}{\alpha}$ and $\frac{\gamma}{\alpha}$ for the parameter values and construct a new endogenous variable

$$y_i = \log n_i + \frac{\hat{\beta}}{\alpha}\log c_i + \frac{\hat{\gamma}}{\alpha}\log d_i.$$

To estimate $\frac{1}{\alpha}$, $\frac{\delta}{\alpha}$, $\left(\frac{1}{\alpha}\right)\log A$, and $\sigma^2_{(1/\alpha)\log u}$, we form the regression of y_i on $\log x_{1i}$ and $\log x_{2i}$. The traffic variables, in this cross-section sample, are regarded as predetermined for the individual road. Our model assumes that roads make decisions about the use of production factors in terms of their own traffic and market prices and that these decisions do not affect their traffic and market prices. This assumption reflects the institutional character of the industry—common carriers required to meet the forthcoming level of traffic.

We must, however, return to our principles developed for cross-section analysis before carrying out the calculations from empirical data. It will be remembered that some variables differ widely among firms in a sample drawn at an instant of time and account for differences in individual behavior, but these same variables may not fluctuate appreciably as averages over time. Such considerations must be brought to bear on our railroad model. Obviously carriers do not operate under identical geographical conditions and this could make for productivity differentials, apart from those taken into account in our Eq. (8.4.1). Our data refer only to Class I roads in a given year, 1936, and do not provide enough independent observations for separate regional models in the type of statistical analysis we want to make. One of the more important regional differences affecting productivity is average length of haul. The western transcontinental roads are obviously in a different position in this respect from that of New England roads. Short hauls are less economical in the use of many production factors. We shall use average length of haul, z_{1i}, as an additional predetermined variable in the production function. There is long historical experience for each road in fixing its length of haul; therefore, we find little objection to the treatment of this factor as a predetermined variable in a cross-section sample for a single year.

Freight ton-miles means different things to different roads. Compared with the outputs of other industries, ton-miles seem to be composed of rather homogeneous units, yet coal carriers have quite different operating characteristics from other types of roads. A fivefold classification into manufactures, agricultural products, livestock, lumber, and mineral products would be adequate for much empirical work, but we have, for simplicity, confined our attention to the distinction between mineral products and all others, because this is the striking difference affecting productivity. We add another variable to the production function, z_{2i}, denoting percentage of freight in the form of products of mines. It, too, is treated, justifiably we believe, as a predetermined variable. In a more extensive analysis one might add other variables of this type, but the main principles we want to illustrate will be made clear in the numerical example using only z_1 and z_2.

In empirical work econometricians rarely have tailor-made data. Usually they have to manipulate and adjust data originally intended for other purposes in order to measure the magnitudes included in the model. Oftentimes the model has to be molded to fit the available data. The present model has the virtue of showing the reader clearly the difficulties encountered in data preparation.

Observations refer to Class I railways of the United States in 1936. Individual companies are grouped into systems of common ownership according to criteria of the Interstate Commerce Commission. We include operations only in the continental United States. This gives us somewhat more than eighty observations. The number varies from equation to equation because some data are missing for individual roads. Our sample includes practically all roads, and for any observation period we shall have only as many entries for a given variable as there are Class I roads. Our sampling scheme, however, refers to the situation in which we conceive the experiment of fixing the same external conditions to the industry and getting repeated sets of observations on all Class I railroads.

The output variables x_1 and x_2 are easily obtained from operating reports. Man-hours of employment is seemingly a straightforward variable, but roads report man-hours for current operations and for capital improvements together. The latter should be excluded from our particular model. Wage payments are, however, charged separately to operating expenses and to capital account. The ratio between these two types of wage payments could be used to split total man-hours into the corresponding parts. We use total man-hours as the variable in the production function n, since over 90% of wage payments are charged to current operations, but later we shall have use for the distinction between the types of wage payments.

Data are reported for the consumption of different types of fuel in the production process, and attempts are made in the reports to convert fuel oil, gasoline, and electricity into physical units equivalent to a ton of coal. Tons of coal equivalents are used to measure c.

The main difficulty in getting data is obtaining a measure of the input of capital services d corresponding to n and c. An analogue to man-hours is train-hours. This measure is a good indicator of the use of equipment. Car-hours to account for varying lengths of trains would be a feasible alternative. The question arises whether train-hours serves as a reliable indicator of the use of way and structures. We observe a strong correlation between train-hours and rail replacement; therefore we use, with many reservations, train-hours as a measure of d.

Wage payments wn and fuel expenditures qc are taken directly from the income statements of individual roads. We derive estimates of w and q from the ratios

$$\frac{wn}{n} \quad \text{and} \quad \frac{qc}{c}.$$

The main operating expense not wholly accounted for by wage and fuel expenditures is maintenance. We use nonwage maintenance expenditures to measure rd, payments for the flow of capital services. We must subtract maintenance wage payments because they are already included in wn. In dealing with an item of the order of magnitude of maintenance wage payments, it is more urgent to distinguish between capital and operating expenditures; therefore, we split maintenance wage payments into the two components in the same proportions as the split for total wage payments. The ratio

$$\frac{rd}{d},$$

where rd and d are our respective indicators of nonwage maintenance expenditures and train-hours, does not give directly a measure of unit capital expenses, but a figure that is only proportional to it. These data have considerably less reliability than those for w, n, q, and c.

There is no particular problem in getting data for average length of haul or percentage of freight in the form of products of mines. Numerous other qualifications about the data could be discussed at length, but we have merely introduced the student to this amount in the present problem in order to give a clear idea of the difficulties encountered in empirical econometric research. We now turn to the actual results and statistical methods used.

The ratio of fuel expenditures to wages should be distributed as v_1, the random disturbance, because the two magnitudes are proportional. The maintained hypothesis will be that $\log \frac{qc_i}{wn_i}$ is normally distributed. For each road, we calculate the logarithm of this ratio and compare the empirical frequency distribution with a fitted normal curve. This comparison is set out in Table 8.1 in a particular manner. We first determine the sample mean and standard deviation of $\log \frac{qc_i}{wn_i}$. The normal distribution is completely specified by two parameters, and we choose as our fitted distribution that normal curve that has a mean parameter equal to the sample mean and a variance parameter equal to the sample variance. We shall use a χ^2 test for the goodness of fit of the theoretical to the observed distribution,

$$\chi^2 = \sum_{i=1}^{m} \frac{(p_i n_i - f_i)^2}{p_i n_i}.$$

The data are arranged in m classes with $p_i n_i$ = theoretical frequency in the ith class and f_i = observed frequency in the ith class. The probability distribution of χ^2 for several values of m is tabulated; therefore, the application of the χ^2 test is greatly facilitated. An unfortunate property of χ^2 tests, however, is that by the choice of alternative groupings of the data into classes, the value of χ^2 and the associated probability can be greatly changed, even from insignificant to significant deviations and vice versa. A method of removing the arbitrariness of the selection of class intervals is to use quantile groupings—percentiles, deciles, quintiles, quartiles, and so on. Quantile points are marked off on the fitted distribution. We then determine the observed frequencies within these quantile limits. The size of the quantile still remains an open choice, but for large samples (200 or more observations) there is a criterion for selecting the quantile size. Because our railroad sample contains only slightly more than eighty observations, we cannot use this criterion. We shall simply choose quantiles that give a reasonable number of groups with a reasonable number of cases per group. It is generally recommended, on the basis of practice, that each class should contain at least five to ten observations. Moreover, there is a problem of "degrees of freedom." We do not enter the χ^2 tables at the value m, the number of classes. We use instead the number of degrees of freedom determined as the number of classes m less the number of parameters estimated from the sample. In a simple fitting of a normal curve, two degrees of freedom are deducted for sample estimates of the population mean and variance parameters. Another degree of freedom is deducted for equating the total frequency of the sample to the frequency of the fitted distribution. Subsequently, we come to a problem involving the loss of additional degrees of freedom.

The data of Table 8.1 tell us that the probability is larger than 0.50 of obtaining a value of χ^2 as large as that computed from our sample, when the true distribution is assumed to be normal. We interpret this result as meaning that there is no contradiction between our sample distribution and the normal hypothesis. A maximum-likelihood estimate of a mean of a normal distribution is given by the sample mean; hence,

$$\text{est. } \log \frac{\beta}{\alpha} = \frac{1}{83} \sum_{i=1}^{83} \log \frac{qc_i}{wn_i},$$
$$\frac{\hat{\beta}}{\alpha} = \prod_{i=1}^{83} \left(\frac{qc_i}{wn_i}\right)^{1/83} = 0.1349. \tag{8.4.6}$$

The likelihood estimate of the variance of a sample mean in normal distributions

TABLE 8.1

Distribution of $\log \frac{qc_i}{wn_i}$, 1936

Quantile	*Theoretical Frequency*	*Observed Frequency*
1	9	8
2	9	11
3	8	7
4	8	5
5	8	11
6	8	4
7	8	10
8	8	9
9	8	9
10	9	9

$\chi^2 = 5.68$,
$P_{\chi^2} > 0.50$, 7 degrees of freedom.

is $\frac{S^2}{N}$, where S^2 is the estimated variance of the sample observations. A range of two standard deviations on either side of est. $\log \frac{\beta}{\alpha}$ forms, approximately, a 95% confidence interval. The antilogs of the end points determine the extremities of a 95% confidence interval associated with the point estimate of $\frac{\beta}{\alpha}$. In our data we find this interval to be

$$0.1277 \leq \frac{\beta}{\alpha} \leq 0.1424.$$

The parallel calculations for the other equation of cost minimization are set out in Table 8.2.

We use only 81 observations to estimate the parameters of this equation, because two cases are extreme outlying observations. Two small freight carriers, with no passenger service, show ratios of 2.18 and 1.19, but the maximum ratio for the remaining roads is only 0.64.

The normal distribution hypothesis is acceptable according to Table 8.2. We estimate

$$\frac{\hat{\gamma}}{\alpha} = \prod_{i=1}^{81} \left(\frac{rd_i}{wn_i}\right)^{1/81} = 0.3124 \tag{8.4.7}$$

in a 95% confidence interval of

$$0.2928 \leq \frac{\gamma}{\alpha} \leq 0.3333.$$

TABLE 8.2

Distribution of $\log \frac{rd_i}{wn_i}$, 1936

Quantile	*Theoretical Frequency*	*Observed Frequency*
1	9	11
2	9	6
3	9	10
4	9	9
5	9	11
6	9	10
7	9	5
8	9	9
9	9	10

$\chi^2 = 4.0$,
$P_{\chi^2} > 0.50$, 6 degrees of freedom.

The estimate of the production equation of the model is obtained from the regression of

$$\log n_i + 0.1349 \log c_i + 0.3124 \log d_i$$

on $\log x_{1i}$, $\log x_{2i}$, $\log z_{1i}$, $\log z_{2i}$. The regression equation for 78 roads producing both freight and passenger service is

$$\begin{aligned} \log n_i &+ 0.1349 \log c_i + 0.3124 \log d_i \\ &= \underset{(0.2404)}{-0.8410} + \underset{(0.0422)}{1.1220} \log x_{1i} + \underset{(0.0208)}{0.1807} \log x_{2i} \\ &\quad - \underset{(0.1057)}{0.3864} \log z_{1i} - \underset{(0.0904)}{0.2788} \log z_{2i}. \end{aligned} \tag{8.4.8}$$

Common logarithms are used in all numerical estimates. The numbers in parentheses below coefficients are standard errors of the estimates. The multiple correlation coefficient is 0.99 and the estimated variance of disturbances is

$$\text{est. } \sigma^2_{(1/\alpha)\log u} = 0.0235.$$

Transforming the regression equation back to the original exponential form of the production function, we get

$$x_{1i} = 5.62 x_{2i}^{-0.16} n_i^{0.89} c_i^{0.12} d_i^{0.28} z_{1i}^{0.34} z_{2i}^{0.25}.$$

An interesting property of this production equation is that the sum of the exponents is greater than unity,[20] indicating that the railroad industry operates at a point of increasing returns to scale.

[20] The excess over unity is statistically significant.

The residual variations in (8.4.8), that is, the difference between observed and calculated values of

$$\log n_i + 0.1349 \log c_i + 0.3124 \log d_i$$

are estimates of the disturbances $-\left(\frac{1}{\alpha}\right) \log u$. If $\log u$ is normally distributed, we should find an acceptably close agreement between the frequency distribution of residuals and a best-fitting normal curve. The normal hypothesis is tested in Table 8.3.

TABLE 8.3

Distribution of Residuals from (8.4.8)

Quantile	*Theoretical Frequency*	*Observed Frequency*
1	6	5
2	6	4
3	5	7
4	5	9
5	5	4
6	5	7
7	5	5
8	5	3
9	5	2
10	5	7
11	5	7
12	5	6
13	5	3
14	5	3
15	6	6

$\chi^2 = 11.84$,
$P_{\chi^2} > 0.10$, 8 degrees of freedom.

More quantiles are used than in the previous two cases, because additional degrees of freedom beyond the customary three are used up in calculating residuals from a regression equation. In addition to a mean parameter, variance parameter, and the total frequency, we must deduct degrees of freedom used up in estimating the coefficients of the variables in the regression equation. We have four variables in (8.4.8); therefore, seven degrees of freedom are used up in the calculation of χ^2, and we selected more quantiles in order to have ultimately about as many degrees of freedom as before. The constant term in the regression equation takes the place of the estimates of the mean parameter.

We have not deducted two degrees of freedom for the estimated values of $\frac{\beta}{\alpha}$ and $\frac{\gamma}{\alpha}$ used in forming the combined variable on the left-hand side of (8.4.8). This is done because we argue that the samples giving rise to the distributions in Tables 8.1 and 8.2 are independent of the sample underlying the regression equation. In other words, we assume that log v_1 and log v_2 are independent of log u. Independence of normally distributed variables is shown by lack of correlation. Our samples show

$$r_{\log v_1 \log u} = 0.14$$

and

$$r_{\log v_2 \log u} = 0.28.$$

The second of these may be just significantly different from zero, but similar tests with samples in another year lead to lower estimates at 0.10 and 0.18 respectively.

Many more aspects, both economic and statistical, could be discussed in an elaborate treatment of the problem at hand, but the example as presented above does lay before the student an illustration of several principles taken up in this chapter. It shows a particular form in which an industry model is cast and the use of some institutional or technical facts about the industry in shaping the equations. Methods of cross section analysis—the study of underlying probability distributions, and the use of additional variables like average length of haul and freight composition to put each individual unit on as homogeneous a basis as possible—are revealed to the student.

Questions and Problems

1. Demonstrate that the usual marginal conditions derived from the production function used for the railroad industry model would not satisfy the conditions of profit maximization in an industry producing joint outputs under perfect competition.

2. Suppose you were given the problem of estimating cost functions for the railroad industry, total expenditures on cost as a function of ton-miles and passenger miles. How could this be determined from cross-section data? Are there any restrictions on other variables in order for a unique cross-section relation to exist between costs and the joint outputs?

3. Describe in detail how you would make a statistical test for the existence of increasing, constant, or decreasing returns to scale in the railroad industry.

4. List other variables you would consider useful in improving the estimated railroad model using cross-section data.

5. POOLING OF TIME SERIES AND CROSS-SECTION DATA

Interesting attempts have been made to combine both time series and cross-section samples to estimate the parameters in a single equation. The principal idea behind these attempts is the following: in a cross-section sample, price and other market variables are held constant. Estimate from the cross-section data the coefficients of variables that change from one individual to another. Substitute these estimates into the structural equation, and estimate the coefficients of price variables from a time series sample. Let us assume a demand equation of the form

$$x_{it} = \alpha_0 + \frac{\alpha_1 y_{it}}{p_{xt}} + \frac{\alpha_2 p_t}{p_{xt}} + u_{it}, \qquad \begin{array}{l} i = 1, 2, \ldots, N \\ t = 1, 2, \ldots, T, \end{array} \tag{8.5.1}$$

in which x = quantity demanded, y = money income, p_x = price of x, and p = general price level. In a cross-section sample at $t = t_0$, we have N joint observations on $p_{xt_0}x_{it_0}$ and y_{it_0} from which we estimate

$$p_{xt_0}x_{it_0} = a_0 + a_1 y_{it_0}. \tag{8.5.2}$$

On multiplying both sides of (8.5.1) by p_{xt} we get

$$p_{xt}x_{it} = \alpha_0 p_{xt} + \alpha_1 y_{it} + \alpha_2 p_t + p_{xt}u_{it}.$$

Because at $t = t_0$, p_{xt_0} and p_{t_0} are constants, we can interpret the coefficients in (8.5.2) as

$$\begin{aligned} a_0 &= \text{est. } (\alpha_0 p_{xt_0} + \alpha_2 p_{t_0}) \\ a_1 &= \text{est. } \alpha_1. \end{aligned}$$

The cross-section sample enables us to estimate the income coefficient in the structural demand equation, but not the price coefficient (unless $\alpha_0 = 0$). The regression of the new variable,

$$\frac{1}{N}\sum_{i=1}^{N} x_{it} - a_1 \frac{1}{N}\sum_{i=1}^{N} \frac{y_{it}}{p_{xt}},$$

on $\frac{p_t}{p_{xt}}$ is then formed to estimate the remaining parameters α_0 and α_2. The time series regression estimates of α_0 and α_2 should take account of the fact that α_1 is not known with certainty. It is estimated from cross-section data with error variance S_1^2. The formula for estimated variance of estimated α_2 is[21]

$$\frac{S_u^2}{TS_p^2} + \frac{S_y^2}{S_p^2} r_{yp}^2 S_1^2.$$

In this expression, S_p^2 is the sample variance of $\frac{p_t}{p_{xt}}$; S_y^2 is the sample variance of $\frac{1}{N}\sum_{i=1}^{N}\frac{y_{it}}{p_{xt}}$, r_{yp} is the correlation between $\frac{1}{N}\sum_{i=1}^{N}\frac{y_t}{p_{xt}}$ and $\frac{p_t}{p_{xt}}$; and Su^2 is the estimate of the residual variance of the time series relation. Thus the usual formula $\frac{Su^2}{TS_p^2}$ is corrected by a term reflecting the error associated with the estimate of α_1. If $r_{yp} = 0$, there is no correction.

A refinement is often introduced by using a nonlinear relation between $p_{xt_0}x_{it_0}$ and y_{it_0} that requires knowledge of additional characteristics of the income distribution in order to estimate the level of aggregate expenditures associated with each time series observation of aggregate income. If only one cross-section sample is available from which to estimate the income distribution, some arbitrary assumptions are usually made about the way the entire distribution changes through time as aggregate income changes.

A variation on the pooling problem for demand analysis arises in connection with the estimation of the *linear expenditure system*. The jth individual's demand for the ith commodity is expressed as

$$p_{it}x_{it}^j = \alpha_i p_{it} + \beta_i(y_t^j - \sum_{k=1}^{n} \alpha_k p_{kt}) + e_{it}^j.$$

It is assumed that the parameters $\alpha_1, \ldots, \alpha_n$ and β_i are the same for all individuals. This is the most general linear demand function satisfying

(i) homogeneity of degree zero in prices and income
(ii) Slutsky conditions on price effects
(iii) consumer budget identity

At the time it was discovered, Samuelson remarked that the α's could be considered as a "necessary" set of goods and that

$$y_t^j - \sum_{k=1}^{n} \alpha_k p_{kt}$$

could be considered as "supernumerary" income, over and above the necessary batch.[22]

[21] J. Durbin, "A Note on Regression when there is Extraneous Information about One of the Coefficients," *Journal of the American Statistical Association*, 48 (December, 1953), 799–808.

[22] The linear expenditure system was first introduced by L. R. Klein and H. Rubin, "A Constant-Utility Index of the Cost of Living," *The Review of Economic Studies*, XV (1947–48), 84–87, and commented on by P. A. Samuelson, "Some Implications of "Linearity", *The Review of Economic Studies*, XV (1947–48), 88–90.

An estimation procedure, derived from a suggestion in another context by R. Dayal, is to determine the α's as the "necessary" batch by reading them off empirical Engel curves from a cross-section sample.

$$p_{i_0} x^j_{it_0} = f_i(y^j_{t_0}) + u^j_{it_0}.$$

The Engel Curve f_i is calculated as a regression estimate obtained from cross-section data on expenditures and income. From *subsistence* income levels set by official welfare agencies or other professional bodies, we can estimate

$$\text{est } \alpha_i = \frac{\hat{f}_i(y_{t_0}(\text{min}))}{p_{it_0}}.$$

The statistical Engel curve is $\hat{f}_i$. The extrapolation of Engel curves to low levels of income should produce some negative expenditure estimates for luxury-type goods. In the *linear expenditure system*, this implies own-price elasticity greater than unity. If the estimated minimum expenditure is positive, own-price elasticity will be less than unity.

The Engel curve could be used to estimate the parameters β_i for the income effects, but the micro relationships in a cross-section may well be nonlinear. It is accordingly suggested that β_i be estimated from the time series regression of

$$(p_{it}x_{it} - \hat{\alpha}_i p_{it}) \quad \text{on} \quad (y_t - \sum_{k=1}^{n} \hat{\alpha}_k p_{kt})$$

subject to

$$\sum_{i=1}^{n} \beta_i = 1.$$

The linear time-series regression is between aggregate or per capita supernumerary expenditure and supernumerary income.

An interesting aspect of this approach is that it turns the pooling procedure around. Instead of estimating income effects from micro cross-section data and price effects from macro time-series data, it estimates the price effects from micro cross-section data and the income effects from macro time-series data.

The pooling principle is admirable, of course, going in the direction of enlarging our sources of basic information. But it does not, in practice, proceed on the basis of a systematic model showing which variables are endogenous, exogenous, or otherwise predetermined. Most applications are not properly formulated in terms of structural estimation. A formal outline of a more adequate model based on pooled data, a time sequence of aggregates, and cross-section samples, follows:

Let x^j_{it} = i^{th} endogenous variable of the jth individual in the tth period, $i = 1, 2, \ldots, G, \quad j = 1, 2, \ldots, N$.

y^j_{it} = i^{th} exogenous variable of the jth individual in the tth period, $i = 1, 2, \ldots, H, \quad j = 1, 2, \ldots, N$.

z_{it} = i^{th} endogenous market variable in the tth period, $i = 1, 2, \ldots, K$.

w_{it} = i^{th} exogenous market variable in the tth period, $i = 1, 2, \ldots, L$.

u^j_{it} = i^{th} random disturbance of the jth individual in the tth period, $i = 1, 2, \ldots, G, \quad j = 1, 2, \ldots, N$.

v^j_{it} = i^{th} random disturbance of the jth individual in the tth period, $i = 1, 2, \ldots, H, \quad j = 1, 2, \ldots, N$.

r_{it} = i^{th} random disturbance in the tth period, $i = 1, 2, \ldots, K$.

s_{it} = i^{th} random disturbance in the tth period, $i = 1, 2, \ldots, L$, $t = 1, 2, \ldots, T$.

The variables are related in four types of equations:

1. There are equations of individual behavior in which economic decisions are made about the x^j_{it} in terms of y^j_{it}, z_{it}, w_{it}. Individuals may, for example, decide about their types of expenditures given their income, prices, and autonomous government policies. Expenditures vary by individual and time; they are included in the x^j_{it}. Incomes similarly vary by individual and time, but each person's income may not be subject to his own decisions. This classification parallels conventional treatment of expenditure and income in the theory of consumer behavior. Individual income corresponds to y^j_{it}. Prices at the individual level are regarded as given variables to which people adjust their behavior, but prices are endogenous magnitudes influenced by the aggregate of individual behavior. This is the role assigned to z_{it} that vary in time, but are the same for all individuals. The w_{it} are more familiar exogenous variables; they are not directly influenced by individual action nor by action of the economy as a whole.

2. There are equations of individual behavior in which individual variables about which people do not make decisions, y^j_{it}, are related to z_{it} and w_{it}. For example, an individual's income is influenced by market prices and government tax policies. This block of equations must also take into account the interrelationships among the y^j_{it} as well as the influence of z_{it} and w_{it} on the y^j_{it}. Individual nondecision variables like age and sex are related to individual income as are prices and tax policies.

3. There are equations of market behavior in which aggregates of individual variables x^j_{it} and y^j_{it} are related to z_{it} and w_{it}. General equilibrium theory provides examples of the excess demand equations. On the one hand, there are equations representing the behavior of individual households and firms. These are covered in 1., but the aggregate of household demand and producer supply are related in market transactions involving prices and purely exogenous variables. These equations have the anonymity of not referring to the actions of any particular individual; therefore, aggregates, say sums, of the x^j_{it} and y^j_{it} may be involved in such equations.

4. Finally, there is a block of equations expressing the mechanism through

which exogenous variables w_{it} are determined. Usually the econometrician is not interested in estimating these equations. He tries to estimate the impact of exogenous variables on the system without trying to explain the exogenous variables themselves.

Greek capitals with Latin subscripts will be used to define matrices of constant coefficients.

$$A_y = \begin{Vmatrix} \alpha_{11} & \cdots & \alpha_{1H} \\ \alpha_{21} & \cdots & \alpha_{2H} \\ \vdots & & \vdots \\ \alpha_{G1} & \cdots & \alpha_{GH} \end{Vmatrix}.$$

Omission of a lower subscript will denote row vectors as

$$x_t^{j\prime} = (x_{1t}^j, \ldots, x_{Gt}^j)$$
$$y_t^{j\prime} = (y_{1t}^j, \ldots, y_{Ht}^j), \text{ etc.}$$

Writing our system in matrix notation, we shall be able to represent the right-hand side of the following equation by the simple matrix product on the left

$$A_y y_t^j = \begin{Vmatrix} \alpha_{11} y_{1t}^j + \alpha_{12} y_{2t}^j + \cdots + \alpha_{1H} y_{Ht}^j \\ \alpha_{21} y_{1t}^j + \alpha_{22} y_{2t}^j + \cdots + \alpha_{2H} y_{Ht}^j \\ \vdots \\ \alpha_{G1} y_{1t}^j + \alpha_{G2} y_{2t}^j + \cdots + \alpha_{GH} y_{Ht}^j \end{Vmatrix}.$$

The formal structure of a pooled linear model is

$$A_x x_t^j + A_y y_t^j + A_z z_t + A_w w_t = u_t^j, \tag{8.5.3}$$

$$B_y y_t^j + B_z z_t + B_w w_t = v_t^j, \tag{8.5.4}$$

$$\Gamma_x\left(\sum_{j=1}^N x_t^j\right) + \Gamma_y\left(\sum_{j=1}^N y_t^j\right) + \Gamma_z z_t + \Gamma_w w_t = r_t, \tag{8.5.5}$$

$$\Delta_w w_t = s_t. \tag{8.5.6}$$

These are the four types discussed and exemplified above.

Aggregative analysis proceeds by summing (8.5.3) and (8.5.4) over all individuals. The equations will involve the same types of variables as those which occur in (8.5.5), and a complete system based on time series aggregates is obtained. Aggregative forms of (8.5.3)–(8.5.4) are the equations of producer and consumer behavior in macroeconomic models, and (8.5.5) attempts to explain market prices and such phenomena.

In a pure cross-section sample, $t = t_0$, we assign constant values to z_t and w_t in (8.5.3)–(8.5.4), and estimate A_x, A_y, and B_y. In current applications of pooling, A_x, A_y, and B_y are first estimated from a cross-section sample. The estimates are substituted in the system, and A_z, A_w, B_z, and B_w are estimated from time series observations. The most general, but complex, approach would be to form the joint probability distribution of x_t^j, y_t^j, z_t, given w_t. This distribution will depend on the unknown parameters, and estimation equations based on sample observations can be derived by the principle of maximum likelihood or some other method of estimation.

The correspondence between individual and aggregative equations in the model (8.5.3)–(8.5.5) is very simple, of course, because the equations have been assumed to be linear with constant coefficients. In more general systems, the aggregation of individual equations is considerably more difficult.

The model (8.5.3)–(8.5.5) is very general, except for the fact that it is presented in static form. Some econometricians have, however, tried to specify the error structure of single equations in (8.5.3) so as to make the estimation problem more tractable.[23] The error term u_t^j for a given single equation (i fixed) is split into components

$$u_t^j = \mu^j + v_t^j$$
$$u' = (u_{11}, u_{12}, \ldots, u_{1T}, \ldots, u_{N1}, u_{N2}, \ldots, u_{NT})$$

a separate individual effect and a residual (joint) effect. This is like our specification in (8.3.7) of a parameter that is constant in time but variable over individuals. We dealt there, however, with only one cross-section or, in (8.3.7″), with two cross-sections. In a more general specification, we assume

$$\begin{aligned} E\,\mu^j v_t^j &= 0 \qquad \text{for all } j, t \\ E\,v_t^j v_{t'}^{j'} &= 0 \qquad \text{if } j \neq j', t \neq t' \\ E\,\mu^j \mu^{j'} &= 0 \qquad \text{if } j \neq j'. \end{aligned}$$

The covariance matrix of error is thus

$$E\,uu' = \Sigma = \sigma_u^2 \begin{Vmatrix} \Omega & 0 & \cdots & 0 \\ 0 & \Omega & \cdots & 0 \\ \cdot & & & \cdot \\ \cdot & & & \cdot \\ \cdot & & & \cdot \\ 0 & 0 & \cdots & \Omega \end{Vmatrix},$$

[23] P. Balestra and M. Nerlove, "Pooling Cross Section and Time Series Data in the Estimation of a Dynamic Model: The Demand for Natural Gas," *Econometrica*, 34 (July, 1966), 585–612.

where

$$E\,u^j u^{j\prime} = \sigma_u^2 \Omega = \sigma_u^2 \begin{Vmatrix} 1 & \rho & \cdots & \rho \\ \rho & 1 & \cdots & \rho \\ \cdot & \cdot & & \cdot \\ \cdot & \cdot & & \cdot \\ \cdot & \cdot & & \cdot \\ \rho & \rho & \cdots & 1 \end{Vmatrix}$$

and

$$\sigma_u^2 = \sigma_\mu^2 + \sigma_\nu^2$$

$$\rho = \frac{\sigma_\mu^2}{\sigma_u^2}.$$

In the single equation case, an Aitken estimator of coefficients in a linear equation can be computed if Σ is known or if it can be estimated. It depends on the parameter ρ. If there are no lagged variables in the single equation being estimated, a preliminary least squares regression estimate of the coefficients will enable us to calculate residuals $(\text{res})_t^j$. The variance parameters, unadjusted for degrees of freedom, would be given by

$$\text{est}\,\sigma_u^2 = \frac{\sum_{j=1}^{N}\sum_{t=1}^{T}[(\text{res.})_t^j]^2}{TN}$$

$$\text{est}\,\rho = \frac{\sum_{j=1}^{N}\left\{\left[\sum_{t=1}^{T}(\text{res.})_t^j\right]^2 - \sum_{t=1}^{T}[(\text{res.})_t^j]^2\right\}}{T\sum_{j=1}^{N}\sum_{t=1}^{T}[(\text{res.})_t^j]^2}.$$

An estimate of Σ can be obtained from estimates of σ_u^2 and ρ; this estimate of Σ can then be used to form an Aitken estimator. In the case where lagged dependent variables are among the explanatory set, however, the first step should not be made in the ordinary way from least squares regression because it will not provide consistent estimates. This is so because lagged values of dependent variables will not be independent of μ^j, the individual effects in the composite error term. In this case, instrumental variables that are independent of both μ^j and ν_t^j may be used for computing initial consistent estimates of σ_u^2 and ρ. These may then be used in the same way as above to form an Aitken estimator using est. Σ.

Questions and Problems

1. The size of the interest-elasticity of personal savings has become a controversial issue in business cycle theory. Can cross-section data on individual households be used to estimate the effect of interest rates on savings? Can a

pooling scheme be devised to assist the measurement of the interest effect on savings?

2. Suppose the expenditure-income relation for a particular commodity to be nonlinear. Describe the data needed to estimate the income parameters from cross-section data and the price parameters from time series data. Show explicit formulas for pooling the two types of data when the income effect is nonlinear.

3. Cite examples from economic theory, or other sources, of each type of equation (8.5.3), (8.5.4), (8.5.5), and (8.5.6). Indicate the detailed variables and economic units involved in each equation.

SUGGESTED READINGS

Arrow, K. J., Chenery, H. B., Minhas, B., and Solow, R. M., "Capital-Labor Substitution and Economic Efficiency," *Review of Economics and Statistics*, XLIII (August, 1961), 225–50. An original derivation and presentation of the class of CES production functions.

Balestra, P., and Nerlove, M., "Pooling Cross Section and Time Series Data in the Estimation of a Dynamic Model: The Demand for Natural Gas," *Econometrica*, 34 (July, 1966), 585–612. Develops new and generalized methods for dealing with the pooling problem.

Durbin, J., "A Note on Regression when there is Extraneous Information about One of the Coefficients," *Journal of the American Statistical Association*, 48 (December, 1953), 799–808. Calculates the effect of error in cross-section estimates on error of time series estimates in the pooling problem.

Girshick, M. A., and Haavelmo, T., "Statistical Analysis of the Demand for Food: Examples of Simultaneous Estimation of Structural Equations," *Econometrica*, 15 (1947), 79–110. An interesting study of a sector of the economy and a useful example of grafting techniques.

Haavelmo, T., "Family Expenditures and the Marginal Propensity to Consume," *Econometrica*, 15 (1947), 335–41. A penetrating article on the relationship between estimates of the same equation from cross-section and time series data.

Hurwicz, L., "Systems with Nonadditive Disturbances," *Statistical Inference in Dynamic Economic Models*, ed. T. Koopmans (New York: John Wiley & Sons, 1950). Statement of problems involved in estimating equations for which the random disturbances are not merely added. Considers several examples of linear systems with parameter coefficients taken as random variables.

Kisselgoff, A., "Factors Affecting the Demand for Consumer Installment Sales Credit," National Bureau of Economic Research, Technical Paper 7 (New York, 1951). A study of installment credit demand containing models of this sector of the economy. An interesting application of grafting techniques.

Leontief, W. W., *The Structure of the American Economy, 1919–1929*, 2nd ed., enlarged (New York: Oxford University Press, 1951). Description of input-output models with empirical tables, containing interesting applications and developments of the techniques.

Marschak, J., "Money Illusion and Demand Analysis," *The Review of Economic Statistics*, XXV (1943), 40–48. One of the original treatments of pooled samples of time series and cross-section data.

Nerlove, M., *Estimation and Identification of Cobb-Douglas Production Functions.* (Chicago: Rand McNally & Co., 1965). A careful statement of econometric models of the firm subject to a Cobb-Douglas technology.

Rubin, H., "Note on Random Coefficients," *Statistical Inference in Dynamic Economic Models*, ed. T. Koopmans (New York: John Wiley & Sons, 1950). Derives maximum-likelihood estimates of single equations, linear with random coefficients.

Staehle, H., "Relative Prices and Postwar Markets for Animal Food Products," *The Quarterly Journal of Economics,* LIX (1944–45), 237–79. Contains interesting examples of estimated demand equations from pooled samples of time series and cross-section data.

Tobin, J., "A Statistical Demand Function for Food in the U.S.A.," *Journal of the Royal Statistical Society*, CXIII, Series A, General, Part II (1950), 113–41. Estimates an equation of food demand from both time series and cross-section data.

9

Special Problems of Econometrics

1. ERRORS OF OBSERVATION AND MEASUREMENT

The main lines of development of econometrics and its applications have been set out in the preceding chapters. Let us now consider a number of special problems, most of which are not fully resolved and leave room for new research. One of the more urgent and interesting problems that we have hitherto consciously avoided is that of observation error.

Anyone who has worked intimately with economic data, especially one who has been engaged in the collection of primary data at the source, cannot avoid being impressed with the presence of observation error. In a double entry bookkeeping system, for example, all accounts are designed so as to achieve balances between receipt and expenditure totals or asset and liability totals. But if all components of the accounts are measured from independent sets of data, we usually find a lack of balance. An important accounting balance or identity derivable from a double entry bookkeeping system and used in macroeconomic models is

$$C + I + G + B = W + P + T, \tag{9.1.1}$$

in which

C = consumer expenditures
I = investment expenditures
G = government expenditures
B = net foreign balance
W = wage payments
P = nonwage payments
T = indirect taxes, less subsidies.

TABLE 9.1

Statistical Discrepancy in the National Accounts of the United States (*Billions of Dollars*)

Year	*Gross national product*	*Statistical discrepancy*
1929	103.1	0.7
1930	90.4	−0.8
1931	75.8	0.7
1932	58.0	0.3
1933	55.6	0.6
1934	65.1	0.5
1935	72.2	−0.2
1936	82.5	1.2
1937	90.4	0.0
1938	84.7	0.6
1939	90.5	1.3
1940	99.7	1.0
1941	124.5	0.4
1942	157.9	−1.1
1943	191.6	−2.0
1944	210.1	2.5
1945	211.9	3.9
1946	208.5	0.1
1947	231.3	0.9
1948	257.6	−2.0
1949	256.5	0.3
1950	284.8	1.5
1951	328.4	3.3
1952	345.5	2.2
1953	364.6	3.0
1954	364.8	2.7
1955	398.0	2.1
1956	419.2	−1.1
1957	441.1	0.0
1958	447.3	1.6
1959	483.7	−0.8
1960	503.7	−1.0
1961	520.1	−0.8
1962	560.3	0.5
1963	590.5	−0.3
1964	632.4	−1.3
1965	684.9	−3.1
1966	747.6	−3.3
1967	793.5	−1.0
1968	865.7	−2.5

If separate data are collected from independent sources for the determination of each of the seven items (retail sales statistics used to estimate C, government budgetary data used to estimate G and T, foreign trade statistics used to estimate B, sample surveys of self employed persons and payroll statistics used to estimate W, and business and financial reports used to estimate P and I), we will find that the two sides of (9.1.1) are not equal, except by chance. This lack of balance in the national accounts of the United States is called the "statistical discrepancy." Its magnitude in recent years is given in the accompanying table.

Hopefully, an error series like this is a random series, but statistical tests of the time series of discrepancy measurements show a significant departure from randomness.[1] The resulting series cannot easily be described in systematic terms, but it does not behave like a random series. The long run of negative values since 1959 is a serious departure from randomness in itself. There is a slight amount of serial correlation in the discrepancy, and significant correlation with exports, government expenditures, and inventory valuation adjustment. There is no significant departure from normality in the frequency distribution.

In absolute value, the statistical discrepancy is substantial in many years, substantial in terms of the number of man-hours of employment or real goods represented by the dollar total. In percentage terms, it reaches an amount approximately 2 percent of gross national product at the extreme. The absolute size of the discrepancy in recent years, although not a large percentage of GNP, is still big enough to obscure the direction of movement of the economy in the short run, say one quarter's movement, or to throw a budget surplus into deficit.

Absolute checks, like those implied by a double entry accounting system, can be made for many statistical series used in econometric studies. In addition, data collectors are well aware of the existence of numerous other errors in the preparation of their results.

Our econometric analysis of preceding chapters has been developed as though we had exact measurements of the magnitudes used in our models. However, when we denote some variable by the simple notation x, we cover up the question of whether the observation has been accurate. More explicit attention would be called to the possibility of measurement error if we were to write, instead,

$$x = (\eta, d), \tag{9.1.2}$$

in which

$x =$ observed value
$\eta =$ *true* value of x
$d =$ error (discrepancy) of measurement.

[1] F. G. Adams and P. E. de Janosi, "On the Statistical Discrepancy in *the Revised* U.S. National Accounts," *Journal of the American Statistical Association*, 61 (December, 1966), 1219–29.

In practical applications (9.1.2) is usually written as

$$x = \eta + d. \tag{9.1.3}$$

Sometimes the expressions *true value* and *error* are replaced by *systematic* and *variable* parts.

An interesting historical aspect of the measurement error formulation is that this scheme originally formed the basis for entry of stochastic or probabilistic elements into econometric models. Econometrics grew from the following type of model:

$$x_t = \eta_t + d_t \tag{9.1.4}$$

$$y_t = \xi_t + e_t \tag{9.1.5}$$

$$\xi_t = \alpha + \beta\eta_t. \tag{9.1.6}$$

The observed variables x_t and y_t were assumed to deviate from true values η_t and ξ_t by the amounts of the random errors d_t and e_t. The true values were further assumed to be *exactly* related by the linear structural equation (9.1.6). The joint probability distribution of d_t and e_t was made to depend on α and β, the unknown parameters, that were then estimated as functions of the sample observations x_t and y_t.

The implications of the older econometric approach are that economic variables are related in exact equations except for errors of measurement. If we could only improve our accuracy of observation, we would find exact, non-probabilistic relations connecting the relevant economic magnitudes. By way of contrast, the more recent approach is to assume that even if all variables could be precisely measured, econometric equations would not be exact. No matter how detailed and complex we try to make our equations we shall find that many variables have not been explicitly taken into account. It is considered to be an inevitable consequence of trying to describe human behavior that we must have resort to stochastic models; this apart from all observation error.

As we shall see below, stochastic models of observation error raise intractable difficulties for statistical inference. Statistical techniques associated with models in which the errors arise from behavior disturbance rather than measurement discrepancy are more straightforward and well defined. This is perhaps one reason, although not justifiable in itself, why emphasis has shifted from the older to the newer type model. For want of better terms we shall call one, the *errors in variables* model, and the other, the *errors in equations* model. Eventually, we must consider the joint model with both types of errors, but the formal statistical difficulties are even greater in this case.

Although most modern work in econometrics has been associated with the errors in equations model, an interesting return to the structure of the errors in variables model is provided by the permanent income hypothesis.[2] According

[2] M. Friedman, *A Theory of the Consumption Function* (Princeton: Princeton University Press, 1957).

to that theory, *measured* consumption and *measured* income are each composed of a *permanent* and a *transitory* component.

$$C = C_p + C_t$$
$$Y = Y_p + Y_t.$$

The transitory components are treated formally as observation errors; they are independent of the permanent components and of each other. The analogy is completed by the assumption that the permanent components are proportional

$$C_p = kY_p.$$

The three equations of the permanent income hypothesis correspond to (9.1.4)–(9.1.6) of the errors in variables model.

From the standard assumption about independence between systematic and error components and also an assumption that the errors are independent of each other, we have

$$E(Y_p Y_t) = E(Y_p C_t) = E(C_t Y_t) = 0.$$

This leads to interpretation of the OLS regression coefficient of C on Y as

$$\beta = \frac{E(CY)}{EY^2} = \frac{E[(kY_p + C_t)(Y_p + Y_t)]}{EY^2}$$
$$= \frac{kEY_p^2}{EY^2} = kP_y$$

where $P_y < 1$. The ratio of the variance of permanent to total (measured) income is less than one, and this biases the OLS regression estimate (C on Y) below the true coefficient k.

Another example in recent econometrics is provided by one of the interpretations for estimation of the distributed lag relation of Chap. 3.

$$y_t = \alpha \sum_{i=0}^{\infty} \lambda^i x_{t-i} + e_t.$$

This equation transforms to

$$y_t = \alpha x_t + \lambda y_{t-1} + e_t - \lambda e_{t-1}$$

or

$$y_t - e_t = \alpha x_t + \lambda(y_{t-1} - e_{t-1}).$$

In this form we see that y_t is measured with error e_t and y_{t-1} with error e_{t-1}. The variable x_t is assumed to be measured without error.

A system of m linear equations in the n variables $x_t (n > m)$ takes the following three forms, depending on whether we assume errors in the variables, errors in the equations, or both types of error simultaneously:

$$\sum_{j=i}^{n} \alpha_{ij}(x_{jt} - d_{jt}) = 0, \qquad i = 1, 2, \ldots, m, \tag{9.1.7}$$

$$\sum_{j=i}^{n} \alpha_{ij}x_{jt} = u_{it}, \qquad i = 1, 2, \ldots, m, \tag{9.1.8}$$

$$\sum_{j=1}^{n} \alpha_{ij}(x_{jt} - d_{jt}) = u_{it}, \qquad i = 1, 2, \ldots, m,. \tag{9.1.9}$$

We have already made extensive investigation of (9.1.8) and will consider in this chapter (9.1.7) and (9.1.9).

The problems raised by the errors in variables model can be brought out clearly in the simplest case as outlined in (9.1.4)–(9.1.6). We have two variables, subject to observation error and related by a linear structural equation. In one approach the true variables η_t and ξ_t are regarded simply as a set of population means, the expected values of x_t and y_t. They are not random variables. They comprise, in the model being considered, a set of $2T$ unobserved parameter values ($t = 1, 2, \ldots, T$). The other parameters we desire to estimate are $E(d_t)^2$, $E(e_t)^2$, $E(d_te_t)$, α and β. Without any loss of generality, we assume

$$E(d_t) = 0,$$
$$E(e_t) = 0.$$

It is instructive to ask whether all these unknown parameters can be estimated from moments of degree no higher than two of sample observations alone. We consider no moments above the second order moments because of the analogy with the normal distribution that is specified completely by first and second order moments.

From the definitions of x and y in (9.1.4)–(9.1.5), we compute

$$E(x) = \eta, \tag{9.1.10}$$

$$E(y) = \xi, \tag{9.1.11}$$

$$E(x)^2 = \eta^2 + E(d)^2, \tag{9.1.12}$$

$$E(y)^2 = \xi^2 + E(e)^2, \tag{9.1.13}$$

$$E(xy) = \eta\xi + E(de). \tag{9.1.14}$$

The time subscript may be omitted because all variables refer to the same time point and all relevant distributions are assumed to remain invariant over time. In making inferences from observed data, we replace expected values by sample estimates; therefore

$$\text{est. } E(x) = \frac{1}{T}\sum_{t=1}^{T} x_t,$$

$$\text{est. } E(y) = \frac{1}{T}\sum_{t=1}^{T} y_t,$$

$$\text{est. } E(x)^2 = \frac{1}{T}\sum_{t=1}^{T} x_t^2,$$

$$\text{est. } E(y)^2 = \frac{1}{T}\sum_{t=1}^{T} y_t^2,$$

$$\text{est. } E(xy) = \frac{1}{T}\sum_{t=1}^{T} x_t y_t.$$

From the linear structural relation

$$\xi = \alpha + \beta\eta,$$

we can write

$$E(y) = \alpha + \beta E(x). \tag{9.1.15}$$

Equation (9.1.15) will be recognized as the condition that the structural equation be satisfied by the mean values of y and x. As in all the other methods of parameter estimation we have considered in this volume, we first estimate β, the slope coefficient, and then use this estimate and the sample means to estimate α in (9.1.15). Elimination of ξ and η from (9.1.10)–(9.1.14) and the linear structural equation leads to the system of two equations

$$E(y)^2 = \alpha^2 + 2\alpha\beta E(x) + \beta^2[E(x)^2 - E(d)^2] + E(e)^2, \tag{9.1.16}$$

$$E(xy) = \alpha E(x) + \beta[E(x)^2 - E(d)^2] + E(de). \tag{9.1.17}$$

The three Eqs. (9.1.15)–(9.1.17) are not sufficient to estimate the five unknown parameters α, β, $E(d)^2$, $E(e)^2$, and $E(ed)$. Even if we assume no correlation between e and d as is often done, we still find too few equations developed from second and first order moments alone to estimate all the unknown parameters.

Many authors have attempted to solve the problem of estimating the linear structural relation between two variables, both subject to error. In every case the proposed solutions add something new to the underlying assumptions in order to obtain definite results. It is clearly accepted that the problem as posed above is not soluble. From the point of view of least squares theory, we may look at the problem in the following way:

Model I. The variable (X) alone is measured without error,

$$d = 0 \quad \text{or} \quad x = \eta.$$

The linear structural relation is

$$\xi = \alpha + \beta\eta$$

$$y - e = \alpha + \beta x.$$

The parameters are estimated by the least squares principle

$$\sum_{t=1}^{T} e_t^2 = \sum_{t=1}^{T} (y - \alpha - \beta x_t)^2 = \text{min}.$$

The result is obviously the simple regression of y on x. In terms of a statistical scatter of sample points in the xy plane, this amounts to finding the line of relationship between the two variables that makes the sum of the squared vertical deviations a minimum.

Distances like that from point A (Fig. 9.1.1) to the line are minimized in the square.

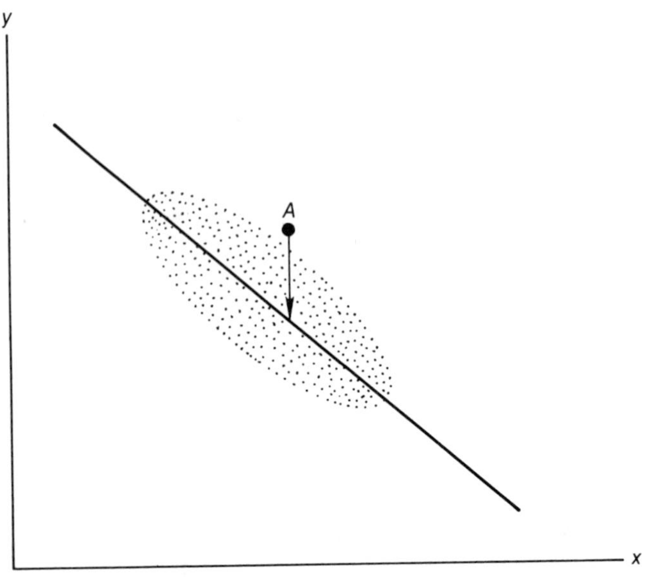

Figure 9.1.1

Model II. The Variable Y alone is measured without error

$$e = 0 \quad \text{or} \quad y = \xi.$$

The linear structural relation is

$$\xi = \alpha + \beta\eta$$
$$y = \alpha + \beta(x - d)$$
$$x = -\frac{\alpha}{\beta} + \frac{1}{\beta}y + d.$$

The parameters are estimated by the least squares principle

$$\sum_{t=1}^{T} (d_t)^2 = \sum_{t=1}^{T} \left(x_t + \frac{\alpha}{\beta} - \frac{1}{\beta} y_t\right)^2 = \text{min.}$$

The result of this minimization is the regression of x on y. Geometrically, it is equivalent to finding the line of relationship between the two variables that makes the sum of squared horizontal deviations a minimum.

In Fig. 9.1.2, the distance from B to the line is a typical horizontal devia-

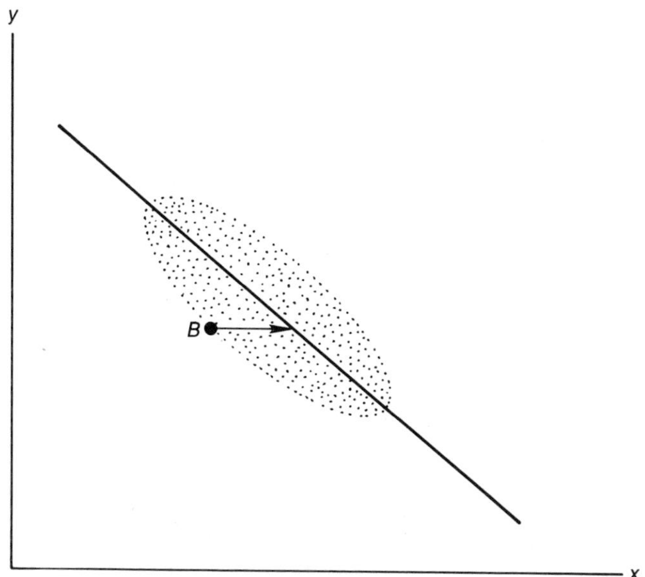

Figure 9.1.2

tion. For the same scatter of points, minimization in the horizontal direction leads to a different estimated line from minimization in the vertical direction.

The treatment of the two special cases in which only one variable is subject to error is clear according to least squares theory. In practice we seldom find these special features prevailing however.[3]

Instead of minimizing either vertical or horizontal deviations of scattered

[3] In the exceptional case in which we are fitting polynomial or other trends to single variables, we do have a situation in which only one variable is subject to error. For example:

$$x_t = \alpha_0 + \alpha_1 t + \alpha_2 t^2 + \cdots + \alpha_n t^n + d_t$$

is the correct model for fitting a polynomial time trend to x_t, where d_t is the measurement error of x_t. The least squares regression of x_t on $t, t^2, \ldots, t^n$ provides a highly desirable estimate of the unknown equation.

sample points about a line of relationship, we might consider minimizing perpendicular (orthogonal) deviations, such as the deviation from point C to the line in Fig. 9.1.3.

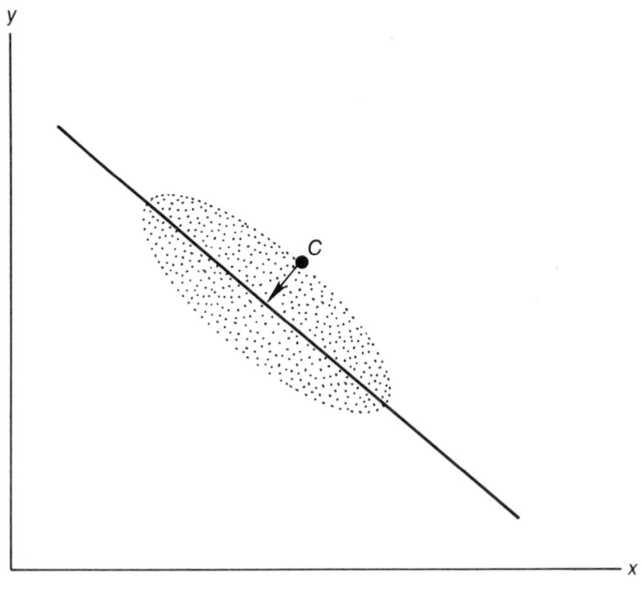

Figure 9.1.3

The orthogonal regression (Fig. 9.1.3) is arbitrary, as are either of the simple regressions (Fig. 9.1.1 and Fig. 9.1.2) when more than one variable is subject to error. We can consider each of these three special regressions as obtained by the selection of a particular direction of error minimization. Associated with each direction is an implicit assumption about the relative importance of the different errors. In the two standard least squares regressions of Models I and II, we actually assume that one variable contains all the error and that its relative importance is consequently infinite. This assumption defines a clear direction of minimization, but it is obviously inapplicable to situations in which a single variable's error does not have infinite relative importance. The orthogonal regression assumes equal relative importance of all errors. The sense in which this assumption is implied will be demonstrated below, but this does not mean that the orthogonal regression cannot be computed unless we have equal relative importance of errors, just as we are not prohibited from making ordinary least squares calculations when the assumption that one variable contains all the error is not met. It is simply that the estimates can be shown to have nice properties when the direction of minimization is appropriately associated with the relative importance of error. We should point out that a criticism has been raised against the orthogonal regression in the present context. It can be shown that the results obtained by minimizing perpendicular deviations are not invariant under a change of scale. That is to say, if we measure the variables in one set of units and calculate the corresponding orthogonal regression, we shall obtain essentially different numerical estimates than if we measure variables in another set of units and calculate the corresponding orthogonal regression.

From the point of view of choosing a direction of minimization appropriate to relative importance of errors, we can see how to obtain a solution to the set of equations (9.1.15)–(9.1.17) that we previously found insoluble. Let us impose two conditions on the variances and covariances of error,

$$E(de) = 0. \tag{9.1.18}$$

$$E(e)^2 = kE(d)^2. \tag{9.1.19}$$

According to these conditions, the errors e and d are mutually independent and the variance of e is k times the variance of d. The ratio of variances, k, is a known coefficient. Equations (9.1.15)–(9.1.17) are now three in number with only three unknown parameters $[\alpha, \beta, E(d)^2]$ if we substitute the conditions in (9.1.18) and (9.1.19). The ratio of variances, k, is said to represent the relative importance of errors in x and y. In effect, we choose a direction of minimization depending on the size of k. If $k = \infty$ we obtain the regression in Model I; if $k = 0$ we obtain the regression in Model II, and if $k = 1$ we obtain the orthogonal regression.

It is not necessary to assume the different errors to be mutually independent. An alternative assumption would be

$$E(de) = k'E(d)^2. \tag{9.1.20}$$

More generally, we can assume all elements of the variance-covariance matrix of errors to be in some known proportion to a single parameter. In our model with only two variables, this can be expressed as

$$\begin{Vmatrix} E(d)^2 & E(de) \\ E(de) & E(e)^2 \end{Vmatrix} = \begin{Vmatrix} k_{11}\sigma^2 & k_{12}\sigma^2 \\ k_{12}\sigma^2 & k_{22}\sigma^2 \end{Vmatrix} = \sigma^2 \begin{Vmatrix} k_{11} & k_{12} \\ k_{12} & k_{22} \end{Vmatrix}.$$

The k_{ij} are known constants and σ^2 is an unknown parameter.

If we replace mathematical expectations with sample moments in terms of deviations from means and substitute (9.1.18)–(9.1.19) into (9.1.15)–(9.1.17), we find that the resulting equation for the estimation of β is (9.1.21)

$$\beta^2 m_{xy} + \beta(km_{xx} - m_{yy}) - km_{xy} = 0. \tag{9.1.21}$$

The definitions of the moments are

$$m_{xy} = \sum_{t=1}^{T} (x_t - \bar{x})(y_t - \bar{y}),$$

$$m_{xx} = \sum_{t=1}^{T} (x_t - \bar{x})^2,$$

$$m_{yy} = \sum_{t=1}^{T} (y_t - \bar{y})^2.$$

There are two roots of the quadratic equation in (9.1.21)

$$\frac{m_{yy} - km_{xx} + \sqrt{(m_{yy} - km_{xx})^2 + 4km_{xy}^2}}{2m_{xy}},$$

$$\frac{m_{yy} - km_{xx} - \sqrt{(m_{yy} - km_{xx})^2 + 4km_{xy}^2}}{2m_{xy}}.$$

Where $k = 1$, these reduce to the expressions for the orthogonal regression. This fact gives meaning to the assertion above that the method of orthogonal regression implicitly assumes equal relative importance of errors. We choose the particular solution that minimizes the sum of squared deviations in the chosen direction from the line of relationship. Inspection of the two expressions shows which value to choose. If the correlation between x and y is positive ($m_{xy} > 0$), the first root is appropriate because it gives a positive estimate of β. Similarly, if $m_{xy} < 0$, the first root gives a negative estimate of β. Equation (9.1.21) is immediately recognized as being close to the quadratic equation of the geometric lag distribution estimate of Chap. 3. The latter is the minimization of the sums of squares

$$\Sigma e_t^2 + \Sigma e_{t-1}^2,$$

corresponding to the equation

$$y_t - e_t = \alpha x_t + \lambda(y_{t-1} - e_{t-1})$$

where it is assumed that

$$\text{var } e_{t-1} = \text{var } e_t,$$

in other words that $k = 1$. The principal difference in the lag distribution case is that x_t is assumed to be measured without error. This difference can be handled below, however, when the errors in variable model is generalized to a multivariate relationship.

The problem can easily be given a direct formulation as a least squares problem. The sum of squares to be minimized is

$$\begin{aligned} S &= \frac{1}{\sigma_d^2}\sum_{t=1}^{T} d_t^2 + \frac{1}{\sigma_e^2}\sum_{t=1}^{T} e_t^2, \\ &= \frac{1}{\sigma_d^2}\sum_{t=1}^{T}(x_t - \eta_t)^2 + \frac{1}{\sigma_e^2}\sum_{t=1}^{T}(y_t - \xi_t)^2. \end{aligned} \tag{9.1.22}$$

We have used the customary notation $E(z)^2 = \sigma_z^2$. The linear structural relation imposes a constraint on the minimization process; therefore we may write out the criterion more fully as

$$S = \text{min.}$$

subject to

$$\begin{aligned} \xi_t &= a + \beta\eta_t, \\ \sigma_e^2 &= k\sigma_d^2. \end{aligned}$$

The unknowns, with respect to which we minimize, are $\xi_t, \eta_t, \alpha, \beta, \sigma_d^2$. The result leads to equation (9.1.21) for the estimation of β and

$$\bar{y} = \alpha + \beta\bar{x} \tag{9.1.23}$$

for the estimation of α. The variance parameter is estimated as

$$\text{est. } \sigma_d^2 = \frac{1}{T(\hat{\beta}^2 + k)}\sum_{t=1}^{T}(y_t - \hat{\alpha} - \hat{\beta}x_t)^2, \tag{9.1.24}$$

where $\hat{\alpha}$ and $\hat{\beta}$ are the estimates of α and β. The mean sum of squares in (9.1.24) is proportional to the mean sum of squares of the residuals from the fitted equation. We are not interested in the estimates of the true values ξ_t and η_t.

A well-known formula from analytic geometry gives the perpendicular distance of the point (y_t, x_t) from the line

$$\alpha_1 y_t + \alpha_2 x_t + \alpha_0 = 0$$

as the absolute value of

$$\frac{\alpha_1 y_t + \alpha_2 x_t + \alpha_0}{\sqrt{\alpha_1^2 + \alpha_2^2}}.$$

The application of this formula to the minimization of the squared perpendicular distance of sample points from the structural relationship gives the orthogonal regression as the solution of

$$\sum_{t=1}^{T}\frac{(y_t - \alpha - \beta x_t)^2}{(1 + \beta^2)} = \text{min.}$$

This is the same thing as minimization of the expression in (9.1.24) with $k = 1$.

By assuming the ratio of variances to be known, we are in a position to give a meaningful interpretation of the variance of residuals. Without knowing this ratio or something else in the assumptions of the problem, we would not have a convenient unit of measurement for the variances of error. This can be seen in the following way:
The linear structural equation

$$\xi_t = \alpha + \beta\eta_t$$

can be rewritten as

$$\begin{aligned} y_t - e_t &= \alpha + \beta(x_t - d_t) \\ y_t &= \alpha + \beta x_t - \beta d_t + e_t. \end{aligned}$$

The variance of residuals from an estimated equation is

$$\frac{1}{T}\sum_{t=1}^{T}(y_t - \hat{\alpha} - \hat{\beta}x_t)^2$$

that is an estimate of

$$\beta^2\sigma_d^2 + \sigma_e^2.$$

We do not know how to apportion this combined variance among the separate variances, σ_d^2 and σ_e^2. Additional information of the form

$$\sigma_e^2 = k\sigma_d^2$$

enables us to make the apportionment and interpret the final result

$$\frac{1}{T(\hat{\beta}^2 + k)}\sum_{t=1}^{T}(y_t - \hat{\alpha} - \hat{\beta}x_t)^2$$

as a quantity measured in the units of d. For these reasons we do not attempt to minimize the constrained sum of squares, S, with respect to σ_d^2 and σ_e^2 as separate unknowns.

We were able to express the problem as the minimization of a sum of squares, only by assuming

$$E(de) = 0.$$

More generally, we may formulate the problem as the minimization of a quadratic form

$$Q = \sigma^{dd}\sum_{t=1}^{T}(x_t - \eta_t)^2 + 2\sigma^{de}\sum_{t=1}^{T}(x_t - \eta_t)(y_t - \xi_t) + \sigma^{ee}\sum_{t=1}^{T}(y_t - \xi_t)^2 \tag{9.1.25}$$

subject to

$$\xi_t = \alpha + \beta\eta_t.$$

where

$$\begin{Vmatrix} \sigma_{dd} & \sigma_{de} \\ \sigma_{de} & \sigma_{ee} \end{Vmatrix} = \sigma^2 \begin{Vmatrix} k_{11} & k_{12} \\ k_{12} & k_{22} \end{Vmatrix},$$

$$\begin{Vmatrix} \sigma_{dd} & \sigma_{de} \\ \sigma_{de} & \sigma_{ee} \end{Vmatrix}^{-1} = \begin{Vmatrix} \sigma^{dd} & \sigma^{de} \\ \sigma^{de} & \sigma^{ee} \end{Vmatrix}.$$

In order to apply these methods that are called methods of weighted regression, we have to know the ratios of error variances (covariances zero), or even the elements of the variance-covariance matrix of errors, apart from a factor of proportionality.[4] Without introducing additional assumptions or without knowing these properties of variances and covariances, we cannot estimate simultaneously from our sample observations, both the parameters of the linear structural equation and the unknown variance-covariance matrix. It must be stressed that in order to perform the necessary computations we have to know certain properties of the variances and covariances of errors in advance, from information outside our sample.

The most frequent situation is that we do not know much about the variance-covariance matrix in advance. In some cases in which new independent samples are repeatedly collected, we can build up some experience about the relative magnitudes of variances and covariances. In other cases the original data collectors may be able to provide rough a priori information. In social accounting schemes, it is usually possible to list a ranking of items by relative accuracy. We should be able to state that such items as government receipts and expenditures, wage payments, outlays on plant and equipment, consumer expenditures, depreciation charges, and value of inventory change represent a hierachy of accuracy from the most to the least reliable. This rough type of information is, however, as much as we do have in advance, and insofar as estimates of structural parameters are sensitive to small changes in the values of assumed relative accuracies, we are not in a good position to apply the methods just developed.

It has been proposed that the sample data be used twice, first to estimate error variances and then to estimate parameters of the linear structural relation. This is not a recommended statistical procedure, but we can present its essence briefly. Each variable is assumed to be expressible as a smooth function of time plus an error of measurement. In particular, the theory is simplest and most directly applicable if the smooth function is a polynomial.

$$x_t = \alpha_0 + \alpha_1 t + \alpha_2 t^2 + \cdots + \alpha_n t^n + d_t. \tag{9.1.26}$$

[4] The term *weighted regression* indicates that the sum of squares or quadratic form to be minimized has components weighted inversely to the size of error variance and covariance.

Differences of the variable x_t are defined as

$$x_t - x_{t-1} = \Delta x_t$$
$$\Delta x_t - \Delta x_{t-1} = \Delta^2 x_t$$
$$\cdots$$
$$\Delta^{n-1} x_t - \Delta^{n-1} x_{t-1} = \Delta^n x_t.$$

If x_t follows the polynomial development in (9.1.26),

$$\Delta^n x_t = \alpha_n(n!) + \Delta^n d_t,$$
$$\text{var}\,(\Delta^n x_t) = E(\Delta^n d_t)^2 = \frac{(2n)!}{(n!)^2} E(d_t)^2;$$

therefore, the variance of $\Delta^n x_t$ enables us to estimate the variance of d_t.[5] In practice, variances of successively higher order differences of the original series x_t are computed until they appear to remain stable, at which stage it is assumed that the variance of d_t can be estimated. The ratio of computed variances of two variables, say, is then substituted into Eq. (9.1.21) to estimate β as a function of sample observations.

The particular scheme using the variate-difference method may be further critized for logical inconsistency. If the variables being studied, x_t, y_t, and others are thought to be related in a system of stochastic difference equations, the mathematical solution of the system

$$x_t = f(t)$$

will not generally be a polynomial as is assumed in (9.1.26) for the application of the variate-difference method. Other approaches, however, may be used for estimating the variances of the error terms. Each variable can be considered to be of the form

$$x_t = \alpha_0 + \sum_j \alpha_j \cos \frac{2\pi jt}{N} + \sum_j \beta_j \sin \frac{2\pi jt}{N} + d_t, \tag{9.1.27}$$

that is, a Fourier series of period N plus a measurement error. Variances of deviations from a fitted Fourier series provide estimates of the variance of d_t.

An entirely different approach to the solution of the problem is to add something to the assumptions other than a priori knowledge of the variance-covariance matrix of errors. The method of instrumental variables discussed in Chap. 4 was originally developed for an errors in variables model. This method can be applied to obtain consistent estimates of the parameters of the linear structural relation without knowledge of the unknown error variances.

[5] The time series, $d_1, d_2, \ldots, d_T$ is assumed to consist of mutually independent terms.

These estimates are consistent but not efficient. An instrumental variable z_t must be found which is independent of d_t and e_t. The estimate of β is

$$\text{est. } \beta = \frac{\sum_{t=1}^{T} (y_t - \bar{y})(z_t - \bar{z})}{\sum_{t=1}^{T} (x_t - \bar{x})(z_t - \bar{z})}. \tag{9.1.28}$$

The instrumental variable z_t may or may not be measured with error. The essential property is that it be independent of d_t and e_t.

A. Wald has proposed another consistent but inefficient method of estimating the parameters of the linear structural relation without making any assumptions about the variance-covariance matrix of errors. In Wald's scheme, the x_t variables are ordered and split into two parts, $x_1, x_2, \ldots, x_{T/2}$ and $x_{(T/2)+1}, \ldots, x_T$. (T assumed to be an even number.) The y_t are ordered according to the associated values of x_t. The structural coefficient β is estimated as

$$\text{est. } \beta = \frac{\sum_{t=T/2+1}^{T} y_t - \sum_{t=1}^{T/2} y_t}{\sum_{t=T/2+1}^{T} x_t - \sum_{t=1}^{T/2} x_t}. \tag{9.1.29}$$

In order to show that this estimate is consistent, the additional assumption is made that the limit inferior (as $T \longrightarrow \infty$) of

$$\left| \frac{(\eta_1 + \eta_2 + \cdots + \eta_{T/2}) - (\eta_{T/2+1} + \cdots + \eta_T)}{T} \right| > 0. \tag{9.1.30}$$

If the η_t variables are chosen at random, condition (9.1.30) is likely not to be met. Wald's additional restriction enables us to estimate the unknown parameters without assuming anything about the variance-covariance matrix of errors. It is not a generally accepted solution to the main problem, however, because of the stringency of (9.1.30).

The Wald solution can be readily shown to be a form of instrumental variable estimator. If we define an instrument variable

$$\begin{aligned} z_t &= -1, \qquad t = 1, 2, \ldots, \frac{T}{2} \\ z_t &= 1, \qquad t = \frac{T}{2} + 1, \ldots, T, \end{aligned}$$

we then see that (9.1.29) can be expressed as

$$\text{est. } \beta = \frac{\sum_{t=1}^{T} y_t z_t}{\sum_{t=1}^{T} x_t z_t}.$$

It is instructive to consider maximum likelihood estimation of the relation between variables subject to error. Two cases may be distinguished: (a) the variance-covariance matrix of errors is unknown, and (b) the variance-covariance matrix of errors is known, either completely or except for a factor of proportionality. The main arguments are unaffected whether e and d are assumed to be independent or dependent. For simplicity of exposition, we shall assume them to be independent.

$$e^L = \left(\frac{1}{2\pi\sigma_d\sigma_e}\right)^T \exp\left[-\frac{1}{2\sigma_d^2}\sum_{t=1}^{T}(x_t - \eta_t)^2 - \frac{1}{2\sigma_e^2}\sum_{t=1}^{T}(y_t - \alpha - \beta\eta_t)^2\right], \tag{9.1.31}$$

or

$$L = -T\log 2\pi - T\log\sigma_d - T\log\sigma_e - \frac{1}{2\sigma_d^2}\sum_{t=1}^{T}(x_t - \eta_t)^2 - \frac{1}{2\sigma_e^2}\sum_{t=1}^{T}(y_t - \alpha - \beta\eta_t)^2.$$

The structural relation has been directly substituted into the likelihood function. L depends on α, β, σ_d, σ_e, and η_t.

In preparing least squares estimates of the parameters, we found that we could not simultaneously estimate α, β, σ_d, and σ_e. Analogous complications arise in maximum likelihood estimation. The likelihood function has no maximum if we attempt to estimate all parameters from the sample data; thus, from another point of view we see that the same results, presented above, hold. Because the η_t are regarded as T unknown parameters, we can define a point in the parameter space at which

$$x_t = \eta_t. \tag{9.1.32}$$

For these points, sample values of d_t vanish. The vanishing of d_t in the sample does not restrict the population value of σ_d. For points at which (9.1.32) hold in the parameter space, the likelihood function becomes

$$e^L = \left(\frac{1}{2\pi\sigma_d\sigma_e}\right)^T \exp\left[-\frac{1}{2\sigma_e^2}\sum_{t=1}^{T}(y_t - \alpha - \beta x_t)^2\right].$$

As σ_d approaches zero, the likelihood function grows without limit. A maximum value does not exist.

The same type of argument does not apply if we assume

$$\sigma_e^2 = k\sigma_d^2,$$

where k is a known constant. In this case the likelihood function becomes

$$e^L = \left(\frac{1}{2\pi\sqrt{k}\,\sigma_d^2}\right)^T \exp\left[-\frac{1}{2k\sigma_d^2}\sum_{t=1}^{T}(y_t - \alpha - \beta x_t)^2\right].$$

As σ_d approaches zero, the likelihood function does not become infinite, because this parameter appears both in the multiplier of the exponent and in the exponent. The maximization of this likelihood function becomes the standard form of normal regression theory.

If we assume complete a priori knowledge of the two variances, it is immediately evident that maximum likelihood and weighted least squares estimates are identical. To maximize L with respect to α, β, and η_t alone is the same thing as to minimize

$$S^2 = \frac{1}{\sigma_d^2} \sum_{t=1}^{T} (x_t - \eta_t)^2 + \frac{1}{\sigma_e^2} \sum_{t=1}^{T} (y_t - \alpha - \beta\eta_t)^2$$

with respect to α, β, and η_t.

All the general principles and basic problems have been conveniently demonstrated with a single equation model with only two variables, each subject to error. We now complete the presentation of the errors in variables models with a discussion of one equation involving several variables and then a system of equations involving several variables.

The multivariate single equation model is

$$x_{it} = \eta_{it} + d_{it}, \tag{9.1.33}$$

$$\alpha_0 + \sum_{i=1}^{n} \alpha_i \eta_{it} = 0. \tag{9.1.34}$$

We shall assume the d_{it} mutually independent for different values of both subscripts. The least squares criterion is

$$\sum_{i=1}^{n} \frac{1}{\sigma_i^2} \sum_{t=1}^{T} d_{it}^2 = \sum_{i=1}^{n} \frac{1}{\sigma_i^2} \sum_{t=1}^{T} (x_{it} - \eta_{it})^2 = \text{min.},$$

subject to (9.1.34). The σ_i^2 are variances of the d_i, and, as recriprocals, are weights in the minimized weighted sum of squares. By straightforward application of methods of finding a constrained minimum, we obtain the result that the estimates of $\alpha_1, \alpha_2, \ldots, \alpha_n$ are a solution of the linear homogeneous equation system

$$\begin{aligned}
(m_{11} - \lambda\sigma_1^2)\alpha_1 + m_{12}\alpha_2 + \cdots + m_{1n}\alpha_n &= 0 \\
m_{12}\alpha_1 + (m_{22} - \lambda\sigma_2^2)\alpha_2 + \cdots + m_{2n}\alpha_n &= 0 \\
\cdots & \\
m_{1n}\alpha_1 + m_{2n}\alpha_2 + \cdots + (m_{nn} - \lambda\sigma_n^2)\alpha_n &= 0.
\end{aligned} \tag{9.1.35}$$

The m_{ij} in the system (9.1.35) are the sample moments

$$m_{ij} = \sum_{t=1}^{T} (x_{it} - \bar{x}_i)(x_{jt} - \bar{x}_j).$$

The errors in variables interpretation of the geometric lag distribution case can be fully estimated from (9.1.35). In this case, $n = 3$ and $\sigma_1 = \sigma_3$, where $x_{1t} = y_t$ and $x_{3t} = y_{t-1}$. The remaining variable is assumed to be measured without error; so we have $\sigma_2 = 0$.
The computational steps are

1. calculate moments of observations in terms of deviations from sample means;
2. solve the determinantal equation

$$\begin{vmatrix} m_{11} - \lambda\sigma_1^2 & m_{12} & \cdots & m_{1n} \\ m_{12} & m_{22} - \lambda\sigma_2^2 & \cdots & m_{2n} \\ \cdot & \cdot & & \cdot \\ \cdot & \cdot & & \cdot \\ \cdot & \cdot & & \cdot \\ m_{1n} & m_{2n} & \cdots & m_{nn} - \lambda\sigma_n^2 \end{vmatrix} = 0$$

   for the characteristic roots $\lambda_1, \lambda_2, \ldots, \lambda_n$;
3. determine the characteristic vector $\hat{\alpha}_1, \hat{\alpha}_2, \ldots, \hat{\alpha}_n$ corresponding to the smallest characteristic root;
4. choose some variable, say x_1, whose coefficient is to be unity and form the ratios $\dfrac{\hat{\alpha}_i}{\alpha_1}$;
5. estimate $\dfrac{\alpha_0}{\alpha_1}$ from

$$-\left(\frac{\hat{\alpha}_0}{\alpha_1}\right) = \bar{x}_1 + \sum_{i=2}^{n} \left(\frac{\hat{\alpha}_i}{\alpha_1}\right)\bar{x}_i.$$

The normalized form of the estimated equation is

$$x_{1t} = -\left(\frac{\hat{\alpha}_0}{\alpha_1}\right) - \sum_{i=2}^{n} \left(\frac{\hat{\alpha}_i}{\alpha_1}\right)x_{it}. \tag{9.1.36}$$

Determinantal equations are usually written with λ subtracted from each diagonal element, while the determinant in step 2 has $\lambda\sigma_i^2$ subtracted from each diagonal element. If we divide the ith row by σ_i and the jth column by σ_j, doing this for all i and j, the transformed determinantal equation will be

$$\begin{vmatrix} \dfrac{m_{11}}{\sigma_1^2} - \lambda & \dfrac{m_{12}}{\sigma_1\sigma_2} & \cdots & \dfrac{m_{1n}}{\sigma_1\sigma_n} \\ \dfrac{m_{12}}{\sigma_1\sigma_2} & \dfrac{m_{22}}{\sigma_2^2} - \lambda & \cdots & \dfrac{m_{2n}}{\sigma_2\sigma_n} \\ \cdot & \cdot & & \cdot \\ \cdot & \cdot & & \cdot \\ \cdot & \cdot & & \cdot \\ \dfrac{m_{1n}}{\sigma_1\sigma_n} & \dfrac{m_{2n}}{\sigma_2\sigma_n} & \cdots & \dfrac{m_{nn}}{\sigma_n^2} - \lambda \end{vmatrix} = 0.$$

This is in a more standard form.

In order to estimate the equation (9.1.34) by the above methods, we would need to know the absolute variances σ_i^2 in advance. Practically the same procedures could be developed if we merely know the ratios of variances in advance. Choose some variance, say σ_1^2, and express all others in proportion to it,

$$\sigma_i^2 = \frac{1}{k_i}\sigma_1^2. \tag{9.1.37}$$

The determinantal equation can then be written as.

$$\begin{vmatrix} m_{11} - \lambda\sigma_1^2 & m_{12} & \cdots & m_{1n} \\ k_2 m_{12} & k_2 m_{22} - \lambda\sigma_1^2 & \cdots & k_2 m_{2n} \\ \vdots & \vdots & & \vdots \\ k_n m_{1n} & k_n m_{2n} & \cdots & k_n m_{nn} - \lambda\sigma_1^2 \end{vmatrix} = 0,$$

and the characteristic roots will be estimates of $\lambda\sigma_1^2$. Because σ_1^2 is a positive constant, we seek the smallest root and the characteristic vector associated with it. The unknown variance parameter σ_1^2 is estimated by

$$\text{est. } \sigma_1^2 = \frac{1}{T\left[1 + \sum_{i=2}^{n}\left(\frac{\hat{\alpha}_i}{\alpha_1}\right)^2 \frac{1}{k_i}\right]} \sum_{t=1}^{T}\left[x_{1t} + \left(\frac{\hat{\alpha}_0}{\alpha_1}\right) + \left(\frac{\hat{\alpha}_2}{\alpha_1}\right)x_{2t} + \cdots + \left(\frac{\hat{\alpha}_n}{\alpha_1}\right)x_{nt}\right]^2. \tag{9.1.38}$$

Because all the ratios k_i are assumed known in advance, this is the only variance parameter estimated by the data. We may, in small samples, subtract n degrees of freedom for the n values of $\frac{\alpha_i}{\alpha_1}$ estimated in (9.1.36). In this case the divisor on the right-hand side of (9.1.38) would change from T to $T - n$.

To determine the characteristic vector in step 3 above, we must solve the system of linear equations in (9.1.35). The simplest method would be to eliminate any single equation from the system, divide through each of the remaining $(n - 1)$ homogeneous equations by α_1. This will give a *nonhomogenous* system of $(n - 1)$ equations in the $(n - 1)$ unknown parameters $\frac{\alpha_i}{\alpha_1}$.

The errors in variables approach to stochastic econometric equations is not confined to the estimation of a single structural relationship. Models containing systems of equations can be estimated by repeated application of the same techniques used for a single equation. In a system of equations we minimize the same sum of squares as previously, but use as constraints the p equations,

$$\alpha_{j0} + \sum_{i=1}^{n}\alpha_{ji}\eta_{it} = 0; \qquad j = 1, 2, \ldots, p. \tag{9.1.39}$$

The final result of this minimization problem is that instead of choosing merely the smallest characteristic root of the determinantal equation

$$\begin{vmatrix} m_{11} - \lambda\sigma_1^2 & m_{12} & \cdots & m_{1n} \\ m_{12} & m_{22} - \lambda\sigma_2^2 & \cdots & m_{2n} \\ \vdots & \vdots & & \vdots \\ m_{1n} & m_{2n} & \cdots & m_{nn} - \lambda\sigma_n^2 \end{vmatrix} = 0,$$

we choose the p smallest roots ($p \leq n$). A separate characteristic vector

$$\left[\left(\frac{\hat{\alpha}_{j0}}{\alpha_{j1}}\right), \left(\frac{\hat{\alpha}_{j2}}{\alpha_{j1}}\right), \cdots \left(\frac{\hat{\alpha}_{jn}}{\alpha_{j1}}\right)\right]$$

is computed for the jth root, $\lambda_j, j = 1, 2, \ldots, p$.

Tintner has proposed that the roots of the determinantal equation be used also to test for the number of independent linear relations existing among x_{1t}, $x_{2t}, \ldots, x_{nt}$.[6] He argues that the quantity

$$(T - 1)(\lambda_1 + \lambda_2 + \cdots + \lambda_q)$$

follows the χ^2 distribution with $(T - 1 - n + q)q$ degrees of freedom. For a given level of statistical significance, successive values of the test quantity with varying q are computed until one is found which is larger than the entry in the χ^2 table for the appropriate number of degrees of freedom. Having found the appropriate value of q, he concludes that the test shows that there are q independent linear relations. q characteristic vectors are computed for the q smallest characteristic roots. The correct application of this type of statistical test, especially when sample sizes are not larger than we usually have in practical time series analysis, depends on prior knowledge of the error variances σ_i^2. When these variances are estimated from the sample as a step preceding estimation of the structural equations, the effective number of degrees of freedom in the χ^2 test is reduced. It also makes the χ^2 test crude, in itself.

If all the equations of the system (9.1.39) are linear with the same variables included in each, we shall lack identification. With identifying restrictions placed on each separate equation of the system, we shall find that the jth equation contains, for example, only n_j variables ($n_j \leq n$). In this case, we must form a different determinantal equation for each structural equation to be estimated. In

[6] G. Tintner, "Multiple Regression for Systems of Equations," *Econometrica*, 14 (Jan., 1946), 5–36.

estimating the jth equation, the determinantal equation is

$$\begin{vmatrix} m_{11} - \lambda\sigma_1^2 & m_{12} & \cdots & m_{1n_j} \\ m_{12} & m_{22} - \lambda\sigma_2^2 & \cdots & m_{2n_j} \\ \vdots & \vdots & & \vdots \\ m_{1n_j} & m_{2n_j} & \cdots & m_{n_jn_j} - \lambda\sigma_{n_j}^2 \end{vmatrix} = 0.$$

The characteristic vector corresponding to the smallest characteristic root is then computed as an estimate of the structural parameters of the jth equation. The same process is repeated for each equation of the system. At each stage, the suggested χ^2 test can be applied to the characteristic roots of each different determinantal equation. It should turn out, in an identified system, by these tests, that only one independent linear relation exists among the variables used.

Identification is an interesting problem in stochastic models based on errors in the variables. The most exhaustive study of identification in such models has been made for a case that differs slightly from that presented thus far. The *true* or systematic parts of observed variables, η_{it}, have, in the preceding pages, been regarded as a set of unknown parameters. Full conditions for identifiability have been developed for a model in which x_{it}, η_{it}, and d_{it} are all random variables. The following theorem has been proved for the two-variable, single equation case:

Let the random variables be defined as

$$\begin{aligned} x_t &= \eta_t + d_t, \\ y_t &= \xi_t + e_t, \\ \xi_t &= \alpha + \beta\eta_t. \end{aligned}$$

If the combined (vector) variables (η_t, d_t) and (ξ_t, e_t) are mutually independent drawings from fixed probability distributions, the combined (vector) variables (d_t, e_t) are independent of (η_t, ξ_t), and the errors d_t and e_t follow a joint normal distribution; then a necessary and sufficient condition for the identifiability of β is that at least one of the two variables, η or ξ, is not normally distributed. Reiersøl has derived other theorems in addition to the above concerning the identifiability of β.[7]

These valuable findings even have some rough application to the model in which η_t and ξ_t are not random variables. In a loose sense, we might say that η_t and ξ_t must not both behave like normally distributed variables, that is, have frequency distributions of the normal type, if β is to be identifiable.

[7] O. Reiersøl, "Identifiability of a Linear Relation between Variables which Are Subject to Error," *Econometrica*, 18 (October, 1950), 375–89.

The more general model containing both errors in the equations and errors in the variables has not been fully developed. This is the equation type in (9.1.9) above

$$\sum_{j=1}^{n} \alpha_{ij}(x_{jt} - d_{jt}) = u_{it}, \qquad i = 1, 2, \ldots, m.$$

The problem in this model is to estimate both the parameter system, α_{ij}, and the separate variances of d_j and u_i. It sometimes happens that the matrix of coefficients α_{ij} can be estimated but the separate contributions to the error variance from σ_d^2 and σ_u^2 cannot. A good reason exists for wanting to decompose the error variance. In any particular problem, we want to know how much of our error is due to inherent behavior disturbance and how much is due to faulty measurement. Eventually, new measurement techniques should enable us to reduce considerably the resulting errors. In prediction problems we are usually anxious to know whether the resulting errors are of one type or the other, because the errors in variables can presumably be reduced through the refinement of our measurement techniques, but the errors in equations are more inherent in systems of human behavior and often cannot be reduced through conscious effort on the part of the econometrician.

On distinguishing among three possible types of models, errors in variables, errors in equations, and combined models with errors both in variables and equations, we find some restrictive cases in which all approaches lead to the same results. Suppose that a single endogenous variable y is linearly related to an exogenous variable z. Suppose further that z is measured without error.

The errors in variable model is

$$y_t = \xi_t + e_t, \tag{9.1.40}$$

$$\xi_t = \alpha + \beta z_t. \tag{9.1.41}$$

Substitution from (9.1.41) into (9.1.40) leads to

$$y_t = \alpha + \beta z_t + e_t. \tag{9.1.42}$$

This derived equation is indistinguishable from the errors in equation model

$$y_t = \alpha + \beta z_t + u_t, \tag{9.1.43}$$

The foundations of (9.1.42) and (9.1.43) are, however, different. In one case, they indicate that improved methods of measurement of y would lead to improved predictions from (9.1.42). In the other case, prediction error is not necessarily reduced by improved measurement techniques. Both (9.1.42) and (9.1.43) are indistinguishable from the combined model with both error types

$$y_t = \alpha + \beta z_t + e_t + u_t. \tag{9.1.44}$$

Without a priori information on the relative magnitudes of σ_e^2 and σ_u^2, we cannot decompose the total error variance in (9.1.44). In this sense, there is a lack of complete identification in the combined model, although all three models result in identical estimates of the structural parameters, α and β.

Matrix notation for the three general types of models in (9.1.7)–(9.1.9) is

$$\begin{aligned} Ax_t - Ad_t &= 0, \\ Ax_t \qquad &= u_t, \\ Ax_t - Ad_t &= u_t. \end{aligned}$$

Denoting the variance-covariance matrices of d and u by Σ_d and Σ_u respectively, we have the following conditions for equivalence between any two of the three models:

$$\begin{aligned} A\Sigma_d A' &= \Sigma_u, \\ \Sigma_u &= \Sigma_u + A\Sigma_d A', \\ A\Sigma_d A' &= \Sigma_u + A\Sigma_d A'. \end{aligned}$$

An interesting point is raised if we consider the corresponding problems in the simplest model with a lagged endogenous instead of exogenous predetermined variable,

$$\xi_t = \alpha + \beta\xi_{t-1} + u_t, \tag{9.1.45}$$

or

$$y_t - \beta y_{t-1} - \alpha = e_t + u_t - \beta e_{t-1}. \tag{9.1.46}$$

By successive application of the difference equation in (9.1.45) to the starting relation

$$\xi_1 = \alpha + \beta\xi_0 + u_1,$$

we build up the general equation

$$\begin{aligned} \xi_t = \alpha(1 + \beta + \cdots + \beta^{t-1}) \\ + \beta^t\xi_0 + u_t + \beta u_{t-1} + \cdots + \beta^{t-1}u_1. \end{aligned} \tag{9.1.47}$$

Let us now multiply (9.1.46) by $y_t = \xi_t + e_t$ and form expectations of both sides of the equation. The result is

$$\begin{aligned} E(y_t)^2 - \beta E(y_t y_{t-1}) - \alpha E(y_t) &= E(e_t)^2 + E(\xi_t u_t) \\ &= E(e_t)^2 + E(u_t)^2. \end{aligned} \tag{9.1.48}$$

In simplifying this product, we have used the following assumptions:

e_t independent of u_t, e_{t-1}, ξ_t, and ξ_{t+1}
u_t independent of lagged values of u_t
$E(e_t) = 0.$
$E(u_t) = 0.$

In a similar way, we multiply by y_{t-1} and y_{t-2} to get

$$E(y_t y_{t-1}) - \beta E(y_{t-1})^2 - \alpha E(y_{t-1}) = -\beta E(e_{t-1})^2, \tag{9.1.49}$$

$$E(y_t y_{t-2}) - \beta E(y_{t-1} y_{t-2}) - \alpha E(y_{t-2}) = 0. \tag{9.1.50}$$

In addition, the ordinary mathematical expectation of (9.1.46) leads to

$$E(y_t) - \beta E(y_{t-1}) - \alpha = 0. \tag{9.1.51}$$

The four Eqs. (9.1.48)–(9.1.51) with expectations replaced by sample moments enable us to estimate α, β, and each of the variances σ_e^2, σ_u^2. The simplest lag model is completely identified, even allowing separability of error variances, although the correspondingly simple unlagged system does not permit separability.

Questions and Problems

1. Derive estimates of α, β, and σ from the model

$$\sigma^{dd} \sum_{t=1}^{T} (x_t - \eta_t)^2 + 2\sigma^{de} \sum_{t=1}^{T} (x_t - \eta_t)(y_t - \xi_t) + \sigma^{ee} \sum_{t=1}^{T} (y_t - \xi_t)^2 = \text{min.}$$

subject to

$$\xi_t = \alpha + \beta\eta_t.$$

$$\begin{Vmatrix} \sigma_{dd} & \sigma_{de} \\ \sigma_{de} & \sigma_{ee} \end{Vmatrix}^{-1} = \begin{Vmatrix} \sigma^{dd} & \sigma^{de} \\ \sigma^{de} & \sigma^{ee} \end{Vmatrix}.$$

$$\begin{Vmatrix} \sigma_{dd} & \sigma_{de} \\ \sigma_{de} & \sigma_{ee} \end{Vmatrix} = \sigma^2 \begin{Vmatrix} k_{11} & k_{12} \\ k_{12} & k_{22} \end{Vmatrix}.$$

The k_{ij} are assumed known.

2. What is the nature of observation error in the collection of economic data? Are the errors encountered in practice likely to satisfy the requirements of the usual stochastic models that state that the errors are independent of the systematic parts of variables, mutually independent in time, and (often) independent of each other at the same instant of time? Is there any reason to expect observation errors to be normally distributed?

3. Could the probability elements of errors in variables models be generated by causes other than observation or measurement error?

4. What is the formal relation between identification criteria in linear systems and Tintner's proposed technique for estimating systems of equations with errors in variables?

2. WEIGHTED REGRESSIONS FROM SAMPLE SURVEY DATA

Methods of weighted regression, as they are developed from models with errors in variables, assign different weights, inversely proportional to error variances, to each variable. Another type of weighted regression is encountered in dealing with cross-section data gathered in sample surveys. Weights are there assigned to each individual and are the same over all variables.

The genesis of weights in sample surveys is different from that in time series models with errors in variables. In sampling human populations, it is often found that some classes of individuals show more variability than others in measurements on certain variables. Estimates of mean values when class variances differ achieve maximum efficiency if sampling rates vary inversely proportional to standard deviations. A concrete example will help to clarify this point. In numerous consumer surveys it has been observed that high income and wealthy people show greater variability in their savings than others. Reasons for this phenomenon are obvious. Low income, poor people are locked as far as savings behavior is concerned. They must spend nearly all their income on current items of consumption and have small savings without much variability about a zero level. High income, rich people have many more degrees of freedom in their savings behavior. They can and do save much or little, depending on particular circumstances of the moment. In order to get an efficient estimate of average savings in the entire population, one should not simply collect data from a strict random sample of the population. A more efficient sampling scheme is to draw individuals from several income classes at different rates, the variation among sampling rates being inversely proportional to the standard deviation of savings in each income class. If the sampling rate in a class is 1: 1000 (one per thousand population individuals), the sampling rate in a class having five times as large a standard deviation should be 5: 1000.

In order to avoid bias in the final tabulations, individuals are weighted down according as they are in classes sampled at a higher rate. Weights assigned individuals in a class sampled at the rate 5: 1000 would be one-fifth as large as weights for a class sampled at the rate 1: 1000.[8]

In econometric analysis of survey data, we must study multivariate relations, and the appropriate sampling scheme will probably not be the same for all variables. However, in practical work a single sample must be selected in

[8] The several classes or strata of a sample do not all respond at the same rate in surveys; therefore, it is necessary to correct the weights in order that they reflect the net effective sampling rate, a combination of original sampling and final response rates.

advance in order to achieve maximum efficiency on some strategic variable or a group of variables. Given survey data that have been collected from a sample drawn at varying rates and given some knowledge about the stochastic structure of the behavior model, the econometrician must devise appropriate methods for parameter estimation.

Different models will be assumed, each of them consisting of a single equation to be estimated from the sample data. Problems relevant to the use of this type of data are adequately delineated in these simple models. The first model we consider is one in which an endogenous variable x is linearly related to a predetermined variable z, with an additive random disturbance in the equation, u. The disturbance will be assumed to follow some probability law and have variance independent of z. As a result of the sample design, we associate a weight w_i with each observation (x_i, z_i). Because the variance of u is assumed to be constant for all values of z, the main use of weights in the present connection is to avoid bias in the estimated equation. The proportional contribution of each stratum in the sample to the estimates of the parameters must be the same as would have been obtained in a complete census enumeration. Bias would not occur, however, if all the parameters of the equation to be estimated were the same for all strata. The equation to be estimated is

$$x_i = \alpha + \beta z_i + u_i, \qquad i = 1, 2, \ldots, N, \tag{9.2.1}$$
$$\sigma_u^2 = \text{unknown constant.}$$

The ordinary approach of least squares theory would be to determine values of α and β that minimize $\sum_{i=1}^{N} u_i^2$. When dealing with weighted data, the corresponding criterion is minimization of $\sum_{i=1}^{N} w_i u_i^2$. Instead of the usual unweighted least squares estimates of α and β obtained as a solution to the equation system,

$$\sum_{i=1}^{N} x_i = \alpha N + \beta \sum_{i=1}^{N} z_i$$
$$\sum_{i=1}^{N} x_i z_i = \alpha \sum_{i=1}^{N} z_i + \beta \sum_{i=1}^{N} z_i^2,$$

we would have weighted least squares estimates satisfying

$$\begin{aligned} \sum_{i=1}^{N} w_i x_i &= \alpha \sum_{i=1}^{N} w_i + \beta \sum_{i=1}^{N} w_i z_i \\ \sum_{i=1}^{N} w_i x_i z_i &= \alpha \sum_{i=1}^{N} w_i z_i + \beta \sum_{i=1}^{N} w_i z_i^2. \end{aligned} \tag{9.2.2}$$

Those individuals who are sampled at relatively high rates are given relatively little weight in the weighted moments of (9.2.2). In terms of deviations from sample means, weighted moments are

$$\bar{x} = \frac{\sum_{i=1}^{N} w_i x_i}{\sum_{i=1}^{N} w_i}, \qquad \begin{aligned} m_{xx} &= \sum w_i(x_i - \bar{x})^2, \\ m_{zz} &= \sum w_i(z_i - \bar{z})^2, \\ m_{xz} &= \sum w_i(x_i - \bar{x})(z_i - \bar{z}_i), \end{aligned} \qquad \bar{z} = \frac{\sum_{i=1}^{N} w_i z_i}{\sum_{i=1}^{N} w_i}.$$

The weighted estimate of β can be expressed as

$$\text{est. } \beta = \frac{m_{xz}}{m_{zz}} = \frac{\sum_{i=1}^{N} w_i(x_i - \bar{x})(z_i - \bar{z})}{\sum_{i=1}^{N} w_i(z_i - \bar{z})^2}.$$

The computations leading to estimates of standard errors of the estimated parameters are somewhat more laborious, especially in multivariate equations. An unweighted least squares estimate of the standard error in the two-variable case is

$$\frac{S_u}{\sqrt{\sum_{i=1}^{N} (z_i - \bar{z})^2}}.$$

In this expression, $\bar{z}$ is simply an unweighted mean, and S_u is the unweighted sample estimate of σ_u. The corresponding expression for the standard error of the estimate of β in a weighted regression is

$$\frac{S_u}{\sqrt{\sum_{i=1}^{N} w_i(z_i - \bar{z})^2}} \sqrt{\frac{\sum_{i=1}^{N} w_i^2(z_i - \bar{z})^2}{\sum_{i=1}^{N} w_i(z_i - \bar{z})^2}}.$$

In this case, $\bar{z}$ is a weighted mean and S_u is the weighted root mean square of residuals from the regression,

$$S_u = \sqrt{\frac{\sum_{i=1}^{N} w_i(x_i - \hat{\alpha} - \hat{\beta} z_i)^2}{\sum_{i=1}^{N} w_i}}.$$

In a multivariate regression

$$x_i = \alpha + \sum_{j=1}^{N} \beta_j z_{ji} + u_i, \qquad i = 1, 2, \cdots, N, \tag{9.2.3}$$

standard errors of unweighted parameter estimates are

$$S_u\sqrt{m^{jj}},$$

where m^{jj} is the jth diagonal element of the inverse matrix of unweighted moments.

$$\left\| \sum_{i=1}^{N} (z_{ji} - \bar{z}_j)(z_{ki} - \bar{z}_k) \right\|^{-1}.$$

The corresponding expression for weighted estimates of standard errors of the multiple regression coefficients are

$$S_u \left[\sum_{j=1}^{n} (m^{kj})^2 \sum_{i=1}^{N} w_i^2 (z_{ji} - \bar{z}_j)^2 + 2 \sum_{j<p} m^{kj} m^{kp} \sum_{i=1}^{N} w_i^2 (z_{ji} - \bar{z}_j)(z_{pi} - \bar{z}_p) \right]^{1/2},$$

Both S_u and m^{kj} are weighted estimates. Many more computations are necessary to evaluate the standard errors of weighted regression coefficients if several variables are used simultaneously, than if the regression is a simple relation between only two variables.

A maximum likelihood interpretation of weighted estimates from the model in (9.2.1) can be given that is identical with weighted least squares estimates. Unweighted maximum likelihood estimates are obtained by maximizing the likelihood function

$$p(u_1)p(u_2)\ldots p(u_N) = p(x_1 - \alpha - \beta z_1)p(x_2 - \alpha - \beta z_2)\ldots p(x_N - \alpha - \beta z_N)$$

with respect to α and β. A weighted likelihood function would be

$$p(u_1)^{w_1} p(u_2)^{w_2} \cdots p(u_N)^{w_N}.$$

For normally distributed u_i, this becomes

$$\left(\frac{1}{\sqrt{2\pi}\sigma_u} \right)^{\sum_{i=1}^{N} w_i} e^{-(1/2\sigma_u^2) \sum_{i=1}^{N} w_i u_i^2}.$$

The maximum likelihood estimates of α and β minimize the weighted sum of squares in the exponential expression.

Efficiency rather than bias is a more important reason for making weighted estimates of structural equations when the disturbances do not have a variance independent of z. Weights are supposed to be designed to correct for differential variances in such a way that the transformation

$$\sqrt{w_i} u_i = v_i \tag{9.2.4}$$

leads to variances σ_v^2 that are independent of z.

Because Eq. (9.2.1) states that we have a linear relation between x_i and z_i, subject to random disturbance, the transformation in (9.2.4) shows that we also have a linear relation between $\sqrt{w_i} x_i$, $\sqrt{w_i}$, and $\sqrt{w_i} z_i$, subject to random disturbance

$$\sqrt{w_i}x_i = \alpha\sqrt{w_i} + \beta\sqrt{w_i}z_i + v_i. \tag{9.2.5}$$

In this equation, the variance of the disturbance term does not depend on z. Least squares estimates of (9.2.5) obtained by multiplying through the equation, first by $\sqrt{w_i}$, then by $\sqrt{w_i}z_i$, and summing over all sample observations lead to the estimating equations

$$\begin{aligned} \sum_{i=1}^{N} w_i x_i &= \alpha \sum_{i=1}^{N} w_i + \beta \sum_{i=1}^{N} w_i z_i \\ \sum_{i=1}^{N} w_i x_i z_i &= \alpha \sum_{i=1}^{N} w_i z_i + \beta \sum_{i=1}^{N} w_i z_i^2 \end{aligned} \tag{9.2.6}$$

The parameter estimates are exactly the same as those in (9.2.2), derived from a model based on somewhat different assumptions. Although these estimates are the same, the underlying probability structure is different. In the former case we assumed that we had N observations of x_i and z_i, representing various sample classes with relative frequencies different from those of the same population classes. In the present model, we simply assume that we have N observations of the variables $\sqrt{w_i}x_i$, $\sqrt{w_i}z_i$, and $\sqrt{w_i}$. The formula for the standard error of est. β is now different.

$$\frac{S_u}{\sqrt{\sum_{i=1}^{N} w_i(z_i - \bar{z})^2}} = \frac{\sqrt{\dfrac{\sum_{i=1}^{N} w_i r_i^2}{N}}}{\sqrt{\sum_{i=1}^{N} w_i(z_i - \bar{z})^2}} = \frac{\sqrt{\dfrac{\sum_{i=1}^{N} w_i r_i^2}{\sum_{i=1}^{N} w_i}}\sqrt{\dfrac{\sum_{i=1}^{N} w_i}{N}}}{\sqrt{\sum_{i=1}^{N} w_i(z_i - \bar{z})^2}}$$

$$= \frac{S_u}{\sqrt{\sum_{i=1}^{N} w_i(z_i - \bar{z})^2}}\sqrt{\frac{\sum_{i=1}^{N} w_i}{N}}.$$

r_i = unweighted residuals from the estimated equation.

The two expressions for the standard error of est. β in the alternative (two-variable) models differ in that one has as the multiplier of $\dfrac{S_u}{m_{zz}}$

$$\sqrt{\frac{\sum_{i=1}^{N} w_i^2(z_i - \bar{z})^2}{\sum_{i=1}^{N} w_i(z_i - \bar{z})^2}}$$

and the other has

$$\sqrt{\frac{\sum_{i=1}^{N} w_i}{N}}.$$

Both of these factors are square roots of the mean weight, the former being a weighted mean and the latter being a simple mean.

The multivariate extension of the present case is quite simple. The parameters are estimated from the customary equations of least squares theory, with ordinary moments replaced by weighted moments. In this respect, the results are exactly the same as in the previous model. The standard errors of regression coefficients are

$$S_v\sqrt{m^{jj}} = S_u\sqrt{\frac{\sum_{i=1}^{N} w_i}{N} m^{jj}},$$

where

$$S_u = \sqrt{\frac{\sum_{i=1}^{N} w_i\left(x_i - \hat{\alpha} - \sum_{j=1}^{n} \hat{\beta}_j z_{ji}\right)^2}{\sum w_i}},$$

and m^{jj} is a diagonal element of the inverse matrix of weighted moments

$$\left\| \sum_{i=1}^{N} w_i(z_{ji} - \bar{z}_j)(z_{ki} - \bar{z}_k) \right\|^{-1}.$$

It frequently happens in the use of sample survey data for econometric models that the individual behavior equations are not subject to additive random disturbances whose variances are independent of predetermined variables, nor can they be transformed into equations with homogeneous variances simply by multiplying each variable by $\sqrt{w_i}$. Neither of the two previous models applies directly. In some instances we know, however, enough properties of the random disturbances so that we can transform the equations into forms more amenable to standard statistical treatment. The variance of the disturbance in (9.2.1) may be proportional to z^2 instead of being independent of z. It then follows that simple transformations change the equation into one that does have a disturbance variance independent of z. If the disturbances satisfy

$$\begin{aligned} u_i &= v_i z_i \\ \sigma^2_{u_i} &= z_i^2 \sigma^2_{v_i}, \end{aligned} \tag{9.2.7}$$

we can divide both sides of (9.2.1) by z_i to obtain $\sigma^2_{v_i}$, that is independent of z_i.

$$\begin{aligned} \frac{x_i}{z_i} &= \alpha\frac{1}{z_i} + \beta + \frac{1}{z_i}u_i. \\ &= \alpha\frac{1}{z_i} + \beta + v_i. \end{aligned} \tag{9.2.8}$$

After having transformed the variables from x_i, z_i, and u_i to $\frac{x_i}{z_i}$, $\frac{1}{z_i}$ and v_i, we now have an equation with the properties specified in (9.2.1). The sample will generally be weighted according to net effective sampling rates; therefore, we must use weighted regressions in the transformed variables in order to avoid bias. We proceed as before in the estimation of (9.2.1).

The realism of this approach can easily be demonstrated by reference to the previously mentioned example of the collection of survey data on individuals' saving, income and other relevant variables. The variance of savings appears to grow proportionally to the square of income; or the standard deviation proportionally to the level of income. Weights used in survey tabulations were not originally chosen from the different sampling and response rates in order to obtain an efficient estimate of mean or other statistics on savings. The weights are often chosen in order to obtain an efficient estimate of mean income and other properties of the income distribution. If in the previous models we let $x =$ savings and $z =$ income, we would find that $\sqrt{w_i}u_i$ is not distributed with variance independent of z_i. It is preferable to use our full knowledge about the stochastic structure of the problem and transform the variables from savings and income to the percentage of income saved and the reciprocal of income. This gives the type of equation in (9.2.8). Calculations made with survey data indicate that the percentage of income saved has nearly the same variance in all income classes; hence the transformation removes the heterogeneity of variances better than direct application of the sample weights to savings and income. Unbiased estimates of the savings-income relation containing the transformed variables must make use of the weights that are in the sample design and affect the data used even though they do not adequately reflect the nonhomogeneity of the variance of savings by income classes. Arguments like these justify choosing the savings-income ratio instead of total savings as the dependent variable in the savings equation estimated from survey data. This choice is frequently made without reference to scientific criteria.

In sample surveys errors of measurement are definitely present, and all variables are not determined with the same precision. A more general model involving errors in the equations, errors in the variables, and weights for differential sampling rates needs further development. A genuine possibility exists that in repeated sample surveys we can acquire enough experience to assign different measurement errors to the several variables involved. In this way we could use a priori values for the elements of the variance-covariance matrix of errors in variables.

Questions and Problems

1. Although three variables x_t, y_t, and z_t are mutually independent, the transformed variables $\frac{x_t}{z_t}$ and $\frac{y_t}{z_t}$ are not, in general, independent. It is often argued that one obtains *spurious* correlation by relating two variables, each of which is divided by a common variable. Are these propositions relevant to the choice of

estimation methods for the model

$$\begin{aligned} x_i &= \alpha + \beta y_i + \gamma z_i + u_i, \\ u_i &= v_i z_i, \\ \sigma_u^2 &= z^2 \sigma_v^2, \\ \sigma_v^2 &= \text{constant?} \end{aligned}$$

2. Suppose that a sampling scheme is constructed with sampling rates varying proportionally to z. Derive weighted estimation equations for α, β, and γ in the model of question one above. How are these estimation equations related to those used for estimating the relation connecting the transformed variables $\frac{x_i}{z_i}, \frac{y_i}{z_i}, \frac{1}{z_i}$?

3. Explain how two methods of estimation have exactly the same equations for estimating parameter values, but different formulas for sampling error (see text above for such models).

3. VARYING THE LENGTH OF UNIT OBSERVATION PERIODS

Much of econometric time series analysis is based on annual data, although on numerous occasions statisticians and economists have pointed out the advantages of obtaining more information from quarterly or monthly data. In rarer instances, weekly or even daily figures have been used. In this section we shall take up, briefly, the problem of varying the unit time period in order to pick out within-year movements of the economy. There are also some virtues in going in the opposite direction and lengthening the unit period beyond one year.

In order to explain the more detailed movements of an economy over quarterly as compared with annual periods, more variables and more parameters will be needed; hence, the degrees of freedom will not be multiplied by four. At least three new types of parameters will be needed in quarterly or monthly models: (a) A new constellation of lags will be required, probably involving more lags and more parameters associated with the lagged variables. (b) Seasonal variables must be added. (c) Serial correlation of disturbances will require added parameters unless the lag distributions in (a) eliminate autocorrelation. An equation of the form

$$y_t = \alpha_0 + \alpha_1 y_{t-1} + \alpha_2 z_t + u_t \tag{9.3.1}$$

may adequately represent some structural aspects of an economy on a yearly basis, and the corresponding type of equation

$$\begin{aligned} y_t = {} & \beta_1 y_{t-1/4} + \beta_2 y_{t-2/4} + \beta_3 y_{t-3/4} + \beta_4 y_{t-4/4} + \beta_5 y_{t-5/4} \\ & + \beta_6 p_t + \beta_7 e_t + \beta_8 a_t + \beta_9 h_t + \beta_{10} z_t + u_t \qquad (9.3.2) \\ u_t = {} & \rho_1 u_{t-1/4} + \rho_2 u_{t-2/4} + \rho_3 u_{t-3/4} + \rho_4 u_{t-4/4} + v_t \end{aligned}$$

may be needed to give a structural representation on a quarterly basis. In addition to the more detailed lag structure of (9.3.2), there are four seasonal variables

$$\begin{aligned} p_t &= 1 \text{ in spring } (\textit{printemps}) \\ p_t &= 0 \text{ in other quarters} \\ e_t &= 1 \text{ in summer } (\textit{été}) \\ e_t &= 0 \text{ in other quarters} \\ a_t &= 1 \text{ in autumn } (\textit{automne}) \\ a_t &= 0 \text{ in other quarters} \\ h_t &= 1 \text{ in winter } (\textit{hiver}) \\ h_t &= 0 \text{ in other quarters} \end{aligned}$$

and four lags in the autoregressive structure of disturbances. There are eleven more parameters in (9.3.2) than in (9.3.1).

An interpretation of lags in annual series is that they approximate an average lag of duration not necessarily equal to an integral number of years. Many lags in economics, technical, institutional, and behavioral, are thought to be considerably shorter than one year; therefore, a single lag in an annually observed variable with a particular coefficient is simply an approximation to a shorter lag structure. In an equation based on annual data, a lag distribution of the form

$$\alpha_1 x_t + \alpha_2 x_{t-1}$$

implies an average lag

$$\frac{\alpha_1(0) + \alpha_2(1)}{\alpha_1 + \alpha_2} = \frac{\alpha_2}{\alpha_1 + \alpha_2} \text{ years.}$$

If this fraction is between three quarters and one year on the average, a quarterly representation of the same process may involve as many as four lags

$$\beta_1 x_t + \beta_2 x_{t-1/4} + \beta_3 x_{t-2/4} + \beta_4 x_{t-3/4} + \beta_5 x_{t-4/4}.$$

The average lag calculated from the quarterly model,

$$\frac{\beta_1(0) + \beta_2(1/4) + \beta_3(2/4) + \beta_4(3/4) + \beta_5(4/4)}{\beta_1 + \beta_2 + \beta_3 + \beta_4 + \beta_5}$$
$$= \frac{\frac{1}{4}(\beta_2 + 2\beta_3 + 3\beta_4 + 4\beta_5)}{\beta_1 + \beta_2 + \beta_3 + \beta_4 + \beta_5} \text{ years,}$$

should be the same as that in the corresponding annual model. It is possible that a fixed and definite lag of a single time unit that is a fraction of one year can be approximated closely by a single quarterly variable

$$\beta x_{-3/4}$$

in place of two annual variables

$$\alpha_1 x_t + \alpha_2 x_{t-1}, \quad \frac{\alpha_2}{\alpha_1 + \alpha_2} = \frac{3}{4},$$

but often an entire distribution of quarterly lags is needed. The distributed lag gives a smoother time path to the dependent variable.

In (9.3.2), a simple type of seasonal variable is used. Each season has an independent additive influence on the economic process. In such cases, four seasonal variables in a linear equation are adequate. Another approach would be to extract seasonal variation from the basic time series in advance of econometric estimation and then determine the estimates of the structural parameters from seasonally adjusted data. This is essentially the method used in the classical time series analysis of economic statistics. In that analysis, each time series is assumed to consist of four independent components—trend, seasonal, cylical, and erratic—that are eliminated, one by one, for separate study. The components may be either additive or multiplicative, and they are supposedly extracted individually by standard methods. A trend-free series is obtained by calculating deviations of the actual series from fitted growth curves. A seasonal index is then obtained by calculating the ratio of the actual observations (trend-free) to a four-quarter (a twelve month) moving average, and averaging these ratios over like seasons in different years. The series, adjusted for trend and seasonal, is then studied for cyclical variation. This may be done according to some comparatively complex method of harmonic analysis (fitting trigonometric functions), by spectral analysis, or by some freehand method measuring peaks and troughs. Deviations from a fitted periodic function would then give estimates of the random components.

The econometric approach in this volume contrasts with the step by step elimination of factors from individual series by estimating all factors simultaneously in systems of equations. Trends will be taken up below. They are represented by special variables in the structural equations. Cyclical properties are derived from the final solution of the lagged equations. The random component is represented by the disturbances attached to each structural equation. It has a further bearing on the cyclical properties of the system. Having considered mainly annual models, we did not have occasion to treat seasonal variation.[9]

We cannot be certain that seasonal variation will always occur additively and independent of the other variables. An essential feature of seasonal variation, as it is introduced in (9.3.2), is that it may be considered as a variable effect on the constant term of the equation

$$\beta = \beta(p, e, a, h) = \beta_6 p + \beta_7 e + \beta_8 a + \beta_9 h. \tag{9.3.3}$$

[9] During the past decade, numerous quarterly (some monthly) models have been built. Some of these used seasonal variables with unadjusted data, and others used prior seasonal elimination.

The interpretation of seasonal indicators introduced in the form of additive dummy variables is not that they are adjustment factors for the dependent variable in a regression; they are the *net* seasonal effects of both the dependent and independent variables.

Perhaps other parameters, in addition to the constant term, are affected by seasonal changes. In that event, we would have

$$\beta_i y_{t-i/4} = \beta_{ip} p_t y_{t-i/4} + \beta_{ie} e_t y_{t-i/4} + \beta_{ia} a_t y_{t-i/4} + \beta_{ih} h_t y_{t-i/4}. \tag{9.3.4}$$

Instead of the single coefficients and variables on the left side of (9.3.4), we would have the four seasonal coefficients and combined variables on the right-hand side. This type of seasonal variation would add much to the complexity of an equation like (9.3.2) and substantially reduce the number of degrees of freedom.

The estimation and computational methods follow in a straightforward fashion because the particular formulation adopted leaves the structural equations linear in the unknown parameters.

The other complication found in quarterly or monthly models is the presence, in increased degree, of serial correlation in disturbances. This problem has already been touched upon in Chaps. 3 and 5, where quarterly and seasonal problems were not considered. As the unit time period is sliced more finely, there is more likely to be correlation between the disturbing factors in an economy during successive periods. In a single equation, such as (9.3.2), the autoregressive equation satisfied by the disturbances is of the fourth order. This fact, combined with the use of added seasonal variables in the basic structural equation, means that the joint estimation of the β's and ρ's will involve the solution of complicated equations.

The serial correlation parameters may be estimated jointly with the structural coefficients through iteration processes, search techniques, or through the direct solution of nonlinear equations by extraction of roots of high order polynomials.

In dealing with serial correlation of disturbances in a single equation, we append an autoregressive equation to the original structural equation. The autoregressive equation involves only current and lagged values of the disturbances in that particular structural equation, plus a nonautocorrelated disturbance. We have already pointed out the possibility of using a more general model in which we have a system of simultaneous structural equations and a system of simultaneous equations with lagged disturbances. A linear system with first order serial correlation in disturbances is (See also Chap. 5)

$$\begin{aligned} \sum_{j=1}^{n} \alpha_{ij} y_{jt} + \sum_{j=1}^{m} \beta_{ij} z_{jt} &= u_{it}, \\ u_{it} &= \sum_{j=1}^{n} \rho_{ij} u_{j,t-1} + v_{it}. \end{aligned} \tag{9.3.5}$$

In this model, disturbance u_{it} depends linearly not only on $u_{i,t-1}$, but also on

$u_{j,t-1}(j \neq i)$. Cross lag correlations between two different disturbances are thus permitted. A complete simultaneous estimation method for all the parameters in (9.3.5), the α's, β's, ρ's, variances of disturbances, and covariances of disturbances, can be developed. The equations providing these estimates are much more complex than the estimation for a system with all values of ρ_{ij} assumed to be zero (nonserially correlated disturbances). The interpretation of limited information maximum likelihood or two stage least squares estimates where lag values of dependent variables are treated as though they are exogenous is dubious from the model in (9.3.5). We cannot ignore restrictions on equations other than a particular one being estimated, because the serial correlation scheme involves all the equations of the system. If we assume

$$\rho_{ij} = 0, \qquad i \neq j,$$

and allow ρ_{ii} to be either zero or nonzero, as the case may be, we can extend the single equation methods to the present model. Substitution of the resulting autoregressive equations into the structural equations leads to the system

$$\sum_{j=1}^{n} \alpha_{ij}(y_{jt} - \rho_{ii} y_{j,t-1}) + \sum_{j=1}^{m} \beta_{ij}(z_{jt} - \rho_{ii} z_{j',t-1}) = v_{it}. \tag{9.3.6}$$

We now apply LIML or TSLS methods to (9.3.6), because the v_{it} are mutually independent in time. (9.3.6) is not linear in the unknown parameters, however, and we must take this into account in developing the estimates.

The annual counterpart of a quarterly model provides an interesting comparison. We can examine the question of whether the more detailed quarterly observations produce a relation that aggregates by time into an annual relation that could have been estimated directly from annual data. Obviously, we cannot infer much about quarterly behavior from annual data, but the reverse inference is legitimate and interesting.

In the simplest case consisting only of unlagged variables, there should be a direct relation between quarterly and annual equations. With no seasonal influences or serial correlation of disturbances, a quarterly equation is written as

$$y_t = \alpha + \beta z_t + u_t. \tag{9.3.7}$$

The corresponding annual model is[10]

$$\sum_{i=1}^{4} y_{t+i} = 4\alpha + \beta \sum_{i=1}^{4} z_{t+i} + \sum_{i=1}^{4} u_{t+i}, \tag{9.3.8}$$

and simple correspondences can be drawn between the parameters of the two

[10] In order to simplify notation, we assume that period $t + 1$ is the first quarter of some year.

equations. With a purely additive seasonal[11]

$$y_t = \alpha + \beta z_t + \beta_1 p_t + \beta_2 e_t + \beta_3 a_t + \beta_4 h_t + u_t, \tag{9.3.9}$$

the derived annual equation is

$$\sum_{i=1}^{4} y_{t+i} = 4\alpha + \sum_{i=1}^{4} \beta_i + \beta \sum_{i=1}^{4} z_{t+i} + \sum_{i=1}^{4} u_{t+i}. \tag{9.3.10}$$

If the coefficient of z_t varies seasonally, the annual equation will have a coefficient which is the weighted average of the four seasonal coefficients.

$$\begin{aligned} y_t = \alpha + \beta_p p_t z_t + \beta_e e_t z_t + \beta_a a_t z_t + \beta_h h_t z_t \\ + \beta_1 p_t + \beta_2 e_t + \beta_3 a_t + \beta_4 h_t + u_t, \end{aligned} \tag{9.3.11}$$

$$\begin{aligned} \sum_{i=1}^{4} y_{t+i} &= 4\alpha + \sum_{i=1}^{4} \beta_i + \bar{\beta} \sum_{i=1}^{4} z_{t+i} + \sum_{i=1}^{4} u_{t+i}, \\ \bar{\beta} &= \frac{\beta_p z_{t+1} + \beta_e z_{t+2} + \beta_a z_{t+3} + \beta_h z_{t+4}}{\sum_{i=1}^{4} z_{t+i}}. \end{aligned} \tag{9.3.12}$$

The comparison between $\bar{\beta}$ and a constant coefficient of $\sum_{i=1}^{4} z_{t+i}$ estimated from annual data is only approximate, of course, because $\bar{\beta}$ depends on the distribution of z_t among the four quarters of a year.

With lagged values of variables, the correspondences between quarterly and annual equations are less direct. To derive an annual equation from the quarterly equation[12]

$$y_t = \alpha + \alpha_1 y_{t-1} + \beta z_t + u_t, \tag{9.3.13}$$

we form the equation for the initial quarter

$$y_1 = \alpha + \alpha_1 y_0 + \beta z_1 + u_1$$

and derive four successive quarters

$$\begin{aligned} y_2 &= \alpha + \alpha_1 y_1 + \beta z_2 + u_2, \\ &= \alpha + \alpha_1 \alpha + \alpha_1^2 y_0 + \alpha_1 \beta z_1 + \alpha_1 u_1 + \beta z_2 + u_2 \\ y_3 &= \alpha + \alpha_1 y_2 + \beta z_3 + u_3, \\ &= \alpha(1 + \alpha_1 + \alpha_1^2) + \alpha_1^3 y_0 + \alpha_1^2 \beta z_1 + \alpha_1 \beta z_2 + \beta z_3 \\ &\qquad + \alpha_1^2 u_1 + \alpha_1 u_2 + u_3, \\ y_4 &= \alpha + \alpha_1 y_3 + \beta z_4 + u_4, \\ &= \alpha(1 + \alpha_1 + \alpha_1^2 + \alpha_1^3) + \alpha_1^4 y_0 + \alpha_1^3 \beta z_1 + \alpha_1^2 \beta z_2 \\ &\qquad + \alpha_1 \beta z_3 + \beta z_4 + \alpha_1^3 u_1 + \alpha_1^2 u_2 + \alpha_1 u_3 + u_4. \end{aligned}$$

[11] If the equation has a constant term, only three independent seasonal dummy variables can be introduced for purposes of estimation.

[12] In the following development, the unit lag is one quarter of a year.

We then sum the four quarterly equations in this form to get

$$\begin{aligned}\sum_{i=1}^{4} y_i = 4\alpha + 3\alpha_1\alpha + 2\alpha_1^2\alpha + \alpha_1^3\alpha + \left(\sum_{i=1}^{4}\alpha_1^i\right)y_0 \\ + \left(\beta\sum_{i=1}^{4}\alpha_1^{i-1}\right)z_1 + \left(\beta\sum_{i=1}^{3}\alpha_1^{i-1}\right)z_2 + \left(\beta\sum_{i=1}^{2}\alpha_1^{i-1}\right)z_3 + \beta z_4 \\ + \left(\sum_{i=1}^{4}\alpha_1^{i-1}\right)u_1 + \left(\sum_{i=1}^{3}\alpha_1^{i-1}\right)u_2 + \left(\sum_{i=1}^{2}\alpha_1^{i-1}\right)u_3 + u_4.\end{aligned} \tag{9.3.14}$$

In a more simplified expression, this becomes[13]

$$\sum_{i=1}^{4} y_i = \gamma_0 + \gamma_1 z_1 + \gamma_2 z_2 + \gamma_3 z_3 + \gamma_4 z_4 + u, \tag{9.3.15}$$

or

$$\sum_{i=1}^{4} y_i = \gamma_0 + \bar{\gamma}\sum_{i=1}^{4} z_i + u,$$

$$\bar{\gamma} = \frac{\gamma_1 z_1 + \gamma_2 z_2 + \gamma_3 z_3 + \gamma_4 z_4}{\sum_{i=1}^{4} z_i}.$$

This latter form would be an equivalent annual approximation. In making any numerical comparison, it would be necessary to preserve the relationships connecting the γ_i to the original parameters in (9.3.13).

In long time series, covering a century or more of quarterly or monthly observations, we could expect to estimate all four types of properties—trend, seasonal, cyclical, and random. An econometric model based on such data would have these properties inherent in it. In the same way that we introduce specific variables to account for seasonal influences, we can also introduce specific trend variables. Even if the data were on an annual basis, or integral multiples thereof, we would still need to consider trend factors, although seasonal influences would then be obscured.

Some time series analyses, econometric or otherwise, have begun by attempting to isolate and eliminate trend variables. Consider the two variables y_t and z_t, each following smooth linear trends

$$y_t = \alpha_0 + \alpha_1 t + u_{1t}, \tag{9.3.16}$$

$$z_t = \beta_0 + \beta_1 t + u_{2t}. \tag{9.3.17}$$

The trend free variables u_{1t} and u_{2t} are assumed to be linearly related

$$u_{1t} = \gamma u_{2t} + v_t \tag{9.3.18}$$

in a structural equation. This latter equation can be estimated either by estimat-

[13] The initial value of the y_t series, y_0, is treated as a known constant.

ing the relation between calculated least squares residuals from (9.3.16)–(9.3.17)

$$(y_t - \hat{\alpha}_0 - \hat{\alpha}_1 t) = \gamma(z_t - \hat{\beta}_0 - \hat{\beta}_1 t) + v_t,$$
$$r_{1t} = \gamma r_{2t} + v_t, \tag{9.3.19}$$

in which r_{1t} and r_{2t} are estimates of u_{1t} and u_{2t}, respectively, or by estimating the general equation by least squares.

$$y_t = \alpha_0 - \gamma\beta_0 + \gamma z_t + (\alpha_1 - \gamma\beta_1)t + v_t,$$
$$y_t = \delta_0 + \delta_1 z_t + \delta_2 t + v_t. \tag{9.3.20}$$

This basic theorem on prior trend elimination or inclusion of trend variables was first proved by R. Frisch and F. Waugh.[14] Their theorem has been extended to the treatment of seasonal variation by M. Lovell.[15] If two seasonal variables y_t and z_t are first adjusted for seasonal variation by computation of least squares residuals (deviations of actual from seasonal) from

$$y_t = \hat{\alpha}_1 p_t + \hat{\alpha}_2 e_t + \hat{\alpha}_3 a_t + \hat{\alpha}_4 h_t + r_{1t} \tag{9.3.21}$$

$$z_t = \hat{\beta}_1 p_t + \hat{\beta}_2 e_t + \hat{\beta}_3 a_t + \hat{\beta}_4 h_t + r_{2t}, \tag{9.3.22}$$

We obtain the same coefficients from the least squares regressions of seasonally adjusted values from

$$r_{1t} = \gamma r_{2t} + v_t \tag{9.3.23}$$

as from

$$y_t = \delta z_t + \delta_1 p_t + \delta_2 e_t + \delta_3 a_t + \delta_4 h_t + v_t. \tag{9.3.24}$$

In studying trends and seasonals, we may thus use adjusted data or use explicit trend or seasonal variables in the equations. One must be careful in using data already adjusted for trend or seasonal variation not to attribute too many degrees of freedom to the sample data. If trend and seasonal variables are used in structural equations, it is immediately evident that degrees of freedom are thereby lost.

Specific trend variables showing the secular effects of particular factors are always to be preferred to anonymous trends in the form of some function of time $f(t)$. In studying consumer behavior, important specific trends are population size, average age of the population, number of persons per family, internal migration, and resources of the advertising industry. Wealth variables,

[14] R. Frisch and F. V. Waugh, "Partial Time Regressions as Compared with Individual Trends," *Econometrica*, 1 (October, 1933), 387–401.

[15] M. C. Lovell, "Seasonal Adjustment of Economic Time Series and Multiple Regression Analysis," *Journal of the American Statistical Association*, 58 (December, 1963), 993–1010.

as opposed to income or flow variables in economic life, move gradually over time and show essentially trend influences in many structural equations. Some trend influences, such as increasing productivity, are difficult to specify in terms of objective variables; hence we do have to resort, at times, to general functions of time in order to express trend forces.

Analogy may again be drawn with the measurement of seasonal variation. Proxy seasonal variables, like those assuming the values either unity or zero in season or out, are anonymous and automatic as are general functions of time to show trend effects. Specific seasonal influences such as temperature recordings, the indexes of rainfall, and the occurrence of Easter can be used, instead of the mechanical variables we considered above.

Another way of studying trends is to change the accounting period toward longer stretches of time, say five or ten year periods. Decade time series would tend to smooth out temporary cyclical as well as seasonal aberrations on the deep seated growth movements of the economy. Decade data over one hundred or more years can be interrelated in macroeconomic models showing such phenomena as population growth, frontier expansion, increasing productivity, and changing tastes. Some variables that are thought to be relatively fixed or exogenous in the short run become genuine endogenous variables in pure trend models.

In some analyses of cross section data, it has been found useful to lengthen the accounting period to time spans as long as five years. In studying investment outlays by individual firms, the lumpiness of this type of expenditure causes large dispersion and obscuring of underlying patterns of relationship in annual data. Individual companies often make an isolated large outlay during one or two years and spend relatively little either before or after this period. By averaging expenditures over several years, we find a considerable decrease in dispersion of the relationship of investment outlays to profits or production. In a similar way, the distribution of individual income approaches a more stable form as ups and downs are smoothed out over several years. Thus in some types of econometric studies we may want to use a relatively long, and in others a relatively short, accounting period. The choice obviously depends on the nature of the problem being studied and the objectives of the analysis.

An analogy to the variation of the unit period of observation is the variation of the grouping of cross-section data, as referred to in problem (2) p. 363, above. Individual sample observations (families, farms, enterprises, and so on) may be related in a single regression equation, or means computed from groupings of the independent variables may be related in the same equation. The estimates of parameters from the grouped data are unbiased estimates (from weighted regressions) of the same parameters that are estimated (unbiased) from the original ungrouped data, but the degree of correlation is much higher for the grouped data, just as it would tend to be for data that are smoothed by time averaging. The basic reason for the increase in the degree of correlation is that the dependent variable computed from group means has much less variation than does the same variable in terms of original, ungrouped observations. J. S. Cramer shows this as follows:[16]

$$y_{ij} = \alpha + \beta x_{ij} + u_{ij} \tag{9.3.25}$$

There are t groups of n_i each; $\sum_{i=1}^{t} n_i = N$.
Total and group means are defined as

$$\bar{\bar{x}} = \frac{1}{N}\sum_{i,j} x_{ij};\ \bar{x}_i \frac{1}{n_i}\sum_j x_{ij}.$$

From ungrouped data, we have for the slope estimate

$$b = \frac{\sum_{ij}(x_{ij} - \bar{\bar{x}})(y_{ij} - \bar{\bar{y}})}{\sum_{ij}(x_{ij} - \bar{\bar{x}})^2} = \beta + \frac{\sum_{ij}(x_{ij} - \bar{\bar{x}})(u_{ij} - \bar{\bar{u}})}{\sum_{ij}(x_{ij} - \bar{\bar{x}})^2}. \tag{9.3.26}$$

From grouped data, the corresponding estimate is

$$\bar{b} = \frac{\sum_{i} n_i(\bar{x}_i - \bar{\bar{x}})(\bar{y}_i - \bar{\bar{y}})}{\sum_{i} n_i(\bar{x}_i - \bar{\bar{x}})^2} = \beta + \frac{\sum_{i} n_i(\bar{x}_i - \bar{\bar{x}})(\bar{u}_i - \bar{\bar{u}})}{\sum_{i} n_i(\bar{x}_i - \bar{\bar{x}})^2}. \tag{9.3.27}$$

If x_{ij} are fixed variates, we have

$$E(b) = E(\bar{b}) = \beta. \tag{9.3.28}$$

The corresponding sampling variances are

$$\text{var}(b) = \frac{\sigma_u^2}{\sum_{ij}(x_{ij} - \bar{\bar{x}})^2}. \tag{9.3.29}$$

$$\text{var}(\bar{b}) = \frac{\sigma_u^2}{\sum_{i} n_i(\bar{x}_i - \bar{\bar{x}})^2}. \tag{9.3.30}$$

The variance in (9.3.30) from grouped data is at least as large as that in (9.3.29) from ungrouped data because[17]

$$\sum_{ij}(x_{ij} - \bar{\bar{x}})^2 \geq \sum_{i} n_i(\bar{x}_i - \bar{\bar{x}}^2).$$

[16] J. S. Cramer, "Efficient Grouping, Regression and Correlation in Engel Curve Analysis," *Journal of the American Statistical Association*, 59 (March, 1964), 235–50.

[17] These are the same expressions that arise in the analysis of variance Chap. 3, p. 113.

The square of the multiple correlation coefficient will be defined as

$$R^2 = 1 - \frac{\sum_{ij} (r_{ij} - \bar{\bar{r}})^2}{\sum_{ij} (y_{ij} - \bar{\bar{y}})^2}, \tag{9.3.31}$$

where r_{ij} is a typical regression residual.
Define

$$C = \frac{R^2}{1 - R^2} = \frac{b^2 \sum_{ij} (x_{ij} - \bar{\bar{x}})^2}{\sum_{ij} (r_{ij} - \bar{\bar{r}})^2} \tag{9.3.32}$$

and $\bar{C}$ as the corresponding transformation of R^2 where the latter statistic is computed from grouped data. Because R^2 is confined to the closed interval [0, 1], C is monotonic in R^2.

$$\frac{\bar{C}}{C} = \left(\frac{\bar{b}}{b}\right)^2 \frac{\sum_i n_i(\bar{x}_i - \bar{\bar{x}})^2}{\sum_{ij} (x_{ij} - \bar{\bar{x}})^2} \frac{\sum_{ij} (r_{ij} - \bar{\bar{r}})^2}{\sum_i n_i(\bar{r}_i - \bar{\bar{r}})^2} \tag{9.3.33}$$

We shall assume

$$\bar{b} \sim b,$$

and

$$\frac{\sum_{ij} (r_{ij} - \bar{\bar{r}})^2}{\sum_i n_i(\bar{r}_i - \bar{\bar{r}})^2} \sim \frac{N - 2}{t - 2}.$$

The latter approximation holds because

$$\sum_{ij} (r_{ij} - \bar{\bar{r}})^2 = \sum_i n_i(\bar{r} - \bar{\bar{r}})^2 + \sum_{ij} (r_{ij} - \bar{r}_i)^2, \tag{9.3.34}$$

and the two terms on the right-hand side of (9.3.34) are estimates of the same residual sum of squares with $t - 2$ and $N - t$ degrees of freedom, respectively. We, therefore, have the approximation

$$\frac{\bar{C}}{C} \sim \frac{\sum_i n_i(\bar{x}_i - \bar{\bar{x}})^2}{\sum_{ij} (x_{ij} - \bar{\bar{x}})^2} \frac{N - 2}{t - 2}. \tag{9.3.35}$$

Although the slopes are not (approximately) affected by the grouping, the multiple correlation coefficient is, according to the approximation in (9.3.35). It usually happens that R^2 computed from grouped data is larger, because the first term on the right-hand side is usually close to unity.

Questions and Problems

1. In some instances seasonal variation can be considered additive, but seasonal influences may be gradually changing over time. How would you introduce seasonal variables in an equation to represent a changing pattern?

2. How would you use trigonometric functions to eliminate periodic seasonal variation in time series analysis?

3. List trend variables that you would introduce explicitly in aggregative econometric models. Classify them as endogenous or exogenous, giving reasons for your choice.

4. From quarterly time series of the interwar period we have the estimated investment equation

$$I = -2.02 + 0.44P_{-3/2} + 0.62P_{-7/2} - 0.05K_{-1} + u,$$
$$u = 0.60\,u_{-1}.$$

The variables are measured in billions of 1939 dollars. From annual time series in the same period we have

$$I = 22.59 + 0.08P + 0.68P_{-1} - 0.17K_{-1}.$$

The variables are measured in billions of 1934 dollars. The index of capital goods prices is 100 for 1939 and 80 for 1934.

In the quarterly equation the lags are expressed in quarters of one year, in the annual equation they are expressed in years. In the former case, quarterly investment is defined as the change in the stock of capital from one quarter to the next. In the latter case, annual investment is defined as the change in the stock of capital from one year to the next. The initial stock of capital is explicitly measured in the annual equation, but not in the quarterly equation. In the quarterly equation it is included in the constant term. Discuss the consistency of the two estimated equations.

SUGGESTED READINGS

Allen, R. G. D. "The Assumptions of Linear Regression," *Economica*, N.S., VI (May 1939), 191–204. An early econometric paper showing the assumptions necessary for estimating the linear structural relation between two variables, both of which are subject to error.

Bartlett, M. S. "A Note on the Statistical Estimation of Supply and Demand Relations from Time Series," *Econometrica*, 16 (Oct. 1948), 323–29. Gives a more refined statistical treatment of Tintner's problem of testing for the number of independent linear relations connecting a set of observed variables and estimating the parameters of acceptable relations.

Cramer, J. S., "Efficient Grouping, Regression and Correlation in Engel Curve Analysis", *Journal of the American Statistical Association*, 59 (March, 1964), 233–50. Develops formulas for the effects of grouping data in cross-section analysis.

Frisch, R. and F. V. Waugh, "Partial Time Regression as Compared with Individual Trends," *Econometrica*, 1 (October, 1933), 387–401. Pioneering study to develop theorem on equivalence between prior extraction of trends in regression analysis compared with inclusion of trend variables and unadjusted data.

Geary, R. C. "Determination of Linear Relations between Systematic Parts of Variables with Errors of Observation, the Variances of Which are Unknown," *Econometrica*, 17 (Jan, 1949), 30–58. Develops results in the method of instrumental variables for estimating parameters of the linear structural relation when several variables are subject to error.

Hurwicz, L. "Variable Parameters in Stochastic Processes: Trend and Seasonality," in *Statistical Inference in Dynamic Economic Models*, ed. T. Koopmans. New York: John Wiley & Sons, 1950. A theoretical econometric treatment of trend and seasonal variation.

Koopmans, T., *Linear Regression Analysis of Economic Time Series*. Haarlem: De Erven F. Bohn N. V., 1937. A detailed mathematical presentation of the errors in variables model for single multivariate equations.

Lovell, M. C., "Seasonal Adjustment of Economic Time Series and Multiple Regression Analysis," *Journal of the American Statistical Association*, 58 (December, 1963), 993–1010. Extends Frisch-Waugh theorem to case of seasonal adjustment.

Morgenstern, O., *On the Accuracy of Economic Observations*. Princeton: Princeton University Press, 1950. An unique study of errors of observation and their influence on empirical research.

Prais, S. J. and J. Aitchison, "The Grouping of Observations in Regression Analysis," *Review of the International Statistical Institute*, 22 (1954), 1–22. An original systematic treatment of the grouping problem.

Reiersøl, O. "Identifiability of a Linear Relation between Variables Which Are Subject to Error," *Econometrica*, 18 (Oct. 1950), 375–89. Gives necessary and sufficient conditions for identification in simple models with observation errors.

Tintner, G. "An Application of the Variate Difference Method to Multiple Regression," *Econometrica*, 12 (April, 1944), 97–113. "Multiple Regression for Systems of Equations," Ibid., 14 (Jan., 1946), 5–36. *The Variate Difference Method*. Bloomington: Principia Press, 1940. *Econometrics*, New York: John Wiley & Sons, 1952. Develops the study of errors in variables models with special reference to applications of the variate difference method.

Wald, A. "The Fitting of Straight Lines if Both Variables Are Subject to Error," *Annals of Mathematical Statistics*, XI (Sept., 1940), 284–300. Presents a simple method of subgroup averages to estimate the linear structural relation and the relative error variances.

Index

Acceleration principle, 12, 165
  identification of, 18, 138
  testing for, 84-85
Adams, F. G., 277, 385
Adelman, F., 241, 253-56, 279
Adelman, I., 241, 253-56, 279
Age distribution, 33, 36-37
Aggregation, 9, 11
  cross-section relationships, 359-63, 376-79
  error in specification, 213
Agriculture, Department of, 22
Aitchison, J., 51, 428
Aitken, A. C., 85
Aitken estimation, 86*ff*, 161
  pooling of cross-sections and time series samples, 380
  three stage least squares, 172-74
  (see also least squares, generalized)
Allen, R. G. D., 427
Almon, S., 100, 129
Amemiya, T., 99
Analysis of variance, 113*ff*
Anderson, T. W., 65, 162, 166, 191, 195
Arithmetic mean, relation to geometric mean, 328, 361
Arrow, K. J., 381
Assets, holding of, 11
Autocorrelation, error structure in
  regression, 88-97
  sampling experiments, 213*ff*
  spectral analysis, 256
  (see also serial correlation)
Autonomous functions, 19-21, 23
Autoregressive structure, in solution and final form, 181, 236-37
  of residuals in forecasting, 271-72
  (see also serial correlation)
Back solution, 290, 293-94
Balestra, P., 379, 381
Bartlett, M. S., 427
Basmann, R. L., 159
Bayes' theorem, 63-64
Behavior equation, concept of, 5, 9
Benster, C. D., 319
Bentzel, R., 197, 224
Bias, sampling experiment, 220
Binary program, 297
Binomial distribution, 45-47, 52
Bivariate distributions, 35-38
  normal, 49
Bodkin, R. G., 126, 332
Borrowing, 11
Brookings Model, 5, 200, 218, 225, 239, 269, 279, 280, 319, 347-48
Brown, J. A. C., 51
Brown, T. M., 178, 181, 195, 264
Budget identity, 375
Burington, R. S., 37
Business-cycle theory, 11*ff*
  (see also cycles)

CES function, 126, 332-33, 339, 381
Central limit theorem, 49
Champernowne, D. G., 51
Characteristic roots, dynamic solution, 181, 235-38, 256-59, 263
  calculation of for LIML estimation, 305-06
  calculation of for simulation, 312
  errors in variable model, 402-05
  principal components, 185, 300-01
Chenery, H. B., 381
Chernoff, H., 165, 195, 203, 222-23, 275

Chi-square distribution, 262
errors in variables model, 404-05
test for normality, 368*ff*
Chow, G., 195, 307, 319
Christ, C., 194
Cobb, C., 4
Cobb-Douglas function, 125, 327, 332, 339, 364, 382
nonlinear estimation of, 206
Cobweb model, identification of, 146
recursive estimation of, 199-202
Cochrane, D., 92
Cochrane-Orcutt method, 92-93, 96, 129
Cohen, K. J., 181
Collinearity
in equation systems, 188*ff*
in testing regression estimates, 82
lag distributions, 97
(see also multicollinearity)
Commerce, Department of, 22, 228
Computation, 281*ff*
Concentrated likelihood function, 147-48, 187, 193-94, 204, 306-07
Conditional probability, 27, 29, 35-37
cross-section relationships, 351
regression theory, 77
Confidence ellipsoid, 84
Confidence intervals, 57-58, 81-83
in cross-section estimation, 370
in forecasting, 278
Confluence analysis, 16
Consistent estimates, concept of, 55
errors in variables model, 399
generalized regression, 87
instrumental variables case, 151-53
lag distributions, 97, 99-100
lagged endogenous variables, 135
limited information maximum likelihood, 165
maximum likelihood, 56, 78, 146
two-stage-least-squares, 159
Constant adjustments, 315-19
Consumer behavior, theory of, 8-9, 11, 23
Consumption function, 171
errors in variables model of, 386-87
Control solution, 241, 251
Controlled experiments, 2, 105
Cooper, R. L., 175
Correlation, defined, 44
regression statistic, 69, 70, 75
Cost function, 11, 322
Cowles Commission for Research in Economics, 175
Cragg, J. G., 214, 219, 225
Cramér, H., 65
Cramer, J. S., 425, 427
Credit, consumer installment model, 335-36
Critical region, 59-61, 81
Cross-section data, 321, 349*ff*
from sample surveys, 409
grouping of, 424-26
Cumulative probability, 32-33
bivariate, 35
multivariate, 39
Pareto distribution, 52
Cycles, cause of error dependence, 88-89
cause of collinearity, 106
component of time series, 422
simulation of, 252*ff*
solutions to dynamic systems, 236-38, 241

David, F. N., 66
Dayal, R., 376
Decision function, 61-64
Degrees of freedom, 68, 69, 77, 80, 129, 183*ff*, 291
errors in variable model, 403-04
in chi-square test, 369-73
in F-tests, 84, 114
in generation of stochastic simulation, 319
in pooled estimation, 380
in recursive systems, 202
in trend and seasonal elimination, 423
with grouped data, 426
with quarterly data, 416
Demand relations, 6, 23, 108, 171, 322-23
estimation of, from pooled samples, 374-76
identification of, 17-18, 145
Density function, probability, 32, 35, 45, 144, 351
Determinantal equation
errors in variables model, 402-05
(see also characteristic roots)
Dhrymes, P. J., 5, 122, 130, 194
Dichotomous classification, 111-12
Difference-differential equation, 14
Diminishing returns, testing for, 84
Douglas, P. H., 4
Duesenberry, J., 5, 200, 218, 225, 239, 269, 280, 347
Dummy variables,
as instruments, 155
in regression analysis, 109*ff*
Durbin, J., 96, 375, 381
Durbin-Watson test, 96
computation of, in program, 299
lag distribution, 102
Dwyer, P. S., 319

ECON program, 297-99

Economic Analysis, Bureau of, 22
Efficient estimate, concept of, 55
  errors in variables model, 399
  generalized regression, 87
  lag distribution, 99-100
  lagged endogenous variables, 135
  limited information maximum likelihood, 165
  maximum likelihood, 56, 78, 146
  sampling experiments, 220
  serial correlation case, 97
  two-stage-least squares, 159
Eisenpress, H., 206, 225, 228, 319, 332
Elasticity, price, 83, 323, 327, 344
  production, 344
Endogenous variables, defined, 133-36
Engel curve, 104, 376, 425, 427
Errors,
  in variables and in equations, 386*ff*
  measures of, in prediction, 275-79
  measures of, in simulation, 242-48
  observation and measurement, 383*ff*
Estimation, principles of, 52*ff*
Evans, M. K., 255, 272, 277, 316, 319
Excess demand functions, 377
Exchange, equation of, 15
Exogenous variable, defined, 133-36
  as instruments, 151-53
Experiments,
  controlled, 2, 68, 132
  nonexperimental data, 2
  sampling, 213*ff*, 270
Extrapolation, 243
  (see also simulation)
Ezekiel, M., 130

F-distribution, 84-85, 114
Factor analysis, 16
Faddeeva, V. N. 319
Family budget, 104, 108
Feller, W., 65
Filtering, 119-27
Final Demand, 340
Final form, 179-81, 234-35, 254
Firm, theory of, 8-9, 20
First-difference transformation, autocorrelation, 90
Fisher, F. M., 143, 195, 200, 225, 347
Fixed proportions, 338
Flow of funds, accounts for, 22
Forecasting, 226, 233
  ex ante or ex post, 241, 277-79
  single period and multiperiod, 268
  (see also simulation, and prediction)
Fortran, 296
Fox, K. A., 129, 206
Frequency distribution, 33
Friedman, M., 386
Frisch, R., 16, 23, 237, 279, 423
Fromm, G., 239, 279
Fuller, W., 99

Gauss-Doolittle method, 282*ff*
Gauss-Jordan method, 293-94
Gauss-Seidel method, 238-40, 275, 279, 313-14, 326
Geary, R. C., 428
General equilibrium model, 337
Geometric lag distribution, 102
  (see also Koyck distribution)
Geometric mean, relation to arithmetic means, 328, 361
Gibrat, R., 328
Girschik, M. A., 333, 335, 337, 381
Goldberger, A. S., 130, 194, 227, 252, 264-67, 279
Goldfeld, S. M., 214, 220-23, 227, 275
Gordon, R. A., 237, 279
Grafting, sector to master model, 325-27, 381
Graybill, F. A., 65
Great Depression, simulation of, 244-45, 251-52
Greenstadt, J., 206, 225, 319, 332
Griliches, Z., 130
Grouping of data, 424-26

Haberler, G., 11
Haavelmo, T., 23, 333, 335, 337, 381
Hart, B. I., 95
Hartley, H. O., 126, 130
Hartley, M., 316, 319
Heteroscedasticity, 102*ff*
  in sample survey data, 415
Hickman, B., 255, 269, 280, 318
Hoel, P. G., 65
Homogeneity conditions, 375
Homoscedasticity, 360
Hood, W. C., 165, 195, 203
Houthakker, H., 175
Howrey, E. P., 180, 254-56, 280
Hurwicz, L., 180, 236, 381, 428
Hypotheses,
  regression case, 80-85
  testing of, 58-62

Identification, concept of, 17-18, 137*ff*
  in cross-section samples, 324-28
  in errors in variable models, 405-07
  in input-output analysis, 342
  in sampling experiment, 216
  maximum likelihood case, 149, 307

Imperfect competition, 330
Income distribution, 36-37, 40, 49-50
  in aggregation of cross-section relations, 361-63, 375
Incomplete systems, 165, 222
Independence, concept of, 28
Input cards, 297
Input-output analysis, 338*ff*, 381
  dynamic case, 348-49
  stochastic case, 344
Institutional relationships, 10
Instrumental variables, method of, 150*ff*
  errors in variables model, 398-99, 428
  interpretation of two-stage-least-squares, 156, 175, 274-75
Interval estimates, 57
Internal Revenue, Collector of, 22
International Bank for Reconstruction and Development, 22
International Monetary Fund, 22
Interstate Commerce Commission, 367
Invariance, property of, 149
  limited information maximum likelihood, 171
  maximum likelihood, 162
  under scale change, 179
Isoquants, 338

Jacobian determinant, 38-39, 144, 150
  in input-output system, 345
  in recursive systems, 197-200
  nonlinear case, 204, 227
Janosi, P. E. de, 385
Jenkins, G. M., 93
Johnston, J., 194
Joint probability distribution, 36-37, 76-77, 332
  cross-section relationships, 351, 359
  errors of measurement, 386
Jorgenson, D., 130, 175, 181, 273

Kalecki, M., 13-14, 19, 23
k-Class estimators, 161
  equivalence with limited information maximum likelihood, 169-70
  degrees of freedom in, 184
  multicollinearity in, 189-94
  specification error, 212
Katzner, D. W., 206
Kendall, M. G., 65, 130
Keynesian system, 15
Kisselgoff, A., 335-37, 381
Klein-Goldberger Model, 180, 226*ff*, 279, 280
  cyclical analysis of, 252-55
Kloek, T., 185, 195
Kmenta, J., 130
Koopmans, T., 24, 165, 195, 203, 428
Koyck, L. M., 97
Koyck lag distribution, 97, 102, 116, 123-24
Kresge, D., 347

Labor, Department of, 22
Ladd, G. W., 214, 224, 225
Lag distributions, 97*ff*, 417
  nonlinear estimation of, 116*ff*
  relation to errors in variable model, 394-402
Least squares, principle of, 66*ff*
  as k-class member, 161
  bias of, 150-51, 243
  computation of, 282*ff*
  degrees of freedom in, 183-84
  errors in variable model, 387, 390-95, 400-01
  estimates from cross-section data, 354-57
  estimates of Klein-Goldberger Model, 228*ff*
  generalized, 85*ff*, 208-10
  iteration of, 175-76
  multicollinearity in, 104-09, 192
  program for, 297-300
  sampling experiment, 218-23
  simulation errors of, 243-48
  specification error, 211
  trend elimination, 423
  weighted regressions, 410-14
Legal relationship, 10
Leipnik, R. B., 195
Leontief, W., 337*ff*, 381
Limited information, maximum likelihood, 161*ff*
  calculation of, 304*ff*
  degrees of freedom in, 184-87
  estimation of food model, 334
  multicollinearity in, 191-93
  nonlinear case, 203, 221
  program for, 297-300
  sampling experiment, 218-19
  serially correlated errors, 420
  specification error, 212
  standard error of forecast of, 266
  use of with cross-section data, 328-31
Linear expenditure system,
  estimation of, 7-8, 375-76
Linear homogeneous restrictions, 142-43, 164-65, 166
Linear systems, 16
  as approximation, 16
Liu, T. C., 143
Liviatan, N., 98
Lognormal distribution, 50-52, 328, 361-62

Lorenz curve, 40
Lovell, M. C., 423, 428

McBride, L. E., 117, 124
McCarthy, M. D., 269, 280, 318
Madansky, A., 174, 311
Main program, 297
Malinvaud, E., 102, 130, 194, 214, 224
Mann, H. B., 135, 179, 196, 272
Marginal cost, 11
Marginal probability distribution, 35, 37
  cross-section relationships, 351
Marginal productivity, 3, 11, 20, 23, 83, 322-23, 327-28
Marginal utility, 6
Market clearing, 8-9, 11
Markoff theorem, 66*ff*, 85, 132
Marschak, J., 24, 382
Master model, 325-27, 330-31
Mathematical economics, contrasted with econometrics, 1*ff*, 25
Matrix multiplication, program for, 295-96
Maximum likelihood estimate,
  autocorrelated error in regression, 92
  calculation of, 306*ff*, 319
  concept of, 53-55
  cross-section relationships, 351-56, 369, 379
  degrees of freedom in, 187-88
  equation system estimation, 146*ff*
  errors in variables model, 400-01
  estimation of lag distribution, 116-17
  estimation of sector models, 332-33
  interpretation of weighted regression, 412
  limited information maximum likelihood estimation, relation to, 166*ff*
  nonlinear regression, 128
  nonlinear systems, 202*ff*, 227*ff*
  recursive case, 198-202
  regression theory 77-79, 80
  relation to 3SLS, 174
  relation to SLS, 178
  sampling experiment, 218-24
  simulation errors of, 244-48
  specification error, 211-12
  standard error of forecast of, 266
Mean value, theorem of, 32
Mennes, L. B. M., 185, 195
Minhas, B., 381
Minimax solution, 62-64
Moments, 40*ff*
  central, defined, 41
Moment matrices, 72-75
  computation of, 285-93
  inverse of, 287-90, 306
  program for, 295-96
Monte Carlo methods, 213*ff*
  (see also sampling experiments)
Mood, A. M., 65
Morgenstern, O., 428
Multicollinearity, avoidance of in lag distributions, 98, 102
  general regression problem, 104*ff*
  in equation systems, 188*ff*
  in sampling experiment, 217
  (see also collinearity)
Multinomial distribution, 52
Multiplier, 226, 241, 251, 334
  balanced budget, 248
  (see also simulation, policy)
Multivariate probability, 38-40

Nagar, A. L., 214, 218, 264-67, 269, 280, 319
Nakamura, M., 178, 190, 195
National income, accounts for, 22
Neiswanger, W. A., 214
Nerlove, M., 364, 379, 381, 382
Neumann, J. von, 95-96
Newton's method, 204-06, 310-11
Newton-Raphson method, 240
Neyman, J., 65, 66, 262, 354
Nonexperimental data, samples of, 2, 131-32, 215
  testing with, 85
Nonlinearity, autoregressive error case, 91
  aggregation of, 359-60
  calculation of maximum likelihood estimates, 309
  equation system estimation, 202*ff*
  estimated Klein-Goldberger Model, 227*ff*
  estimation of, by TSLS, 221-23, 275
  estimation of demand relation from pooled sample, 375
  forecast error, 268-70
  lag distribution case, 102
  regression analysis, 116*ff*
  sampling experiments, 213*ff*
  serial correlation case, 207
  simulation, 234, 238-40, 255
  solution form, 181, 273
  stochastic simulation, 252-53
Normal distribution, 47-50
  bivariate, 49
  errors in variable model, 388, 405
  least squares regression theory, 76-77, 80, 401
  maximum likelihood estimation, 56-57
  measurement error, 385
  reproductive property, 78
  sampling experiments, 213*ff*, 269-70
  simultaneous least squares, 178
  tests in regression theory, 80

Normal distribution (*cont.*)
use of in forecast error, 262
use of in railway model, 368*ff*
use of in stochastic simulation, 318
Normal equations, 72-74, 76-77, 293
autocorrelated error case, 94-95
instrumental variables, 151
lag distributions, 118-19, 120, 122
limited information maximum likelihood, 167
maximum likelihood case, 308-11
nonlinear estimation, 126-27
recursive case, 200
3SLS case, 311, 319
two-stage-least-squares, 158
Normalization, rule of, 149
computation of maximum likelihood estimates, 309
errors in variables model, 402
for simulation calculation, 313-14
in input-output system, 345
instrumental variable case, 154-55
iterated least squares case, 177
limited information maximum likelihood case, 167-68, 305-06
sampling experiment, 216
Norman, M., 228, 244, 297

Odeh, H. S., 264-67
Orcutt, G. H., 92, 180, 234
Ordinary least squares (OLS)
(see least squares)
Orthogonal regression, 392-95
Orthogonal transformation, 179
Otsuki, M., 280

Parameter Card, 297
Pareto distribution, 51-52
Pascal distribution, 124
Pearson, product moment formula for correlation, 70, 75, 76
Permanent income hypothesis, 386
Point estimates, 57
Poisson distribution, 47, 52
Policy, analysis of, 248*ff*
Pollak, R. A., 8
Polynomial lag distributions, 100-01
Pooling of samples, 322, 374*ff*
Power of test, 59-60
Prais, S. J., 428
Predetermined variable, defined, 133-36
as instruments, 151-53
Prediction, 260, 267
accuracy of, 275-79
ex ante or ex post, 277-79
multiperiod, 271-72, 273
one period, 263
Prediction (*cont.*)
with serially correlated errors, 271-72
(see also forecasting and simulation)
Prediction-realization diagram, 276
Principal components, 184-86
calculation of, 300-03
use of in estimation of Klein-Goldberger Model, 228*ff*
Probability, 25*ff*
conditional distribution of, 27, 29, 35-37
cumulative distribution of, 32-33, 35, 39
density, 32, 45, 76-77
distributions, 31*ff*
element of, 32
joint distribution of, 36-37
marginal distribution of, 35, 36-37
Probability integral transformation, 40
Production function, 3-5, 11, 20, 23, 171, 322-23, 327, 332
railway services model, 364-66, 371
relationship of to input-output analysis, 342, 346-47
Profit, maximization of, 8
Propensity to spend, tests for, 84
Pseudo sample, 269

Qualitative variables, regression analysis of, 109*ff*
(see also dummy variables)
Quandt, R. E., 214, 220-23, 227, 275

Railways, production model of, 363*ff*
Random parameters, 354, 382
Range, as measure of dispersion, 42, 47
Rectangular distribution, 45
Recursive system 197*ff*
calculation of for simulation, 312-15
Reduced form, 16, 150
role of in identification, 138*ff*
use of in limited-information-maximum likelihood, 162, 165-66, 168, 177
use of in two-stage-least squares, 157
Regression analysis, 64, 66*ff*
Reiersøl, O., 405, 428
Reproductive property, normal distribution, 78
Returns to scale, railways, 371
Risk function, 62-64
Root mean square error, 220, 275
Rubin, H., 162, 165, 166, 191, 195, 203, 222-23, 275, 375, 382

Saito, M., 255, 347
Sample survey data, 409*ff*
(see also cross-section data)
Sampling experiments, 213*ff*

Sampling rates, in weighted regression, 409, 415
Samuelson, P. A., 375
Sargan, J. D., 92
Savings function, interest elasticity of, 380-81
  estimates from sample survey data, 415
Schink, G., 270
Scott, E. L., 354
Search method, estimation of serial correlation, 92-93, 96
  estimation of lag distribution, 119-25
Seasonal variation, estimation of, 111-12, 416-24, 427
Serial correlation, errors in, 350
  distributed lag case, 98, 99, 102
  induced in final form, 180, 236-37
  in equation systems, 207*ff*
  measurement errors, 385
  regression, 80, 272
  specification error, 213
  stochastic simulation, 255
  with quarterly data, 416
Set theoretic approach to probability, 25, 28
Shan, S. K., 320
Shinkai, Y., 347
Simulation, 226, 233*ff*
  programming of, 311*ff*
  stochastic, 252*ff*, 316-19
Sinusoidal limit, 238
  (see also cycles)
Slutsky, E., 236-38
Slutsky equation, 7, 9, 375
Small sample properties, 213*ff*, 270
Solow, R., 124, 130, 332, 381
Solution form, 181-83
  programming of, 311*ff*
  use of in prediction, 273
Specification error, 149-50
  in equation system estimation, 210*ff*
  system experiments, 213*ff*
Spectral analysis, 253-59
Spurious correlation, 415
Stability condition, tests for, 84
Staehle, H., 382
Standard error of forecast, 260*ff*
  use of in measuring prediction error, 277-79
Standardized variable, 48
Statistical discrepancy, 384-85
Steiglitz, K., 117, 122, 124
Steiglitz-McBride method, 117-19, 124, 125
Step size, iterations, 128, 310, 314
Stochastic relation, concept of, 4, 10
Stock-adjustment, 104
Stone, J. R. N., 16
Strotz, R. H., 24
Structural equation, concept of, 5, 9, 16, 20-21
  relation of to reduced form in covariance of error, 265-66
  role of in identification, 144
  role of in limited-information-maximum-likelihood, 162, 169
Stuart, A., 65, 130
Subgroup averages, method of, 154-55, 428
Summers, R., 214, 216-20, 223, 225
Supernumerary income, 375-76
Supply and demand, law of, 336
Supply function,
  autonomy of, 23
  derivation of, 20
  food model, 334
  identification of, 18, 145, 322
Survey Research Center, 361

t-distribution, 80-85
  t-test, collinearity case, 108-09
Taubman, P., 279
Taylor expansion, nonlinear estimation case, 126-29
  simulation of nonlinear system, 239-40
Tax laws, 10
Technical coefficients, 338
Technological relation, concept of, 5, 9, 20
  interpretation of input-output parameters, 343*ff*
Tests, for regression, 80*ff*
  for serial correlation of errors, 96
Theil, H., 159, 161, 172, 175, 195, 196, 266, 276, 280
Three-stage-least-squares, 172*ff*
  degrees of freedom in, 184-87
  equivalence with TSLS, 183
  multicollinearity, 189-94
  specification error, 211-12
Tinbergen, J., 11, 24, 180, 234
Tintner, G., 195, 404, 409, 428
Tobin, J., 382
Tolerance interval, in forecasting, 262, 277-78
Torrance, C. C., 37
Transformation, of probability, 33-35, 37-40, 76, 144-45
  linear, 179
  orthogonal, 179
  probability integral, 40
Transition probabilities, 51
Treasury, Department of, 22
Trends, cause of error dependence, 87-88
  cause of collinearity, 105
  component of time series, 422
  elimination of, 423-24
  simulation of, 253

Two-stage-least-squares, 155*ff*
  as instrumental variable method, 155-59, 274
  as k-class estimator, 161
  calculation of, 303*ff*
  degrees of freedom in, 184-86
  equivalence with 3SLS, 183
  estimates of Klein-Goldberger Model, 228*ff*
  iterated, 175, 181-82, 273
  multicollinearity in, 189-94
  nonlinear case, 203, 221-23
  program for, 297-99
  recursive case, 199
  relation to three-stage-least-squares, 172-75
  sampling experiment, 218-23
  serial correlation, 208-10, 420
  simulation errors of, 243-48
  specification error, 212
  standard error of forecast of, 266
  use of with cross-section data, 328-31
Type I (II) error, 59, 81, 83, 85

Unbiased estimation, concept of, 53-54
  generalized regression, 86
  regression analysis, 67*ff*
  serial correlation case, 97
Uniform distribution, 45
United Nations, 22
Utility function, 6, 23
Utility, maximization of, 8

Variate-difference method, 398, 428

Wagner, H. M., 214
Wald, A., 65, 135, 179, 196, 272, 399, 428
Wales, T. J., 8
Wallis, W. A., 262, 277
Walrasian system, 131-32, 136
Watson, G. S., 96
Watts, D. G., 93
Waugh, F. V., 423, 428
Weighted regression, 307, 401
  from grouped data, 424
  from sample survey data, 409*ff*
Wharton Model, simulation of, 255-59, 272, 277, 279, 280
Wilks, S. S., 65
Wold, H., 97, 175, 196, 197, 216, 224, 227

Yancey, T. A., 214

Zellner, A., 172, 175, 196